Sabbath Bloody Sabbath
The Battle for Black Sabbath

Garry Sharpe-Young

ZONDA BOOKS

Zonda Books Limited, New Plymouth

SABBATH BLOODY SABBATH: THE BATTLE FOR BLACK SABBATH
By Garry Sharpe-Young

ISBN 0-9582684-2-8

Copyright © Garry Sharpe-Young, 2006.

First published in 2006 by Zonda Books Limited, New Plymouth, New Zealand.

Find us on the World Wide Web at www.zondabooks.com

First Edition, March 2006.
Second Edition, August 2006.

All rights reserved. No part of this publication may be reproduced, stored in a retrieval system, or transmitted in any form or by any means, electronic, mechanical, photocopying, recording or otherwise, without the prior permission of the copyright owner.

While every precaution has been taken in the preparation of this book, the publisher and author assumes no responsibility for errors or omissions, or for damages resulting from the use of the information contained herein.

National Library of New Zealand Cataloguing-in-Publication Data

Sharpe-Young, Garry.
Sabbath bloody Sabbath : the battle for Black Sabbath / by
Garry Sharpe-Young. 2nd ed.
Previous ed.: 2006.
Includes index.
ISBN 0-9582684-2-8
1. Osbourne, Ozzy, 1948– 2. Black Sabbath (Musical group)
3. Rock groups—Great Britain—Biography. 4. Rock
musicians—Great Britain—Biography. I. Title.
782.421660922—dc 22

Contents

Preface	v
1 Sabbath Bloody Sabbath	1
2 Killing Yourself To Live	9
3 The Reluctant Wizard	27
4 "It's A Band"	43
5 An Englishman's Castle	63
6 Hair By Sarzo Of Cuba, Way To Go	81
7 Enter Jake	93
8 Born Under A Black Moon	101
9 Carmine Feels The Noise	113
10 Headless	119
11 Zero The Hero	125
12 Jesus Christ, Supertzar	133
13 The Ultimate Din	147
14 'Seventh Star'—Hughes Next?	157
15 Gillen Not Gillan	171

16 Blacky Sabb: Caribbean Speedballs	**185**
17 Idolatry	**199**
18 No Rest For The Headless	**215**
19 A Last Tyr Goodbye	**233**
20 No More Dio	**247**
21 Vai–able Options	**255**
22 Skol?	**265**
23 A Forbidding Farewell	**271**
24 Reunion	**279**
A Discographies	**305**
A.1 Black Sabbath	305
A.2 Ozzy Osbourne	308
A.3 Dio	310
A.4 Bill Ward	312
A.5 Geezer	312
A.6 Tony Iommi	312
Index	**313**

Preface

Acknowledgments

This book could not have been written without the generosity of the following Black Sabbath and Ozzy band members and associates:

Don Airey, Tommy Aldridge, Carmine Appice, Jimi Bell, Lindsey Bridgwater, Bruce Brookshire, Jo Burt, Paul Chapman, Terry Chimes, Malcolm Cope, Laurence Cottle, Fred Coury, Bob Daisley, David DeFeis, Ronnie James Dio, David Donato, Jeff Fenholt, Steve Fister, Lita Ford, Kelly Garni, Ian Gillan, Brad Gillis, Ray Gomez, Rob Halford, Frank Hall, Gary Holt, Glenn Hughes, Bill Hunt, Ron Keel, Lee Kerslake, Blackie Lawless, Alvin Lee, Tony Martin, Kyle Michaels, Neil Murray, Terry Nails, Geoff Nicholls, Graham Oliver, Dave Potts, Bobby Rondinelli, Rudy Sarzo, Carl Sentance, Paul Shortino, Eric Singer, Phil Soussan, Dave Spitz, Dana Strum, John Thomas, Bernie Tormé, Pete Way, Terry Horbury and Steve Vai. All the interviews with the above were conducted solely for this work.

I would also like to thank the members of Ozzy's band that, although wishing to remain anonymous, also contributed greatly.

All these people gave generously of their time over many, many hours of interviews.

Tony Iommi, Geezer Butler, Randy Castillo, Ray Gillen and Cozy Powell were interviewed by the author over the course of two decades of Rock n' Roll. A nod of appreciation goes out to Gloria Butler and Albert Chapman too.

The following people helped enormously: Wendy Dio, Claudia at Niji, Shell at Caramba, Roisin, Gabrielle Hughes, John Baxter at EMAS Management, Steven Warner, Dan Spitz, Richard Galbraith, Matt Sampson, PG Brunelli, Robert Ellis at Repfoto, Wolfgang Rott at CMM, Olly Hahn at SPV, Rupert at Assassination Music, Joe Siegler at www.black-sabbath.com, the Sleeping Village website, Roland Hyams, Jayne Andrews, Jon Hinchliffe, Jimmy Phillips, Drew Thompson, Michael Davis, Eric Parmeter, Ray Luzier, Howard Garolsky, Bob DuPerry.

Writing this book brought back some wonderful memories of Birmingham circa '87–'90. Salutations to Rob Bruce and Rich Bitch Studios, Terry Lee and Simon at Light & Sound Design, Gary "I'm (still) only in it for the glamour" Rees, Nikki, Nigel, Fats, Mr. Bilge, Phil Mogg, Bethina, John & Dee, Dave Juste, those Starfighters—Burtie, Rikdiculous, Stevie & Margaret, Redvers & Jaimie. Special mention must be made for the late Lynn Bruce, a true friend to many Birmingham musicians.

For friends and sources of inspiration. Mum, Grace-Anne, Kerr, Krystan, Kjaric, Peter, Chris, Stevie, Phillip, Lucy, Louise MacPherson, Simon & Diana, Debbie, David Borgioli-Jones, Gregg Russell, Andy Southwell, Andy Pyke, Andy Dawson, Nell Sully, Michael Langbein, Bernard Doe and Grant Pease at Zonda Books.

Introduction

This is the story of two genuine giants of Rock, pitched in battle over two decades. This slugging match provided the world's music media with acres of juicy newsprint and gave fans some quite incredible moments of artistry. The timespan of this book is 1979–1997, with an added reunion history leading up to December 2005. Black Sabbath, Ozzy and Iommi, finally gave up the struggle and relented to the inevitable in 1997.

Tony Iommi, one of the most influential guitarists of our age. A man who is as cardinal as he is condescending, Iommi's status is comfortably within the elite echelons occupied by Beck, Clapton, Page, Blackmore and Hendrix. Without Tony Iommi, thousands of guitarists who have forced their attentions onto us over the past two decades would probably never have picked up their first instrument in the first place. He is largely unaccredited, yet Tony Iommi virtually single handedly invented the Metal riff. Although the arch spellbinder Jimi Hendrix had paved the way with his mercurial zest, Jimmy Page had skryed his malevolence and mystique it was to be Tony Iommi, stacking notes in unfamiliar yet bludgeoningly hypnotic patterns, that crafted the bombastic beast known today as Heavy Metal.

Ozzy Osbourne is undoubtedly an enigma. Too often dismissed by the ignorant as an ailing buffoon, this self-deprecating giant of the scene has played an equally large part in shaping Heavy Metal. Quite frankly, removing Ozzy Osbourne from the equation and the Hard Rock movement might just collapse like the walls of Jericho. Although the general public knows Ozzy as the Prince of Daftness, the bat biting, ant snorting TV antihero, those with a musical persuasion know that contribution to the Heavy Metal genre is simply staggering. Once all the questions as to Ozzy's abilities remain unanswered the cold truth is that there is nobody else on the planet that could have fronted Black Sabbath's 70s glory years. Detractors might want to indulge themselves in Black Sabbath's first illustrious quartet of albums to rediscover the sheer unbridled power of Ozzy's vocals.

Between 1979 and 1997 Black Sabbath's fortunes peaked and troughed like a Himalayan survey map. The ride was so erratic most failed to stay onboard. Indeed, only Geoff Nicholls completed the journey from start to finish. Somehow, a white knuckled Tony Iommi, sole possessor of the trademark 'Black Sabbath', hung on for grim death and press-ganged more passengers to climb aboard at every junction. At times Black Sabbath was populated with the very elite of the Rock cognoscenti, at others Iommi fronted up a gaggle of equally talented but relatively anonymous players.

Quite how Tony Iommi managed to craft the superb slices of art that were 'Eternal Idol', 'Born Again', 'Seventh Star', 'Headless Cross', 'Tyr' and 'Cross Purposes' throughout this turmoil is a testament to the man's tenacity. His creativity failed him only at the very end, 'Forbidden' landing leaden like a maggot bloated hog carcass in a mediaeval gutter. Sabbath fans could sense the end had been and gone as soon as they clocked the cartoon cover art. One suspects that if only the band had been allowed to just get on with it then this album too would have ranked amongst the best Metal has to offer. By that stage though, Iommi was dealing with two opposing messages, one surreally whispering 'Aerosmith / Run DMC' whilst the other was screaming 'Ozzy!'

In early 1979 though all these tribulations, and more, lay in the future.

To learn about Black Sabbath's earlier history, pre-1979, I recommend you read the excellent 'How Black Was Our Sabbath' by Dave Tangye and Graham Wright. Please note that the introductory chapter of this book is intended just as a reminder of the 70s glory years, leading into some of the offshoots and branches that would figure later in the story.

Ozzy, despite a knack for discovering some of the very finest guitarists of the age, had simply been unable to replace the riffmeister Tony Iommi. When such figures as Randy Rhoads, Jake E. Lee and Zakk Wylde do not suffice then, with Iommi, you are simply dealing with the irreplaceable. For Tony Iommi's part he too endeavoured to fill the awning gap left by Osbourne by drawing in vocalists of superhuman quality. However, the talent levels of Dio, Gillan, Hughes and Martin, amongst others, could not quash the legend of Ozzy.

I had my first biography, 'The story of the Ozzy Osbourne band', published just as 'The Osbournes' TV series broke big. Although my book had been finished months previous to this, the then publishers delayed and the book was distributed only after every other publisher on the planet had put out their quick fire, cash-in Ozzy titles. The American distribution, what there was of it, was pathetic to say the least. It was frustrating dealing with emails from people who simply could not get hold of the book.

Assured that U.S. distribution had been secured, the same company released my next biography 'Black Sabbath—Never Say Die'. Only upon release did I discover that there was, in fact, no North American distribution whatsoever. They also forgot to edit it.

Due to multiple breaches of contract by the original publishers the rights reverted back to myself. My lawyer suggested I put the two books together, add new interviews, and get the damn thing distributed properly. This is the book you now hold. If it was a record it would be a re-mastered compilation, with bonus tracks.

Contributions

Whilst writing this book it quickly became apparent that the Sabbath / Ozzy story unfolds into a never-ending saga. Every time I thought the darn thing was finished, something else arrived in my inbox or someone else telephoned. Therefore, I'm planning on periodically updating this book every few years or so. If you have anything to contribute, if you're a musician that features in the story, or have photographs you want to share please get in touch. Which brings me onto further projects ...

There are further Sabbath titles underway. If you have pictures or stories from all periods of the band's history please drop me a line.

Garry Sharpe–Young, March 2006.
garry@rockdetector.com

Overview of Chapters

Chapter 1, *Sabbath Bloody Sabbath.* The classic four. Early outside dabblings with Necromandus. The first 'Blizzard of Ozz'. Dirty Tricks & Ozzy.

Chapter 2, *Killing Yourself To Live.* 1979. Black Sabbath implodes. Geoff Nicholls and the World of Oz. Quartz. The induction of Ronnie James Dio. The making of 'Heaven And Hell'.

Chapter 3, *The Reluctant Wizard.* Randy Rhoads—Katzenjammer Kids to Quiet Riot to Blizzard Of Ozz. Enter Bob Daisley. 'Heaven And Hell' sees release. Lee Kerslake joins Ozzy.

Chapter 4, *"It's A Band".* 1980. Blizzard Of Ozz record debut. Black Sabbath tour behind 'Heaven And Hell' in Europe and USA. Exit Bill Ward, enter Vinny Appice. Blizzard adds Lindsey Bridgwater. The making of 'Diary Of A Madman' and 'Mob Rules'.

Chapter 5, *An Englishman's Castle.* 1981–1982. Ozzy tours the USA with Rudy Sarzo and Tommy Aldridge. Black Sabbath's 'Mob Rules' tour. UFO and dwarf abuse. The death of Randy Rhoads. Bernie Tormé.

Chapter 6, *Hair By Sarzo Of Cuba, Way To Go.* Bernie Tormé hands over to Brad Gillis. Things get wild with Pete Way. Bridgwater is back.

Chapter 7, *Enter Jake.* 1983. Studio capers with 'Live Evil'. 'Speak Of The Devil'. 'Holy Diver'. The Costa cheesegrater. Ozzy recruits Jake E. Lee.

Chapter 8, *Born Under A Black Moon.* "Gillun joins Sabbuf". 'Born Again'. 'Bark At The Moon'.

Chapter 9, *Carmine Feels The Noise.* Carmine Appice joins Ozzy. Don Airey replaces Lindsey Bridgwater.

Chapter 10, *Headless.* Ron Keel. Sabbath search for a singer.

Chapter 11, *Zero The Hero.* David Donato. The missing six months. Geezer quits. Live Aid 1985.

Chapter 12, *Jesus Christ, Supertzar.* Jeff Fenholt—was he or wasn't he?

Chapter 13, *The Ultimate Din.* Fred Coury demos with Ozzy. Randy Castillo, Phil Soussan and John Sinclair complete the band. 'The Ultimate Sin'.

Chapter 14, *'Seventh Star'—Hughes Next?* Glenn Hughes, Dave Spitz and Eric Singer 'Black Sabbath featuring Tony Iommi'.

Chapter 15, *Gillen Not Gillan.* 1986. The 'Seventh Star' tour. Ray Gillen. The Geezer Butler band. 'Eternal Idol' rehearsals.

Chapter 16, *Blacky Sabb: Caribbean Speedballs.* Recording 'Eternal Idol' in Montserrat. Gillen out, Spitz out. Badlands. Zakk Wylde joins Ozzy. Jimi Bell and Geezer Butler.

Chapter 17, *Idolatry.* 1987. Tony 'The Cat' Martin. The 'Eternal Idol' tour. South Africa. Terry Chimes and Jo Burt.

Chapter 18, *No Rest For The Headless.* 1988. Lita Ford and Ozzy's biggest single. Cozy Powell and Neil Murray. 'Headless Cross'. Sabbath in Russia.

Chapter 19, *A Last Tyr Goodbye.* 'Tyr' to 'Dehumanizer'. No more tours, Ozzy "retires".

Chapter 20, *No More Dio.* 1992. The 'Dehumanizer' tour and Costa Mesa. Rob Halford sings for Black Sabbath. Cozy Powell's Hammer. Ray Gillen contracts AIDS.

Chapter 21, *Vai–able Options.* 1993. The Ozzy / Steve Vai X-Ray project. Bobby Rondinelli. 'Cross Purposes'.

Chapter 22, *Skol?* Joe Holmes replaces Zakk. Alex Skolnick and the secret gig. Geezer's 'Plastic Planet'.

Chapter 23, *A Forbidding Farewell.* The 'Forbidden' album. Bobby Rondinelli rejoins. 'Ozzmosis'

Chapter 24, *Reunion.* 'Eighth Star'. 'Black Science'. Ozzy, Tony, Geezer and Bill reunite. The death of Cozy Powell. 'Ozzfest'.

Ozzy with Sabbath in 1978. Pic: Rich Galbraith.

Chapter 1

Sabbath Bloody Sabbath

Cited by most to be THE original Heavy Metal band, Black Sabbath has had an unquestionably massive influence on the genre and has sold countless millions of albums. Black Sabbath, steered into their chosen doom / occult leanings by bassist and songwriter Geezer Butler, impose an enormous legacy upon the Heavy Metal scene. Guitarist Tony Iommi has laid down many of the classic all time riffs and is a versatile Blues inspired musician revered as a guitar hero despite having lost some fingertips in a 1966 machine accident, which nearly put paid to his chosen career. With such a huge profusion of Metal in all its myriad of genres pouring out onto the market these days, it is often all too easy to forget exactly why, when and how the whole landslide kicked off. Just thirty seconds into the opening track off 'Black Sabbath' will bring you back to your senses with a refreshing clarity.

The aural superstructure of Black Sabbath was shaped by the quite sublime rhythm section of Messrs. Butler and Ward. Too often portrayed by the pompous and the ignorant as bludgeoning, bumbling barbarians these two provided a mainframe on which the Sabbath classics hung that is sometimes menacing, often subtle and delicate. Quite simply, Butler and Ward are superb musicians. Black Sabbath's ill earned reputation for wallowing in a murky, Neanderthal soup of simplicity is blown away by anyone adventurous to actually purchase and listen.

Until 1978 the band was fronted by the irrepressible Ozzy Osbourne. Now renowned as one of the true legends of Metal from his Black Sabbath years and his subsequent, massively successful solo career Osbourne's trademark vocal style and outrageous on and off stage behaviour have gained the Brummie true Rock idol status.

Manifested during 1967 in Aston, deep in the heart of industrial Birmingham, a skinhead singer then known as Ozzy Zig, guitarist Anthony Frank Iommi, bassist Terry 'Geezer' Butler and drummer Bill Ward first united, albeit briefly, under the name Polka Tulk Blues Band. Osbourne's first attempts at singing came just after leaving school when, together with guitarist Jimmy Phillips, he founded the short-lived act The Prospectors. Previously, Iommi and Ward had been part of The Rest, a proto-band fronted by erstwhile Method Five vocalist Chris Smith. The group later changed its name to Mythology.

Osbourne and Butler, the latter a rhythm guitarist at this point, were members of Rare Breed, an act that lasted a mere two gigs. Antecedent to this, Osbourne had stints with local bands The Black Panthers and Approach as well as having served a short term in the foreboding Winson Green prison for burglary. It was during his incarceration at Her Majesty's pleasure that the singer gave himself his now famous 'Ozzy' and smiley face tattoos by rubbing floor cleaning paste into his skin.

The catalyst came for the quartet joining forces when Mythology lost both singer and drummer. With the acquisition of Osbourne and Ward, Mythology changed its title to Music Machine, drawing in saxophonist Alan Clark and Jimmy Phillips on slide guitar. Before long the Handsworth based Music Machine became the Polka Tulk Blues Band and had been whittled down to a quartet, with Butler adopting a new role as bass player by crudely taking two strings off his lead guitar. Phillips meanwhile would go onto become a keyboard player, performing with a variety of diverse Birmingham acts such as Purple Onion, Frog and Magic Roundabout. Within a short space of time the revised band had altered their moniker to the truncated Polka Tulk before another name change was enforced, the foursome evolving into Earth.

Contracting a management deal with Jim Simpson (who later was to manage fellow Brummies Judas Priest) the band got into the grind of playing the Rock and Blues clubs. Their first taste of Europe came when Simpson booked a tour of Germany. These shows included a date at Hamburg's infamous Star club (the once famous haunt of The Beatles), before getting the band in a four track studio to record their first demo. This recording, featuring the tracks 'Song For Jim' and 'The Rebel' in 1969, enabled the band to gain a deal with the then 'Pro-

Mythology 1968 featuring Tony Iommi (back).

gressive Rock' experimental label Vertigo Records, an arm of Fontana Records. Earth had already put in an appearance in the capitol with a batch of gigs at the legendary Marquee club in March of 1969.

Upon signing they were to discover that another act called Earth had just released a single in Germany, thus necessitating a name change. According to legend it was a Dennis Wheatley novel that inspired Butler to come up with Black Sabbath. Despite the deal, Black Sabbath were financially in difficult times and it was at this point that Iommi actually left to join Jethro Tull for all of two weeks, to replace the departed Mick Abrahams.

Although Iommi's stay in Jethro Tull was brief he did appear with the band at the legendary Rolling Stones 'Rock n' Roll Circus' film session. However, he was soon back in the fold and Black Sabbath recorded their first Rodger Bain produced album for a miserly £600 on a four track machine. (Interesting to note as an aside, that the engineer for the first two albums was none other than 'Colonel' Tom Allom, later to find fame as a producer for Judas Priest).

The band's first product as Black Sabbath sunk without trace. A single, 'Wicked Woman (Don't Play Your Evil Games With Me)', a cover of the Minnesota band Crow's track, had seen a release in January 1970. However, in February, the album 'Black Sabbath' emerged upon an unsuspecting world. Laden with many what are now widely regarded as all time classics; such as 'Black Sabbath', 'The Wizard' and 'N.I.B.' The latter was allegedly at the time thought to be 'Nativity In Black' but actually a strange reference to the shape of Bill Ward's beard! The album's almost Neanderthal bludgeoning heaviness and thick industrial riffing took Rock fans by storm. Quite simply the band had delivered a unique brand of Hard Rock on the unsuspecting masses. The debut reached Number 8 in the British charts with virtually no assistance from radio airplay.

Live dates to promote the album saw the band opening up proceedings in Cardiff. The British tour would include such salubrious venues as the East Ham Dukes Head, Salisbury's Alexis Disco and the Croydon Greyhound. Black Sabbath would venture into Germany, appearing at festivals alongside Rory Gallagher, Deep Purple, Free, Status Quo and Black Widow. The band also played later British shows including a support to Pink Floyd. The group returned to Germany in August.

Shortly after wrapping up recording for their second album in June of 1970, provisionally titled 'War Pigs', again with Rodger Bain, in August 1970 Black Sabbath played the 10th Plumpton Jazz and Blues festival alongside Humble Pie and Yes. Prior to the album release the record company changed the album title to 'Paranoid'. The record company objected to 'War Pigs' due to the prevailing Vietnam war and also as there was a feeling 'Paranoid' could be a possible hit. The 'War Pigs' title itself had been changed, the original composition entitled 'Walpurgis'.

The single 'Paranoid' reached Number 4, (which still remains Black Sabbath's biggest single hit to date), with the album reaching the dizzy heights of Number 1! The album, with the now more renowned classics such as 'Hand Of Doom', 'Faeries Wear Boots' and 'Iron Man', had Black Sabbath exploring a much more varied field of interests than its predecessor's predilection for the occult.

In America the second album reached Number 12 and settled in for a long chart stay, eventually clocking up a sixty five week residency. The band's first American shows also occurred, with support slots to Leslie West's Mountain prior to a headline tour.

There would be virtually no respite for the quartet as live promotion for the sophomore outing saw the band back on the road in the UK during September starting off in Wales yet again—this time at the Swansea Branwygn Hall. Three shows in Switzerland were undertaken before a short burst of live activity in the low countries and by October Black Sabbath were putting in inaugural gigs in Scandinavia. The close of the month witnessed another first as a Philadelphia appearance signaled the start of a long trail of roadwork in the United States. Black

Sabbath's first American trip would also see a run of three San Francisco Fillmore West gigs opening up for Arthur Lee's Love and the James Gang. As 1971 drew in so did another stream of British dates. Black Sabbath would prove nowhere was safe with gigs in New Zealand and Australia upfront of a return visit to America and then Europe once again.

With the album's success came a valuable indicator to the band of the international potential of Black Sabbath. In a rather messy legal wrangle, the band wriggled out of their management contract with Jim Simpson and signed up to Wilf Pine and Patrick Meehan, both of whom had been previously with the Arden Management company.

August 1971 saw the release of the last Rodger Bain produced Black Sabbath album 'Master Of Reality'. The record peaked at Number 5 in the British charts, but provided the band with a strong "out of the box" seller in America, being certified gold before its release.

The band backed up this success Stateside by a lengthy bout of touring, which by this time was beginning to take its toll both mentally and physically on the individual members. 'Volume 4' (originally to be titled 'Snowblind') gave the band another top ten British album and featured the classic ballad 'Changes', featuring Yes keyboard player Rick Wakeman, alongside the more brutal 'Snowblind'.

Black Sabbath made another trip to New Zealand in early January 1973 gearing up for the by now familiar American dates. An Italian tour was completed and by March it was back for another round in Great Britain. Quite surreally Black Sabbath would also make their presence felt at the Cascais Jazz Festival in Portugal.

The band returned to America to work on 'Volume 4's follow-up but found for the first time their flow of ideas had ebbed. Relocating to rehearse in the suitably spooky setting of a Welsh castle dungeon Iommi came up with the classic riff for the track 'Sabbath Bloody Sabbath' and the creative juices started to flow once more. In late 1973 Black Sabbath released the renowned 'Sabbath Bloody Sabbath' album to worldwide critical acclaim.

For live work, keyboard player Jezz Woodruffe was added and Black Sabbath put in one of their most important American appearances at the California Jam festival in 1974 alongside Emerson Lake & Palmer and Deep Purple playing to an audience of over quarter of a million people.

However, touring excesses and managerial nightmares had taken the band to breaking point, with Iommi and Osbourne becoming ever more confrontational. By now the band had shifted their business affairs to the notorious Don Arden. 1975's 'Sabotage' kept the flame alive and the band put in another enormous American tour supported by Kiss. The 'Sabotage' album included a rarity for the band as initial copies included an unaccredited track 'Blow On A Jug'. This was actually Bill Ward singing the Nitty Gritty Dirt Band track captured unawares by a studio engineer. Later pressings do not include this moment.

The compilation 'We Sold Our Souls For Rock n' Roll' charted well too, but many thought the 1976 experimental effort 'Technical Ecstasy' to be way below par. The album did include a first for the band though as Ward took lead vocals for the first time ever on the track 'It's Alright'. American dates saw the band on the road supported by the unlikely duo of REO Speedwagon and The Ramones. Then the unspeakable happened. In the middle of rehearsals Ozzy left.

With the inevitable disintegration of Black Sabbath in the late 70s Ozzy had motivated himself to set about creating a fresh band. Ozzy's personal assistant at the time was Dave 'Tang' Tangye, who also happened to manage Cumbrian heavy Rock band Necromandus. Created under the original name of Hot Spring Water the quartet comprised of vocalist Bill Branch, guitarist Barry Dunnery, bass player Dennis McCarten and drummer Frank Hall. A name change to Heavy Hand led eventually to Necromandus, a fusing of Nostradamus and Necromancy.

Frank Hall's first memories of Ozzy Osbourne date as far back as 1969. Black Sabbath would often play the gig circuit around the Lake District and it would be at one of the bands very first gigs that Ozzy came to the fore. "I first clapped eyes on Ozzy at the Towbar club in Nethertown in Cumbria" the drummer recalls. His memories of an Ozzy pre the fame and adulation about to break upon Black Sabbath are in stark contrast to the onstage persona that would come to be known by millions. "I remember talking to Bill Ward who told me "He's not long been out of prison" to which I replied "Better to break into music than houses I suppose!" Ozzy was a dramatic figure. He was really like a wild man. Onstage he used to whip his head up and down really, really fast and put his finger in his ear while he sang! I noticed he soon stopped doing that! The thing was though is that he was in fact a really friendly bloke, actually quite shy and nervous."

Ozzy's evolving dress sense, rarely captured in photographs during the formative years, would also give cause for concern. "In the early days he would always go onstage barefoot. God knows why. He certainly had a presence all of his own. I don't know why I remember this but he was wearing black corduroy trousers at that first gig. His hair was this long brown shaggy Rod Stewart kind of cut, spiky on top." This is not to say Frank too would not get caught up

Classic Black Sabbath—Ozzy, Geezer, Tony & Bill.

in the Rock n' Roll image stakes. "I had very long black hair and I would wear a black raven's feather in it" he admits. "People would say 'What tribe are you from?'"

Tony Iommi too would make an impression for reasons out of keeping with his media persona. "Tony is a great practical joker" Frank confides. "Both he and Ozzy are very, very funny but in different ways. Tony would often wind Ozzy up by putting eggs in his bed every night." (As we shall see this jape would pass from victor to victim in later years).

Besides playing together on the live circuit the band already had a strong Black Sabbath connection having cut a 1973 album 'Orexis Of Death' for Vertigo Records during 1973 with Tony Iommi at the production helm. The Black Sabbath guitarist also had Necromandus signed up to his Tramp agency. Also involved with the agency were Judas Priest manager Dave Corke, one of the undisputed maverick legends of Rock management, and Norman Hood. Necromandus would tour the Midlands area with Judas Priest as support band. "Judas Priest had Al Atkins singing back then" Frank Hall affirms. "They did a lot of gigs with us and they had this great drummer, a black guy called Chris Campbell. Their manager Dave Corke would always buy my clothes from me for some odd reason. I would walk into the agency office with a pair of jeans and a denim jacket and Dave would say "How much do you want for those?" So I'd sell them and walk out virtually naked. Dave was a Hell of a character. Once he organised this freshman's ball gig with Necromandus, Vivian Stanshell and Keith Moon. As you can imagine it turned into a night of absolute lunacy."

The Necromandus album has been a constant source of fascination for Black Sabbath fanatics. Frank unveils the makings of a bona fide lost classic. "There were two attempts at making the album. The first was at the Marquee Studios at the back of the Marquee club and the second was in Blue Mink's Morgan Studios. The first time we came out with some pretty scrappy songs so Tony Iommi more or less said 'Go away and come up with some better songs.'" The material Necromandus came up with was strong. Hall describes the bands music as 'Progressive Rock' not too far removed from today's acts such as Spock's Beard or Dream Theater.

Finally getting down to recording Necromandus found they were not the only ones ensconced in Morgan Studios. "Yes were there recording 'Topographic Oceans'." Hall recalls. "I saw Jon Anderson walking in the middle of the street one day and told him "You're from The Warriors!" I used to go and see him with that band before he joined Yes. As you can imagine he was quite surprised. Well, Jon and I got talking and he introduced me to Rick Wakeman." The world renowned keyboard maestro was doubling up on duties at the time recording for Yes

Necromandus, managed and produced by Tony Iommi and featuring three members of the original Blizzard Of Ozz.

and mixing his own solo work 'The Six Wives Of Henry VIII'. Necromandus were on the night shift starting work at 9 in the evening and emerging as dawn broke at 5 o'clock in the morning.

Frank was forthright in his approach to Rick. "Necromandus had this one track which I really thought could benefit from an outro using cellos, violins and keyboards so being cheeky I asked Rick if he would do it. I really got into his ribs about it, really pestered him but in the end it turned out he wanted to do it anyway. "Yes" he said "I'll do it for a crate of Guinness!" Rick actually thought it was a good idea."

This union never transpired though as Frank relates. "When I told Tony that Rick wanted to put piano on this song he simply didn't believe me. Tony's first question was "What does he want." He thought Rick would charge us megabucks. I told him he only wanted a crate of Guinness but it just didn't happen because Tony thought I was only joking and naturally thought too much money would be involved. I'm sure Rick would have done it for the beer."

The focal point of Necromandus was always guitarist Barry 'Baz' Dunnery. Although never to break into the public arena, Dunnery's talents left many open mouthed in astonishment. "He was incredibly fast" reckons Hall. "I remember Steve Howe being very impressed as Baz was going through his legato runs and speed picking. I'll never forget that look on Steve's face, like, fucking Hell! What's he doing?"

Ozzy's reputation for targeting guitarists with exceptional abilities was evident even then. With Black Sabbath on a global commercial high the singer had nevertheless earmarked Dunnery as Frank Hall explains. "Everyone knows Baz's brother Francis from It Bites but believe me Baz leaves his brother standing. Baz was, and is, a fantastic guitarist. Both Ozzy and Glenn Hughes really rated him. Ozzy, I'll never forget, really tried to push Baz. He told Baz that he had the world at his feet."

Iommi himself would guest on one track though putting guitar down on 'One Fine Lad', a song about army life. However, Frank has some problems with remembering which song was which because, for a reason the drummer never discovered, all of the song titles would be changed. "The first Necromandus single was to be 'Don't Look Down Frank', a song about me. For some reason, that title got changed to 'Nightjar'. All the titles were changed."

With Black Sabbath riding high internationally, an Iommi production credit, a guitar hero in the making and signed to a major label it seemed as though the future looked bright indeed for Necromandus. It was not to be. 'Orexis Of Death' was shelved. The reasoning behind the decision remained a mystery for nearly three decades. "The album was axed because Baz left the band" Frank sighs resignedly. "He said that he didn't want to go but he felt he had a conflict with the musical direction of the band. This was our big chance. We just couldn't understand it at all. We were devastated."

With Dunnery out of the picture Iommi thought Necromandus was dead in the water. "We offered to try and get another guitarist as good as Baz but Tony thought this would be unlikely. He was right. We tried to get someone to keep the band going and get the album out but it was just impossible. Then of course Black Sabbath got back out onto the road so Tony was busy with that and the whole thing was just forgotten."

Frank though was picked out by Glenn Hughes, vocalist for renowned Funk Rockers Trapeze. "Glenn was always asking for Necromandus to open for Trapeze. He asked me to consider joining the band because he could see things were shaky with Necromandus. I was just so low and disappointed by the whole thing at that point I went back home."

The 'Orexis Of Death' album would remain consigned to the vaults until the late 90s when curiosity regarding all things Doom prompted its semi-official release on a series of small labels. With Necromandus consigned to the history books Hall travelled back up to his native Cumbria soon reforging links with Dunnery in a band called Nerves. At first a covers act Nerves, with Steven Hatfield on keyboards and Don McKay on vocals, would evolve into the hard edged R&B outfit Tantrum. Hall's musical career gradually fizzled out and the drummer would find himself working on a building site to make ends meet. Returning home from work one day in 1976 he would be given a jolt to see a familiar car outside his house.

"I recognized it straight away" he declares. "It was Ozzy's Range Rover. I got inside the house and there in my living room was Dave Tangye—Ozzy's P.A, Baz and one other guy." Frank and Dave Tangye went back a long way. "I actually got Dave the job with Ozzy" Frank maintains. "Ozzy asked me one day if I knew of someone to mind him and I suggested Dave straight away. I told Ozzy he was totally trustworthy and you can rely on him. Dave became Ozzy's P.A. and minder for many years."

Dave Tangye broke the news. Frank remembers the exact words. "Right, Ozzy wants a guitarist, bassist and drummer and you lot in Necromandus are the likely candidates." Piling into Ozzy's car the new recruits journeyed down to Staffordshire and Ozzy's home at Bullrush Cottage. Enter Blizzard Of Ozz . . .

The original incarnation of Blizzard Of Ozz was in an enviable position. Ozzy was a globally known figure and with Baz Dunnery the quartet was blessed with a world class guitarist. Frank Hall had many reasons to be optimistic. "Ozzy had a lot of offers on the table from a few record companies. The potential was just huge at that point because the press would jump on any new Ozzy album. Ozzy was really keen to show the world how good Baz was too. The band was called Blizzard Of Ozz right from the start. There was one label in particular who were talking about very large advances, not just for Ozzy, but for all of us."

The musical persuasion of the inaugural Blizzard Of Ozz was not what the average Black Sabbath fan would have ever anticipated though as Frank elaborates. "Necromandus was always a kind of progressive, Jazzy type Rock band. I suppose you could put us in the same camp as GreenSlade or Gentle Giant—that type of thing. We didn't actually change much when we worked up the songs with Ozzy. Some of the material was extremely complex, lots of time changes and it sounded great. Ozzy of course wanted heavyweight detuned guitars all the time but the combination really was striking."

The band spent over a month working up new songs and gathered together some 15 or so, enough to be whittled down for a full album's compliment. The chaotic circumstances prevailing in Ozzy's personal and business life would take their toll though. "Ozzy was having a really hard time dealing with a lot of Black Sabbath stuff, his personal life and management troubles too. He had an awful lot to contend with." Frank confirms.

Naturally these early sessions would be peppered with famous Ozzy tomfoolery. "It was a fun summer!" the drummer laughs. "I don't know how we managed to get so much work done actually. Ozzy would often seek what he called "Inspiration" at his local pub the 'Hand & Cleaver'. By the time he got back around 11 at night he would want to rehearse!

I remember one night Ozzy got really bothered by rats. He had this old dog kennel thing at the back of his house and he was obsessed with the idea it was full of rats. Well, he had been talking about rats all day and then suddenly I saw him marching off to this kennel with a can in his hand. "Where are you going with that petrol can John?" I said. Before I could stop him he had covered this thing with petrol and set light to it. Now, Ozzy was growing a beard at the time and he was standing far too close to this building when he lit it. Boof! It went up in flames and the flames all blew back on Ozzy. When turned round he had singed all his beard and eyebrows!"

Frank would witness another Ozzy trick that had the band members fearing for their singer's life. "There was a field at the back of Ozzy's place that he rented out to the local football team. In the corner of this field was a large pond. Well, one day Ozzy got into his Range Rover and, God knows why, drove straight into the middle of this pond! Ozzy thought it was hilarious until he realized the car was stuck in the mud. Not only that but it was sinking with Ozzy in it! I mean—it was going down fast! We thankfully got him out but it he had to wait for his car until the farmer pulled it out in the morning with his tractor."

The band did manage to prevent one of Ozzy's potentially near fatal exploits though. "We were having this big barbecue one day" Frank reminisces. "Ozzy is a great cook and would come up with these fantastic curries. God knows what he would put in them because we would feel stoned for days afterwards! Anyway, we were eating and this helicopter was flying low over Ozzy's house which really bothered him. I seem to remember he thought it was the press trying to get some pictures. Ozzy, as I'm sure you know, loved shotguns. So, he marched into his house and got out this Remington pump action shotgun and started to fire at the bloody helicopter! We just managed to stop him but he did get a few shots at the thing."

All these exploits (and many more besides) were naturally having a serious effect on the work schedule. "Baz got very disillusioned with it all. We spoke one night and agreed to move out. It was a shame because the music was great—I could still sit down and play it. Ozzy was obviously having to deal with too many things at once. Baz was being approached by other bands at the time—he was asked to replace

Peter Banks in Flash. Some friends of mine from Barrow In Furness knew Phil Collins well and had recommended me for the position in Genesis. They liked my Jazz Rock style but of course I was with Ozzy at the time and had to decline the offer."

The Blizzard Of Ozz split up. McCarten joined Birmingham band Grit while Dunnery and Hall refounded Nerves up in Cumbria. There was little in the way of hard feelings though and Hall, along with his parents, would be invited to Ozzy's house for a mammoth celebratory bash in honour of the Queen's silver jubilee in 1977. This is when the drummer would discover Ozzy had other strings to his bow besides singing.

"For that party the house was totally crammed. Hundreds of people" he recounts. "My Mum and Dad were in awe. My Mum always tells people that she slept in Ozzy's bed. She did actually, Ozzy let her have his big four poster covered in carved gargoyles for the night. That day I found John in his sitting room. Now he had this very impressive and extremely expensive Steinway piano in there. Ozzy showed me that there were more ways than one to play it. I couldn't believe my eyes when he climbed up on top of it. He stood on it and urinated inside it. He was playing the strings by directing this endless stream of urine trying to get a tune! We were in absolute hysterics and I was pushing against the door as hard as I could praying my Mother wouldn't try to come in!" Beat that Keith Emerson. In later years Dunnery would become a member of the Electric Light Orchestra offshoot Violinski whilst Hall journeyed through many acts and has played most recently with Jazz band The Children. By 2002 he would be touting his own project The Binmen led by former Sweet singer Malcolm McNulty.

Meanwhile, with the Necromandus musicians no longer on the scene, Ozzy had another stab at reforging the Blizzard Of Ozz. His manager, the ubiquitous Don Arden, had discovered that a band an acquaintance of his handled business affairs for were in limbo. That band was Dirty Tricks, signed up to Polydor Records, Argent's manager Roger Myers and just having completed a run of three albums, the first of which happened to be produced by Rodger Bain, the man responsible for the early Black Sabbath albums. The band comprised of vocalist Kenny Stewart, guitarist John Fraser Binnie, bass player Terry Horbury and drummer Andy Bierne. The group had returned to the UK from a lengthy bout of touring in America supporting a series of major acts such as Blue Oyster Cult and Cheap Trick to record their third album. Arden played Ozzy these new Dirty Tricks tapes, for the Tony Visconti produced 'Hit And Run' album, to favourable response and a meeting was duly arranged.

Dirty Tricks bassist Terry Horbury takes up the tale. "Dirty Tricks had split really but the three of us, myself, John and Andy stuck together planning on starting another band. Our manager had decided he wanted out of the business but unfortunately would not let us out of contract so we were in an impossible situation. It wasn't just that. Punk and New Wave had come in and really set us back too. For Dirty Tricks to do a gig we'd need our full crew, etc. which was costly but these new bands would just turn up and plug in. Basically we were in a jam. What happened though was that we got the call to meet up with Ozzy. We first met him in Don Arden's office in London, we all had a banter then arranged to travel up to Ozzy's house near Stafford to get some songs together.

So, we all went up to Ozzy's place. I think all in all we stayed there three weeks. I remember that almost as soon as we arrived Ozzy seemed distracted by something outside the window. Next thing we knew he's grabbed this shotgun and then we see he's crawling along the hedgerow like a commando. Well, after a time he came back with this dead partridge he'd just shot. He just stood there with a big grin on his face dripping blood all over our guitarist's wah wah pedal. That was our Ozzy greeting if you like."

Dubbed 'Atrocity Cottage', Ozzy's abode, at the end of Butt Lane in Ranton, was strategically positioned within short walking distance of a pub, the Hand & Cleaver. "It was quite a house" relates Horbury. "In the yard Ozzy had this big bus he had bought. He was in the middle of turning it into a tour bus. He's ripped out all the seats and was painting it black inside and out. Ozzy had Marshall amps and cabs everywhere, which for poor musicians like us were the holy grail, but he was using them for tables! Oddly though, despite the Marshalls everywhere else, he had no P.A. set up in the actual rehearsal room. What he did have in there was a Revox tape recorder, a microphone and a large stuffed bear which looked like it had been attacked a few times!"

There would be no hint of the former material in use as this new proto Blizzard Of Ozz started from scratch writing new material. "It was a bit like an old Blues session really because the only way Ozzy could record was through this Revox. We'd be blaring away and we could see him singing, reading ideas from his lyric books he had, but not hear him. It was only when we played the tapes back we got the full picture." Terry remembers distinctly the name 'Blizzard Of Ozz" being mentioned as the moniker for the band. Pointedly no Black Sabbath material was attempted. "I don't ever recall doing any Sabbath songs. Ozzy said that we would probably do 'Paranoid' as an encore or something but he wanted all new stuff. I think all in all we got about half a dozen songs together. It was good stuff, just good solid Hard Rock. I've still got tapes of the rehearsals."

The problem was that, to be truthful, Ozzy really wasn't in the best shape to get a band together at that time. We would be ready to work at 10:30 but Ozzy wouldn't wake until midday and then he'd go down to the local pub until 4. Glenn Hughes came round once while we were there. I'll never forget it." Glenn Hughes, a man fully deserving of the appellation 'legendary' for his works with Trapeze, Deep Purple and subsequently Black Sabbath, expands upon the historical tradition of friendship and camaraderie that placed him in the frame at that juncture. "Trapeze and Black Sabbath had been on the same circuit locally for years. All around the West Midlands Trapeze would be playing the exact same clubs as Black Sabbath so we had known each other for years and years. That whole crowd—John Bonham, Robert Plant, us and Black Sabbath. Although the music was very different, because we had that loose Funk thing going on and Sabbath was kind of ultra heavy we had a basic respect for each other. Because the bands were so different we could afford to be friends too because Trapeze was no competition to Black Sabbath but we had common bonds. We all hung out together, I would go to Ozzy's house, he would come to my place and we were just good friends. I lived in Penkridge in Cannock and Ozzy lived just down the road. As the years went on I always kept an eye on what they were doing just because they were local."

Glenn is happy to add some depth to these recollections. "Yeah, I was around at Ozzy's house a lot in '77 when he was first trying to put that Blizzard Of Ozz band together. We spoke quite a bit about forming a band too but I don't think we could ever really get beyond the fact that we were both singers so could not find a way of making it work. I was also working on my solo record 'Play Me Out' too, I had just come out of this huge Rock band Deep Purple and really wanted to do my own thing. I could see Ozzy needed to go it alone too but I guess he was looking for some support from a friend. We were both young then and, in truth, both completely screwed up too."

Horbury is in agreement that the prevailing circumstances did not lend themselves to the discipline of creating a new band unit. "With Ozzy it's just so easy to forget because he was full on all the time. Every five minutes he would tell us a hilarious story about his past. One of the few I remember was that apparently one day Ozzy and Geezer were standing next to each other at the urinals having a piss. Ozzy, for some reason, had a can of silver spray paint in his pocket so he whips this out and sprays Geezer's manhood with it! Of course Geezer couldn't do anything because he was in mid stream so just had to stand there while he was sprayed silver! We'd get about a hundred stories like that every day. So much so that we actually had some serious discussions between the three of us just what we were letting ourselves in for!

Ozzy was having a real hard time of it really. Money was a big problem, Ozzy even told us it would be a good idea if we all signed on the dole in Birmingham!" The three musicians suggested to Ozzy that rather than travelling to Staffordshire it would be more practical to pursue matters in London. "Ozzy thought this was a good idea too so I went ahead and booked a month's rehearsal at The Tunnel studios for us" relates Terry. "The day before we were scheduled to go in I phoned Ozzy to make arrangements and he simply said "Oh, I've just rejoined Black Sabbath." So that was that."

After their Ozzy adventure the Dirty Tricks musicians would all follow differing paths. Binnie wound up with the much vaunted Rogue Male. Horbury and Bierne would work with Alvin Lee for a while before the bassist hooked up with German ex-UFO guitarist Michael Schenker then the Steve Zodiac led Vardis. He would also become acquainted with another figure in the Ozzy saga—Bob Daisley.

"There was a time when Bob was in Uriah Heep but had got the call to go back to Ozzy. We were trying to work out a plan for me to temporarily fill Bob's role in Uriah Heep while he sorted out the Ozzy thing. Although I would have loved to have done I was committed to another band at the time so it never happened."

Matters have come full circle for the Dirty Tricks trio now playing in the same band with their erstwhile frontman Kenny Stewart once more but under the guise of Stairway To Zeppelin. Horbury has adopted the persona of 'Tom John Jones', Binnie is 'Jimmy Beige', Bierne's alter ego is 'Monty Dick' with Stewart playing out the role of 'Robert Planet'.

Chapter 2

Killing Yourself To Live

Although deeply wounded by two below par albums in a row and disharmony among the ranks, Black Sabbath still held a lofty position, particularly on the U.S. touring front. Although lowly chart positions had directly mirrored fan confusion over the band's recent musical output touring receipts were still strong as the faithful knew that Black Sabbath could still deliver a live show like no one else. Like an insatiable and irresistible black hole Ozzy was duly sucked back into the Götterdammerung of Black Sabbath's dying star, ousting his temporary replacement former Savoy Brown and Fleetwood Mac man Dave Walker, to rerecord the vocals for the 'Never Say Die' album.

Black Sabbath had actually got on with the business of recording with Walker while Ozzy had taken his leave. Although without question a vocalist of some repute, Walker was the first to face the insurmountable obstacle placed in the way of all pretenders to the Sabbath throne. Simply put Black Sabbath don't need a lead vocalist—they need Ozzy Osbourne.

Before he officially joined Black Sabbath, in mid 1979, keyboard player Geoff Nicholls had also, at Tony Iommi's request, been asked to help out with the fleeting Dave Walker incarnation of Black Sabbath. Although the union was brief it did manage to produce one local Midlands TV appearance, parading a formative version of 'Junior's Eyes' as well as the old warhorse 'War Pigs' on the 'Look Hear' programme in January of 1978. Also generated would be a set of demos for what was proposed as the next Sabbath album. Geoff believes the presence of Dave Walker's partner at recording sessions in Wales precipitated the end of that particular alliance. "Dave Walker had his wife there so I could see the writing on the wall. Black Sabbath was always a boy's club. Always a bad move bringing your bird down to the studio!"

The Quartz man, struck by the trappings of success Black Sabbath was obviously still enjoying, also noted that no matter the pedigree of the vehicle the practicalities would be the same. "Sabbath had so much money. Even Lez the roadie had a Lamborghini! The trouble was it was always stuck on his driveway ramped up with the wheels off which I always found funny. Tony had a Ferrari, which was so bloody sensitive he had to keep calling mechanics out to it every other day. When it ran right it was a dream machine but the slightest unbalance and it just wouldn't go."

Black Sabbath Mk II soon floundered. Caught on the hoof, studio time intended for cutting tracks with Walker in Toronto was hastily rescheduled to accommodate the returning Ozzy. Here the band started from scratch, the material demoed with Walker being deemed completely unsuitable for Ozzy.

With such constraints and still dealing with the tumult of the previous months it is quite remarkable that 'Never Say Die' turned out as respectable an album as it undoubtedly is. The lyrics to the eminently catchy 'Hard Road' probably being a bit more poignant to the band's situation than many outsiders would have dared guess. The record fared well in the UK and Europe but would wallow in the lower reaches of the American Billboard top 100.

With Ozzy back in tow the band staggered through a subsequent world tour. On home turf the band had been supported by the electrifying spectacle of Van Halen and Ozzy was not shy in his praise for the Americans. Sabbath, anaesthetised by their own excesses, had looked slow and awkward in comparison to the exuberance of David Lee Roth and the sheer wizardry of Eddie Van Halen. Their work ethic had not been tempered though and the U.S. tour actually played out for an impressive catalogue of dates.

A bruised Black Sabbath retired to California ostensibly to work on a fresh album but came up against an unassailable brick wall of apathy. In May of 1979, matters got confusing. Nobody quite seems to know if Ozzy jumped, was pushed or just fell off. The labyrinth of the inner circle became too involved. Rather like the motorists curse that is the infamous spaghetti junction, sprawling atop their hometown of Aston like some monstrous intestinal explosion of concrete and steel, relationships degenerated into

Advert from 1978 featuring Van Halen.

a tangled mess. The familiarity of drink and drugs, often admitted with candour, numbed both senses and perceptions. Ozzy was gone ...

1979 saw Black Sabbath at a crossroads. It was a bleak, lonely landscape and someone had stolen the signpost. What's more, the devil had already done a deal for their souls a long, long time ago. This time they were on their own. Behind them was a decade where the band had literally reshaped Rock n' Roll, playing louder and uglier than everyone else, defying all the naysayers with a catalogue of landmark albums. As the eighties loomed, whether he realised it or not, guitarist Tony Iommi's career had just turned on its head. The four Astonians that had made up Black Sabbath had, bar the odd expected spat that is par for the course in Rock n' Roll, had been bonded by a rare friendship for ten long years. Bearing in mind subsequent admissions this solidity would be all the more remarkable. In that time the band had sold millions, shocked millions, played to millions and, as time would reveal, had placed their trust in individuals that had duly squandered millions. As the seventies withered, the sheen had dulled on the Sabbath machine enough for Ozzy to pull the big red handle marked 'eject'.

The three remaining musicians, Tony Iommi, bassist and lyricist Geezer Butler and drummer Bill Ward, faced a challenge of titanic proportions. Geezer soon backed out too leaving the guitarist facing the unavoidable question. Was Black Sabbath dead?

Joining Black Sabbath on this journey into the unknown would be two figures both equally influential in the reshaping of the band. One, Ronnie James Dio, would be lauded as a virtual savior whilst the other, Geoff Nicholls from the Birmingham Heavy Metal band Quartz, was, despite being the staunchest of allies, to remain a figure of mystery.

Nicholls loyalty would, for the most part, remain unsung for two decades. Yet he, alone amongst all the guitarist's comrades in arms, would never falter. Although a pivotal figure, appearing on every tour and every album, Geoff Nicholls developed anonymity into an art form of the highest order. Rarely would he intrude upon the stage, official band line-up credits or photographs.

Geoff Nicholls involvement with Black Sabbath cannot be underestimated. Many insiders cite him as Tony Iommi's confidante and unwavering 'right hand man'. Although known for his evocative keyboard work, he is a gifted, multitalented musician, having contributed both rhythm guitar and bass to the band when needed. His impact can be felt deep into the very core of Sabbath too as many of the lyrics and melodies can be attributed directly to him.

Black Sabbath and Quartz had numerous affiliations stretching back over many years, with Iommi acting as producer for the fellow Brummies, Black Sabbath tour manager Albert Chapman handling Quartz's business affairs and even Ozzy helping out in his own way. Quartz would enjoy a run of albums, producing a catalogue of work now highly sought after by fervent NWoBHM collectors. It would be a local record store's makeshift label; Reddington Rare Records, which had released their opening single, a raucous cover version of Mountain's 'Nantucket Sleighride'. The band also contributed the track 'Back In The Band', written by Nicholls about Ozzy's return to Sabbath for 'Never Say Die', to the highly influential EMI compilation 'Muthas Pride'. Heavy touring had placed the band on the starting blocks for a deal with MCA Records just as the UK Hard Rock explosion was set to be triggered. Things looked good for an emulation of the success enjoyed by their close friends, local heroes Black Sabbath. Although bona fide stars, the likes of Ozzy Osbourne and Tony Iommi regarded Quartz as equals and if a flight case needed hauling or an amp head fetching everyone mucked in.

"Ozzy used to carry our gear around just like a

Quartz. Geoff Nicholls, Malcolm Cope, Taffy Taylor, Mike Hopkins, Derek Arnold.

regular roadie" observes Quartz drummer and bandleader Malcolm Cope. "He was always really down to earth like that. When we would rehearse he would always help load the gear in. We got very close to both Tony and Ozzy. When we toured together Ozzy would actually spend most of his time in the Quartz van rather than the Sabbath bus. Geoff and Tony got on like a house on fire from day one. Tony really respected the way Geoff worked at things and the way he tried to get things just right. Geoff has always been like that. He can play most instruments and really has the knack of putting a good song together—riffs, melodies, chord patterns and lyrics. Most musicians contribute just their bit but Geoff could do it all."

Tracing back in time Geoff describes his very first footsteps into the Rock n' Roll arena. "I was a guitarist for many, many years" he explains. "In all of my bands before Black Sabbath I played guitar and, in fact, I originally joined Black Sabbath as a rhythm guitarist. I must have been about 13 or 14 when I started to learn and it was actually a bit of a competition between swimming and Rock n' Roll at one point. I was a keen swimmer and used to take part in these contests all over the country. I was amassing quite a collection of trophies and medals too so it really could have gone somewhere."

The lure of the chlorine was to lose out when faced with the furtive prepubescent pleasures of air guitar. "Swimming was a big thing for me, but on the other hand, I was getting myself obsessed with guitar. I admit I did pose in front of the mirror with the old broomstick in my hands pretending to play 'That'll Be The Day'! People like Chuck Berry, Buddy Holly, Django Reinhardt and the Elvis songs were a real inspiration at first. I think the bug really got to me when I heard Hendrix. I knew then that I wanted to play a heavy style of guitar and I started to look for heavier bands. It took me quite a while because there were so few people into it."

As stated, it would take many years of trial and error on the Pop circuit though before Geoff was able to pursue the heaviness he desired. Nicholls' inauguration into performing live took place at the Settlement Club in Birmingham, as part Colin Storm & The Whirlwinds. "That was quite a good little Rock n' Roll band" he muses. "It was all pink and purple suits, all the Teddy Boy gear. He was actually a great singer too." From there he would move onto The Boweevils. "I guess this was the stage that the Blues guitarists, people like Robert Johnson, were coming into play. What I would call Heavy music hadn't really started then so everybody was playing Blues, Jazz and Pop. It was a nice melting pot of styles, which actually had a huge impact upon the music scene for many years to come. Most of those guys that went onto the very big bands came through that period. It just doesn't exist now. People always seemed surprised to find that most Heavy Metal bands started off as Blues bands. Black Sabbath started as a Blues band and if you know your stuff you can still hear it. You don't see that anymore unfortunately."

Good fortune came Nicholls way when he joined The World Of Oz in 1968, just after the band had scored a sizeable European hit single with 'The Muffin Man' / 'Peter's Birthday' (Deram DM 1987—1968), the A side being an adaptation of the familiar children's nursery rhyme. The band comprised vocalist Christopher Robin (a.k.a. Christopher Evans of The Mayfair Set), guitarist and keyboard player Geoff Nicholls, former Zeus bass player Tony Clarkson and drummer Rob Moore.

"The World Of Oz had just given their keyboard player the boot and they were kind of a local band. I knew two of the guys already. I remember seeing an advert looking for a guitarist, in the Birmingham Mail or something like that. Anyway, it was a Birmingham telephone number, which is why I phoned. I auditioned and got the job."

With Nicholls breaking his recording duck with the prophetically titled band The World Of Oz, he cut his debut eponymous album for the Deram label (Deram SML 1034—1969). A quirky slice of light Psychedelic Pop Rock, produced by Wayne Bickerton and topped off with liner notes from one Jonathon King, the album is now highly sought after on the collectors market. So much so that bootleg fakes were to appear as recently as 1998.

Touring was prolific, partnered up with Grapefruit, signed to The Beatles Apple label, and a Carnaby Street clad pre-boogie Status Quo. "We would tour Europe and keep swapping the billing around depending on whose single was doing the best in each particular country" Geoff relates. "It got quite competitive but in a very friendly way. The World Of Oz had a big hit single in Holland so we topped the bill over Status Quo there." In evidence Geoff dug out the Dutch charts from his attic, proudly displaying The World Of Oz at No. 6 (it was to rise to No. 4) with the Rolling Stones 'Jumpin' Jack Flash' languishing at No. 14.

"We did all those classic gigs, like the Star Club in Germany. I can remember we were booked in there originally to do two 45 minute sets so we thought, OK, we'll put in a drum solo, a guitar solo, play a couple of songs twice and we'll be fine. We can get away with that. When we got there we discovered to our horror we had actually been booked for eight 45 minute sets over two days! We weren't too happy because we had a song in the charts at the time and really didn't think they should be treating us like that. The problem was we were staying in a hotel that had made us hand over our passports, basically because they didn't trust us, so we were stuck. We had absolutely no money but there was no way we were going to play eight sets. We nicked our passports back from behind the till and bogged off!"

The World Of Oz ultimately found themselves in a dilemma they could not extricate themselves from. "We weren't really a Pop band" Geoff motions. "Musically we were quite adventurous but the thing was though that they had recorded the album to appeal to the kiddie market. From our point of view it wasn't supposed to be like that but they ended up putting all these strings on it and putting it out in an album cover that had the tin man and the Lion from 'The Wizard Of Oz' on it. All for kiddie appeal."

The World Of Oz had one last gasp. A followup single, 'King Croesus' (Deram DM 205—1968), had suddenly taken off in California but the band disintegrated and was unable to capitalise on it. "The single was selling 100,000 copies a week in the U.S. but the band fell apart" Geoff says resignedly. "There were lots of rows, threatening letters and then it just collapsed."

Not one to have his ambitions thwarted Nicholls next move was to team up with cabaret Beat act Johnny Neal & The Starliners. This band that gave him another hint of Pop success, winning the Hughie Green fronted TV talent show 'Opportunity Knocks' on a number of occasions. "Because we won this thing like 5 or 6 times we were asked to play on the 'All winners' show which was a very big thing" he expounds. "They gave us a great big backing band and even the two girls that did Tom Jones backing vocals. They looked amazing and sang wonderfully. We had a single out at the time called 'Put Your Hand On Your Hand' (Parlophone R 5870—1970) which was doing very well for us too. The trouble is we were doing a lot of Cabaret type stuff and my heart really was getting more and more into the heavy stuff. That's where I really wanted to go. I can remember I met up with some of the guys that later became Quartz at Bloomers Cavendish. It was a bit of a leap of faith because with Johnny Neal I was earning good money."

Before the band evolved into Quartz the group had been operational on the club circuit for a good few years, releasing Pop-Rock influenced material under the quirky band title of Bandy Legs. This unit included personnel from bands such as Copperfield and The Lemon Tree. "That band was a bit of a Birmingham 'supergroup' at the time because we collected up different quality players from a lot of different bands" Geoff outlines. "Our drummer Malcolm Cope came from a Jazz band for example. We

Bandy Legs—Geoff Nicholls centre.

The Quartz twin axe attack, Geoff Nicholls and Mike Hopkins.

all had this common aim to put something together that was a bit heavier than what we had all been involved with previously. The bass player built a studio in his garage and that's where we got started. Initially of course we just got together to see if we were all keen, have a bit of a jam and get the feel. It sounded really good though so suddenly we had a band." Bandy Legs released three singles 'Red Ride' / 'Don't Play Games'. (WWA WWS001—1974), 'Silver Screen Queen' / 'Lonely Girl' (Pye 7N45449—1975) and 'Bet You Can't Dance' / 'Circles' (Jet 783—1976).

"We knew the Black Sabbath guys because we were all local. Bill Ward used to live near me and I would very often see him waiting at the bus stop. Tony Iommi was always hanging around the music shops with his long hair and these big leather boots he used to wear. We all knew each other. We were quite envious though because we had all been playing music to make money, the Pop thing but what we really wanted to be playing was that kind of heavy Sabbath thing. We admired them greatly for that because as an up and coming musician you are constantly torn between fame, 'Top Of The Pops' and money or playing the kind of music you really wanted to. Sabbath were doing just that and they changed the way a lot of bands approached their careers."

Tony Iommi, spotting some potential in Geoff and Malcolm's new project, put the band on as support to Black Sabbath's UK tour. Guesting for the Sabbs had the band toughening up their own sound considerably and Bandy Legs did not quite have that Heavy Metal ring to it. By this stage the two groups friendship had sparked Iommi's benevolent streak. "Tony got involved helping us sort out a publishing problem we had" Quartz drummer Malcolm Cope acknowledges. "From there he offered to produce the album. Bandy Legs wasn't a very suitable name because our music had changed so much, especially after supporting Black Sabbath. I think the manager at the record company suggested the name Quartz."

Duly renamed as Quartz the group certainly started to make inroads into the Hard Rock fan base around the country. The band wanted to be seen as an act with major potential and a great degree of attention was given over to not just the songs but the image and stage sets. The very name Quartz fired their imagination when it came to the latter as Geoff remembers. "We made this huge Quartz logo that would light up. It didn't matter where we played, we wanted the audience to get a good show. We made the logo out of a huge sheet of plywood, made the letters out of mirror glass, drilled lots of holes in it and put these great big lights behind it so the whole thing lit up. We would use this thing everywhere, even if we were playing in a pub."

Quartz was on the rise and having Tony Iommi acting as producer on their album lent extra kudos. "Working with Tony as a producer on our debut record was great, very different to some of the big name producers we had used in the past" reckons Malcolm. "With Tony things weren't so rigid. He encouraged us to experiment quite a bit, which made us come up some good ideas too. Tony put guitar on two tracks on the record and even played his flute on 'Sugar Rain'. He's a great flute player. Not many people know that."

Contracts kept any notion of actual performance credits out of the public arena as acknowledged by Geoff. "It happens so many times. Tony had produced the record and he was obviously going to play on it too. It's just that we couldn't say that at the time for legal reasons. He did quite a bit on the record actually, a couple of solos. Ozzy sang on 'Sugar Rain' too. Again, we weren't allowed to credit him."

It would not only be the Sabbath duo that featured on the record. Tony's friend Brian May of Queen fame was invited down to the recording studio. "Tony asked Brian to mix one of the album tracks because he was impressed with the way Queen did things. The trouble was that, as we discovered, Queen tracks are heavily edited so that's what Brian tried to do. The result was a load of edits that just ended up as a big pile of tape on the floor! So Brian never in fact got to mix anything. I can remember us all looking at this wasted tape and saying 'So, that's how you get the Queen sound then Brian'. He didn't know whether to laugh or apologise. Birmingham humour can be very dry."

The Queen man would get to add a splash of that famous hand made guitar onto the track 'Circles', once more featuring a certain Mr. Ozzy Osbourne on backing vocals. "Ozzy tried to put some harmonica on too" laughs Malcolm. "It didn't work though and I think that ended up on the floor too or we just didn't mix it in. It might still be on there though, I'll have to dig it out and give it a listen."

Black Sabbath collectors will need to do their own spade work. 'Circles'—a rework of an earlier Bandy Legs tune, inexplicably never made the album, only appearing as the B-side to the subsequent 'Stoking The Fires Of Hell' single (MCA 642—1980).

Malcolm Cope would have another brush with Ozzy a few years later. "Ozzy had just left Sabbath and was trying to put together his own band. He asked me to join but I wasn't too sure. Ozzy was a big name and everything but it looked a bit shaky to be honest. He wasn't in the best shape to be putting a new band together. Besides, Quartz was my band, we had a major deal with MCA and things were bubbling very well for us so I declined." Ozzy would then draft the members of Carlisle act Necromandus for his first stab at a solo act. This Northern act already having Sabbath ties as Iommi had produced an album for the group, subsequently and sadly shelved. Another brief alliance put Ozzy together with Londoners Dirty Tricks.

Back with Quartz, the recording process with Tony Iommi also offered Geoff Nicholls an opportunity too. One he would take. "I worked very closely with Tony in the studio on that Quartz album and I think he was impressed by the amount of work I put in to get things just right. I put a lot of effort into getting the lyrics down, getting the melodies sorted out—that kind of thing."

Malcolm ventures a rather more unexpected catalyst to Nicholls lengthy and ongoing membership of Black Sabbath for the former Quartz man. "Tony and Geoff got very close personally. Whenever Black Sabbath went off on tour to America Geoff helped Tony out by looking after his father's chickens until he came back. He obviously did a good job!"

Quartz.

With Ozzy having recorded and toured the 1978 'Never Say Die' album Black Sabbath, promptly found itself stranded high and dry for a second time. Before Ozzy had bailed, the group had got down to collecting ideas together, which included a fledgling variant of 'Children Of The Sea', for a proposed tenth anniversary album. Some of the early prototypes of tracks, such as 'Children Of The Sea' and a very formative version of 'Lady Evil', were caught on tape during rehearsals with Ozzy. Nicholls had lent Iommi his Teac tape machine and when he retrieved it from the guitarist he discovered those rehearsal sessions still in place. During these work outs Ozzy cut his ties. Tony, Bill and Geezer persevered, inducting Ronnie James Dio, before Geezer too threw in the towel.

With the band in dire need of a rebuild before too long Tony Iommi was on the telephone to his friend Geoff. "Tony phoned me up and asked me to go over to California to help them out with some songwriting. He had got Ronnie already by this point and I was asked to come in as second guitarist. Before Ronnie joined there had been some talk of getting David Coverdale or even Robert Plant involved after Ozzy had left. I know that Tony thought that only a big name could replace Ozzy. Coverdale was approached I know that."

Tony Iommi, speaking in 1986, verified the approach to the former Deep Purple frontman. "Yes, we did ask David Coverdale. There was a conflict of schedules I think. He was up for it but the timing was wrong. I've asked David a couple of times actually and each time he had only just signed up for something else."

This raises the question of another former Deep Purple man Glenn Hughes, long term friend of Iommi's and another singer of high repute. Was he considered for 'Heaven And Hell'? Glenn Hughes scotches the idea of any proposals put his way. "No, not at that time. I was hanging around quite a bit with Ronnie while they were making 'Heaven And Hell'. Great record. But no, I was never asked by Tony at that time." If the approach was not made it was at least discussed. Geoff Nicholls believing Glenn Hughes to actually have been first in line over Ronnie but with the band hoping for an eventual reconciliation with Geezer Butler the problem of Glenn's singer / bassist role nixed the proposal. So Ronnie James Dio it was. "Glenn and Ronnie were very good friends at that point" says Geoff. "I don't know if Ronnie knows this, if Glenn and Ronnie ever discussed it, but Tony Iommi was very keen on having Glenn front the band. The thing that decided it was that Tony also wanted Geezer back badly. That was always a priority for him. Because of that Glenn simply wouldn't fit in."

Ronnie James Dio is the only man besides Ozzy Osbourne that has fronted a platinum version of Black Sabbath. He has a loyal, even fanatical, worldwide fan base and is one of those rare singers to have been granted with truly Olympian vocal chords. Born Ronald Padova, probably back in a time when Messerschmitts ruled the skies of Europe, he had brought his talents to bear on school outfits, including Ronnie and The Red Caps who actually went so far as to release a single, 'Lover'/ 'Conquest' in 1958. The sixties had Dio fronting Ronnie Dio and the Prophets, a band in which he not only sang but played piano, bass and trumpet. In 1967 a fresh project, The Prophets were to release a string of singles and one album 'Dio at Domino's' on Lawn Records in 1963. The Electric Elves (latterly Elf) was forged with Dio's guitarist cousin and latter-day Rods mentor David 'Rock' Feinstein.

Ronnie had discovered his natural talent at an exceptionally young age. "I was asked to sing two songs in a church play" he registers. "I must have been just 8 or 9 and I really didn't want to do it. I had never sang in my life and I was really forced into it. Anyhow, afterwards all these people kept coming up to me and saying 'Wow—what a great voice!' I had no idea and, to be truthful, and no interest or inclination towards singing. I think at the time I just thought OK, now point me in the direction of the baseball pitch!"

Sport would slowly but surely lose out to music though. The young Dio tried his hand at a whole variety of instrumentation. "I'm incredibly lucky that the natural rhythm of music is ingrained in me. I'm known as a singer but I can play guitar, bass, keyboards as well as trumpet, French horn and a bit of saxophone. Actually, scratch saxophone. You really don't want to hear me abusing that instrument! Drums too, far too noisy. Actually I always sucked

Elf 1972.

Elf 1974—Carolina County Ball.

at drums so kind of neglected the percussion side of things. When I write songs, even with Sabbath, I have always been able to put my input into the guitar and bass side of things."

Despite his dexterous command of numerous instruments it would be as a lead singer that Ronnie James Dio really struck out. "I realise I have a gift and I'm fortunate enough to be able to use it too. There are people out there who can match and surpass me but never apply their skill. That's all I did really, applied myself the best I could with a bit of imagination. I was bright enough to use what had been given to me. In my early bands all the other singers sucked so it kept falling back onto me so I started to get a reputation. I started off just like every other singer in the business. I took my inspirations from others and crafted it into my own thing and pretty much stuck with the same formula. Although my voice has developed over the years, strangely it seems to get stronger every year, if you listen back to older records you can hear the method is exactly the same. It works for me anyhow."

With the whimsical Elf, Dio began to break into the big league supporting Deep Purple and issuing consistently better albums. He would, along with Elf in their entirety (minus their redundant guitarist, naturally) be plucked from obscurity and groomed for stardom by Ritchie Blackmore. Commencing with 1975's 'Ritchie Blackmore's Rainbow' and edifying 1976 outing 'Rainbow Rising' albums, the Dio era Rainbow, which found the singer's sense of majesty and grandeur coming to the fore, would provide a reliable barometer of what was to come for Black Sabbath. Dio capped his Rainbow years with 1978's 'Long Live Rock n' Roll'. Dio had always imbued his projects with Gothic kitsch and mediaeval romanticism with such familiar imagery as dragons and rainbows. Dio branded Black Sabbath as his own simply by steering the band towards more malevolent and brooding lyrical themes. Quite deliberately, Osbourne's replacement was his complete and unequivocal antithesis and as such would over the next few years provide the fuel to a publicly played out feud unparalleled in Rock n' Roll.

Antecedent to his Sabbath alliance Ronnie James Dio had the foresight to jump from Rainbow before he was pushed. The Blackmore / Dio alliance had been creatively fruitful indeed, indeed many cite this period as the pinnacle of Blackmore's musical accomplishments, but the errant guitarist had his heart set on radio play. The band assembled in Connecticut for rehearsals, and it was at these sessions the change of tack was brokered.

"After the 'Long Live Rock n' Roll' album Rainbow was really being steered into a completely different direction. A direction I really didn't want to travel down" acknowledges a recalcitrant Ronnie. "Ritchie wanted success with singles and on the radio. At first I was writing new songs in the familiar fantasy areas, which had served us very well, but then Ritchie tells me he wants to hear something simpler. I didn't quite get it at first but then he made it clear he wanted love songs, relationships, more boy / girl type material. That just isn't me. I've never done that and never will, so I could see this was being engineered. If I didn't write the songs Ritchie wanted I would soon be surplus and out.

It all came to a head when I was told Ritchie was leaving the band. When I questioned this I asked 'OK,

Rainbow featuring three future Black Sabbath members, Ronnie James Dio, Cozy Powell and Bob Daisley.

who else is leaving the band?' It seemed as though Ritchie and Cozy were sticking together and the rest of us were out so it was a less than subtle way of forcing us out. My manager at the time, Bruce Payne, confronted them about this and said to them 'Look, it doesn't look like you are leaving Ritchie, rather Ronnie is being fired'. They finally admitted it. And that was it. I was given the elbow."

Ronnie James Dio portrays the closure of that particular Rainbow chapter thus. "Ritchie had decided in his own mind that the Pop audience was for him, which was not what the rest of the band was into at all. Y'know, it was Ritchie's band—we all knew that—but there was a group of musicians there that had achieved quite a bit, well—a lot, and then Ritchie just decides to change his mind and play something else. I had in mind my own band, I was very keen on the band philosophy of pulling together and striving for a common aim. Ritchie went off and brought in some Russ Ballard songs. I can't imagine I would have been happy doing that kind of stuff."

Dio wasted no time in pulling together a new project. Although never given a name the vocalist accepts this was the beginning of the Dio band. "That was the very start of it. The first steps to carrying my own burden and controlling my own destiny." His former Elf colleagues, keyboard player Mickey Lee Soule and drummer Gary Driscoll, got together with Ronnie to work up fresh material. New musical gear was purchased and installed into a new studio in a basement—which then flooded. "I saw this as the hand of doom telling me my timing was off on this one!" laughs Ronnie.

Whilst still in Connecticut, Ronnie James Dio received his first communication from Tony Iommi. A mutual friend based in Los Angeles acted as go between. "It was quite funny" relates Ronnie. "This woman was always getting Tony's name wrong. She rang me up and says 'Is it OK if I give Tommy Iommi your number?' I said 'Yeah—give it to Tony Iommi too!' So, Tony called me and tells me he heard I was no longer with Rainbow and would I consider working with him. The original conversation was to put me together with Tony, Bill and a bassist and keyboard player of my choice. It sounded cool to me.

We spent quite a number of weeks just talking on the telephone; both really excited about the prospect of putting this new band together. Then the calls just stopped. I did a little digging because I was keen but after speaking to Tony's Mum I realised it wasn't happening. He didn't want to talk so rather than sticking my nose up someone's butt I got on with my own band."

Dio, Lee Soule and Driscoll, deciding their venture needed to be centred in a more favourable atmosphere, relocated to Los Angeles. Dio would be hedging his bets though. Approached by Blood, Sweat & Tears guitarist Al Kooper he found himself involved in another proto-band. The union with Kooper also numbered the highly respected Doobie Brothers and Steely Dan guitarist Jeff 'Skunk' Baxter along with Little Feat drummer Richie Hayward. This Progressive Rock inclined yet untitled unit got through just one rehearsal before a chance meeting with Tony Iommi brought Dio's involvement to a conclusion.

"I was having a drink at the Rainbow Bar & Grill when I noticed Tony Iommi sitting at another table" says Ronnie setting the scene. "He was with Sharon Arden and she came over and asked me if I wouldn't mind coming over to their table for a drink and a chat. Now, I felt like telling him to shove it up his ass but I didn't. We talked for a bit and Tony asked if I would like to come to their house in Bel Air to discuss things further and check out their studio. When I arrived I discovered they had set up a studio in the garage. Everyone was there except Ozzy.

Now remember, I hadn't been asked to become involved or anything, I was there to look at a studio as far as I was concerned. Before I knew it the instruments had been strapped on and they started to play this song. Tony says 'Do you think you can do anything with that?' No problem I thought. I put myself in the corner for five minutes and then we jammed through 'Children Of The Sea'. We pretty much got it nailed first time. I think they were quite stunned. They were bloody happy anyway."

Matters then got more convoluted. Tony Iommi revealed they were having problems with Ozzy. Ronnie, understandably, voiced his concern. "I told them straight this was not the reason I came down to meet them and I wanted no part in any of that stuff. I didn't want to be replacing anybody and I knew the situation. Those guys went a long, long way back.

I didn't want to come into a situation only to find I was booted out shortly after because of old loyalties. I told them, sort whatever you have to sort out then call me. If it's complicated—count me out." Next day Tony Iommi telephoned Ronnie. The message would be succinct. "I've fired Ozzy. Are you still interested?"

Initially Geoff Nicholls was led to believe his jaunt to Los Angeles was more by way of a favour. "Provisionally this was supposed to be just for two weeks but very soon after I got there Tony asked if I wanted to join the band full time. Of course, I was very interested because Tony was just great to work with and with Ronnie he had a fabulous voice, but told him I had to go back to the UK to tell everybody what was happening, make arrangements, etc. Tony said 'No, you have to stay here'. So I did. Two weeks somehow turned into twenty years!"

The original formula blueprint for the reconstituted Black Sabbath was to have Geoff Nicholls backing Tony Iommi on second guitar, an interesting turn of thought from Iommi who had not worked with another guitarist onstage since Jimmy Phillips in the pre-Sabbath Polka Tulk Blues Band some twelve years previous. Black Sabbath did rehearse as a two guitar unit. "In the studio both Tony and I would be blaring out of a 4x12 stack each and it was sounding really good" confesses Geoff. "That was how Tony was thinking, two guitars. It worked quite well because of course I could thicken up the riffs and when Tony went into a solo there would be no drop in power."

Nevertheless, slotting into this formative line-up, by necessity Geoff found at first his skills on bass had become a priority. Some idle meanderings on this instrument would unwittingly provide the catalyst for one of the greatest Hard Rock songs of all time. "They already had 'Children Of The Sea' by then. Geezer wasn't there by that point so I had to play bass at first to start getting the songs worked up. The very first song we did was 'Heaven And Hell' Not bad for a first go eh? Tony had a riff which he put over my bass line. I had used a very similar chugging bass line in Quartz for 'Mainline Riders' so I just did that. I was just messing about with this bass riff and suddenly everything started to build up from there. It was very, very simple but it really worked."

Crafting the title track provided a moment of alarm for Geoff Nicholls though when in mid flow Tony Iommi promptly fell asleep on him. "I had only just joined the Sabbs and in the first few days Tony and I were both sitting in the sofa in the living room at home, playing guitars on little amps, trying out ideas for what later became 'Heaven And Hell'.

Tony started to feel a little unwell so I asked his roadie, Roy Lemon, to fetch some antibiotics in a bottle by his bed. So Tony takes two tablets from the bottle, swallows them and we carry on working on the song. It was sounding really good and we both knew this was a great idea that was developing. About twenty minutes later we started to run through the ideas again in order to record it when all of a sudden there was an almighty clunk, banging and lots of feedback! Tony had passed out. His head had fallen back on the sofa, his guitar was still screaming yet he was fast asleep!

We tried to wake him but all we got out of him was a mumble. The roadie had given him sleeping pills instead of antibiotics! That was Tony done for the rest of the night but what a great song we had to work on the next day."

Was Geoff aware that that bass line had been later attributed to Geezer Butler? "Nah, no way" he objects. "Geezer wasn't even there. I can remember the first studio jam of that song as clear as day. It was all very spontaneous too. By the time Tony, myself, Bill and Ronnie had finished we had this song that was eight and half minutes long! It worked though and we all had some big smiles on our faces that day."

Ronnie James Dio holds similar affection for the song. "That is such a great song. We all just loved it, loved playing it too. We got so into that song because ideas and creativity was just flowing out of all of us at that point. It just came to us. We never got tired of it and we would play it for hours and hours. I think we were maybe thinking 'Is it really this good?' I had the lyrics, the mood and melody for that and I had a very firm concept of how I wanted the song to end up. Tony's riff was just great. We had to keep pruning the song back too because it was really growing."

Geoff was as equally enthusiastic. "'Heaven And Hell' sounded just great so we taped it. We played it to the manager, Sandy Pearlman, and he said 'Fucking hell boys—that's great!' He absolutely freaked. We had to cut it down from the eight and a half minutes and change the arrangement a bit but it still ended up a bloody epic. Afterwards Geezer told me he would never have played that riff on the bass because it was so simple.

It's a good way of working though and it's how I work on keyboards too. Get a simple bass melody line down and then you can move the chords around and create a song. It's always a good point on which to start a new song at and build the guitar riff and the vocals on top. A great melody is the most important thing because without that the song will never be any good. It was funny though Geezer saying that about 'Heaven And Hell' because he was right, he would never have played that bass line, which of course means that 'Heaven And Hell' might never have happened in the first place. It was me messing

Geezer's 'Henry' devil.

about on the bass that started the whole song off."

With a working demo in the can Black Sabbath still did not have a full compliment of band members. They were also undecided on another critical issue. Were they to call the band Black Sabbath or something else entirely? Geoff gives some insight into the thoughts of the band members at the time. "There was talk of calling the band something else" he readily admits. "There were pros and cons for staying as Black Sabbath or going off on something completely new. As far as we knew Ozzy was planning on going out on tour with a band called 'Sons Of Sabbath'. That was his original idea because he legally could not tour or work as Black Sabbath. At the time the name 'Black Sabbath' was owned by Tony, Geezer and Bill. These days of course, it is owned solely by Tony Iommi. This question kept coming up in later years too of course—is it Black Sabbath?

Well, Tony felt the songs we were coming up with were good enough to stand up on their own without the name Black Sabbath. It's interesting to think that the 'Heaven And Hell' album would certainly have done that. It was more than strong enough to sell in its own right. I guess that's part of the reason Tony called me in originally as second guitarist. There were lots of changes being proposed. At the end of the day though I just think keeping it as Black Sabbath was easier all round. It made life more difficult for Ronnie though as is well known. He took a lot of flak for replacing Ozzy which he probably would not have received if it had gone out under a new band title."

With Geoff intended as second guitarist / keyboard player Ronnie James Dio put forward his former Rainbow ally Craig Gruber to occupy the bass position. Prior to this, with the band having relocated to Miami for final preproduction on the album, Fran Sheehan of multi-platinum Pomp Rockers Boston tried out for the vacancy. Ronnie James Dio too spent some time manning the bass helm. "At rehearsals I would very often play bass but of course I had no intention of carrying on with that. I was asked if I knew of any bassists and as it happened I had only just spoken to Craig Gruber."

Gruber got through the auditions but Geoff believes Tony Iommi was never really convinced. "Craig's playing was good but not exactly amazing. He was an OK guy, I guess he would have been good enough but there was a feeling that he wasn't able to fit into the unit. Tony's philosophy at the time, and always a good one, was that everyone had to give everything to the group. He wanted dedication, which is why I suppose when I told him I had things to sort out back home he said 'No'. It was the group or nothing in his eyes. There was a strong kind of family thing and Tony wanted people he knew personally too. Craig couldn't give that so we met up with Geezer in Miami, played him the stuff and he loved it. He was back in so it was the old team again."

When asked if any of Craig Gruber's bass work made it to the final cut of the 'Heaven And Hell' album, a continual subject of speculation amongst Sabbath fans, Geoff replies with a flat "Absolutely not." Ronnie simply speculates that Craig lost his position for being "too American."

Geezer Butler, although having opted out, was never believed by Tony Iommi to have placed himself beyond reach. There would be an open channel of communication between the two. "When Ozzy left, after the 'Never Say Die' tour, I left too" motions Geezer. "I think Tony started working with someone else but he kept phoning and telling me that it wasn't the same so in the end I went back to work on the 'Heaven And Hell' album. I'm glad I did because I was really proud of that record. I think we came up with something very special there."

"Tony asked me my opinion on getting Geezer back and I was all for it" allows Ronnie. "After all, this was Black Sabbath so it made sense. Tony was quite miffed that Geezer had left in the first place. The choice was either that or myself or Geoff playing bass, neither of which was a viable option. Craig Gruber was a helluva bass player but simply didn't fit in. Just one of those things. Having Geezer back in the band was a good move on Tony's part."

With Ronnie James Dio's vocal stylings having stamped such an indelible mark on Rainbow there were obvious detractors—Ozzy chief amongst them— that foresaw a 'Black Rainbow' album looming. Intended as a put down by Ozzy the prospect of a 'Black Rainbow' had fans contemplating whether such a grandiose vision might not have been such a bad thing but Ronnie disagrees. "Yeah, 'Black Rainbow', that came from Ozzy. I guess we knew that one was coming. I didn't see it that way. Everyone

Ronnie James Dio fronting Rainbow. Pic: Rich Galbraith.

was very free with their ideas back then and people were just so enthusiastic for the whole album that all of that was encouraged. I saw it as a team effort and everybody involved really pulled out all the stops for that record. That includes the producer Martin Birch who deserves a lot of credit for the way 'Heaven And Hell' turned out.

I know I had a lot more input into the songs themselves than Ozzy had ever done before. Songs are very precious to me and I can't just come in and compromise like that. It's important to me to give my all to a song. The band got pulled into a different direction that is for sure but I think that was just as much Tony and Geezer's decision as mine. I don't see too many similarities with Rainbow there. I felt that Tony, Geezer and Bill all put much more effort into 'Heaven And Hell' than they had done on a lot of those early Sabbath albums. It made a big difference."

How did Ronnie view the individual contributions of his band members? "It was democratic. Everyone worked together as a band during that record. Tony came up with some wonderful riffs, which were a pleasure to sing over. I think some of his very best work is on that record. Bill made a major contribution too. Bill is often overlooked because he has been out of the public eye for so long but he really did make a major contribution to those songs."

Summing up, Ronnie is happy to pinpoint 'Heaven And Hell' as probably his favourite record out of the entire Dio catalogue. "That album is very important to me and I place it at the very top when it comes to personal achievements. There was so much more to 'Heaven And Hell' than just the record itself. The fans got the musical message but for the band it represented so much more. Black Sabbath was in a tremendous mess and was virtually rebuilt from scratch during that period. It was a big challenge and the stakes were high, especially with it being called Black Sabbath too. Both Tony and I had a vision with 'Heaven And Hell' and we saw it through. Pride played a big part in the way we were thinking then. For the most part it was Tony and I that wrote that record.

Tony asked me in and was hoping, I think, that I could give my all to the band and get it back up from the floor. He certainly needed somebody involved that not only shared his vision but could bring onboard that extra element. With Ozzy he never had that input because he wrote the music, Geezer wrote the words and Ozzy just sang what he was told. Tony was looking for an artistic partnership. Well, we did that and so much more. We knew the songs were special, we could feel it despite being so close to them. I am immensely proud of that record."

As it happens, Dio's perceived public anathema of all things Ozzy was a little more flexible than might be imagined. This is illustrated amply by a revelation courtesy of Geoff Nicholls. "At one stage Ronnie wanted to rerecord the song 'Black Sabbath'. He was deadly serious about it too. It wasn't just an idle thought either; the band sat down and discussed it as a serious proposition. This was when all the discussions were going on as to whether we should call it Black Sabbath or something else so I guess Ronnie gave us his answer to that question there."

"I thought it made sound common sense to call the band Black Sabbath" gestures Ronnie. "I left the decision up to them but I believe that my opinion carried some extra weight because my viewpoint was looked upon as an outsiders, possibly how the fans would think. I can remember when I told Tony this he looked at me and said 'Do you really think so?' The moves to rename the band were certainly there but it just made no sense to me. They needed some reassurance on the name issue that's for sure. There were pros and cons to it. The down side was that the last two Sabbath albums had stiffed big time. There were serious problems inside the band, which were becoming visible to the fans because Billy was singing half of it. Black Sabbath wasn't exactly flying high at that point and the label, quite frankly, didn't even give a shit.

On the positive side the band did have a great tradition, Tony had an ever better one and keeping the name would give us that little extra edge. Tony, I felt, had always had greater aspirations musically than he was able to show with the old Sabbath. I think that because a lot of it was so basic he never received the same degree of respect of, say, Ritchie Blackmore or someone like that. That same kind of respect that he enjoys today. He wanted to show what he could really do this time. Keeping it as Black Sabbath would mean more people would listen.

Because of the way Warner Bros. were treating us at the time, or rather ignoring us shall I say; that little extra edge with the name might have proven just enough to give us the jump start. We had to take the leap off the diving board anyway so, fuck it, let's call it Sabbath and dive off the top board and catch more people in the opening splash. Overall though we just knew we had a great album that was worthy of the name. We knew those songs were special."

Inquiring fans have often wondered if there is more material from these sessions is lying in dusty vaults somewhere, reels of audio treasure waiting to be unearthed for future rarities collections. Geoff doesn't believe so. "In those days, to keep an album sounding 'heavy' on vinyl you had to limit yourself to 20 minutes per side. It was a very creative time so there were lots and lots of ideas being worked on at various stages. It came to a point in the process where you had to add all the times of the songs up and make sure you had the correct length of material for the album. We already had two epic type long songs in 'Heaven And Hell' and 'Die Young' by that stage too. That's when you have to choose which songs to finish and which stay as just ideas. Those ideas sometimes get worked on later or are just forgotten. I'm pretty sure there are no complete songs from back then waiting to be discovered."

The record was laid down in bulk at Miami's Criteria Recording Studios before being polished off in France at the Ferber complex in Paris. This initial switch in recording venues, from California to Florida, had been dictated by forces within the management sphere of operations. The band had only recently broken off engagements with Don Arden, the proverbial fans had been turned on and the manure duly tossed into the air. "It was quite funny looking back because Sabbath had got messed up in that whole split between Don and Sharon. The house where we were staying, rented by Don, suddenly lost all of the furniture! These guys just came in one day and repossessed everything. That's why we moved out to Miami."

Ronnie James Dio in Tulsa, 1980. Pic: Rich Galbraith.

Heaven and Hell 1980.

Prior to this relocation Ronnie James Dio received his first taste of Tony Iommi's wicked sense of humour. The guitarist, having gone for a walk in Bel Air, had found a large dead snake. The requisitioned reptile was duly tied to the inner passenger door of Ronnie's car in such an ingenious, spring loaded fashion that when the singer opened the driver door the snake 'jumped' at him. Needless to say Dio received quite a shock. Dio got his own back, locating his very own deceased serpent to secrete in Tony Iommi's toilet bowl!

The East Coast would give the band a far from pleasant welcome. As Black Sabbath flew into Miami, the Florida coast was hit four square by hurricane David. "Bloody scary I'll tell you!" Geoff reckons. "As soon as our plane landed they closed the airport so we were stuck. We had arranged to rent a house from Barry Gibb of the Bee Gees but because of the hurricane that had been flooded. We spent a few days in hotels before stopping at Barry's place. They were really nice people. Very generous to us, the whole family."

At these closing sessions the last song 'Neon Knights' was introduced to cap the proceedings. "When we had finished off in Miami we had got ourselves to Christmas so it was time for a break" observes Nicholls. "The plan was to mix the album in London but then Tony had to get out of the UK for tax reasons so we both had a week's holiday in Jersey. After that some thought was put back onto the record and we came to the conclusion we needed a faster paced track because the album as it stood was all fairly mid tempo. The band joined back up together in Paris to record 'Neon Knights'. That was probably the only real band writing effort on that entire album because Geezer was involved by that stage. Tony came up with this little riff and Ronnie quickly sorted out some vocal melodies for it. They got stuck in the middle though so I came up with the chords for the solo part. All in all a team effort."

The sessions would not be over until a certain band member had become the unsuspecting victim of some in-house pyrotechnics. Bill Ward very nearly came a cropper when Tony Iommi decided to give his band mate a foretaste of Beelzebub's burning pit. Geoff Nicholls can hardly contain himself in regaling the author with this sorry tale of Ward's misfortune. "This might sound very bizarre, but Tony Iommi was always setting fire to Bill. Just one of those daft things we used to do to pass the time. We were doing some overdubs at the studio one day when Bill walks in and Tony says, very casually, "Can I burn you today Bill?" Now, Tony was always setting Bill's beard and hair on fire. Bill replied, just like a normal everyday conversation, "Not now Tony, maybe later" and with that he went off. Sometime later he wandered back in and tells Tony "I'm going now. Do you want to burn me or what?" So Tony gets this lighter fuel, pumps it all over Bill then sets fire to him!" On previous occasions the lighter fuel, quite a neat party trick, had looked spectacular but had evaporated within seconds. This time the flames seemed to be more tenacious.

"Before we knew it Bill's trouser leg was totally on fire. He started to jump up and down, screaming like a lunatic. I was trying to put him out by rolling him around and rather stupidly beating him with a rolled up newspaper. Meantime, Tony was laughing his head off and squirting even more lighter fuel on him! Bill was doing the whole dying fly bit with his legs and arms.

We finally put him out. We hadn't realised though that he had been wearing these nylon socks that had melted in the fire and tore all his skin off. Bill went to hospital to get treated and sometime afterwards Bill's Mum phoned Tony up and called him a 'barmy bastard!'"

As recording drew to a closure the band put their minds to more serious matters, namely the forthcoming live strategy. Despite Geoff Nicholls having been utilised as a jack of all trades in the sessions Tony Iommi mooted a proposal to get back to the original proposed format of two guitars for live work. According to Nicholls, quite incredibly, something as mundane as a lack of basic equipment on the day would dictate the band's makeup for the next twenty years. The band was set up with full P.A., Tony Iommi going through a customary 4x12 stack and Geezer Butler utilising a 200 watt bass amp. All that was left over for Geoff Nicholls to fashion a sound out of was a tiny Fender Princeton. It was no contest. "Consequently nobody could hear me because I couldn't compete on the volume obviously" sighs a resigned Nicholls. "So when Tony went into a solo, I would riff but you couldn't hear it. Ronnie got into a real state about this saying "This ain't gonna work!" He couldn't see such a basic thing that if I was given a 4x12, like we had tried out before, it would've sounded great. Even on the very last Black Sabbath shows I did, with Ozzy, I would play rhythm guitar with a 4x12. Ronnie just didn't get it though and was adamant it was not going to work. Tony just gave in to keep the peace. Personally I don't think he should have given in because his original plan for the two guitars sounded bloody amazing."

According to Ronnie James Dio the twin guitar theory was always a non flyer. "Tony Iommi needs to operate solo. He's singular and it sounded a lot better with one. It was tried out with Geoff on second guitar but it all got a bit mushy. He's a very fine guitar player but Sabbath really didn't need two guitars. Tony couldn't deal with it, with Geoff blazing away on guitar too. Tony actually came to me one day and told me he didn't want to hurt Geoff's feelings but of course, Tony being Tony, he didn't want to tell him. I think Bill and I told him the second guitar was a no go and that he could still contribute musically through the keyboards. And that worked out just fine as background filler, a C here, an F sharp here. There was call for sound effects too—wind, bells, thunder and lightning.

Black Sabbath didn't need a keyboard player as such, by that I mean someone like Tony Carey or Jon Lord with all the inversions and mastery of their instrument. That was why there was no sense in putting Geoff on the stage because it was just background filler. The addition of keyboard textures contributed a lot more than having two guitars."

The 'Black Rainbow' doubts then began to mould the visual aspect of the band line-up. So prevalent was this concern that the Rock public would perceive the band in this manner, the vacillation within the band eventually impacted further on Nicholls' role. "A decision was made to keep everything streamlined as just singer in the centre with guitar and bass to either side" Geoff motions. "Ronnie didn't want me onstage because he thought the press would then compare us to Rainbow and he was very keen to avoid that. Tony Iommi went along with it too, he was worried about the same thing too. He argued that with Ronnie being a new singer the emphasis needed to be totally focused on him and having keyboards would act as a distraction. I didn't like it but I felt I would play ball in the best interests of the band and sort it out later."

As 1979 dawned Los Angeles was a seething hotbed of Hard Rock bands. It was a unique primeval soup fired by the inspiration of the 70s Rock leviathans, the over the top exploits of Kiss and the latter day heroics of Van Halen, whilst still smarting from the bruises left by Punk. Within this maelstrom of talent and determination band members switched allegiances in order to place themselves in the right camp while bands scrabbled to find ever new and daring stage shows and images to set them apart from the crowd.

This new generation would include names such as Snow, London, The Boyz and Mickey Ratt. Later evolutions would foster Ratt, Dokken, Great White, Mötley Crüe, Quiet Riot, Poison, Warrant, L.A. Guns, Faster Pussycat, Guns n' Roses and W.A.S.P. along with a labyrinthine web of offshoots, predecessors and descendents. Within this den of madness, and oblivious to all but a chosen few, sat Ozzy Osbourne in self-imposed purgatory. He had finally severed his ties with Black Sabbath and was determined to erase the memory of the last decade. Into this void would walk Dana Strum.

Strum was racing on the treadmill of the Los Angeles rat run with his act Badaxe. The band differed from the melting pot of other desperate souls in that the group was firmly rooted in a more rustic traditional earthiness akin to the pioneering British acts and in particular Black Sabbath. The act shunned the prevalent Glam trend and went for a back to basics long hair and jeans look.

Along with the pivotal figure of Strum, Badaxe comprised of drummer Steve Ward, guitarist David Carruth and a succession of singers. The mic was initially in the hands of Toronto born Stacey Morland who then relinquished his role to Bob Geadreau out of Phoenix, Arizona. Badaxe's last line-up was fronted by Louie Merlino. Recordings were undertaken for an album but this never surfaced. However, a 7" single for a Canadian label Earth Breeze in 1978 'Cry For Me' / 'All You Can Stand' did emerge and would come to the attention of Billboard magazine that singled out Badaxe for their 'Pick Hit'.

The group gigged hard pulling off many notable supports and guest slots to such diverse artists as Judas Priest, Black Oak Arkansas, Starz, The Dogs, Eddie Money and Michael Des Barres Silverhead. They would also make it onto celluloid featuring in the Emilio Estevez movie '17 And Going Nowhere' and one of their amateur video clips would earn the director Mark Goldberg a UCLA Jim Morrison award. All in all though, Badaxe was not in the commercial boat. Yes they wanted to break it big time like every other hungry eyed band but they could not compromise on the music. Strum himself is philosophic. "Mainly it was a very Sabbathy trip but a kinda American version. We were not set out to be a hit type of act at the time although maybe now twenty years later it might have been."

It was probably their marked rawness that brought Badaxe and in particular Strum to the attention of Jet Records Pat Sicillano. Scouting for talent to build a band back around Ozzy the enterprising Sicillano had marked Strum out giving him the address of Frank Zappa's Hollywood studio where the label was setting up sessions in order to entice his royal Ozzness out of his self imposed exile.

A week later Strum received the call to attend. "I got a phone call telling me at what time to arrive but not what we would be playing or doing. I always thought that was odd but I knew most of the Black Sabbath stuff anyway and I figured who gave a fuck ... Badaxe was very 'Black Sabbathee' and I was totally into it".

The first meeting with Ozzy was to provoke a wave of conflicting emotions that would become a part of Strum's life for the next few months. The sense of disbelief at the opportunity afforded to him was triggering instincts in Dana that had him mentally shouting "Wow! It is him ... Ozzy!!!" but the pragmatist soon took over. "This was not the glitz and dollars and fun that anyone would think." There was work to be done.

Strum's sensibilities were assailed further when he walked into Zappa's studio startled to see the renowned figure of former Thin Lizzy guitarist Gary Moore performing. The scenario was somewhat surreal. Being invited to try out for Ozzy was hard enough to take in but being confronted by one of the greats of Rock guitar set the bass player's mind reeling.

Moore's status within Rock echelons was undoubtedly of the highest ranking but the Irishman came with baggage and a reputation. Like Ozzy the effects of the demon alcohol had generated Moore as much media print as his guitar abilities. On top of this his clashes with Thin Lizzy mentor and driving force Phil Lynott had boiled over into expensive mid tour walk outs. In spite of all this Gary Moore was an awesome lead guitarist and at this stage in his life was slowly shaping his life and career back together again. On paper the union of Moore and Ozzy, both Jet Records artists, had huge potential.

Strum notes that Moore's playing ability was "unreal" but he could detect a severe clash in styles finding it hard to imagine Moore as part of any post Sabbath outfit. Nevertheless the trio, together with more than one drummer that have drifted into the annals of time, jammed whatever came into the sphere of operations. Pointedly there was never any attempt at or discussion of any Sabbath run throughs. Although the mood overall was relaxed Moore and Ozzy simply didn't gel.

From the outset Ozzy's state of health had made an obvious impression on Strum and signalled a quick mental game of questions and answers to assess the situation. "He is a bit fucked up—what to do? Fuck it—I love the music. I know it will be a good thing." He surmised. Strum was committed and hoped the relaxed rapport struck up with Ozzy was an indicator that he had got the gig.

Shortly after this jam Moore would go his own way and forge an alliance with ex-Deep Purple vocalist Glenn Hughes and drummer Mark Nauseef for what was to become G-Force. However, Hughes departed and bassist 'Willie Dee' (actually erstwhile Captain Beyond frontman Willy Daffern) and vocalist Tony Newton brought the band up to strength. G-Force would be short-lived. So, after a stint with the Greg Lake Band—including an American tour—Moore set about constructing a new solo band. This would instigate the recording of the 'Corridors Of Power' album, a record that would seriously push Moore's name to the fore and kick start a lengthy and productive run of albums built on a stable career path. Meantime, Strum's colleagues in Badaxe went their separate ways. Carruth later coming to attention in the Betsy led Bondage Metal band Bitch whilst Ward teamed up with Drastic Action. Merlino would figure later in the Strum saga.

Although the first sessions had ruled Moore out of the picture Ozzy was keenly impressed by Strum and invited him over to his residence at the Le Parc Hotel in West Hollywood to discuss further plans. The singer's room was a stark visual clue to the overall chaos surrounding Ozzy that Strum would in time have to weave together into some kind of grand plan. "It was a wreck, beer cans, dope smell, piles of dirty clothing, old food and pizza boxes. Nothing too incriminating out in the open—he was smart. It looked like Oz had been having some good Rock n' Roll fun in a high dollar hotel!" Fortunately the hotel, used to the eccentricities of bored Rock stars, let it all pass as long as the bill was paid.

It was here that the bass player learned that although Jet Records had given Ozzy a list of potential guitar recruits there was no band as yet. The pair talked of future plans and the evening rounded off with Ozzy stating "Kid, you got the job." Strum responded boldly enough to surprise Ozzy that he was sure he knew who the right guitar player for his band was.

"That night was odd, not just because I had just got the Ozzy gig." Strum was totally convinced of his choice and although Ozzy questioned his judgement Strum would not be deterred. It was a big risk. Here he was, a relative unknown, telling Ozzy Osbourne a cast iron, true as they come Rock n' Roll legend in no uncertain terms that someone equally obscure was the man to resurrect his whole career. So convinced was Strum that he describes this conversation in almost fatalistic terms. "A strange feeling came over me in that I knew the guy that I had told him should be the guitar player. It was Randy Rhoads and I was certain of that. I really saw it happen very clearly in my head. Like it was just a fact in time that was meant to be. I had no doubts."

Strum may have felt the firm hand of destiny placed on his shoulder at that point but Ozzy and the as yet unaware Randy Rhoads were oblivious at this point. It would transpire that not only were both parties ambivalent about the union but as it turned out Strum had to fight tooth and nail to make it happen. Strum's conviction was reinforced by the fact that he personally had nothing to gain short term from hooking Ozzy up with Randy. The club circuit at that time was a vicious back biting pit of aspiring broke musicians who would trample on anyone and anything to make it to the top. Landing the gig with Ozzy Osbourne was a one way ticket to superstardom and Strum was putting forward an arch rival for the position.

"All of the Hard Rock bands were kinda fighting each other for that magic record deal. Badaxe and Quiet Riot were not the best of friends." Quiet Riot was led by one Kevin DuBrow, a man who by his own admission later in life bad mouthed colleagues, compatriots and rivals to such an extent that his own band became alienated within the scene. In a matter of years Quiet Riot would rise meteorically scoring an American number one album and for an all too brief moment eclipse all but the very biggest of established bands.

However, like a wounded bird in flight Quiet Riot's demise though was as ungraceful as it was sickeningly swift and on the way down all the spitballs that DuBrow had flung out with abandon over the years were fired back twice as hard. It was an ignominious fall, the revenge made sweeter for those bands and musicians that had suffered DuBrow's scorn and derision were seemingly all on a rise. As Quiet Riot crashed into the gutter the newly platinum bands like Ratt, Mötley Crüe, Dokken and Great White could hardly contain their glee. For now though Quiet Riot's ascendancy was in the future and Strum faced an uphill task in contacting Randy. "I had a trip to break through which was to get hold of Randy without anyone really catching wind".

Dana Strum set about his mission with zeal drawing up a candidature of possibles for Ozzy. It was a short list headed by Randy but also including George Lynch of The Boyz and Carlos Cavazo of Snow. Both Lynch and Cavazo were players of stature and both would go on to achieve acclaim; Lynch with Dokken and, paradoxically for Cavazo, Quiet Riot.

From an acquaintance at the Starwood Club Strum got a contact number for Randy at his mother's music school in Burbank. Once the deal had been put to Rhoads, Strum was taken aback by the guitarist's response. "Randy was not really into the idea and he didn't like Sabbath that much. He was kinda into Glam Rock and fancied himself more of a Mick Ronson, T-Rex or Brian May of Queen type of vibe."

Strum's sense of purpose took over once again. "At this time I felt myself almost telling him that he had to try, it would be great." He also informed him of his opinion that 'Because of Quiet Riot's trip that he was held back and very under rated." The guitarist then awkwardly confessed that he had never auditioned for anyone before and simply would not know what to do. The pair discussed one of Randy's solos that had impressed Strum at the Starwood Club. "I told him that would be a great start and we could just go from there." Further conversations throughout the day finalized the details of the audition. Strum still had his "strange feeling" but little would he know that his campaign to unify Ozzy and Randy had only just begun. "I knew that this was to be a very meaningful day in Rock history, I will never forget." Not knowing the tribulations he still had to face Strum set up the meet.

Although this was without question a pivotal juncture in Ozzy's life he was far from fighting fit and not exactly in the best shape. He was physically heavy and the blitz of drink and drugs that had numbed the immediate wrench of leaving Sabbath had now become his own personal ball and chain. Strum still had in his memory the images of Sabbath in their prime and resolved himself to better times to come convinced that if a good band could be assembled Ozzy's renaissance would be inevitable.

"Despite Ozzy's condition I always thought it would work out" he confides. "It just needed time. He might have had times where he did not really know what to think. He was a bit unclear a lot of the time and much later I would understand just how meaningful Sharon's role in his life would be."

For the time being though Strum simply had to deal with Ozzy's troubles often acting as a sounding board. "I didn't do drugs and drink much at all at that early point in my life. Our meetings at the Le Parc Hotel would often turn into talks about life and booze. More than once in the apartments across the street we heard someone playing 'Iron Man' kinda out of nowhere. It was really funny shit from day one. He really was like a 3 ring circus all of the time."

In the midst of this somehow the true spirit of Ozzy managed to break through. "One night in the hotel he kinda came up with a few melody lines" says Strum. "I knew then and there that the magic Sabbath sound was something other than the killer guitar and bass riffs. The vibes and melodies were all Ozzy. I was really happy as I had learned what I thought to be true was a fact. Ozzy was the centre of that great sound I loved".

Often the singer would share tales of his past with

Dana who was enthralled by stories of Ozzy's pre Black Sabbath bands, his job at an abattoir and his exploits stealing televisions. The two even discussed a wild scheme to start an agency with Strum slated as 'Super agent'. Weighed down though he was by emotional, alcoholic and chemical shackles the atmosphere around Ozzy was nevertheless electric. "One night he went out and yelled at the sky in Hollywood and it seemed to make it rain" Strum recalls. The magic was tangible and the excited American was honoured to be chosen as the wizard's apprentice.

This was the Ozzy that Strum drove around to check out the guitarists on the agenda. By now Strum had realized that not only was he Ozzy's bass player but his driver and all round organizer as well. Even the normally patient hotel staff were getting irate at the sheer volume of calls Strum was patching through and receiving in his efforts to assemble a band. Typically the auditions were an enlightening experience. "We saw a few real freaks" Dana admits. "One guy kept singing Hendrix songs while he played the guitar and Ozzy kept saying "No, just play—I'm the front guy!" It was crazy".

Interestingly, number two on Dana's list of three was blissfully unaware of the proceedings. Ensconced in his pre Dokken band The Boyz the band's manager had neglected to inform George Lynch that there was an interest in him from the Ozzy camp. "He was never told that I ever thought that he should be my second shot" Strum relates. "Oh boy was he upset!"

Another applicant was the towering tattooed figure of Chris Holmes later of W.A.S.P. infamy. Strum is diplomatic "That just was not right . . . ."

In between viewing each candidate Strum drove Ozzy in his Triumph TR7 sports car to the next audition all the while attempting to convince his employer that Randy Rhoads was the man. "It was kinda nutz. I think that he thought that I was selling him a friend." Little did Ozzy know that Strum's intentions were totally altruistic and that he and Randy were for all intents and purposes adversaries on the circuit. Having his nerves assaulted by American hopefuls Ozzy simply wanted to go home. "Let's just go to England" he told Strum. "We can find a real bloke." His colleague maintained his stance "I kept on with the fact that he needed to see Randy".

Ozzy's daily ritual was still revolving liquid sustenance and the evenings would invariably be spent at the notorious Rainbow Bar & Grill on Sunset Boulevard. "Ozzy kinda liked the circus of that place I guess that it made him feel at home. There were very many wild cool nights, after all he was Ozzy so anywhere we went . . . I was new as hell to all of that. Don't forget, I was young, dumb and full of cum" Strum fondly remembers. "Really each day at

Geezer Butler. Pic: Rich Galbraith.

that time in his life was kinda get up, get high, get drunk and . . . who knows . . . "

Ozzy could hold his own though in the face of the public. Strum has recollections of being extremely nervous when Jet Records laid on some premature media interviews. "I took him to the interviews and we both kinda sat there. I wondered what he was going to say being that there was no band and no songs. He did just great."

Chapter 3

The Reluctant Wizard

Randall William Rhoads, the youngest sibling to brother Doug and sister Kathy, was born on December 6, 1956 at St. John's Hospital in Santa Monica, California. His mother Delores was left a single parent when his father, a music teacher, bailed out on the relationship. This severing of ties would provide Randy with an extended family of two half brothers, Dan and Paul, in later years.

Both Randy and Kathy would take up folk guitar from a very early age, the youngsters getting to grips with an acoustic Gibson belonging to their Grandfather. Their musical environs would be fashioned by the fact that Delores was the owner of the North Hollywood music school Musonia.

Prompted by his mother, in an effort to instill a practical knowledge of sight reading, Randy also took up piano lessons. Randy though had set his sights firmly on the guitar, despite the fact that his semi-acoustic Harmony Rocket's sheer size when compared to the waif like Randy presented physical challenges all of its own.

Randy's close friend Kelly Garni would also get sucked into this pursuit of Rock music. The two had met when just 11 at Junior High school and were both fired by a love of Rock music. It was a glue that would create a friendship for life. Garni has vivid memories of the Randy he was first drawn to.

"There was just something about him that stood out, he really had a presence about him. At school Randy actually had a big problem with it. He actually looked feminine so other kids would give him a hard time over that. The thing was though, that he had this Mozart like talent. We both wanted to be Rock stars, even at 11, it's all we ever spoke about." The two budding stars resolved to learn the craft of playing music and form a band as soon as they were able.

"When we first met Randy only knew rhythm, no lead. I would spend every day hanging around his house just learning. It was quite a house—his mother played, his sister played and his brother played too. Of course I wanted to join in so Randy said "How about bass?" I would play the root notes to his rhythms, runs and patterns."

Randy was eager to add lead playing to his skills and this is where tutor Scott Shelly comes into the picture. "Randy worshipped Scott" Kelly confides. "He learnt how to play lead from Scott and add it to his rhythm playing so pretty soon he was playing both rhythm and lead over my bass runs. Music just took over our world. We both cared about little else and as fast as he was learning guitar I was learning bass. I don't think his mother knows this but we would both cut school and jam at my house all day. When Randy's mother left for work at the music school about 3 o'clock we would grab our amps and haul them 2 or 3 blocks to Randy's house to carry on playing there. Nothing would stop us except the 'Beverly Hillbillies'. When that came on TV we dropped everything!"

In their early teens the duo graduated from theory to application bowing in with a debut act Violet Fox. With Randy's brother Doug on drums Violet Fox's ambitions flickered for a matter of months but it was enough to set Randy and Kelly onto the path of Rock n' Roll.

Sojourns ensued on the Burbank party scene with further acts including Mildrid Pierce and The Katzenjammer Kids, the latter with drummer "Rubberhead." "We were performing as a band by the time we were 13" admits Garni. "Often it would just be grabbing whoever was available to act as a drummer and we'd just play these surfers big backyard beer bashes, mostly without a singer. I think we got through about 4 or 5 guys on drums." These proto bands would fuel their live sets with covers by the likes of the Rolling Stones, Mountain and Alice Cooper.

"Randy was a major, major Leslie West fan. Not enough is said about that" reckons the bassist. "Mountain was a major influence on Randy. We also did a lot of Rolling Stones—stuff like 'Street Fighting Man' and 'Sympathy For The Devil'. Also at that time Alice Cooper was very big for us both. We both loved Alice and Randy was especially taken with Glen Buxton's style of guitar playing. Randy loved to make weird noises on the guitar and he was fired up to do that by Glen Buxton's Alice Cooper records. Alice Cooper was the very first gig we went to, supported by Black Oak Arkansas. It's interesting that not many people have picked up on that, even the guitar magazines, which I think is because of the Ozzy / Sabbath association. Randy's inspiration really came from Leslie West, Glen Buxton and Mick Ronson."

Next in the trail of fledgling bands would come Smokie. Still just 13, Rhoads and Garni had elevated their status to the Hollywood club scene and would be patronized by KROQ radio anchor Rodney Bingamheimer performing on a regular basis at the DJ's club. "That was a great club, great for us too because Rodney was very influential on the scene" Garni maintains. "Everyone in the club was only 15 or 16 but everyone got served liqueur. We had this huge Transsexual guy 'Smokie' as a singer. He couldn't sing a note but he looked incredible. On drums there was a guy named John Barber."

Smokie would be perfectly poised to capitalise on the latest influential wave to hit America—Glam. "We really got into it—Slade, Mott The Hoople, David Bowie. We'd start to play all their songs. Randy really got off on Mick Ronson. If you've ever seen the 'Ziggy Stardust' video you can see it all—Randy looks exactly like Mick Ronson from that video, the hair, the clothes, the Les Paul—even Randy's facial features."

Ultimately Smokie bit the dust, unfortunately in less than salutary tones. "Basically 'Smokie' didn't have all his faculties" Garni says bluntly. "In fact, he was crazy and violent with it. We had to get rid of him because he got violent with us—he was a big guy and, remember, we were still just kids. From then on we had a few singers—Cagey, Glenn, all of these when the band had no real name as such."

In 1976 the band Little Women would provide a useful step up to a semi-professional outfit in search of more than just a good time. Rhoads and Garni were No. 15 and more enthused about the prospect of Rock superstardom than ever before. Trouble was they had no frontman. The story of just how Kevin DuBrow enters the scenario has been elaborated on time and time again albeit with less and less reliability. DuBrow is a pivotal figure in the saga as it was his drive and ambition that would, as Kelly Garni recognises, push Randy Rhoads into the public arena by way of his first recording contract.

"Randy and I were at our good friend Hillary's house" relates Kelly taking up the tale. "We had been partying pretty hard, hadn't slept at all and it got to early morning. I heard Hillary in the next room talking to someone on the phone about a singer, a guy who sounded like Rod Stewart. Of course I caught this because any mention of a singer was useful so I asked Hillary "Who was that guy? Tell me all about him." I got a name and number and called him. I said 'We've got a band ... of sorts. I think we should meet.'"

Bearing in mind Garni and Rhoads were too young to drive a friend drove the pair over to Kevin DuBrow's house. There they were treated to a 8mm film reel of Kevin performing live with guitarist Stan Sobel of The Dickies. Trouble is there was no sound. "He was dressed up just like Rod Stewart, even had the scarf!" Garni laughs at the memory of it. "Both Randy and I thought this was really silly and, in truth, we weren't very impressed. We both kept looking at the door wondering how we were going to get out."

The budding musicians may have crossed DuBrow off their list but the singer had other ideas. "He would not leave us alone" Garni records. "Kevin would just keep phoning us day after day after day. In the end it just became too much so we gave in and invited him around to audition in the garage at our house. Well, he was just horrible. He was like the worst singer you ever heard in your life. We told him not to call us anymore but still he persisted."

Figuring DuBrow's persistence must surely account for something, and still lacking an all important frontman, Rhoads and Garni relented—again. "We thought if the guy is that keen to promote himself it can't be all bad. Kevin is certainly not what you would ever call shy. Randy and I spoke about it and thought, well, perhaps we could try and teach him to sing. Kevin was a big Steve Marriott fan so we agreed we would try to teach him to sing in that style. To his credit Kevin got it down pretty good—he really worked at it. Then of course, as soon as he had his foot in the door, he took over everything. Kevin wanted to be a Rock Star more than any of us."

With DuBrow now affirmed as frontman the trio drafted drummer Drew Forsyth from an earlier Rhoads / Garni combo Mildrid Pierce. The band was complete. DuBrow suggested the name Little Women. After a matter of weeks with this handle the band switched to Quiet Riot, the name prompted once more by Kevin after hearing Status Quo's guitarist Rick Parfitt describing the band's sound.

DuBrow's Gung-Ho attitude soon snared management, of a sorts, for Quiet Riot. "Actually this guy was a coke dealer who put some money into us" laughs Kelly. "He was actually pretty helpful, got us our first gigs and arranged our first recordings, got us from the embryo into the carriage so to speak. Unfortunately he had a tendency to violence so our parting with him was very bitter."

The singer would then strike a deal with a more soundly based management set up—the Toby Organisation run by David Joseph and Warren Etner, business advisors to Angel. "The new managers really got things moving for Quiet Riot" motions Garni. "They refined us from the raw product that we were." However, the Toby Organisation had a game plan set out for Quiet Riot that was not in keeping with the band's ideal path of career enhancement. Ready to Rock the band would be dismayed at some of the image moulding they would undergo as Kelly Garni explains.

"We were a hard Rock band but they had different ideas. Some of it was just plain goofy. They wanted to portray us as innocent little schoolboys but with a mischievous side to our nature. They even got me to dress up in a sailor suit. This period is actually pretty interesting because it's where Randy's trademark bow tie comes from. They kept telling us to think like The Knack! They had plans for a TV show and everything. Randy and I just wanted to play more spookier, menacing stuff like Alice Cooper but every time we tried they would say no." What the Toby Organisation did achieve was a record deal. Unfortunately it was in the wrong country.

Quiet Riot was rejected by every major American label without exception. The band put in a seemingly interminable round of showcases at the Starwood Club to no avail. Refusing to acknowledge defeat Joseph and Etner spread their net further and following a few trips to the land of the rising yen and snared a deal with CBS in Japan. Quiet Riot would then enter into a four year period of life inside a bubble. The band had a debut album out but no one could buy it in the stores. Their reputation as a live act was also being bolstered by a rapid climb up the ladder at the Starwood Club. Starting out booked by Michelle Meyer as an opening act Quiet Riot soon elevated themselves from amateur night on a Sunday up through the mid week rankings to rapidly score a regular residency. And that's where they got stuck.

"We spent four years languishing at the Starwood Club" says Garni resignedly. "At the time it was great because we packed the house every night we played but we couldn't break out of it. It's great to be playing in front of a thousand people who come back to see you week after week but we were going nowhere. We were also broke."

There were other gigs, such as at the Santa Monica Civic guesting for Angel, but in reality Quiet Riot were anchored at the Starwood Club and with a very short chain. There were internal problems too. Garni and DuBrow were growing farther and farther apart. The frustration of their treadmill career predicament and an ever growing resentment building between bassist and singer triggered Garni's next move.

"I'd had enough. I'd only ever known music. I was 19 and had no money. The lifestyle was getting to me too" he readily admits. "I had an ever growing problem between Kevin and I. It wasn't just his fault, I was drinking a lot, I said stupid things, got thrown in jail. Kevin had his hands full with me. I was constantly provoking him."

Eventually the atmosphere had worsened to such a degree that the two could not even bear each other's presence in the same room. Garni had been seriously considering a career in the emergency services and, after the conclusion of a band meeting, it was time to jump. "I became a Paramedic which I stuck at for ten years and loved every minute of it. I kept my friendship with Randy. Nothing could change that."

Randy and Quiet Riot persevered, enlisting a young Cuban by the name of Rudy Sarzo to fill the void left by Garni's departure. A second album for the Japanese market came and went. Quiet Riot was treading water, still waving, not yet drowning...

Came the day of the first Ozzy / Randy / Dana tryout at Dirk Dalton's studios all was not going to plan. Strum has a vivid recollection of the day. "Ozzy had a few drinks and kinda did not want to go. I kept telling him he had to go. Trust me. This is the guy!" However, despite the pair getting to the audition Ozzy's mood could not be lifted. "You could see he was as frustrated as Hell. He hated life, he hated LA and he missed England and his home."

About 10 p.m. the studio rear buzzer rang and Randy made his way in with Strum helping set up his gear—a small old Gibson amp, a dist box and an echoplex. "Randy was nervous because he still did not know what to play. I assured him it would be fine." Unbeknown to Randy Rhoads he was not the only one whose nerves were on edge. Dana Strum was deeply concerned. "Ozzy was in the lobby drinkin' and gettin' pretty fucked up. I was concerned that he might pass out and not get all of this. I was freakin'!"

Strum set about getting Randy into action before his boss flaked out. Wisely he had set the studio up prior to the guitarist's arrival. "I got a sound on Randy, just so that we could hear him, he still kept telling me that he did not know what to play. I played a bit of bass with him to relax the vibe and told him the Starwood solo would be the shit. This was the first time I had played with him and he was ... great!"

The bass player rushed out into the lobby and could not believe his own eyes when he found Ozzy sound asleep. He was not prepared to come this far though to simply let the opportunity slip through his fingers. "I woke him. He was fucked up and asked me to take him home, just take him home" he relates. "This was a crazy night. I had a guy who wanted to go home and a guitar player that did not really want to try!"

Strum was now in real fear of losing his own position but felt there was no turning back now. "I got Ozzy up and told him firmly that he had to at least see this guy." A degree of self preservation also crept in as Strum admits. "I also told him that I live in Los Angeles and he can't do this to me."

Somehow Ozzy, with Strum's physical assistance, made it out of his torpor and into the studio room. Desperation had by now set in. "I sat him down. I told Randy, who had no idea how fucked up Ozzy was, to play."

Randy replied "Like what?"

"The Starwood solo trip—just play!!" ordered the exasperated Strum.

"I fucking cranked the big speakers in that place. Ozzy's eyes opened and he listened, looked at me and laughed." The bass player recalls.

"Have him come to the hotel tomorrow" beamed Ozzy. "Tell him he's got the job".

Later that night Strum got on the phone to Randy still trying to convince him to join the band.

Dana Strum, according to Kelly Garni, is correct in the assumption that Randy was far from keen on the proposed alliance. "I can't think of any other way to say this but Randy and I both had the same opinion of Black Sabbath—we thought they were fools. In truth Randy thought it was just silly and had very little musical interest there" explains Garni in terms which may come as a jarring shock to Ozzy fans.

"Randy came from a fairly religious background and had a big problem with all the black magic stuff. It was against everything he believed or had been taught. Musically we thought Black Sabbath was music for old farts, the kind of people who sat around all day and smoked pot—old hippies. I can't express it in any other terms, we thought it was downright silly. This might sound odd because we were both heavily into Alice Cooper. But, Quiet Riot was going nowhere and Randy was sick of having no money ..."

Fortunately, and in spite of Randy's misgivings, the relationship between the three personnel did solidify. More significantly, and in spite of the guitarist's wariness of the whole 'dark' side of Black Sabbath, Ozzy and Randy would quickly develop a unique friendship. Rhoads did turn up at the Le Parc as instructed but his appearance was not all Strum or Ozzy expected. The bassist met Randy, clad in a polka dot shirt and rings, in the rain outside the hotel and took him up to Ozzy's room.

Randy was offered a beer but declined in favour of a diet coke. "Oh no, not another one" sighed Ozzy resignedly. Randy's unusual choice of attire provoked another question that needed settling and a less than tactful Ozzy was as forthright as ever. "You're not gay are you?" Randy stared at Strum in disbelief. "No doubt he wondered why he was there again" Strum laughs. "No doubt!" The guitarist, probably wondering what on earth his hairdresser girlfriend Jodi would make of this madness, was simply dumbstruck.

Subsequent interviews given by Ozzy suggest that Randy's reply offered that, although he wasn't gay, he was Catholic. It broke the ice and soon plans were made for another jam session. This time Randy suggested he knew of a great drummer—Frankie Banali.

Making his departure Randy and Strum discussed details such as pay, the name of the band and other details. He also reminded Strum that he still had commitments teaching at his Mom's music school.

The second workout took place at Mars Studios. Strum had organized everything as was becoming the norm. Badaxe roadie Bill Birch was conscripted to help move Randy and Dana's gear as both only had small cars. Banali brought his own drums along. It was the first time Strum and Banali had met and while the trio were setting up their gear they listened to an R&B band rehearsing next door. They were surprised to find out the soulful tones were that of Glenn Hughes.

Ozzy was late and so a relaxing jam ensued. Strum has fond memories. "We jammed and played riffs, some of my stuff, some of Randy's. 'Crazy Train' vibe stuff. The magic was unfolding big time." When Ozzy finally arrived so did Jet Record's owner Don Arden. This notorious and powerful figure in the music industry was also Osbourne's official manager. The comfortable atmosphere evaporated but soon the four were so deep in the music that Arden's presence was soon forgotten.

Strum is effusive. "Ozzy sang kinda any lyric he thought of just to get a feel. He really is a gut feeling type of guy. It was fun for all of us and Randy played fucking great. He was on fire. You had to know that this was it. History!" Sitting in the same room Strum's friend and roadie Bill Birch must have been one of the happiest men on the planet.

Further run throughs would take place after this event but without Banali who, coincidentally, hooked up with Quiet Riot. Many of the riffs and formative ideas which would eventually surface on the first Ozzy album were worked out during these sessions in the studio and in Ozzy's hotel room.

Outside of the studio Strum's role as general organizer was being stretched to the limit of his capabilities. "There were lots of phone calls to keep it going. Randy was still not certain, my band was pissed and Kevin DuBrow was pissed. The truth was though that Randy was having mixed feelings about Quiet Riot and did not like the band's last album. He hated the guitar sound big time. Professionally he felt really bad about it." To this day DuBrow has not forgiven Strum for poaching his star guitarist.

The next move was a relocation to England but concerns over the whole financing of the endeavour were raised by Randy who wanted to know who was going to pay for everything. Strum was just in it for the experience. "At this point none of us had a dime. All my phone bills, my time and Randy's time were on us" he states matter of factly without any trace of bitterness. "My vibe was to just let it roll but I later felt that Don Arden did not feel the same way. I was to learn more about that later but at that moment I just wanted to be in the game. I loved Black Sabbath and the music that Ozzy did and that was it. The dollars did not matter because I loved the shit. It was a treat."

Dana Strum believes that his energetic stage performances and his general gung-ho manner in getting things done did not put him in Don Arden's good books. There is even a suggestion that Strum by necessity had taken too much control of the situation and Arden felt he needed to regain the initiative. The bass player began to get a sense of foreboding that, in his words, he "was in the wrong place at the wrong time".

"I'm a strange guy to be a bass player really. In fact I make a better manager or producer" he confesses. Although these qualities and skills would come to the fore with Strum's very public success in his later acts right then and there the people pulling the strings were sensing potential trouble. Not only was Ozzy's new bassist playing the four string role but getting intricately wrapped up in the day to day affairs of running the star's life. Dana was making the phone calls, Dana was driving the car, arranging the meets, placating the nervous, enthusing the faithful and smoothing the rough edges.

Within this whirlwind of activity Strum first met Don's daughter Sharon who was then in the employ of her father and working at Jet Records. Outside of his adventures with Ozzy Strum was earning by editing and cutting radio spots. Sensing all was not well within the Ozzy camp he was also getting plans in mind for a new band just in case. "There were many phone calls and lots of work still for Ozzy and Randy but the more the cards played out I felt I was about to be the low draw."

Ozzy journeyed to England on his own whilst Randy and Dana waited anxiously. Randy had actually been prevented from travelling by not having a passport. High and dry in Los Angeles and with no word from England or Jet Records Strum tried to convince the guitarist that Ozzy would get in touch. The call eventually came—but only for Randy.

Undaunted, Strum simply got on with matters in hand and duly assembled Modern Design in union with former Buffalo, New York native and former Cheater and Bang Bang guitarist Ron Mancuso. Modern Design's original vocalist, Strum's erstwhile Badaxe colleague Louie Merlino, relocated back to New York and was replaced by Mark Free. Ultimately the group, although having made sizable waves, was short-lived. Mancuso would reunite with Merlino to create Beggars & Thieves (the same band that would also include a later Ozzy player—bassist Phil Soussan). Mancuso also laid down guitars on Vanilla Fudge's comeback album 'Mystery'. Free would be involved with Signal, Blue Murder, Black Roses and Unruly Child before taking the Rock star reinvention process to the nth degree by becoming a woman—Marcie Free.

Post Modern Design, Strum put his energies into a hot new act centred on ex-Kiss ultra speed guitarist Vinnie Vincent. Eking a living as a session player, Vincent Cusano, to give Vinnie his real name, had played on 70s Disco king Dan Hartman's popular 'Instant Replay' album before teaming up with songwriter Felix Cavaliere in the group Treasure, recording an album for Epic in 1977.

Prior to joining Kiss, Vincent had been working with the former New England trio of bassist Gary Shea, keyboard player Jimmy Waldo and drummer Hirsh Gardner in the Los Angeles based Metal band Warrior, recording some impressive demo material. It would be his high profile union with the legendary Kiss though on the 'Lick It Up' tour that Vincent gained his kudos. In helping to form what was to become the Vinnie Vincent Invasion Strum had at last found the vehicle to deliver in the public arena.

Signing a deal with Chrysalis Records Strum and Vincent pulled in Houston, Texas born ex-Nitro drummer Bobby Rock. The band had all but chosen to work with Greg Bissonette until Rock auditioned. Bissonette wound up getting a gig with David Lee Roth. Vocal duties were performed by onetime Journey and Channel frontman Robert Fleischman.

Upon the album's release it was immediately noticeable that the soberly dressed Fleischman stuck out like a sore thumb surrounded by band mates who favoured, upon the hair extension sporting Vincent's instigation, a rather over the top Glam image. It was no surprise to learn that the group would be hitting the road with a completely different singer, adding former X-Cursion vocalist Mark Slaughter in place of a departing Fleischman. Interestingly, Randy's friend Kelly Garni, upon relocating to Las Vegas, had also been a member of X-Cursion.

At first, as the band hit the road opening for Alice Cooper, confused fans believed that Slaughter was actually Fleischman wearing a wig, but quickly became to warm to the man. Slaughter made his Vinnie Vincent Invasion recording debut on the 'All

Systems Go' album of 1988. The group would fall apart on tour as Vincent became embroiled in a series of lawsuits. The group officially split in August 1988 and Dana Strum immediately threw himself into production work on demos with Los Angeles outfit Brunette. Bobby Rock wound up working with Nelson.

Strum extended his reach as a producer laying claim to records such as Detente's 1986 outing 'Recognize No Authority' and Sweet Savage's debut the same year. By 1989 Strum, retaining ties with Mark Slaughter had geared up to launch his new venture Slaughter. The band immediately hit the big time in 1990 with the release of their debut album 'Stick It To Ya' and the smash hit single 'Up All Night'. This debut was followed by the even more successful 'Fly To The Angels', both reaping the benefits of heavy exposure on MTV in the United States where the group was to tour with Kiss.

The band had convened in Los Angeles whilst Slaughter and Strum were producing demos for the North Carolina outfit White Heat (who became platinum act Firehouse once signed to Epic Records). The duo met guitarist Tim Kelly, a veteran of a number of local bands in Philadelphia at Cherokee Recording Studios. Houston resident Blas Elias was then added after auditioning for the position.

Due to the band's success on the road Chrysalis Records opted to release a live mini album, appropriately titled 'Stick It To Ya Live' and containing five tracks. Slaughter toured America during 1992 opening for Ozzy Osbourne in support of 'The Wild Life' album. Strum's services were later hastily employed in the Vince Neil band when an inter band fist-fight saw the rapid mid tour exit of previous incumbent Robbie Crane.

With many of the 80s era Rock acts becoming the victims of a general major record company cull Slaughter responded by considerably toughening up their sound for the 1995 outing 'Fear No Evil'. And whilst other acts floundered amidst the Grunge revolution Slaughter resolutely set about a seemingly inexhaustible touring schedule. Slaughter's 1997 album 'Revolution' saw the band seemingly drifting into a 60s era Psychedelia direction.

Sadly, Tim Kelly was killed in a car accident on February 5, 1998. Kelly, who was driving from Baghdad, Arizona to Kingman was involved in a collision with an oncoming semi-articulated truck that had jackknifed in front of him. Kelly was taken to hospital but died from head injuries sustained in the accident. Kelly had played his last shows with Slaughter at Detroit's Harpo's club on November 14 and 15, 1997.

Slaughter was expected to continue, although initial reports suggested that Tim Kelly would not be permanently replaced. As it transpired Jeff Blando eventually fulfilled the position. The band, still a major draw, put in a series of shows toward the end of 1998 as part of 'The Rock Never Stops' American tour alongside Firehouse, Warrant and Quiet Riot.

Although prioritising Slaughter, Strum had widened his tally of production credits to include Kik Tracee's 1991 'No Rules' session, China Rain's 1992 opus 'Bed Of Nails', Sister Whiskey's eponymous 1993 record and Mark Hafer's 1998 album 'Wanna Get High?' The man, along with Slaughter, also worked on the original Firehouse demos and has sessioned for Danny Spanos and Rod Falconer.

Strum's formative years with Badaxe and his endeavours with Ozzy Osbourne have given the bassist an experience rooted in practicality that would bode well for throughout the 80s and 90s. Known in the business as a man of sharp practice he owns his own digital studio and touring production company.

"The world of Hard Rock and those that stake a valid claim in it is and always was small. It's like the porn industry. The same people over and over. So, I learned, over and over" he motions. "I never really fitted into many of the circles. I wouldn't kiss ass to get a deal or play at fake friends just because I wanted to make it. I've been a slave to my trade. I would not trade a day for the way I have had to work my way up through the music business. I've loved it all and it's made me a stronger person—no silver spoon shit with me."

The rewards for Strum have been rich indeed. Now a native of Las Vegas Strum resides in a palatial self designed retreat somewhat reminiscent of a Spanish castle. Over the main fireplace hangs a swordfish coated in dollar bills, a win in a bet Strum had with an attorney. All in all a home of a bona fide Rock star. "I love it all, the music, the vibe, the women and the Rock n' Roll life. I don't regret a day."

The next bass player in line to enter the saga would prove to be over the unrolling years an ever reliable foil for Ozzy Osbourne. Although Bob Daisley and Ozzy have had many spats and altercations over more than a decade the Australian four stringer's talents both musically and as a songwriter would see him playing a sometimes pivotal role off and on over the next decade. Daisley's dues were paid with Stan Webb's illustrious Blues Rockers Chicken Shack although he was for a while at his own admission tempted away for a spell by the bright lights and quick success of Pop music for a while.

"I joined Mungo Jerry in 1973" Bob readily confides. "Remember them? It was actually the management who thought I would be right for the job. We had a couple of hit records, 3 I think, and I did 'Top Of The Pops' and all that. Although it was fun it wasn't credible so I went back to Chicken Shack to play some serious music. Those were great times. We had Robbie Blunt on guitar then from Silverhead, Well, that all ended for me in '75 when Luther Grosvenor alias ... Ariel Bender! He had a good track record with Mott The Hoople and Spooky Tooth at the time. On drums was Paul Nichols of Lindisfarne. That's how Widowmaker came together. That was a great band although Steve Ellis had a severe drinking problem which messed things up quite a bit. We got in John Butler for the second album."

The band would land the honours of opening for The Who on a series of mammoth dates across the UK when Roger Daltrey had caught the bands appearance on the TV show 'The Old Grey Whistle Test'. Bob explains how these prestigious showcases came about. "Steve Ellis knew Roger Daltrey and of course Roger knew of Steve's drinking problem. So, when Roger saw Widowmaker on the TV he phoned to Steve congratulating him for getting his act together and for putting together such a good band."

Widowmaker also famously supported Uriah Heep on their UK 'High And Mighty' tour which is where Bob came across Lee Kerslake. With Hawkwind man Huw Lloyd Llangton on guitar an American tour would lead to the final disintegration of Widowmaker but offered a fresh opportunity for the bassist. At the close of the tour in Los Angeles Daisley's colleague from Mungo Jerry guitarist Dick Middleton hooked up a meeting with a friend of his. "Dick introduced me to Ritchie Blackmore who told me he was looking for a bassist" Daisley reveals. "The auditions were held at this huge film studio I seem to remember. Well, anyway, I was told I had got the gig but I wasn't sure I wanted it. I was really wary of being a side man but I spoke to friends who convinced me it was a good step up and would do my career some good. After all, Rainbow was an arena band. As it turned out I had a great time with Rainbow."

Bob Daisley became a member of Rainbow when many would judge the band to be at their creative peak. "I did the 'Long Live Rock n' Roll' album and the following world tour which went everywhere." Daisley put in his live debut with Rainbow at the Swedish capitol of Stockholm before trekking around America, Japan and Europe. The band was riding on a high but famously Rainbow's tradition of instability would present itself. Rainbow vocalist Ronnie James Dio offered Bob Daisley his opinion on the circumstances unfolding and a lot more besides.

"There came a time when Ronnie took me aside to tell me that in his opinion Ritchie was considering changing players and that he in turn was looking to set up his own band. Would I be interested? Well, of course I was. Ronnie has a world class voice

Bob Daisley (left) backstage with Rainbow. Pic: Rich Galbraith.

and Rainbow was looking a little shaky for all of us except Ritchie. So I went back to my home in London and waited on Ronnie who told me he was lining up a deal and it was all looking good. Ritchie did of course get his new people in as Ronnie predicted. I hung on and spoke to Ronnie numerous times who was saying "Hang in there, we've got a guitarist, we'll fly you over when we're ready." I was still hanging around until I finally read in a magazine that Ronnie had joined Black Sabbath! Well, all I could think of was thanks a lot Ronnie!"

What happened next would turn out to be one of those strange twists of fate. "It was ironic" Bob relates. "Soon after that episode I met Ozzy at a gig in London. I had gone to see Girl at the Camden Electric Ballroom and Arthur Sharp, from Ozzy and Girl's record label Jet Records, introduced me to Ozzy. We got chatting and that's when he told me he was getting a band together and it was arranged that I should visit Ozzy at his house."

The initial conversation did soon manifest itself into a trip to Ozzy's house in Staffordshire for the bass player. "Ozzy's house was set up for auditions as he had a kind of rehearsal studio built onto the side of it" Daisley recollects. He would be surprised to discover he was not the first to arrive. "There were two different guys there already—a red haired guitarist and a drummer. To this day I don't remember who they were, we were never properly introduced. I think Ozzy just said "Meet Jim" or something like that. Well, we started to play a bit and afterwards Ozzy took me into another room and asked me what I thought. Frankly my honest opinion was that these guys were not really good enough and I said so. Ozzy thought about it a bit and then marched into the studio and said "It's not working out guys. Pack up your gear and go home." I was stunned but they just did as Ozzy ordered. They just left without saying a word. Never did find out who they were."

At this stage Ozzy resolved to get a serious band together and Randy was flown over from Los Angeles. Further sessions were held at Ozzy's house where songs were starting to get knocked into shape. By now Ozzy and Randy were beginning to develop a close friendship that was becoming apparent to all. Randy and Bob too enjoyed a moment of synchronicity when, just as they were finishing a song, the pair said simultaneously to each other "I like the way you play".

An old friend of Ozzy's called Barry Scrannage (more popularly known as 'Spencer') was helping out on drums and a lot more besides. "Spencer was a useful bloke to have around" opines Bob. "He was our general helper, our roadie, our drummer and our driver. In fact we used him a bit like a drum machine. He was never at any stage discussed as being the drummer for the band though."

There have been tales filtering through the years that this unit of Ozzy, Randy and Bob with Spencer on drums actually gigged. The truth, according to Daisley, is that one jam session was put on for the locals in order to test out the new songs. Bob brings to mind the event that sparked the rumours. "We were working up these songs at a place in Ilkeshaw owned by Transam Trucking. It was a really nice live in situation and we had use of this proper rehearsal studio in a big barn like building" he describes. "Because we had got to know quite a few people down at the local pub we invited maybe 8 or 10 of them back. Spencer sat in and played drums. We needed to see what it felt like to play these songs in front of people so that's what we did. It certainly wasn't a 'gig' in any sense."

This 'public jam' did not go without incident though as the bassist reveals. "I remember one local kid was pissed and got really mouthy. In fact he soon got to be a pain in the arse. He got really pushy and actually tried to get into a fight with Ozzy. It was quite funny because Ozzy broke a cup over the kid's back and told him to "Fuck off!" There was a bit of a scuffle and this troublemaker was thrown out. Well, later, I went and found Ozzy and he was sitting in front of this open fire drawing himself a fake black eye with an eyebrow pencil!"

Spencer and Ozzy, although long time compatriots, would during this time have their fallings out. Daisley summons up an altercation between the two which set Randy Rhoads into a state of panic. "Ozzy and Spencer had gone off to a neighbour's house while Randy and I stayed back at Ozzy's house. Well, they came back arguing, obviously having had a few drinks. I don't know what the reason was but Ozzy was really annoyed at Spencer for insulting his neighbour somehow. Ozzy got so angry he picked up this piece of wood and started to chase Spencer around and around his yard! It was really funny but Randy took this deadly seriously and ran up to his room. All we could hear was the noises of him barricading himself in his room by pushing all his furniture in front of the door! Randy didn't live that down for a long time."

In the midst of all this male bonding and with auditions taking shape it seemed as though Spencer's role in the whole situation became a point of contention. "Spencer was never the drummer for the band at any stage" states Bob categorically. "We never told him he was the drummer either. He was very useful to have around, driving to London for us, running errands and so forth and we did use him to lay down a beat so that Randy, Ozzy and I could work up the songs.

Jet Records were paying us a living wage at the time from our advance, just £100 a week I think. I remember that Spencer got his envelope and it had written on it 'Roadie's Wages' with about £50 or something in it. He was pretty pissed off with this and threw his money into the fire. He may have thought that he was in line to be the drummer but I don't understand that because we were actually auditioning drummers for a long time so he knew the score. Spencer still stayed with us for quite some time afterwards as our helper."

With Randy, Bob and Ozzy now really beginning to work off each other the proto-band now began an earnest search for a drummer. It proved to be a more arduous task than any of them could have possibly imagined. The efforts extolled in structuring a new band were put sharply into focus when the rejuvenated Ronnie led Black Sabbath released 'Heaven And Hell' in April of that year. The record not only achieved a No. 9 placing in the UK, the highest for any Sabbath album for the past five years, it was already being heralded as a classic. Iommi had also persuaded Geezer Butler back on board. Ozzy was truly out on his own.

'Heaven And Hell' broke free in May of 1980.

Producer Martin Birch had been called in by Ronnie James Dio, the singer being justly impressed with Birch's work with Rainbow. All the promise of Dio's tradition with Rainbow's career peaks with 'Stargazer', 'Gates Of Babylon' and 'Man On The Silver Mountain' was undoubtedly fulfilled. Indeed, Dio made such an authoritative stamp on the album it took many unawares. Fans of Rainbow's darker moments, such as their monolithic mythology fuelled 'Stargazer' could not believe their luck.

Besides bearing the title of Black Sabbath on the sleeve, a wry depiction of poker playing angels taking a cigarette break, the album bore very little relation to the tired latter day Ozzy era albums 'Never Say Die' and 'Technical Ecstasy'. Those records had been like watching an ageing, overweight, punch-drunk prize boxer vainly launching blows that all missed the target. Fans and media alike had felt a degree of betrayal at being offered such third rate product. 'Heaven And Hell' was an entirely new beast, one which had broken evolutionary laws by leap frogging and bypassing accepted genetic norms to emerge as undisputed king predator.

Dio was to be the complete antithesis of Ozzy. The American brought with him a whole realm of magic, mystery along with an accompanying and quite enthralling method of delivery. Quite simply Ronnie James Dio was one of the very finest singers of the age, not only possessing the range that has so captivated Blackmore, but also a character that imbued his songs with a sense of very real majesty. A bard out of step with time, Dio's audiences should rightly have been the courts and palaces of feudal Europe. Ever noticed that all doorways in castles are vertebrae crunching challenges for twentieth century tourists? Ronnie James Dio would have sailed through with ease, his mediaeval stature in perfect harmony with his surroundings. Dragons and kings were but second nature to him.

The album sleeve credits took due consideration for the complete cortege of players. On the surface it looked harmoniously democratic but Ronnie James Dio was, in truth, somewhat rankled. "I didn't agree with that. You look at the album and it credits everybody but the truth was that 'Heaven And Hell' was written by Tony Iommi and Ronnie James Dio. The thing was, Geezer wasn't even there. He had left then came back again just before the album was recorded so pretty much all of those songs were written in between. How can that be that he gets a credit—part of my credit—for writing a song when he wasn't even there? Geezer left the band, people don't know that but he did, and got rewarded just the same.

It was like this. Two people wrote 'Heaven And Hell', in the main. You wouldn't know that by looking at the album sleeve though. To my way of thinking the people that grind these things out of their minds for days upon end, agonising over each turn of phrase to get that track just right—the people with the talent, had their contribution belittled. It all looked equal but it wasn't. Geezer's contribution was minimal.

What I would say is this; take my vocals, my melodies off the songs and then take out Tony's guitar parts. You won't be left with half a song to credit that's for sure. I just never understood it. It was alien to me. It would make my skin crawl to claim credits for something I had not done."

Geoff Nicholls, who would get involved in the lyrical aspect of Sabbath's song-writing in later years, describes how, from his point of view, the form of the album was conjured up. "Ronnie did all of the lyrics for 'Heaven And Hell'—everything. It was very much his baby in that respect. That might sound a little odd because of course Geezer had been responsible for virtually of all Sabbath's words before but this was Ronnie's thing 100%. There was never any talk of changing this or that because Ronnie had done such a perfect job. He was very clear about what he wanted and put an enormous amount of work into those songs.

All of the main guitar riffs came from Tony but a lot of the structuring of songs I had a big hand in. Not 'Children Of The Sea' because that was in place already but certainly a lot of the other stuff. Geezer came in right at the end."

The musical environment into which 'Heaven And Hell' was plunged could certainly have not been more conducive. The full gale of the NWoBHM ('New Wave of British Heavy Metal') movement was in full flow, thrusting up eager new talent such as Iron Maiden, Saxon, Def Leppard, Angel Witch and Diamond Head. All of the NWoBHM frontrunners had some grain of Black Sabbath's genetic code in their makeup somewhere.

This British renaissance of interest in all things loud, leathered, long-haired and preferably drenched in patchouli oil was no mere fad. It would help fuel Rock n' Roll throughout the next decade. Established acts, that had been rubbing shoulders with Sabbath for many years, such as UFO, fellow Brummies Judas Priest and AC/DC, would all be given a welcome, second wind toward the close of the decade. Because many of these bands already knew the ropes they were poised to make maximum capital out of this good fortune. In the UK, 1980 was a very heavy year indeed as Black Sabbath, Motorhead, Judas Priest, Iron Maiden, Thin Lizzy, AC/DC, Rainbow, Whitesnake, Gillan and Saxon all scored large on the charts.

However, even this sudden geysering of Metal

could not mask the pedigree of 'Heaven And Hell'. Giving muscle and sinew to Ronnie's visions Iommi, Butler, Nicholls and Ward had gone above and beyond all expectations. Recent history in the Ozzy led song-writing department had not augured well, with the last real Sabbath classics being dispensed during as far back as 1975. The band had dug deep and pulled out not one classic but a whole fistful. The album opened with the blistering pace of 'Neon Knights', a stampeding rhino of a track that, in an age that was yet to know the meaning of the word 'thrash', sprinted along at an unheard of thundering pace. Bravely released as the album's inaugural single 'Neon Knights' bulldozed its way up to a creditable No. 22 in the UK charts.

Importantly, 'Heaven And Hell' saw a nostalgic regression to the glory days of complete album packages. The sharp difference here was that 'Heaven And Hell' was for its time a thoroughly modern record, the troglodyte hammerings that had hewn out seventies outings replaced by an air of cool sophistication. It was no vicarious impostor. Indeed it bore the brand of Black Sabbath with an obvious pride. The whole edifice hinged around the Wagnerian scale of 'Children Of The Sea', the Goliath like title track and the menacing 'Die Young'. Even humbler tracks such as 'Lady Evil' and 'Lonely Is The Word' would have proven life savers if included on Sabbath's more recent Ozzy led antecedent works.

The tsunami waves that reverberated in the Rock scene from the impact of 'Heaven And Hell' were of so great a magnitude that Black Sabbath would be treated to a double dose of chart action in the UK. Within a few short weeks a collection of rustic live Ozzy era tracks had been cobbled together and pumped out as 'Live At Last'. The marketing teams rubbed their hands with glee as this second rate set of tapes, lambasted by both Iommi and Osbourne camps, made its way to No. 5 in the charts. On the singles front, with 'Neon Knights' having already raided the charts, the hoary old warhorse that was 'Paranoid' was dragged out and shoved back into the arena during August, climbing all the way to No. 14. 'Heaven And Hell' was not finished yet though and the sprawling 'Die Young' duly signalled the third Black Sabbath presence in the single charts that year in December.

The huge success of 'Heaven And Hell' would mask some very real business concerns that preyed upon the band. The album was in fact the band's last with their existing Warner Bros. contract. If the experiment had failed Sabbath would be in search of another home and, as it transpired, there were many at the label that thought 'Heaven And Hell' was one huge belly flop waiting to happen. The label had effectively washed their hands of Black Sabbath. That is until they were deluged with surprise reorders. "It had been a battle" concedes Ronnie. "With 'Heaven And Hell' being the last album under contract for Warner Bros. nobody from the label really cared. They certainly had not bothered to find out what we were up to in the studio when we were recording it. Their indifference gave us the attitude of "we'll show the bastards!" and it did well to bond us together.

One problem we had was that we were basically managing ourselves for a time, which is something labels hate. They think, rightly or wrongly, that all musicians are stupid. When Sandy Pearlman came in things started to happen. Our attorney suggested him and he certainly greased the wheels for us. Our world certainly became a lot easier to live in once Sandy arrived. Labels like to deal with the old boy network and Sandy fell straight into that. He had scored some considerable success with Blue Oyster Cult too. Everyone knows Blue Oyster Cult was more than a bit of a Black Sabbath copy really, even the name, so he was happy to get his hands on the real thing at long last.

When the album came out Warner Bros. did not really get behind the record like they should have. Pretty soon though the word of mouth started to really push the record. As soon as they realised there was a big buzz on the album the Warner Bros. machine kicked into gear and took over."

Ronnie attests that partly responsible for the rapid build up in sales was the habit sound engineers at live gigs got into of playing 'Heaven And Hell' before gigs. This was certainly a key factor in building the record's momentum as anyone attending concerts in early 1980 will verify. "I think that when the record came out the quality of the songs and the production really took people by surprise. 'Heaven And Hell' was a true 'street' record, by which I mean it sold by word of mouth" says the singer. "What we heard from the feedback to the label and management was that people were listening to the tracks on the radio and at gigs through the PA and asking "Who the Hell is that?" When they were told 'Black Sabbath' they couldn't quite believe it. We knew this was happening because we heard versions of the same story again and again."

Bob Daisley's memory of the pressure bearing down from Black Sabbath and of those initial auditions is that of urgency and frustratingly dealing with a seemingly endless run through of musicians who simply were not what they were looking for. "We tried out a German guy who was very good but just not quite right. There was a guy from Birmingham, Kelvin 'Yatta' Yates, and a bloke who played for Wings—Geoff Britton. We tried out Dixie Lee from Lone Star for about a week I think. Dixie was the guy who we used to record the demos at a studio in

Tony Iommi. Pic: Rich Galbraith.

Birmingham for the American label. He was so upset that he apparently cried when Ozzy told him he had not got the job."

Frankie Banali, who had bashed the tubs the one time in Los Angeles when Randy Rhoads first tried out with Ozzy and Dana Strum, was also approached by Randy but had prior recording commitments in Germany. The bands frustration was evident toward the tail end of these tryouts. By now the trio was ensconced in the legendary surroundings of Rockfield Studios in Monmouthshire. They had been endeavouring to finalize the band for three months. Next on the list was Dave Potts, previously with the highly rated late 60s band Skip Bifferty and also Ten Years After.

"All of us were really frustrated by it" sighs Bob. "We had been through at least 40 drummers and nothing was close. We nearly picked Dave Potts but I think Ozzy told him he had got the job to close the issue rather than because he was right for the job. Don't get me wrong, he was a very good drummer, but again just not right."

Producer and bass player for Ten Years After Leo Lyons had given Dave Potts the nod that he would be receiving a call in regard to the Ozzy vacancy. Dave remembers the occasion well. "I was told by Arthur Sharp, who I had been aware of since the early days when Don Arden was my manager in Skip Bifferty. "It's an audition and it is not an audition. We don't want to insult you." He explained I had to go down there for a week. If things didn't work out obviously I would come straight back but if they did click we would let it go and see what happened."

Potts recollects his initial jam with Ozzy, Randy & Bob. "We sat down the first day and discussed what we should do. Should we play a Black Sabbath number or something and they said "No, we'll do a jam." So, we did a 12 bar shuffle. And of course, I can excel in a shuffle and I knew that so when we were playing I was giving it a bit and Ozzy went 'Oh fucking hell! You're the drummer!'" Taken aback the drummer advised caution. "The trouble is that was a very impulsive thing to do and I think I said to Ozzy hang on we are going to need a few days."

Dave, who was using a kit previously owned by the renowned Cozy Powell, is philosophical about his week spent with the proto Blizzard Of Ozz in the Welsh hills. "I think Bob and Ozzy were prepared to work with me but I am not so sure about Randy. I hadn't been in a band for a while and I only had the double bass drum kit about a year so I don't think I was up to full speed with it like I was later with Praying Mantis. Randy being the best player probably spotted there was a little more work needed."

Nonetheless the Osbourne / Rhoads / Daisley / Potts quartet stuck at it for the allotted time. "I stayed there for the whole week but I think my drumming wasn't as good as that first session" Dave concludes. "We used to go running into the nearby town, which I guess was Monmouth. We would run into the town as if we were going to keep fit and then we would have a drink and run back. As a little team with Ozzy and Bob Daisley we hit it off. We would all have a drink, even Bob who was always looking after his health, and then run back to the studio afterwards. That last night I was with them they got me absolutely blitzed. It was a good laugh. So, it was a good relationship but to be honest sitting down at the kit I worked out after about three days that I wasn't going to get the gig but we were definitely going to have a bit of fun. If I had gone in there at the level I was at with Praying Mantis I think I would have been the drummer but because I had been inactive for a while I could see something was lacking."

Out of the seemingly endless stream of drummers the band auditioned Bob Daisley records his meeting with Dave for another reason beside the fact Ozzy told the sticksman he had got the job. "Funnily enough we were terrified of him!" he admits sheepishly. "We knew he was a karate expert and as soon as he was told he was in we knew it was a mistake. Ozzy, Randy nor I, would dare not tell him! What made it worse was that afterwards Dave went upstairs after we had told him he was in and then came down smelling of cologne and said "Right, let's go out and celebrate" That night we had a good time but we were all secretly feeling awful because we knew that although we had told Dave he was in actual fact he wasn't."

Dave's known martial arts skills also weighed heavily on their minds. Looking back Bob finds it amusing now but at the time it was a serious concern. Ozzy, Randy and Bob even resorted to theoretical pythonesque methods of informing the hapless drummer of the reality of his perceived tenure. "We discussed stupid things like standing a long way from him and shouting "Dave—You're not in!" then running off!!" Bob laughs with the memory of it. "In the end we all got together with him and told him that although he was a good drummer—which he was, that deep down inside we all felt it wasn't right. It turned out OK."

Dave Potts walked off to a career with NWoBHM pomp rockers Praying Mantis, later laying down his sticks to manage the band and also look after the business affairs of Clive Burr's Escape. Meantime a relieved Ozzy, Randy and Bob were happy to emerge from Rockfield without bruising and all limbs intact.

Dave Potts path would cross once more with Ozzy's. "Around 1980 I bumped into Ozzy in John Henry's Studios. Ozzy came over to me. He remembered me which is not unreasonable after a week together but he also asked "Have you still got that blue Ludwig drum kit?" I was rather stunned because I couldn't have told you what drum kit I had when I auditioned. Ozzy has got a very good memory for a lot of things. You know Ozzy is a crazy guy but underneath it all he is a very sensible guy. When I first met him and saw all those tattoos all over his knuckles I thought "Fucking hell." You know I was going with the first impression but it was completely wrong."

Bob Daisley too kept up with Dave. "I developed a good friendship with Bob Daisley" Dave affirms. "Back in the days of Praying Mantis I had bumped into him and he had taken me to some Buddhist classes and introduced me to that way of thinking. He absolutely amazed me. You look at him and think he is just another Rock n' Roll guy but there is so much more to him."

What made the whole auditioning process irksome in particular for Ozzy was that his personal choice was unavailable. "Ozzy really wanted Tommy Aldridge" Bob affirms. "They had met when Black Sabbath had done a lot of touring in America with Black Oak Arkansas during the mid 70s. Ozzy really rated him but he was tied up." Indeed, approaches had been made surreptitiously to Tommy Aldridge who, while filling in at the time with Gary Moore had been in the employ of Canadian master guitarist Pat Travers since 1977. The American drummer recalls a scouting expedition from the Ozzy camp during this period. "I was approached to join early on by a representative of Ozzy and declined as I did have a commitment with Gary Moore at the time" he recounts. "I remember we were in rehearsal when Ozzy and Randy came down. Randy was a fan of Gary's and it was at that time that I heard Randy play … Wowski! I thought to myself that it would be nice indeed to someday work with him. Little did I know at the time that it would come to pass. That was the first contact I had regarding possibly working with Ozzy."

Whilst the fledgling unit was focused on tracking down a drummer there was another musician who entered the frame during the Rockfield sessions. Stourbridge based keyboard player Bill Hunt was a teacher by profession but had solid Rock credentials under his belt. Hunt had been a member of Clem Clempson's post Bakerloo progressive Rock act Hannibal. The band, whose business affairs were handled by Black Sabbath manager Jim Simpson, had released one now extremely rare Rodger Bain produced album and toured as support to Black Sabbath on early German dates.

Switching to, of all things, the French horn the versatile musician had been involved with the debut Electric Light Orchestra line-up and later as a pianist maneuvered over to Roy Wood's Wizzard prior to entering the teaching profession. The call from Ozzy Osbourne would come not only out of the blue but at a typically ungodly Rock n' Roll hour. "I got a phone call from Ozzy at 3 o'clock in the morning!" Bill Hunt recalls vividly. "He said "My mate Spencer has been bending my ear about you"."

The keyboard player actually took a day off work on a Monday to journey down to Monmouth. "Well, I had heard about Ozzy's reputation of course so I had already had a couple of pints to give me Dutch courage by the time I arrived. When I got there only Spencer was there. He said "They're all on this health kick and they are out running." Seeing as they were out jogging Spencer and I went down the pub."

With the return of Ozzy, Rhoads and Daisley the group settled down in front of the TV. Hunt remembers some disparaging remarks from Ozzy regarding the late Ayotallah Khomeini were curtailed by Randy and Bob's eagerness to get back to work. "I really wasn't there long enough to judge anyone's true abilities" Bill maintains. "What I do remember was how keen Randy was, He was a really nice lad. Very eager and enthusiastic."

A jam ensued with Hunt taking on the keyboard role. "Randy and I tried a few things I had been working on, just chord patterns really. Then Bob came in and we were all just jamming. Well, Ozzy heard this and thought it sounded like something they had been working on called 'Mr. Crowley'. It was a similar feel and similar key. That's as far as it went really."

Bill's jam session did leave a little but important legacy with the Ozzy crew as Bob Daisley relates. "Bill actually instigated the intro to 'Mr. Crowley'. He was playing around with this keyboard chord progression, piddling about with some rough ideas. It was just a small part but that would become the opening sequence to 'Mr. Crowley'."

Bill did not return the next day. "I had a young family and different pressures to the other guys. It would have been a bit of a luxury to hang around waiting for something to happen. If I would have known of course … Anyway, we just jammed and left it at that but looking back it was a huge privilege." Bob backs this up. "Bill was a decent enough bloke but we weren't seriously looking for a keyboard player at this stage. I think he was a bit older than us too. Randy must have been 22 or thereabouts, I think Ozzy had just turned 30. Bill had short grey hair so Ozzy called him 'Grecian 2000'! We were actually much more concerned with getting a drummer to put the actual core band together."

Bill would return to teaching but later would become involved with another West Midlands legend Slade. Hunt co-wrote songs for both Slade and Dave Hill's later offshoot Slade II. In later years Bill, courtesy of Dave Hill, would have the opportunity to meet Ozzy again at the Castle Donington 'Monsters Of Rock' festival. Watching the show from side stage Bill was taken aback to recognize his 'Mr. Crowley' contribution still in place. "I was really surprised when they did 'Mr. Crowley' because that little chord progression was still there which was nice to hear. I was quite chuffed actually!"

With keyboards temporarily put aside and Aldridge firmly out of the equation Daisley describes Lee Kerslake's arrival as being a godsend. "Lee was the last drummer we auditioned" Bob advises. "He came in at a very difficult time as the record company was straining at the leash. If Lee had not worked out they would have to get someone like Cozy Powell in or another session drummer. Time was running out."

The unstoppable march of old father time was not the only thing preying on the musicians minds. That Summer, Black Sabbath was enjoying a renaissance bout of sell out shows and their single 'Neon Knights' was also floating in the top thirty. 'Heaven And Hell' was also making a strong showing giving Tony Iommi his best American chart placing since 1975's 'Sabotage' and, to rub salt into the wound, passing the million sales mark with consummate ease.

Fate would intervene to redress the balance and swing the pendulum of luck back in Ozzy's favour though. In what must have been galling to Iommi's new ratings though was that in July a less than welcome collection of poorly assembled live tapes of Ozzy era Sabbath had usurped even 'Heaven And Hell'. The downright shoddy 'Live At Last', using material from as far back as a Manchester Free Trade Hall gig in 1973 and roundly panned by critics as well as band members past and present, nevertheless struck gold at No. 5. Even Ozzy anthem 'Paranoid' was dusted off for another stab at the singles charts and catapulted its way to No. 14 in August. If Ozzy needed any motivation it had was arriving in spades.

1979 found Lee Kerslake divorced from Uriah Heep after a mammoth eight year run. During that time Kerslake had seen Heep achieve dizzying heights of success internationally with the seminal and undeniably grandiose 'Demons And Wizards' and 'Magicians Birthday' albums. The band had made huge inroads into such traditional territories as America and mainland Europe, but would also be of bona fide superstar status in such remote climes as Australia and Asia. However, during the mid seventies the Uriah Heep institution had hit troubled times with fracturing line-ups and the tragic death of their New Zealander bassist Gary Thain.

Kerslake, along with mentor and guitarist Mick Box, had remained a stabilizing influence weathering the many storms that assailed the band but by the time of the 'Fallen Angel' record of 1978 Kerslake's tenacity had been tested to the limit. Friction between band members and record company boss and manager Gerry Bron about the musical direction of the band had been slowly but surely pulling the band apart for many years. Eventually, giving it all up as a thankless task, the drummer walked intent on proving his ability as a songwriter and arranger with an ambitious solo venture.

Not one to remain, idle Kerslake was quick to assemble a union with Manfred Mann bass player Colin Pattendon and the then unknown vocalist Pete Cox. "This was of course years before Go West you understand" the man enthuses. "He had a phenomenal voice even then. I had about twenty or so of my songs, all good strong melodic Rock stuff, and we were shaping up for a solo album. I really needed to prove a point after having been hassled so much in the past. I'm not just 'the drummer' y'know and in Uriah Heep there was this big battle going on between Ken Hensley and Gerry Bron as to the arrangements and the songs. It had been going on for too long and it was beginning to affect the band's success. One day I had a big argument with Bron and just left."

The proto-band, it never did reach the naming stage, was in the midst of assembling a finely crafted Rock package centred on compositions of Kerslake's when the drummer received a call from an old friend.

Kerslake takes up the tale. "A very old friend of Uriah Heep's named Ossie Hoppie called me up one day. Ossie is a big promoter in Germany and has been for donkeys years, all the bands know him as someone to be trusted. Well, he'd read an article in a German magazine about me leaving Uriah Heep and was surprised to say the least. When he gave me the message I nearly fell off my chair."

By now a seasoned veteran of behind the scenes skullduggery and the inner machinations of major Rock bands Lee was understandably cautious if not more than a little curious. 'When Ossie asked me if I'd be interested in working with Ozzy I have to admit my first reaction was no bloody way!! I'd been ripped off to buggery already and wanted nothing to do with that side of things any more. Once bitten twice shy y'see."

"Of course I wanted to work with Ozzy and when I heard Bob Daisley was involved too it began to look very attractive. The business side of it was a major worry though. Ossie explained that this was a brand new thing and that all the band members would be in it together—that it was a proper band and not just a bunch of backing musicians for Ozzy. That I liked.

Well, I left it with Ossie and told him that I'd play it like this—they can audition me at the same time I audition them. Ossie relayed the message, got back to me and we went from there."

Kerslake was sent a rough demo tape, which included an early work out of 'Crazy Train', and arranged to meet the Ozzy trio at a rehearsal studio in London where Lee's kit was already set up. Ozzy, Randy and Bob were apparently in defeatist mood having spent many fruitless months searching for a drummer. The prospect of a session with Lee had lifted their gander somewhat. Bob and Lee had known each since Daisley's old act Widowmaker had opened for Uriah Heep whilst Randy was a keen Uriah Heep fan. Lee remembers his introduction to Ozzy. "He was very frustrated at not being able to find a drummer. He actually said 'Fuckin' 'ell, 50 million drummers we've been through! Not one of 'em had a chance!' It was quite a challenge but I knew I could click in with Bob straight away."

"When I listened to the demo tape I knew that this was just my style" relates Lee. "I knew Dave Potts had a try out before me but there was another guy on the tape, I don't know who that was. Anyway, this demo had 'Crazy Train' but with a strange kind of Disco drum beat that didn't fit at all. To me it was obvious what I should do." The atmosphere in the studio changed as soon as the former Uriah Heep man began to play. "I remember Randy and I looking at each other instantly as soon as Lee started" says an excited Daisley. "Randy was very excited and so was Ozzy. We all thought the same thing. Fuckin' Hell—This is the guy! I'm sure we told him so too."

Lee describes what happened from his vantage point. "We had this little cassette player to play back the demo so we gave it a quick listen then got on with it. Randy went into the 'Crazy Train' riff and I just put down what I thought would work."

"Bob looked at Ozzy and gave each other a big smile but Randy leapt about four foot in the air! 'We got one' he shouted. It was really funny, he was so excited he simply couldn't contain himself. 'Oh Man! At long last we got one!' he kept shouting. Ozzy and Bob looked relieved and happy that this was obviously going to work but Randy was just over the top. I remember Ozzy had this big fox fur coat on and he said to Bob and Randy "Are we happy now?" We were all grinning like little kids." This moment became imprinted in Lee's memory for more reasons than one. "Well, we all knew there and then. Ozzy shook my hand and said to me "Here's my hand, here's my heart, 'till we're dead, 'till we part." That was good enough for me. I was in."

"Lee was absolutely perfect" records Bob Daisley. "It was all sorted out there and then. Myself, Ozzy and Lee went out to a Chinese restaurant afterwards to celebrate." It must be remembered that Lee Kerslake was walking into an already entrenched trio. Of course Bob Daisley was a known quantity to Lee while Ozzy's reputation was legendary. But how did Lee take to Randy? "The only thing you can say about Randy is that he was very, very special. A lovely, lovely guy." Lee states emphatically. "He was truly gifted, quite simply a fantastic natural player. The things he could come up with were mind-blowing. His capabilities seemed to know no bounds."

As the quartet got into serious rehearsal they naturally began to gel musically. "Randy was just amazing. I'd come up with something on the piano and Randy would just put down something that was near perfect. Bob would get himself out of bed and start scribbling down lyrics. We created some real magic. It's a very rare thing. He could play the blues phenomenally. Some of the stuff just blew me away."

By the stage that Lee became involved, Ozzy, Bob and Randy had already put together nearly a complete album's worth of material. "I just put my oar in a little bit on the arrangements, little directional ideas and of course put my drums down. We did do some more writing though to include one of my ideas in a new song called 'No Bone Movies'. Mainly though, the album was about there but ideas were already flowing for the next record. Creatively it was an amazing time."

Bob backs this feeling of comradeship up too. "In fact we were so keen on it being an equal unit that when Lee joined we wrote another song, all four of us as a joint effort, to make it fair. 'No Bone Movies' was written as an intended B-side but in the end it made it onto the album." The title of 'No Bone Movies' passed most British fans by but the American audience got the reference straight away. Notions that the song is about pornography prove correct as Bob explains. "We all went to see the porn film in London" he candidly admits. "Me, Randy, his girlfriend Jodi, Ozzy and Sharon. I kind of got, er ... inspired! It was Randy who was partly responsible for the title because, being American, he called porn 'bone movies'. You have to remember that when we were writing and recording the album we had no idea of how big the album would become so I thought 'No Bone Movies' was obscure enough to be kind of hidden for an English audience."

Geezer in action—Heaven & Hell. Pics: Rich Galbraith.

Chapter 4

"It's A Band"

With the set up of the band now cast the quartet began looking at other areas needing attention. The first matter that needed resolving was what was the band going to be called. "It was very much a four way band" observes Bob. "That was the deal and it was clear to everyone. The problem was that the record company, as they do, insisted on just calling it 'Ozzy'. We told them in no uncertain terms that this was a band and not a solo artist. Ozzy wanted this too. Ozzy fronted the band and came up with vocal melodies, Randy was the guitarist and riff writer, I wrote both music and lyrics and Lee was a drummer with proven writing abilities too."

Rehearsals began apace at Clearwell Castle and Rockwell Studios to work up the album songs. The band was kicking around proposed names for the band but none memorable enough that Lee can recall. "It was around this time that Blizzard Of Ozz was decided on though" he remembers. Jet Records though were insistent on promoting the act as a solo venture. "They kept up with this campaign but we said no. The band is called Blizzard Of Ozz. You can put 'featuring Ozzy Osbourne' on the first couple of albums to start with but it's a band."

Bob is also very clear about how the band name came about. "Ozzy's Dad thought of Blizzard Of Ozz. Ozzy told him he was starting a new band before he left Black Sabbath the very first time, in 1977, and his Dad suggested it then. Ozzy even got tee shirts made up with it on." Ozzy himself was by all accounts feeling trapped in a self made dilemma. Lee maintains that Ozzy was raring to get working again but also in some trepidation at the prospect. This is an aspect of Ozzy's character often voiced by the man himself over the years. "He was a little lost if you want the honest truth" Lee reckons. "A lovely warm hearted bloke was Ozzy, I'm sure everyone will tell you the same, but he was really struggling with himself. He was in a rush to get on the road but scared shitless of it at the same time. He also had a lot of problems at home. He'd often be forced off onto a tangent by outside distractions."

The band's rhythm section would often play on Ozzy's fears and found his trusting nature an Achilles heel that was too tempting to ignore. "We used to go for a good long walk around the country fields before we went into the studio" Lee laughs. "We would start work about midday and work through until two or three in the morning then. Anyway, Ozzy would be so easy to wind up. Both Bob and I were in on it. We once started talking about the news and saying 'What are we going to do about the country?' Ozzy would be listening to this wondering what on earth was going on. 'What do you mean?' he would say. 'The news, didn't you hear about the invasion? The outbreak of war. We're at war again, they're coming over right now'. Ozzy believed it totally 'What are we going to do?!!' he said. You should have seen the look on his face. He was so terrified he literally ran back to the studio! When he found out it was only a joke he said that when we had told him he nearly had a heart attack. He's a very funny guy. That was an example of how little things really bothered him. The big things he could handle easily with no problem. Ozzy was a very funny, warm guy to be around. All four of us actually got on really well. It was a great team."

When the foursome got into the studio the feeling that something special was on the cards really began to materialize. "We'd be rehearsing songs and I'd notice riffs and for the first time in a long time I was thinking this is really, really good" Lee recalls. "We would chop and change things all the time to get things right. Randy had ideas just pouring out of him and Bob and I totally understand how the other was thinking. There really was a unique magic. When Ozzy started to put down the vocals I said to Bob "Bloody Hell, this is going to be a fuckin' fantastic album!" We all knew it."

The first album was required quickly although proceedings at Ridge Farm Studios did not start according to plan. "We were working with Chris Tsangarides as producer but after a week we dispensed with his services" Bob states. "We had a talk and said "Fuck it—we'll do it" and decided that we were working so well together anyway that we didn't need

Blizzard of Ozz. Bob Daisley, Lee Kerslake, Ozzy Osbourne, Randy Rhoads.

a producer so we just kept the engineer which was Max Norman."

What really began to strike home at this point was the burgeoning talent of Randy Rhoads. An obviously impressed Daisley is quick with praise. "Randy, you could tell, was going to be a major talent. He would play an absolute blinder of a solo and then double it note for note exactly. Everything was completely worked out to the finest degree in his head. That's a rare talent." Outsiders were equally enthralled. "People came down from the record company on a pretty regular basis" says Bob. "You could tell they could sense the band chemistry. It's either there or it's not. When they heard Randy you could see they were thinking what planet is this kid from? We were all very proud of the magic that we had. We had certainly stumbled onto something unique."

The band was complemented in the studio by the highly regarded figure of Don Airey lending his keyboard talents. Airey's CV reads like a who's who of Rock starting with Cozy Powell's Hammer then Babe Ruth and includes performances with Rainbow, Whitesnake, Colosseum II, Gary Moore, Uli Jon Roth and Jethro Tull. Airey first came to prominence in the Rock world (previously he had his own act touring globally on cruise liners!) with Cozy Powell's Hammer in 1974 before joining the esoteric Jazz Rock outfit Colosseum II recording the 'Strange New Flesh', 'Electric Savage' and 'Wardance' albums. The man also found time to collaborate with none other than Andrew Lloyd Webber on his 'Variations' theme for the television arts programme 'The South Bank Show'. Next port of call was with the ex-Thin Lizzy guitarist Gary Moore one of his credits including the arrangement on a track titled 'Biscayne Blues' which was to evolve with the addition of Phil Lynott's vocals into the famous 'Parisienne Walkways'.

Airey was jettisoned from a fragmenting Colosseum II in 1978 briefly uniting with Black Sabbath for their 'Never Say Die' album prior to a reunion with Cozy Powell in Rainbow. Airey would also find time to aid Gordon Rowley's Strife with their 'Back To Thunder' effort. Airey's tenure in the notoriously volatile Rainbow lasted for three years and two major international albums 'Down To Earth' and

'Difficult To Cure'. During time out keyboard contributions were added to the Michael Schenker Group's remarkable debut. It was while still in the employ of the mercurial Ritchie Blackmore that Airey got the call to embellish Ozzy's inaugural outing.

Although a session player for the recording Airey's invaluable contributions should not be underestimated. The haunting monolithic cathedrals of sound that makeup the intro to 'Mr. Crowley' were in the main arranged by Airey. Although he cannot recall the inspiration for the tune the practicalities of composition are still clear. "I sent the band out of the studio for half an hour while I dreamt it up and recorded it" Don reveals. "When they came back it was all done." Airey would also add his deft touch to the overall atmospherics of the album by donating the instrumental passage in 'Revelation Mother Earth' and the outro to 'Suicide Solution'.

The lyrical content of 'Suicide Solution' would become the subject of heated debate in later years accused as they were of leading directly to the deaths of three American teenagers. The first of these occurred in October 1984 when a 19 year old, named in court as John M.' shot himself in the head whilst apparently listening to the song. The teenager's body was found still with headphones on.

"Ozzy set the ball rolling for that song by coming up with the first line 'Wine is fine but whiskey's quicker' which inspired me to come up with the rest of the words" records Bob. "I've seen mentions in magazines previously which say that the song is about Bon Scott. That's bullshit." Quite a paradox then if Ozzy penned the opening line reflecting on the late AC/DC singer's alcohol related death only to have Daisley wrap the song up with words a little closer to home. "I wrote the words about Ozzy and the state he was getting in after leaving Black Sabbath" Bob states emphatically. "Basically Ozzy was drinking himself to death when he got booted out of Sabbath and the lyrics were my way of telling him to stop before it was too late. I came up with the title as a bit of a play on words—'Solution' being the solution to a problem but also with the double meaning of a liquid solution. It was me saying to Ozzy, look—stop: you're killing yourself." As for suggestions hinting at hidden vocal lines or subliminal messages? "There's nothing there, that's absolute rubbish" Bob defends. "Totally untrue. Who on earth would be so stupid as to write a song telling people to kill themselves?"

The slurred narrative entangled in the outro to 'Crazy Train' has lent itself over the years to many over eager theories as to the exact 'meaning' of what Ozzy is saying. In actual fact it isn't Ozzy at all as Bob Daisley explains. "We had this young kid helping out in the studio as a bit of a roadie. Well, he was talking about how much he could drink so of course we took him down the pub. After a pretty heavy drinking session we ended up literally carrying this lad out. Well, we got back to the studio and after he came to he started telling all these silly stories in this funny voice. I remember he had a really odd laugh." The sozzled youngster's guffaws made such an impression on the assembled musicians they decided to capture it for posterity on tape—but not before subjecting the hapless individual to a practical joke of the highest order. "We put raw eggs in his bed!" Daisley laughs. "Of course when he got in they all broke. In the morning he was telling us this story and he was talking in such a strange manner, a bit like a madman actually, we got it all on tape. So, what you hear at the end of 'Crazy Train' is not Ozzy but this young kid answering our question—what was in your bed? 'An Eeegggg!!!!'"

Whilst 'Blizzard Of Ozz' was being crafted, 'Heaven And Hell' was demonstrating its staying power. Not only had the album broke big, its tenacity was alarming Mr. Osbourne. Black Sabbath was experiencing a true groundswell of renewed fan support that would fuel a quite colossal world tour. The live promotion for 'Heaven And Hell' commenced in Aurich, North Eastern Germany on the 17th of April. The group had completed mixing of the album in London before jumping straight into rehearsals in the capital city prior to crossing the channel. The show, although somewhat of a tester for a string of further German gigs, the UK and ultimately the grand prize of North America, was given due importance by the band members. "That Aurich show was nerve wracking for Tony, Bill and Geezer because Black Sabbath had never really done that much live work in Europe. Most of it had been in the USA, which of course would change in the next few years" offers Geoff Nicholls. "I remember it being an excellent show. Everything went according to plan because each of us individually was so tensed up and focused on making it happen. It was on the second or third gigs that we started to fuck up a bit because we had got more relaxed. Mainly stuff to do with timing. Most of the songs Tony started us off with a riff so that was fine but on others I started with thunder, lightning and bells so I had to make sure everyone was ready. Otherwise it was Bill's job if the song started on drums to make certain everyone was on cue. Very difficult at times because you couldn't hear a bloody thing—it was all visual."

Ronnie James Dio, besides providing his vocal skills also took this opportunity to add his own little visual moniker. The 'Devil's horn' symbol made by raising the index and little fingers and holding the middle and ring fingers onto the palm. According to European mediaeval folklore subtleties regarding

Black Sabbath, Oklahoma 1980. Pic: Rich Galbraith.

the position of the thumb whilst holding this symbol are of paramount import. With the thumb held under the fingers it is the sign of the horned God Cernunnos, with the thumb above the fingers and the extended digits pointed towards a person it is a device for cursing an individual. Wherever he places his thumb, and whatever the intention (if there is any whatsoever), Dio audiences can rest easy as his digits remain pointed skyward, cursing only those hapless supertrouper operators and riggers high in the light rigs above his head. Dio's neat little bit of digital sigilism became his trademark and would, spreading far beyond the confines of a Black Sabbath or Dio concert hall, sweep into nearly every Heavy Metal gig from that point onward.

A puzzling part of the show was to be the inclusion of the classic song 'Sabbath Bloody Sabbath'— without vocals. Latter day Sabbath singer Tony Martin explains the reasoning behind this. "That song is pitched very high and to do it night after night for Ronnie would have probably fucked his voice up for the rest of the show. I could manage it OK but it was a tough one. It's an odd one. The fans always want to hear it because of that famous riff but it's a real bastard!"

As part of the stage show Black Sabbath took out their famous flaming cross for this run of shows. Naturally, as with all stage effects, it was not totally reliable giving the band members much hilarity. "Ronnie delivered this big speech mid way through 'Heaven And Hell'" Geoff records. "Well, sometimes this 'speech' just went on and on and on... it started to get a bit bloody presidential. He would come with all of this stuff like "Can you feel the power of the cross? Feel the force of the cross!" And all of this nonsense. We always had a good giggle at it but Ronnie was into it. When Ronnie gave a cue the big cross at the back of the stage was supposed to burst into flames. It looked quite spectacular actually. This one time Ronnie was really playing up on his speech and it was really dragging out. We were all looking at each other wondering when he was going to end. He got his just desserts though because when he pointed to the cross it didn't explode into fire but just gave this farty little fizzle. We all burst out laughing and so did the entire audience! Ronnie was furious! He went absolutely apeshit afterwards!"

The German tour would see the group cautiously

Black Sabbath, Oklahoma 1980. Pic: Rich Galbraith.

Heaven and Hell tour pass.

testing out the band unit, set list and stage show at relatively small towns such as Oldenburg, Kaunitz, Fallingbostel and Rendsburg besides putting in a solitary Austrian gig in the capital Vienna. This dash of dates closed in Germany at the Landschut Sportshalle on April 26th. A welcome burst of shows then broke out across the UK supported by London gals Girlschool. Black Sabbath was given a rapturous, sell out and well deserved reception in their home country. At their run of sell out Hammersmith gigs some good friends from Brum would be made welcome but did little to foster favour with Ronnie James Dio.

"At one of the Hammersmith Odeon gigs all four members of Led Zeppelin showed up to watch the show" records Geoff. "It was great to see them. They loved the show and wanted to see what was happening because they were talking about going back on the road together. I think that was the last time all four were seen out in public together. John Bonham, not known for his diplomacy, came back to the dressing room to tell the band he really enjoyed the show and said to Tony "What a great singer ... for a midget"! Ronnie was standing in the dressing room at the time as John just kept on making less than kind remarks about his stature. It was getting seriously embarrassing. Eventually he was politely asked to leave and Ronnie's minder got him out. Ronnie was not amused!"

Nevertheless, in spite of Bonzo's misgivings over the singer's physical presence the spectre of Ronnie James Dio cast a very large shadow indeed over Europe that year. Dio dominated proceedings on one continent as the band, eyeing the lucrative market over the Atlantic, got itself in good shape for a U.S. invasion. Throughout June the band blitzed German soil once again, this time playing in the major cities with guests Shakin' Street.

The 'Heaven And Hell' album would rapidly sell over one million copies in the USA, soon becoming one of Warner Bros. highest selling Rock catalogue albums ever. The band would also match that figure in concert attendances. "We started off in North America with a couple of small gigs, Bethlehem, Pennsylvania was one. I guess the first proper big gig would have been Los Angeles at the Forum. Besides the regular shows that had 4,000 or 5,000 people we did a whole series of enormous outdoor festivals, 80,000, 50,000 people a night. Things like the 'Day on the Green' in San Francisco. It was an incredible summer" records Geoff Nicholls. Sabbath would perform at both the gargantuan 'Day On The Green' festival in Oakland alongside AOR giants Journey, Molly Hatchet and Ronnie Montrose's Gamma as well as the 'Summer Blowout' event a day previously, once more with Journey, Molly Hatchet and guests Cheap Trick.

Snagging the midsection of the Black n' Blue dates was the yapping Yorkshire terrier that was Saxon. The band's now widely acclaimed 'Wheels Of Steel' album had just broken huge in the UK and Europe, putting Saxon at the very forefront of the NWoBHM movement. As their introductory tour to break North America the group had hopped from one historic tour to another. Commencing with Rush, which often put them in front of audiences exceeding 20,000, the band then jumped over to AC/DC's mammoth 'Back In Black' shows. Their third round of supports put

Tony Iommi, Tulsa, Oklahoma 1980 'Heaven And Hell' tour. Pic: Rich Galbraith.

the Northerners in front of equally huge crowds as part of the Black Sabbath / Blue Oyster Cult extravaganza. For Saxon guitarist Graham Oliver, a man responsible for some breathtaking heavy riffs himself, it brought a very special moment in his life.

"Quite simply I got to meet Tony Iommi which, for me, was a big thing because I had been waiting to meet him for years for a very special reason. Back in the early days of Saxon, when we were called Son Of A Bitch in fact, I had an accident that nearly stopped my playing career. We were waiting to go to a gig, the 6th of October I remember. It was a very windy day. Anyway, this gust of wind blew this door shut on my hand. It was horrible, I lost the top inch of my first finger on my left hand. As you can imagine I was devastated."

It would take three painful months before Oliver picked up a guitar again. "It was a long process, relearning how to play. It's actually still a painful memory just thinking about that day." He confides. The Saxon guitarist was given hope with the knowledge that another guitarist had suffered a similar injury and had gone on to achieve remarkable results— Tony Iommi. "It was quite funny because I must have been 22 years old or something at the time. I was desperate to meet Tony to talk about this injury and ask him how he coped." Oliver and fellow Saxon guitarist Paul Quinn got to Sabbath's dressing room at the Sheffield City Hall but the youngster balked. "Paul kept trying to make me go in and meet him but I was too scared to go into Sabbath's dressing room!"

Fast forwarding to 16th August 1980, Saxon hooked up with Black Sabbath at Kalamazoo Wings Stadium in Michigan. Also on the bill was Sammy Hagar. Riot had been due to open the show but withdrew, paving the way for Saxon. This was the tail end of the Black n' Blue dates, Saxon pairing with just Black Sabbath initially, then with both the Sabbs and Blue Oyster Cult and finally out for a final run allied solely with Eric Bloom & co. The guitarist remembers the shows being afforded ecstatic reactions from fans. "Both Black Sabbath and Blue Oyster Cult were huge. Both had that kind of mystery to them too and the crowds were huge. What I did notice that Sabbath were pulling in a lot of new fans too."

Oliver was not going to let this chance slip. "I finally got to meet Tony and he was absolutely fantastic, a perfect gentleman" Oliver expounds. "I told him my story, about what had happened and how I was too scared to go and talk to him and he said "You should have come in, I would definitely have made time to talk to anybody with that kind of story." Anyhow, he was great. He got his guitar tech to go back onto the stage and get all of his false finger tips, he's got loads of them. So I sat there trying all of these things on. Tony said, if any fitted I could have them. Tony's injury is different to mine though, he has lost the tips of his fingers whereas I lost a good inch of just the one.

I think we do both do very well for being considered relatively hot shot guitarists. The worst thing, and I'm sure Tony must have gone through this, is that you can do things in your mind that your disability will not allow you to do on the guitar. So you compensate, relearn. For example I can't do first finger vibratos and I have to skip fingers on certain things.

Tony is actually a very unorthodox player. He flicks from strings to accommodate his handicap, which is obviously something I notice being in the same boat. I once saw him do this great, long guitar solo—something he doesn't usually do onstage—and he was coming out with the most amazing stuff. He introduces lots of different styles, there was even a bit of flamenco in there I swear! Tony is very rooted in the Blues. He is a marvellous guitar player. In fact it goes beyond him being just a great guitar player because obviously he has to pull something extra special out from his boots too. The other thing that

Tony Iommi on the 'Heaven and Hell' tour. Pic: Rich Galbraith.

makes him quite amazing in my eyes is that he is on his own up there, everything rests on him. If you just think about the riffs that he has come up with. I don't think any other guitar player, even Jimmy Page or Ritchie Blackmore, has that many classic Heavy Metal riffs to his name. Tony is certainly a one off."

Another round of the 'Heaven And Hell' tour would go down in Rock n' Roll folklore as documented by one of the support bands Molly Hatchet. Good God fearing Southerners, the Hatchet men, having performed in dry conditions earlier in the evening, would be stupefied by the site Black Sabbath having to deal with their own personal rain cloud. The way they told it somebody upstairs was far from happy and had pinpointed the band for a personal downpour. It is not entirely myth. "Yes, that did happen" recounts Geoff Nicholls. "I remember it well. It was in Phoenix and the day had been bone dry. I think we went on at 9:30 p.m. because there would have been an 11 o'clock curfew. It was quite spooky actually because as we were getting ready I could see these two huge black rain clouds heading our way. They came suddenly out of nowhere. Just as we started up, literally as I hit the bell and did the thunder effects this lightning cracked open from the skies and the rain just pelted down. It was right on the money too—exact timing so all in all a bit bloody eerie. We made a joke out of it by saying big G. was handling the stage effects out front but, I tell you, it was very bloody weird. It would happen a couple of times afterwards too. Maybe someone was keeping an eye on us and just giving us a reminder not to get too cocky!"

Freak weather aside, the band discovered that festering personality clashes between Dio and Ward had whipped up into an internal storm. By the time the band had reached Kansas the drummer announced he was to quit. A marooned Black Sabbath languished in the sun, unable to proceed for a few days before Bill was persuaded back and the tour recommenced. Within a matter of days though he had really had his fill and walked for good. "Bill packed it in at Denver. He just said "That's it guys" and off he went, just like that" says Nicholls. "We went back to Los Angeles, rehearsed with Vinny for two days then got ourselves back on the road. It was a quick turnaround." Bill Ward's prior performance at the Bloomington Metropolitan Sports Center in Minnesota on the 19th August would be his last showing with Black Sabbath for five years.

The next scheduled gig, at the Bonneville Salt Flats in Salt Lake City, presented a dilemma. Fervent negotiations were underway in an attempt to lure Bill back but to no avail. Nicholls explains just why the band's gear was set up on stage yet the band didn't play. "You have to remember there are a lot of legal and financial implications to things like this. The crew set the gear up because we were trying our best to get Bill back. If the gear had not been set up I guess the band could have been put into a very sticky situation. We were all hoping Bill would make it back for the show but he was adamant."

Ronnie James Dio attributes Bill's exit to alcohol. "Bill was a great guy but he was drinking himself stupid and there's no way to brush over that fact. The way I saw it his vision and been clouded because he was imbibing so much. Remember, Bill had been at it a long, long time. He hated travelling and flying totally freaked him out so life on the road was torture for him. All he could do was drink. Bill tried to get around his problems by travelling in a bus with his brother Jim acting as the driver. He took his wife and son Aaron out with him too. But it was still difficult for him, criss crossing America, and I think mentally and physically he had enough."

As mentioned previously Bill Ward gave his decision in Denver. That gig was scrapped with the

Geoff, Bill & Geezer bid farewell. Pic: Rich Galbraith.

promoter less than amused. "When we told them Bill had quit the promoter ordered everyone he knew not to let us out of town!" scoffs Ronnie. "He had put the word out to all his people, the limo companies, everybody. We all just got in taxis and buggered off. What could we do? We made the gigs up to him later." The Black Sabbath collective attempted to sway Ward's decision with a lengthy meeting in an Albuquerque hotel. This effort at persuasion would fall on deaf ears.

Cozy Powell would be offered the drum stool at this stage as he confirmed in 1990. "Yeah, I wish I'd taken it now but I was busy. It took Tony too long to ask me again!" Geoff Nicholls recalls Cozy's name cropping up too. "Yes, Cozy was approached but there has always been a bit of a problem between Ronnie and Cozy. Basically they never liked each other, so that would have been difficult. At the time we were really trying to build a kind of family unit and the last thing Tony wanted was to have another band fall out. The priority was to keep the band as solid as possible. Ronnie knew Vinny so that was taken care of that way. It maintained the harmony."

Vinny Appice's inauguration with Black Sabbath was set in Hawaii at the Honolulu Stadium on the 31st August. Opening act would be Southern Rockers Molly Hatchet. Vinny would mark a visual as well as an audible change as Geoff Nicholls remembers. "The thing was that Bill had an enormous fuck off drum kit. I mean, this thing was huge, all set up on this massive drum riser. He had a massive gong up there too. So when Vinny came in to play with us he had to set his kit up on Bill's old riser and there was virtually nothing of it! He had one bass drum and a couple of toms and that was your lot! Vinny's set up looked like a toy compared to Bill's. He did look quite odd up there I have to admit!"

The 'Heaven And Hell' tour, interlocked with management stable mates Blue Oyster Cult, wound on, traversing throughout the expanses of the American heartlands. The impetus granted by increasing week on week sales of 'Heaven And Hell' fuelled an expedition that had enticed out the old guard and legions of eager new fans alike. Many of these gigs would draw capacity audiences, most often Sabbath trouncing an increasingly unsteady Blue Oyster Cult. This is not to say Black Sabbath was having everything their own way. The Milwaukee Mecca Arena show on the 9th of October would go down in history, but for all the wrong reasons. Ronnie James Dio first realised they had a situation when Geezer failed to start the intro to 'N.I.B.'. "In between the songs the lights dimmed and at that precise moment Geezer had been hit on the head by something from the stage. Of course I didn't know this so after waiting a bit I walked over to his side of the stage and he was there, concussed with his hand up to his forehead—blood everywhere."

Geoff reveals just what the projectile was. "Some nutter had thrown a brass cross at him! It had come very close to hitting him in the eye. They chucked it just as the lights went down so nobody saw it coming. Geezer was in a bad way. I don't know why on earth they did it, whether it was a lone lunatic or what. It had been an odd day. The audience was very into the whole Ozzy vs. Ronnie thing I remember and there had been a lot of local media rubbish about the old devil worship too. A bit more than the regular crap we had to put up with. Just as we were trying to deal with Geezer one of our road crew, Fergie, got hit by a bottle. It was like a bloody battleground."

Ronnie documents what happened next. "Unfortunately the tour manager took it upon himself to take this out on the audience. Of course they hadn't seen what had happened so when they heard this guy calling them "assholes" and saying we were pulling the show they went crazy!" Black Sabbath suddenly found themselves locked into a very frightening situation. "That crowd just tore the venue to pieces" Geoff states. "The chairs were all made of old cast iron and wood and they ripped these things to pieces and were chucking them at us. We suffered a lot of damaged equipment. I remember looking out and seeing all these thousands of chairs flying through the air. There was not a lot we could do because even the security was being attacked. We looked at each other and Tony said "Fuck this—let's get out of here!" They got Geezer and Fergie to hospital but only just."

"We got out of there by the skin of our teeth" reckons the singer. "I think the entire Milwaukee police force turned up to try and restore order but by then it was too late. The venue had been ripped to pieces. We had flight cases with bits of iron chair parts embedded in them. It was a very dangerous moment."

Over on the opposing team, Bob Daisley has vivid memories of just how influential the success of 'Heaven And Hell', and Black Sabbath's renaissance in particular, was on the newly constituted Blizzard Of Ozz band. "Ozzy was very bitter about Ronnie. It must have been a huge slap in the face for him because here was Ronnie, technically a much better singer than Ozzy, taking over his band and having this massive success. It wasn't nice for him. I mean, you can't say with singers whether someone is better than another because you are dealing with matters of personal preference but the cold fact was that Ronnie was technically superb. You just couldn't deny it. Ozzy might have been a better singer for Black Sabbath because his voice and character suited the band and he certainly had stamped his trademark on there over many years but Ronnie had just blown all of that away. At times Ozzy would get exceptionally low about just how big and how fast Black Sabbath had got without him. That is why things got so bitter and personal because Ronnie was so good. Hence the dwarf and all the ridiculous comments in later years. Ozzy could verbally have a go at him for being short or having a big mouth but he wouldn't dare start slagging Ronnie off for his vocal abilities. When you look back at all those things that were said the bitterness really comes across. A lot of it is so over the top it was, I'm sure, designed to grab the headlines away from Dio."

So pervasive was 'Heaven And Hell' itself the album even managed to squirm its way deep into the lion's den of Ridge Farm Studios. "Someone had the record there in the studio while we were recording the 'Blizzard Of Ozz' album" admits Bob. "I remember it being played. It could well have been Randy who got hold of it. I know Randy thought it was a bloody good record. That was the problem, it was so good. It would have been daft to say it wasn't. Let's face it, the last two albums Ozzy did with Sabbath were crap and that band was on its way down very fast. Ronnie turned the whole thing around. 'Heaven And Hell' was a great, great album and we were all very much aware of that. It didn't influence the rest of us either musically or emotionally, not one tiny bit. Ozzy of course was really worked up about it because it was so close to home for him. It was very personal. Ozzy is big on self doubt, always has been. The rest of us weren't bothered. We had a whole set of songs which we had a gut feeling about and that sounded nothing like 'Heaven And Hell' so it was no competition in our eyes. Randy, Lee and I knew we had something very, very special with the 'Blizzard Of Ozz' album but Oz was totally preoccupied by what Tony Iommi and Ronnie James Dio were doing.

There was one particular incident I remember as clear as yesterday. The three of us, Ozzy, Randy and myself, were in a black London taxi going down the Bayswater Road. As usual we were heading down to Westbourne Grove for a curry. I think we might have just finished the album and Ozzy was really down about everything. What he could not understand was that the rest of us in the band were so upbeat. He kept on saying "Do you think it's good enough?", "Are my vocals alright?", "Are the songs good enough?" Stuff like that. When he starts there is no stopping him.

I looked him straight in the eye and told him "It doesn't matter what Black Sabbath are doing. Our record is going to be a big success. Don't worry about it." I just knew. People might think I'm a bit barmy but I had a huge faith in both the Blizzard albums because my Mum was a psychic. She told me they would be big. I think Ozzy just thought I was saying that to de-stress him but it was the truth. As it turned out I think just about all the Black Sabbath fans that had bought 'Heaven And Hell' ended up buying 'Blizzard Of Ozz' too and then when it started to snowball Ozzy started to bring in a whole new audience too." The poignant Ozzy ballad 'Goodbye To Romance' would harbour some of these feelings. "That was the whole point of that song, I wrote it about Black Sabbath because Ozzy always referred to the split as a divorce. He used those kind of terms, like it was a marriage breaking up and not a band.

That would never leave him though. Just before every album he ever worked on he would throw a wobbler. I think he might have felt very alone outside of Black Sabbath because those people were who he had grown up with, had his success with and in the end had sacked him. Part of that was probably the reason he was so keen at working with the very best musicians he could get hold of. To give him his due he did himself a big favour by pushing himself away from the Sabbath sound. Funnily enough Ronnie did the same with Sabbath, with his own ideas, so you had two branches of Black Sabbath as it were with very different sounds. The new Ozzy record didn't sound like Black Sabbath and even the new Black Sabbath record didn't sound like Black Sabbath!

The best thing for Ozzy at that time was that myself, Randy and Lee wrote him a bunch of songs that had practically no Black Sabbath influence whatsoever. I had never listened to a Black Sabbath album in my entire life honestly. That was probably a good thing. Especially with Randy Rhoads sounding absolutely nothing like Tony Iommi. Randy didn't like those old Sabbath albums at all. He couldn't bear to listen to them. That set Ozzy's career up really because the Sabbath fans always had an emotional attachment to Ozzy and I think they were relieved to see he had done something so completely different."

Fans, in fact, got the best of both worlds. Two bands of equal repute would both be cranking out Black Sabbath numbers. Ozzy may have scoffed at Ronnie James Dio's interpretation of 'Iron Man' but he didn't have it all his own way with that particular song either. "One of the funniest onstage moments I had with Ozzy was with the song 'Iron Man'" Bob Daisley recounts. "Randy had just cranked up his

Ronnie James Dio, Tulsa, Oklahoma, 1980. Pic: Rich Galbraith.

guitar and Ozzy puts these effects onto his voice for the vocal intro. Just as he got to the words "I am Iron Man" I handed him an old steam iron I found in the dressing room. I thought he would laugh but he got really pissed off about it!"

Once the 'Blizzard Of Ozz' album was nailed the band's thoughts turned to live promotion. With Don Airey committed to American touring with Rainbow the search was on for a replacement in order to replicate the intricacies and fills laid down in the studio for the live environment. Jet Records placed an advert in the 'Melody Maker' classifieds requesting, surprisingly, the services of a keyboard player cum rhythm guitarist. "I was 22 at the time and I really fancied joining a Rock n' Roll band and touring America. I had my classical training and had gone through Cambridge to get my music degree. Up until then I had been playing in a Folk Rock band—7 people in the back of a transit. I think I was just eager to go to the States really." admits an aspiring Lindsey Bridgwater. "As soon as I saw the advert I thought that's for me! Jet Records sent me the tape and I was immediately impressed."

Expecting a bludgeoning Heavy Metal album Bridgwater would be taken aback to hear a guitarist free forming in ecclesiastical Hypo-Dorian and Mixolodian modes. "I loved the guitar playing and the fact that songs such as 'Mr. Crowley' had a lot of classical influence, almost Vivaldi in structure really appealed. I sat at home and scored everything then went to the audition and played it all note for note. They were surprised to say the least." Lindsey recollects the competition on the day. "I was quite surprised. There were some people there who were simply there to say they had played with Ozzy. A lot of the stuff was quite complex, 'Revelation Mother Earth', 'Mr. Crowley', etc. No one I heard that day quite managed it."

After impressing the band on the ivories Lindsey was keen to show he could fulfill the full criteria required. "I picked up Randy's guitar and hacked away on a few chords but it became quickly apparent that Randy could pull off all the guitar parts live so any rhythm guitar from me simply wasn't needed" Lindsey explains. "The way Randy could switch from lead to rhythm and vice versa really showed his virtuosity—in fact his ability knocked you flat. On the albums there was an awful lot of guitar, sometimes 7 or 8 tracks with electric overlaid with acoustic and then lead too. When I first heard it I remember thinking "How the Hell are we going to do that live?" but as soon as I heard Randy play it became obvious. Randy could do it all. He was such a dynamo live. You wouldn't believe some of the things he could do."

Rehearsals upfront of live shows took place at the converted church that held Nomis Studios. UFO were sharing the same facility and Paul 'Tonka' Chapman, a guitarist of no mean standing himself, had heard Ozzy had got himself a new wonder kid. "It was the talk of the building when we arrived. Everyone was talking about Ozzy's new guitarist." He maintains. "UFO was in there writing I think and Ozzy was rehearsing. They were right at the end of the complex next to this coffee shop thing they had so of course being nosey I went down there for a look. Well, when I got there I found this tiny little guy with blond hair playing this big classical acoustic guitar. He had his music stand set up and he was playing 'The Deerhunter'. You must be Randy." I said and of course we got talking. Everyone else, typically, was down the pub."

UFO bassist Pete Way has memories of the same period. "Randy was a massive Schenker fan, he knew all the UFO songs. He was an absolute sweetheart of a guy. Ozzy kept talking to me about his 'secret weapon'. This is before I'd heard Randy and I didn't work out what he meant. I thought "What is he talking about?" Paul had burnt his fingers I remember. He'd fallen asleep with a lit cigarette and was so out of it he was still snoozing when the cigarette burnt into his fingers! Ozzy was a bit alarmed at this when Paul showed him and to take his mind off the pain he invited us to see his 'secret weapon'. We walked in and there they were—Randy, Bob, Lee and Ozzy—although you couldn't hear Ozzy at all."

Paul elaborates. "Now, I'm used to loud music but they were unbelievable! They had a full P.A. set up so it was bloody loud when Randy, Bob and Lee were playing but every time Ozzy sang the red warning light came on to indicate an overload so Ozzy looked like he was just mouthing the words. It was totally deafening!" Pete was dumbstruck. "I knew what Ozzy meant by 'secret weapon'. Randy was just unreal."

"The Nomis rehearsals were great fun. It really was an inspiration being able to appreciate just how good individually everybody was" affirms Bridgwater. "For the most part Randy, Bob, Lee and myself would just run through the set. Randy was such great fun to work with because he was not your run of the mill guitarist, quite unlike anyone I have ever played with before or since. Bob and Lee of course were extremely professional—absolute top class musicians. Both had success in their own right and I suppose they took me under their wing a bit.

I think after the first album had been done keyboards came as a bit of an afterthought. Initially I was kind of an extra really and it took a while to find my feet and become a valid member."

Bridgwater also backs up the feeling of camaraderie present at the time. "It was never Ozzy and a group of session musicians. Not only did everyone believe it was a band but, more importantly, it felt like a band. They had all written the tracks, Bob more so than most. Lee was highly skilled with arrangements, Bob contributed the words and lots of chord progressions and Randy had the riffs. Ozzy was kind of seen as the guiding light—he would show everyone the direction in which to go. There was no drunken debauchery, none of that. Quite unlike the image portrayed to the outside world we just got on with the job night after night getting the set absolutely right."

Ozzy debuted the Blizzard Of Ozz with two low key anonymous club gigs in front a favoured few. The exact venues would pose a memory test for the rhythm section. Lee thinks they were in the far flung climes of Cromer in Norfolk and Skegness. Daisley is unsure of their whereabouts but ventures "Blackpool was one I'm sure." Completists might wish to note that the bands recently inducted member Lindsey Bridgwater confirms the first gig was Blackpool, the second West Runton near Cromer.

The band went out under a pseudonym to keep the media at bay. "David Arden at Jet came up with the cover name Law, not The Law but simply Law" relates Daisley. "Of course people locally soon found out who it was. I remember Roy Wood from Wizzard came to the first gig. We signed a lot of autographs too. What was funny was that Ozzy, Lee and I were known to the kids from Black Sabbath, Uriah Heep and Rainbow but Randy was pretty much left alone as no one knew him."

Blizzard Of Ozz road tested much of the debut album packed out with Sabbath staples such as 'Children Of The Grave' and 'Iron Man'. With such high profile players this brace of supposed low key gigs turned out to be anything but. The grapevine had resulted in hundreds of fans crammed into the tiny venues as Bridgwater recalls. "I was staggered. The gigs were packed out. I don't know how they got to know it was Ozzy. Strangely for us, the band, we only then really appreciated how big this whole thing could be. It was awe inspiring seeing this devotion to Ozzy at first hand."

Bob has reason to remember a small incident afterward which in some small way would signal the misapprehensions that all the band members would be forced into coming to terms with as the band profile grew. "After the gig we did these signing sessions and this kid brought along a Black Sabbath album for Ozzy to sign. Just as he was leaving this kid said to Ozzy 'Are you still into black magic?'"

Lindsey Bridgwater confirms this. "This chap—who looked a little strange—sidled up to Ozzy and took him to one side. He said he was into black magic and didn't know what to do about it. Ozzy's advice was to change to Milk Tray! It was absolutely wonderful how Ozzy dealt with that one. He didn't belittle the kid in any way just put him in his place." Standing next to Ozzy, Daisley took all this in too. "You should have seen this poor kids face! He soon got the joke though and all the kids standing in line had a good laugh too."

The following full scale British tour, kicked off at the Glasgow Apollo on September 12th 1980, saw Ozzy welcomed back as an all conquering hero. 'Blizzard Of Ozz' crashed into the UK charts peaking at No. 7 on 20th of September and lending a huge boost. Even a reissued 'Paranoid' made it back into the charts but not everything was complying with the grand plan.

"At Hammersmith Odeon there was a plan for Ozzy to rise out from under the stage during 'Crazy Train'." Recounts Lee Kerslake. "Well, we had to do this on a fork lift truck to make it work. When Ozzy came out of the smoke from the floor in his white tassels flashing his peace signs the crowd just went into uproar. What people don't know is that there was a plan for me too. They were going to put a pyrotechnic device under my seat and blow me up! The idea was for the explosion to go off and I would be launched into the air by the aid of wires and four roadies. We had half of the Electric Light Orchestra crew on the road with us then, great guys. The problem was that we tried it at rehearsal and not only couldn't the block and tackle lift me up but it took eight roadies not four to get me off my seat!"

Uriah Heep fans will know that Lee's stature could never be described as sleight. Indeed, the very day we conducted the interview the Sun newspaper had a light hearted jibe at him for eating too many pork pies! "It's taken me years to get into this shape" laughs the self deprecating drummer.

Support band for the tour were Welsh veterans Budgie enjoying a second wind of popularity with their 'Power Supply' album. Strange to imagine now but Budgie's addition to the billing actually brought so many of their fans to shows it was only after their confirmation a lot of the shows sold out. Lindsey Bridgwater would double up each night performing with both bands. "I did both band's sets. I would come off after Budgie, grab a half hour break then go straight back on with Ozzy. It never seemed like hard work.

John Thomas, Budgie's guitar player, was absolutely smitten by Randy. The whole band was just in awe of him. The two guitarists got on great and I remember John trying to glean as much as he could from Randy "What's that progression?" or just simply "How do you do that?" They got on famously." As Bridgwater recalled Budgie's guitarist John, or J.T. as he is more commonly known, would click instantly with Randy, both as a musician and as a friend. "That tour was the best I have ever done" J.T. records. "I've known Ozzy for years and he was keen for me to meet Randy so he introduced us both backstage at the first night, the Glasgow Apollo. We hit it off straight away, Randy knew all about Budgie. Well, we both picked up guitars and didn't put them down from that point on!"

J.T.'s recollection of watching his first live performance of Randy Rhoads is crystal clear. "He totally knocked me back. I can remember telling everyone—this guy is just brilliant. He looked an absolute star. He was an absolute magician on the guitar. His approach was just superb, he didn't play 'dark' like a lot of players then. Randy was very melodic. Absolutely perfect for Ozzy. I know Randy pretty much impressed the world. That's how good he was."

The two six-stringers bonded like glue. "We met at the Glasgow show and by the second night I was staying in his hotel room. We couldn't be separated. We just played and played and played. Randy stayed over at my house when there were any gaps in the tour. My memories of Randy are the two of us sitting in front of an open fire just playing guitar all night long. He was a total genius and such a beautiful person with it. A lovely, lovely guy."

Whilst staying at J.T.'s house, Randy would witness the Budgie guitarist's Rock n' Roll method of dealing with bad neighbours. "We had these people

Rare home snap of Randy Rhoads with Budgie's J.T.

next door who kept throwing dogshit over my fence. I saw them do it" J.T. laughs. "One morning, I got up really, really early. Randy was still in bed. Well, I got two Marshall stacks and put them right next to their fence, turned them up full bore and started to play 'Crazy Train'!! Randy ran down into the garden terrified. I think he must have thought it was an horrendous nightmare or something. I forgot all about the neighbours when I saw Randy though—this skinny little guy, hair everywhere, shaking and holding tight onto his hot water bottle! I could not stop laughing. I never got any more neighbour trouble by the way."

Randy would be enthralled by J.T.'s huge Gibson collection and his intimate knowledge of guitars. This would lead to a small disappointment for the young American though. "Randy had this white Les Paul he was very keen on" J.T. motions. "He asked me how old it was so I told him—1972. He was gutted. "I thought it was a 1963!" he said. That little incident really, really upset him. You have to remember, he was very young. He loved going through my guitars—I had hundreds of them. He would open up each case and either say "Wow—great" or "That's crap!" He wanted to play them all."

In the midst of the run of UK Blizzard Of Ozz dates it was decided that a live version of 'Mr. Crowley', already making a radio impact in America, should be issued as a single. A mobile recording studio was dispatched to capture the song on the British tour. However, the record company was keen to make this single release doubly collectable by including an unreleased track. With no excess material left in the can from the 'Blizzard' sessions the band were faced with a challenge coming up trumps with 'You Said It All' in record time.

"We wrote that track in one afternoon during a soundcheck, at Oxford I think" observes Bob. "It was quite funny how it came together. Lee had the vocal melody and Randy put down the music. All very quick. After I had recorded this on tape from the desk I came up with the lyrics back at the hotel." But where was Ozzy? "While we were writing the song Ozzy was sound asleep underneath the drum riser!" Bob laughs heartily. "We recorded the song that night with Lindsey on keyboards. I suppose what we should have done was to record Ozzy's snoring for the intro!" The track would remain a highly sought after rarity. With the exception of the single B-side it would only resurface on the Japanese compilation album 'The Other Side Of Ozzy Osbourne', noted not only for the inclusion of 'You Said It All' but also the even scarcer 'You, Looking At Me Looking At You' studio outtake.

Meantime, Black Sabbath's ever extending live schedule saw the band hitting Japan, Geezer Butler hitting the wall and Tony Iommi's dinner hitting the toilet bowl. The group had started off on 16th November with a run of five Tokyo gigs, which included matinee performances due to excessive demand. The guitarist would not make it to the fifth show. "Tony got very serious food poisoning in a fish restaurant" Geoff Nicholls confirms. "It was one of these pick your own live fish type of places and I guess he picked a bad 'un. When it came to sound check he fainted, actually collapsed on stage in front of me, so the show was off. It was pretty nasty so I was quite surprised to see him recover so quickly to do the rest of the tour. Later on Geezer got drunk and punched a wall. He made a big mess of his hand. So, all in all Japan was quite memorable!"

In a heady year which had truly seen the band conquering the globe Black Sabbath closed out 1980 with four Australian gigs in Sydney. The band would not see the like again, the seeds of discontent were sprouting . . .

The UK Blizzard Of Ozz dates led straight into preproduction for a second album. "David Arden wanted another album quickly. The first record was selling much faster than anyone had anticipated and he wanted a follow-up straight away" Lee emphasizes.

The 'Diary Of A Madman' album was cut swiftly after the debut as the label needed it ready for an American tour. The first album sales were going through the roof but it was initially released only in Europe. Indeed, 'Blizzard Of Ozz' would have to wait until March of the following year to see an American release. The songwriting came thick and fast at that point. Lee was now able to lend his arranging talents fully and ended up contributing melodies to about six songs. At the close of 1980 the Blizzard Of Ozz was back in the studio, once again with Max Norman acting as engineer.

Lee recalls this hectic period. "With 'Diary Of A Madman' we just clicked. We matched and progressed from what we had done before and took it to a whole new level. Those songs just flowed." Bob remembers the sessions for another reason. "During the 'Diary' sessions Ozzy had his car, a classic green Mercedes, just repainted and restored. He had parked it on this dark country lane just outside a pub named 'The Plough' near Ridge Farm Studios." Ozzy's choice of parking would not prove opportune. A red Mini smashed into the back of it causing major damage. "You can imagine, he was really pissed off" records Bob. "Well, I didn't know this yet and I had just bought a new car—a red Mini! So I see Ozzy in the pub looking really pissed off and was telling him about my new car. When I told him it was a red Mini I'm absolutely certain he thought that I had smashed his car up!"

Car crash coincidences were not the only mysteries to be dealt with. One of the album songs had been laid to bed minus a suitable title and this simple practical point would engender a little fable all to itself. Lindsey Bridgwater for the first time unveils what he believes to be the true meaning of the track 'S.A.T.O.' The exact nature of the title has been expounded and hypothesized upon over the years with various theories claiming to be authoritative. It has been credited from to anything from Ozzy (then still married to his first wife) extolling his clandestine love for Sharon by cryptically putting his love's initials into a song title—wrong, or some devilish combination of mystically charged ciphers—equally wrong. Other combinations include 'Sailing Across The Ocean' and 'Saturdays And Thursdays Only'.

"Ozzy told me this himself" states Lindsey. "They had this song but no title. To close the issue they took the first letter of everyone's first name who was in the office at the time—Sharon, Arthur Sharp from Jet, Thelma—Ozzy's then wife and Ozzy himself—S.A.T.O. Simple as that."

Or is it? Bob Daisley is certain Lindsey has got it nearly right. "It was Sharon, Adrian—Sharon's then boyfriend who worked in the office, Thelma and Ozzy. The song lyrics I wrote about a particular Buddhist doctrine. It's based on one of the teachings which was titled 'A ship to sail across the sea of suffering'." Arthur or Adrian? Such is the heady brew of neological esoterica that fuels The Cult of Ozzy ...

Having launched such a successful rejuvenation of the band Black Sabbath felt the pressure to come up with a product equally spectacular as 'Heaven And Hell'. Momentum was everything. In truth, the follow-up album 'Mob Rules' was to be the equal of its illustrious predecessor but that is exactly where the critics had a problem, believing the record to have almost duplicated 'Heaven And Hell'.

Warner Bros. had re-signed the band—and Ronnie James Dio. "I got signed up for a solo deal when Black Sabbath signed back to Warner Bros." the singer confides. "I guess they thought they were onto a good thing with me. 'Heaven And Hell' could well have been their last Warner Bros. record but it did so spectacularly well they soon asked for another contract. The turnaround was huge. I mean, before 'Heaven And Hell' nobody at Warner Bros. gave a shit about the band. They were over and out and their last two Ozzy records had been dreadful. Of course they were smart enough to realise I had played a major part in that rejuvenation so I got signed for a future solo record too. This would soon become a bone of contention with the others as things developed. I never wrote any solo material whilst I was with Sabbath—none. I have been accused of that but it never happened. Basically I viewed my solo deal as useful money in the bank. As it happens it turned out very useful later."

The actual recording process of the 'Mob Rules' record would be far from in keeping with the re-debut though. Geoff Nicholls reveals strong tensions had now surfaced. "Ronnie wanted things much more his own way this time. That is the truth of the matter. I guess he felt that because 'Heaven And Hell' had been such a success he should take more control this time around. On the previous record we had captured a very real magic and that team spirit seemed to have evaporated. To give you an example, Ronnie insisted on doing all the vocal harmonies himself, whereas previously I had been involved in that too. I don't think the songs were as strong as before either. I remember being disappointed with 'Country Girl' because I thought that was a great riff Tony came up with but then Ronnie added these very twee lyrics. It sounded like a bit of a beerkeller song to me actually. That wasn't very Sabbath at all."

Dio does not rebuke such suggestions about his authoritative manner, claiming the force of his will was required. "I did come on a bit dictatorial for 'Mob Rules' because the situation needed it" he says candidly. "I would have denied it to myself at the time but looking back I can get a clearer picture of the way I was thinking. There was a certain amount of familiarity amongst the band, our little foibles were beginning to niggle at each other—mine included. Our personal glitches were starting to irritate quite seriously so there was a notion of 'let's get this bastard thing over with!' We needed some focus."

Ronnie believes that Martin Birch did not possess enough authority to take the whip hand. "Martin was actually wavering. He was dealing with this bunch of strange people—myself included—and unable to deal with it. He was fantastic at capturing the sound we made, a great, great engineer, but he couldn't steer the ship. It was his job as a producer to do that but he just couldn't handle us. The band also had another attitude to deal with too because Vinny Appice was in there as a foreign element. Geezer loved playing with Vinny but he would drive Tony nuts with all his fills and busy stuff. Vinny would drop in a fill and Tony would shit himself! 'What the hell is that?' he used to shout. There were a lot of minds wanting to be heard, wanting to contribute including Vinny. Sometimes it did mean someone had to say 'Vinny, you're just the drummer—shut up!'

I tried to avoid taking a direct control because I was concerned with gently keeping everyone pointed in the right direction. Even then I was concerned with them thinking I was more of a control freak than they already thought I was! So, I would make suggestions in order to get the best contributions from everybody. I didn't shout at anybody because that just doesn't work with musicians. Someone had to take charge and get the job done." With Geezer and Ronnie's prosaic skills available one wonders why the bassist deferred. "The truth was that Geezer didn't like writing lyrics" states Dio matter of factly. "He actually said to me beforehand 'You're going to write the lyrics right?' When I said 'OK' he replied 'Great! I fucking hate writing lyrics!' He told me he was sick of Ozzy getting them wrong all the time."

The catalyst for 'Mob Rules' lay in the animated movie 'Heavy Metal'. The band had been asked by Warner Bros. to submit a track for the battle sequence in the film and accepted the challenge. The title track was conceived and recorded at Startling Studios, Tittenhurst Park, in actual fact the former residence of John Lennon and Yoko Ono. The Beatles frontman had operated the studios as Ascot Studios but when Black Sabbath took residence the house, whose expansive grounds boasted a guitar shaped lake, had come under the ownership of another Beatle, Ringo Starr. The band were travelling back to the UK from North America for these sessions when a disc jockey informed them mid flight that John Lennon had been shot dead. It was 8th December 1980.

"Recording there was a very strange sensation I have to say" says Nicholls. "Obviously there was the famous white room with the piano where he had recorded 'Imagine' but there was a huge, ceiling high church organ too so I was in seventh heaven with that thing, a pool, gazebos and everything. Stunning house. Being in there so soon after he died was a little spooky. Even odder was the fact that I slept in their bed. It had light switches on either side that said 'John' and 'Yoko'. A real once in a lifetime experience."

It is common knowledge amongst Sabbs fans that this original version of 'Mob Rules' was recorded at Startling Studios. What many are unaware of is that much of the intro and outro keyboard work on the movie is also Sabbath stamped by Geoff Nicholls. "There was a lot of keyboard work I put down for that film around the 'Mob Rules' song. A lot of the special effects noises, the spaceship coming down and the atmospherics around the horse on the mountain and the glass city. That's all mine too."

Heavy Metal soundtrack with the original 'Mob Rules'.

Once the movie work was fulfilled Black Sabbath launched into yet another UK tour, supported by AIIZ, which took the band throughout January of 1981. Demand for tickets on the prior 'Heaven And Hell' dates had been so strong a further sojourn across home turf was warranted. Once again Black Sabbath filled the hallowed portals of Hammersmith Odeon four times over. Consensus was they could have crammed the place eight times or more if they had really felt like it.

With the song 'Mob Rules' in the bag Black Sabbath relocated to the USA with a proposal to build their own recording studio. An interesting undertaking to be under consideration because it so obviously demonstrates that there was a common aim of longevity between the band personnel at this juncture. The fundamentals of this endeavour were to save themselves considerable money of future recordings, the band reckoning on having the studio paid for relatively quickly. A desk was purchased, at great expense, and studio space acquired. Upon completion the band duly entered their new domain to rerecord the song 'Mob Rules'. There would be one small glitch. "It sounded absolutely fucking crap" proclaims Nicholls. "They soon jacked that idea in and went to the Record Plant to record the album properly. The studio was ditched."

Ronnie James Dio illustrates the thinking behind this move in some detail. "To do the 'Mob Rules' album we got $500,000. I think that's what it was. Anyway, Sandy Pearlman had an idea to invest that for the band's future so we found a studio that needed a new desk. So, Black Sabbath brought a Trident desk, which was something like $280,000, and had it installed in the studio. The deal was that the band would record their next three albums there at no cost. See, how it works is that for each album in the chain the label gives you more money so by taking a stake in the studio we potentially would have a lot more free capital to invest in other areas or stick straight in your pocket. It was good sound commercial thinking but unfortunately it all went wrong because once we started we soon realised we could not get a decent guitar sound in the place. In point of fact it was so horrible that it was beyond fixing. Suddenly the investment was looking like a huge mistake. Now, this is where some typically Sabbath thinking came into play. Because we couldn't use that studio they said "OK, we'll go somewhere else." Well, fine, but what about this desk we've just bought? They took the decision to go anyway and we left our brand new gear in the other studio."

Obviously the band had every intention of retrieving their investment. It would not be as simple as they thought. "Sabbath sent two guys down, Paul Clark and someone else, to get this desk" relays Ronnie. "The next thing they know they are surrounded by a full SWAT team with rifles pointing at them! As soon as they turned up with the truck for the desk the studio owner called the police and told them a robbery was happening! The guys put against the wall and everything. Finally they convinced the police that the owner had concocted this fake robbery. Sandy took the fall for that whole episode at the end of the day and we had to eat the cost of the desk. It could have been good for us but it turned out typically Sabbath!"

To clear up a point of confusion repeated in error throughout various Black Sabbath tracts the song 'Mob Rules' was recorded three times: once at Aston, a second aborted attempt and then finally for the album itself with Martin Birch. The version of the song that appears in the 'Heavy Metal' movie is not a remix, as is often cited. It is a completely different recording. This is clarified by Nicholls. "Birch didn't want to work on remixing anybody else's recordings. At first the song 'Mob Rules' was intended just for the movie but obviously with that kind of promotion it just had to be included on the album too. We rerecorded it at the Record Plant from scratch."

The 'Mob Rules' album cover was a post apocalyptic nightmare scenario of sack clothed, faceless slave raiders. Wielding whips and obviously awaiting their

Mob Rules.

next victim for a lashing, this picture, painted by the artist Greg Hildebrandt and titled 'The Crucifiers', was uniquely disturbing. Almost as soon as it hit the record racks murmurs filtered through that all was not appeared with the 'Mob Rules' artwork. People began to say they could see the word 'Ozzy' depicted in the cobbles below the artist's signature. Dismissed by the band and treated as an aberration of unlucky and coincidental brushstrokes the supposed moniker was hushed down.

History is littered with visual subterfuge ranging from Leonardo Da Vinci all the way down to the famous shagging dogs hidden behind bushes on 1940s biscuit tins. There are very few artists that don't enjoy a personal joke at their clients expense. The name 'Ozzy' is there clear as day and has been subtly masked by filling in the 'O' and blending in the last two letters. The stark 'O' and 'Z' with the less refined second 'Z' and 'Y' are seemingly no accident. However, oddly enough it appears that the original version of the painting, executed prior to Sabbath's commission, also includes this same device. Strange indeed. Also to be taken into account here are the surreptitious clues secreted into future sleeve artworks. Black Sabbath album covers were rarely 'just' a good picture.

With the 'Diary Of A Madman' record finished Lee Kerslake took a well deserved holiday to Lanzarotte blissfully unaware of the cogs turning silently in the inner workings of the machine. "I got back from Lanzarotte and found a message on my answer machine saying I was no longer in the band. What a way to go eh? Sharon had phoned my ex wife to tell her" sighs the drummer resignedly. "Bob Daisley got the same treatment. It got taken away from being a band to becoming just Ozzy. Randy was totally gutted. He phoned me and we spoke at great length. He wanted to leave and work with Bob and I but I persuaded him to stay. He was in a unique position and I told him so. I'm glad I did but of course I can't help thinking that if he had of left he might still be alive. Things like that you can't even think of. At the time I was very glad he stayed."

Such a blow has naturally left a sharp imprint on Bob Daisley's memory too. He was staggered to discover that out of the blue both he and Lee Kerslake had been fired. "It was very simple" he motions. "I got a phone call from Sharon and she just said "You and Lee are out"."

When asked if he knew of the reasoning behind such a decision Bob has no hard and fast theories but hindsight has naturally opened up a few avenues of thought. "Ozzy was very keen on getting Tommy Aldridge into the band which is something I never understood. Tommy is a great drummer but Lee was his equal and actually much better suited to the band. Tommy was actually turning up to quite a few gigs too. I remember him being at the Brighton show. Sharon and Ozzy asked me to go along to see him play with Gary Moore at the London Marquee. Sharon said to me "Isn't he a great drummer." I had to agree but I also made it clear what I thought. "So is Lee" I said "And he's better for our band too." It was not the answer they wanted to hear but I could not see the sense in changing the band around for no gain. They kept on at me though but I kept making it clear that I was not going to agree. In the end I guess I stood my ground too much."

Tommy Aldridge bears witness to the same event. "I do remember Randy, Sharon and Bob coming to the Marquee club and going out afterwards. I don't remember attending any of their shows however that's not to say I didn't. I was working with Gary Moore at the time and trying to establish more of a 'freelance' direction. This was shortly after my departing the Travers camp and was a bit disillusioned regarding the 'band' thing at the time. I was trying to maintain my 'independence' ... I suppose until something came along that really struck my fancy."

Asked to expand upon the contrasting styles of the two drummers Daisley describes the differences as such. "Lee is more hard Rock n' Roll—a bit more like a bull in a china shop. Tommy is fancier than Lee but has got a pair of very fast feet. He's well known for his double bass drumming." Also perplexed by the whole situation would be Lindsey Bridgwater. "I simply didn't understand—not that it was my place to you understand. Bob and Lee were the absolute backbone of that band and they were co-writers too. However, Ozzy had always wanted Tommy—it was no secret. The two have totally different styles, Tommy is a lot busier whereas Lee is just Rock solid. He could say a lot with very little if you know what I mean."

With the benefit of hindsight, Bob Daisley also believes that both replacements were American is significant. "Randy called me a few days later to say how sorry he was that I was no longer in the band which was good of him but then again I think they really were after an American band. In the end Lee and I had too much to say for ourselves I suppose. I guess Randy suggested Rudy Sarzo from his Quiet Riot days and Tommy was obviously first choice for Ozzy."

With these Machiavellian manouevres taking place behind the scenes at centre stage the 'Blizzard Of Ozz' album was eating into the American Billboard charts satisfying it's appetite with over a million registered sales. Before it had its fill Ozz mania had seen it engorged with a double helping of platinum pie and like the twisted bastard brother of Oliver it was still yelling for "More!"

It was not only the unforeseen revolving door policy in the personnel department that grieved Daisley and Kerslake. "When 'Diary Of A Madman' was released Lee and I were bloody angry. It was no longer Blizzard Of Ozz it was just Ozzy and we were virtually erased. Our names are there but only in the smallest of fine print and only listed as songwriters. Rudy Sarzo and Tommy Aldridge were credited but never played a note on that record. 'Diary Of A Madman' was recorded by Ozzy, Randy, Lee and myself but anyone buying the album would never have been able to figure that out. It really was insulting. Even the production credits changed. Lee and I were left out there too. I really could not see the point of that."

Tommy Aldridge, quick to praise his predecessors, confirms that rather like embarrassing Russian political figures airbrushed out of official photographs the departing Brits were scheduled for retrospective revision. "Though I've never had the opportunity to tell him, Lee should be very proud of those records" he states for the record. "I remember someone (who shall remain nameless) trying to get me to rerecord the drums. I declined saying I couldn't improve upon what he did. I didn't know it at the time but I was being approached not to 'improve' but only to 'replace' his performance. I didn't know why but can only imagine. By the way, the person who made this request is no longer associated with Ozzy."

Aldridge, the Nashville born mop topped drummer with the fastest feet in the West had honed his skills with perhaps the original Southern bad boys Black Oak Arkansas. The initial Black Oak Arkansas roster included vocalist Mangrum, guitarist Reynolds, guitarists Stan Knight and Harvey Jett, bassist Pat Daugherty and drummer Wayne Evans. However, Evans was replaced by Aldridge during 1972 as he took his place on tour that summer during which the live set 'Raunch And Roll—Live' was captured.

Officially Black Oak Arkansas had debuted with

self titled effort in 1971 produced by Iron Butterfly men Mike Pinera and Lee Dorman. The album struck an immediate chord with the American Rock public; especially the renewed attitude the band gave the Guy Mitchell hit 'Singin' The Blues'. The band had kept up a hectic schedule of recording and touring throughout the 70s outpacing many of their rivals. Highlights included a British tour opening for Black Sabbath, although the good ol' BBC mysteriously banned the 'High On The Hog' album's 'Jim Dandy To The Rescue'! It was on this encounter that Aldridge first came into contact with Ozzy Osbourne.

With a true Dunkirk spirit prevailing Lee Kerslake did not have long to ponder on might have beens. Ossie Hoppie, the same man who had discovered his departure from Uriah Heep post 'Fallen Angel' now found out that Lee was a free agent once again. Mick Box was straight on the telephone excitedly relaying plans to re-form Uriah Heep. Once the drummer had established that certain people were no longer involved he jumped at the chance. His next action was to phone Bob Daisley. "Do you want to join Uriah Heep?" he inquired. "Not 'arf!!" came the reply. The circle had been closed.

The pair would retain their partnership for what would turn out to be Uriah Heep's 1982 renaissance album 'Abominog'. The record pulled Mick Box's boys back from the brink and the fresh look Pete Goalby fronted Heep found renewed international audiences and revitalized album sales. Also a member of the reforged Heep was erstwhile Heavy Metal Kids keyboard player John Sinclair, himself later to figure as a long term player in the Ozzy story in later years. Daisley would stick with Heep for the follow-up 'Head First' effort in 1983 too though in spite of this Daisley's career with Ozzy was far from over. Indeed, it had only really just begun.

'Diary Of A Madman' was released on the 7th of November 1981 peaking at No. 14 in the UK album charts. The very next week Black Sabbath's 'Mob Rules' hit No. 12. To the eager fans happy to fork out for both releases the sheer level of quality evident on both records portrayed a keen sense of competition. Once again, both camps had come up with bona fide classics. 'Diary Of A Madman' arrived in the stores complete with the brand new band members names emblazoned on it as a statement of intent: Ozzy Osbourne, Randy Rhoads, Rudy Sarzo and Tommy Aldridge. It was a fearsome combination.

Bassist Rudy Sarzo had been handpicked for Ozzy by Randy Rhoads. The guitarist had known Sarzo since he had supplanted original Quiet Riot bass player Kelli Garni for the second Japanese release album, 'Quiet Riot II', released by CBS in 1979. As an aside, Garni, the ousted partner, kept it in the family by later joining Randy's brother Kelle Rhoads

Diary of a Madman.

act Emerald. Just previous to lining up for Ozzy's band Sarzo had actually been working with whiter than white pompsters Angel.

Joining in the fray was Don Airey. The keyboard player had been unable to tour with Ozzy up to that point or contribute to 'Diary Of A Madman' as he was serving out a touring term with Rainbow. A well timed telephone call secured his recruitment. "Ozzy phoned me up in November of 1981 and asked me to take over from Lindsey in the live show. I said I wouldn't do it if it meant playing offstage. He phoned back five minutes later and asked me to join the band as a full member."

The man remembers being instantly struck by the unbridled power of the band that he had just joined. "When I heard Randy, Rudy and Tommy playing together I thought they sounded like Cream. Tommy did deservedly have a fantastic reputation at this point."

It would also be Don's first experience of working with Randy Rhoads outside of the studio confines and in the live arena. "The way Randy played, needed a much different approach keyboard-wise to say working with someone like Ritchie Blackmore or Gary Moore. It had to be sparse, with sound FX, etc. Anything vaguely avant-garde he really liked. We'd play the gig tapes back in the bus, and if he went "Wow!" I'd keep that bit in. He turned me on to a lot of diverse stuff—18th century guitar music, obscure film soundtracks, records by pianists Katia and Marielle Lebeque, Ravel and Debussy. I remember his favourite chord, which was the one in the film 'Carrie', when the hand comes out of the grave—we'd play that bit of the video over and over again."

Tommy Aldridge too has his own recollections of the first time the unit gelled as the new Ozzy Osbourne band. "I had never worked with Rudy Sarzo before but Randy had and Rudy was there on Randy's recommendation. I believe that Lindsey

Bridgwater was present at this time as well. It was, I thought at the time, a relatively tight rhythm section. It worked well around Randy which I felt then and still do that he was the catalyst. He was certainly my motivation for being there. Not to discount Ozzy of course but my interest was predicated strictly on working with THAT guitarist. I only remember it to be very exciting working with Randy. The better I got to know Randy the more I realized just how very special he was. It was exciting to be part of that."

The new grouping faced an uphill struggle. Not only did they have to mentally lock as a band but quickly get down pat on a whole slew of material written and performed by those they had so recently supplanted. Aldridge enjoyed the challenge. "As far as learning Lee's parts . . . some of it was necessary. First off . . . they're cool parts, some of them being 'thumbprint' parts. Meaning they need to played note-for-note. I was impressed with his playing on that record. I've kicked myself in the butt more than once for not being on that record. But again, I am the worst copy drummer but try to remain faithful to the music."

Bob Daisley's legacy also weighed heavy on his replacement Rudy Sarzo. In a '20 questions' interview for the infamous 'Metal Sludge' website on 31st July 2001, in which the bassist is asked to grade other musicians, Sarzo's admiration for his predecessor is clear. "Awesome bass player. I had the time of my life playing his bass lines live, because of course he recorded 'Blizzard Of Ozz' and 'Diary Of A Madman'.

'Diary Of A Madman' was in the can before Tommy Aldridge and I joined the band, so we first joined the band tour in '81 for 'Blizzard Of Ozz', we went out there, then we took a break, then we went to Europe and started the 'Diary Of A Madman' tour. And let me tell you, his bass lines are world-class. So as a recording artist I definitely give him a 10. As for rock star appeal, oooh. You know he comes from a whole different 70s tradition. More of that very grounded, you know, type of bass player." Rudy finished by giving Daisley 6 points out of 10—losing marks due to lack of 'Glam' MTV appeal!

In the same Metal Sludge interview Sarzo is also keen to verify the speculation that it was Randy Rhoads that secured the Ozzy position for him. When talking about the guitarist Sarzo had this to say: "The fondest memory is actually the fact that if it wasn't for him, I wouldn't be here. He was completely, 100% responsible for me meeting Ozzy Osbourne. You know, the fact that he helped me through the early days. 'Cause, I mean, Sharon and Ozzy are wonderful people. But they can be pretty wacky! (laughs) And I got thrown into that, that, world, you know. It was like going on the biggest roller coaster ride of your life, you know. I went from sleeping on the floor, on Kevin's floor (Kevin DuBrow—Quiet Riot), in his apartment. We were sharing a, a . . . you know, I was living with him, at his place, and I didn't even have a bed. So I had a sheet. So, I was sleeping on this sheet, and I got a call to audition for Ozzy, and Randy really helped me out a lot. He's the one who told Ozzy, "This is the guy." So my fondest memory was that if it wasn't for him I'd . . . be playing conga drums in a Salsa band in Miami."

Ozzy on the 'Diary of a Madman' U.S. tour. Pic: Rich Galbraith.

Chapter 5

An Englishman's Castle

Launching in Towson, Maryland on April 22 1981 Ozzy proceeded to pursue a mammoth 14 month globally encompassing tour. Ozzy's support bands for these U.S. gigs were Brummie natives The Starfighters and Pomp Rockers Magnum. The former of these acts was fronted by a notorious hard drinking character named Steve Burton. More commonly known as 'Bertie', he had as legend would have it recently turned down an offer to join AC/DC as replacement for Bon Scott. That was not the only AC/DC connection as guitarist Stevie Young's obvious family resemblance betrayed what was the cousin of Angus and Malcolm. The quintessentially British Magnum were Jet Records stable mates.

Initially the band was in the odd position in America of promoting the debut album almost a year after its recording. These inaugural Stateside shows, some supported by Def Leppard, ranged from crammed theatres packed to the gunnels to gigs with attendance's so poor that, according to later interviews given by Sharon Osbourne, the band sometimes had to fight to just get paid for their efforts. It would be during this period of dogged persistence that the Ozzy legend was kindled.

At the band's stop off in Las Vegas Randy Rhoads would be reunited with his old friend Kelly Garni. "We met up the night before the Vegas show on that very first tour and we had the best time ever" the bassist remembers fondly. Worryingly the guitarist would reveal to Garni some of the more disturbing aspects of touring with Ozzy. "Randy was really bothered by the whole satanic thing. Y'know, he told me had guys coming up to him backstage with goats heads and stuff which really scared him."

Come show time Garni and his partner received the best seats in the house. "Randy arranged it so that my date and I could watch the show from backstage. We sat on a road case in the wings just ten feet away from him. It was really funny because we were both pulling faces at each other. Afterwards we hung around to try and catch him again but they just got mobbed by fans so that was the last time we actually met. He would write me letters after

Ozzy & Randy. Pic: Rich Galbraith.

that or phone now and then but often he was either tired or sick. Randy got sick a lot, he suffered from anaemia."

Black Sabbath too were swinging into live action, embarking upon an equally gargantuan world tour in Canada, Quebec's Coliseum being treated to the opening blast of 'Mob Rules' era Black Sabbath on the 15th of November 1981. This first leg would cover the North American East Coast concluding in Chicago on the 21st February. Confident that the Dio fronted band had by now proven itself adequately only six songs from the seventies version of Black Sabbath actually made the song list. Opening to the sinister strains of 'E5150' the band indulged themselves and their audience with 'Neon Knights', 'Country Girl', 'Children Of The Sea', 'Turn Up The Night', 'Voodoo', 'Slippin' Away', 'Falling Off The Edge Of The World', 'The Mob Rules' and naturally 'Heaven And Hell'. The sets climaxed with the warhorses

Ozzy & Randy. Pic: Rich Galbraith.

Mob Rules tour pass.

'Paranoid' and 'Children Of The Grave' but overall the band seemed keen to stamp a renewed authority on the proceedings and their newer material was certainly up to the task.

Special guests by way of a kind payback would be Alvin Lee, the man who had so inspired Iommi and Butler in their formative years. Lee had put together his Ten Years Later band which incorporated former Rolling Stones guitarist Mick Taylor. He acknowledges the gigs were by way of a favour. "I'd known Tony, Ozzy and Geezer from the very, very early days. Way before they were even called Black Sabbath. We bumped into each other a lot at places like the Blue Boar and I jammed a few times around at Tony's house. Never recorded anything though which was a shame. I guess we just didn't think about doing it at the time. It was great to see them get their success because Tony is such a sweet guy. I never understood all the black magic stuff though. They were just normal blokes yet they were attracting all these bizarre Voodoo type people. Tony had a great sense of humour, always playing jokes. I remember he was really into cars and one day he took me for a drive in this brand new Lamborghini he had just bought. It was the model with the engine right behind the cockpit so you couldn't hear a bloody thing. Tony was trying to play me music on the car's 8 track but even Black Sabbath couldn't compete with a Lamborghini engine!"

Tony Iommi is known for his passion for expensive motor cars. Over the years the guitarist has indulged himself in several Rolls Royces, Porsches, Jaguars, Corvette Stingrays and Lamborghinis. At one point the guitarist owned a special edition Ferrari Dino, one of only six in the world. His collection of speed machines aside, Iommi remained very much rooted in the real world. Alvin, personally invited by Tony and Geezer for these gigs, was struck by just how casual Black Sabbath was in dealing with success. "It was nice touring with them because they were just so down to earth, being Birmingham boys n' all. My one overriding memory of that tour is how much curry we ate! They had Indian curry on their rider every night, which was bloody marvellous. I was in their dressing room practically every night stocking up on curry and having a good old banter. Nothing seemed to phase them, they were so laid back." Those with a culinary persuasion might wish to know Black Sabbath's tastes in curry were nothing if not regimented. Tony favoured the absolute hottest variety, Geezer was a strict vegetarian whilst Geoff and Vinny went for mild chicken. Such is the sustenance of success.

Alvin remembers how this nonchalant attitude cost the band dearly. "I remember they take a long time to set up the stage after we had finished our set. It took about an hour because they had to lay all these carpets down and they even had a roadie whose job it was to spray fake cobwebs on the monitors. I always thought this was funny because the only people who could see them was the band.

Anyway, this one time the boys were there waiting backstage, chatting away over a curry and the tour manager (probably Paul 'Disco Dancer' Clark) comes

Mob Rules tour pass.

Mob Rules UK tour programme.

in and says "When you're ready lads." They carried on talking about cars, had another drink. Fifteen minutes later the tour manager comes back and says again "When you're ready!" Well, they carried on talking and I'm thinking about all the people outside waiting. So I found this tour manager and said to him "Listen, I don't think they realise they should be going on now." He says "Oh, I see." I told him to go back in the dressing room and say "Time to go on—now!" Well he did this and the boys stopped their chatting, casually picked up their gear and wandered off to the stage. They didn't know they were supposed to be going on at all! They were too busy grooving. The thing is, on those big shows going overtime costs the band a lot of many, many thousands of dollars. I wonder how much money they lost that way. I think before I told this bloke to be a bit more forthright they were very often late onstage.

I know there was one city where they cost the locals a lot of money. They had this huge bloody great cross that stood at the back of the stage with a million bloody lights on it. It looked amazing but one night they switched it on and they blew out the electricity substation in the city! All the power and the lights in the venue went out. Of course, the crowd started to get a bit rowdy because everything stopped. The doors of the arena were electric too so everyone was stuck there. When they got the power up again someone explained they had blown the substation and everyone cheered. They thought that was bloody great!" Lighting designer Martin Nicholas, an immensely likeable and affable chap whose skin hosts a veritable aquarium of Japanese tattooed fish, had earlier fitted the cross light rig with a larger fuse to prevent the device blowing out. Trouble was when it did eventually give up the ghost it had juiced itself up to such a degree it took half the city with it.

Black Sabbath's festivities for the dawning of new year 1982 were played out in style as new year's eve signalled the inception of a celebratory four night run at London's Hammersmith Odeon venue to kick off another triumphant British tour. Such was the band's lofty standing in their home country at this juncture that the bastion of Heavy Metal gigs, Newcastle's City Hall, welcomed the band for a three night stand there too. For the British shows Sabbath had trimmed their set considerably, disappointingly omitting 'Turn Up The Night', 'Voodoo' and 'Falling Off The Edge Of The World'.

With the conclusion of British dates, and eager to sink their teeth back into the American pie once again, the band then launched into a second round of shows to promote the album. Hooking up with Sabbath at Greensboro, North Carolina on the 16th of February was the high energy Southern Rock n' Roll band Doc Holliday who would take on the mantle of opening act as the tour wound its way through Florida and Georgia. This second leg of U.S. shows was originally scheduled to commence earlier that month although dates had been postponed due to the death of Tony Iommi's father. When the tour got going again fans found 'Voodoo' reinstated in the set.

Fronting up a band of no small repute themselves Doc Holliday's frontman Bruce Brookshire recalls being quite taken aback by the headlining act's initial handling of their guests. "Our first Sabbath show was in Greensboro, NC. I remember standing on the main floor of the Greensboro Coliseum about 25 feet from the stage watching Sabbath do their sound check. Inside of ten minutes, a roadie came out and said that we would have to move, as we were not allowed to watch their sound check. We wondered if this was how we were to be treated every night. Greensboro was almost like our home town, we were living in Raleigh at the time, and we knew that we would have a very sympathetic audience that night. Sabbath's crew let us use probably 50 out of the 400 lights available and turned off most of the main PA during our set. They were taking no chances with this Southern Rock band..."

The two bands did warm to each other though and the regime was soon relaxed as the tour progressed. "By the end of our tour with Sabbath, we were friends, the crew and band were very kind to us, we used over 250 lights each night and they gave us the whole PA to use, and a very large section of stage" Bruce determines. "Ronnie Dio and I talked about writing songs together many nights, but I never followed up on it. I often wonder what we could have written together. It was surely a missed opportunity for me. Later on, a guy we met on the Sabbath crew, Dave Hulme, became our manager for some years. Dave is still a good friend."

The Black Sabbath and Doc Holliday package wound its way up country to the North East, taking in cities such as Binghamton, Rochester, Syracuse and Providence. "These were real Sabbath strongholds, and their most loyal fans. We were glad to expose ourselves to these crowds, 'cause we knew we would sell albums if we could just get out there and show the people what we could do."

One persistent member of the Sabbath crowd though would make it clear he was not to be won over though and Brookshire still rankles at the fact he was unable to exact his revenge. "I don't remember where it was exactly, but here's the scene: We are using by now, about 250 stage lights and I'm the lead singer, so I have at least four Supertrouper spotlights on me nearly the whole set, beaming from all corners of the coliseum."

To his horror Brookshire saw as clear as day, and silhouetted for the entire crowd to see by his own spotlights, a raised arm right in front of the photographers pit—a defiant middle index extended skyward. "This kid's flipping me a bird! He is obviously a big Sabbath fan, he's got the Levi jacket with all the patches sewn on it, and he doesn't like this Southern band opening up for his heroes! We think nothing of it until the next night, different town, and he's there again! With his finger up in there air for all to see! And then the NEXT night! This guy is following the tour, bound and determined to show his disapproval of the Southern rock band to everyone he can!" The Doc Holliday crew concocted a plan to fix their finger friendly foe once and for all. A ramp was built out

Madison Square Garden.

over the pit with Bruce vowing "I'm gonna run out there and boot him. After three of four nights, when we finally build the ramp, he doesn't show up! Never did get to kick that little shit..."

The 'Mob Rules' tour would, courtesy of Black Sabbath, realise a personal dream for the Doc Holliday gang with a performance at New York City's most prestigious live venue. "I remember when we flew to NYC to do Madison Square Garden, Ronnie took me aside and said "OK, we got you here, now it's up to you what you do with it." He was always very kind and supportive of us. Tony and Terry were rather shy and we didn't get to know them as well as Ronnie.

Vinny seemed like a regular guy then, but he played the rock star completely years later when I saw him, saying "we had a lot of opening acts, what makes you think I would remember you?" Years do different things to different people.

Ronnie remembered us years later at a Dio show and welcomed us in his dressing room. Ronnie is a class act all the way. He didn't have to do the things he did for us, and he didn't have to be so gracious, but that's the kind of guy he is".

Brookshire was to discover further Black Sabbath connections when in the studio with Doc Holliday. "The fellow that produced our first album, Tom Allom ('Colonel' Tom Allom—later famous for producing platinum albums for Judas Priest), was a young engineer on the first Sabbath LP. He told us that the studio owner would come in during those sessions and give him only one bit of instruction—"Boost at all frequencies" That gave us a laugh every time!"

For Ozzy Osbourne, a further extended bout of dates officially plugging 'Diary Of A Madman' solidified another hit album and a constant stream of sold out, hysterical gigs that featured an elaborate medieval castle stage set and a bizarre dwarf named 'Ronnie'. By now the 'Blizzard Of Ozz' album was racking up sales of over 6,000 units a week.

The second leg of the American tour would commence at San Francisco's Cow Palace on the 30th December 1981. At that inauguration gig Randy Rhoads would be presented with a notable award from 'Guitar Player' magazine for 'Best New Talent'. Earlier Randy had picked up a similar award from the influential British 'Sounds' Rock weekly being voted by fans as 'Best New Guitarist'. A brief respite from America was the welcome slot alongside Motorhead at the Port Vale 'Heavy Metal Holocaust' festival when Ozzy stepped in at the last minute to wryly supplant none other than a baulking Black Sabbath. Indeed, Motorhead would open for Ozzy in the States after both Def Leppard and UFO had enjoyed stints on the tour.

The 'Diary Of A Madman' trek was fuelled by persistent Ozzy outrages that outranked even his infamous biting the head of a dove episode the year before. One famous episode included biting off the head of a bat tossed onstage at a concert in Des Moines on January 20th 1982. What Ozzy thought was a rubber toy hospitalized the man as the dead animal carried the risk of a rabies infection. According to myth the fact the creature was flesh and blood only became evident to Ozzy once he'd taken a bite which duly startled the bat into action.

On the road for this second round of dates was a guesting UFO, a valuable addition being a major draw in their own right. Ozzy would get on famously with bassist Pete Way but found frontman Phil Mogg a little aloof. UFO guitarist Paul Chapman was glad to meet up with Randy Rhoads again. The sheer size of the Ozzy show though would strike the Welshman as ambitious. "When we started the tour I thought the Ozzy production was too big for someone I didn't think was doing that well, what with the castle and the dwarf and everything but as the tour got into gear their bet paid off. I got on fabulously with Randy straight away. He was a great guy, not really a party type person.

I was endorsed by Washburn at the time and throughout the tour I kept having these guitars arriving. One day two acoustics turned up so Randy and I spent a good long time playing together. I remember I had just written 'Profession Of Violence' and he said the chords were really cool. I've always been slow at reading music but he was well up on it. He wanted to construct the chords for 'Profession' because I didn't know the name to one of the chords! He showed me how to build complex chords from major scales, using triads and compounding 3rd in-

Randy Rhoads. Pic: Rich Galbraith.

tervals. Consequently, the chord turned out to be an E7th, (inversion) starting on the third (G#), and not the root (E). That's when he showed me all about triads and chords, compound inserts, sevenths and ninths, his knowledge was quite unbelievable really. His grasp of scales was way ahead of its time. I mean, the song 'Diary Of A Madman' is a Hungarian minor scale. Nobody did that back then. He was the first." These reminiscences are not just a distant memory for Paul. "I teach now and my students of course want to know all about how the first two Ozzy albums were put together. I teach so much of Randy's stuff now."

Another character in Ozzy's entourage also evokes crystal clear memories for the UFO guitarist but for quite different reasons. Ozzy's stagehand and willing 'victim', dwarf John Allen, was introduced cruelly as 'Ronnie' prior to each ceremonial mock execution. Paul recalls Allen's diminutive stature providing no obstacle to his willingness to party. "He passed out once on our tour bus. I was the last one still awake and had to lock up. The thing is, it had been snowing constantly for about five or six hours while we carried on drinking inside. So, at about 4 a.m. I tried to wake him up but he was completely out cold in an alcoholic stupor. I put him over my shoulder while I tried to try to lock up at the same time. Suddenly he woke up and obviously being drunk and

Randy Rhoads. Pic: Rich Galbraith.

confused, not knowing where he was, he decided he didn't like being on my shoulder and jumped off. The problem was that he landed in a snowdrift that was deeper than he was tall so I lost him! There I am—drunk, searching for an even more drunk dwarf in a snowdrift in the middle of the night.

I just couldn't see him so he panicked, not comprehending the swift change in body temperature I suppose, and started howling like a madman. It was pitch black and all I could hear was this screaming but I just could not find him. Well, although he was small he made a hell of a noise and by now lights were starting to come on in the hotel. I had visions of the police arresting me for "dwarf abuse"!. Anyway, I did find him and bravely rescued the little fella. I got him into the hotel lobby where he rather ungratefully started swearing very loudly at everyone!" Paul duly adopted UFO strategic manoeuvre No. 1. "At that point I ran away!"

For Don Airey embarking on the American tour would be also prove unforgettable experience. He soon struck up a keen friendship and working relationship with Randy Rhoads. The keyboard player had also become aware of Randy's future aspirations to back out of life on the road in order to attain a music degree. "It was very much in the air and we often talked about it" he motions. "He wasn't particularly enamoured of the Rock n' Roll lifestyle and had some pretty serious long term musical goals. Mind you, this is not to say he couldn't create havoc with the best of them! If you ever saw soft furnishings and the like floating past your hotel window that would be Randy just tidying his room up!"

Don was also witness to the lighter side of the young guitarist. "He had some very engaging traits. If you were in a restaurant or coffee shop with him and there was a lull in the conversation he'd just pull out his portable television, plug it into the nearest socket and just watch cartoons. He had a very infectious laugh and before long we'd all be watching and laughing along too. Then he'd order a round of Long Island ice teas and time would just fly! I knew he collected a lot of train stuff in Europe. He was also an audiophile, very knowledgeable about speakers, record decks, etc. and was always on the look out for additions to his system at home."

The camaraderie of the road though would be put under severe strain by the explosion of adverse publicity surrounding Ozzy. On top of the regular round of meet and greets and the unceasing barrage of the press Don found himself in the middle of a band that was the focal point for unwanted attention too. "It was a frenetic time" he admits. "As there were so many journalists, photographers, radio DJs, competition winners and record company people continually joining and leaving the entourage life on the tour bus became very difficult. Also there were the various religious organisations in individual towns trying to get us banned from their city limits. The Daughters of the American Revolution tried to stop us playing in Texas. The mayor of Odessa, Texas succeeded in exhorting his constituents to use their God given right as Americans to take a gun to this son of Satan (yes—Ozzy!). I got the distinct impression the FBI were harassing us through the local unions."

When time and energy would allow band members would visit local clubs. Randy in particular was keen on jamming with any band on the night that would have him. Don has fond memories of one night when the group's long hair combined with the guitarists ready wit nearly provoked serious trouble. "Tommy, Randy and I went to a club out in the sticks near Beaumont, Texas and sat in the corner listening to a very bad country band." Randy's boyish looks and blond mane obviously found favour with the clientele as Don elaborates. "A lot of the rednecks were coming up and asking Randy to dance. Randy took it all very well and his put downs to these guys had Tommy and me in stitches. We eventually made

Randy Rhoads. Pic: Rich Galbraith.

a hasty exit when one of them finally caught on to his wisecracks."

The singer would then stumble onto a God given publicity magnet quite by accident. Ozzy was caught quite literally with his trousers down pissing on the Alamo! Ozzy was fortunate to get away with a class C misdemeanour. Arrested and booked only for public intoxication, which carried a maximum fine of $200, Ozzy evaded the count for which he could easily have been charged for. The Alamo is categorised as a shrine and to the letter of state law Ozzy unawares had actually been guilty of 'Desecration of a venerated object'. UFO were travelling to the San Antonio gig by bus when they heard an announcement on the radio. The DJ told his listeners the gig was in danger of being cancelled because "Mr. Osbourne is in jail at the moment!" "All Hell broke loose on that tour" sighs Paul Chapman "I'm pretty certain Phil went to jail on that tour too for mooning the Police Chief's daughter!"

With each successive show scaling renewed heights of excess some gigs still stand proud for Airey. Following Ozzy's national media 'splash' resulting from his spending the proverbial penny on America's holy of holies Fort Alamo the singer aired his grievances to an enthralled audience in San Antonio, Texas. Don remembers the content of Ozzy's ramble in detail.

"Ozzy gave a ten minute speech in the middle of the show that would have earned him a presidential nomination!" he enthuses. "Tommy Aldridge put a towel down as a pillow in front of the drums, lay down and went to sleep for the duration." Ozzy did not confine his outburst to the Alamo incident. Don catalogues other heartfelt topics Ozzy felt in need of sharing his views on with the crowd. "The importance of Rock and Roll, Peace and Love in the modern world, the effects of pollution on the planet, the effect Ronald Reagan was having on the planet, Ozzy for President, the price of food, the criminal justice system, you name it, he talked about it, and not in a shy way! It was marvellous."

A beachside Corpus Christi gig would go down in the annals of Ozzy folklore too quite predictably for all the wrong reasons. UFO's bus arrived following a day off and the band stumbled off into the early morning Texan sunshine. Paul Chapman recounts the tale. "I had literally just stepped off the bus when I hear Ozzy shouting "Hey Tonka!" I looked around and saw him in this bar. It was totally empty except for Ozzy sitting at the end of the bar next to a cash register. Now this was at 8:30 in the morning so he must have been there all night right? "Come and have a Bloody Mary" he shouted over. Oh Lord I thought but of course I joined him. So we had a drink and then he spotted Pete Way so then it was no stopping us. We had downed about six double Bloody Marys before Ozzy suggested we all go to this seafood restaurant for something to eat, his argument being we couldn't drink on an empty stomach. Well I was fucking plastered and just wanted to go to bed but somehow we made it to this restaurant were Ozzy just ordered absolutely everything off the menu—lobster, prawns, everything—and a bottle of Remy Martin! It was the middle of the afternoon by now and we were still drinking. Pete and I were wondering who was going to pay for all this because Ozzy had spent all his money earlier. Then I saw Sharon's head sticking around the edge of the door. We'd been caught like naughty schoolboys. Ozzy was literally dragged out by the scruff of his neck and we didn't see him again until the gig. Meantime we just about persuaded this waiter to cancel Ozzy's huge food order."

Upon arriving at their originally intended destination of the venue that evening UFO found much to their surprise that their dressing room had been relocated. "The roadies were more than a bit pissed off!" states Paul. "We had been put right on the other side of the arena." Seeking an explanation Chapman ventured off to find Ozzy and was met with an unexpected sight. "There was this huge black bouncer blocking the way to Ozzy's dressing room and yellow 'Do Not Cross' tape hung across the corridor. I showed this guy my pass but he told me nobody but nobody gets past. Well, I could see past this guy and there was Ozzy, dressed up in his stage chain mail with a big pot of coffee—and he was jogging! Sharon had a stopwatch and was making Ozzy jog—very slowly I might add—gulp down some coffee, then jog back again on a circuit then have more coffee. It was intense!"

Sharon Osbourne's radical quick fix did not apparently produce the desired effect though. Paul spotted Ozzy just as the lights lowered for the start of the show. "Ozzy was walking down these steps holding this big black crucifix with mirrors on that he used. Well, he saw me and Pete and said "Hello" but as he did he tripped and fell down the stairs! Oh my God I thought! The intro tape was running and Tommy was on his kit. Pete and I were thinking fucking Hell he's broken his neck. It was a long fall. But Ozzy got up and walked over to his mic for the start of 'Over The Mountain'. He starts to sing 'Over The ....' He didn't reach 'Mountain'. It was like watching a cartoon. He got the first two words out then just fell over straight as a board backwards! The band was still playing and Sharon ran over frantically. Even the little dwarf John Allen ran up in his monks costume and was fanning Ozzy with a towel. Ozzy was out stone cold."

And the dastardly UFO duo? "We ran away!" Paul reveals. "We were seriously blamed for that whole day even though it wasn't our fault. The tour changed completely for us after that." The Corpus Christ audience received ticket refunds and the gig was later rescheduled at the close of the tour.

For Don Airey another landmark gig stays sharp in the memory purely for an artistic bearing. "The other standout one was Knoxville Tennessee, Randy's last gig, for no other reason than that at this point the band was beginning to sound very cool." Knoxville proved a welcome marker for Paul Chapman too. The UFO man had his home in Florida and was looking forward to a well earned break with his family. UFO and Ozzy would split from the other acts and were scheduled to join Foreigner and Bryan Adams for two Florida gigs at the Orlando Tangerine Bowl and the Miami Orange Bowl. However, Paul had promised to arrange a favour to Randy earlier.

"Randy had a really bad problem with his wisdom teeth and he really needed to see someone about it. His toothache was so bad his face had swollen up and he was in quite a bit of pain. Playing loud music wasn't helping him either as the vibrations got straight to the teeth. There was no dentist or doctor on the road with us so I said I would sort out a dentist for him when I got back home. It was pretty easy to do because I lived there and Randy really was in agony with his teeth so it needed to be sorted.

We left Knoxville pretty early, our tour manager John Knowles got the bus packed while we were playing and then we were straight off. As we left Ozzy's intro music was on and I saw Randy walking up the ramp to the stage. "See you at the hotel" I said. "OK" he replied. I'd previously arranged to meet Randy at the International Hilton so we could get his teeth problem fixed."

The next morning Paul had breakfast by the hotel pool and waited for Randy to arrive, looking through the yellow pages to find a local dentist. "I waited, and waited and waited. We swam in the hotel pool to kill some time. Well, of course this was my day off remember but by midday I was saying to my wife 'Where the fuck is he?'" UFO's keyboard player Neil Carter had just got back to the hotel after picking up his wife Sue from the airport. When Paul set eyes on them in the lobby the first thing he saw was that both were openly crying. "Haven't you heard?" said Sue. "That's when they told me" says Paul. "I couldn't take it in. What was Randy doing in a plane? It didn't make sense."

Randy Rhoads died on the 19th March 1982. It is often unfortunately overlooked that Sharon Osbourne's friend Rachel Youngblood died in the same plane crash, as did the pilot Andrew Aycock.

Early that morning Aycock had taken Rhoads and Youngblood up in a small single engined 1955 Beechcraft Bonanza F35 aircraft. There was talk that the plane, belonging to Jerry Calhoun, was taken by Aycock from its owner's hanger without permission. The band's bus, with the Osbourne's and Rudy Sarzo still sleeping onboard, was parked near to a house by the airstrip.

There is some conjecture that Don Airey was taken for a flight prior to Rhoads and Youngblood. Airey witnessed the events unfolding as Aycock 'buzzed' the bus no less than three times before coming around for a fourth attempt. Crash investigators believed that on this last pass the aircraft, which was deemed to have been travelling at no less than 10 feet off the ground and at speeds of some 140 mph plus, hit the back end of the bus with it's left wing. The Bonanza's main body missed the bus, severed a pine tree and crashed into the garage attached to the house exploding on impact. The only substantial part of the aeroplane to survive the accident was the left wing which had hit the bus.

Subsequent toxicology reports on Aycock showed traces of cocaine. Randy Rhoads report was clean. Poignantly the guitarist's autopsy makes mention of Rhoads jewelry, a gold ring and a gold crucifix inscribed 'R.R.' With Randy went a spirit that beckoned a new era of Rock guitar. More significant though was that Ozzy had lost a dear friend and rare ally.

UFO's tour manager John Knowles hastily resched-

The Prince of Darkness. Pic: Rich Galbraith.

uled UFO's plans. They were still to undertake the next days gig and an evening soundcheck was put in place. For Chapman it would be an unpleasant experience.

"The atmosphere was ghastly. Behind me I had all of Randy's gear, his white Marshall stack. All of Ozzy's crew, all strong experienced guys, were just losing it. What made it especially eerie was the fact we were sound checking at night in a stadium. Normally of course it's in the day but there we were with everyones mind on Randy and everything we were playing, instead of being absorbed by the crowd as normal, was just drifting off into the night. We were all in tears. We just couldn't help it. Next day when we played the actual gig Ozzy's crew were taking down his gear while we did our set. It was just devastating. We did the next day in Miami too

then took a week off."

Somehow, within the maelstrom of recording, promotion and touring, material was also being compiled for a project that although alluded to has to date not been readily acknowledged as one of Rock n' Roll's great 'What ifs? That of the Randy Rhoads solo album. The guitarist had been embarking on a quest of self improvement with the ultimate goal of striking out from the confines of Rock n' Roll. It is well known that Randy would seek out classical guitar tutors at every opportunity. Indeed, Ozzy often expressed his wish for his star guitarist to do his own thing. Lindsey Bridgwater confirms Randy's motives. "Randy was working hard on a solo album" the keyboard player agrees. "Randy really was very classically influenced so we had an empathy there. We would often jam with him on guitar and me on

Randy Rhoads. Pic: Rich Galbraith.

piano. He felt the need to learn. We worked on a few things that ultimately were not to find themselves on the 'Diary' album simply because they weren't suitable for Ozzy. It was actually rare to see Randy without a guitar. If he had of lived to complete his own album it certainly would have been a revelation. Of that I have no doubt. There was one track in particular which I helped him transcribe. I wrote it down after he died because it was still fresh in my memory. I still have the manuscript."

Randy had been due to fly back to England to stay with his friend J.T. "Two weeks before he died he phoned to say he was coming back over, he was going to spend a week at my place. I had a 1958 Gibson ready for him." One wonders if Randy and J.T.'s fireside sessions resulted in anything more creative than just jamming? "We wrote a song together" J.T. affirms. "I've still got it. It's very typically Randy in style. I thought about using it for Budgie later on but the only person who can really finish it is Ozzy. It's an Ozzy Rock song. I took the news very, very badly. In truth I have not been even though it is nearly twenty years ago. God knows what he was doing in that plane, he was absolutely terrified of flying.

Randy changed Rock guitar forever, I think that is often overlooked. Ask any serious Rock guitarist and they will tell you the same. The thing is, that what he played in private was a million times better than the Ozzy stuff. I know that sounds ridiculous but it's true—I've seen it. His mastery of the guitar was just unique."

Randy's life long friend Kelly Garni reveals just where Randy just might have been heading. "We spoke about forming a band together after he had done the Ozzy thing. Randy was planning on studying classical guitar in England and after that really keen to do a heavy keyboard orientated thing, we were both big Deep Purple fans, something like that or like a heavier Boston or Styx. That's the way he was thinking then."

Two decades later an Ozzy confidante would observe "You could see that Randy's influence had simply just stayed there with the band. That chugging rhythmic guitar style of 'I Don't Know' and 'Crazy Train' virtually defined the sound of Ozzy and none of the guitarists afterwards could really step too much out of that mould. Each new player had a dynamic new approach but they had to incorporate aspects of Randy's style. Randy had really defined what an Ozzy riff was. Everyone involved was very conscious of this and you could see it still there many, many years later—right up to 'No More Tears' that Randy style is still there."

Ironically it would be one of the humblest characters on the Rock n' Roll circuit that would be chosen to full the awning void left by the passing of Randy Rhoads. Irishman Bernie Tormé is a talented guitarist with great character and renowned for some particularly wild axework and theatrics. Such showmanship brought him close to 'guitar hero' status whilst in Gillan. Tormé first made his name as guitarist with Irish bands Wormwood and Urge, prior to relocating to London forming Scrapyard in 1976. A Hard Rock trio of Tormé, bassist Bernie Hagley (also playing with Vanity Fair at the time) and drummer Roger Hunt, Scrapyard gigged solidly throughout the London area. Hagley was to depart and the band was swiftly brought back up to strength with the addition of former Zzebra bassist John McCoy. However, this union lasted only a matter of months with Tormé striking out on his own as The Bernie Tormé Band. McCoy meanwhile soldiered on with Paul Samson on guitar as Scrapyard became McCoy.

Playing Hard Rock but with a Punk image—Tormé having cut off his long hair to keep in vogue—the band managed to release two singles and contribute tracks to the Punk compilation album 'Live At The Vortex'. The Bernie Tormé Band, still a trio format with the guitarist augmented by bassist Phil Spalding and drummer Mark Harrison, put in some British supports to Gillan, the headline act now featuring McCoy on bass. An album was recorded for Jet Records but remains unreleased. Disillusioned, Tormé took up his old colleague John McCoy's offer to hook up with Gillan. Spalding joined Punktress Toyah then Mike Oldfield, Original Mirrors and the platinum supergroup GTR led by guitarists Steve Howe and Steve Hackett. Harrison went on to The Nipple Erectors and Dirty Strangers.

With Gillan, Tormé would elevate himself to guitar hero stature courtesy of UK top ten albums 1980's 'Glory Road' and 1981's 'Future Shock'. The guitarist locked in neatly into the band unit with his quirky rogue gypsy image proving a perfect foil for the veteran ex-Deep Purple man and the undoubtedly eccentric McCoy. However, in spite of sell out tours, hit singles and numerous TV appearances the Gillan ship was financially shaky and it was this factor that prompted the split. Tormé's replacement would be the able ex-White Spirit man Janick Gers, later of Iron Maiden, but in truth the quintessence of Gillan was absent from that point as sliding chart positions and album sales were to testify. After his split from Gillan in 1981, Tormé joined the warhorse Rock act Atomic Rooster, appearing on their 'Headline News' album and undertaking two tours of Germany and Italy.

Although the Atomic Rooster position had not been widely recognised in the UK itself Tormé's status post Gillan remained intact and many eager fans were keen to see which direction the Irishman would take next. Bernie explains his musical and career environment at the time of receiving the Ozzy offer. "I'd spent from the previous September, a couple of months after I left Gillan, till I got the call to join Ozzy sorting out financing to complete the 'Turn Out The Lights' album and bring in a producer on it. So, over that timescale I had managed to buy back the tapes from Ian Gillan's studio, got a publishing deal which financed the completion of the album at the Marquee studios with Nick Tauber producing, and got it signed to record companies in both the UK and Germany for an April/May release."

Bernie's band, the Electric Gypsies, had a finalized roster of former Bethnal bass player Everton Williams, second guitarist Bob Andrews and drummer Mark Laff. The latter two being veterans of Generation X.

Essentially the Electric Gypsies project was in the starting blocks, primed and ready to go when David Arden put in the call. "I had also sorted a UK tour that was due to start on 20th April." Explains Bernie. "At the time of the phone call to join Ozzy we had never done a gig together. I had really worked my ass off to get the Electric Gypsies thing off the ground: if I had been offered the Ozzy situation a month or so after leaving Gillan, it might have been completely different. But at the time I was offered it, I had already taken a different route: I had already put an enormous amount of work, time, and my heart into getting out there and playing and promoting a record again." There were other considerations to take into account too. "I also hadn't played on stage since the previous July, apart from doing a short Italian tour, during February I think, with Atomic Rooster, which was incidentally a gas. On that tour I was standing in for John Cann, who hadn't wanted to tour when the other two, Vincent Crane and Paul Hammond, did. I agreed to do other stuff with them on a longer term basis after the tour, but it was a very loose arrangement at that stage. It wasn't clear that there would be any subsequent touring or recording at all."

Don Airey was delegated to put together a rapid audition structure and recalls Bernie Tormé being at the forefront of his mind to handle the enormous task fate had dictated him. "It was a heartbreakingly awful time" the keyboard player confides. Nevertheless Don set about his task suggesting former Gillan guitarist Bernie Tormé. "It was just what the circumstances dictated. I had seen Bernie with Gillan I think and thought he had the off the wall quality that Ozzy liked."

Bernie thinks that besides Don's recommendation Ozzy and Sharon may have been present at one of his earlier gigs too. "I was also told by Phil Banfield (Ian Gillan's manager) that Ozzy and Sharon had also been at an Aylesbury Friars warmup gig for a Gillan tour in '80 or '81 and had seen me play. I had never met them at that time so I don't know how true that is. I never asked." Tormé's diary records the necessary expedition of events over the next few days. "Randy died in Florida on Friday 19th, I was approached to go out to replace him on Monday 22nd, early afternoon as I remember" he observes. "I flew to Los Angeles on Friday 26th after a ticket cock up of the 25th. I auditioned on the 27th and 28th, and was asked to do the gig on the 28th. We flew to New York on the afternoon of 29th, and I'm sure that the day of Randy's funeral was the morning of the 29th. Point I'm trying to make is that I was there, auditioned, committed and in place before Randy was laid to rest. So the decision to carry on and approach me must have been made between Randy's death on Friday 19th and Sunday 21st. With the time difference and the need to track me down that would be just enough time to contact me on the 22nd. It must have been a very quick decision to ask me."

On paper the process looks to have been a whirlwind of activity with decisions being made quick-fire and acted on expeditiously. The reality from Bernie's viewpoint was a multifaceted emotional dilemma with implications for his long term career. Over the ensuing years Bernie's take of this traumatic period has not been given full vent. Indeed, interviewed for a previous book, the guitarist asserts his then freely given observations were twisted to such a degree that they ended up far removed from the truth. Naturally Bernie is keen to once and for all set the record straight regarding the circumstances of teaming up with Ozzy and the actual events. Bernie recalls the first telephone conversation:

"The gist of it was something like:

D: "Hello Bernie, its David Arden from Jet here, how are you?"

B: "Hello David I'm fine, how are you?"

D: "I suppose you've heard about the death of Randy Rhoads—Ozzy's guitarist, well the band are in the middle of a big U.S. tour they need to complete. Can you go out and replace him?"

It was as I remember as blunt and short as that. I didn't understand what he was talking about at first, I hadn't heard about Randy's death. This also probably makes me sound like a complete idiot, but I didn't know much about Ozzy's doings at that time, I hadn't been a great Black Sabbath fan and hadn't really followed his career. I hadn't heard 'Blizzard Of Ozz' or 'Diary Of A Madman'." The call was such a shock to the system David Arden had to repeat his message before Bernie grasped exactly what was being relayed to him. "It was a very difficult conversation to get dropped into out of the blue. They had a really huge problem, since everyone found it very hard to carry on. I asked when and for how long they would want me, and when he said from tomorrow for probably two months I said no, I couldn't.

I've got to say that I really felt for their position, I really would have liked to have helped them, it sounded just awful, but I could not see how. I said I couldn't do it because I had an album out the next month and a tour starting, and that I was committed to doing that." Over the course of this initial conversation and subsequent other telephone exchanges Bernie Tormé began to realise the only answer David Arden would accept was 'Yes'.

"David really presented it to me as if it was me or nothing, the tour would collapse and the world would come to an end, and while that was nice for my ego, it obviously wasn't the case. I was sure they could find someone else. I thought it was just the usual record company bullshit. I mean also this was not Ozzy or Sharon or even Don on the phone, none of whom I had ever even spoken to: it was all second or third hand, and I felt I was not getting anything like the full picture. I did feel that if it was all that important that I did it, Sharon or Ozzy or Don would have been on the phone. But David did make me feel that I would have liked to help them out if I could, but as I said I really didn't see how I could without destroying everything I'd been working for, and I was not going to do that. Again fairly dumb, but I also didn't know how big Ozzy was in the U.S. at that stage, I thought he was probably playing Agoras and suchlike, not Stadiums."

As outlined previously Bernie's short but vitally important tenure with Ozzy has all too often been portrayed in ways at great variance to the truth. Naturally such accounts had not gone unnoticed by Bernie who maintains that the reasoning for the brevity of his stay and his initial acceptance of the position has never been adequately explained. "There were three reasons why I did not want to get involved initially, apart from the fact that I thought it was logistically impossible from my end. Two of these reasons were probably unfair in retrospect, the third was something that was personally important to me, and meant I would only go as a stand in to help them out of a jam. Reason one was that I had been signed to the Ardens and their record company Jet Records from the end of '77 till mid '79, (when I was in my Punk band period). I had a certain amount of not very positive experience dealing with the Ardens at that time (I don't include Sharon in that, I had never met her until I went to do Ozzy's thing).

I was not keen to work for them again. I would not want you to think that I'm implying they were dishonest or whatever, that was not my problem when working for them. It was just that you never knew what was going on, or where you stood, everything was done behind your back and you were the very last person to know about it, especially if it was bad news and concerned you. There are a lot of famous apocryphal stories about them. I don't know if any are true or not, and I don't really care, there's two sides to every story, but I found they were hard people for me personally to deal with, and I was not keen to do it again. So when David phoned me my immediate reaction was "Oh no, not them, what do they want"."

The second reason Bernie baulked at the initial prospect he believes may be incomprehensible to most. He simply did not want to tour in America again. Gillan's 1980 promotional jaunt to the States only held bad memories. "Most people hear the words 'American tour' and think wow, wouldn't it be great, hold me back!" The reality, as Bernie relates, was somewhat different. "It was one of the least enjoyable periods of my life, of all our lives in fact. As well as being a total disaster, it was absolute complete fucking Hell. I got food poisoning and nearly died of it, and when I wasn't almost dying I felt like a total alien." The guitarists creative environs in Britain were infused with the rich mixture of Punk, Glam and NWoBHM. His perception of America though shocked him. "At that time a 1974 time-warp still reigned supreme in a large part of America, mixed with a sizeable sprinkling of right wing Christian intolerance. I spent my life avoiding getting beaten up."

Bernie's shock of multicoloured hair, pointed Cuban heels and deliberately torn black jeans exemplified his Romany raggamuffin Punk image and in the UK had made him a focal point of the Gillan band. America had different ideas. "Tommy Aldridge subsequently said to me on the bus "Boy, if you walked through Dallas lookin' like that you would die!" I felt like a Martian in Tesco's. So when David mentioned the words 'American tour' I thought "Oh no, find someone else." I'd like to say that I don't hold that view at all now, I love America. Satellite TV and MTV in particular and time in general changed it totally for the better."

There was a further overriding factor as to why Tormé felt reluctant to take up the offer. "The third reason, the most important one, and the one I still hold to was that I did not want to step into a dead mans shoes. The only reason I could see for doing it was to help out, help them to finish the tour. People are different and for me it's the most important thing that I treat people with respect, there's not a lot of it in the music business or the world, and that for me was the best way of my showing my respect. To a person, not to a guitar player. I don't expect anyone else to understand that, I couldn't really give a fuck if they do or not. I definitely don't expect them to agree with it, or to live by it, we're all different, we've all got different reasons: but for me it is important, and I tried to live by it. I don't think anyone did understand that."

David Arden's dogged tenacity eventually won the day. "I agreed on the third call" admits Bernie. "Following the previous telephone conversations I sat down and thought about it hard. I was so gobsmacked by David's call that I phoned a couple of people to ask what they thought, the consensus seemed to be that I ought to try to do it. Phil Banfield Ian Gillan's manager phoned me (David Arden had called him), and said I should do it, but I still couldn't see how. I felt in the circumstances I would like to help out if I could, I just couldn't imagine the Hell Ozzy, Sharon and the band and all involved must have gone through. It must have been truly awful. Totally tragic for the families of the people killed. Horrific. I phoned David back and said I'd love to help but I really couldn't see how, since I couldn't afford to delay my album and tour and let people down. David started saying please think again, oh and by the way the money is £ X,XXX per week."

As much as Bernie would like to say the fiscal aspect of the offer held no bearing he is brutally honest with himself. "Let me put this way, I was very hard up at the time. I'd as yet had no Gillan royalties, publishing or otherwise, and £ X,XXX was probably more than I had earned in the previous six months. Times were very hard and the Tormé coffers were totally boracic. Black holes even. I've never thought of myself as someone who does things just for money, you wouldn't be a musician if you did, but this definitely stopped me in my tracks and made me go "hmmmmmm, maybe there is a way round … hmmmm." Typical, terrible really. I was a rabbit trapped in the £ X,XXX a week headlights."

David Arden then told Bernie the gig was his. No auditions necessary because the band were familiar with his playing already and knew he could cut it. Bernie was sceptical to say the least. "I found that very difficult to believe. I said to him the last thing I wanted to do was to go to Los Angeles for a gig I wasn't really after in the first place and waste at least a week having managed to reschedule all my shit, and then have the whole thing fall through. Well possible. In the music business you never believe anything will happen until you've had the hangover. David was adamant, no auditions. I still didn't believe it."

Tormé then had a desperate dash to reschedule not only his plans but those of others who were relying on him at that point. The diplomat in him came to the fore as he managed to assuage his label boss Nick Raymond at Kamaflage/DJM and put back the release date of the Electric Gypsies album and inform his band there would be a delay. They were understanding in the circumstances. "My agent, Albert Samuel at Smash, was a quite a bit less happy, but agreed, though I had to agree to do the same gigs for a lot less money later in the summer. I talked to my band who were OK about it too."

A phone call was also put in to Phil Banfield who offered some sage advice. "He made the very practical suggestion that since there were, according to David, no auditions, and since I was having to move a lot of things around to do it, I should ask for a weeks pay cash up front before I left, just to protect myself and find out if I was being told the truth about the pay. That seemed like a good idea, since I was personally 100% certain there would at least be auditions, and that made everything else look a bit questionable too." Bernie had one condition as a proviso on the whole affair. "I also said I wanted to take a roadie, which he was also not happy about, but he agreed to, and that subsequently turned out to be a major mistake on my part. The guy got up the band's and Ozzy's crew's noses and I got a lot of grief for it, I wished afterwards I hadn't taken him."

Bernie got back in touch with David Arden, his welcome news relayed with a sting in the tail. "I said I could do it, I had managed to move things around, but it would have to be only a couple of months. He was really pleased, and confirmed it was only a couple of months till they finished the tour. I then said that I had been advised by Phil Banfield to require a weeks pay cash up front to protect myself.

There was a long silence at the other end of the phone, but he did agree. He didn't sound very happy about it. I was happy with his agreement, that made it sound as if the money amount was true, but as it eventually turned out the £ X,XXX per week was all bullshit."

Bernie acknowledges that David Arden's persuasiveness and unwillingness to accept a negative answer won him over. "I was blagged into it by him making me feel that they really needed my help, the 'no one else would do' sketch." He readily admits. "That appealed to my ego, even though it wasn't true, and I did want to help them out if I could. Temporarily. The money I was offered made it possible for me to do that, to move things around and keep people happy."

The following day Bernie travelled into the Jet offices in London to arrange shipping and carnets for getting his gear to America. He would also pick up copies of 'Blizzard Of Ozz' and 'Diary Of A Madman'. When he got home and put the albums on his record deck he was staggered.

"I was totally blown away, I loved the albums"

he readily confesses. "Randy's playing, the songs, everything. Totally brilliant. Not what I expected at all. I also realised I was going to have to work very hard to try to get a handle on all of that material and the superb guitaring." At this stage Bernie still had no idea which songs made up Ozzy's live set and he still had not spoken to Ozzy or Sharon. "I spent all the next day (the 24th) playing the albums, trying to learn what I could, mostly just arrangement of songs progressions and riffs. It was pretty hard to take in all of the details and nuances in a short space of time."

The adventure would get off to a false start before Bernie had even set foot on an aeroplane. "I was supposed to be going on the morning of the 25th: the weeks pay cash up front hadn't arrived. I phoned David who said it was being couriered across, and could I go to the airport and phone home to check it had arrived, otherwise I'd miss the flight. I sort of smelt the inklings of a rat, but I agreed."

Bernie and his roadie made it to the airport on schedule but would receive an unpleasant surprise when they attempted to pick up their tickets. Mistakenly only one way tickets had been arranged and without being American citizens or green card holders their flight would have been to no avail. U.S. Immigration would have automatically turned the two men back on a return trip at the airline's expense.

An angry guitarist called home to relay the news to his wife. "She told me that the courier had indeed arrived, but only with a cheque for only £XXX. I was convinced at this stage the whole thing was indeed bullshit, so I phoned David at home and said "Terrible mistake mate, one way tickets and no £X,XXX cash. I'm going home, if you want me to go, sort it out." He sounded a bit crestfallen, and said it would be sorted. I went home with absolutely no conviction that it would be, and very pissed off that I had rescheduled my album and tour for what looked like a waste of time."

Finally Jet Records solved the ticket and money problems and the procedure started for a second time. "I didn't listen or learn any more music until the money in advance surprised me by arriving late that afternoon. Then I started work on it all for an hour or two again. I flew out on the 26th. I met Don Airey that night, only met the others the next day at the first auditions."

Coping with the grief of losing a dear friend the Ozzy band and organization had no inkling of the shenanigans Bernie Tormé had just endured simply to get him there.

As predicted Bernie arrived to find that contrary to David Arden's assurances auditions were indeed taking place. Rudy Sarzo's brother Robert, later to make his name with Hurricane, was one of the applicants. Don Airey confirms this. "Rudy Sarzo's brother Robert auditioned. Gary Moore and Michael Schenker were asked but had said "No." Pat Travers had been very supportive on the phone, but his kind offer of help wasn't taken up. Pat had phoned a couple of times, very genuinely concerned on a personal level at what had happened." Bernie Tormé was aware of the potential Pat Travers union too. "Pat was very keen to help, but when it came to it his management demanded silly stuff like equal billing and a lot of money."

John Sykes, making a name for himself with Tygers Of Pan Tang, was also flown in for an audition. His services were requested once he had landed back in England but the six stringer declined, eventually hooking up with Thin Lizzy. UFO bassist Pete Way recalls the possibility of a union with Michael Schenker. "Ozzy called me asking for Michael's number. I think Peter Mensch was involved somewhere in there too. They never rehearsed together though. Y'know, Michael has been asked to play for everybody—Aerosmith, the Rolling Stones—everyone, but he's such an individual and not necessarily the person you really want in your band! Ozzy and Michael? It's just too different and wouldn't of worked. The thing with Michael is he's so fuckin' eccentric. I can say that because he's my best friend. Phenomenal, phenomenal guitarist but not right for Ozzy. Later Michael did have a few regrets though, he said to me he'd wished we'd have both done the Ozzy thing. Now that might have worked!"

There were other hopefuls as Bernie verifies. "I don't remember the names of the others, the names didn't mean much to me at the time, and I was very jetlagged and tired, I don't think I'd slept much since agreeing to go. I'd had a lot to sort out and think about." Bernie dutifully auditioned and then waited on the band and Sharon to come to a decision. After some discussion Sharon broke the news that the gig was his. "I was really pleased, I really liked Ozzy and Don was a real nice guy. Tommy didn't really talk to me much, but it didn't matter, he was a real hero of mine and I was a bit overawed. Rudy was superb. But reality kicked in almost immediately, and this is all Gods honest truth: Sharon then said the pay was $XXX a week. I sputtered "but, but, David said it was £X,XXX..." Sharon said "David's on drugs, he doesn't know what he's talking about." I said 'oh ...'"

Bernie then informed Sharon of his advance and was told it would be deducted from his weekly pay until the advance was cleared. "I contemplated saying fuck it and letting Robert do it, but I liked everyone and wanted to help and not kick them in the teeth, it was such a tragic situation. And I had never asked for the £X,XXX per week in the first place, its only money after all. But it did leave a bit of a strange taste. Even at a glance it was very obviously heavy metal sideman situation, it was not a band: that was clear by the fact that the rhythm section had changed, and that Tommy and Rudy hadn't played on the records up to that date. Basically it was Oz plus backing band. Of course there's no reason that it should be a band, it was just that I've never really had much desire to operate as a mercenary hired gun, its not what I get off on, I like bands."

The Ozzy band got back to work once more, with UFO still retained as openers, at the Leigh U Stabler arena in Bethlehem, Philadelphia. If anyone noticed that date was April 1st the subject was not raised.

Chalking the experience with the wages up to experience the guitarist got down to work plotting the set with Don Airey. "Initially Don spent quite a few hours teaching me the songs we auditioned on: he helped me a lot" he confirms. "Since he doubled a lot of Randy's licks and solos, he knew what Randy played. This was both a blessing and a curse, since it meant I had to really stick to a fairly exact game plan, and not really play it the way I would have liked. I would have preferred not to do that, I did not want to imitate. But that seemed to be what Ozzy initially wanted, he seemed very paranoid about my not playing stuff exactly like Randy, and honestly even if the notes were exactly the same, I wouldn't, probably couldn't play it identically, ever. But I could understand why he felt like that, I just didn't find it much fun or easy to do initially."

With just two days rehearsal in the bag the band set out to re-launch the tour in Bethlehem, PA. Bernie's first opportunity to perform the entire set came with the gig soundcheck. Learning the show was more than enough to contend with and teething practical problems with sound and guitars were to be anticipated and dealt with. It was to be another equipment issue that brought home to him the very reason of his being there in a way he could never have envisaged.

"My gear hadn't arrived for that gig: I had one Strat I brought from the UK, one I'd bought in Los Angeles, and a hired plank with a Fender sticker and strings on from SIR in New York. I needed at least three since 3 or four tracks were de-tuned for Ozzy's voice. Really for safety I needed 4, but my other was still in transit, so I prayed I wouldn't break a string on the de-tune. Luckily I didn't."

Bernie's out of reach guitars were not specially customised but they were trusted and familiar. "They were just very good instruments, their tremmy arms didn't make 'em go out of tune. They were a lot older, worn in." Instruments and the power that fed them raised further difficulties. "I've never been much of a

Bernie onstage with Ozzy. Photo supplied by Bernie Tormé.

one for guitar technology, I like the classic Strat Tele and Les Paul sounds too much. Strats are my fave, because you can get more sounds out of them. Ozzy didn't like Strats at all, he was a Gibson man. I had nightmares with my sound on that tour incidentally, the amps never sounded right, a bit weedy, but there was bugger all I could do about it. No one on the crew knew why."

These sound problems were not an 'Ozzy' problem though, more an Anglo-American mismatch as Bernie outlines. "They had sounded dire in the U.S. when I toured it with Gillan too, I only found out later that I needed a voltage regulator / stabiliser. British Marshalls, especially old ones, don't like the unevenness in U.S. power, which is multiplied in the amp due to U.S. power being 110 volts, and that's even more of a problem if you have a big show, huge PA and a huge lighting rig drawing lots of power."

And then came the horrifying realization that something else was missing from the equation.

"My pedals also hadn't arrived, and a Strat directly into an un-souped Marshall superlead sounds a bit like a distorted banjo" Bernie states. Still cased up with his guitars in the gear cases there was only one set of pedals available at such short notice—and they belonged to Randy Rhoads. "I really did not want to use them, it seemed like desecration" Bernie dictates. "A guitarists gear is very personal, its part of them. I used Randy's pedals for the soundcheck. I could just about deal with that. At that time mine were being flown from Los Angeles to New York, some of the crew were trying to get them from La Guardia or wherever in time for the gig. It didn't happen, and the situation came up, 8,000 people in, and I either had to use Randy's pedals or no gig. No one was happy about it, me probably least, I hated doing it, and again it left me feeling depressed about the situation. I felt that really this was a gig that someone else ought to be doing, not me."

"The first gig. That's unforgettable. Very mixed emotions and mixed up memories about that. Everyone was under a great amount of stress, looking at it in retrospect it must have been the make or break as to whether it would carry on or not. Ozzy was very supportive, very helpful for the whole gig, took a lot of pressure off me. It was not the same situation as Brad's. I suppose with Brad they were really putting him on the spot, with me on that first gig they must have been more concerned with what was going on in their own heads and hearts. They probably really were not that concerned with me, just so long as I didn't make a total balls of it."

With the full gamut of emotions for all concerned strictly on overload the very last thing Bernie Tormé, already dealing with unfamiliar guitars and pedals that had a life of their own, was a further set of technical difficulties outside of his control to contend with. "I was pretty scared, I wasn't really at all sure of what I was doing, and in that stage setup that was not a good way to be. The onstage sound was absolutely crap. I could hardly hear a note I played, I had set up my 3 amps and 5 cabs back of the stage behind the portcullis, and they may as well have been back in England, I couldn't hear a fucking thing without standing close to it. Mind you that may have been a blessing. I couldn't hear Don or Rudy at all, they may as well not have been there."

What the guitarist could register though was not exactly beneficial in attempting to construct a cohesive aural platform on which to work. "All I could hear was Ozzy wailing like the back end of Concorde, and Tommy's snare, no bass drum, no hi-hat, no toms" he reveals. "A very uphill journey soundwise, and the most difficult thing was not getting totally lost on stuff like 'Believer' or 'Steal Away The Night', which I had problems remembering at all at the start." With the gig in full flow Bernie's focus was shifted away from getting through the show as Randy's chorus pedal repeatedly turned itself off and on. "It didn't scare me, I'm not scared of that sort of shit, sometimes it just happens. Something trying to say something. But because I didn't feel good about using the pedals, it was a bit freaky. Some of the crew noticed it too."

As the tightly rehearsed show raged around him Bernie's peripheral vision began to digest the strangest of surroundings with the show and the antics of the dwarf all registering. "I made it, but it was all just approaching OK, nowhere near good. I didn't think I did much of a good job that first show, but the bootlegs of it were much better than I expected. It sounded OK." With the gig over Bernie informed the others of his pedal problems. "They seemed to think I was crazy, they said if it happened it must have been condensation on the switch. Maybe it was, but I've been using pedals now for 33 years, it's never happened to me any other time." Much to Bernie's relief his personal pedals arrived just as the gig ended.

Despite the spectacle for those who had just come off stage the event was eclipsed by a huge burden of grief. "Ozzy and the band must have been going through Hell" Bernie acknowledges. Indeed, less than two weeks has passed since Randy's last gig in Knoxville, Tennessee and Bernie maintains that some of the crew were openly crying. "It must have been so hard for them to go on stage. And every time they looked over and saw me they must have wished to God I wasn't there and Randy was still there. You try to put yourself into their position and feel what they felt, but you can't. That gig must have been the biggest mountain they ever had to climb, I've no idea how they did it."

Some encouragement came from a welcome and respected source. "Tommy said afterwards that I must have had the biggest balls in the world to do that gig, but the worst thing I could do was hit some bum notes, so fucking what, I hit a few, probably more than a few, but I got through it with no disasters. But what Ozzy and the band did that night really needed the biggest balls in the world. I am very proud of having helped them to get through that gig. I am glad I had a chance to do that."

Watching side stage Paul Chapman could not quite believe what he was seeing. "I had known Bernie for quite some time and it was very weird watching him up there. I was standing next to the monitor desk with Sharon and I'm not ashamed to say we were both crying. What was uncanny was that Bernie looked like Randy—the hair, the clothes, everything. Randy used to wear these purple waistcoat kind of things and they had dressed him up the same. I just thought Jesus Christ they've tried to clone him. It was bizarre. I tell you, I'm sure Bernie won't mind me saying this—he was losing it. He was so nervous. I really felt for him. Somehow, God knows how, he managed to pull it off and put on a good show. Amazing."

Chapter 6

Hair By Sarzo Of Cuba, Way To Go

With his first taste of fire out of the way Bernie attempted to settle into the touring routine. However, despite his guitar style remaining intact his trademark image would be in for a battering of the first order. "The first and only time in my life that I have ever been in a band and been told what clothes I had to wear and that I had to have my hair cut. Hence in any of the pictures of me with Ozzy I've got this ridiculous retro pudding bowl un-Tormé like wighat on. Dreadful. Sharon demanded it and since no hairdresser was around Rudy Sarzo did it! Rudy, you're a great bass player, I love what you do, but never take up hairdressing!

Anyone who knows me or the bands I've been with over the years would probably agree that while I've often looked like a total cunt, I've always had a pretty strong visual image. Its part of what you try to express as a performer. If I'd wanted to be told what to wear I would've joined an Irish Show band years ago. It seemed to me to be pantomime, plastic and a bit corporate, and I thought Ozzy's music and the band were so strong that it was unnecessary. It was a bit like having my mum telling me what to wear again, very weird, and a bit sad in the circumstances, like clinging on to something that really didn't matter at that point anyway."

As Paul Chapman has already pointed out the style gurus would have designs on Bernie's wardrobe too. "Because I was quite a bit bigger at 6 foot than Randy, I was also told to wear Rudy's spare clothes. Rudy was approximately my build. It didn't feel quite right to me: I think the fact that a different person to Randy was playing should have been made clear, and no attempt should have been made to make the actor less important than the role. It was a bit like a soap opera when one actor dies or leaves and someone comes in and wears the same clothes and says the same things: that didn't seem right to me, it seemed creepy. It seemed to me to be a denial of something. The production and show was no way as important as Randy's death and absence, and trying to make it look as if not much had happened seemed to me to be out of balance. And that is not a judgement of anyone, because there was a lot of paranoia and even panic floating around at the time, and paranoia and stress are not conducive to making the most balanced choices. I don't think it was the right choice, but I can see how it happened."

On the positive side though Bernie Tormé had at least reconciled himself with the fact that he was playing alongside some of the greatest Rock musicians in the world. Of his fellow band members Tormé has only the greatest respect. "Tommy Aldridge was a real hero of mine, I was aware of the things he did with Black Oak Arkansas and I'd heard his solo and I just loved his playing. I get off on drummers, and he's one of the best. I wish I'd been able to hear more of him on stage. He's such a great player. Rudy Sarzo I didn't know, but he was absolutely awesome, great bass player, solid and clever."

Don Airey I was obviously aware of with Rainbow and various other bands, but actually working with him you released how brilliant he is, he underplays his ability for the benefit of the song and the other players. Total opposite to me! Great to play with." Bernie relates to Don as being quite a lynchpin in the live show. "The keyboard interplays were pretty much left intact, which left me struggling to keep up with Don on a few occasions, it was good discipline, but it did not leave me playing to my strengths, which is very much doing it off the top of my head. That's when I feel I'm best."

Bernie got on with the task in hand but describes what should have been a process of gradual easing of pressure as operating in reverse. "For me the first few gigs were all a bit one step forward followed by two steps back. The only part of the set that I could relax on was the guitar solo bit—I'd been doing that for years with Gillan, I could have done it in my sleep. So I did my routine, I can't remember if I did the very hokey Hendrix play with the teeth thing that night or the night after, but anyway, because I was relaxing I probably played for 2, maybe 3 minutes. I needed it for my sanity. The audience dug it, lighters up everywhere. After the gig that night or the next night Sharon came up to me and said the guitar solo was too long, it had to be more like Randy's, under 60 seconds. That was hard work man, because I wasn't Randy.

They were very worried and paranoid at that stage, very understandably so, but it made it very difficult for me. Maybe they thought I was trying to make a name, score points or something, maybe they thought I was a bit too 60s Strat/bluesy not classical like Randy. I don't know what they thought. I was just relaxing at the guitar break truck stop, after driving at about 200 miles an hour on a very twisty road with no idea of what was coming next. Anyway it was their show, so they called the shots, but I felt it to be an added stress, I needed that bit to catch my breath."

Miscommunication, whether deliberate or otherwise, put both Bernie and Sharon Osbourne awkwardly into an unclear situation not their making. Bernie describes the moment the two parties realised he had never wished to be involved long-term. "Again, David Arden did not appear to have passed on my lack of desire for the long term gig on to Sharon or the band, who appeared not very happy when I said that I had to get back after a couple of months. Sharon especially, understandable since she was manager didn't seem too happy with that."

The guitarist would also be surprised when talk turned to future plans. "Ozz discussed writing with me, which obviously would have been only in a long term situation. Then Sharon started talking about extra gigs in Alaska and Hawaii, which were as I remember 4 or so months away. This freaked me, but obviously they were not going to change stuff around to suit me. I think Sharon found it ridiculous that I wanted to go back and do my own crummy tour! I was also always really uncomfortable about the fact that there was no mention of Randy's death during the show: I know that Ozzy couldn't have done it without breaking down, and that alone made it impossible, but I would have been far happier if it had been mentioned. Having come from Gillan, and having had a bit of a name in the UK, the possible reverse situation would cross my mind, if I had been killed and someone had replaced me and the band had continued touring within two weeks. In those circumstances I would have liked a mention, so its absence in Randy's case always made me very uncomfortable. I know Ozzy couldn't have done it, but I wish it had been possible."

A familiar scenario in the Rock world is that of outright hostility from the fans to any new recruit, especially one that has been deemed to have unjustly taken the place of a perceived hero. Randy Rhoads—a genuine hero not a product of media myth, had been cruelly taken away and here was a total unknown occupying his space. The fans had brought their tickets to see Ozzy and Randy after all but the expected antipathy gave way to respectful appreciation. "The audiences were just great, very supportive, you couldn't ask for better" outlines Bernie. "I personally got no shit at all, or none that I was aware of, which was not the case when I joined Ian Gillan, where there was a lot of the "Blackmore" shit initially."

Paul Chapman backs this up. "Bernie got accepted pretty well. Poor guy. I really felt for him. I couldn't have done it I tell you. At Madison Square Garden he was so incredibly nervous. The gig was packed out too, an element of morbid curiosity I suppose but Bernie I have to say did a fantastic job. People forget that, they think "Oh, Bernie the guy who stood in for Randy" but they forget the fact that he's a great soulful guitarist. Not many I know could have stood that kind of pressure."

Musically, as others in this book have testified, the complexities and structure of the songs demanded respect. Bernie records the task he had in front of him. "I was continually terrified I was going to get lost, and because of the sound it could well have taken till the beginning of the next song to find out where I was! So I really only started getting into enjoying specific songs with which I felt at ease and more confident. 'Mr. Crowley' was probably first, then I don't know and 'Flying High Again'. I loved 'Over The Mountain', but that scale in the beginning of the first verse was a nightmare at first. Out of seven gigs I probably got it right twice! I never really got into 'Revelation Mother Earth', 'Goodbye To Romance', 'Believer' or 'Steal Away'. I got to love 'Crazy Train'. Initially I found that really quite hard. I majorly hated 'Iron Man'. Beyond me why anyone likes that. My kids love it!" In spite of the intensity of the songs and the production Bernie still manages to put this light hearted observation on his onstage surroundings. "Tommy was a half a mile away up the great pyramid of Cheops, Don was like the house elf occasionally sticking his head out the castle window to empty the slops, I couldn't see him or hear him. Rudy would be thundering away in his own world on the other end of the football pitch going through the book of heavy metal bass player poses. Other than that it was keep rolling at all costs and stay out of Ozzy and the dwarfs way! Occasionally Oz communicated by pulling my hair or looking in panic at me because I probably had this "what the fuck happens next?" expression on my face, but he was mostly really tied up with the audience, it was a full on show.

I had to regiment myself to do the shows, there was no choice in the circumstances. I did loosen up as time went on, but I did need to know what Randy had done to begin with. Knowing that, on some tracks I had started to go away from it, doing my own bits in places. I suppose 'Mr. Crowley' was the first track that I tried to stamp some identity on, but I was never really happy with the hammer on solo, I'd have liked to have built on that. I am much more of a free form player than Randy was, playing the same thing tends to bore me a bit, and then I don't play quite as well, quite on top of it, I need to be on the edge to play well, and with repetition or a formula I'm not on the edge. Some people shine at that, but its not my strong point. Randy was definitely out of classical and Spanish, and amazing at it too. That was not my school."

Contending with more than most could endure Bernie's senses were assailed when Ozzy pulled the same trick on the Irishman as he had on Randy night after night. Problem is that no one had deigned to tell Bernie what was coming. "All I thought was "Aaaaaargh—what the fuck is happening!" Its a strange thing that I didn't try to sock him or something, that's probably what you would normally do if someone pulls as hard as they can on your hair. I suppose I must have realised it was not serious, but the initial thing was that it was."

Understandably though, the overwhelming thoughts were of Randy and a sense of unreality at dealing with the practicalities of getting through the shows and ultimately the tour. A musician lives for that moment onstage, that brief burst of artistic freedom and fulfillment of ego but in these uniquely crushing surroundings the work ethic quashed any such luxuries. "I don't think that enthusiasm or euphoria came into it when I was there" Bernie says unashamedly. "It was get the job done and do it as best you can, I think for everybody in the band. I don't think they really wanted to play at all at that stage. But if you play you sometimes get lost in it, you forget and if that happened they probably looked up and expected to see Randy. It must have been hard."

For obvious reasons the outlandish excess and vivacity one would normally associate with Ozzy Osbourne was stark in its absence. The sheer weight of losing Randy was heavy and all pervasive and the guitarist found himself in a surreal icy world that had echoes of a mobile Rock n' Roll Berlin bunker. "Ozzy's dressing room was not exactly a barrel of laughs" Bernie says somberly. "Sharon didn't allow any alcohol (or other recreational substances obviously) at all in the dressing room, or on the bus for that matter. Not even a can of beer. It was like an old peoples church outing or something. Very Rock n' Roll. No one was very happy, that's obvious in the circumstances. Rudy sat and practiced with his Roland bass synthesizer in one room, doing awesome Stanley Clarke impressions, amazing slapping from Hell, really stunning stuff, while Ozzy and Sharon sat in the other room and moaned about him making a racket. It was all pretty grim. I understand they had a lot on their minds, but I couldn't deal with it, it was a wasteland that dressing room, about as inviting as a night on the Siberian tundra."

"I had a bit of a brain problem about all of the "not being allowed to": I was Irish, I was 30—Randy had died the day after my 30th birthday, and I could not quite mentally accept being treated like I was a 10 year old kid. I'm from Dublin, its part of my culture that I like a drink. It was like trying to deprive a Rasta of his ganja. I couldn't spiritually connect with the source without my Guinness. Anyway I found it all a bit tense. I have a total aversion to being told how to live my life, that is not what I got into playing Rock n' Roll for. I don't get fucked up, I don't let people down onstage, but I don't regard it as part of any gig being told how to live offstage."

With alcohol strictly off the agenda, Bernie sought solace elsewhere. In dire need of a watering hole and lighter company Don Airey suggested the guitarist introduce himself to some fellow travellers. "Don told me to go down and say hello to UFO in their dressing room. It must have been the second or third gig or so. Pete, Paul, Phil, all of them, they were all great, gave me a few cans of beer, made me feel at home and human: a few beers and a bit of a laugh, it was all I needed, it saved my sanity for quite a few days. I love them to death, great bunch."

It must be remembered that although Ozzy was topping the bill UFO were far from a support band more onboard as special guests. The bands support in certain areas of America was of arena headlining status built on a steady upward climb of album sales topped by the awesome live outing 'Strangers In The Night'. With these Ozzy dates UFO were promoting the more refined 'The Wild, The Willing And The Innocent' record. The bands capacity for worship of the golden can and subsequent offstage tomfoolery was already legendary. "I got on well with them, loved watching them too, tottering about the stage." Bernie remarks fondly. "Great band, really entertaining, right up my street."

With Bernie in place to plug the gap the race to find a permanent replacement was feverish. Down in California Brad Gillis was pushing his band Ranger. Although history records that Ranger would evolve into the multi platinum success story of Night Ranger at the time Gillis and his colleagues were finding it tough going. It was an all too familiar tale of record companies being too blind to see the gold beneath their feet but for Gillis it was no less than frustrating.

"We had spent a couple of years getting demos together and playing around the Bay Area honing our live show." He relates. "It was kind of a problem, getting a record deal, because we were a little heavier than normal, with songs like 'Don't Tell Me You Love Me' and 'Can't Find Me A Thrill'. I actually started another band called the Alameda All-stars. We were playing locally around the San Francisco Bay area and we were doing Ozzy, Blue Oyster Cult and Bad Company tunes around the night club circuit, trying to keep myself busy, keep my chops up. Meanwhile, Night Ranger kept trying to get a record deal. We were actually doing 2 Ozzy songs at that time."

Brad became aware of the tragedy of Randy's death in the same way as most Americans. "I'd heard on the radio that a plane crashed and Randy Rhoads was killed. That totally blew me away. I couldn't believe it." It was all the more poignant for Gillis as not only being an aspiring Rock guitarist he had been a fan. Brad had caught the Ozzy show at the "Day In The Green" outdoor festival in Oakland a matter of weeks beforehand. "In the back of my mind, I thought 'Gee, I wonder who they're going to replace him with?' Anyway, I'm doing this Alameda All-stars gig, doing my Ozzy tunes and this guy came in, a friend of mine, checkin' me out."

The friend was Preston Thrall, brother of the renowned guitarist Pat Thrall. "Pat Thrall played with Tommy Aldridge in the Pat Travers. Tommy Aldridge was of course playing drums with Ozzy Osbourne at the time. Anyway, there's the connection. After the Alameda All-stars show that night, Preston comes up and said "Man, I should let my brother know you would fit right in and to get a hold of Tommy about landing you the gig with Ozzy." I thought "Sure, that's going to happen." I said 'Well, go ahead and we'll see what happens.' That was a Friday night."

Unbeknown to Brad wheels were set in motion immediately upon Preston Thrall's recommendation. "Sunday morning, I get a phone call, early in the morning, waking me up and there is this English lady saying, "Bradley?" I'm like, "Yeah ..." She says, "This is Sharon Arden, Ozzy Osbourne's manager and we'd like to know if you'd want to fly to New York to audition for the band?" I'm going 'Who is this?'"

The guitarist had quickly but wrongly surmised he was the victim of a prank call and he was being well and truly wound up. "She says, "No, it's Sharon. Would you like to talk to Ozzy?" I said "Yeah! Put Ozzy on the phone!" This English man's voice says, "Hello Bradley?" and you know when you talk long distance, or at least back in '82, there was a delay in the phone line? I could tell it was long distance." Reality sank in and the full enormity of the telephone call was beginning to strike home. Gillis concluded he really was in conversation with Ozzy Osbourne.

"After speaking with him after a minute or so he says, "Get a piece of paper and a pencil and I want you to write down the songs that I want you to learn." All of a sudden, I started believing that it was Ozzy and I started trembling. I thought, 'Oh My God! This is for real!' I got a piece of paper and he named all the songs and said, "Would you be available to fly out on Tuesday?" Here it was Sunday morning and I said, "Oh yeah. Sure. I don't know if I can learn 19 songs by Tuesday" He says, "No, no, no, learn what you can. Come on out and you can work out here." Sure enough they send me a ticket to fly me out on Tuesday. I ended up getting all the albums because back then, there were no CDs! I found all the songs and started learning the material".

By the next Tuesday as planned Gillis found himself in New York. He had been told that Bernie Tormé was deputizing but assumed he would be thrown into a cattle call audition process. He was wrong. The night of his arrival Ozzy Osbourne was playing at the prestigious Madison Square Garden with a reluctant guitarist who in all honesty just wanted to go home. The gig Randy had so looked forward to but never got to see.

"Oh how I wished I would've done that gig" recalls an awestruck Gillis. With the enormity of the situation bearing down on him the guitarist joined the entourage. However, his first impression left him a little disconcerted. "A limo driver had picked me up at the airport and took me to the Helmsley Palace Hotel" he remembers. "I went to check in and there's no room under my name! They gave me a one-way ticket and I had $150 in my pocket, and the room was $135. So, I had to pay cash for it. That left $15 in my pocket!" Maybe this was all an elaborate hoax after all.

Concerned he duly checked in awaiting some recognition of his arrival. "There was no one around from the Osbourne entourage because they were all at Madison Square Gardens. I, basically, just went to my room and waited. Sure enough about midnight, I get a phone call from the road manager saying, "Hey! Come on up and meet Ozzy." I thought, "Wow, this is it ... Cool." I went up to the penthouse and there were press, media, radio, and rock stars everywhere!" This initial impression reinforced Brad surmised that he was about to be put through his paces in a tough process of elimination. "By the looks of it, it pretty much looked like there were about 20 or 30 long-haired musician / guitar player types in there, auditioning for the gig. I was thinking; Oh great! Competition—a big auditioning process. I met Larry McNinny, the road manager, and said "You know I had to pay for my own room!" and he handed me five crisp $100 bills and said "This should keep ya happy." I said, "Yea, that'll work"." At least fiscally now relieved the guitarist laughed and asked

SABBATH BLOODY SABBATH: THE BATTLE FOR BLACK SABBATH

Brad Gillis and Ozzy Osbourne.

the obvious question. "How many people here are auditioning?" He replies, "No, no, it's just you Brad." I said, "Really?" He said, "Yeah. If you can't cut the gig, then we'll send you home and get somebody else." Well, no pressure there!"

Then came Brad's first meet with Ozzy himself. The urgency of the situation dictated the pair got down to business without delay. "I went downstairs and grabbed my red Strat from my room and came back up to the suite. He takes me up to the penthouse bedroom suite. He sat on the floor and I sat on the end of the bed." Now was the moment of truth. It must have been a heady mixture of nerves and bravado swirling inside Brad's imagination at that precise moment. "He said, "What song do you want to play?" I said, "Well, 'Flying High Again'" and so he sang it and I played my guitar, no amp at all. I came to the solo, played all the solo parts and he jumped up, gave me a big hug and said, 'Bradley, I love you. Pull me through!'" The mood in the room lifted immediately to one of sheer relief. Not just for the guitarist either, he had already got a sense of the anguish his new employer was enduring. "He was having a hard time, you know, going through the tragedy of losing Randy Rhoads."

Now officially 'in' Brad Gillis then set about applying his craft to his new found surroundings. "I hung out for four or five days on the road around the New York area, sitting in my room everyday, with a live Randy Rhoads tape that the sound man had recorded a few weeks before Randy's death, so I could check out all the segue ways in between songs." Due to the time constraints it was to be a steep learning curve. Consequently Gillis applied both determination and discipline.

Tommy Aldridge had a unique perspective on events and recognised the enormous burden from Tormé's shoulders. "I really felt for him. He was trying so hard to cram everything in. There just wasn't enough time. He was so stressed and rightfully so.

Randy was a small dude but boy did he leave behind a massive pair of shoes. These were all quite capable guitar players but the situation really exacerbated the pressure. It was a terribly stressful time for everyone. Brad was recommended to me by Pat Thrall and he was the one that knew Randy's parts the best. That was one thing that was imperative ... Randy's parts were to be performed note-for-note ... or as close as 'someone else' could play them."

Bernie Tormé describes the moment he surmised a successor was waiting in the wings. "I think someone had told me about Brad initially, and he came up to me and said "Hello" when we were having breakfast someplace, maybe Rhode Island, maybe New Haven. I know I bailed out just after Madison Square Garden, because we were staying at the Helmsley Palace in New York at the time. I really was not enjoying it, and I think I was aware of Brad being carried as an insurance policy at that point. I think they were very worried that I would just say fuck it and leave, because that's what was said I had done in Gillan, coupled with my lack of enthusiasm for the long term gig. Of course there was no way I would have done that. Initially I think I felt a bit unhappy about him being there, but really it was par for the course in the situation, and after I saw him playing somewhere backstage I realised that this could lead to a situation that made everybody happy."

Tormé is quick to give Gillis credit due. "We never jammed, I think we did a bit of widdling around together backstage, his four note hammer ons blew me away, he, like Randy was much better at those than I was at that time. He was a nice guy. He obviously had not been around the block too many times. Bright eyed, keen, and bushy tailed! Very straight and to the point, which I liked. A good guitarist."

With Brad Gillis in place and Bernie Tormé treading the boards there were however still other names under consideration as Don Airey confirms. "Ray Gomez played with us in New York, and maybe Earl Slick was in there somewhere." Bernie Tormé backs up the keyboard player. "I was told by Don after the Madison Square Garden gig on the 5th that he had auditioned Earl Slick at the venue on the afternoon of the gig. They didn't let me go to the venue to soundcheck because of this, which really pissed me off majorly at the time."

Oblivious to the media circus surrounding the Ozzy circus Ray Gomez relays the tale from his standpoint. "One morning, I got a call from a writer, a guy who wrote for a New York magazine". Gomez qualifies. "It was a very strange thing. He asked me if I would like to play Madison Square Garden with Ozzy Osbourne!" As if this wasn't enough his friend then dropped a further bombshell "You'll have about

36 hours to do it he said. Apparently Ozzy wanted a change. I think Rudy, maybe someone else, strongly suggested to call me."

It was actually Tommy Aldridge who put the word in as he reveals. "I suggested the call to Ray" says the drummer. "I do remember Rudy and I getting together with Ray at some point. It's a bit sketchy actually!" The guitarist's retained knowledge of his pre Ozzy collusion with Sarzo and Aldridge is more than a bit fuzzy too. "I think I hung out with Rudy and Tommy more so than jammed. We almost played on a couple of occasions. Could've been for a project called Taxi I think." Whatever the circumstances of previous liaisons or proposed projects Ozzy's rhythm section had good cause to suggest Gomez.

Born in Casablanca of Moroccan descent and having been touted as a Jazz guitar child prodigy in Spain, Ray Gomez was much in demand behind the scenes during the 70s. An attempt at forming an ill fated 'supergroup' with then future Ozzy drummer Carmine Appice and ex-Yes man Bill Bruford had faltered but studio credits with John Lennon, Stanley Clarke, Herbie Hancock and Narada Michael Walden had bolstered his reputation. Striking out on the solo trail, Gomez launched a 1980 album 'Volume' which was involved in a CBS promotion alongside the debut Joe Perry Project album. Upon their release in Britain buyers purchasing either record were entitled to a free cardboard guitar at the point of purchase! The album featured Rick Derringer, Axis and Black Sabbath drummer Vinny Appice and Soul man Narada Michael Walden on drums. Will Lee and Blackjack's Jimmy Haslip supplied bass. By the time of 'Volume's release Gomez had already established an enviable repute among fellow musicians.

Don Airey confirms that Ray Gomez was under serious consideration for the Ozzy post and simply describes the guitarist as "A wonderful player." The possible inclusion of Gomez was not as outlandish as it seemed at first. "All the Rock guys knew of the Fusion players" Ray states. "I'm a Rock Blues Fusion guy so it would of worked no problem. Also, I was told that Randy used to really like my playing a lot. That was very nice to hear."

Next came the meeting. "I was asked to call the Waldorf Astoria hotel in New York. I spoke to Sharon and she invited me to dinner with Ozzy and Rudy. We just hung out really. Ozzy was, er ... out there. I don't know if he actually ate—there was some Brandy on the table for sure! It was a surreal event." Ray recalls the practicalities of the issue. "I was asked to learn a full set of high energy material in basically 24 hours. I said I'd give it a shot but it was tight. The playing style was not much of a problem it's just putting out that Rock energy, that balls to the wall Rock sound. The energy and the sound of what I was doing was similar. It was not a loose Blues gig there were a lot of structured riffs to learn. It was all pretty much arranged."

As it transpired the Ozzy camp weighed up the risks and opted for Gillis. "They worked it out with Brad" relates Ray. "It was a tough thing but I think it just settled. In the end I think there was no guarantee it would work, the risk was too great. I did start learning songs though just in case." Ray had thought that his meeting with Sharon and Ozzy had, according to plan, remained a closely guarded secret. However, when in the studio recently Ray received a shock from an arranger programmer and bass player working for producer Jack Douglas. "He asked me if I had played with Ozzy Osbourne" says Ray. "I thought this was a very odd thing to be asking so I asked him why. He replied he had heard that I was going to play with Ozzy at the Madison Square Garden. How he knew I don't know. The funniest part was that he had bought tickets for the gig! "I bought tickets" he said "Ozzy with Ray Gomez. I would have paid to see that! It would have been a trip." As it was of course he went to the show and I wasn't there!" So what did Ray think of the show? "I didn't go to the gig" he confesses. "I was so stressed I just went to bed!"

The actual Madison Square Garden gig itself would become a permanent fixture in Bernie Tormé's memory not due to the scale of the occasion but because of a near fatal incident involving Sharon Osbourne. With the show about to commence the band members were positioned behind swift drop kabouki curtains behind their own portcullis. Ozzy was underneath the central pyramid awaiting his grand entrance. Bernie takes up the tale. "So, I'm trapped in the portcullis, the intro music is playing. They had a kabouki curtain hanging up. I've had no soundcheck due to massed guitarists being auditioned before the gig including Earl Slick, so I'm not a happy camper. Sharon goes in front of my portcullis into the pyramid to give Ozzy a kiss. It was actually nice how caring and loving and supportive Ozzy and Sharon were to each other all that time."

With the intro tape still rolling a foolhardy individual in the audience launched a maroon firecracker onto the stage. The device bounced off the boards and hit Sharon Osbourne foursquare in the neck and exploded on impact. "All I know is the bang and flash" recollects the Irishman. "I haven't seen Sharon, who has just come out of the pyramid. So we're about ten seconds to kabouki drop, thirty seconds to portcullis lifting time, and I see three or four crew carrying a prostrate Sharon about three feet in front of my portcullis with blood pumping from her throat. They carry her off. Man, I thought she was dead. Bang, the show starts. 'Over The Mountain' . . . I spent the entire show looking at Ozzy wondering if he knew his missus might be dead when he came off stage. He knew nothing about it. But there was no time to say or do anything till the show was over, it was such a tight show." Thankfully Sharon, although her injuries required stitches, was relatively unharmed. "It looked worse than it was. And Madison Square Garden was a great show incidentally, I really enjoyed it, even with the above having gone down. I played OK too."

As the tour rumbled on Brad Gillis had imposed upon himself an intensive and perfectionist regime. "I was inside my room, oh geez, 12 hours a day just playing my guitar and learning all the riffs. On the fifth day Ozzy came up to me. "Let me know when you're ready 'cause Bernie wants to go home." he said." Brad told Ozzy he was.

Don Airey tries to convey the sense of relief the American guitarist lent the band. "Brad appeared as if by magic, in Providence, Rhode Island—he somehow knew all the songs, was very cool and did a lot to relieve a very traumatic situation."

It had taken only four gigs: Bethlehem, Boston, New Haven and New York Madison Square Garden for Bernie to convince himself beyond doubt that he could assist Ozzy no more. He called Ozzy and Sharon in their hotel room the day after the Madison Square Garden gig and requested a meeting in his room. "I said that I didn't feel I was the right person to do the gig, I wasn't enjoying it, and I wanted them to find an alternative, and as soon as they had, I wanted out. I found it very difficult to verbalise a precise reason why I did not want to stay, I still do, it was just a lack of happiness with the overall vibe, that's always difficult to justify." Bernie believes Sharon, no doubt having seen this conversation as somewhat inevitable, took the news better than Ozzy.

The guitarist then relays how the discussion got a little odd. "Sharon said something strange about it being understandable because it was not my type of music. I've still got no idea what she was talking about, maybe she was just trying to grease the wheels and not hurt Ozzy, maybe she was remembering the Punk band I had on Jet in '77, no idea really." Mystified, Bernie bit his lip. "It was a bit bizarre, funny even, cause I loved the music, it was right up my street, a bit like Gillan with tunes and fewer keyboard solos. Very close to my ideal stuff. Anyway, I dorked a bit at that, and then thought that I would grease the wheels and agreed. Not really my kind of music? What the fuck, there didn't seem to be much to be gained in arguing the point at that stage. It was a bit like we were speaking a different language. Ozzy probably thought I wanted to go off and study ukulele or something, funny in retrospect. Apart from that they were very understanding and kind."

The meeting closed with due thanks on both sides and a touch of characteristic modesty from the singer. "Ozzy said that he was very grateful to me, he said that I had really saved the tour and his career. He was just great about it, really appreciative. It was very nice of him to say that, but looking back it obviously was not true. Ozzy's pretty indestructible, and people love him to an unbelievable extent. That was so obvious at the gigs, that's what kept him going, and if it hadn't been me it would have been someone else, maybe a few days later, whatever, but the fact is the thing was going to carry on, that had been decided before I was even asked."

Three further gigs would follow: Providence Rhode Island, Buffalo and Rochester. Glen Falls was scheduled but cancelled. "Having told them I wanted to leave, everything seemed to go into very slow motion. They didn't seem to want to audition Brad and make the jump for ages. It was almost as if while I was prepared to stay they went around auditioning everyone possible, but after I decided I wanted to walk the plank they got temporary regrets, cold feet, whatever, wanted to hang on to the devil they knew. Brad was hanging around for quite a few days. I really had to almost talk Don into giving him a try. I suppose the band were not keen to go through all of the shit of someone new again. Don tried to talk me into staying."

Unbeknown to Bernie, his successor had been decided upon much earlier although, as Brad admits, the learning curve was as steep as they get. "I only had a chance to play six or seven songs at the soundcheck with the band, before my first gig in Binghampton, New York, sold out with 7,000 people." Brad recollects nostalgically. "All the other songs, I'd never even played with the band before that first night."

Bernie Tormé backs this up and concedes, citing caution, he had been asked to wait side stage just in case. Nobody need have worried. "The band eventually auditioned Brad just before the Binghampton gig, they were happy, and I stayed for the first gig in case he didn't cut it on stage. It was quite a little gig, no stage show, and he was excellent, closer to Randy than me. More West Coast technique than Irish/British filth. Perfect."

Fortunately the American newcomer's debut gig came without the added burden of a Bernie Tormé style image makeover. "When Brad did his first gig I think he cracked that one and wore a white boilersuit!" Bernie laughs. Besides his fashion statement Brad's first test under fire was particularly memorable. "That was quite an experience. I screwed up on one song called "Revelation Mother Earth." I went into the fast part too soon and Ozzy looked at me with that evil look like "You screwed up!" I caught myself and got back into place and finished out the night, and did well!"

With the gig wrapped up and a huge weight lifted from many shoulders by Brad's performance that night Ozzy would bid farewell to Bernie Tormé. "Ozzy came up to me and asked me how much money would help me set up my band and tour in the UK. He had mentioned something about it beforehand, but I hadn't really taken it seriously. I said I really didn't know, and he asked if $ XX,XXX would help. I was totally gob-smacked, and said yes, of course."

The singer took Bernie to the coach that provided the on the road base for the tour's accountant and promptly requested a cheque made out to Bernie for $ XX,XXX. "The guy looked at Ozzy and literally said 'You can't do that'" recalls a staggered Tormé. "Ozzy repeated it, getting a bit pissed off, and the guy wrote me the cheque. I could not believe it. A real gentleman. I then asked him if I could buy the blue green Strat off him, which Ozzy had paid for in Los Angeles as a spare, (it cost about $2,000, it was a '64 L series). He just told me to take it as a present. Unbelievable." Bernie Tormé flew home on April the 14th.

Seven gigs, a fortnight out of his life all held in a maelstrom of raw emotion without precedent. Bernie tries to encapsulate the overall experience thus. "I really don't think I was the right guy for them to ask. I was really uncomfortable about my replacing Randy, it seemed to me that what I was doing didn't show sufficient respect from me for him as a person or for his death. People are different, and I could not get away from feeling that at the time, and I still couldn't. It may not have bothered many, but it did bother me. In contradiction to that I was very glad to help Ozzy and the band get over what has to have been one of the most difficult points in their careers, if not in their lives. And I was very proud as a gunslinger to be asked, and to pull it off. But the only way I could personally reconcile the irreconcilable was to be temporary, and I probably used a lot of peripheral shit to justify that, the way you do. Looking back on it, none of that peripheral stuff was very important after all, it could all have been put on hold."

Misconceptions regarding the terms and conditions of his tenure added to a liberal sprinkling of plain old bad journalism would hound Bernie during and after his experience with Ozzy and the guitarist feels he was treated unfairly for not persevering. "I got quite a lot of shit at the time back in the UK for not carrying on, in the press and personally. People seemed to think I was being big headed and arrogant not carrying on, but that was a load of bollocks. It was like how dare a humble worm like me say no to the great Ozzy. But it wasn't at all like that, obviously it would have been a better career move to stay, I had no illusions about that, but I just couldn't do it, it wasn't for me in the great scheme of things."

Contact between the Osbournes and Tormé since has been fleeting although Ozzy has in various interviews freely voiced his admiration for Bernie since and has not held back on his praise. "I met Ozzy again a couple of times in the 80s, not too long after, at Liverpool when Pete Way was playing bass... and again at a drinking club in North London—Ooops! I bumped into Sharon about a year ago at a 'Kerrang' magazine do, I went up and said hello, I think she thought she'd seen a ghost, she seemed very nervous, nice to see her again though."

With just under a years worth of touring with the Ozzy Osbourne band stretching before him Brad Gillis would soon get into his stride. "I started touring and did better and better every night." The guitarist states emphatically. "I got more comfortable with the material and learned how to swing my guitar neck back and forth and play at the same time. Rudy taught me. After about two weeks of touring and playing, we did a live broadcast from Memphis, Tennessee, the "King Biscuit Flour Hour—Live Ozzy Osbourne" and that's when the whole country was able to hear me, the fans and my friends back home. That's when I started getting a little respect. I kicked butt that night. I played very well and after that, things went smooth."

Taking over from Don Airey on keyboards came the familiar figure of Lindsey Bridgwater, recalled for service with Ozzy for the second time. Don Airey would go on to make his mark as a session man extraordinaire. By 1985 he was back helping out Gary Moore for his 'Out In The Fields' record. The man would also figure on outings by Phenomena, Yugoslavians Wild Strawberries, German Metal band Sinner's 'Comin' Out Fighting', Zeno, Helix's 'Wild In The Street' and Alaska's 'The Pack' before hooking back up with Tommy Aldridge and Rudy Sarzo laying down work on Whitesnake's masterful '1987' album. The same year had Airey conducting live duties in America with Jethro Tull. His session work continued unabated. Airey notably performed on Judas Priest's 'Painkiller' and even wrote the British Eurovision song contest winner for Katrina And The Waves before ultimately enrolling into Rock institution Deep Purple.

During the interim, Bridgwater had once again found a port of call with Welsh veterans Budgie. The revival in their career was buoyed by their signing to RCA Records and the strength of their album 'Nightflight'. The follow-up, 1982's 'Deliver Us From Evil' produced by Don Smith and featuring keyboard contributions from ex-Cockney Rebel, 10CC and Camel man Duncan MacKay increased their profile. Budgie hit the road with vigour Bridgwater assuming MacKay's position for live dates, most notable being a successful string of shows in Poland during 1982. The keyboard player would then be re-summoned to the Ozzy camp.

Bridgwater readily confides that he got off on the wrong footing with Brad Gillis. "It was never going to be the same experience again after Randy Rhoads had gone. Brad was doing a great job but I admit I initially approached this new band all the wrong way. I was still carrying too many memories of Randy. I remember starting to show Brad some pieces and he turned to me and said something like "No, you've got to play them this way." I was really resentful because Randy had showed me those parts. I was too territorial. Although I admitted my actions were immature the thing is the memories of Randy and I working out those parts was still with me. Brad did a fantastic job all round but Randy could never really be replaced by anyone."

Bridgwater would view his 1982 Ozzy campaign in a different light to his erstwhile tenure. "I wanted to be more involved this time around simply because I loved the music. Coming in to fill Don's place was odd because he was a star in his own right and had been more forthright in his approach and so had made it easier for me second time around. He actually took the keyboard role to another plane altogether.

So, I kind of felt the need to co-ordinate everybody which of course I could fulfill because I had been once around the block already. I think for that second time I became more of an integral part of the rhythm section, part of the machine. Gradually I came to the fore. I even would go out and take my bow at the end of the evening!"

"I loved the 'Diary Of A Madman' album personally" states Lindsey Bridgwater. "For a musician to listen to it gives a different perspective of course but it truly is a wonderful record. I was only sorry we never got to play more songs from it" The Ozzy live show would include 'Over The Mountain' and 'Flying High Again' as staples with 'Believer' also getting an airing. "We rehearsed the title track a few times" reveals Lindsey. "I had got some nice choir effects for it and when we did it I thought it sounded fantastic. I think it strained Ozzy's voice too much though and it would have been too punishing for him to sing it night after night."

There would be another new face in the entourage too, that of the renowned UFO bassist Pete Way. Recently having split away from his immediate post UFO project Fastway, a union with ex-Motorhead guitarist 'Fast' Eddie Clarke, Way clambered onboard for Ozzy's European dates. His reputation preceded him, Way probably having done more to add sheer bravado to the normally staid role of the normally steady plod of the bass man's duties than anyone else.

Way, since the age of sixteen, had been recklessly cavorting across UFO arena stages putting in poses hardened yoga instructors can only dream of and in states of chemical inebriation that would have the Surgeon General reeling. Despite all this Pete Way laid claim to having played a major hand in crafting some of British Rock's greatest recordings such as 'Phenomenon', 'Obsession', 'Lights Out' and the seminal 'Strangers In The Night'. He would pull all this off garbed in some of the most outrageous custom striped or diamond backed stage uniforms and perform the role with such abandon that a UFO show would often have the audience wondering just who was going to fall over first. Would it be Way, Mogg or Tonka? Very often it would be all three.

Way believes he first hooked up with Ozzy backstage at an early UFO show in Birmingham but would cement their friendship at the Nomis rehearsal studios upfront of the debut Blizzard Of Ozz dates in 1980. "Ozzy is the same character as I am essentially" reckons Way. "So, when we got to Nomis and found the Ozzy band there we just had a great, great time. Ozzy is such a great, great man. He shares the same love of Rock n' Roll as I do so we clicked instantly. It was an odd combination of bands in there at the time and at any one time you would see the pool table with The Clash, Elvis Costello, UFO and Ozzy's band on it. Actually, I spent a lot of the time in a daze thinking 'Fucking 'ell—I'm drinking with the God of Rock n' Roll'!"

The camaraderie set in place at Nomis would be rekindled two years later. In a shock move Way, after 13 years, had spectacularly quit UFO disgruntled with his perceived taming of attitudes displayed on the 'Mechanix' album. A high profile union with erstwhile Motorhead guitarist 'Fast' Eddie Clarke resulted in Fastway but with CBS pouring in the readies and fan anticipation from both Motorhead and UFO camps riding high Pete Way received a rude awakening one day with a knock at the door. "There was a lawyer standing there from Chrysalis Records telling me I could not sign to CBS. They placed an injunction on me so I was stuck. I'd enjoyed working with Eddie, I'd co-written the Fastway album, rehearsed the songs and CBS had put in big money but I couldn't do a thing. I had to sign off on everything."

Seemingly stuck between the proverbial rock and a hard place an unexpected telephone call saved the day. "It was Ozzy. Out of the kindness of his heart he simply said "Come and play bass with me." So that's what I did. I didn't expect a salary or anything.

I think Sharon was interested because I had proven writing skills with UFO which may have come in handy later. I was just relieved. The God of Rock n' Roll had taken pity on a poor destitute bass player!"

Pete believes Ozzy's call to arms was purely altruistic. "Maybe Ozzy thought I looked better naked than Bob Daisley? I dunno, I was the wrong man for that band. I'm not an Ozzy player and really, the only reason I was there because both Sharon and Ozzy have a big heart. The very last thing Tommy Aldridge needed to deal with was me—not that he made it easy for me though. In truth I didn't play the Ozzy songs very well. Brad was a great guitar player—very, very underrated. He's a very talented man and a nice guy too. I tried hard but we had just one day rehearsal for me to learn the songs and the rest of it was catch up in hotel rooms with Lindsey. He was a cool guy, focused on the job of teaching me but Tommy, well, I guess he resented having a junkie for a bass player and who can blame him. At the time I thought that he could have given me more of a chance, I could really have used his coaching but looking back I guess I can see it more through his eyes."

Stylistically too Pete maintains the pieces simply didn't fit. "Onstage I would just be doing my best but I was struggling. I was totally addicted to heroin at the time. My style is more Sid Vicious than Geddy Lee, I'm not precious about the craft, I'm into the Rock n' Roll. Anyway, it was enough for me to share the same stage as Ozzy. Just seeing him working the crowd. That was just awesome."

Bridgwater's overriding memories of his second term of Oz duty with Pete Way are ones of musical achievement and friendship. "Brad had got comfortably in the role very quickly. He really had developed his own niche and was excelling at it. Pete, having come in at what seemed like very short notice, was doing his very best in a very short space of time. He was a lovely guy, very professional. I never really understood this thing about him being the wildman. I suppose he must have been because even Ozzy said to me once "If you think I'm wild you should see Pete in action."

All I ever saw of him though was the perfect gentleman. We would often spend nights in hotel rooms going through the songs piece by piece. Pete really wanted to get it right. The songs were a lot more complex with more time changes than what he had been used to with UFO. With the way Randy wrote, being so brimful of ideas, there were probably as many riffs in one Ozzy song than on an entire album from another band." Way was in fact enduring a tornado of activity at probably the lowest physical ebb of his life. The bassist had ignited a blitzkrieg of activity by his bailing out of UFO then Fastway and the press were now eager to learn of any inevitable Ozzy / Way shenanigans. To top it all Pete found the time to produce albums for two tear away acts Cockney Rejects and Twisted Sister. All this whilst dealing with a major habit.

Way, even after all these years, is still keen to express his thanks to Ozzy and Sharon for the lifeline they threw him in 1982. "Sharon was fantastic. I wish she was looking after me now. Although I don't think I'd marry her!" he laughs. "I totally admire that woman for everything she's done not just for Ozzy but Rock n' Roll in general. She's the Hillary Clinton of Rock. Sharon totally took the stress of Ozz. They've both got great vision and, although you hear about all the business side with them, really the reason they do it is because they just have a great love of Rock n' Roll. The thing I learnt is that they really look after the people who matter. If you're there for them they'll return the favour one hundred times over. Y'know, Ozzy rides greatness, he really does. He's like me in one sense—we're both sentenced to play Rock n' Roll. I'm just totally honoured I got the chance not to just drink with him but play with him. I had a totally awesome time and they paid me very, very well for the privilege."

With the closure of the European dates Way took his own path, creating one of Rock n' Roll's most suitably titled bands—Waysted. Debuting with the 1983 opus 'Vices', Waysted, fuelled by the bass player's full blown heroin addiction, proceeded to somehow stumble and falter through a succession of quality albums. Even hindered by the big H Way could still come up with the goods though and the 'Save Your Prayers' album remains one of British Hard Rock's greatest, if overlooked, moments. Waysted opened though with the Chrysalis 'Vices' album. It would chart in the UK but stall in America. For the second time Ozzy became benefactor. "The first Waysted album was dead and buried in America" confides Way. "Ozzy and Sharon gave us an American tour. Just gave it to us. We didn't have to pay a dime, it was simply a huge favour to me."

Fast forwarding to 1984 Waysted were on tour as guests to Iron Maiden in the UK. It was in the midst of this venture that Ozzy would cross paths with Way and Paul Chapman once more. "I remember it like yesterday" Paul Chapman regales. "I've every cause to! We were playing Hammersmith Odeon with Maiden and, unbeknown to us, it happened to be Sharon's birthday and so Ozzy was celebrating. Somehow—don't ask me—Ozzy went out in Birmingham for a few drinks with Noddy Holder and Don Powell from Slade and ended up in London. Of course, they went to the pub but ran out of money. Ozzy went to see his accountant Colin Newman to get some cash. Now, this is the bizarre bit. Ozzy went to a costumers and got himself dressed up in red wellys, a Dolly Parton dress, a blonde wig and a German Helmet. On this helmet he had painted "OZZY" in nail polish. He also went to a butchers to get a rabbit. So, Ozzy marches into his accountants office and bellowed "Where's Colin?!" and started to swing this rabbit around. Unfortunately the butcher had put the creature's guts in a bag which flew out and splattered everywhere! Colin gave him £500 to go away so they went back to the pub!!"

Ozzy's next move would be to reacquaint himself with some old friends. Paul recalls the moment he realised Ozzy was in town. "The next thing I know is we are backstage at Hammersmith Odeon waiting to go on and suddenly we here "Where are they?" from down the hallway. We recognised it as Ozzy's voice straight away. When he burst into our dressing room though we just couldn't believe what we were seeing. Well he sat down and told us what had happened at Colin's office and then he says "Are we going to play 'Paranoid'?" Our jaws dropped. I think we tried to get out of it by saying we didn't know it but Ozzy would have none of it. "It's bloody easy" he said, 'Just follow me'."

Rejigging their set list to include 'Paranoid' as an encore, Waysted went about their business onstage. Ozzy's impatience to perform got the better of him though. "We planned on doing 'Paranoid' last but right in the middle of our set Ozzy marched onstage—in the middle of a song!" The dumbfounded audience took a while to register who this strange character was, still in dress, wig and helmet, who had barged into Waysted's set.

"When they realised it was Ozzy the place just exploded" Chapman records. "So, we stopped what we were doing and played 'Paranoid', very badly—I'd never played it before in my life. Things just got more surreal from that point on. Ozzy tried to grab me and lift me in the air but, as anyone who knows me will tell you, I ain't called 'Tonka' for nothing! It was hilarious! Obviously he was used to just picking Randy up off the floor and swinging him around but me he couldn't budge. He didn't give in though so we just stood there for what seemed like an age, me trying to play a song I didn't even know and Ozzy grunting and groaning trying to lift me up! Well, anyway, Ozzy finally did give up and for a grand finale got his knob out and started to wave it at the audience!"

With the privileged Hammersmith Odeon reeling from one of the most bizarre Rock n' Roll performances ever the musicians realised that the night was still young though and Ozzy had further plans. "I was already in big trouble by that point" Chapman reveals. "My son had been born just days before and I promised my wife I would not go out. Well, Sharon was trying to find Ozzy by phoning everywhere but all he wanted to do was to go to his accountant's house to get some more money. I talked him out of it and in the end he fell asleep on my sofa. In the morning he was gone, but only after he had thrown up all over my floor!"

With both bands proudly in delivery of worthy slabs of vinyl and both acts also having launched into extensive world tours there would be some post tour calculations to be made. 'Diary Of A Madman' had made a big dent into the Billboard top twenty running out of initial momentum at No. 16. 'Mob Rules' would just scrape into the top thirty. Like two screaming leviathans pitched chest to chest in a clash of wills 'Diary' and 'Mob Rules' slugged it out for over a year. Both Ozzy and Sabbath had taken casualties. Although Osbourne's position, having so cruelly lost the gift of Randy Rhoads, looked the more perilous his career had reached a turning point. When the dust settled and the soundscans were totted up it was without question Ozzy, another two million sales under his title belt, hailed as the victor.

Chapter 7

Enter Jake

Dio stepped out onstage for the 'Mob Rules' tour's final gasp at the Hoffman Estates Poplar Creek Music Theatre, Illinois on 31st August 1982. A full decade would elapse before he was to share the stage with Messrs. Iommi and Butler again. Although, judging by barbed quotes circulating in the Rock media shortly after, it would seem a ten year hiatus would be thought of by the band members as being on the generous side. Black Sabbath was to go to war with itself.

The manufacture of the live album, culled from taped shows in Texas at San Antonio, Dallas along with Seattle, Washington would soon spill into farce. The stories that made the British press conjured up a Keystone Cops display of professional ineptitude. Various factions were accused of surreptitiously pushing up levels on their instrument or vocal, only to have them reduced and other desk knobs raised, creeping back into the studio to get their desired personal levels up again, and so on and so forth. What made the stories doubly worse was the veracity of them.

"I'm afraid so" admits Geoff Nicholls sheepishly. "The stories that got into the press were pretty accurate. It didn't do much for our credibility but it was all true." Iommi, Butler and Nicholls would convene during the day with engineer Lee DiCarlo. What they didn't know, for a long time, was that Messrs. Dio and Appice were conducting a night shift of their very own. Setting their fader levels in the evening, Iommi and colleagues would be perplexed to find they had all changed come the morning. It was almost as if a mischievous gang of leprechauns had been in and run riot on the mixing desk every night.

"What we didn't know at the time was that Ronnie was writing up his solo record at the time too. It got a bit comical really because this thing of them creeping in at night went on for quite some time. Basically Ronnie was pushing his vocals up. What he forgets though is if the vocals go up the rest of it loses the heaviness and starts to sound small in comparison. The engineer was put in an impossible position because he was trying to please everybody. This whole farce went on for about ten days until, finally, Tony Iommi said to him "Look Lee, tell me what the fucking hell is going on here?" Lee then threw his arms up and blurted it all out. Tony was livid and shouted back at him "I'm the one who's fucking in charge here!" That's when Tony found out and that's when he fired Ronnie."

Black Sabbath had certainly divided into two camps. Ronnie James Dio maintains that separate factions would indeed inhabit the studio at different hours but puts forward an opposing reasoning behind the manouevres. "Vinny and I would go into the studio and wait for Tony and Geezer. This is where it started. They simply didn't turn up but this is where all the rumours of sneaky sessions came from. There was no sneakiness—we were there on time, they weren't. Because they wouldn't turn up obviously we got with working in the meantime. Studio time is expensive and I'm not about to sit there and waste those dollars. If they're not there what did they expect? We were making an album.

Anyway this went on for three or four days. We would go in and they still weren't there. It became an absolute nonsense. That drove it home to me right there. Something had come to a head and it was that whole avoiding confrontation thing which Geezer and Tony specialise in. Eventually Geezer phones me and says 'I don't think this is working out. We really want Tony to produce the album on his own'. Now, I know this kind of cryptic talk, so I say 'So, if you don't want me involved with this album are you saying it's over then?' and Geezer says 'Well, er ... yeah, I suppose so.' They could never just tell you straight. It was all a device to force me out. I called Vinny and said 'I'm out of Sabbath. I've been given the elbow. Do you want to be in a band with me?' Vinny says 'Absolutely!' No hesitation. So then we had the start of Dio."

Band splits are often ugly affairs. Creative personalities are emotive, highly strung and have egos that are easily bruised. A quite vicious war or words ignited across the Rock media before both parties retired from the arena to lick wounds and regroup.

Behind the scenes though, the divisions were handled in proper fashion. "Black Sabbath didn't screw me" offers Ronnie. "Although things got nasty on the pages of magazines we all just got on with it in the correct manner soon enough. All the blabbing in the press was just superficial really and something we needed to get out of our systems. I had a great attorney and good friends but nobody in the band was looking to screw me out of any money. It was all professional and decent. There have been bands I've been involved with where I was screwed and it took years of legal work to get paid but with Sabbath it was all as it should be. Actually, my success with Black Sabbath gave me the profile and financial means to get the money I was owed from earlier bands."

Nevertheless, the cut off from Black Sabbath was about as clinical as it could get. Dio and Appice, with the exception of Ronnie's attorney who had made the break with them, were out on their own. "Besides my attorney we didn't take anyone else with us. It was interesting because a band and crew is more like a family organisation. There is great camaraderie if you are part of the team but once you're out you are really out. You become a pariah and all the people who probably would like to give you a call don't because they fear losing their jobs. I considered I lost a few good friends there."

Prior to formulating his next band endeavour the singer had a brief window to reflect upon his term of office with Black Sabbath. "Immediately after being given the boot from Sabbath I was filled with both optimism for my new band and sadness for what had just happened. I wasn't happy with the way everything ended but I could feel proud of what I had achieved. It was pretty remarkable and had given the career I had for the future a big leap ahead of the competition. I gave as much to Sabbath as Sabbath gave to me, probably more so."

In the unceasing battle for the fan's loyalty towards the two Black Sabbath camps Ozzy stole a march on his erstwhile colleagues. In a simple manoeuvre designed to both fulfill a recording contract he was eager to sever ties with and deliver a thundering statement of intent Osbourne conjured up a double live album all of his own. Sabbath was given a sound drubbing, caught in a classic Blitzkrieg pincer movement. In simple terms the 'Speak Of The Devil' live record, titled 'Talk Of The Devil' outside of America and recorded 26th and 27th September at the Ritz venue in New York, would trounce 'Live Evil'. Recorded with Randy Rhoads second tour replacement Brad Gillis, the record comprised solely of Black Sabbath tunes. Gillis, often sorely overlooked in the annals of Ozzdom, rampaged through the Sabbath classics. Most fans saw it for exactly what it was, a challenge to Iommi and Butler as to the legitimacy of their claim to the name Black Sabbath.

Tommy Aldridge records some swipes in his direction as part of the fall out. "I did hear that after doing the live album of Sabbath material that I recorded with Ozzy that Butler and Iommi weren't impressed with the performance. That was certainly their prerogative as it was their material. I've always been hired to play the way that I play and not try to 'copy' someone else. With the greatest respect to Bill Ward, I chose to play those songs, while still trying to faithfully represent them, in my own style. I think they were maybe a little offended by that. That's unfortunate but ... you gotta like what you like."

The crafting of 'Speak Of The Devil' though was apparently not a spontaneous decision as discussions with Randy Rhoads confidante Kelly Garni revealed. "Randy spoke to me about this, it was a big ticker for him. Ozzy had wanted Randy to do an album of Black Sabbath songs but Randy really didn't want to do it. He objected because he was actually really bothered by playing that stuff. I'll never forget when I saw him play live with Ozzy he warned me that he was going to be playing some Black Sabbath numbers. I can quote him word for word "OK, Don't laugh, we do a couple of Black Sabbath songs." He hated telling me that, he had this embarrassed grin on his face and he was looking down at the floor all embarrassed. Well, I did laugh at him!"

Offered up in the November of 1982, 'Speak Of The Devil's targeting was as precise as any Gulf War smart missile. It strode defiantly into the Billboard top twenty with ease. Whereas 'Speak Of The Devil' had the testicular fortitude of a herd dominating warthog, both in terms of sheer audacity and aural sonic capacity, 'Live Evil' was neutered before it even hit the racks in the stores. The public bickerings of the now rent asunder Sabbath merely provided the coup de grace. The tired results of their labours lumbered out in January of 1983. As a newly shaven headed Ozzy took to the live circuit once again, 'Live Evil' plateaued at No. 37 in North America. In short, Ozzy's amateur, makeshift and last minute cobbling together of a live album had given him a life saving ark to bob happily on the waves. The mighty Sabbath machine had painstakingly constructed a leviathan, poring over the mixing minutiae and conducting war games with flying faders. Somewhat pompously they had cracked the champagne bottle on the bows of their very own Titanic.

Although the original plans for Ronnie James Dio and Bob Daisley to form up a new band post Rainbow had faltered, with Dio joining Sabbath and ironically Daisley teaming up with Ozzy, the singer still had a keen eye for the bassist's talents. "Ronnie came over to my house in London just after leaving Sab-

Ronnie James Dio.

bath" Daisley recalls. "So Ronnie, Vinny Appice and I went for a curry and some beers down Westbourne Grove. I remember it very well because the curry was fantastic, a place called the Al Kayam. Anyway, they had asked me out to see if I wanted to join Ronnie's new band, Dio. It came at the wrong time though because I was working with Ozzy on 'Bark At The Moon'." With Daisley otherwise engaged Dio and Appice picked up another former Rainbow man Jimmy Bain and, together with Vivian Campbell from the NWoBHM band Sweet Savage and ex-Magic and Rough Cutt member Claude Schnell on keyboards, crafted the band Dio.

As a signature to Warner Bros. with two prominent albums under his belt Ronnie James Dio assumed a degree of open armed enthusiasm would come his way from the label. Quite bizarrely the organisation took some time to even realise Ronnie was recording at all. "The first Dio album became exactly the same as 'Heaven And Hell' unbelievably" the singer sighs. "For three weeks nobody even bothered to come down to the studio and check it out. It was kind of amusing and alarming at the same time. Eventually someone from the label called my manager Wendy and inquired 'Is Ronnie in the studio recording an album?' Wendy says 'Yes, and he's using your money to do it!' They say 'Oh, we didn't know. Who's producing it?' This is when it gets interesting. Wendy replies 'Why, Ronnie is of course'. Warner Bros. just went 'Oh ...' After that they started to move and wanted me in their offices at 10 sharp next morning to meet Ted Templeman.

So, I turned up at 10 as arranged as Ted turns up at 10:15. The first thing he says is 'Which idiot arranged this meeting for 10:15 in the morning?' When we got down to the talking Ted says 'Are you doing a record?' and I say 'Yeah'. 'Who's producing it?' he asks. 'I am' I told him. After that, Ted gets up and says 'Great! See ya!' Ted's a musician, he knew the score."

Dio's secret weapon for 'Holy Diver' was guitarist Vivian Campbell. The guitarist lent Ronnie's tunes a distinctive edge. Riffs were piled on aplenty and the solos were miniature melodic masterpieces. The Irishman was quite a find. Before Campbell came onto the scene and the band got into the studio proper, Dio and Appice had formed up two tracks, 'Don't Talk To Strangers' and 'Holy Diver', in the shed-come-makeshift studio at the back of the singer's house. Vinny had laid down the drums for these demos whilst Ronnie took on vocal, guitar and bass responsibilities. Although they were rough the pair had an inkling that something special was developing with these two unfettled gems. "Although we had cranked these tracks out we then realised we needed to get a band together" records Ronnie. "We flew to England because I had always admired English guitarists. People like Blackmore and Tony Iommi just have that bit of quirky uniqueness that I was looking for."

The duo scoured the clubs hoping to locate a six stringer with the X factor but remained unfulfilled. It was starting to look as though their quest was in vain. "We couldn't find anyone in the clubs so we thought we would ask around. Jimmy Bain told us he had a couple of tapes so he came over and we listened to cassettes of John Sykes and Vivian Campbell. Both were amazing players but Vivian stuck out a bit more. It was unique and even had a little bit of Chuck Berry in there, which I liked. The guy was flying by the seat of his pants, he pulled off some unexpected, quirky stuff and I liked that attitude. Jimmy called him and we arranged a jam. Jimmy took it on himself to bring his bass and kind of made the assumption he was in too! Thank God actually. Vivian was just great. Once we had a band we flew to Los Angeles to start writing and recording."

Dio's inaugural outing, the glorious 'Holy Diver' album, was a sharp statement of intent and an album of such magnitude it succeeded in carrying many Black Sabbath fans along with the new project. Indeed, 'Holy Diver' would be seen by many as more of an example as to the natural evolution of Black Sabbath had Dio stayed the course than Sabbath's own follow-up 'Born Again'. The record charted satisfyingly in the USA, peaking at No. 56, but broke into the top twenty across much of Europe. As well as delivering an album of world class Dio also aided their cause enormously with an electrifying performance at the annual Castle Donington 'Monsters Of Rock' festival. These shows, illustrating a pattern throughout Dio's career, paid equal homage to Dio's liaisons with Black Sabbath and Rainbow as well as fresher material.

With Gillis re-prioritising Night Ranger, to subsequent huge success it must be said, the Ozzy band

Holy Diver.

was in need of fresh blood. Jake E. Lee, or to give him his real name Jakey Lou Williams, had been raised in West Virginia by his American Naval officer father and Japanese mother. In later life the Williams family had relocated with the military to Imperial Beach, California. His musical upbringing had centred upon the regime of enforced piano lessons but his elder sister would lure the young Jake into the big bad world of Rock n' Roll with her album collection. Sadly for Jake his sister would lose her life in a motorbike accident.

At school Jake had been an outsider, his untypically long hair and obsession with guitar playing setting him apart from the other kids. His first band Teaser, named after the Tommy Bolin album, was conceived at the Mar Vista High School. Legend has it Lee would be expelled from school for a series of misdemeanours including punching a teacher who objected to the loudness of his guitar playing by pulling the plug on his guitar amp. As Teaser elevated themselves from school gigs to dates on the local San Diego club circuit Lee would strike up a rapport with Enforcer guitarist Warren De Martini. Another encounter came with Stephen Pearcy, lead singer of Mickey Ratt.

The late 70s found Lee experimenting with a number of Jazz Rock Fusion bands and whilst pursuing this avenue the guitarist would audition for a new band Jerry Goodman, violinist with the Mahavishnu Orchestra, was assembling. Lee didn't get the job. Before long Jake, shifting bases to Hollywood, was in the ranks of Pearcy's band which in time had evolved into simply Ratt. Club gigs at such infamous venues as 'The Roxy', 'The Whiskey' and 'The Troubadour' ensued but Lee would decamp, suggesting his friend De Martini as an able substitute.

Lee had a fleeting tenure with the Greg Leon Invasion. The band was centred on guitarist Greg Leon who had claims to fame with early incarnations of both Dokken and DuBrow, the name assumed by Quiet Riot after the departure of Randy Rhoads to Ozzy's band. Jake would soon take a career side step. Rough Cutt frontman Paul Shortino (himself prove positive to the adage 'All roads lead to Rome'—he later fronted Quiet Riot!) records the sequence of events. "Almost all the members of Rough Cutt were in Ratt at one point. We were rehearsing at the Starwood Club when it was closed down." The incarnation of Rough Cutt that Jake would join numbered Shortino, guitarist Bob Dalilis, bassist Joe Cristo (real name Cristofanelli—an ex-Ratt man), keyboard player Claude 'Steel' Schnell and drummer Dave Alfred. "Dave said he knew a guitar player that would be great for the band" records Paul. "Jake had just quit Ratt and was looking for a new project. Dave asked him to jam with us and the next thing you know, Jake is in the band!"

With former Rainbow and Black Sabbath man Ronnie James Dio taking the band under his wing for both production and career guidance Rough Cutt entered the studio to demo. Two songs from these sessions, 'A Little Kindness' and 'Used And Abused', would surface on the 1983 Backhouse compilation 'L.A.'s Hottest Unsigned Rock Bands'. "Jake's style of guitar was so different from a lot of players out there. Jake has great vibrato and technique and is a great showman" rates Shortino. "Ronnie was thinking of using him for his record. We were playing the Hollywood club circuit at the time and Jake had heard Ozzy was looking for a guitar player. Jake asked Wendy Dio if she could get him an audition for the spot and she did. Jake got the gig and the rest is history. He was offered a great spot with a 'Rock legend'. It was a great move for his career. In my heart, we parted as friends and I could only wish him good fortune."

Managed by Wendy Dio's Niji organization Rough Cutt's future held promise. A collection of strong riff heavy songs and the characteristic vocal chimes of Paul Shortino made the band an exciting proposition. With such an obvious talent Lee's obvious next step would be Dio itself. Lee and Ronnie worked up material for what would eventually emerge as the debut Dio record 'Holy Diver' before Irishman Vivian Campbell took the reins.

Jake E. Lee's enrollment into the Ozzy stable came courtesy of another player that had already featured significantly in the Ozzy timeline—original bass player Dana Strum. "I got a call from Sharon and Ozzy's attorney Fred Ansis" relates Strum who felt at the time he was being treated with kid gloves. "I was treated very nice. Sharon had done her best to make all of the past bad vibe just go away. As it stood she knew that I was 'un paid' in a sense." The call came out of the blue. Strum recalls that hearing of Randy's death he cried himself to sleep and felt a heavy burden of misplaced guilt. The memories that came flooding back of earlier times at the Le Parc were now being put sharply into focus. Strum was soon to find himself back in familiar territory. "Sharon put me onto Ozzy who asked if I had any great guitarists up my sleeve. Mike Jensen, long time Ozzy PR man, got me involved in the pitch to do a Los Angeles guitar round up. It felt like time had stood still."

Strum's enthusiasm took over and he got to work. "I thought that George Lynch was the guy and called him." This is when George learnt that his manager at the time of Ozzy's first guitarist auditions had never brokered the subject of Dana and Ozzy's interest in him. Other potential recruits lined up were Mitch Perry of Steeler, Spencer Sircombe of The Sharks (later Shark Island) and Jake. Initially the hopefuls were told by Strum that the position was for a fill in musician to keep Ozzy out on the road but in reality Ozzy had asked to check out their writing credentials for more long term plans. "I worked with each guy on the phone" Strum recalls. "I could prep them for what was to be a fill in spot to keep Ozzy on tour as well as to go on and write. Ozzy was very concerned that any new guy should be a good riff writer as well." Once worked out and ground rules established the bass player set up studio sessions in North Hollywood.

Strum was not originally slated to play at the session but having organised the whole event and being a bass player Ozzy got the jam rolling. "Ozzy said to me—"Get up there. You know you want to" Strum remembers. "So we—George, Ozzy, Tommy and me—jammed to 'Crazy Train and 'I Don't Know' and some more fun shit. It was the second wave!" Decisions were made and Strum was instructed to deliver the good news. "I was told George had got it. I was even told to tell him he had it and that he was going to England or on the road. George had quit his job and was into doing it big time."

"George Lynch was on fire" he exclaims. "A great player. But, the other standout guy was Jake. He was late and with a girl in tow but none the less he was damn good. He played a number of styles that shocked me. From his background you just would never have thought." It was a delicate situation. George Lynch had not only believed he had got the gig but had been told so. "It was a good bit late and no one in the room was thinking other than George had got it. That included George and his then wife Christy who was also there. Then Jake showed up. Ozzy and Sharon liked his image and vibe, the whole Crue / Ratt type thing. Jake played very well and the night got very odd. I was told that George might not be they guy. Ozzy, Sharon and Tommy kinda seemed to fancy Jake and his whole trip and vibe."

Tommy Aldridge confirms this rapid decision change "Jake was the guy. Jake's playing was / is unique and he really was the only one that could really do the job. It's unfortunate that we didn't find him sooner." George Lynch was far from amused to find out he had lost out. "George was shocked, very pissed and very upset" Strum recalls. "This was the worst thing for him." Strum was facing the déjà vu of acting as ringmaster once again. "Hook up master to Ozzy again—how strange that was!"

His previous experience with Ozzy had fired off Strum's natural drive to organise and involve himself to the fullest. He still felt he had responsibilities. "I was a bit worried that Jake would not have the songs or riffs to bring to the party so myself, Jake and Ron Mancuso (Modern Design's guitarist) spent a few nights working things out. We put down what would later become three of the riffs for songs on the 'Bark At The Moon' album. It was a trip but more than that a way to secure Jake a gig and write some Ozzy stuff from afar. We actually swore Jake to keep this between us. Jake was the right guy for the gig and we just wanted to give him the best shot plus Ron and I still loved the music. Money? What money?"

Matters got deeper than even the music. "I got very involved with Jake" Strum confides. "I even discussed with him his name change, organised the PR shots and set up an article with the LA magazine 'Music Connection' titled 'From nothing to the U.S. Festival.' I spoke with Jake a lot during the making of 'Bark At The Moon'. I even arranged to rent a car for Jake and his girlfriend Sharon. I would regret that—the car was destroyed and totalled!" Jake was immediately flown to England to begin rehearsals with the Ozzy Osbourne band for the European leg of the 'Speak Of The Devil' tour.

Taking over Pete Way's mantle would be the relative unknown figure of Don Costa. If Pete Way was 'wild' Costa was, according to the media, virtually a basket case. Costa had paid his dues with a proto version of W.A.S.P. upfront of stints with Hollywood acts Dante Fox and Damien. Soon the press was releasing lurid tales of Costa's exploits, the most memorable being that the bass player would take a cheese grater onstage to shred his knuckles and belly with, inviting girls in the audience to lap up the blood. It was perfect Ozzy fare.

Whatever the realities of Costa's onstage exploits behind the scenes his apparent primeval nature continued apace. "Our sound engineer Chuck Weissner would record every gig for us on tape so the band could listen back to it later that night" records Lindsey. "Jake in particular was very aware of whose shoes he was filling and really was keen to get everything just right. Jake had enormous ability and great flair but he was always willing to listen and learn. It

Jake E. Lee. Pic: Rich Galbraith.

Jake E. Lee, Tommy Aldridge, Ozzy Osbourne, Don Costa and Lindsey Bridgwater.

was the norm for us all to listen back to the shows to see how we could improve and make things better."

One night the keyboard player got more than he bargained for though. "So, one night Don Costa was listening to a tape on the bus. I said to him "Is that a tape of last night?" He looked up and said to me "Yeah, Wanna listen?" So I listened but it wasn't a tape of the concert. It was an 'In flagrante delecto' recording he had made of his previous night's conquest with this girl screaming and howling in ecstasy! "No you idiot, I meant the show!" I said. "Yeah right," OK . . . I thought. Don was a big hit with the ladies and virtually every night would get at least one, often more, back after the show. What they did not know was that he had a tape recorder under his bed and recorded every one of them for posterity! I think he had rather an interesting little audio library accumulating." Indeed, Costa subsequently used record of one such conquest as a novel outro to an M-80 album.

"In many ways Don was a typical never-been-out-of-America kind of guy" Lindsey Bridgwater observes. "I remember one occasion, we were in Paris driving around the Arc De Triumphe. Someone was telling him about how inside the monument there is a flame kept perpetually burning in honour of the French soldiers that had died in the two world wars. Don, quite genuinely, said 'They have wars over here too?' A thousand years of European history had simply passed him by. The thing you have to remember about Don Costa was that underneath all the madness he was a great player" maintains Lindsey. "I don't know why he went. Was he pushed or did he fall? Sometimes it felt like not a case of if but when. I think in the time I worked for Ozzy over three years we had eight different line-ups. The whole band was in a constant state of flux." Costa would briefly hit the limelight post Ozzy with M-80, a union with guitarist Niki Buzz. After just one album Costa decamped, never to be heard of since.

The Ozzy Osbourne band would, in sheer terms of numbers, peak in 1983. The band was invited to perform at the gargantuan U.S. Festival in San Bernadino to over 400,000 people—Jake E. Lee's American concert debut. The U.S. tour would see the Ozzy rollercoaster helter skeltering at an alarming speed visiting many cities twice performing in open amphitheatres. Demand for tickets in New York was so great the band played the Palladium twice in one night.

Public acclaim though did little to dispel the cloak of suspicion surrounding Ozzy though as Bridgwater elaborates. "Ozzy certainly eclipsed Black Sabbath for attracting the religious zealots out of the woodwork. It was odd for me because in between times I was playing organ in church. It didn't affect me, I just saw through it all. Ozzy though, it did get to. Sharon had to keep him on the rails. I don't think I could have summoned the strengths Ozzy found to get through all that side of things. His professionalism was there at all times, he kept his stamina and energy up while being in the eye of a hurricane really. It must have been bloody hard work being Ozzy. The outside world had a very distorted view of us whereas in actual fact it was just 5 blokes getting on with business. That tour was hardly the orgy on wheels many might have supposed." The band, on a second leg supported by Def Leppard, had grown in stature so rapidly that by the time a return to New York was made it would not be the Palladium but the 17,000 Nassau Coliseum that welcomed them to a capacity crowd.

Chapter 8

Born Under A Black Moon

Back in the UK on the opposing camp, Tony Iommi responded to the exit of Dio and Appice by re-enlisting Bill Ward and, controversially, pulling in former Deep Purple singer Ian Gillan. The singer had a huge reputation having fronted up one of the very few bands to have eclipsed Black Sabbath itself. Although Gillan was a grade A pedigree Rock star the weight of opinion both in the industry and amongst fans was that the huge stylistic differences between Sabbath and Purple could not be bridged. Nevertheless, it all made sense to the money men as Iommi had succeeded in securing the most well known British singer after Robert Plant. This next chapter of the band was to signal the onslaught of press diatribe that would dog it for the next decade.

According to quotes from Tony Iommi in the 'Born Again' North American tour programme other vocalists had been considered and auditioned before Ian Gillan's name was put forward. This admission has intrigued fans but it has been next to impossible to get any kind of verification of this from the band until now. In actuality Arthur Sharp at Don Arden's office, a man who had previously sang for the Nashville Teens so knew a thing or two about vocals, was delegated to sift through prospective candidates. (Although Arthur's skills failed him when he rejected the Jet Records artist Madam X's proposed second album demos—the singer was Sebastian Bach, later to go multi-platinum with Skid Row).

Geoff Nicholls confirms this modus operandi. "Yes we did audition quite a few singers after Ronnie left. Nobody really famous I don't think. The way it worked was that, rather than wasting the band's time in the studio by dealing with people individually, chatting, etc., the management gave them a backing track of some of the songs which they had to sing on. They then filtered out the unsuccessful ones and the downright silly ones so we could meet up with just the good ones. I remember we auditioned Nicky Moore from Samson because his tape was excellent. We had a good jam with him. He had a phenomenal voice, absolutely brilliant but he just didn't look the part, which was a shame. Great, great singer. There was a guy from Wales too. (John Sloman of Lone Star). I'll tell you who else sent a tape in—Michael Bolton! Imagine that? Wonderful voice but obviously completely wrong for what we were doing."

David Coverdale was also back on the Black Sabbath wish list. "Tony Iommi and I met up with David and Cozy Powell at The Rainbow club to talk about getting them into the band at that point" reveals Geoff. "We had a good chat and we kind of agreed in principle that it could work. Tony has always been keen on working with David. Anyway, we left it awhile and the next thing we hear is that they had gone off camping on Dartmoor and were getting Whitesnake back together."

Speaking to 'Sounds' magazine in August of 1983 Gillan had this to say. "At the time I wasn't considering anything other than what I was doing. Then I had this trouble with my voice, which meant I had to take six months rest without singing after the last Gillan tour. The split was purely a medical thing. I've read a few things in the press where Mick (Underwood) and John (McCoy) have said 'it was all a farce and just an excuse to wind up the band'—which is a load of bollocks, quite frankly. I could authorise ANY of the specialists I saw to release their reports if you like. I had huge nodes on my vocal chords and they were badly inflamed, and I was only able to get through the last Gillan tour by adapting the way I was singing. When we finished at Christmas I was very, very sad indeed; I had a lousy Christmas, and nothing was further from my mind than Black Sabbath."

The actual process of Ian Gillan's inauguration into Black Sabbath has, like so many stories associated with the band, been elaborated on and twisted over the years. The essence of the tale, that of the singer offering his services in an Oxford pub whilst under the influence of the demon alcohol, is basically correct though as Ian affirms. "This is what really happened. Tony phoned me and suggested we have a talk so we agreed to meet up halfway between where I was living, in Reading, and where Tony was in Birmingham. It wasn't actually in Oxford either, it was a pub called The Bear in Woodstock. Now, some of my memory of that day is very good because I actually had a car crash on the way up there, some bugger rammed me up the arse, so I arrived in an L shaped car and not in the best of moods. The other thing I remember was that Tony's greeting to me was 'Cor, you're a big bugger aren't you?'

Meeting in a pub turned out to have its merits of course but we all got along so famously that we just got totally pissed, I mean, we were under the table and having a great time. We overstayed our welcome because by 7 o'clock the manager was wanting to open up the restaurant and basically kicked us out into the street. So, as you can imagine, as to what we actually spoke about the memory is a little fuzzy. Somebody must have taken me home and the first phone call I received was from my personal manager Phil Banfield who said, almost word for word "If you're going to make career decisions do you think we could consult on them first?" Of course I had absolutely no idea what he was talking about until he explained. "Apparently yesterday you agreed to become the new singer for Black Sabbath!" Somehow the press had got hold of it and phoned Phil before I had even got out of bed!"

Black Sabbath was now, once again, under the protective wing of Don Arden. They had broken away from the Arden stable for the Dio endeavour, having their affairs handled by Blue Oyster Cult manager Sandy Pearlman, but had been drawn back like the death star's tractor beam back into Arden's empire. Gillan had heard all the stories but was unconcerned. "Don Arden? I have a lot of time for Don. He is from that old school of managers who will threaten to break your legs if you don't do as he says but he gets things done. You might not like the way he gets it done but it's done nevertheless. Sure he can lose his temper. Actually he threatened to break my legs once. Why? It was personal, we got it sorted out the next day. I have a lot of respect for him, had some good times with Don. He's a great guy. One thing you should make very clear. Don Arden didn't manage Black Sabbath. He owned Black Sabbath"

A fable has sprouted since those days that the alliance of Gillan with Iommi and Butler was never actually intended to be presented as Black Sabbath but was to be projected as a new Hard Rock 'Supergroup'. This postulation has been taken as gospel and expanded upon over time but, according to Ian, has little credence. "I have no idea where this 'Supergroup' idea came from, certainly not from any of us" he counters. "All that 'Black Purple' and 'Deep Sabbath' stuff was bloody nonsense. From our first conversations we were very clear about discussing myself joining Black Sabbath and there were never any talks I was party to that put forward the idea of creating a new group. The timing was spot on for me because after the Gillan thing I had got wind of a mooted Deep Purple reunion but that was going to take some time as everyone was deeply involved with their various musical enterprises. The guys had started to talk about it though and it looked like it could happen. Basically I needed to fill in the time between so Black Sabbath was a perfect opportunity."

Geezer Butler, speaking in 1997, did not quite see things the same way. "That 'Born Again' album with Ian Gillan. That wasn't supposed to be Black Sabbath. That was the manager and the record company insisting we use the name and I was opposed to it but they are the ones who can turn the tap off when it comes to paying for everything so it became a Black Sabbath album. It wouldn't be the last time that happened either."

Geoff Nicholls too saw things in sharp contrast to Gillan. Is this another case of a singer not being in the loop? "Geezer's right about that" the keyboard player says backing up his band mate. "That album was designed as a new 'supergroup'. They didn't want to call it Black Sabbath at all because, well, it was Ian Gillan wasn't it! How could that be Black Sabbath? It's possible Ian might not have been put in the picture about all of that, that's for him to say. Well, anyway, the record company got their way again and so Black Sabbath it was. It's all about selling albums at the end of the day and that is, as an artist, an argument you will always lose with a record company. Geezer was very pissed off about that I can tell you."

For many onlookers, especially hardened fans of Deep Purple and Black Sabbath, the Gillan–Sabbath collaboration seemed at best an awkward fit. One of the leaps of faith both sets of fans were asked to accept was that Gillan could place himself lyrically into the Sabbath world populated by demons, dragons and other such devilry. To be blunt, Gillan was more than comfortable when warbling on the tried and tested subject matter of wine, women & Rock n' Roll. It was a literary chasm as deep as it was wide that he had to bridge. The UK Rock media of the day scoffed. 'Gillun joins Sabbuf' proclaimed a notice written in deliberately childlike crayon script in one of the better known London Rock mags editorial office. Nobody, it seems, was taking the venture too seriously.

Questions were raised in pubs across the length of breadth of Great Britain and heated arguments ensued. Would Gillan wear a cross? Would he (even could he?) sing 'Iron Man'? How on earth could he bottle that famed ribald onstage humour. After all, if Gillan had famously observed there was 'No laughing In Heaven' just how on earth was he going to cope in Hell?

Seemingly, the singer simply did not see a problem and viewed the entire enterprise in more basic terms. "That's just the press again isn't it?" Ian ponders before explaining his take on the perceived mismatch of styles. "Look, we just look to make the music with people who can play well and have some credibility. I never saw any dark side to Black Sabbath at all. It never entered my head. Maybe when they were 18 or 19 or something it was there but that is just a tag they have to live with. The reality is very different. You know, a very wise lady who used to manage one of the bands I was in during the 60s once said to me "Be very careful about how you make your first big success because you will be judged by that for your entire career. Nobody will ever see you for anything other than what you did the first time." I think that about sums up Black Sabbath."

His predecessor Ronnie James Dio found the alliance surreal to say the least. "I was expecting them to try and patch things up with Ozzy or go for a certain type of singer but never in a million years would I have guessed Ian Gillan. The guy's voice is just too distinctively un-Sabbath. Ian Gillan has an amazing voice for Deep Purple. That fact is beyond question. It was never going to work with Sabbath and I remember thinking some clown in a record company who knows nothing about music is responsible for this. Everyone knew there was no way in Hell it could last."

Although the collective media, many fans and even former Sabbath personnel found the prospect of Ian Gillan with Black Sabbath too much of a stretch of the imagination to even contemplate. The Devil and his minions never figured highly, and then only allegorically if ever mentioned, in the Deep Purple and Gillan catalogue. The singer himself had no such qualms. "I never contemplated not joining the band for any reason. Tony asked, I said yes. The whole thing was very attractive, nothing scary or spooky at all. Tony and Geezer are both great players who have had a great deal of deserved success. Of course I had heard Black Sabbath on the radio and I was familiar with the music in that way but I never sat down to listen to them to unearth any 'hidden' meanings in the songs or any of that crap. This goes way back to all those guys like Buddy Holly, Chuck Berry, Elvis and back further to all the original Blues players which is where Heavy Metal comes from. If you believed everything you read they were all supposed to be in league with the devil. It's just bollocks. Tony is supposed to be the Godfather of Grunge but as a musician he's a Blues man through and through. He has written a hundred world class heavy Blues Rock riffs and inspired literally thousands of bands so all credit to him for that. I'm pretty sure the devil had

Ian Gillan in Dallas. Pic: Rich Galbraith.

no hand in it though. I certainly never saw him. The bogeyman with Black Sabbath doesn't exist, it's just a Rock n' Roll band like the rest of us."

Keen to find evidence of Gillan's ill fit the official press photographs would be seized upon as damning indictments of the singer's lack of suitability. Iommi and Butler were fashioned in the expected black leather, Ian more casual and looking like he had just stepped out of, er ... Gillan. "I never stuck to the dress code because that just wasn't me" he states. "The boys never presented me with an inauguration crucifix or anything. I think the only thought I had about any 'image' for me fronting the band was to remind myself to buy a pair of black leather trousers but that was only because I needed a new pair of pants to wear onstage."

The singer did admit to contemplating a fashion left turn, actually trying on some of Tony's stage wear but thought better of it. "The press made a huge thing of it of course, because I wasn't wearing the black uniform. I recall reading all this garbage about how I was breaking the Sabbath tradition and that the fact that I was wearing denim and the guys were wearing black leather was evidence of my unhappiness with the whole thing. Totally untrue. In actual fact we never, ever discussed it, not even in social conversation. I don't think the level of respect from the fans or the press would have gone up if I had walked out onstage dressed head to foot in black swinging a crucifix. In fact I think I would have been a laughing stock. It was very simply a case of Ian Gillan singing for Black Sabbath. No big deal."

Working up the material that would be offered to the expectant public, Tony Iommi, Geezer Butler and Ian Gillan spent a month long period in a small Birmingham studio crafting songs with Iommi's old ally Malcolm Cope of Quartz on the drums. "I'm pretty sure all the songs we worked on ended up on the album" reckons Malcolm. "We worked up quite a bit of music before Ian came on the scene and when he arrived I can remember him writing up lyrics in the studio. I just kept all of the drums really simple because I knew Billy was coming in to do the actual recording. Bill wasn't in the country, he was stuck in America for some reason, so Tony asked me down to get all the songs ready for the album." It would only be after the tracks were hewn to a state of readiness for recording that Bill Ward was flown over from North America. "Bill arrived to do the actual recording and I stayed on throughout the album helping Bill out. I would drive him around, get him whatever he needed, sort stuff out for him. Bill was always a lovely bloke. Bill put down the drums just great, no problem there. He had some emotional problems at the time though I remember."

As already illustrated Cope and Iommi had been friends for many years and it was only natural for the guitarist to call on Malcolm for these sessions. Ian Gillan sums up his disappointment upon hearing Bill's news. "Bill came to us half way through doing the record and said "Look guys, I don't think my health is up to it and I can't do the tour. I'll let you down if I try to carry on." So we completed the record and Bill did a wonderful job on that. The guy was just very ill at that point and did the right thing by being completely honest with us and taking time out to get himself sorted. I thought he did a fantastic job on the album and it was a big shame we couldn't take him on the road. Lovely guy. The plan from day one was to do a world tour with Bill Ward on drums. He was never signed on to session just for the album. He was in the band. We all really wanted it to happen with Bill but the timing was wrong for him."

"The 'Born Again' album was a bit of a difficult one. Quite strange in a way because we really did not want to call it Black Sabbath" said Tony Iommi nearly a decade after the event. "We all had our problems and Bill's were getting the better of him. He had kicked the bottle but the alcohol was back in the picture in the studio so he had to go and sort himself out. He knew it and, credit it to him, he admitted it and did the best thing. There was a lot of booze around unfortunately." Bev Bevan, longstanding friend of Tony Iommi's, and known for his successes with The Move and Electric Light Orchestra stepped into the breach. "There was never anyone else in the frame other than Bev. Tony and Bev are good friends from way back. I believe the whole thing took just one phone call. Sorted." Ian reckons.

The question has to be asked though—why not Malcolm Cope? He was there, had worked up the songs so knew the material intimately and was an old ally. "I don't know really" Malcolm ponders. "I would have still been busy with Quartz at that time and Bev was a big name too. I never really thought about it actually. It wasn't only Tony that knew Bev, I knew him too. Bev used to actually manage me back in 1968. I was in a band called Stacks and he was still in The Move. We all knew each other. Bev was a name though so I think that was probably it at the end of the day."

Ian Gillan certainly gave everything he had on 'Born Again' and delivered his most aggressive vocal performance to date. Many of Gillan's admirers cite 'Born Again' as the pinnacle of his vocal achievements, the singer giving his vocal chords little in the way of respite ranging from throat tearing howls to the stratospheric choral wails of the title track. Tony Iommi too seemed to have been lent further inspiration, both on the riff front and with a collection of commendable lead solo performances. The album certainly hangs together well as a complete piece of work. It even contained a gaggle of tracks that almost warrant the title of classic in the mechanical drive of 'Zero The Hero', the unique British schoolboy humour evident on 'Disturbing The Priest' and the quite wonderful vocal performance of the title track. The two instrumental interludes, 'Stonehenge' and 'The Dark', appeared to provide a lineage to some very similar, subterranean sonic experiments Geezer had dabbled with in the 'Mob Rules' sessions.

The faster paced 'Trashed', hung on Geezer's inventive bass lines and topped with a starkly Luddite Iommi riff, seemingly captured a page out of Gillan's mental scrapbook of drunkenly careering cars around the Brands Hatch circuit in a dream state, was indeed a cerebral cut and paste job. "That could have been quite nasty and it was a bit of a wake up call. Hilariously funny afterwards but scared the living daylights out of me at the time. Richard Branson had a go kart track at The Manor which I decided to tackle in a car. That's why I mentioned Brands Hatch in the lyrics because I was on a bit of a fantasy trip. Unfortunately I was blind drunk. I hit this pile of Tyres and before I knew it I was completely out of control and rolling upside down. In my drunken haze I realised I was in fact heading towards the swimming pool. Luckily the car ground to a halt a matter of inches before the water. Good job too because I was properly strapped in and in my inebriated state it took what seemed like forever to get out of the thing. If I'd have gone in the drink that might have been the last of me. I can't imagine what I was thinking. I can imagine the obituary 'Deep Sabbath singer dies in drowning incident on go kart track' That could have been historical."

In a somewhat diplomatic exclusion from Ian he failed to mention that the totalled car was not his but belonged to a certain Mr. Ward of the parish. The band had decided to forego the expense of hiring cars and shelled out for a batch of Ford Granadas for transportation. Purchased from road crew-cum-car dealers the idea was to sell the cars on at a profit after the tour. Understandably the drummer was not best pleased to discover his brand new investment upside down. "Ian was very lucky that day" reckons Geoff Nicholls. Apparently when the overturned Granada finally ground to a halt it was not only precariously close to the swimming pool but also the local canal, where Gillan had his boat moored. "Ian was so unbelievably drunk. If he had actually gone in the canal we would not have been able to see him because it was so dirty. The water was pitch black and covered in green scum. He was so close to the edge but he miraculously walked away without a scratch. Bill was not too pleased but he decided to get his own back."

Having walked away from the car crash unscathed the singer still had a mind for yet more pranks. It would be his undoing. Gillan found a ladder with which he intended to climb in through Tony Iommi's bedroom window and create some further mayhem. Instead he drunkenly lurched through the window, smashing his head on an iron radiator on the way down. "There was blood everywhere!" laughs Geoff. "We thought he must have come a cropper in the car but he was completely uninjured. Then he goes and smacks himself on the head trying to ransack Tony's room. I could not believe how pissed he was that night. I don't think he felt a thing. Funnily enough, while we were recording, Ian chose to live in a tent in the grounds. On more than one occasion though Tony and I caught him creeping back into the house to sleep late at night. Anyway, Bill and Paul Clark got together, blew Ian's tent up and sank his boat!" The singer's temporary canvas abode would not be the only item on Black Sabbath's detonation list either. "We had a lot of fun at The Manor" continues the keyboard player. "They planted a concussion bomb in the lake too. Some of the record company A&R people came down with the management to listen to the music and see how we were getting on. When they were invited down to the lake the bomb was exploded to give them a fright. Well, of course, they absolutely shit themselves! It was like a bloody depth charge going off in a war movie! It also stunned all the fish in the lake, which all floated up to the surface."

Still the band had not finished with their waterborne pursuits. "A few days later some of the crew were fishing in the lake and one of the guys, who shall remain nameless, started to throw a javelin in to try and spear the fish. He didn't have any luck but a few days later everyone noticed the water level in the lake had dropped a lot, revealing that it was a man made lake. The javelin had punctured the canvas base! Branson must have loved us."

As well as incurring the wrath of the Virgin magnate Black Sabbath upset a prominent part of the local population. This tale is related on the song 'Disturbing The Priest'. In an effort to gain a chunkier guitar sound Tony Iommi had a speaker stack set up not just in the regular studio but also in an outhouse in the house grounds. With Sabbath very often recording into the small hours, these riffs from the outhouse, unconfined by studio soundproofing, blasted out into the clear Oxfordshire skies. The band also had another method of noise pollution at their disposal in the form of the studio's resident Irish Wolfhound. "This dog used to howl its head off because he wanted to be let out for a piss!" relates Nicholls. "One of us would eventually get around to it at about four or five in the morning." The combination of late night riffing and early morning howling soon produced an unwelcome visitor. "After a few days we got a knock on the door from someone at the local clergy saying that we were disturbing the local priest. He couldn't get a good night's sleep. I think we may have had an official letter to that effect too. We thought they had a bloody cheek because after we had gone to bed they used to wake us up with their church bells!"

'Digital Bitch' did not let the side down either when it came to aural overload. The latter would provide a historical pinpoint for the pace of change within the recording industry. Ian Gillan explains the background thinking to this track. "That whole song was just euphemistic. It was a nascent era of computers being heralded as a new, great age that was dawning. As musicians we felt it too because of the digitalisation of the recording studio. It was all new to us and seemed very important, probably more so than it was in hindsight. It tickled me thinking about this because the same thing happened when we were writing 'Space Truckin' some thirty years ago. Then it was the space age that was promising a grand new age. It just so happened that computers were the revolution when we did 'Born Again'. It certainly was a big change for musicians used to cutting everything onto tape in good old analog. Basically 'Digital Bitch' is the classic rich girl / poor girl story

Black Sabbath with priest disturbing Wolfhound.

given a twist from the time. It's not one person, I never do that, my stories might involve collections of people but never anything you could pinpoint on one person. Just like 'Woman From Tokyo', same thing." Another, more wholesome, woman was also to find her way into the 'Born Again' lyric sheet courtesy of the melancholy 'Keep It Warm' written by Ian for his then girlfriend, and later wife, Bron.

Geoff Nicholls lends some behind the scenes detail to his contributions to the 'Born Again' album. "I worked on the whole album from the powerful choirs in the main riff of 'Zero The Hero' to the swirling drum fills in the verses of 'Disturbing The Priest', which were actually done by keyboards. I wrote 'Stonehenge' too. It was my concept. I had just come back from visiting Stonehenge and had this inspiration for an ethereal idea, originally for Tony to play over. Geezer was messing with a pedal board though and added some things on top, Bill put a water bell on it and it didn't need anything else so Tony never actually played on it. That other little instrumental filler, 'The Dark', was Geezer's thing."

The band completed recording at The Manor played out and somewhat porked out too. Richard Branson's 24 hour on hand cook had noticeably increased the band's waistlines. "We all had to go on a major diet when we left that place!" laughs Geoff.

Diplomatic to a tee, Ian Gillan told 'Sounds' magazine in 1983 "There was a bit of a cock-up with the studio time when we finished the album and I had already planned a short holiday—and it was great to be able to just go away knowing that Tony and Geezer would be at the mix." However, as that statement was being broadcast other, less savoury, remarks were apparently being uttered out of press

ear shot. Before long, word got out in a subsequent 'Kerrang' magazine article that Gillan in fact hated the mix.

Questioned in later years regarding the sonic quality of 'Born Again' the man had another story to offer but was still typically blunt. "It's crap. There is no other word to describe it" states Ian firmly and with no less rancour than his first whispered protestations to 'Kerrang' back in 1983. "When we finished the album I stood behind the desk at The Manor in Oxford and gave it one final listen and it was fucking great. It wasn't just great, it was monstrous. I remember the smiles in the room. I took a cassette of that mix, which I thought was final. That's what I was told. The next thing I hear is that Geezer is unhappy because he thought the bass wasn't loud enough. So, he took it down to London, remixed the whole thing and from that point on radio refused to play it. It was bloody awful plain and simple—a total fucking disaster. The band was great, the record was great but it was issued to the public in a form that was wrong. It was crap and you have to lay the responsibility for that firmly on Geezer's doorstep."

There is an opposing side to this supposition though, with Geoff Nicholls defending Geezer Butler's role in the final mix. "First of all, it wasn't Geezer that remixed it" he states for the record. "It was in fact the whole band, after Ian had taken a break. Tony Iommi was in charge just as he always has been. Tony has final say on everything despite what anyone else says. He is the decision maker. The tracks were adjusted because at that time American radio had this nasty habit of compressing the hell out of everything so you needed to present the sound of the album in a certain way to cope with this. If you didn't do it there was a great danger of the thing sounding shit on U.S. radio. I do remember that we also suffered from a batch of crap studio tapes, which didn't help. The record was finished, sounded great in the studio but when you played it on a normal cassette player in the car it sounded dreadful. There was a lot of work done on it after that."

The 'Born Again' album, it is true, manages to portray an almost primitive, garage like quality that could either be considered 'raw' and befitting or just plain bad. It would obviously strike a lot deeper into the Rock n' Roll conscious than at first admitted. As is now widely recognised, Guns n' Roses either borrowed heavily from 'Zero The Hero' for their 'Paradise City' hit or Slash was struck by the unnatural rarity of creative lightning striking twice. Those cheeky chappies The Beastie Boys too bounced all over the charts in later years with 'Fight For Your Right To Party' brazenly sporting a riff that could have been simply stripped straight out of 'Hot Line'.

If the final mix had raised Gillan's mood to near

boiling point the package it was delivered in blew more than a few gaskets. "The baby. That was Don Arden's idea. Perfect isn't it?" Ian's famous 'Kerrang' magazine quote, "I saw the cover then puked, then I heard the record then puked" has become legendary. Looking back, did he really feel so disgusted? "I think I was" he reckons. "I was certainly very, very disappointed because the record I had made was absolutely bloody fantastic and it had been ruined behind my back. So when I saw the cover I just thought this has to be a joke. C'mon, somebody tell me this is a joke right? But it wasn't. It was the real thing.

I can remember looking at this thing. A bright red baby with fangs, two horns and long fingernails and just thinking to myself that this about summed the whole thing up. It was just so Black Sabbath. I would have been happier if Don had put a lump of cheese with two horns on it for the cover because at least they would have been honest. It was just so unclassy. In a way it didn't matter what the songs were like, how good I was onstage or anything because it all just boiled down to that baby. That's all people would remember. Everywhere I went promoting that record, all I saw was that fucking baby. Strangely though, over the years that cover has become almost as famous as some of the well known Sabbath album covers because it was just so awfully bad. What was absolute rubbish twenty years ago is now an ironic classic. I've come to accept the baby in my life now. It's been a struggle." Cheese had not only been present in an allegorical graphical sense as the schoolboy pranks continued unabated. "Tony placed this lump of mouldy cheese under Bill's pillow" giggles Geoff. "It was there for weeks and Bill never noticed!"

For the ensuing world tour Black Sabbath's stage set, a beast of literal monolithic proportions, would go down in history. Known at the time to have been a right royal cock up, the fibre glass menhirs that adorned the stage of the Reading Festival would become immortalised by the makers of the spoof movie 'Spinal Tap'. Here's how it happened according to Ian Gillan. "We did stage rehearsals at Light & Sound Design in Birmingham. While we were there the production designer asked us if we had any ideas about a stage show. It really was a case of us all looking at each other with blank faces and going "I dunno", "I dunno", ... So then Geezer said "Yeah, I've got an idea. What about Stonehenge?" So the next question was "How big?" to which Geezer famously replied "Life size of course." That's how we ended up with a plastic Stonehenge stage set so big we couldn't use it anywhere. Spinal Tap, those clever fellas, simply turned the thing upside down. Well, we started rehearsing at the NEC in Birmingham and

Geezer Butler. Pic: Rich Galbraith.

this Stonehenge thing arrived. As the crew were loading it in you could see it was just ludicrous. The bloody things were 40 feet high. I don't think anybody was laughing at the time. It wasn't just the fact that they were so big, you were also bloody nervous in case one of the bloody things fell on top of you."

This most controversial of Black Sabbath formations tested the water in the icy climes of Scandinavia, opening up the proceedings in Oslo at the Drammenshalle on the 18th of August supported by up and coming Danes Pretty Maids. Captured by the clandestine microphones of eager bootleggers Sabbath were ambitiously blending a collection of tracks to appease fans of both new and old standing. From 'Born Again' the band ploughed through the less than obvious 'Hot Line' along with 'Born Again', 'Zero The Hero', 'Disturbing The Priest' and 'Digital Bitch'. Besides traditional Ozzy era fare would also sit 'Heaven And Hell' and the cuckoo in the nest that was 'Smoke On The Water'. Gigs on these dates would see the welcome addition of 'Rock n' Roll Doctor' and the quirky 'Supernaut'.

With 'Smoke On The Water' in the set rumours filtered through of the possibility of Bev Bevan's heritage with Electric Light Orchestra somehow being represented. Word was that ELO's 'Evil Woman' had been rehearsed and, perhaps, even performed live. The quite comprehensive bootleg tape trail failed to capture it either in sound check or a live gig situation and Ian Gillan finally wishes to lay this apparent myth to rest. "I don't ever remember us ever discussing doing any ELO songs or rehearsing any. More press speculation I think. Bev was just the drummer you know, just like I was just the singer at that point. I think I would have remembered doing 'Evil Woman'. One of us might have said it as a joke and then it got blown up as these things do. Contrary to what people may think or have read being a part of Black Sabbath for me was in many ways a lightening of the load because I purposely did not get involved in any 'band' discussions. I left all of that up to Don, Geezer and Tony. It was their thing. I was just there to turn up, sing, entertain the audience and that was it."

Geoff Nicholls though does broker some previously undisclosed information that runs contrary to Ian's memory and pushes the pendulum arm back into the 'supergroup' direction. If 'Deep Sabbath' was ever going to plunder the classic Purple material one song had, by its very title, to be top of the list. "We messed around with 'Black Night' too" he divulges. "We just jammed it, played it at sound checks quite a few times but never live onstage. It was on the list of possibles sure."

And 'Evil Woman'? Fact or fiction? "I think with the ELO songs it was much more of a mess around. Yes, we had a crack at a few. It was more of a mess around kind of thing. Tony would start a chord sequence and we'd all jam along until we couldn't remember how it went and some really horrible chords would make us all fall about laughing! It was all done in a joking about kind of way. If we had managed to get one of them right it may well have turned up in the set. 'Black Night' was talked about a few times and would have fitted in really well." One left of centre track that did occasionally work its way into the live set though would be totally unexpected. "We did a full length version of the Shadows song 'Apache' a few times live" discloses Geoff. "It was quite funny because the kids loved it in Europe but they were very bemused when we did it a few times in America."

A short burst of dates into Sweden, adding 'Keep It Warm' into the set at the Johanneshoves Isstadion in Stockholm, Finland and Denmark was all that was to prepare them for their real baptism of fire at the Reading festival on the 27th, or to give the event its proper title the 23rd Annual Jazz, Blues & Rock Festival. Paradoxically, as Sabbath ushered in their new age a spent Thin Lizzy would top the bill on the other night to signal the end of their reign, Phil Lynott's words to 'The Sun Goes Down' proving prophetic and deeply moving. The gig itself comprised a diverse billing of acts spanning the likes of the ascendant Marillion, Ten Years After, fellow Brummies Magnum, Mama's Boys, Hanoi Rocks, Heavy Pettin', Lee Aaron and bludgeoning Canucks Anvil plus an eclectic cast of Pop and Indie bands. The festival organisers must have been rubbing their hands with glee with the realisation they had captured two pivotal moments of genuine Rock history.

Most UK press reports of the Reading show would emerge as cursory, dismissive or both. Scorn would be poured upon the band's bare faced cheek in cranking out 'Smoke On The Water' but on the day the massed ranks of fans lapped it up. When Iommi launched into Ritchie Blackmore's most famous of riffs, which upon analysis bears common traits with the mightiest of Tony's own distinguished offerings, the Hampshire night sky was bathed in applause and ecstatic cheers. As the lights dimmed over the silhouettes of the menhirs of a synthetic Stonehenge fans straggled back to their tents side stepping camp fires and passed out revellers, knowing they had been blessed. British fans would not witness the like again.

Ian Gillan has this observation on the inclusion of the Deep Purple set closing standard. "That was totally Tony's idea. He loved the song and thought we should give it a go. We thought it was no big deal, we even still do it to this day! Sometimes if I'm around I'll get up on stage and do 'Smoke On The Water' with Tony and he'll jam with us too. There was no sinister 'Deep Sabbath' plot going on for sure. Tony simply said "How about this then?" and that was it."

From there Black Sabbath crossed the Irish Sea to Dalymount Park in Dublin to headline a further outdoor event topping a thundering evening of Motorhead, Twisted Sister, Diamond Head, Mama's Boys and the vibrator wielding Canucks Anvil. The group would spend much of September proffering their wares in mainland Europe maintaining the set intact with the exception of a relegated 'Keep It Warm'. Ian Gillan grants that, for some reason, Black Sabbath lyrics would have trouble registering. "I kept on forgetting the words. I don't know why because I have never had that problem before or since. Those songs just didn't want to stick."

Stuck out on stage with the memory banks flashing a blank warning Gillan resorted to doing what he did best. "He kept on bloody screaming all the time" says Geoff Nicholls with good humour. "Whenever he forgot the words he would fill the space and just go "Aaarrrghhh,haaaa..." really high. It wasn't an occasional thing though, it was every bleedin' show. Tony and Geezer had words with him actually. Tony said "Stop the bloody screaming and just learn the fucking words!" He never did get them though. He even forgot the words to 'Smoke On The Water'!

I loved working with Ian, he was a real character. Sometimes we all used to fall about laughing at his antics onstage. Some nights, because of the smoke,

Geoff Nicholls.

Ian would not see his own monitors, trip over them and fall flat on his face. We all used to howl at that. He also had these Congo drums. His timing on them was crap but it was so very funny to watch. He tried to put them in the middle of the stage so eventually we got one of the roadies to tie string to them and slowly pull them away from the centre of the stage. He would keep trying to play them as he followed them offstage! Ian soon got the message though."

Winding their way through Spain, the Low Countries and Germany Black Sabbath brought along for the ride West Midland kinsman Diamond Head, pushing their grandiose 'Canterbury' album, as openers. One of the German dates on the 'Born Again' jaunt would go down, for Geoff Nicholls at least, as the very worst gig of his life. Most concerts simply blur to hardened road veterans but this particular show will stay with the keyboard player forever more. "Usually if you have had a crap day you can look forward to the gig and forget everything for a while" he surmises. "This gig, somewhere in Southern Germany, was just the absolute worst. Most of the German gigs had been just great but with this one everything that could go wrong did. Firstly, it was fucking freezing and it had taken hours to get to this dump, which was in the middle of nowhere. It was a really horrible bus ride over bad roads so as well as being cold there was no chance of sleep. We all turned up grumpy, tired and in a very bad mood. We got to the motel and it was the poxiest place you could imagine. The rooms were so small you didn't even have enough floor space to open your suitcase. The toilet was outside too and the walls were so thin you could hear people breathing next door I'm telling you. Oh well, I thought, let's just get to the gig."

It got worse. Much worse. "I walked into the gig and found they had set my keyboards up in the fucking dressing room!" he exclaims in disbelief. "I couldn't fucking believe it. So I started to think—is this a joke? But it wasn't. The stage was small but not that bloody small. They seriously thought I could play the gig in the dressing room and do harmony vocals from there too. It was impossible because of course I provided a lot of cues and intros for the songs so how could I do that if I couldn't see anyone? I went apeshit and pushed all my gear onto the stage. When the gig started everything broke down. Ian forgot his words again and his voice went, Geezer was doing his nut, Tony lost his monitors, the whole sound system was fucked. Fortunately we only ever had one gig like that!"

Suitably limbered up and with teething glitches ironed out Iommi and co. braced themselves for the big prize, North America. Rehearsals for this leg took place at the Maple Leaf ice hockey Stadium in Toronto during October, the tour set list simply adding the Dio era tour de force 'Heaven And Hell' to the song roster. Unfortunately, the opening night of the tour would see the resurrection of something Ian Gillan had been vainly trying to shut away behind a locked door in the recesses of his mind—Don Arden's baby. "I noticed this dwarf hanging around on the day of the show which obviously piqued my curiosity. When we got into the production rehearsal this dwarf was there again. What happened was so mind boggling that we all had to pinch ourselves afterwards to make sure we had really seen it with our own eyes. The rehearsal involved an intro tape of a new born baby, but distorted and flanged through the PA to sound utterly horrible. The dwarf then appeared dressed in red exactly like the baby on the album cover, complete with yellow horns and fingernails, and crawled about on top of Stonehenge before standing up and with a scream falling backwards onto a pile of safety mattresses. It actually got worse though.

The baby's screaming stopped and an ominous bell began to toll and a line of roadies, dressed in monks robes with cowls pulled down sombrely shuffled onstage. I can imagine those roadies all having a good giggle under their cowls. This was the cue for the band to go on. All we needed at that point was a bearded lady, a couple of elephants and a high wire act and I think we could have got that down to perfection. Don Arden thought it was just wonderful but Bev and I voiced our concerns that the whole thing was deeply disturbing and actually in very poor taste. Don basically told us it was show business and to shut up and get on with our jobs. When Don Arden tells you to shut up and get on with it that is exactly what you do so that was that."

The mischievous inclusion of a dwarf in the band's show was an obvious snub to a certain ex-singer. "I bet Ronnie was fuming!" laughs Geoff Nicholls. "First Ozzy had taken a dwarf out on the road with him and then Black Sabbath did the same! He was getting it from both ends." The gig itself will remain forever etched on Ian's memory. "It still staggers me to this day actually. It was a big gig and there were a lot of people there to see us. The screaming baby tape began to roll and the dwarf-baby appeared on top of the monoliths. He fell off on cue but then kept on screaming! The mattress wasn't there. Someone had moved it. We never saw him again."

Geoff Nicholls has this same bizarre episode imprinted on his frontal lobes too. "Just like Ian says the dwarf was prancing along on top of Stonehenge, like he was supposed to. What was supposed to happen next was that the front of house lights would go off and he would take a dive. However, the back lights were supposed to stay on so he could see where to fall. The problem was that nobody had turned the back lights on in the first place so that when the cue came all of the lights went off and he couldn't see a thing. It was pitch black so of course he fell off in the wrong place. We all heard this tremendous screech of "Aaaarrrggghh!" It wasn't part of the show. He had really hurt himself but I don't think anybody cared because it was just so, so funny!"

With his opening Black Sabbath show off to literally a flying start Ian Gillan soon surmised he had problems of his own to contend with. "As the show started the stage was pumped with dry ice. I realised that if that smoke reached my cue sheets I was scuppered but that is exactly what happened. They were very important because, and I don't know why, I had great difficulty in memorising the Black Sabbath songs. I had a book of lyrics made up and hidden behind two monitor wedges at the front of the stage. The idea was I could turn the pages with my feet. I had even rehearsed this at home and it worked out fine. Before I knew it the music had started and I was deep in a dry ice cloud trying desperately to find my notes. The footlights came on and just made the fog thicker so I was totally lost. I was ducking in and out of the dry ice like an idiot, trying to sing the first song but completely having lost it. I ended up racked with laughter."

At the Montreal Forum gig the opportunity was taken by director Lyndsey Clennell to collect two promotional videos of 'Trashed', not actually performed that night but spread to radio as a single, and 'Zero The Hero'. Footing the bill for these Canadian shows and their inaugural foray into the USA, marked by a gig at the Buffalo Memorial Auditorium, New York on the 27th, would be Quiet Riot.

The tour was heavy in all departments with the exception of one. Although the sheer tonnage of riffage, wailing, and rumour mongering was unquestionably as monumental as the megaliths that were hauling in the back of their (often unopened) trucks every night question marks hung over Bev Bevan's suitability to the proceedings. Black Sabbath fans were accustomed to Bill Ward, a man who in the finest traditions of Black Country industrial heritage hit things bloody hard. But Bev Bevan? Mr. Blue Sky? Ian Gillan posted this anecdote on his official website regarding a conversation with a later drummer of his, the notorious Y&T monster skin basher Leonard Haze.

"Man, I came to see you with Black Sabbath in '83. I thought, what's this Bev Bevan from ELO playing drums with Black Sabbath? That can't be right."

I explained that Bill Ward had some health problems and that Bev had stepped in at the last minute, he was a good friend and a nice guy.

"Yeah" said Lenny, "he plays like a nice guy."

Although Black Sabbath's tour was doing some serious business, enough to add a second leg into the following year, back home in England unsubstantiated whispering told of dissent in the ranks. Black Sabbath had shuffled the set around, now opening with the unexpected maelstrom of 'Neon Knights' utilising 'Children Of The Grave' as a closing tune and by all accounts were having a ball onstage. This gossip would slowly gain ground to such an extent that casual biographers have often assumed this perceived tension was concrete and have gone on to describe the U.S. tour in such terms. Once again Ian Gillan squashes this as fabrication.

"There were all these rumours flying around that I hated every minute of it. Nothing could be further from the truth because the year I was involved in Black Sabbath was, to my memory, one long party from start to finish. We became good friends and had a great, great time. Tony is a very funny guy and Geezer is just off this planet. It makes me laugh how the media build up these feuds and push these stories when very often nothing could be further from the truth. We all got along just fine, in fact, much better than that. There never was any animosity, I was having a ball. All those guys I love to bits, Tony, Geezer, Ozzy and Ronnie. We had Ronnie out on the road with us just recently (with Deep Purple) and whenever we sit down to have a chat all we can remember is all the good times we had. The rest are just minor incidents the press just love to latch onto. The truth is I had a big smile on my face for the greater portion of the time I was singing for Black

Ian Gillan on the 'Born Again' tour. Pic: Rich Galbraith.

Sabbath."

Ian is keen to address what he sees as misapprehensions, often repeated in print, that he was either fired or quit the band. Wild speculation according to the singer. "I agreed to join Black Sabbath for one album and one tour. That was the agreement acknowledged by everybody, before one single note was recorded. Everybody knew this when the whole thing was decided upon and I certainly don't recall anybody ever suggesting the band be called anything else. All these things were just made up, supergroups, Deep Sabbath, playing ELO songs,... All just garbage.

I never viewed Sabbath as a long term thing. How could I? Myself, Tony and Geezer all knew that once the world tour was over I would be teaming up with Deep Purple. Of course, I read in the press that I had walked out but that was just conjecture. I made a deal and I stuck to it. We all parted on amicable terms. Would I have stayed on if things were different? If Deep Purple wasn't happening I would have seriously considered it but that was the situation so that, even hypothetically, is something I don't know. There was certainly nothing amiss with the relationship between the band members. Working with the boys was a blast, I had a seriously fun time but the Purple thing was always there from day one and pretty much on schedule for when I came out of Sabbath. It all slotted in very nicely as it happens."

The vocalist's line though is not endorsed by Geoff Nicholls. "I remember this very clearly because it all tied in with this new thing that Geezer had" he recalls. Butler, apparently, had issued a dictat that he was not to tour for any period longer than six weeks. "Geezer wanted this and he got his way. Tony and I just wanted to tour non stop but Geezer said no. So, that's what we did. We did six weeks then had a break. That was intended to be for two weeks, then a further leg in the USA was due. The shows were all there and mapped out. Trouble was, Ian Gillan didn't come back. Someone, somewhere lost a lot of money on gigs that should have happened but didn't.

If Gillan was always intending to go back to Purple then we were all unaware of it. That includes the crew who went out on the road with us. Anyone will tell you that the crew know everything, sometimes before the band. Possibly it was a big secret Tony and Geezer kept to themselves, but I can't see it. We were on a roll. We were all raring to go, keep the momentum building because 'Born Again' was selling very well, it wasn't slowing down and we were drawing some pretty big crowds. An extra six weeks of dates to big audiences would have sold us a lot of records. The video for 'Zero The Hero' was just out too so when Ian left they stopped pushing that. The promotion for 'Born Again' was never finished and it cost us."

Tony Iommi also saw things differently too. Speaking in 1986 he remembered the 'Born Again' tour as a confused period. "The tour was a bit up and down, because we had the people coming to the shows and buying the record but the press was really letting us have it. First there was a big stink because we played 'Smoke on the Water', which I really enjoyed playing, then they really didn't like Ian being there for some reason. For us it made sense, and the fans loved it too. It was just the press really. The Stonehenge disaster didn't help either."

Was the guitarist aware Deep Purple was beckoning for Gillan? "Oh yes, of course we knew. Actually, we might have known before Ian! We knew Deep Purple was getting back together a long time before it was in the press but Ian was being tight lipped. The band was still good, the shows were great and Ian certainly kept everyone's spirits up. It was quite funny about the Deep Purple thing actually because we knew that he knew and he was trying to guess if we knew."

With Ian Gillan having flown for the glory of a resurrected Deep Purple, Tony Iommi and Geezer Butler engaged in talks with Ozzy to try and entice him back into the fold. Meetings took place between the musicians and a union was apparently agreed in principle but would be blocked by the powers that be. "Just after Ian went we all agreed to get back together" says Iommi. "We were all keen but we couldn't work out the business side of things in the

Bob Daisley. Pic: Rich Galbraith.

end."

In 1983 Bob Daisley received a surprise telephone call. "It was Ozzy" says Bob. "He was in a jam and needed a writer for his next album 'Bark At The Moon'. It must have been a bit humbling for him to call I suppose. Well, in spite of everything we had remained friends and so I took up the offer. The album led to a full world tour with America and Japan. I like Tommy Aldridge as a bloke. He was good to work with, a great, great live drummer but I still didn't believe he was right for the band. That should have been Lee there. In fact this showed up in the studio too because we used to get the drums down a lot faster with Lee. I thought Jake E. Lee did a phenomenal job filling Randy's shoes. He had started off trying to make his mark under this huge shadow cast by Randy and really did well. The pressure really was on him but he stuck to it and did it in his own style too which greatly impressed me. We wrote quite a bit together." One unused song Jake E. Lee brought along for use on the album was entitled 'The Rapture'. Written when still a teenager, Lee had the song worked up, although Ozzy apparently could not find a suitable vocal melody to tag onto it.

Whilst still in the employ of Ozzy the bassist was thrown in at the deep end for an intensive fortnight with a mutual friend of both Daisley and Ozzy when he guested for Gary Moore's live band temporarily. "I did the 'Emerald Aisles' video" laughs Bob. "Five days to learn 14 songs from scratch and then be filmed playing them! That was a tough one but we pulled it off. Fantastic shows and Gary was a really nice bloke. Of course he knew the score with Ozzy but said to me "If ever you're not with Ozzy give me a call." Well, later I did make that call and I stayed with Gary off and on for quite some time." Bob would over the years, at the last count, feature heavily on six Gary Moore albums including 'Victims Of The Future', 'Run For Cover', 'Wild Frontier', 'After The War', 'Still Got The Blues' and sessions on 'After Hours'.

Following the 'Bark At The Moon' sessions Aldridge would find himself replaced by the legendary moustachio'd figure of Carmine Appice as the drum stool position became more like a game of musical chairs. Daisley succinctly wraps up the occupancy for the next term. "They let Tommy do the album, then fired him—got Carmine Appice in then fired him halfway through the tour and got Tommy back in!"

'Bark At The Moon', hit the racks in December of 1983. The album needed to fare well as back in the parallel universe of Black Sabbath their latest release 'Born Again' had tested fans loyalty to near breaking point and won through. The 'Bark At The Moon' album would provide Ozzy completists with the challenge of attaining both the European and American versions the two territorial variants differing in both artwork and song content. The U.S. version has the Ozzy logo in yellow and red whilst the Euro outing is in yellow and blue.

The track 'Spiders' replaces 'Slow Down' for America and vice versa for the rest of the world. Strangely 'Forever' was re-titled 'Centre Of Eternity' for the U.S. market. If fans were not confused enough the two pressings came with completely different track orders. A 12" single of the title track was released in the UK upfront to promote the album. This release too proved collectable as a limited run silver vinyl edition with an unreleased tongue in cheek track 'One Up The B Side' and the American album track 'Slow Down'.

'Bark At The Moon' fared well gaining a foothold inside the Billboard top twenty. In the UK the title track single, backed by a video in which Ozzy is garbed in full blown movie style werewolf disguise, gave Ozzy his biggest solo single success to date. 1983 was also notable for an Ozzy recording that would largely go unnoticed by fans but by warrant of association prompt a media furor a decade later. Ozzy had donated a lead vocal track to the song 'Shake Your Head (Let's Go To Bed)' for the Was (Not Was) album 'Born To Laugh At Tornadoes'. Apparently unbeknown to Ozzy he had replaced an earlier session singer's track that Don Was had felt was lacking the correct feel—that of Madonna. Underneath Ozzy's vocal, Madonna is still quite audible. The track would resurface in the 90s on the compilation 'Hello Dad, I'm In Jail', Ozzy's track still in place but Madonna's contribution supplanted by that of actress Kim Basinger.

Chapter 9

Carmine Feels The Noise

Next in line for recruitment into Ozzy's band was the highly respected figure of drummer Carmine Appice, a man as well known for his trademark moustache as his undeniable percussion abilities. For the first time Ozzy was inviting into the fold a 'name' artist. Appice came to prominence some two decades earlier with the pioneering Rockers Vanilla Fudge. Appice joined the Fudge in December 1966 when, then still operating under the handle of The Pigeons, his predecessor Joey Brennan had left to join The Younger Brothers Band. Bassist Tim Bogert, having been impressed with a drummer he had seen playing a gig at New York's Headliner Club took his band mates to see the guy play and the trio quickly invited the aspiring Appice into the fold.

With Appice in the group a record contract with Atco would follow after Shangri-Las writer / producer George 'Shadow' Morton had caught a live version of The Pigeons new take on the Supremes 'You Keep Me Hangin' On' after being invited down to a gig by manager Phil Basille. Morton cut the track with the group and emerged with the deal from Atco's Ahmet Ertegun and the song was released as the group's first single in the Spring of 1967 backed with an adaptation of La Belle's 'Take Me For A Little While'. Just prior to its release the group had dispensed with The Pigeons name and had become Vanilla Fudge. The group's debut album appeared later in the year and was supported by gigs with Mitch Ryder, Blue Cheer and British imports The Yardbirds as the record began to shoot up the charts in America. Vanilla Fudge' also made something of a minor impact in Europe as well.

In February 1968 the second album, 'The Beat Goes On', appeared and Atco then reissued the 'You Keep Me Hanging On' single (with a new B-side) which reached Number 6 in the States as the buzz on Vanilla Fudge just grew and grew. The band's third album, 'Renaissance', was issued not long afterwards as the quartet continued a hectic touring schedule that saw them play date after date in North America and also venture over to Europe. Vanilla Fudge had a major breakthrough on the American West Coast opening up for the Jimi Hendrix band. The group would also play support on British outfit Cream's farewell American tour in the Autumn of 1968.

In December 1968 Vanilla Fudge played a show in Boston opened up by a new British Rock outfit due to have their debut album released in the new year. The band? Led Zeppelin. The groups would subsequently tour America together throughout 1969. Indeed, members of Vanilla Fudge would figure highly in the incident involving members of Led Zeppelin, a red headed groupie called Jackie and a Red Snapper fish that, Rock n' Roll legend has it, took place in room 242 of the Edgewater Hotel in Seattle, Washington during July 1969.

In February of that year Vanilla Fudge released the 'Near The Beginning' album. A self-produced affair, the album nevertheless featured only four songs, with the entire second side devoted to a live recording of the 'Break Song'. However, by the following year the Vanilla Fudge was history. With Appice and Bogert keen to work on a band project with ex-Yardbirds man Jeff Beck, the group released the swan song 'Rock & Roll' album in September 1969 and played their last show on March 14, 1970 at manager Phil Basille's Action House club. Following the break up of the band assorted former members of Vanilla Fudge went off in a variety of directions.

With the Boogie driven Cactus, Bogert and Appice debuted with an eponymously titled album on Atlantic in 1970. They went on to release five more albums before finally teaming up on that pipedream project with Jeff Beck, as Beck, Bogert & Appice, to cut two albums for Epic in 1973. Beck had quit by the time the 'Live In Japan' album emerged in 1974. A second studio album was recorded without Beck, but never released. Appice enjoyed a quite illustrious career since Beck, Bogert & Appice broke up. After playing with KGB and on an avalanche of hit albums with Rod Stewart in the late 70s and early 80s—Appice actually co-wrote Stewart's huge international hit 'D'ya Think I'm Sexy?' the drummer recorded with guitarist Rick Derringer in the D.N.A. band project. He was in the midst of a run of drum

Carmine Appice, Oklahoma '84. Pic: Rich Galbraith.

clinic master classes in Europe when the world of Ozzy collided with his.

Carmine expands upon how he landed the position with the Ozzy Osbourne band. "I was in the south of France doing some drum clinics and a friend of mine called me and told me Ozzy had fired Tommy and I should call Sharon in London as they needed someone fast. So, I called Sharon and I went to London straight from France and had a meeting and a play. No audition—just a Hang! After few days Ozzy and Sharon told me I was in and we were in business." Implanting Appice into the band necessitated some long distance learning sessions as Carmine reveals. "I went to England to rehearse but in order to get my work visa I had to leave. So, I ended up writing charts for the show and practicing in LA at my house listening to a tape of Ozzy live with Tommy on drums. In actual fact I had only two days of real rehearsing with the band in England." Musically, an outsider might believe interpolating Ozzy's material with Appice's established trademark sound might be difficult for the drummer to accommodate. "My style was a little heavier, less notes and Funk Rock sort of overtones. Tommy plays a bit faster and maybe not as Funk Rock at all. It's hard to describe the difference. I originated my style." When asked if any adaptation to his recognised style took place to fit the Ozzy material Carmine has this to say. "Maybe a little ... but Lee the original drummer of the Ozzy band played like me so the songs were already in my style so I think Tommy had to adjust more than Bob did. I just played whatever happened each night. I had light cues worked out for different parts of the solo but each solo was a little different." The drummer records his impressions of his band members with obvious respect. "All the other musicians were top of the line all of them, the best in their field. I thought Jake was great. In Rough Cutt he was great! He had a great feel and he was killer on stage. I know that Sharon and Ozzy were pushing Jake's image hard to break the Randy thing. Jake just went along and played great and got on with the business of playing. Jake's a unique player. He had a great stage presence and for me the way he played chords using his thumb differently was unique.

I struck up a friendship with Jake as we were the only two American guys in the band and my roadie Andre was the 3rd American so we had some things in common. At the time it was my first bus tour and I couldn't sleep on the bus so we would both stay up all night watching movies on the bus together." Appice's rhythm partner Bob Daisley too comes in for praise. "Bob was better than ever. Bob has got a great groove and sound. He's an easy going guy,

Ozzy 1984. Pic: Rich Galbraith.

flows with any situation. He comes up with melodic bass lines that become hooks for the song. He doesn't overplay. Bob Daisley is the meaning of the saying fat bottom groove." Conversely Daisley has this take on Carmine. "Carmine was very clever on the drums. Too clever sometimes!" he laughs. "He would put a lot of Funk stuff in but in general he was more like Lee than Tommy in style. Carmine would do a lot of drum clinics in the afternoons before a gig so when we played live we could hear all these extra little fancy bits creeping in!"

The European dates, with San Francisco's highly respected Y&T as opening act, would peak with a gargantuan Metal festival in Dortmund, Germany. Featuring the cream of the Heavy Metal world—Iron Maiden, Judas Priest, Def Leppard, MSG, etc., many thought Ozzy's was the standout set. "The Dortmund Festival really stands out" confirms Appice. "It was televised and the band was great. The audience went nuts. I had a great solo that night too which was televised all over Europe."

Carmine's tenure would be interrupted abruptly. The departure was so swift it would come mid tour with a reinstated Tommy Aldridge waiting in the wings. "I left the band because Sharon fired me" Carmine readily admits. "She said my name was too big and they wanted more of a back up player. At the time I was doing a lot of press for the tour and the fact that I was doing master classes at music stores five times a week and receiving lots of press for it. Sharon didn't like that. I was also getting mentioned too much on MTV. JJ Jackson would say "Here are the Ozzy concert dates with the Legendary Carmine Appice on Drums." Sharon didn't like it. In fact she told me I need to start my own band. So, I did. I started King Kobra straight after Ozzy."

Appice maintains the band knew the score before taking him on. "I talked to Sharon and Ozz before I joined and told them I did get a lot of Press in the U.S. and that I did clinics and Master Classes while I was on tour which generated a good amount of press. That same year Ozzy was in 'Oui' Magazine in the U.S. Everyone was in it. Besides Ozzy there was Motorhead, Mötley Crüe, Joe Perry and me. We all had 5–10 pages in the mag and we were on a Calendar each on a different month. My issue sold over 3 million copies and Oui gave me a big party and an award for the issue. So I talked about press, bringing up that mag and all. I also ran a drum contest and got press that was covered by national TV in the U.S. and MTV. So, I guess at the time I joined nobody cared but afterwards in the U.S. it got ... weird!"

The omnipresent Daisley had seen the writing on the wall. "Tommy Aldridge turned up for the show in Dallas, his hometown. I could see exactly what was going to happen. Within a few days Carmine had been fired. We did a day's rehearsal with Tommy and then carried straight on as if nothing had happened." Another casualty, albeit unexpected, was Lindsey Bridgwater. "I had done the European dates in the beginning of 1983 with Jake and Don." He relates. "We actually spent quite some time working through the songs. Both Jake and Don were very professional and had done their homework so it was only really topping and tailing to get the songs just right for the road. I didn't have to teach them anything really." Bridgwater would commence the American dates but would not complete the full run. "I left halfway through the U.S. tour. I took it on the chin really but I was very sad to leave. Don completed the tour." Tommy Aldridge's last Ozzy gig would come with the Brazilian 'Rock In Rio' event in front of 300,000 South American fans.

The album ballad 'So Tired' would have two shots at the British charts. Originally launched in March of 1984 it oddly sank without trace. Revamped less than two months later and bolstered by a welcome inclusion of three live tracks—'Bark At The Moon', 'Suicide Solution' and 'Paranoid', recorded in Salt Lake City, Utah on March 18th, an Ozzy Osbourne logo textile patch and another limited 12" coloured

Ozzy & Jake. Pic: Rich Galbraith.

vinyl (this time gold) it hit the top twenty.

After his second Ozzy experience Lindsey Bridgwater was inducted into a potentially exciting band unit led by erstwhile Mott The Hoople and Bad Company guitarist Mick Ralphs. Anticipation was high and although an album, 'Take This' issued in 1983, materialized circumstances around the group were less than stable. The band was scheduled to tour but these plans would wither away leaving a clutch of London gigs as a legacy. "Mick put a lot of his own money into the project" Lyndsey recounts. "We were all put on retainers. The band was hot to trot but sadly it all fell apart when Mick joined Dave Gilmour's band."

Years later Bridgwater would again tread the Rock n' Roll boards as part of former Wings and Moody Blues guitarist Denny Laine's band for touring in Poland and Russia. In 1984 the keyboard player put in a worthy six month spell with the musical 'Blood Brothers'. Occasionally the inkling for Rock still drags him back into the arena, as witnessed by a recent live sojourn with the regrouped cult 60s act Quatermass.

During 1997 Mick Underwood reconvened Quatermass roping in former Deep Purple, Warhorse and Fandango bassist Nick Simper. The initial line-up of this fresh attempt also included the familiar face of guitarist Bernie Tormé and Stonebird vocalist Bart Foley. Both were to opt out and in their stead came former Raw Glory and Northstar guitarist Gary Davis and frontman Johnny Haywood. The band, prompted by Japanese interest, recorded a 1997 al-

Don Airey, Bob Daisley, Ozzy Osbourne, Carmine Appice. Pic: Rich Galbraith.

bum 'Long Road'. Although keyboards for the album sessions were handled by none other than Don Airey for live work as the band went out on a spring '98 European tour the keyboard position was given over to Lyndsey Bridgwater. These days Bridgwater's preoccupations are mainly in the classical field. "I'm rediscovering my classical roots actually" he opines. "Most of the 90s has been spent with the Philharmonic orchestra. I have an absolute passion for Covent Garden but I keep my feet on the ground with a London Blues band too."

And, there is of course the question that Lyndsey cannot avoid, the one that has been passed into Ozzy folklore and handed down in less than hushed tones by successive band members down the years. Is he the man Ozzy got to stand on one leg for the entire duration of a show? Lyndsey stalls. "Ah ... er, ... it was a wind up. I think that could well be me" he offers somewhat sheepishly. "In Ozzy's world it was all a bit surreal at times and I probably am guilty of losing my powers of judgement at times. There was occasion that I put my hand in my pocket to discover Ozzy had peed in it! And, of course, I famously had my eyebrows shaved off too. I endured quite a bit of teasing initially because I was young and sensitive back then. I think the incident in question got exaggerated hugely though. I'm not sure if I even did stand on one leg at all but, yes, the roadies had told me they had an earthing problem onstage. They explained to me that I would be OK if I just kept the one leg off the ground in order to avoid forming a circuit and getting electrocuted! I don't think I actually did it although the memory is a bit fuzzy so possibly I did. I do recall thinking that this must be another bloody wind up."

Ultimately Bridgwater is philosophical yet generous about his tenure with the Ozzy band. "I wanted more for sure but it just wasn't my time" he muses. "In truth I never really seized the opportunity that Ozzy gave to me. There are no regrets, no rancour, no bitterness. Just lots of very pleasant memories. Ozzy actually sent me a letter much letter saying thanks for the good times. I have very fond memories too so I was very happy to receive that." Whilst performing harpsichord in a live performance at the Vatican for his holiness the Pope John Paul's 80th birthday celebrations Bridgwater would be struck by the irony his particular wheel of fortune had circumvented.

With the Ozzy 1983 experience over, the rhythm

section of Tommy Aldridge and Rudy Sarzo's next move unfortunately engendered more anticipation than hard results. On paper the Driver concept seemed a sure bet for success but as the drummer explains the whole venture was stifled by a lack of real band stability. When the debut album emerged it pointedly made no reference to a band unit, only 'Project Driver'. "It was around this time that Rudy Sarzo and I started toying with taking a shot at putting something together. He had just finished up with Quiet Riot and we were both feeling bold. We started auditioning guitarists and singers in LA. After a few months of this our enthusiasm started to wane. There seems to be a large pool of 'journeyman' musicians whose lot in life seems to be applying at auditions. We seem to keep seeing and hearing the same guys. We even resorted to flying people in. We were becoming more discouraged with every passing day. We did manage to come across Tony MacAlpine and did a couple records with him but it ended up being a project . . . not the band that we were hoping to build."

With Driver consigned to the history books Aldridge's next port of call would, quite incredibly, grant both the drummer and Sarzo a degree of adulation surpassing that of even Ozzy. Former Deep Purple frontman David Coverdale had enjoyed acclaim in Europe and Japan with his classy, Blues based Rock outfit Whitesnake. In America though Whitesnake had struggled and by the mid 80s the singer had opted for a radical rethink completely rebuilding the band from scratch. "During this time I was hanging out with John Sykes. He and Dave Coverdale were in town looking for a rhythm section and Rudy and I were looking for a guitarist and singer. I actually met with them to discuss possibilities but they had decided on a bass player and at that point were only interested in my services. I cannot say it wasn't tempting but Rudy and I had a commitment and I am nothing if not loyal. I suppose I made the right decision as we were both asked to join later though it would have been a real blast to have played on that '87 record. Not that I could have done a better job than Aynsley Dunbar, mind you. His drumming is stellar on that record and I seriously question that it could be improved upon. I speak mostly to the opportunity missed. Sometimes you get the bear . . . sometimes the bear gets you."

Sykes would soon be out of the picture and would forge ahead with his own Blue Murder project. Undaunted Coverdale assembled what was thought to be by many a perfect video presentable band as their record company geared the band up for a massive push on the American market. Alongside Coverdale, Aldridge and Sarzo Whitesnake now boasted the guitar partnership of former Sweet Savage and Dio guitarist Vivian Campbell and "The flying Dutchman" Adrian Vandenberg. Not only were the level of talents assembled for the new look band extreme but so was the image. Honed for the video age the band appeared to have spent as much time preparing their image and hair as their music. The landmark '1987' album, which had keyboards courtesy of ex-Ozzy man Don Airey, gave Whitesnake the major success in America the band had strove for so long. In spite of the fresh look given to the band the album contained many songs co-written by Sykes and featured his guitar parts too as well as a rerecording of 1980's 'Fool For Your Loving'. A massive American tour capitalized on a clutch of American hit singles including the Number 1 ballad 'Here I Go Again'.

The ex-Ozzy rhythm section's tenure with the revitalized Whitesnake would put the duo in front of enormous capacity arena crowds promoting escalating sales of the '1987' album. 1989's 'Slip Of The Tongue', although giving the band a top ten U.S. album, saw the band struggling. Coverdale had added former Alcatraz and David Lee Roth guitarist Steve Vai to the line-up and many purists felt Vai's quirky individualism sat ill at ease with the band's traditional hard blues. The follow-up tour also struggled to sell out the same venues earlier dates had packed with ease. Ultimately the Whitesnake hit machine faltered and Aldridge and Sarzo were free agents once more.

For Sarzo it would be the familiar climes of Quiet Riot that would prove welcoming. Aldridge would feature on the highly regarded if overlooked House Of Lords album 'Demons Down' before hooking back up with Sarzo once more with the Manic Eden project. As with Driver, the Manic Eden endeavour, a union of Aldridge, Sarzo, fellow Whitesnake colleague Adrian Vandenberg and vocalist Ron Young promised much but failed to really gel. The album crept out to little fanfare. Tommy Aldridge would ultimately swap the perceived madness of Ozzy for madness of an altogether baser distinction—Ted Nugent.

Ian Gillan shook hands with Iommi and Butler, capping the North American tour at Springfield Civic Center, Massachusetts on the 4th of March 1984 and side stepped straight into the extravaganza of the long planned Deep Purple 'Perfect Strangers' reunion. Black Sabbath would be once more on the search for a singer. Bev Bevan too was caught in reunion fever, teaming up with the ill-fated Electric Light Orchestra II venture. Naturally the way was smoothed once more for the re-entry of Bill Ward, the drummer having made solid progress in his long running battle with the bottle.

Chapter 10

Headless

Adopting a new policy the band opted to seek out an unknown. Fronting up the band with established veterans had kept the Black Sabbath profile high and the PR companies in business but had also made the group a juicy and obvious target for cheap media wise cracks. To the outside world the odd barbed comment and snide jibe must have seemed as ineffectual as peashooters at a bull elephant hide but to the inner circle every word stings. Even the Led Zeppelin members had tortured themselves out of all proportion to the actual gravity of the problem with the very same curse. In short, empires of platinum albums and record breaking tours mentally crumble with one, well aimed journalistic broadside. Bringing in new blood would hopefully rid them of that baggage.

In the Spring of 1984 Los Angeles radio proclaimed with great fanfare that Sabbath had found their man. But had they? Originally hailing from Nashville, Tennessee, Ron Keel had made an indelible impression on the Metal underground with his act Steeler. Keel was lanky, loud and hungry for fame. Fortunately for the singer he stood apart from the swarm of Metal vocalists on the circuit by possessing a certain rustic character to his voice. In short Ron Keel had an edge. The group had debuted with a self-financed single, 'Cold Day In Hell', and it was this track they contributed to the first pressing of Brian Slagel's first 'Metal Massacre' compilation. Keel had been born in Georgia but had moved to Phoenix, Arizona as a child before moving back to the East Coast to wind up in Nashville where he put Steeler together. The band that recorded the single comprised a line-up of Keel, guitarist Michael Dunigan, bassist Tim Morrison and drummer Bobby Eva.

After relocating to Los Angeles, Steeler signed to Shrapnel Records and label boss Mike Varney subsequently helped reshape the group by bringing in Swedish protégé Yngwie Malmsteen. The rhythm section was also superseded by bassist Rik Fox and drummer Mark Edwards. Fox had turned down an earlier offer from veteran whiter than white Pomp act Angel. Produced by Mike Varney, Steeler's debut album featured Le Mans vocalist Peter Marrino in a backing vocalist capacity. Steeler made significant waves on the international Rock scene with export copies in high demand. As a bona fide cult album European fans (the author being one) would be happy to fork out extortionate import prices to hear for themselves if the Californian graffiti that proclaimed Malmsteen as "God" was indeed true. Although an unashamed showcase for Malmsteen the cohesive quality of the album would be one the Swede would struggle to attain in his future career. Overshadowed by the furor of the six-string Scandinavian was the undoubted quality of the songs and Keel's vocal abilities. The group would soon suffer the loss of Malmsteen to his next staging post Alcatrazz and Rik Fox was to leave along with Edwards. Mitch Perry, Greg Chaisson and Bobby Marks replaced them respectively before the group ultimately fragmented. As for the Steeler personnel, following his departure from Steeler, Rik Fox helped to found W.A.S.P. with Blackie Lawless and later formed Sin before being ousted by his band mates who promptly renamed the group Jag Wire. The bassist subsequently attempted to form a band with erstwhile Alien vocalist Frank Starr. Edwards skills would post Steeler be employed with Riot, Burning Starr and Lion.

Having been forced into the sidelines by Malmsteen's presence the vocalist found an easy remedy in order to draw the spotlight back onto the right target by founding a band entitled, naturally, Keel. Fuelled by the legacy of Steeler interest in Keel's new act was keen and he would make rapid progress in convening and promoting this new venture. However, upon a tip off from producer Spencer Proffer it appeared the possibility of landing a bigger fish might be within his grasp. Proffer was hot property, having production credits on the multi platinum 'Metal Health' album of Quiet Riot. Quite sensationally this Los Angeles act, that of course had up until that juncture only merited recognition by their inclusion of a pre-Ozzy Randy Rhoads, had bulleted to national stardom with an infectious brand of gumby Pop Metal. Their star would burn bright if all too briefly. Before their implosion, Quiet Riot had eclipsed all before them.

Proffer and Keel had united to cut demo recordings at the producer's own Pasha Studios in Hollywood. In parallel Proffer was also in negotiation with Black Sabbath as Ron Keel recounts. "Spencer had just signed on to produce Black Sabbath's follow-up to 'Born Again'. Ian Gillan had just left the band. Spencer had heard my voice on the Keel demos and brought me into a meeting concerning the vacant position in Sabbath. I was of course very excited. The opportunity to go from a struggling unsigned LA musician to be the vocalist for one of rock's legendary bands was a dream come true, and I'd be lying if I said I didn't want it. Seeing Sabbath on 'Don Kirshner's Rock Concert' TV show when I was very young was a pivotal moment for me; Sabbath records always had a place on my turntable and I never missed a Black Sabbath concert when they came to my town. I remember once, my father found my hidden Black Sabbath concert tickets and tore them up and threw them away, thinking I was going to be attending some sort of Satanic rally or something, he didn't know it was a rock band." Moves were made to tie up this potential synergy quickly. "I signed a management contract with Spencer Proffer, giving him the rights to negotiate with Black Sabbath on my behalf" affirms Ron.

Rumours in circulation at the time sought to brush off any linking of Ron Keel and Black Sabbath, with one widely promulgated myth, especially in the European Rock press, scurrilously trying to present the connection as nothing more than a mix up. The fable that a cassette of two singers, one on each side but incorrectly labelled, had led Iommi and Butler to believe they were listening to Ron when in fact it was another candidate is common knowledge. There is some truth in this as Geoff Nicholls verifies. "Ron Keel had sent this tape in and I remember it being OK. Tony Iommi phoned him up and it got quite funny because Tony was talking to Ron about this one particular song on which he really liked the singing style. Ron, credit it to him, admitted that he hadn't sang on that song. It was another singer! So yes, there is some truth to that rumour. Ron was still worth checking out though."

Ron Keel goes some way in explaining how the mix up occurred. "Spencer set up a recording session where I was to put my voice on three songs he had handpicked for the new Sabbath album. These were not written by Tony, this was outside material, and I'm not sure who played on the demo. It was not typical Black Sabbath, but commercial eighties metal. The songs were called 'Hunger', 'Metal Victory' and 'Running Wild In The Streets'." In actual fact these tracks, unknown to Ron at the time, had been put down by another of Spencer Proffer's acts of the time, the Canadian Metal band Kick Axe noted for their infectious radio hit 'Heavy Metal Shuffle'. Two of these songs, 'Hunger' and 'Piece Of The Rock', would subsequently turn up on a King Kobra album.

Behind these sessions was a familiar and trusted face on the Californian Metal scene Dana Strum. Antecedent to this Sabbath hook up Strum had proven his worth to none other than Ozzy Osbourne having introduced the double O to Randy Rhoads. Indeed, Strum had originally been slated to form up a proto Blizzard Of Ozz and was later instrumental in the co-ordination and organisation of later Ozzy auditions. Strum was no slouch in the musical department either, at that stage part of the Vinnie Vincent Invasion, setting himself up for platinum success with Slaughter.

Dana still has a good recollection of how the recordings were conducted. "I was asked to do the Black Sabbath vocal audition tape by Spencer, he owned and produced out of Pasha Studios. Later I took that studio from him and prior to that Slaughter cut the drum tracks for our first three albums there, as did Mötley Crüe, Quiet Riot and Ted Nugent. It was known for great drum sounds. The vocals were all recorded on a 24 track tape that we made a copy of. Then, each singer, such as Ron, was recorded as though he was the singer on the tape." Coincidentally, Strum was juggling this project with another incestuous link in the chain. "Meantime, at the same time, I was producing a Ronnie Dio management project called Burn, from Philadelphia."

Ron Keel has a sharp memory for the day itself. "When I walked into the studio, Jake E. Lee was there—I believe Spencer or Dana had requested him to come in and give me a pep talk. Jake shared with me what it had been like for him, getting the gig with Ozzy, what I could expect, advice and insight, and I really appreciated him taking the time to come in and have that talk with me right before the session. Dana Strum in my opinion did a great job producing the vocals on that demo session. He worked me very hard, pushed and pulled me into doing some amazing screams and I remain very proud of my work on that session. I still have a copy of it, and have resisted all requests to make copies of it or even play it for anyone including my wife and band mates. It's a very special piece of my history which I will keep all for myself."

Although singers were in the frame Ron Keel it seems had been singled out for special attention as Dana confirms. "Ron Keel was not just a given. Both Mikey Davis (engineer) and I both thought that Ron would be great due to his range and so on. It was Mikey Davis who had contacted Ron for the audition. Ron was great, great attitude and very hungry. We used just the basic guitar / bass / drums, the Sabbath vibe, to have Ron sing to... and he kicked ass! Great stuff. I wanted the best and nothing but the best out of anyone that I worked with. He was just great and all of what we did should have landed him with a great spot to do the gig. The shit was raw, loud and crude. The tapes were very good and he did have a trip and a half. Many LA guys names were mentioned, we recorded a few during that time but we all figured Ron stood a great shot at it."

The tape was duly dispatched to the Black Sabbath camp and, as hoped for, Keel's promise had obviously shone through. Ron records the next stages of his adventure. "Tony Iommi and Geezer Butler heard the demo and apparently liked it. Arrangements were made for us to meet, and I went to their hotel in Los Angeles. For several days we hung out, talked about music, snorted cocaine and drank a lot. Tony was dating Lita Ford back then, and she would hang out with us from time to time. Tony gave me a song list of classic Sabbath tunes, a killer set that began with 'Neon Knights'. I made a tape of all the songs in order, and spent every day rehearsing with the tape blasting through my PA system while I sang along and choreographed my stage moves."

One of Keel's proposed visual enhancements was to drop to his knees and cross himself "with the sign of the Devil." The singer was as enthusiastic as he was optimistic. "I was determined to knock them on their ass at the very first rehearsal. I was anxious for this to happen, because I knew once we played together it would be a done deal. Unfortunately Bev Bevan, who was their drummer at the time, was involved with other commitments and could not participate. They discussed the possibility of getting Bill Ward back. Tony was very gracious and treated me great." Ron was given a dose of reality though as "Geezer made it clear that I was to be a hired gun and what they really wanted was to get Ozzy back."

Although it seemed as though Black Sabbath was beckoning Ron Keel still had domestic matters to attend to with his own band. This first incarnation of Keel boasted Boston born ex-Steel Assassin guitarist Marc Ferrari and Phoenix native David Michael–Phillips, who had played in an early incarnation of Icon, on guitars along with erstwhile Metal Beast bassist Kenny Chaisson, the brother of onetime Steeler four stringer bassist Greg Chaisson. Assuming the drum role would be Ron Keel's former Steeler colleague Bobby Marks. Judging it only fair to keep his band members in the picture he made a decision to inform them of current events.

"I called a band meeting with my guys in Keel at our rehearsal room, and told them that it looked like this was going to happen for me. The plan was to go on with our debut show, at Perkin's Palace

Bev Bevan with Sabbath in 1983. Pic: Rich Galbraith.

in Pasadena, which was about a week away. They understood this was an opportunity that I had to pursue, and they had great attitudes and a work ethic, which would later propel the band into the upper echelon of 80s Metal acts. I stressed to them that this was still strictly confidential, that no announcement was to be made until everything was finalised." His honesty would prove to be his undoing. "And then as soon as the band meeting was over, I got in my car to go home. Blasting over the radio was an announcement that 'Ron Keel has just become the new singer for Black Sabbath!' Then I got home, turned on MTV, and there it was on the MTV news 'Ron Keel has just become the singer for Black Sabbath!' I don't know who leaked the news but it wasn't me. Immediately it was in all the rock magazines and various industry publications." Although seriously undermined by the premature announcements Ron Keel was still a viable contender and, as promised, Geezer and Tony showed up at Keel's debut gig.

"The time came for the debut Keel show. Tony, Geezer, and Lita came to the gig together, came backstage and hung out before the show. I never spoke to them or saw them again" he says philosophically. When analysing the reasons behind Keel's deferment the singer opines "Granted, there is a world of difference between a Keel concert and a Black Sabbath concert. There was nothing dark or evil about Keel. Our shows were full of smiles, high fives, and rock anthems with a predominantly positive message. Had I been onstage with Sabbath, I would have been the devil in black leather but that wasn't what Keel was about and perhaps Tony and Geezer didn't see what they wanted to see at that gig. It was a great show, the first in a long line of kick ass Keel concerts, and the beginning of something very special in my life and career."

Black Sabbath had, in point of fact, been patrolling

the clubs of Los Angeles in search of a suitable singer for some time. Nobody had been impressive enough on the stage to warrant further communications. Hence the cassette cattle call. "We must have seen tons of singers recommended by all kinds of people" reckons Geoff Nicholls. "We were always at clubs checking these guys out but nobody came close. The problem with most of them was a simple lack of range. We wanted to walk into a club and hear the next Dio, the next Glenn Hughes, the next Rob Halford but we couldn't find anything." He details the required criteria the Californian hopefuls fell short on. "Tony wanted someone who looked the part, could command an audience and sing with a full range. Virtually every singer we saw lacked the very top range. They really struggled with that. The Black Sabbath range is very varied. You need a lot of strength. Ozzy had got that power, well, in the studio at least. A lot of singers would not have been able to sing the material. Power in all ranges—that was the common tie between all the singers Black Sabbath worked with. That's why later Tony then kind of gave up on the search and started checking out English singers again." Dana Strum maintains Ron Keel was under serious consideration for the vacancy. "I never really cared for Keel (the band), no real songs in my opinion, but Ron had great drive and one Hell of a flyin' voice. Great Rock attitude as well. I am not certain as to why he never worked out. As we all know there is a great deal to being and staying in a band, not just your voice as many figure."

With Ron Keel no longer in contention the arrangement between Spencer Proffer and Black Sabbath deteriorated and plans for involvement behind the desk of the next record stalled. Geoff Nicholls believes the proposed Proffer / Sabbath alliance was never destined to come to fruition. "It was a familiar scenario actually. The band had meetings with lots of producers over the years. Some of the very biggest names too but a lot of them never 'got' what Sabbath was about. A lot of these people told Tony Iommi the same thing, like "I love Sabbath, I really understand the band and how you need to sound" and all this bollocks but they never did. Very often producers suggested doing cover versions, which always went down like a lead balloon. Quite a few times the subject of rerecording 'Paranoid' cropped up I remember. Tony Iommi has always worked in a certain way and it's a manner most producers don't like to work."

Over the years the band had learned to be wary of record company decision makers, A&R gurus and prospective producers. Finding people to work closely with saw Sabbath, like so many major Rock artists, fostering an almost impenetrable inner circle of confidantes. It took a lot to break in. Nicholls

Ron Keel. This picture taken just one day after his Sabbath "auditions".

records just one instance, which illustrates the basic lack of respect the band would sometimes be afforded. A supposedly hot new Warner Bros. executive made his presence felt in the recording studio, introducing himself as a longstanding Sabbath fan. "This really young guy came down to the studio to show his face and listen to the new music. After introducing himself he proceeded to tell us the things he was going to do and what else he had been involved in. He also told us he knew what we needed because he was a fan and had listened to all of the old stuff and had ideas to help us.

Tony gave me one of his looks so I knew what he was planning. He plays this Warner Bros. guy a tape and the guy sat there, listened and made notes. When the tape had finished he started to make some comments, that he liked the stuff but he would like to make some changes and he suggested this and that. So, Tony looked at him and said "Have you really listened to our old albums?" The guy said "Yes, of course, I always do my homework." Tony, very casually, replied "Well, you must have some cloth ears then because we've just played you four songs from some demo from the management company. They are not our songs and they don't sound anything remotely like us!"" The humiliating coup de grace was that, in his naivety, the A&R 'expert' had failed to notice Black Sabbath are not in possession of a female singer. "Needless to say he got thrown out on his arse! One of the top guys came down after that. I don't know what happened to the guy in question. He's probably one of the top people in the music industry now no doubt."

So, this was the climate of suspicion any eager producer had to break into. The latest in line would also fall at the first fence. "With Spencer Proffer, he was being really pushed on us because of the Quiet Riot thing. Somebody high up thought he could do the same for Black Sabbath. Tony was never really convinced and when Spencer presented these tapes of other people's songs he wanted Black Sabbath to record that was it—all over. Proffer wanted the band to cover other material, which was, in fact, totally crap. I remember us listening to these songs and not believing what we were hearing. I think Tony said something very close to "What the fucking hell is this? This is just shit!" Basically what he wanted us to record was a very bad copy of the Black Sabbath sound by a band that had no clue at all. Spencer Proffer shot himself in the foot there."

With Keel's name often brokered in the Sabbath rumour mill the singer, describing himself as "a small thread in the tapestry that is Black Sabbath's history", is happy to put forward his view of his part in the complicated labyrinth of eighties Sabbath. "The question remains: was I actually 'in' Black Sabbath? The bottom line is: there was never a contract between the band and me. I never performed live or appeared on a Black Sabbath release. Tony himself told me I was their man, but my belief is that the only singers that were ever truly 'in' the band were Ozzy and Dio." In a nutshell, Ron Keel, never physically auditioned for Black Sabbath, never jammed with the band, never rehearsed, performed live or recorded.

Ron Keel himself was far from out for the count and would force a sizeable impression upon the Rock world with Keel. The band debuted with the 'Lay Down The Law' album, generating an appreciable degree of underground Metal fervour. The record created excited praise amongst the Rock press and, matching its Steeler predecessor, reaped healthy import sales into Europe prompting the interest of Kiss leader Gene Simmons and, in turn, the A&M affiliated Gold Mountain Records. A deal was secured and Simmons produced 1985's 'The Right To Rock'. 1986's 'The Final Frontier', the band's first for MCA Records, saw no let up in style or hard rocking intent. The album was, once more, produced by Simmons and toured hard to promote its release included support shows, ironically enough, to Dio in Britain prior to opening for Krokus in America. 'Calm Before The Storm' too made solid progress before the band, despite boasting a solid fan base, splintered. Ron would reinvent himself in more ways than one, fronting up an otherwise all girl band Fair Game. Although this band made a media splash concrete achievements were limited and the singer relocated to Nashville where, re-billed as Ronnie Lee Keel, he embarked upon a Country & Western career. True to form, Keel would make a significant impact on the Country scene too with the album 'Western Country'. Latterly the man is fronting up a reconstituted Keel as well as the commendable Iron Horse.

Would Ron Keel have ever worked out as vocalist for Black Sabbath? It is difficult to pass a judgement even in hindsight. Keel is known for a distinctive, upbeat style as displayed on the Keel albums, which would not sit easily with Sabbath. There is no Keel material on the open market that bears even the slightest affinity to Black Sabbath. The acid test is of course that audition demo. The one major stumbling block for Ron Keel's inclusion in the band, not to be xenophobic but realistic, is his downright lack of Englishness. Black Sabbath is a quintessentially British band and even the American singers that have adopted the mantle, most noticeably Ronnie James Dio, have approached the group with traditional, classic Rock themes. The obviously Italian blooded Dio is steeped in European mythic folklore and legend that transferred from Elf to Rainbow to Sabbath relatively smoothly. Even the latter day Ray Gillen was self-schooled in the traditions of Rodgers, Plant, Hughes and Gillan.

Black Sabbath required a lead vocalist that was in possession of both power, "across all ranges" as Geoff Nicholls has already indicated, and clarity of diction. The latter criteria appeared to come more naturally from English born singers. Ronnie James Dio agrees wholeheartedly with this theory. "To sing for Black Sabbath you have to have a presence to your voice, a natural power and the ability to sing your words clearly. The Sabbath catalogue is pretty varied and there are not too many singers who can cope with it. A lot of American singers do not sing clearly, it's true. I got my diction from trumpet funnily enough. If a certain note was supposed to be there, I wanted to make sure it was crystal clear. I applied that same way of thinking to my singing. In that way I suppose I am quite an 'English' style of vocalist. Tony Iommi is the same when it comes to a guitar solo or a riff— you can hear every note." One striking point about this whole episode is that if the union had transpired Ron Keel would have quite potentially breathed new life into the band being by far its youngest singer since Ozzy had first trod the boards.

There would be another contender who came under serious consideration. Geoff Nicholls can only remember the vocalist's Christian name, as well as some other, rather odd bodily characteristics. "There was another guy we tried out before David Donato.

He was an American guy, funnily enough as short as Ronnie, but he had this huge voice. He owned a recording studio and was also a karate teacher. The thing was, his name was David but he insisted on being called "Da-Verd." We were doing some song-writing up in my hotel room and he kept on correcting me every time I called him David.

Anyhow, the tapes he submitted were great but we needed to hear him sing live in rehearsal. What did it for us was that we were watching him from behind whilst he was singing and he had this thing about wiggling his bottom whilst he sang. We were in hysterics, literally crying with laughter. Well, he knew something was up and kept looking around suspiciously and we would all rapidly adopt stony faces and look away. As soon as he turned to the front and started singing again, this little bum started to wiggle and we would all be rolling in tears again. Of course, when you're playing live you need to be concentrating on the show—not your singer's bum! Geezer stopped laughing, finally saw the serious side, and said "This is not very fucking Heavy Metal is it?" There is no way we could have done a full gig with the guy!"

Chapter 11

Zero The Hero

In mid 1984 the British 'Kerrang!' magazine ran a major feature on the new Black Sabbath—Tony Iommi, Geezer Butler, Bill Ward and David Donato. Although the central interview of the issue, the tone of the article was sneering to say the least. The quotes taken from the new frontman seemed overly confident and the whole thrust of the article put David Donato's ego, at least to the reader, on a par with the size of his now infamous lion's head belt buckle. The next mention of this version of the band revelled in its collapse; the interim has over the years simply become a void. Naturally the story presented to the public and the reality was at odds. Strangely, many Sabbath biographies have dismissed this chapter as merely another aberration, as if Iommi and co. had somehow been duped into undertaking an obviously organised official photo shoot with someone they had met minutes before then dismissed as soon as the magazine hit the news stands. Other accounts have expounded even more nonsensical 'facts'. Steven Rosen's book 'Wheels Of Confusion' states "... just prior to Gillan's membership, vocalist Dave Donato filled in on some live dates." Absolute garbage of course, not only is it historically arse about tit, to coin a delightful English colloquialism, but it is factually wrong on the issue of live dates to boot. It is statements such as these that have sullied this vitally important sector of the band's history.

With the exception of promoting his post Sabbath White Tiger project David Donato has not spoken about his term of office at the Black Sabbath microphone stand. What follows is the unravelling of events in the aftermath of the unsuccessful search for a singer at the Pasha Studios sessions. David Donato's first forays with potential fame came courtesy of Armageddon in the mid seventies. Armageddon was a band initially assembled as a classic Rock 'Supergroup' uniting the troubled Keith Relf of Yardbirds and Renaissance repute, Steamhammer guitarist Martin Pugh, Relf's Renaissance comrade in arms Louis Cennamo on bass and Bobby Caldwell from Captain Beyond on the drums. Although having released a now highly collectable, solitary album,

Neil Citron's Headshaker with David Donato second from right.

this act then stalled by the departure of both Relf and bassist Louis Cennamo. The exiting duo founded Illusion but this band too came to an end in 1976 with untimely death of their singer.

Despite the setbacks and Relf's tragedy there were plans to persevere and record further material as the inaugural Armageddon album had sold respectable quantities in North America. The remaining band members, Pugh and Caldwell, set about formulating a fresh band structure. Enter David Donato. A man with a formidable set of lungs and looks to match, Donato had fronted acts such as Virgin, Hero and subsequently Headshaker on the California club circuit working with drummer J.R. Saenz, bassist Mike Christie and guitarist Neil Citron. To make ends meet Donato used his image to sustain his true passion. "Yes" he admits "I was doing a lot of modelling at the time in order to feed my addiction for singing. There was no ego involved. It was actually my singing instructor who suggested it as an easy way to make money. Just stand there and get paid—good job! It was good money and allowed me to get on with what I really wanted to do. The band I was in was doing OK, we were playing regular and building up a good vibe but like everyone else I was always searching for the next thing.

Hero. Mike Christie, Neil Citron, David Donato, J.R. Saenz.

"I auditioned for Armageddon over a period of a month and a half at the A&M studios" he explains. "I wouldn't say I was actually in the band but we certainly got to work together for quite a period. I was constantly on the lookout for a better gig and this situation just presented itself. Keith Relf had just passed away so it was a heavy scene but the music was great, very inspiring. I remember the guys in the band told me how Keith had really bad asthma so he sometimes really struggled to get through a set. Musically Armageddon was definitely my thing, certainly not radio music in any sense, heavy, complex stuff that suited my voice well. More Progressive Rock and I fell right into that. It just didn't work out I guess."

With the Armageddon liaison not coming to fruition Donato got back on the circuit in a band with Saenz once more and former Hero colleague Neil Citron on guitar. By 1984 the trio had been joined by a figure of international renown, Glenn Hughes. "It wasn't a band as such, all four of us were between things and we really enjoyed just playing good music with each other" reckons David. This project got into the studio to put down some demos with producer Andy Johns, before Mark Norton replaced Citron. "Glenn is of course phenomenal, he's like a white Stevie Wonder. We did a lot of acoustic, soulful stuff together. Together we complimented each other very well vocally. Some great stuff but it was all just for fun really, there was no determined direction or plan. Looking back, maybe if we had got organised it could have been a great band. A great collection of talent. J.R. was a fantastic drummer, really, really good and Mark was a speed demon on guitar. But, like I said, we were just having a blast jamming with each other."

Donato's longstanding alliance with Norton though would be rudely interrupted when the guitarist was plucked from club land and put into the spotlight with the self styled greatest Rock n' Roll band in the world—Kiss. "Mark copped a gig, the Kiss gig. He was afraid to tell us" recalls David. "We knew he was going for the gig, and were outrageously hoping for the guy but when he got it he couldn't tell us. He actually cried, that's how much it got to him. I really felt for him because he was really eaten up by the whole thing. Actually though, it made me even more determined to push myself forward."

David's drummer J.R. was close friends with fellow sticksman Randy Castillo, the late musician having his own Sabbs connection as he was later to find fame as a member of the Ozzy Osbourne band. It was this acquaintance that provided the key for the singer. "J.R. and Randy were best buddies. They were very close and had even both made the journey from New Mexico to Los Angeles together in a van with the sole purpose of becoming Rock stars. It was Randy, who was playing in Lita Ford's band at that time, told me about the opening with Black Sabbath."

The timing was good as the singer was beginning to believe a break would never come his way. His resolve was reinforced by Rainbow frontman Joe Lynn Turner though. "I was so fed up with not being able to find a gig. We were at a party with Randy Castillo. Well Joe's Italian and I'm Italian so we got talking. He gave me some great advice 'Don't you ever fucking give up' he said 'The minute you give up you'll miss the best gig of your life'. Joe was right of course." As luck would have it Donato would chance a meeting with Lita Ford at a party. "As you know, Lita was dating Tony so I asked her straight, 'how do I get a tape to Tony?' She gave me the management address and instructed me to write very clearly 'c/o Tony' on the package. She said that way it would be guaranteed to reach Tony unopened. Her advice was good and I got a call back from Pat Sciciliano, Don Arden's assistant, asking me for an audition".

Unbeknown to David his acquaintance Glenn Hughes had also smoothed his path by putting the word in on his behalf as the former Deep Purple star divulges. "I used to party with Dave, he's a nice guy and a good singer. I thought he would be worth a shot for Sabbath, he had all the right characteristics, so I told Tony Iommi to check him out."

Practicalities became the order of the day for David once he had learned there was an opening in the band. "I was asked to learn a set list of ten songs but I knew 99% of it already because I was a major fan" he freely discloses. "There was only one off the 'Born Again' album, 'Disturbing The Priest'. I auditioned with Tony, Geezer and Bill and that was that. I was in. Sciciliano told me, exact words 'They love you'. I then went for sushi with Tony and Geoff Nicholls so I figured that was a good sign.

David Donato brought many attributes to the table.

Hiding identities before the launch. Donato, Iommi and Geezer.

Donato and drummers, J.R. Saenz, Tommy Lee of Mötley Crüe and Rick Allen of Def Leppard.

Not only could he sing with the power and style required but he unquestionably looked the part too. "Vocally my timing was good. Personally I was into that Dio and Gillan type of style so that was a big plus for them. In my club days I was a Robert Plant clone—happy to admit it. I was also big on Ronnie James Dio, even back to the old Elf days. Lots of power and melody I like to think. I had done my modelling so for that I obviously I had to look good. I was 6 foot 2 inches and kept myself in good shape. I certainly have a presence. It's like Halloween every time I get on stage. From that point on we just rehearsed at the Rockhouse. I remember the Olympics were happening at the time and Bill and I would travel into rehearsals together, driving past the Coliseum, because we lived very close to each other, Bill on Seal Beach and me on Huntington Beach. This went on for a good many months. Just solid rehearsing." For Donato this would be an opportunity to witness some of his favourite musicians at close quarters. "Tony is a stylist completely on guitar. When you hear a riff of his you know exactly who it is and there are very, very few guitarists you could claim that of. It's interesting the Heavy Metal label the band has because Billy always said they were a Blues band. They knew all of that old stuff, had a great knowledge of it."

This observation about Sabbath's Blues heritage is poignant. Often overlooked it is vital to the understanding of Black Sabbath's immensely successful formula. They didn't title their fledgling act The Polka Tulk Blues Band for nothing. Geezer Butler backed this up, taking a momentary dip back into time when asked a question on the musical values of his 1997 solo record 'Black Science'. "I like to experiment, we all do. When I think of the hours and hours we have spent just jamming along in the studio. That's how we relax, have a good old blast with your mates and forget about everything else. If we could get paid just for that I would be very happy. Sometimes you forget why you're there. Oh, we have to make an album? Rehearse for a tour?

Most of our stuff goes back to 12 bar Blues really. Our younger fans find that surprising sometimes. When we were kids we started out playing along to those old records in just the same way people like Jimmy Page did. Back in those days that's how you leant to play. We taught ourselves. All our early gigs were Blues songs and that is what we were—a Blues band. We would be happy to just jam instrumentally for ages. I suppose the transition to Heavy Metal was through Tony and I developing these very simple three chord Blues riffs into something of our own. It was like, OK, where can we go with this? Alvin Lee of Ten Years After had a big effect on us too. Alvin was doing the same thing, taking the Blues but turning it around into something different. It's the same for Led Zeppelin, Jethro Tull and Deep Purple too, all those bands of that period, just expressed the Blues differently. Its all a tradition of the Blues so give us half the chance and we'll spend all day playing Willie Dixon. People seem surprised by that but I tell them, Heavy Metal would not exist without the Blues. Black Sabbath would not exist without the Blues."

Tony Iommi, talking to the author backstage at the Leicester De Montfort Hall in 1986, would acknowledge the Blues as central to the very essence of Black Sabbath. "When we started both Geezer and I were playing guitar and we learned everything we knew from the Blues. Anyone who was serious about an instrument was either learning Blues or Jazz. The Blues is a great place to start, to build on and find your own style." Did Tony find a grounding in the Blues the reason for a dearth in quality of latter day Rock acts? He was diplomatic. "I would recommend it to anyone. Don't pick up a guitar and try to play my riffs. Get hold of some old Howlin'

Wolf or Willie Dixon records first. That's the way to start. Ask Jimmy Page, Brian May, Rory Gallagher or Gary Moore or any of those guys. The thing is there are so many bands around today I can't keep up. There were not that many bands around and it was very creative because everyone was trying to find something different. Everything was based on the Blues though—everything.

It really was inspiring, listening to what Jethro Tull, Taste, Cream, Traffic or Ten Years After were doing. There wasn't the huge numbers of bands around then either so if somebody made a really good record everybody picked up on it really quickly. You were very conscious about trying not to sound like anybody else too. That was OK if you wanted to be a Pop star but if you thought you were serious you had to do your own thing. That doesn't seem to happen so much anymore. I don't actually listen to much Heavy Metal at all, which might sound a bit strange. Americans in particular find it amazing I don't spend all my time listening to Black Sabbath albums. Instinctively if you put most bands of a certain age into a rehearsal situation the first thing they will play will be the Blues. When I'm at home I'll still listen to my old Blues records, Hank Marvin or Frank Sinatra."

Really? Frank Sinatra? "Yeah" he replied with a straight face. I thought that was a joke? "Oh no, I love Frank. He's the best."

Tony Iommi's affection for big Frank, often hinted at by way of jocular remarks from other band members in interviews, is very real. Black Sabbath drummer Bev Bevan once revealed to the author that Iommi's home listening consists almost exclusively of Sinatra and The Shadows and that Heavy Metal is conspicuous by its absence. Once some Sabbath fans received a rude reality check by pulling up at a red light on Sunset Strip in Los Angeles and discovering the car parallel to them contained Messrs. Iommi and Nicholls. The four Metal types, obligatory joint in hand and blasting out 'Paranoid' no less, sat open mouthed and incredulous next to the Sabbath duo, relaxing in their open top Corvette Stingray matching the volume with Sinatra's 'My Way'. "As soon as they recognised us they just could not believe the music Tony was playing" laughs Nicholls. "We told them that 'My Way' was a song off the new Sabbath album. They were so stoned I think they believed us!"

David Donato of course would be privileged to catch these moments of musical inspiration and relaxation first hand. "I have some great memories of walking into rehearsal, watching them do an orchestral warmup. They loved the old Blues stuff and those guys just had such a mastery of their instruments. The three of them were great; they just blew me away every day. Sometimes I would just sit and watch them play the Blues. They would just be away in another world. Wonderful times. It gave me every reason to be the best I could be." The now infamous photo session that appeared in the Rock magazines was taken a couple of months into David's employ. "Those pictures were taken before we did the demo. I remember going back and forth to Tony and Geezer's places writing up new songs at the time."

Rehearsals would then lead onto the next logical platform of demoing up new material. "We did what was, in my opinion, a way premature recording with Bob Ezrin" affirms David. Bob Ezrin ranked as one of the true elite in Rock production. Known for his attention to detail and enthusiasm for large scale projects the man had a track record of the highest repute, having worked on classic albums by artists such as Alice Cooper, Pink Floyd, Lou Reed and Kiss. Ezrin can lay claim for the sonic values of Kiss' 'Destroyer', Alice Cooper's 'Billion Dollar Babies' and 'Love It To Death' and was known in the business as a bona fide hit maker. "He came in and I remember nobody in the band really seemed to know why. Maybe it was a management or label thing. I don't think the band was ready with new songs. Anyway, we cut some tracks, one called 'No Way Out' which lyrically was about Sabbath really. Like, there's no way I can quit this legend. I felt honoured to be there, with those guys and I wanted to express that in a song. The opening lyrics went "Let the story be told, history unfolds, And visions of the mind, fade to black." I was very conscious that this was Tony, Geezer and Bill I was working with—the original Sabbath. That was really exciting for me. Later I heard that same riff on a later Sabbath album, in a different song. Some of the vocal melody line was still there too! Its no big deal, everybody does it. Copies, borrows, remembers—whatever." Indeed he did. 'No Way Out' underwent a number of transitions over a period of years. The band obviously knew they were on to a good thing with this song, it mutating from 'No Way Out' to 'Black Fire', then 'Power Of The Night' and 'Rise Up' until it finally ended up as 'The Shining' on the 1987 'Eternal Idol' album. It is quite possible a number of singers had a stab at the track on its protracted journey to acetate.

"Another song we did was called 'Don't Beg The Master', that was something Tony and Geezer wrote and I came up with the title. Very Sabbathy. Another title being kicked around was 'Dancing With The Devil'." The fourth track would be a laid back number entitled 'Sail On'. The upbeat 'Dancing With The Devil' became a close contender for future reworks but, ironically, Tony Iommi's skill at precision riffing proved its undoing. Paradoxically the main riff was so strong that no matter what the band did with the track it always failed to gel into a full blown song.

Geoff Nicholls remembered that, from Tony Iommi's point of view, it would be these tapes that planted the seeds of doubt. Black Sabbath brought Bob Ezrin into the situation, both to gauge his methodology as a potential producer as well as to get a feel for Donato's vocals on tape. Only 'No Way Out' progressed in any form beyond this point. The keyboard player has this to say on the Ezrin sessions, interestingly choosing very similar words to the singer. "David Donato was a great guy, we all got on with him but it was too premature I think. When the band rehearsed they were just having a good time and, of course, Black Sabbath rehearsing is bloody loud so we couldn't really get a feeling for Dave's voice. With that kind of studio rehearsal vocals have no chance in competing with guitar, bass and drums. He had a good voice, don't get me wrong, but I think the Ezrin tapes showed Tony that it might not have been quite what he was looking for. David had a great bottom end, very rich and full voice. I think the top end was the problem. Tony wanted an extra bit of zaz in there. That's not to say David might not have been able to give Tony what he wanted. He certainly had the power. Remember that any singer who spent any degree of time with us in the studio had already beaten off hundreds of other singers to get there. David Donato was good. As usual, there was a lot of behind the scenes stuff going on as usual."

It is worth underscoring the singer's concerns over the state of readiness of the band as they recorded these demo tracks. "Everything was way premature" he maintains once more. "It was odd for me because this was Black Sabbath, the whole thing was pretty overwhelming for me. These guys, like Purple or Zeppelin, were my heroes and I was working with them. The whole thing though was pretty undirected and when Bob Ezrin came in Tony and Geezer just said this is some material just to get started, just to get something down. It was all pretty loose and I think I would have preferred if they would have had a bunch of songs written for me to just sing on. Mark was enduring the opposite with Kiss. That was very regimented, they told him change your name (he became 'Mark St. John'), dye your hair, lose some weight, play like this. In a way I think I would have preferred that but it was very relaxed. I was given a writer's contract. I would rather they said 'Here's a song, sing it'. But it didn't work that way. We were building stuff up from scratch totally. There was nothing there, no songs at all. We would just jam and see what developed."

And then came that article. 'Kerrang' had landed an exclusive but had, according to David, been exceptionally selective in their use of editing. "I spoke a lot about how honoured and privileged I felt to be in the band and they never printed a word of it. Y'know I never saw that feature at the time but just recently I saw some stuff on the Internet about me which was just horse-shit, just a misinformed guy talking shit about me! All that 'Donut' stuff... I don't even like cake!" he laughs. "All we ever eat in rehearsals was Kentucky Fried Chicken. Tony and Geoff loved it, we ate it on a daily basis. After each rehearsal we would look at each other and one of us would say 'Shall we get some more of that chicken?' It became a ritual." Of course the strictly vegan Geezer would never have participated in such arcane practices.

Geoff Nicholls believes it was the magazine that had pushed the band into an interview sooner than they would have liked. "That magazine, 'Kerrang', jumped the gun. They wanted a Black Sabbath story and they got one. It was way too early and of course it didn't do anybody any favours." This, of course, does not discount the fact that the management could have simply denied the request and begs the question—why the photo session? Besides the huge furor generated by the 'Kerrang' article the Sabbath camp shied away from the press. "It was all pretty tight lipped" David reckons. "No announcements were made and the only stuff I saw was accidental. I remember playing a board game with my girlfriend at the time. We had the TV on and my picture flashed across MTV but that was about it. There was also a strange thing on 'Nightflight', a report saying that Phil Mogg of UFO was in line to sing for Black Sabbath. As I was working with the guys in the studio every day I kinda just said 'oh yeah?'"

All told David calculates he was with the band some six months. He believes the alliance fell apart not from any lack of faith in his abilities but a split amongst the core members. "We kept up with these rehearsals at the Rockhouse for quite some time. Then I was called by Pat Sciciliano to come in to pick up a cheque. I was on just rehearsal pay at that stage but it was odd, to be asked to collect my cheque. So, I asked him what was going on to which he replied 'We're not gonna work for a while'. Of course I said 'Does this mean I'm fired?' Pat said 'No, they think you're great. You are not the problem. The guys are just not working.' The story I was then told was that Geezer and Tony had got involved in a managerial dispute, which, at the time I was unsure of. In fact I thought it was bullshit, but later events kind of confirmed for me that Pat was giving me the real story."

When David actually received that telephone call he was at his friend J.R.'s house. Randy Castillo was also there. "It was very funny" laughs David. "This is a wonderful memory I have of Randy because he asked me what had happened when I got off the phone so I told him 'They asked me to come in and get my cheque'. Randy looked me straight in the face, real close up and said 'Welcome to the world of getting fucked Dave!' Then he gave me a big hug and a handshake and we all had a good laugh."

Although David's accounts of that half year with the band once and for all determine what was really happening during this critical period what was to follow provides ample evidence that it was not his vocal talents that were found wanting and that Pat Sciciliano's reasoning was truthful. Not one to rest on his laurels the singer hired rehearsal space opposite the 'Guitar Center' in Los Angeles and convened a new band unit with guitarist Lanny Cordola ("He was just a kid back then, recommended by Mark who was his guitar teacher") and Barry Brandt of Angel fame. "I wanted to call the band The Void because we were going to ... fill the void. The other guys found it too negative though!"

Donato's days under the Sabbath umbrella were not yet at an end though. Four months went by until one day Gloria Butler, Geezer's wife and manager, got back in touch. "Gloria called me on my birthday. Both Mark and Randy Castillo were at my place at the time." The vocalist relates. "She said 'Terry wants you to come back and do some work with him. Can you come?' So, I spent two or three weeks working up new material with Geezer, very heavy stuff. They took it to Warner Bros. and apparently they said 'This sounds like the last Black Sabbath stuff'. Of course it was, because it was me singing again and Geezer wrote a lot of that stuff too.

We spent quite a bit of time in Geezer's basement studio in St. Louis. Me, Geezer, his nephew Pedro Howse on guitar and a local drummer who was given a hundred bucks! It was very, very good heavy stuff. This was going to be The Geezer Butler Band. When I got there some tracks had lyrics; some didn't so we got them all finished. There was a song called 'Mr. D-He' which was what Geezer's little son called the Devil, a very powerful 'Neon Knights' type of song. We also did 'Looking Back' which Geezer wrote, 'Street Wars' and 'Inner World'. I loved Tony's playing but being with Geezer was a lot of fun I have to say. For some reason I think the record company wanted these songs rerecording again so we went to Malibu Middle C Studios and redid some vocals. I didn't question anything, just did the job. Geezer said he loved the songs, they were great. We were just there to fix 'em. Getting invited back by Geezer made me feel very good."

This variant of The Geezer Butler Band, one of many aborted attempts at getting a solo venture for the bassist off the ground, never got past these demos for a proposed album. Pedro Howse, who had been treading the boards in Midlands club band Crazy Angel previously, would bond so tightly with Butler to the extent that he would be used on all of these tryouts right up to and including the G//Z/R albums in the mid nineties. Backtracking once more to the Donato fronted venture the whole project had the typically English working title of 'Bob's Your Uncle'. (So typically English in fact that it was only in 2002 that David Donato got to know the meaning of the phrase!). "We just lost contact," says David. "They were in St. Louis, then England and it kind of drifted. We kept in touch for a good while."

Wishing to strike while the iron was hot David lost no time in making the most of his Sabbath credentials and Mark Norton's status as a Kiss member by formulating White Tiger. Directly due to the central characters recent associations with major status acts the resulting album was given high priority in magazine review columns. "We both had a reputation at that point so White Tiger made sense. We certainly both had the ability too. Unfortunately for us the production of the final album was just terrible, it was barely listenable. Everybody said the songs were there, the musicianship was there but ... so it was disappointing. We got Michael Wagener to remix just the one song, which sounded amazing. Trouble was there was no money for him to do the rest. Years later we heard he would have done it for free! So, White Tiger didn't happen. I think we got big in Sweden though!"

White Tiger wrote a second album but would grind to a halt. Fans were simply of the misapprehension the band had simply vanished although behind the scenes work was in progress. "Mark and I wrote another album. It was good stuff. Mark is a speedball on the guitar, the guy can do anything on the neck, he's like an Allan Holdsworth kind of player but I was maybe looking for something a bit more like a classic four piece, Sabbath kind of thing. Mark was amazingly fast but sometimes a slow hand approach is good too y'know? Anyway, we had this album, 'On The Prowl', ready to record. We heard a rumour of an offer to our managers, which was apparently refused. We were never made privy to it. That's how White Tiger ended."

And then, David Donato, drops off the face of the earth ... Only of course he didn't. There was a chance to audition for Michael Schenker but a former singer delivered some timely and sage advice. "Gary Barden, who is a great singer and a lovely guy, looked me straight in the eye and said 'Don't do it'." His next port of call would be high profile yet strangely muted. Hooking up with fabled Kiss drummer Peter Criss and his constant ally guitarist Mark St. John, ex-707 guitarist Kevin Russell and bassist Joey Mudarri, the singer fronted a 1989 outfit billed Keep. However, for this venture Donato went under the assumed name of Michael McDonald in an

Not Rob Halford, but David Donato in 2002.

attempt to deflect the awkward Sabbath connections. Changes in the line-up then saw the introduction of St. John and new bassist Jim Barnes, the latter subsequently superseded by St. John's brother Michael Norton in January of 1990. This incarnation of Keep recorded demos at Sound City Recording Studios. Keep would put in just one live performance, at the Guitar Center music store in Lawndale, California on 2nd May 1990.

It seems Black Sabbath kept him on their Christmas card list and one year, out of the blue, an anonymous package of backstage passes for the local Ozzfest event arrived in the mail. The Donato myth has been fuelled by his lack of musical appearances since the eighties but the singer has led a more than content lifestyle since those days, simply swapping one passion for another. "Musically, nothing much. I build custom motorcycles from the ground up, Harleys mainly, some other funny stuff too. It's very rewarding. I also busy myself with art, along with bikes and music I have always involved myself in art. All my life I have hung around with Rockers, bikers and artists. I still look the part, I can still sing with the same power and sometimes I will sit in with some local groups just for fun."

Ozzy Osbourne. Pic: Rich Galbraith.

Chapter 12

Jesus Christ, Supertzar

David Donato's clarification as to the parting of ways between Tony and Geezer toward the end of the year illustrates how and why Iommi found the opportunity to embark upon a solo album. As it would unfold, the powers that be were to ultimately deny him this chance. Piecing together a rhythm section for getting down on tape his initial ideas for this proposed solo album was no tall order, Tony merely borrowed bassist Gordon Copley and drummer Eric Singer (real name Eric Mensinger) from his girlfriend Lita Ford's band.

Singer's debut behind the drum kit in public was a sixth grade band The Axe. He had taken up drums a year earlier at his school in Cleveland, Ohio. "We had a few bands before The Axe but we never had a singer so we would jam out these Black Sabbath songs but with no vocals. As it turned out it was good training." He was already deeply embedded in Rock culture, not just as a musician but as a die hard fan. "I was just so into it" he gushes. "Buying records, Rock magazines, everything. What is just so strange to me now is that all the people I have worked with were once on posters on my wall. I would spend hours playing the records and just dreaming what it might be like to be on stage with these people, just fantasies back then but ... what I'm trying to say is that I was a major fan! It actually blows my mind. Still to this day I remember that the guys I am playing with are the same people who made the records that I bought back then.

I went to see Kiss when I was 16 years old, I saw Black Sabbath with Ozzy and I was obsessed by Queen. That whole period was just such a great, great era. I've never lost that fan feeling despite my achievements. It is probably strange for the audiences we play for to think that the guy they are watching play drums is thinking the same thoughts as they are. They're all out front thinking 'Wow—that's Gene Simmons on stage in front of me!' and I'm at the back going 'Wow, that's Gene Simmons on stage with me'. It really is the coolest feeling to have night after night. I'm working with heroes."

Although intent on the life of a Rock n' Roll star, no matter how far down the personal yellow brick road that appeared to the teenager at the time, Singer disciplined himself in the craft of percussion by performing in an altogether more salubrious type of ensemble. "I was part of a big band, playing anywhere for anybody, ballrooms, debutante parties, bah mitzvahs. It was actually great because we would cover the whole gamut from Cole Porter to Count Basie. I learned a lot of valuable stuff there." Before long the budding drummer had made the leap in the dark required, it seems, by every eager Rocker keen to make an impression on the American Rock scene. Breaking away from his last Cleveland act Taskmaster, an outfit that subsequently evolved into Beau Coup, found himself manning drums for Los Angeles based Icebreaker during 1983.

Icebreaker, and Singer in particular, soon made an impression in spite of the intensity of the competition. "We were in the same position as all those LA bands back then" Eric recalls. "We were hustling with our flyers and I guess we looked pretty typical, even though we thought we were very individual! Y'know, spiked hair and the full Heavy Metal regalia. Those were crazy times, Crue and Ratt were huge and there was a sense that a lot of other bands would follow."

It would be the legendary figure of Vanilla Fudge and erstwhile Ozzy Osbourne drummer that gave Singer his first step onto stardom. "Carmine had these "Drum battle" contests. They were pretty famous all over the country. Well, I had entered in Cleveland but didn't win. When I was in Los Angeles I went along to the 'Drum Battle' there, at the Hollywood Palace, I gave it another shot and came in third. There were lots of celebrity drummers acting as the judges so third to me was very cool. Anyway, some girl had seen me play that day and put me forward for this Playboy sponsored 'Women Of Rock' event. It was quite funny, because with Playboy's name involved you start to think, but it was explained that there would be filming that involved "Some nudity—but no fucking!"

So, I found myself part of this 'band'. Kurt James

from Steeler was the guitarist—that guy could fuckin' play I'm telling you. He was just great and on bass was Ray Marzano, from Lita Ford's band. That is really how I hooked up with Lita because Ray told me Randy Castillo was no longer in the picture and he told her about me. I auditioned and got the job." This is, of course, where Singer became acquainted with Tony Iommi, the Black Sabbath guitarist and Lita Ford being a well known item on the scene. Naturally Iommi took a hand in Lita's creative endeavours too and at that juncture was assisting with demos for an album with the projected title of 'The Bride Wore Black'. This album, unfortunately shelved, did include musical contributions from both Tony Iommi and Geoff Nicholls.

"I remember the first conversations with Tony that led up to Black Sabbath" the drummer maintains. "Obviously we were working in the studio together on Lita's songs so he had become familiar with my style and got to know me as a person. One day he told me he was thinking of putting together a solo record. This was very early stages as he had no band at all at this point. Because Tony and Lita had a thing going it was agreed that Gordon Copley, our bass player, and myself could be loaned out to cut some demos. It was no big deal then although obviously it became a big deal later. As things went on we learnt Tony had in mind to use Jeff Glixman as a producer and he wanted different singers involved. I remember the names Plant, Coverdale, Halford and Hughes mentioned. That was the initial plan."

Amongst those names, Led Zeppelin's Robert Plant, Whitesnake and Deep Purple veteran David Coverdale and Judas Priest singer Rob Halford, one looked a likely and compatible match. Rob Halford was a fellow Brummie and, like Tony Iommi, had built his band up to multi-platinum status on the global arena with a series of groundbreaking albums such as 'Unleashed In The East', 'British Steel', 'Screaming For Vengeance' and 'Defenders Of The Faith'. Halford had set himself apart from the regular Rock crowd by having the distinction of virtually inventing the leather and studs uniform, complimenting the theatrics by making his stage entrance astride a Harley Davidson. Besides the theatrics Rob Halford also lay claim to the ultimate in Heavy Metal frontman accolades. He was unquestionably the best technical singer on the world circuit, boasting a range that by rights should have seen him spirited off into an undercover government secret weapons programme long before. When Halford opened his mouth even continental shelves quivered.

Halford has a vague memory of some connection with Tony Iommi at this point in time, illustrating how the original concept never got beyond the drawing board. "I think we were working on the Judas Priest tour for 'Turbo', which for us was another hugely successful album, our third platinum record in a row. I think Tony had got it into his mind but had been unable to follow it through. Actually it is all kind of lost in the memory banks. I think we spoke but how far it got I can't remember."

Glenn Hughes grants that, based upon these initial conversations, he found the prospect extremely exciting. "I thought Tony had a great idea" he concedes. "When I was first approached the way Tony mapped out the whole project, using Ronnie and Rob, I found very appealing. Those are two singers and people that I truly respect. Rob Halford and I have known each other for years and years. Same as the Sabbath thing, we're all from the same region. Great guy, great voice. The idea of singing with Rob I liked a lot. We have actually sang together quite a bit but only in the shower. Not naked I stress! Ha, Ha—Rob will laugh at that. Backstage the showers are usually the best place you can get the acoustic sounds to have a good old screaming match. Rob is just the best y'know? He has that voice, that whole 'Metal God' thing going on which is just great but let me tell you—that cat can really sing. I mean really sing. There is so much more to Rob than people have got to hear yet. So yeah, Ronnie, Rob and myself—great idea. You can see why I wanted in."

Rob Halford was a good choice for other reasons too, the Judas Priest man too expressing the ties lent by common roots. "I just recall that it was exciting because I had grown up in the same area as Tony and the guys, we kind of started off around the same time too. So there was an affinity. I think Black Sabbath started in around '68 or '69 and that's when the very first version of Judas Priest, with Al Atkins on vocals and Congo Campbell on the drums, was going too. It was all an embryonic Heavy Metal melting pot, quite unique in the world. If memory serves the first time I saw Black Sabbath was at Mothers club in Erdington." This venue was to mark a keen and lasting impression on the fledging singer, it even being mentioned in the track 'Made In Hell' from Halford's monumental 'Resurrection' album some thirty years later.

As coincidence would have it Mother's Club played an important part in Glenn Hughes' early Sabbath connections too. "It would have been around the 'Paranoid' era I guess. Mothers Club was quite a hub of activity. A lot of musicians who later made a name for themselves started out there. During that time it was a meeting place for people like the Sabbath guys, Bonzo from Led Zeppelin was down there a lot. Trapeze would play there and Bonzo often came down to check us out. That whole area of the West Midlands was, for some reason, extremely special. It has often been overlooked that Ozzy, Tony,

Geezer, Bill, Bonzo, Plantie, myself, Rob Halford and those boys all came from this quite small region. I remember the first time we got to play together. Trapeze opened the show for five bands at the Bull Ring in Birmingham. Sabbath were top of the bill. We all chatted quite a bit then and hung out but the next thing for me was Deep Purple and we met up again at the Cal. Jam in '74. Ozzy and I were staying at the Beverley Wilshire and we became very good friends. There was a lot of partying going on and I hit it off with both Tony and Ozzy."

The proposed union with Ronnie James Dio, David Coverdale and Rob Halford would not transpire though. Halford was wrapped up in ongoing turbotronics and Coverdale was just about to construct his all conquering '1987' album. All the big names were out of play. It is now that one of the biggest question marks that shadows Black Sabbath looms large. Propagated and expounded upon by a variety of sources, even the very involvement of the next singer to step up to the microphone was in doubt at one point. The annals of Rock n' Roll are littered with lurid claims, clandestine jam sessions and secret auditions. There are anecdotes aplenty that add intrigue to the stories released to public and media by the PR machines who would have you believe that, of course, this latest album is their best, the drummer left because of musical differences and the band actually likes playing smaller, more intimate venues.

For ardent followers of Black Sabbath their own personal 'Is Elvis alive and well and selling fish & chips on Clacton on Sea?' is the notoriety afforded a now famous TV evangelist Jeff Fenholt. Did a born again preacher that now plays into millions of American TV screens every week really sing for Black Sabbath? Debate on this issue is heated. Probably due to the impact of organisations such as Tipper Gore's Parent's Music Resource Center and a whole swathe of religious bodies upon Rock n' Roll, and particularly Heavy Metal, during the eighties, feelings run very high. Christianity and Metal have never sat easy together and the acceptance as fact that the Lamb of God breached the inner sanctum of Babylon and survived unscathed is perceived as an awkward embarrassment at the very least.

There are many Black Sabbath fans who will vehemently voice the opinion that Jeff Fenholt auditioned once, didn't get the job and since then has been bitterly exacting revenge. Tony Iommi is simply dismissive only deigning to deliver a wry 'Who?' when asked. There are other weighty sources that totally deny Fenholt's participation. The excellent, usually authoritative but unofficial www.black–sabbath.com website run by webmaster Joe Siegler has this to say "Just for a second, assume that Fenholt was working with Iommi (which everyone I have spoken to or emailed about this issue says he wasn't), but assume he was for a second. Black Sabbath didn't exist during this time period, and even if Fenholt was involved (which he wasn't), it wasn't Black Sabbath, so his claim of being a former Black Sabbath vocalist is doubly inaccurate. Please note that I do not consider Jeff Fenholt a member of Black Sabbath!!" This statement by Joe is not down to any malicious agenda, simply an acknowledged expert struggling with a dearth of facts. A latter day Black Sabbath drummer Bobby Rondinelli holds an opposing view. "Jeff is a great guy and a long term friend. He was there and it's about time the truth came out. I don't know why they deny it. He's a cool singer."

In an ironic twist the Jeff Fenholt issue has become such a point of rancour that it is held up as tantamount to some kind of heresy to even mention the man's name. The entire episode is marked by one clear factor and that is that presumptions, testimonies and vitriol are being served up by people who quite simply are not privy to the facts. What is without doubt is that, even putting aside the Sabbath episode aside for one moment, Jeff Fenholt is a colourful character. His own story is one of sinning then being saved, of stalking the stages in the lead role of 'Jesus Christ Superstar' whilst believing he was in a state of possession. His biography tells of a child moulded by abuse at the hands of his parents and an out of control youth. He says that after witnessing his friend and band mate Gary Driscoll, the former Rainbow drummer subsequently had his life, and indeed his skin, torn from him in a Satanic ritual. Driscoll was murdered in a most brutal fashion in his Ithaca, New York apartment during 1987, police believing the incident in some way drug related. (One high profile musician interviewed for this book seemed to scoff at Beelzebub's claims on this particular tragedy but did more than hint, tongue in cheek, that he recognised the dastardly handiwork of Ritchie Blackmore!)

Information, misinformation and speculation regarding Jeff Fenholt abound on the World Wide Web. During August of 2002 Internet reports even stated Jeff Fenholt was killed in a car crash. Jeff Fenholt himself is seemingly not shy of self promotion, operating a website, publishing books and recording albums in a variety of musical favours on top of his television exploits. There are many who claim Fenholt's modus operandi, extolling the virtues of God through such mediums, masks more sinister motives. There was even a San Francisco stage show 'Salvador Dali Talks to the Animals in the Heaven on Top of Heaven' that saw Vince Camillo playing the part of Fenholt, conversely playing 'Jesus Christ Superstar', caught in a bizarre courtship with Salvador Dali's widow Gala. Fiction or fact? One senses a Hollywood movie in the making here. Two established facts here are beyond reproach. One is that Jeff Fenholt is a gifted singer with an accredited Rock n' Roll history and that secondly he was, somehow, to some degree, involved with Tony Iommi. The critical question is, if Jeff Fenholt merits his placing in the picture, was this Black Sabbath? Many say no, Jeff Fenholt says yes and Tony, unfortunately, has to date never publicly expanded upon "Who?" Ultimately one suspects there are many truths here, the credence held by both camps equally sincere even if never the twain shall meet.

Although probably an unknown to many of Black Sabbath's followers, particularly in Europe, Jeff Fenholt already had a rich Rock heritage by the point his path crossed with that of Tony Iommi. The singer had worked with some of the very finest players in the business and was certainly no rookie. Indeed, despite being presented by some factions as an irrelevance in the Black Sabbath saga, Jeff Fenholt in actual fact was as far removed from the anonymous glory hunter he is often portrayed as could possibly be. The singer had already hit the very top echelons of his profession long before becoming embroiled in the machinations of Sabbath.

His first public port of call though would be as a teenager with Columbus, Ohio act The Fifth Order. Jeff elaborates on his introduction into the world of music. "When I was 15 years old, we recorded the song, 'Goin' Too Far', which became a number one regional hit, and appeared somewhere between 40 and 60 on the national charts. I toured throughout the Midwest with The Fifth Order for two years." Over this period Fenholt got to perform nation-wide sharing stages with such diverse artists as the Four Tops, Bob Seger and Tony Knight & The Pack (later, of course, to evolve into the mighty Grand Funk Railroad). Regionally the band could hold their own too and rose to such a status that they could draw healthy crowds to headline gigs. The band, who reaped a further hit with the song 'A Thousand Devils', also scored valuable TV coverage, appearing on shows such as 'Shindig' and 'Hullabaloo', a precursor for a later and hugely successful television career for the singer in later life.

Moving on from The Fifth Order Jeff Fenholt opted for a change of tack, attending the Ohio State University on a vocal scholarship. The singer's plans to gain an educational foundation would be foiled though. "I lost my voice scholarship because of drugs. While I was on tour with the Ohio State University men's ensemble, singing for the U.S. Senate and in the rotunda, an alum caught me smoking marijuana with a colleague and reported me to the dean. I was summarily dismissed and my voice scholarship was revoked. Although I was not formally expelled from the university at large, without my scholarship, I was financially unable to continue my education."

Things took a turn for the positive though when, during that same year of 1971, his talents were requested for the touring company of the renowned flower power musical 'Hair' as an understudy to the lead. Whilst on this tour Fenholt scored a recording contract with Columbia Records as a singer / songwriter.

During this period Fenholt met up with Robert Stigwood on the West Coast. Stigwood's reputation for his deep involvement with The Beatles business affairs and as manager for both The Bee Gees and Eric Clapton presented Jeff with the opportunity to take the next step up. "He asked me to come to New York and meet Andrew Lloyd Webber and Tim Rice. Peter Brown, the former head of Apple Records and Beatles' manager, signed me to a personal management contract." Following the death of Brian Epstein fellow Liverpudlian Peter Brown, having worked closely with the Fab Four since 1962, had taken on the responsibilities of managing The Beatles individually and acting as overseer of Apple Records. Brown's patronage bore solid results almost immediately, Jeff Fenholt scoring a radio hit with a cover version of the Graham Nash song 'Simple Man'.

Next in line would be one of the mightiest challenges available to a performer. Oddly enough it is a role that two singers connected with Black Sabbath would come to make their own, that of the lead role in the tour de force stage show 'Jesus Christ Superstar'. "Tim and Andrew asked me to sing the part of 'Jesus' for the world premier of 'Jesus Christ Superstar' in Pittsburgh, Pennsylvania. The album in England had already become a hit and was climbing the charts in America. Ian Gillan had performed the part of 'Jesus' on that album. For reasons unbeknown to me, Ian was unable to perform the part in concert, and therefore, I got the call. I toured approximately 60 cities in 90 days to sold out arenas and stadiums." Fenholt's portrayal of the Messiah was deemed to have been such a success that he was invited by Robert Stigwood to open the show on New York's Broadway Mark Hellinger Theatre on October 12th 1971. Being the first time a Rock musical had broken into Broadway 'Jesus Christ Superstar' made headlines around the world garnering some of the biggest ever ticket advance sales Broadway had ever seen. It would also ignite a furor of protest from Christian movements opposed to the quite unique adaptation of Jesus' life. "We were thrilled about all the people protesting around the nation and in New York. This only heightened our visibility and increased the buzz, which we gladly took advantage. I did a national television interview with Phil Donahue discussing

Jeff Fenholt on the cover of the October 25, 1971 issue of 'Time' magazine.

the show and the controversy."

The show ran for over 700 performances and made a star of its lead actor, Jeff Fenholt. Clad in a huge Sci-Fi silver mantle that would make even Grace Jones think twice, he graced the cover of the fabled 'Time' magazine that same year. Despite this enormous triumph eventually the singer decided to give it another shot with a traditional Rock n' Roll band. It was far from an easy road though Having cut loose from 'Jesus Christ Superstar' in February of 1973 Fenholt was to struggle through the rest of the seventies, success which was always within his grasp, constantly eluding him. "I struggled with the demons of drugs and alcohol. I signed recording agreements with Capitol, RCA and Polydor. My dysfunction led to my dismissal at all three labels."

Finding himself in California, Fenholt would unite with Armageddon. As relayed earlier Dave Donato had enjoyed a fleeting tenure with Armageddon as the band was coming to terms with the death of Keith Relf. Years would pass before attempts would be made to re-activate the group. Jeff Fenholt picks up the story here. "I joined the Rock group Armageddon in approximately 1980. I replaced Keith Relf as lead singer. Keith had died of a heroin overdose. I was introduced to Martin Pugh, the lead guitarist of Armageddon, by Bruce Payne, Ritchie Blackmore's manager. We worked off and on writing material for over a year. We decided to resurrect the band in Los Angeles in 1983 with some of the original line-up, and a bassist from Eastern Europe by the name of Chrys, minus Keith."

The road would not be an easy one to tread. Armageddon, and its individual members, had deep rooted problems and the task ultimately proved too arduous. Jeff illustrates some of the internal and external pressures being brought to bear. "Drugs and heroin were rampant at the time. After several stop, starts, A&M Records decided to forego working with the group any further. Larry Mazar, later Kiss' manager, who was my manager at the time, took over the group and got us a recording deal with Capitol Records. While we were in the midst of recording our album, I left because of personality disputes ... fist fights, etc. A classic case of tremendous talent destroyed by drugs and dysfunction. My understanding is that at that point, the album was shelved and the group later completely disbanded."

Nevertheless, Jeff Fenholt would still be in demand and that same year he received word of a further project. A telephone call from Bruce Payne put the singer in touch with a new band proposal incorporating the erstwhile Elf and Rainbow rhythm section of bass player Craig Gruber and drummer Gary Driscoll with Blue Cheer's veteran guitarist Andrew 'Duck' McDonald. Driscoll had also added stints with Dakota and Starcastle to his credentials following his dismissal by Ritchie Blackmore. Gruber had just recently been involved with the early stages of the 'Heaven And Hell' pre-recording line-up of Black Sabbath. The foursome soon got to work, ironically deciding upon the band title Bible Black.

"During this time, I got a telephone call from Bruce Payne, informing me that Rainbow had fired Dio. They asked me to join Rainbow and I turned them down. I was told later that Ritchie Blackmore was listening on the other line, waiting to hear my excitement. As I recall, I was somewhat inebriated at the time, and said something to the effect of "I'll have a think on this and get back to you." This apparently really set Ritchie off. Roger Glover spent a week at my house writing music with me. We discussed the possibility of my joining Rainbow, but by that time, Ritchie had retracted his offer and the door was closed. Light another match to drunken dysfunction." Undaunted, Bible Black hit the road in New England playing to large clubs and concert halls. Jeff Glixman was pulled in to add his craftsmanship to demo recordings. The band recorded five songs at Glixman's studios in Buckhead, Georgia. The band found gaining a record deal though was tougher than expected. Bible Black began to spiral downward as Jeff recounts. "The drinking, drugs and violence were again getting out of hand. The band was partying non-stop. My wife sued me for divorce at which time, I quit the band, returned home and saved my marriage."

Jeff gave Rock n' Roll another chance, forming up a band with the Rondinelli brothers Teddy and Bobby. Drummer Bobby, previously with a band known oddly as Samantha, had recently come to the fore with Rainbow, gracing the 1981 record 'Difficult To Cure' and the follow-up 'Straight Between The Eyes' a year later. This second sojourn had proven lucrative, the album not only being Rainbow's biggest selling opus in North America but also spawning their biggest radio hit 'Stone Cold'. Soon making an enviable reputation for himself as a drummer with both a deft touch and an ability to purely pummel when the need arose, Rondinelli had also marked himself out on the touring circuit as the possessor of a wicked sense of humour. The new group, simply billed as Rondinelli, drafted Mountain's Felix Pappalardi to act as producer. Besides the weight of his name Pappalardi brought with him not only his instrumental prowess but also his proven organisational talents, he had during the 60s handled business affairs for Cream, and his repute as a producer.

Here the vine of Black Sabbath weaves in once more. Bobby, some years subsequent, adding Sabbath to his list of high profile appointments alongside a current long term employment with Blue Oyster Cult. Bobby confirms his affiliation with Jeff Fenholt. "I was still in Rainbow at the time but myself, my brother Teddy, Felix and Jeff were getting together this new band. It sounded great and Jeff is a great singer. I like the guy a lot. We had always skirted around each other on the live circuit, always talking about getting a band together and with the Rainbow situation closing we were finally able to do it. We did a lot of rehearsals, a lot of jamming. Good times." All the promise though would come to a sudden and dramatic halt. "Felix Pappalardi, Bobby Rondinelli and his brother, Teddy, and myself went into the recording studio to begin recording what was my dream project." Jeff relates. "While we were working on this project, Felix was murdered. We were devastated."

Pappalardi was killed by his wife Gail with a fatal shot to the throat on April 17th 1983. The pair were both keen gun enthusiasts and Gail had claimed that Felix had been shot accidentally when her husband had been showing her how to clean the weapon. Although prosecution lawyers tried to reinforce an assertion that the shooting was in actuality a revenge slaying for Felix's known indiscretions with his mistress Valerie Merians, the wife of the Rock star was acquitted.

With Bible Black regrettably consigned to the Rock n' Roll history books and Rondinelli rolling on with a new singer by the name of Ray Gillen, yet another example of the tantalising Sabbath spider web in operation, Fenholt extricated himself out of the East Coast scene. "Jeff went to California after Felix was shot by his wife" explains the drummer. "We spent, like, a year at least trying to find another singer. Getting nowhere. We auditioned so many singers you would not believe, most of it a complete waste of time and very frustrating."

Gillen was doing the rounds of the New York clubs fronting up an act named Harlett. "Someone told me this guy was good so I called him. By then, we had gotten fed up with auditioning all these losers but the recommendation for Ray was very strong so he seemed worth a call. The thing was, I called him and said 'Hi Ray, this is Bobby Rondinelli . . . ' and he hung up! I'm thinking what the . . . ?! So, I call up again and he hangs up on me a second time. I called him again and I said 'Look, if you hang up on me one more time I'm not going to call you back OK?' to which he replied 'Enough George!' Turns out the drummer in his band, George, had been talking to Ray the night before about me, and he thought the whole thing was just a big wind up.

So, when Ray realised it really was me, I told him about the gig and asked if he was interested. 'Yeah' he says 'but can I just come along?' I told him no, he had to send a tape because we were not into wasting any more time auditioning people, so send a tape. 'OK' he says. The tape never arrived. A few weeks later he phones up and says 'Did you get the tape?' Of course, I hadn't got it so we spoke and he suggested he come down and sing for us anyway. The minute he opened his mouth we knew. He could sing great and we were knocked out. That's when he told us he had never sent the tape!"

Jeff Fenholt relocated to Palos Verdes, California in the summer of 1984. Next on the agenda would be Joshua. Comprising musicians with personal Christian values the band's public message was simply one of Rock n' Roll, albeit aided by the quite unique talents of the Greek born former Blind Owl lead guitarist Joshua Periah. With the young Swedish guitar guru Yngwie Malmsteen taking speed guitar to stratospheric new levels the search was one for even faster fret fiends and Periah more than fitted the bill.

Joshua's aptly titled mini-album debut 'The Hand Is Quicker Than The Eye' scored a deal with major label Polydor resulting in the 'Surrender' album. This record threw down the gauntlet had drew much appreciation for its melodic Rock stance and Periah's super speed dexterity, some journalists even branding the guitarist as the fastest in the world. When Jeff Fenholt teamed up with Joshua they had dispensed with singer Steve Fontaine, he would go onto

Ringleader and a fleeting shot with Uriah Heep, and were building up to their second album. The recording process for this record would be expeditious. "We wrote all of the music in two weeks. Recorded all of the tracks in four days and were finished" Jeff records. "I chose not to tour with the band. I had become a Christian by this time and found it refreshing to work with guys that were clean and sober. Joshua was a secular band comprising Christians. I did not leave Joshua to join Sabbath; I left for other reasons."

Joshua was on the receiving end of some weighty offers from European labels. The guitarist returned to North America, explaining what happened next on his personal website. "Coming back to LA with advances made the victory bittersweet, when Jeff Fenholt told Joshua he would remain with Josh, but wanted the other band members to be replaced, by friends from the 70s rock group Rainbow. Joshua told Jeff he couldn't dump the other band mates that way, so Josh declined. Respectfully, Fenholt left."

This then, is when Black Sabbath rose large on the horizon. Both industry and fan perception as to the band's status at that point was still reverential. The Dio triumvirate of albums and 'Born Again' had all been records of major impact. The group was still striving to maintain their Britishness and had made approaches to Steve Marriott of The Small Faces to take up the position of singer. These talks never came to fruition though. Geoff Nicholls gives some consideration to Tony Iommi's thinking at the time. "Tony really wanted an English singer and there was talk of Steve Marriott. I know the guy had a great voice and I think that might have really worked well. Another guy who was considered was Bob Catley from Magnum, because we were still thinking it was going to be an album of different singers, with all different styles. Then Tony got hold of a cassette of Jeff Fenholt, I think through the producer Jeff Glixman, and he was knocked out by Jeff's vocals. I remember when Jeff first came down because he was obviously very wealthy from the 'Jesus Christ Superstar' thing. He told us how much he was paid and I can remember thinking 'Fucking Hell—that's a lot of money!' That I do remember because it was more than any of us were getting at the time! We did wonder about the money thing because he was so obviously well off. He wasn't an unknown, which is how he is often spoken about, at least in the things I've read. If anything he was doing us the favour! He came with a voice, a look and a reputation."

This is how Jeff describes his induction into the Sabbath camp during the December of 1984. "Don Arden, Black Sabbath's manager, called me. He stated that Tony had gotten hold of a Joshua tape and had flipped over my voice. How Tony got that tape; to this day, I do not know. Don asked me to come to his office and meet with him concerning Black Sabbath, so I did. We spoke for several hours. Shortly thereafter, he called me and told me that Tony wanted to meet me for cocktails and/or dinner. I went to the Chateau Marmont and met Tony for the first time."

This initial meeting, probably to establish Fenholt's basic character and persona, went without a hitch according to the singer. "We got along great; lots of laughs. I got together with Tony several times after that and we had dinner and talked. I visited with him and his girlfriend, Lita Ford, several times in their hotel suite. Tony asked me to sing lead on his solo project, to which I agreed. It was my understanding that I would write all melodies and all lyrics. As a Christian, I insisted upon this. No audition was required. We broke camp for the holidays. Tony returned to England."

True to his word Tony Iommi picked up where they had left off. "Upon his return to LA in January, he informed me that we were going to use Lita Ford's rhythm section; Eric Singer and Gordon Copley" Jeff explains. "We all went into the Cherokee Recording Studios in January and began laying tracks. By the end of a couple of weeks, we had about six or eight rhythm tracks laid down."

As a Christian, albeit admitting he was struggling with this aspect of his life during this period, one wonders just how the vocalist reconciled himself in allying himself with such a band as Black Sabbath. The band had after all always been high on the anti-Rock fundamentalist hit list for over a decade. "With regard to a Christian joining Black Sabbath, though I was a believer, my lifestyle didn't necessarily reflect it at that time. I was struggling to balance two worlds. I felt that Tony was not a bad person; though he did have some bad habits. With regard to old Sabbath lyrics being sung onstage; I figured I would cross that bridge when I came to it. Quite frankly, the subject never came up."

Here are Eric's memories of Jeff Fenholt's introduction. "We were at Cherokee Studios. Somehow we just found this guy. I don't know how, possibly on a recommendation to Tony because I don't recall any audition as such. So, there he was and the initial instincts were very good. Jeff looked great, actually he looked a lot like Robert Plant. He had a great set of pipes too, he could definitely sing to the quality Tony was looking for so his input at first was very encouraging. We all got along fine and when he first went into the vocal booth he did great. He sang his ass off and put forward a lot of lyrics, 'Star Of India', some Blues stuff too."

These first tryouts held a purpose beyond ascertaining the qualities of Fenholt's vocal character. Geoff Nicholls tells how Tony Iommi used these early jams to find out the potential scope of Jeff Fenholt as a possible writer. "When you first ask a singer in it has to involve so much more than just whether they look the part and can hit the notes. This is the same for any new singer you try out. You keep stuff back deliberately, such as lyrics, idea and vocal melodies because you really want to see what they come up with first. A vocalist can inject his own ideas and take the song somewhere else. If it doesn't work then we can come in and start guiding with the original ideas. Jeff had some nice ideas.

'Star Of India' was a good example. That was Jeff's title. We were just talking about the Indian feel of the song which sparked that one. 'Through The Eye Of The Storm' was another one of Jeff's and we had a very commercial Van Halen type of song, which was very good but a bit too poppy for Sabbath. Jeff came up with a lot of sound lyrical stuff. I remember working with him on the very original version of 'No Stranger To Love'. We were in my hotel room at the Merlin and I was just chunking out some riffs, I was actually trying to get a Foreigner 'I Want To Know What Love Is' type of vibe going. Jeff heard me messing about and said 'I've got an idea for that!' and we started working. He had a lot of good stuff."

Some of those proposed lyrics clearly did impinge on Jeff's beliefs though as he recalls "Tony and I had many heated discussions about wanting more Sabbath-like lyrics on the tracks. Case in point, Tony had written a lyric titled, 'Defiant and Damned' and I refused to develop it and I refused to sing it."

Eric Singer does not recall theological issues intruding into the studio. "I've got nothing against the guy personally. His religious agenda? I find it contradictive but that's just my opinion here. He was always pretty straight up with me, he seemed an OK guy. I can't remember the religion thing ever coming up while we were working with him at all." Geoff Nicholls is in agreement here and cannot remember any religious issues impinging on the sessions. "I didn't know Jeff was religious then. He kept it to himself and I can't ever remember it being talked about. The first I knew about all of that was when I saw him on TV quite a few years later."

Jeff also reveals that this line-up was very nearly bolstered by a particular high-ranking individual. "Geezer Butler was living with his wife in the Midwest at the time. He came into the studio with us for one day and never returned. It was my understanding that Tony and Ozzy were at odds and that Geezer had aligned with Ozzy. Tony and I proceeded on." This brief visit from the bassist was actually held in much more significance than Jeff would have realised as Geoff Nicholls details. "When Geezer came down he was there to listen to the stuff. He said he liked it so then there were talks about getting him back into the band, which didn't work out. Geezer left to join up with Ozzy soon after, I think this is the period when Tony Iommi actually bought the name 'Black Sabbath'. Before, it was the three of them, Tony, Geezer and Bill, but from that point on Black Sabbath belonged to Tony Iommi."

What Jeff Fenholt describes as happening next is crucial to the understanding of these sessions. "Gordon and Eric were not asked to return to the studio. Tony and I continued in the studio, often times accompanied by Geoff Nicholls on keyboards. I am not certain of this point, but I think Bobby Clearmountain was running the boards. Whoever it was, quit because of all night sessions and the many, many times Tony and I didn't show up as scheduled. During this time, Don Arden informed Tony that this needed to be a Black Sabbath project not a solo project."

If this is correct then Jeff Fenholt clearly believed, and was told, he was singing on a Black Sabbath project. Bearing in mind that Tony Iommi had only just legally secured the name as an asset this is none too surprising. This is a matter of dispute with most biographers and commentators who maintain that the recordings only came under the wing of the Black Sabbath name tag after Glenn Hughes had much later wrapped up his vocals for 'Seventh Star'. Rock n' Roll history is littered with accounts of musicians entering the studio not yet having decided upon a project title. It is, of course, noteworthy that Jeff asserts both Eric Singer and Gordon Copley left the proceedings at this juncture, Eric to return at a later date after Jeff had backed out too.

"Now that it had been established that I was singing lead on a Black Sabbath project, I was determined to maintain my own personal vocal style, yet stay within the Sabbath tradition" the singer says. "My vocal style at that time was heavy rock with a Blues foundation. I was not concerned about covering Ozzy music or Dio, the only thing that I was concerned with was making the best album we could make."

Eric Singer refutes Fenholt's version of events strongly. "I was always involved from the beginning. Gordon Copley went with Lita to Hawaii to write and removed himself from the project. Dave Spitz was then brought in and did all the Cherokee bass tracks except on 'No Stranger To Love'." This is where the controversy hinges. Jeff Fenholt saying that at some point only he and Tony carried on the recordings, during which time he was told it had become a Black Sabbath project. Eric Singer denies this, stating that he was present throughout the entire recording process and that the suggestion of the Black Sabbath handle only came much, much later.

Tony Iommi works up his new rhythm section of bassist Dave Spitz and drummer Eric Singer. Note Lita Ford's drum kit still in use.

Intriguingly, Jeff makes mention of something that, if published, might confirm the 'band' status for the recording unit at the time. "The only photos that were shot of me with Tony and the band were shot in the studio by a photographer who was brought in to shoot the session." These pictures, apparently taken by a close friend of Tony Iommi's, have never surfaced.

In the singer's take on this period Tony Iommi and Jeff Fenholt soldiered on but the rate of progress would be slow. Jeff records that by May of 1985 only 3 or 4 finished songs, with Iommi acting as producer, had been committed to final tape. "The dysfunction was obvious to all. I telephoned my friend, Larry Mazar, and asked him if Jeff Glixman could come in and help us sort this out and finish the project. Glix agreed." This solution to re-energise the recordings did not materialise in the fashion anticipated though. "When the three of us went into the studio together, Tony and Glix paired off" predicates Jeff. "Glixman started criticising my work ethic. It had been my hope that Glixman would help make things better and from my standpoint, it didn't work out that way."

Geoff Nicholls has his own conception on the work accomplished during this period and his working relationship with Jeff Fenholt. He is surprisingly candid about his admiration for the singer. "I liked Jeff. He was, in truth, a great singer too." He goes on to make some comparisons here. "A bit like Ray Gillen I felt. Jeff was very much a vowel singer like that, in a way a lot of Americans are. I know Tony found that difficult with Jeff just in the same way as he did with Ray. It's just a particular way in which Americans, in the main, tend to sing. He had a good range to his voice, it was a very full, bluesy voice. The guy was a bloody good singer and nobody could deny it. If it had worked out and Fenholt would have done the album and toured I don't think he would have let the side down vocally."

In relation to the difficulties Jeff encountered with producer Jeff Glixman the keyboard player has some observations too. "I would say that was right in one sense because it was Jeff that suggested bringing Jeff Glixman in the first place but it kind of backfired on him in a strange way. When we did some recording though, Glix pulled Jeff Fenholt up on his diction. That was a big concern I seem to remember. It gets back to that unique Englishness of Sabbath I guess. Tony Martin and Glenn Hughes were always superb at diction and you could hear and understand every word. I think it might be just an American thing. Anyhow, it's quite possible Jeff Fenholt wasn't told this. Overall Jeff Fenholt was very good. I liked the guy and had some good times with him writing songs. I remember going through 'No Stranger To Love' with Jeff and that was sounding great. It was my song and I was really happy with the ideas and vocals Jeff was suggesting for it. The one funny thing that was going on in the studio was that we had too many Jeffs!" he says in jest. "Maybe that was the reason? Too many Jeffs!!"

The actual catalyst for Jeff Fenholt's departure lay in an incident with Don Arden. What follows is an incident the singer has never related publicly before. "I genuinely liked Don Arden, who was managing Tony at the time; however, Don was highly volatile. After I had laid down the first three tracks with Tony, Don Arden showed up at the Cherokee Studios with a huge black guy named Bob Street. Don said that he wanted to hear the music! So, Tony played him the cuts. At the end of the first cut, I asked Don what he thought ... to which Don replied, "Not bad." They listened to the second cut and Don just sat there and I said, "What do you think of that cut?" Don said once again "Not bad" to which I said back to Don, "What's that ... your stock answer?"

The next thing I knew, Don had me by my shirt collar, slammed me against the wall and growled into my face, "I don't give no fucking stock answers to nobody, you piece of shit." When Don let go of me, I tried to leave the room but Bob Street wouldn't let me. I was more emotionally hurt than physically shaken and I actually stood there in shock. At that point, Don came over and hugged me and started patting me on the cheek and said, "Come on, what's a little argument between friends? You're a great singer. I'm sorry I got a little rough with you but you're a big boy ... you can take it. Come on, let's be friends." I remained in the session for the rest of the night but obviously had learned never to talk down to Mr. Arden again. That is why when I decided to leave the band, I waited until Don was out of town and scheduled the meeting with David Arden as a courtesy to let them know he was leaving for South America. Needless to say, I was scared of Don.

After leaving Black Sabbath, I joined with Rudy Sarzo, Tommy Aldridge and Craig Goldy to form a Rock group. Rudy Sarzo told me that when they were putting their band together and looking for a lead singer, they had made some inquiries to try to find him to see if I was happy in Sabbath or would consider their band. Rudy told me that Don Arden personally called Rudy and told him that if he even so much as made contact with me that Don would have Rudy's arms and legs broken. Apparently, that scared the ever lovin' hell out of Rudy, but apparently not enough for Rudy to contact me after I departed from Sabbath. Don is apparently the wrong guy to play around with."

Bassist Rudy Sarzo, of course known for his multi platinum work with Quiet Riot then Ozzy Osbourne, reinforces this story. "Tommy Aldridge and I had set up this group and at first Sharon Osbourne wanted to get involved in the management side of things. At that time, although Ozzy as obviously her prime thing, she was branching out too, working with us and Lita Ford. Anyhow, this was during her fall out with her father Don. Sharon suggested we try to get hold of Jeff Fenholt to sing for the band and gave me Jeff's number. So, I call him up and he says "Thanks but I'm working with Black Sabbath right now." I had no idea! After that I call I get a return threatening call from Don, basically saying leave his artist alone—in the Don Arden way!"

The singer goes some way to illustrating his mindset at this difficult time. "I was sad that the whole Sabbath thing fell apart because I genuinely wanted the tour and hoped for the remuneration that would follow. At the same time, I was incredibly relieved once I was out of the band because being clean and sober and fully aware of what was going on around me, the paranoia and negative influences surrounding Tony and the Sabbath stigma were next to personally unbearable."

Jeff Fenholt and Tony Iommi duly parted ways. "At that point, I informed Don Arden that I was leaving for South America for a four week solo tour. Don then informed me that Black Sabbath was reconvening with the original members and they were going on without me. We shook hands and that was it. Shortly thereafter, the original members of Black Sabbath performed at Bob Geldof's Live Aid. It is my understanding that hopes of a Black Sabbath reunion were thwarted; at which time Tony went back into the studio with Glixman and Glenn Hughes to complete the 'Seventh Star' album."

During the nineties a bootleg CD of Jeff Fenholt's recordings 'with' Black Sabbath saw active distribution on the Internet. For anyone familiar with studio

The 'Black Sabbath Seventh Star Demos with Jeff Fenholt' bootleg.

procedure it is obvious that the recordings involved are not audition tapes but working demos, some close to completion, others caught on tape in a very embryonic 'jam' stage. Jeff himself says "From the beginning, it was my understanding that we were recording final album tracks. Several of the same tracks that I sang on wound up on the Black Sabbath 'Seventh Star' album with Glenn. Obviously, these were not demos or audition tapes."

The songs titled by Jeff Fenholt as being cut in these sessions are 'Star Of India' (evolving into 'Seventh Star'), 'Dark Side Of Love' ('Danger Zone'), 'In The Eye Of The Storm' ('Turn To Stone'), 'Rock The World', 'Lock Myself Away', 'Don't Turn Away' and 'Love Has No Mercy'.

The CD comprises these first four tracks plus 'Take My Heart' ('No Stranger To Love') and 'Love On The Line' ('Heart Like A Wheel') a variety of jams and improvisations before a Blues number 'The Thrill Is Gone'—with Lita Ford, and closes out with further short jams. "As you know, Lita was Tony's girlfriend at the time, I found her to be not only gorgeous but highly intelligent and very sweet." Says Jeff. "She asked me to come into the studio and listen to some of her vocals and I did so. As I recall, one thing led to another and I did a bit of jamming with her." However, those interested in these recordings should tread carefully as there are two versions in circulation, the latter featuring material that, although taking some of the titles given by Fenholt, certainly do not include Tony Iommi's guitar work. The status of these tracks remained somewhat of a mystery until clarified by Jeff Fenholt, who finally explains the stark contrast in guitar. "'Star Of India', 'Dark Side Of Love' and 'In The Eye Of The Storm' are songs I recorded with Tony, Eric and Gordon Copley. 'Rock The World' was one of the cuts I did with Rudy Sarzo, Tommy Aldridge and Craig Goldy." (The later Driver project.) The other, non Iommi, tracks will be dealt with as the timeline unfolds.

What is clear from these leaked Iommi recordings is that all of the songs were changed substantially for the final album recordings. Whilst the basis of the songs have been retained, (they are undoubtedly the same songs) vocal melody lines, all of the lyrics and even song structures have undergone a significant overhaul. Jeff Fenholt remarks that "While I was in the band, I wrote all of the melodies and lyrics you have heard me sing. I must say, though I have only listened to the album with Glenn one or two times, I noticed a lot of my melodies being used and even a few lyrics for which I was not given credit." The question of lyrical credit is still open as none of the tracks that can be compared with the available bootleg material match.

Eric Singer sees things very differently and offer his opinion on why Tony Iommi decided to scrap the Jeff Fenholt material. "I think the thing was that although at first Jeff did great Tony wanted everything to progress, especially on vocal melodies. That was it really. Vocal melodies. Tony is a great melody man. That gets forgotten a lot because a lot of people just think of Black Sabbath in very basic terms. Actually all those great songs are built upon a really strong root melody, which mainly comes from Tony. For a song to really work the musical melody has to be matched by a complimentary vocal that takes it up that next step. You think of Kiss, those guys are just melody machines. Ozzy and Ronnie did it for Sabbath in different ways, both of which worked. Jeff just couldn't nail it."

Singer raises a valid point here. Riffs, no matter how loud or aggressively pitched, are in essence melodies given form. A successful melody makes a great song, the strengths of which can be transferred to any instrument and any style. Tony Iommi's knack of mastering the riff has been complimented by a range of singers that have spanned the spectrum in terms of lifting those songs up to a higher plane. Ozzy had a habit of happily, some might say lazily, following the riff. Listen to 'Iron Man' for damning evidence. However, he would also be able to bring a song to conclusion with simple yet effective melody patterns that harked back to The Beatles, a craft he has polished with each successive solo album release. Ronnie James Dio embellished songs with his own unique wizardry, able to weave a more complex, if equally successful, series of hook lines.

Melody is the great decider for all great music. A song is a hook, a memory that lasts. Indeed it has been proven time and time again that vocalists with awesome talent and guitarists blessed with supernatural gifts are nothing without the song. Why Sabbath songs survive and prosper to this day is down to melody pure and simple. Even Einstein would have forgone the challenge to construct a successful song formulae without this mercurial ingredient.

Eric illustrates the point as evidenced by the frustrations of the musicians in the studio. "I think Jeff thought the melodies were fine but they just didn't cut it. Jeff was asked to go home and work on them but they never got better. He could jam great but when it came to the actual thing it just never seemed to work. We were actually all quite dumbstruck because it was an odd situation, very weird. I don't remember a decision being made about Jeff as such, it just all kind of petered out. So, what we got recorded with Jeff was a set of ideas really. These demos obviously later got onto the tape trading market. Nothing vocally or lyrically was used. When Glenn came in we started from scratch."

Meantime, as Jeff Fenholt was on tour in South America, a reception whipped up by a local promoter provided the catalyst for the polemics to come. This is how the singer recalls the sequence of events. "I had mentioned to my promoter that I had just left Black Sabbath as lead singer. The man who introduced me to the crowd took it upon himself, unbeknownst to me to introduce me as the former original star of 'Jesus Christ Superstar' and former lead singer of Black Sabbath. In subsequent interviews, I was asked about my involvement with Sabbath. I didn't give it much time, but simply said something to the effect, "I sang with Sabbath for several months and left and I am now doing Christian music." My concerts in South America were taped by a Christian organisation. Without prior notice to me, excerpts of these tapes were aired throughout the U.S. on national television. From that moment to now, people have mostly been interested in my 'Jesus Christ Superstar' background, but the Sabbath issue does come up. Since I did, in fact, sing with Black Sabbath, even for a short time, I have no problem discussing the topic. I was with the band from December '84 through May of 1985. Nothing more. Nothing less. Anything beyond that is definitely blown out of proportion."

Here Jeff reiterates that he sang with Black Sabbath. This is the raw point of contention. Surely his claims would hold more veracity if he were to simply say he demoed on tapes for Tony Iommi? Fans would have little to get worked up about if that were the case. The central issue that makes Fenholt such a pariah in the Rock community is that he consistently claims it was Black Sabbath that he sang for. Possibly, (and this is purely hypothetical) regaling an audience of Christian fundamentalists unfamiliar with Heavy Metal with tales of being saved from the clutches of Tony Iommi would simply sail over their heads. It is worth pointing out here though that Fenholt's personal ministry does not exactly go after 'soft' targets, his literature making appeals to society's fallen.

Using the very words 'Black Sabbath' though can tap into a direct emotion. For the ignorant, Black Sabbath is Hell, Beelzebub, Satan, Lord of this world. The distinction is simple. To the ignorant Tony Iommi is just a talented unassuming Brummie muso with a quirky penchant for a cowboy moustache. Black Sabbath though is nothing less than the Devil incarnate. This is, of course, just speculation based upon the hearsay that Jeff Fenholt has used the Black Sabbath connection for self-glorification. Although; there's the rub. Has he?

Much, if not most, of Jeff Fenholt's mentions outside of this work regarding Black Sabbath are rather humble. There are no lurid claims and, indeed, everything seems very matter of fact. Geoff Nicholls caught one of Fenholt's TV performances and, far from being offended, found it mildly amusing. "I just turned on the tele and there he was. It was cool to see him still singing so well and obviously enjoying some success. It's not my thing but he sounded sincere. OK, he said he was in Black Sabbath. It didn't annoy me or anything. Tony might have told him that, Don might have told him that. Who knows? I don't see why it is such a big issue actually. There are other people that have done a lot worse."

Jeff Fenholt says he was told by Arden and Iommi that he was recording a Black Sabbath project. It is possible that Eric Singer may not have been kept in the loop on this or that, as so often happens, minds were changed. Some of the biggest household names chronicled in this book were, at times, kept very definitely out of the loop. If there is one industry that specialises in keeping its operatives in the dark it is Rock n' Roll and, as many band members interviewed for this work have testified, the Black Sabbath inner circle perfected that Machiavellian art form to a fine degree. Some of the musicians interviewed for this book have often voiced the opinion they felt like carthorses fitted with blinkers. It is eminently feasible that Eric Singer, Jeff Fenholt and Glenn Hughes are all telling 'their' truth, all with equal veracity and conviction. All the conversations held with the author were sincere. The trouble with Black Sabbath is that there has always been more than one truth in operation at any given time.

The question remains. Was he wasn't he? On reflection Jeff Fenholt, until the disclosures afforded by recent discussions, had seemed a lone voice. It could well be that his account is truthful and, it has to be said, his communications with the author seemed utterly sincere. Not once did Jeff ever mention his faith or suggest anything outlandish. Unfortunately for him, prior to this book no one else ever come forward to back up his claims and he is to this day,

assailed by an army of detractors. What must not be overlooked is that he has too much intimate knowledge, plus the solid evidence of circulated tapes, to be pushed into the glory seeking loony league. The 'Seventh Star Demos' bootleg holds greater probity than the shroud of Turin, the weeping Madonna and all 38 of St. Benedicts atrophied fingers combined.

To be objective, it must be pointed out though that most people offering their opinion on this contentious issue have no first hand experience or evidence on which to base their assertions. Tony Iommi (to date) refuses to discuss the subject. Eric Singer, a reliable, credible witness who was there, contradicts the vocalist totally. "He was never in the band. You know how I know? Firstly there was no band at that stage. We were working on Tony's solo record. I was there so I know. It was an odd period because it seemed as though Tony was almost treading water. He was between Sabbath and just aiming for a solo record. Nothing was set in stone and we were all kind of waiting for something to happen.

You know, if Jeff had nailed those melodies he might have hung in there but, who is to say? Too many ifs you see, if he had delivered what Tony wanted that record might still have been Tony's solo record. Nobody ever discussed Sabbath at the time we were demoing because that was something decided upon by other people much later down the line, probably after Glenn Hughes had put down his final vocals."

What is the drummer's perspective on the fan curiosity regarding Jeff Fenholt's time in the studio? "Ha, well I can give you Tony's take on the whole thing! He doesn't give two flying fucks about it. It really was no major deal. The guy came in, sang for a bit then went. It just didn't work. I don't know why really. Jeff was cool, he wasn't an asshole or anything. Probably Tony just thought it wasn't what he was after."

Geoff Nicholls has a different perspective. "Yes, that was Tony's solo record" he maintains. "But, and this is a big 'but', all the way through the Sabbath history there have been talks going on about is it or is it not Black Sabbath. Jeff Fenholt may well have been told it was a Black Sabbath album at that time. Tony may have told him that for some reason best known to himself. That I just don't know. Ian Gillan has said he was only ever singing for Black Sabbath but I remember very clearly that 'Born Again' was designed as a brand new group. Different people are told different things. Certain people are given information and others are not. I don't think Jeff would lie. I actually don't think it's too big a deal. Could I have imagined him onstage with us? Yes I could because he had the look, the voice and the credibility. It might have been quite interesting

Jeff Fenholt in 1986.

actually. Put it this way—he got past the auditions and into the studio. There are many, many hundreds of very capable singers who never get to that stage. The guy was there, he sang great but it didn't work out. It happens a lot with bands.

I didn't think it was Black Sabbath at that point. As far as I was concerned I was working with Tony on a solo record. I guess when fans hear 'Seventh Star' it sounds very much like Black Sabbath, but it really wasn't in those stages. I believe the very first suggestion that the Black Sabbath name be used came much later when we had submitted the track 'No Stranger To Love' to the record company."

Speaking after the event, on the 'Seventh Star' UK tour Tony Iommi put these troubled times into perspective. "For a long time I had been thinking about going solo, putting the Black Sabbath name to rest for a while because Bill had gone, Geezer had gone and getting some stability was proving difficult. I thought I had the chance to make a bit of a break and make a couple of records before getting Black Sabbath back together again later on. 'Seventh Star' was supposed to be my first solo record but then it seemed as if everyone wanted it to be Black Sabbath."

Returning to the USA after his run of South American concerts Fenholt found that his work with Iommi, ironically in much the same manner as David Donato before him, had brought him to the attention of another link in the Black Sabbath chain. This is the source of the remainder of the bootleg recordings. 'Lock Myself Away', 'Don't Turn Away' and 'Love Has No Mercy' were all recorded for Geezer Butler.

"After I left Black Sabbath, Geezer and his wife called me several times and asked me if I would sing on his project. He told me that he was impressed with my vocals from the day he came into the studio with Tony and me, and that now that Tony and I had separated, he wanted to know if I would work with him. The manager of Iron Maiden, Rod Smallwood, was representing Geezer at the time. Geezer laid the tracks in England. Rob's associate called me and scheduled me to go into the studio and lay down some demos. I did so. I recorded the three rough demo tracks in approximately two hours. Geezer did not attend the session, as I believe he was in England at the time. Shortly after that I jumped on board with Driver and stopped communicating with Geezer."

The singer had received a further call from Rudy Sarzo. A new project entitled Driver, also numbering another ex-Ozzy man drummer Tommy Aldridge and the guitarist Craig Goldy, was in the making. "I had dinner with them a few times and decided to rehearse with them" Jeff recounts. "They were all great guys and there were no hard drugs in the band.

John Dempsey, a big shot at Columbia, signed the group. After three months or so, Dempsey was no longer with Columbia and we, being his pet project, were having a hard time dealing with his departure. At the same time this was going on, I was getting calls to do major venues around the world performing Christian music."

"Jeff was a real find for Driver" reckons Rudy Sarzo. "After first approaching Jeff when he was with Black Sabbath Tommy and I had built up the band with Craig Goldy and Jeff Scott Soto as vocalist. The problem was with Jeff Scott Soto he had just come out of Yngwie Malmsteen's band and, because of all the extended soloing and instrumental stuff that Yngwie does, he really had not sung too much. We wanted a singer that could commit to a full live show and at the time Jeff Scott Soto couldn't manage it. Driver was then being managed by Alex Koshan and he recommended Jeff Fenholt. We spent about a year working with Jeff and I have to say that, out of all of the singers I have ever worked with, Jeff has the very best voice. The guy can sing incredible, totally natural with real heart and emotion. Basically the guy has a gift from God so it was understandable Sabbath wanted him."

Ultimately the Driver project stalled. "We had a deal on the table but basically Alex asked for too much money" explains Rudy. "A great shame because the buzz on the band was huge and it has always been a regret of mine that we never cut an album with Jeff." Sarzo and Aldridge stayed united and hopped onboard Whitesnake, touring the monumentally successful '1987' album. Although Sarzo put in the hard yards on the live front, it had been the reliable Neil Murray, post his brief Ozzy stint, that had hewn out the low end architecture in the studio. Craig Goldy teamed up with Dio, the guitarist keeping in contact with Fenholt subsequently putting in appearances with the singer in various Christian based media.

Chapter 13

The Ultimate Din

Although nowhere near approaching the fragility surrounding Black Sabbath, Ozzy too was in the midst of carefully rebuilding his band. Auditions to pull in a new drummer were held in Los Angeles to which Randy Castillo—complete with a broken leg, attended. Eric Singer would also try out and as Bob Daisley sheepishly admits "Apparently I was the one who said Eric wasn't good enough! Eric told me this many years later but I don't even remember him being there."

The then future Black Sabbath drummer confirms his audition for Ozzy's band, and the reason he did not make the grade. "That's right. That was third time round for me and Bob. I auditioned with Bob and Jake E. Lee at Mates Rehearsals before. In truth I hadn't prepared myself properly for that one. I had pleaded my case with Sharon to be given a try out but, in truth, I didn't know the songs. I remember Bill London, from the Robin Trower band, was also trying out that day. In the end I jammed two songs with Bob and Jake. Ozzy said he liked the way I hit the drums really hard but I just didn't know the stuff. A valuable lesson in preparation."

Sandy Gennaro of Blackjack and the Pat Travers band was also among the hopefuls who nearly secured the position. Coincidentally Gennaro had replaced Tommy Aldridge in the Pat Travers band in 1980. Another face was even more familiar as Daisley recounts. "Bill Ward came down too. Not for an audition but just for the crack. He came down and we said, fuck it, let's have a play. We had a good time with Bill. That was a good session." The welcome diversion of Ward's jam could not allay the very real work at hand though. Bob recalls just how gruelling the auditioning process was and how his normal conciliatory nature was lost toward the end. Each candidate had four tracks to run through, 'Over The Mountain', 'Crazy Train', 'I Don't Know' and 'Flying High Again'.

"Jake and I were doing the auditions while Ozzy watched. It was drummer after drummer after drummer, day after day after day. After the first twenty or so it got a bit of a chore. Up until then we had been very professional, very polite telling the unsuccessful applicants "Thank you, we'll let you know" or "You're not quite what we're looking for" but it was disheartening going through four songs with a drummer who you knew after a few seconds wasn't good enough." With patience at a low ebb, Bob concedes the latter auditionees fell foul of his and Jake's frustration. "If they didn't get the fill intro to the first song 'Over The Mountain' right we would just stop them right there and say "Sorry—Next!!" It got that frustrating."

It was with some degree of relief that Fred Coury was finally chosen. Earlier in life the young Coury had in fact nearly railroaded himself from his chosen destination of Rock n' Roll to the world of sport. He had been attending hockey training school but the impact of his first ever gig in Toronto featuring a line-up of The Who, Heart and the J. Geils Band had captured his imagination and kindled a new ambition. "I went home and told my Mom I wanted to be a Rock n' Roll star" he laughs. His Ma replied "That's sweet," and Fred Coury was on his way.

Coury, still only 18, had only previously plied his trade with Chastain, appearing on their 1985 release 'Mystery Of Illusion'. Hooking up with Chastain had been on personal recommendation from renowned bassist Billy Sheehan to Mike Varney, Shrapnel Records boss. It would be Varney who would put Coury up for the Ozzy position. At this stage enter the familiar 'Mr. Fixit' figure of Dana Strum again. This time though his instincts for a good Ozzy man would fail him. Or maybe it's just guitarists?

"I was practicing 8 hours every day learning all the Ozzy and Black Sabbath songs I could in time for the audition" states Fred. "I would just go in there and play and play and play all to try and get the Ozzy gig. One day I came out of the studio and I saw this guy who I recognized. "Wow, it's that Dana Strum guy!" I thought. This was like the first real Rock star I had ever met. He was there doing preproduction for some other band and asked me what I was doing so I told him that I was trying out for the Ozzy gig.

"Give it up" he said. "You're not gonna get it. I know the guy who's gonna get it." I was crushed. It just destroyed me."

Come the day of the audition Fred sensed all was not well. Fred knew the owner of Mates Rehearsals where the tryouts were taking place. As he went in his acquaintance told him prophetically "I have a feeling you're the guy." Lifting his confidence somewhat his friends portent then fell flat as the reality of the situation dawned. "Everyone wanted Randy Castillo. He was the guy" he confides. "Everyone knew it was Randy's gig but he turned up with a broken leg in this big plaster cast. Well, he played and was still great but he had this cast on. What could they do? In the end I was the first runner up so I got the gig."

The youngster, aware of Randy's position within the camp, still had to go through with the audition. He hadn't spent time on those gruelling learning sessions to give up now. A sarcastic yet truthful observation from Bob Daisley jangled his nerves a bit more to add to the tension. "Bob told me that I was born the year after he first started playing bass guitar. That made me feel just great!" Fred listened as drummer after drummer were put through their paces. "I noticed that Ozzy never sang with them. When it was my turn I did a few songs and then Ozzy wanted to sing! I was actually having a ball because believe it or not this was the very first time I had played with monitors. I would hit the drum and hear it come back at me. I'd never heard that before! The mix was great and it made a world of difference."

The over eager teenager was keen to show the by now weary auditioning team just how much he had learnt. "I suggested this Ozzy song, or that Sabbath song because of course I knew all of them. I had learned every damn Ozzy song—every one! Every time I suggested a song to play they didn't know it so I would start them off and we would try them out. It was surreal. We were there for about an hour and when I finished I turned round and there was every other drummer all standing at the back of the room. I was blessed that day."

The new team of Ozzy, Jake, Bob and Fred would then enter the studio in London. Bob Daisley has cause to recollect this period well. "I was writing lyrics sitting at home in my garden" he muses. "Ozzy would send me a backing track with any old stuff on it. The tapes would have all Ozzy's phrasing and vocal melody ideas down and then I would put lyrics in to fit, to make the songs make sense. During this writing period Ozzy and I had a fall out though. The record company wanted to hear how the songs were sounding so we went into a studio. I put the bass on the demos but, as I said, Ozzy and I fell out, we were at lock and horns."

However, a later contact would set the pattern for the next few years. "Ozzy called me again less than six weeks later wanting some lyrics for 'The Ultimate Sin'" Bob confides. "Of course I ended up doing it. I did some demos and wrote the lyrics for 'The Ultimate Sin' album which was a bit of an odd one because I don't think anyone in the band really liked it. I know Ozzy doesn't rate it—he calls it 'The Ultimate Din'! Ozzy and I had a verbal fallout though and Ozzy told me that we could not work together. So be it I thought and left."

Coury too would move on after laying down his demos. Shortly after Fred was flicking through 'Circus' magazine when he spotted his name. "It said I had worked with Ozzy on preproduction. How cool is that? It looked great on my resume!" The drummer would get another surprise just as Cinderella was getting into gear. "I picked up the phone one day and it was Ozzy calling from out of the blue. "Best of luck with the new band" he said. The nice thing was he really meant it and he had taken the trouble to call me after he had heard about Cinderella. That was awesome. Sharon and Ozzy treated me so well during that time I worked with them. They're very awesome people."

As for Dana's advice? "I kinda proved him wrong in a way I think but it bugged me for nearly 15 years!" confesses Fred. "Then recently Cinderella and Slaughter played together and he remembered and apologized to me for that!"

Next occupant of the Ozzy Osbourne drum stool would be Jimmy DeGrasso. His tenure would be brief, lasting from March until April of 1985. The veteran bassist Neil Murray would be on hand for a few days too at this juncture, just prior to rejoining Whitesnake. Post Ozzy DeGrasso would of course make his name with Alice Cooper and Megadeth.

In the midst of this period of confusion for both parties, Tony Iommi and Ozzy Osbourne would both be plucked out of their respective studio tribulations for an event which was to delight Black Sabbath fans worldwide. As part of the Bob Geldof instigated 'Live Aid' famine relief event many major Rock n' Roll acts had been persuaded to perform live for what was to be the world's biggest musical TV event. Geldof was a somewhat unexpected figure to galvanise the cream of international Rock talent. It had been many a year since his band the Boomtown Rats had scored any hits but once the Irishman had made his mind up the music world, beaten into submission by Geldof's guile and sheer guts, backed him to the hilt.

Naturally a plethora of the old guard, most noticeably Robert Plant and Jimmy Page, buried their differences and re-formed for this unique occasion. The very biggest names on the scene signed up to pledge their support. Amongst them was Black Sabbath.

SABBATH BLOODY SABBATH: THE BATTLE FOR BLACK SABBATH

The band, a true re-formation of Ozzy Osbourne, Tony Iommi, Geezer Butler and Bill Ward, marched out onstage in Pennsylvania at the Philadelphia JFK Stadium on the 13th July 1985. Notwithstanding the 90,000 punters packed into the arena Sabbath played out to an audience of many, many millions on TV. Running through just three numbers, 'Children Of The Grave', 'Iron Man' and 'Paranoid', it was to be the Sabbath collective's first association since the close of the 'Never Say Die' tour in December of 1978.

Upon close inspection fans, eager for a full blown reunion, gained some encouragement from the performance. Ozzy, managing to melt his mid 80s bleached perm into a lank, sweaty mess in about 30 seconds of onstage exertions, looked to be having a ball. Millions of global viewers caught the childlike smile on a mascara blurred, beaming face and wondered if this was a signal of greater things to come. Tony Iommi grinned with obvious glee and Geezer wasn't far behind in the visual appreciation. Tony Iommi found the event bewildering. "It was something that I think nobody could have possibly said no to. It made our lives, our bands and our silly arguments all look as insignificant as they actually were. Nobody went into it thinking about a re-formation. It was such a great pleasure to play with Ozzy, Bill and Geezer again. I don't think we played spectacularly well but the day wasn't about that. The four of us actually had a very good time. Being there was the important thing. You have to wonder though if we made any difference to the situation in Africa. I hope we did but time will tell I guess."

Backtracking slightly to June of 1985 future Ozzy bassist Phil Soussan had chosen to take up an offer from none other than Led Zeppelin guitarist Jimmy Page. These sessions would transpire to become the basis for Page's collaboration with former Free singer Paul Rodgers and the band known as The Firm, this unit being handpicked by former Led Zeppelin tour manager Phil Carlo. Soussan was involved with the band prior to the inclusion of eventual incumbent Tony Franklin and during this period would work with former Uriah Heep drummer Chris Slade and Rat Scabies of The Damned.

"Phil Carlo at Swansong called me to tell me that Jimmy had wanted me to jam with him. Chris Slade came by and played for one day but although he would end up eventually being the guy Jimmy wasn't sure. We played with Rat and that line-up lasted quite some time." Soussan had previously come to public attention with the Swansong signed Wildlife, a classy melodic hard rock act whose inaugural line-up comprised of brothers Chris and Steve Overland, bassist Nigel Widowson, keyboard player Mark Booty and drummer Richard Plumb. Widowson was supplanted by Bob Skeat whilst Plumb lost his spot to former Hotline drummer Pete Jupp.

The veteran Bad Company drummer Simon Kirke had replaced Jupp who joined Samson for their 1983 album. By early 1984 Kirke was out and replaced by Jeff Rich, formerly with Judie Tzuke. This last incarnation of Wildlife also saw the inclusion of former Cuddly Toys and Reflex bassist Phil Soussan. Promise was high but ultimately though Wildlife would flounder. The Overland brothers and Jupp re-emerged with Illegal Tender, a short lived outfit that included Soussan and Rich. Illegal Tender broke apart as Soussan joined the much vaunted solo artist Robin George's band. Rich would of course found a more prominent haven in Status Quo. Undeterred the Overlands together with Jupp formed the highly rated AOR act FM.

The early 1985 band Robin George assembled for touring comprised of Phil Soussan, former Magnum drummer Kex Gorin and Alliance keyboardist Eddie George. The latter was soon to depart for Magnum, although his stay in that particular outfit was extremely brief to say the least. Eddie George was not only succeeded in Robin George's band by Mark Stanway but the latter also replaced him in Magnum as well, Mark opting to rejoin the group after a period spent away from the ranks. In addition, George added second guitarist Huw Lucas, ex-Korea and Trouble, to the band now known as Dangerous Music after the album title.

Following a series of low key British club gigs the band supported the German guitar maestro Uli Jon Roth across Europe in February. However, Stanway was taken ill midway through the tour and his place was temporarily filled by Alan Nelson. With the tour dates completed Soussan was keen to jump ship. Little did he know that he would be abandoning this vessel to work with one of the very biggest names the Rock world had to offer.

At this particular career crossroads Soussan was still hedging his bets with Robin George too but an unexpected call would take his career into an altogether unexpected direction.

During the mid eighties the then fledgling Channel 4 TV station was bravely testing the early evening with a weekly Heavy Metal show dubbed 'ECT'. Often disastrous live performances set in a pseudo sci-fi panorama by bands such as Rock Goddess, Warlock, Magnum, Madam X and Rogue Male made it for strangely compulsive viewing. One such performance by Robin George's band would catch the eye of someone just a little more influential on the night of broadcast.

Phil Soussan takes up the story. "I'd been with Robin for quite almost a year and for various reasons it really was time for me to move on. We had just done the live TV show 'ECT' and it was actually really good. Afterwards I went back home and got a phone call from Lynn Seagar who worked for Sharon Osbourne. She told me there was someone who wanted to talk to me and next thing I know I'm talking to Ozzy on the phone! Well, Ozzy told me he had just watched the show and he wanted to meet up to discuss something. He was in Spirals bar, a place I knew well." Spirals bar was actually owned by a mutual friend of both Ozzy's and Phil's the comedian TV host of 'Candid Camera' Arthur Atkins. "So we arranged to meet that night. I did warn him though that I was with a few friends and they would be coming along with me."

The friends were the noted guitarist Lawrence Archer (a.k.a. 'Florence') latterly of Wild Horses and Stampede (and later of UFO) and the Scottish singer Fin of erstwhile Ozzy bassist Pete Way's chaotically charged act Waysted. This troupe set out on their destination by way of a few other drinking establishments and before long the bass player's phone was ringing again. "It was Ozzy" Phil relates. "He was a bit angry too. "I'm still fucking waiting" he said." Soussan hurried up his colleagues and they eventually made it to Spirals where a worse for wear Ozzy was indeed waiting albeit less than patiently.

"Ozzy was with Lynn and Arthur. We had a good long conversation even though he was pretty drunk" the bassist recalls. "He spoke about fame and fortune and that he really wanted me to join the band and record the next album." The young bass player was already aware that both Bob Daisley and Fred Coury had vacated. "I knew Randy Castillo was involved so I was definitely up for it." Soussan and Castillo actually already knew and respected each other from the drummer's days working with Lita Ford. Indeed Soussan and Ford had even dated on occasion. The Ozzy offer seemed like a logical if admittedly valuable step up. Soussan had actually picked the drummer up from the airport for his first Ozzy audition up in Scotland.

However, as is seemingly typical in any scenario involving Ozzy matters took a bizarre turn before the night was out. "This guy that Lawrence knew turned up at completely the wrong time. His name was Dominic, Dominic Dibbs I think, and he was eccentric to say the least. Unbelievably he would tell people that he was the reincarnation of Ozzy Osbourne come back to earth—this being even though of course Ozzy was still very much alive. The thing was, he did actually look like Ozzy too. He would wear the clothes and the eye makeup and say he was Ozzy. Well, there I was talking to Ozzy when Dominic comes in! The two of them sat facing each other having a real go at each other. They were having this contest trying to see who could eat the most rose petals!!" This consumption of flowers in an attempt to determine who indeed was the 'real' Ozzy did not resolve the issue though. "They then had a big altercation—the real Ozzy Osbourne and the reincarnation of Ozzy arguing! We were pissing ourselves!"

Phil Soussan left the surreal world of Spirals bar that night not knowing quite what to make of it all. As it would turn out it was indeed to signal the inception of a rollercoaster time with Ozzy. The next day though would give him a foretaste of what was to come.

"Sharon phoned me up" Phil states. "She told me everything that Ozzy had said the night before was a load of rubbish and that I was not being asked to join the band. It had all been a big mistake."

Chalking his episode in Spirals up to experience a few weeks elapsed before Soussan paid a visit to Brighton, staying the weekend with friends, his host being his Swansong Records colleague Phil Carlo. As coincidences go the next one would take some beating. "This was about three weeks after first meeting Ozzy." Soussan remembers. "I had walked into a shop in Brighton and quite unbelievably there was Ozzy!" The singer was quite taken aback. "He was as surprised as I was I think. In fact he even asked me if I was following him! (Later he told me that he was convinced that I had been following him!) It was a seaside joke shop and Ozzy was stocking up on an industrial quantity of those little glass stink bombs. He loved to torment people with those."

It emerged that Ozzy's band was rehearsing just up the street. The conversation did not take long to get around to the subject of that previous inebriated offer. "Well, now he was sober and he asked if I would like to come up and have a play—that night! I quite literally ran to get back to London, grab my guitar and get back down to Brighton. I also had to learn a tape too before going along that night." Phil soon was made aware of the situation with the band. "They had been trying some American guy but it wasn't working out. Anyway, we played and they ended up keeping me around for quite a while." The 'American guy' was in fact former Steeler member Greg Chaisson. The band had rehearsed up in Scotland with Chaisson for a fortnight.

Phil would then bump into Ozzy tour manager Jimmy Ayers when the pair travelled back up to London. "Well, he told me straight that the band was unsure about me because I played with my fingers and not a pick. They liked me but didn't like the fact I used my fingers. It was just a style of playing I had fell into really. I could play with a pick fine and told Jimmy so. He replied that, in his opinion, he thought

I would get the job if I used a pick. It was odd though because none of the band had ever mentioned this." One wonders if this was because the reliable Bob Daisley used a pick. It is a point Geezer Butler has mentioned previously in interviews. Phil Soussan believes it is simply down to the nature of the songs. "Yes, Bob uses a pick but it's the songs. In general they are a lot more aggressive than Sabbath, less pedantic. Sabbath have this kind of dull pounding style. It's about definition and speed with Ozzy."

The young bassists next session with Ozzy's band proved a revelation. "I started playing as normal and then later I said 'Shall I use a pick?' and the whole mood changed! 'A pick? Oh yeah!' It was just what they wanted but they hadn't told me. A few days later, my birthday in fact, Ozzy came to me and said "Happy Birthday—by the way—you've got the gig if you want it." I actually told him I'd think about it but of course very quickly afterwards said "Yeah, sure—great!" I was in. It was all very surreal how it turned out from delivering Randy for his audition to a few weeks later being on the chopping block myself."

Barry Evans, previously bass tech for Neil Murray in Whitesnake, was assigned to Phil—apparently Neil had occupied the bass slot as a friendly fill in just prior to Phil's induction. The esteemed rhythm man describes his fleeting tenure. "I never really joined the band at all, I just helped them out. That's how I viewed it—just helping. Someone called me up and asked if I would like to rehearse with Ozzy for a few days to tide them through as they had no bass player at that point. It was Ozzy, Jake E. Lee and Jimmy DeGrasso on the drums. They were just trying out some songs, pretty casual actually.

I ended it actually because I got a call to go down to the south of France to join David Coverdale and John Sykes to put together the Whitesnake '1987' album. I said 'Look Ozzy, I'm sorry but I've got to disappear'. That was that." The new band, with Soussan now installed, set about putting down a series of basic demos on a four track recorder as pilots for the next album. "We were rehearsing songs for the album without the vocals at first" admits Phil. "Bob Daisley was still writing the lyrics while we were sorting out the music."

In spite of these delays the demos would be accepted and for 'The Ultimate Sin' the esteemed Ron Nevison was picked as producer. Nevison had made his name with such seminal works as UFO's mighty live opus 'Strangers In The Night' and as producers go was very definitely in the A league. However, things would not turn out as the band imagined. "When he arrived it was obvious he had not given the tapes a listen at all" records a miffed Soussan. "It was actually pretty insulting and we were rightly pissed off. Well, he went away and listened to the tape but when he came back he had the nerve to say he wasn't going to record the album unless he could hear a single. He actually seriously suggested we try having a go at 'Born To Be Wild'! You can imagine Ozzy's reaction. It really was quite amazing but Nevison was being serious. We actually kicked around a few suggestions for cover versions until Randy and I were asked if we had any songs."

As it turned out the bands newest recruit did have a song. "I'd had this song that I had written at the end of the band Wildlife. I had the music, melodies and a title and then Chris Overland came in and added some lyrics to it. It Became 'Shot In The Dark'," he motions. "Ozzy didn't think the lyrics were appropriate so I rewrote them and we sped it up quite a bit too and Ozzy put his ideas in too and it ended up great." The Ozzy band retired to the Townhouse Studios to start proceedings for the album recording but encountered problems from the off. "It was very, very difficult working with Ron" Phil states emphatically. "The truth of it was we thought he was just bloody lazy. The band and the producer fought about a lot of things.

Really Ron just wanted to spit it out. For the band it was like pulling teeth. The atmosphere in the studio was so adversarial that it did succeed in unifying the band and made us a tighter unit. I even had to go back and rerecord all my bass parts because they weren't recorded correctly in the first place." One wonders just why in such an apparently hostile atmosphere Nevison's services were maintained but Phil maintains the producer had status. "He had been very lucky and had been involved in some pretty big albums around that time. He was the 'Hot guy' and it was felt he could be an asset. Sharon did mention though that she was not afraid to do whatever she would have to do however."

With relationships in the studio straining matters would take a turn downward to a new low. "I know Ozzy was insecure about the album because it was the first one he had done without Bob Daisley" Soussan records. "What really got to us though was when we found out that Nevison actually wanted Randy and I out. He went to Sharon and told her the rhythm section has to go! He also said that Jake didn't take direction very well! Sharon, bless her, in her own particular manner told Ron to sack the singer too and start his own band!"

With Ozzy's band in a constant state of flux from year to year it would be quite remarkable that the next player to enter the fold would tenaciously hold onto his position for a marathon 15 years. Keyboard player John Sinclair is not what you would call a high profile figure mainly operating hidden from view side-stage but still fulfilling the same valuable role as occupied by Don Airey and Lindsey Bridgwater.

John's first footsteps into the world of Rock n' Roll came with his appearance on a solo album by Larry Page on the now highly collectable Penny Farthing Records. The ambitious ivory tickler was just 19. From there, in the grand tradition of British Rock upward career moves, Sinclair answered a 'Melody Maker' advert and found himself working with Jackie Lynton. A well known and much loved figure on the Blues Rock scene Lynton had strong connections with perennial Boogie Rockers Status Quo and as such the young keyboard player undertook his first major touring schedule as support to the mighty Quo. A series of Jackie Lynton gigs at London's Marquee club would dictate his next port of call. A mysterious hooded figure in the audience would turn out to be Gary Holton, lead singer of the Heavy Metal Kids on a less than innocuous mission to check out Sinclair's skills.

Holton's sense of theatrics was in keeping with his character both on and offstage. The savvy Londoner had as a youngster played the 'Artful Dodger' in the West End stage performance of 'Oliver!' and that persona of the likeable cheeky ne'er do well had stayed with him. At that moment a prescient Holton was fronting a boisterous bovver boy band titled The Heavy Metal Kids. Popular in the London area the band, who would stage manage fights as part of their live set, had found themselves on the nation's television screens courtesy of a BBC documentary on youth violence. The only flaw in Holton's plan being that in 1973 when he launched the band Punk hadn't happened yet and The Heavy Metal Kids were out on their own.

Two albums with Danny Peyronel had preceded Sinclair's term and following the sophomore effort 'Anvil Chorus' The Heavy Metal Kids had reportedly split. The group duly regrouped but minus Peyronel who had taken up a high profile position with UFO and thus leaving a vacancy to be plugged by Sinclair. Although original guitarist Cosmo was in the frame upon Sinclair's induction he would later make way for a new face in the form of Barry Paul. Sinclair would record the 1977 Mickie Most produced 'Kitsch' album with The Heavy Metal Kids. A much underrated album which included a daring look at the world of sniffing speed with the track 'Chelsea Kids'. During the mid seventies the band supported Uriah Heep across mainland Europe and Sinclair soon struck up a valuable and lasting friendship with Lee Kerslake and Mick Box. The keyboard player would break away from anarchic The Heavy Metal Kids journeying to America to earn his crust with session work. Kerslake would often stay over when Uriah Heep hit the States.

Meantime, chirpy frontman Gary Holton embarked on a solo career which saw a brief tenure in the Damned in late 1978 and a European released album. Holton would also hit the British charts in 1984 with his version of 'Catch A Falling Star'. The singer had found fame as a TV actor alongside Jimmy Nail, portraying the king birding, Cockney carpenter Wayne in the ITV series 'Auf Wiedersehn Pet'. Sadly, at the height of his acting career, Holton died in tragic circumstances in 1985 during filming of the second series.

Back in Los Angeles a band of expatriates called Lion was next on the agenda for Sinclair. Lion, fronted by singer Gary Farr of Gary Farr & The T-Bones, the group included the seasoned drummer Eric Dillon, a veteran of Fat Mattress, Hemlock and Savoy Brown, ex-Mahatma bass player Steve Humphries and former Jess Roden Band guitarist Steve Webb. Later Lion pulled in guitarist Robin Le Mesurier, the wayward son of 'Dad's Army' actor John Le Mesurier. An album on major label A&M 'Running All Night' arrived in 1980 but made little impression. The sojourn in Los Angeles would also afford Sinclair to get involved in the session world and his deft touches would grace albums by the likes of The Babys, The Outlaws, Starship and Eddie Money.

Kerslake, then still stinging from his ousting from the Ozzy camp, would call John to participate in the Uriah Heep 'Abominog' resurrection. In the thick of it with a major status band Sinclair's talents would come to the fore and much of the high class work that made 'Abominog' and its successor 'Head First' was the product of Sinclair's songwriting skills. In later years Sinclair would witness such unsavoury objects as snakes and cows heads thrown onstage by over zealous Ozzy fans but it was with Uriah Heep ardent fan fervour resulted in one truly dangerous missile. A particularly enthused Hammond organ finale was brought crashing down to earth by a soggy but still lethally hard white cabbage launched from the audience.

The keyboard player would then find himself inducted into a world more bizarre than any Rock n' Roll adventure—Spinal Tap. This is where reality intrudes into the fantasy world of the movies. Rehearsing songs of such pedigree as 'Sex Farm', 'Big Bottom' and 'Stonehenge' the Spinal Tap actors had in true method acting style adopted English accents in initial meetings and auditions with people outside of the project. The Spinal Tap actor Christopher Guest had been fishing for genuine Rock n' Roll stories to spice up the film and a Uriah Heep American Air Force base gig stood head and shoulders above the rest. The bands promoter had put the gig in as a last minute stop gap when a previously scheduled date had fallen through.

'Spinal Tap' would elaborate this tale into one of the movies most cringe worthy moments. Bob Daisley has vivid memories of the event too. "We turned up at this gig and they had written this huge sign in glitter on the hall." The portent of doom must have been striking as the band members read the herald 'The Uriah Heep show. Sold more records than ABBA!' "It happened exactly the same as the movie—as soon as we started to play all their air traffic control commands started to come out of the sound system." Daisley still has hysterics when relaying the tale of a Hard Rock bands worst nightmare. "The whole audience was in uniform and all the women looked like Dolly Parton." Uriah Heep opened with a steaming Metal riff and were met with stony silence.

Besides inspiration for story lines John Sinclair would contribute 'keyboards and musical styling' for which he is credited for in the movie. He also appeared in the pilot to the movie. The keyboard player was then asked to commit to filming of the actual movie but found himself between a rock and a hard place with Uriah Heep. This presented Sinclair with a dilemma. Uriah Heep had just completed the 'Head First' record, an important stepping stone on from the rejuvenation given the band by 'Abominog'. However, Bob Daisley had left the fold for another term with Ozzy and Trevor Bolder had stepped in on bass. With a world tour imminent Sinclair's loyalty had to remain with his band rather than an uncertain movie. The movie 'This Is Spinal Tap', a sharply observed parody documenting the exploits of David St. Hubbins, Nigel Tufnel and Derek Smalls would go on to become one of the true great cult movies of all time. It remains as a steadfast and ever popular antidote to the biggest Rock n' Roll ego.

In 1986 Sinclair found himself back in the UK. Unbeknown to the keyboard player a good friend, Mick at the Rock n' Roll security company Artist Services had mentioned Sinclair's abilities to Ozzy's tour manager Jimmy Ayers. His former Uriah Heep colleague Bob Daisley, back and forth with Ozzy beforehand, had also suggested the same name on a few occasions. 'The Ultimate Sin' was wrapped up recording wise by the time Sinclair became involved and after a quick audition the keyboard player was invited on board—a stay that would last fifteen years. Sinclair's task was to add colour and depth to the whole proceedings. Being out of sight from the main show apparently holding no qualms for him. The keyboard player would lend colour and depth to songs such as 'Perry Mason', 'No More Tears' and of course 'Mr. Crowley'.

With the album cut and laid to rest the band geared up for what would turn out to become a monstrous world tour. "We began rehearsals at a big warehouse near the Ace café off the North Circular Road. We set up the whole stage in there and had full production rehearsals. I remember one day Vince and Tommy from Mötley Crüe came by to see us" recollects Phil Soussan. The infamous Crue singer and Soussan would immediately hit it off leading in time to a working collaboration in the future. For now though the Ozzy band was primed and ready to roll.

"Then we went straight out and played our first gig in Dublin" Phil Soussan reminisces. The bassist has vivid memories of the opening night, his debut as a public member of the Ozzy Osbourne band. "The Irish crowd was nuts—they went ballistic. The album had just come out and was shooting up the charts. After the show it was just incredible. I've never been so exhausted after a gig. I was just drained, physically tired. I couldn't hear for two days after that gig. At the time I didn't think it was that loud but it must have been. After the gig everyone else was running around but I just sat at the hotel with a hot chocolate. Not very Rock n' Roll but I was beat."

The musician's head was swimming with the enormity of it all. "I was nervous but not in the manner of stage fright or anything. I just wanted to prove my point and make a good impression. It was very taxing, there was a lot to remember musically and we had done no warmup shows. For Randy and I we also had some very big shoes to fill too so the pressure was on big time. That early on we couldn't take anything for granted. We thought we had done a good job but I do remember actually looking around for approval after the show. It was a big sense of relief really, the same I'm sure for Randy."

'The Ultimate Sin', in spite of production upheavals and what is now reflected upon to be a fairly nondescript set of songs by Ozzy's previous high standards would nevertheless prove to be a steadfast hit. The catchy 'Shot In The Dark' single had given the band a bona fide hit and as such the album a good initial impetus. Not only did it climb high in the charts internationally but it kept on selling making the world tour ever drawn out as new legs were added to fulfill demand.

The era in which the album was launched was at the height of the Los Angeles Glam rock renaissance as spearheaded by Mötley Crüe, Hanoi Rocks and Dokken. Ozzy himself would not go unaffected by this focus on image. At the time the singer's flowing sequin silver cloaks and designer bleached hair seemed the norm for an international rock star. "We were all into it" Phil Soussan readily admits with no hint of shame. "Those cloaks were actually Ozzy's idea. He'd been to a Diana Ross concert and had seen her in a glittering coat. He called Fleur Thiemeyer, our stage clothes designer and said "Get me a glittering silver coat just like Diana Ross." I think everyone

The Ozzy band backstage 1986. Jake E. Lee, Randy Castillo, Phil Soussan, Ozzy Osbourne and John Sinclair.

at the time thought it looked quite good. Ha Ha!!! The whole band at that point was quite glammed up actually."

Phil would find guitarist Jake E. Lee a hard character to fathom. "Jake was a great guitarist no doubt. He had the showmanship, the stage presence, charisma and the right look too" he recognizes. "He was a genuine loner though. I travelled on the same bus as him throughout that whole tour and must have had at the most three conversations with him." Metallica would open up for Ozzy for the first two American legs of the tour. "At the start Metallica nearly got thrown off the tour because of a barney Ozzy got into with Lars Ulrich over an altercation between my bass tech Barry and Lars ... but it didn't last. We all got on pretty well" Soussan reveals. The untimely death of bassist Cliff Burton led to Blue Oyster Cult stepping into the breach before a final spree with Queensryche.

In the UK the multi platinum then red hot Ratt, one of Jake E. Lee's previous acts, would act as openers with Leicester's Chrome Molly fulfilling support duties for three gigs. Shows in Australia were scheduled in but aborted when Ozzy lost his voice due to vocal nodes. Doctor's advice kept Ozzy maintaining a no talking regime for two weeks.

The Ozzy Osbourne band would also find themselves playing a special one off gig in the capitol city. Not at Hammersmith Odeon or Wembley arena though but at the rather less salubrious surroundings of H.M.P. Wormwood Scrubs! Talk about a captive audience. For security reasons the band would even have to rehearse within the confines of the jail. With the multitude of gigs that have drifted into the misty annals of time Phil Soussan has good reason to have the memory of this particular event etched on his brain. "We had found ourselves locked up in a prison having rehearsals with some of the inmates on several occasions, one guy I think called TJ was really cool, he was a guitar player who had a tragic turn of events in life and found himself behind bars for 25 years."

Another inmate and willing helper would make an impression but for another reason entirely. "While we were rehearsing one other older inmate would make us endless cups of prison tea which we would down. At one point Randy asked what his crime had been and we were told that he had poisoned his entire family—wife, kids, the lot!! Somehow the tea took on a strange mental aftertaste!" One wonders how Ozzy was feeling at the prospect of performing a gig to some of Britain's most hardened criminals.

Ozzy's period of incarceration at Her Majesty's pleasure whilst a truculent teen banged up for minor misdemeanours paled in comparison to the sentences being endured by the majority of the inhabitants of Wormwood scrubs. Phil recalls the gig itself. "The day of the gig we were locked in this big hall with 300 hard lifers and only about 10 guards ... halfway through the set this big guy jumps up on stage and sticks his shoe on his head and starts dancing around. This was the guy that had tried to decapitate the cop in the Brixton riots ... all of a sudden I realised that if there was a riot here we would have been toast!!"

Ozzy would pop up in some unexpected places too. The 1986 teen horror flick 'Trick Or Treat' included both Ozzy and Kiss mainman Gene Simmons in extended cameo roles. Ozzy ironically portraying the anti-Rock n' Roll Reverend Aaron Gilstrom.

Back on the open road and with the world tour winding ever onwards Phil Soussan was feeling ill at ease within the camp. "There were days when I never really knew whether I was in the band or not. I was young though, only 24–25 and naive enough to just go along with it. I never really felt there was a unified focus within the band despite Randy and I being tight. You got the impression that it was our privilege to be there which of course it actually was but we were there for all the right reasons. Musically as a band we were very strong."

As strong as they were the Ozzy Osbourne band and their organization could not control everything though. The centrepiece monolithic green Ozzy statue that descended on stage revealing the real flesh and blood Ozzy to the awaiting masses would prove temperamental. "It got stuck in the air once" Soussan laughs. "When they finally got it going only two of the three motors started lowering with the net result being that the whole thing started to tip over! Ozzy was carrying a cordless microphone that was switched on and all you could hear over the music was Ozzy yelling across the arena "Help! Help! Get me out of this fuckin' thing! Aaarrrggh!" And all that from the Prince of Darkness."

As the tour reached Japan tensions within the band would come to a head. "Sharon asked me to take Ozzy out for a drink in Tokyo" Phil recollects. "Well, of course he got plastered. At one point we ran into some of the crew who ran away from us like we had some terribly contagious disease. They were the smart ones!" The battle hardened crew obviously made a wise decision. "We ended up in a Japanese Beatle bar with the owner bringing us litre bottles of saki. Every time Ozzy looked away I would pour it under the table to stop him drinking it but the guy would then come out with another one! All this to Japanese renditions of 'Lucy In The Sky With Diamonds', 'I Want To Hold Your Hand' and other favourites!

We finally left and I tried to drag Ozzy back to the hotel despite his resisting. At one point he wanted to sit down at a roadside soup kitchen and have yet another drink. He slipped off the seat and cut his arm. When we got back to the hotel a very pissed off Sharon took delivery of her husband. All I heard when the door slammed was crashing and yelling, fighting and banging. The next morning the two of them were sitting in the hotel lobby—dark glasses, bruises, black eyes and hair missing. It was funny!" Ozzy's reluctant drinking partner's amusement at the sight of two of the Rock world's most esteemed figures in such a state of dishevelment did not last for long though. "I was told, in front of everyone, that I was fired!" Naturally the musician took this quite literally. "I guess they held me responsible. I went upstairs and started to pack my bags but then they changed their minds."

With 'The Ultimate Sin' breaking the million sales mark in America alone (it would eventually go double platinum) and giving Ozzy huge international sales patterns too the climax of such a successful world tour would turn out to be unintentionally a muted affair. Originally the band was scheduled to close in Tyler, Texas but public protest had forced the cancellation of this event. Therefore the original penultimate gig in Corpus Christi would end up being the final show. "The last night of the tour was a great anticlimax" Phil Soussan states. "There were no parties—it was just like any other gig." Of course, being Ozzy even this dampened atmosphere could not go unmarked. The bass player recalls an odd character forcing his presence upon Ozzy over breakfast that day.

"It was about 9:30 in the morning in a crowded hotel coffee shop with all of us quietly eating breakfast. This guy jumps up next to Ozzy with a bible in his hand and starts chanting "Behold—Satan!" over and over again." According to Soussan Ozzy simply turned to their uninvited guest and said dryly "Look, I'm not Satan. I'm just trying to eat me scrambled eggs."

1986. Randy Castillo and Phil Soussan travel by luxury limo . . . .

. . . and by private plane.

Chapter 14

'Seventh Star'—Hughes Next?

Back in the studio the recording line-up shifted its axis a number of times over this period with the opting out of both singer Jeff Fenholt and bassist Gordon Copley. Other side attractions were also impinging upon the schedule as Eric Singer divulges. "Lita was getting bummed out in a major way. There were disagreements with the record label and suddenly it looked as though 'The Bride Wore Black' would never happen. There was a lot of bullshit going on and I know Lita was frustrated as Hell with the whole thing. Gordon and I were still part of Lita's band whilst we were recording with Tony so it was a little weird. Then it started to look as though Black Sabbath was happening and Lita's record had been cancelled. This obviously created a lot of schism between her and Tony naturally. Lita was very unhappy.

The bass thing was strange. Gordon had done a lot of writing with Lita. He was playing with Tony on loan, just for the demos. When Glenn came onboard he was originally there to act as singer and bass player. As you know, Glenn is just great on bass. Then there was a decision made that Glenn should just sing, this is where Dave Spitz came in. Jeff Glixman put his name forward and Tony dug him as he had lots of the right influences and looked good. It wasn't so simple getting Dave into the band though because he was with White Lion and they had just been offered a long term major label deal. Dave made the decision to skip White Lion and join us. Sadly the future didn't unfold for him the way he had hoped. He was a great guy, I liked him."

With Jeff Fenholt no longer involved the material, by necessity, had to be drastically revamped as is confirmed by Geoff Nicholls. "We couldn't use any of Jeff's stuff because of the obvious legal implications that would entail. That was in actual fact a bugger for me because what he had come up with was good and it was hard to mentally shake that off and write it all again from scratch. The point I would like to make about 'Seventh Star' is that I wrote a good 75% of the lyrics and melodies for that album. Glenn came in and sang it all and it was a real treat for me to guide him through that. To have such a world class voice singing something you have written was just brilliant for me I can tell you."

Although Glenn Hughes was the high profile entrant bassist Dave 'The Beast' Spitz would also be coming onboard to bolster the ranks and load in some necessary ballast. Hughes reputation as a bassist meant that anyone covering the Black Sabbath bottom end had to be amongst the very best and Dave Spitz was equal to the challenge. The obvious question needs addressing first—why 'The Beast'? Dave is happy to oblige. "My 'Beast' nickname has been around since I was 12 or 13. It originated from Steven 'Pee Wee' Weiss, up in White Lake, New York. Pee Wee was infamous in the community for naming everyone, and members of their families. Actually, before Beast, I was dubbed Piggy from a very early age. Piggy was transformed into Beast, and it was so perfect for me that it has survived until this day. It works because I'm very primal; my hair is dark and grows out of every pore, my voice is extremely deep, I'm well endowed, and of course, I beat the crap out of my basses. In fact, on my older Spectors and my Kubicki basses, I have actually worn holes above the pickups as deep as 3/4" into the wood."

A native of Haverstraw, New York—the famous Civil War site on the Hudson river—Spitz had fallen into Rock n' Roll at a young age and found himself unwilling to extract himself. His musical talent had been initially nurtured by household echoing to the strains of his father's Jazz, big band and Sinatra collection and his Mom's piano playing. The young Spitz, whipped into shape quite literally by the conducting rod of a certain Mr. Buck, had first performed live as a clarinet soloist in 4th and 5th grade, competing in county and state wide events.

Spitz worked up his first attempt at a band unit with friend and guitarist Jay Reilly. "I was getting into the heavy music, I knew I wanted to play guitar. Also, my mom forbid me to play drums. So, my folks bought me a cheapo acoustic 6-string. I actually took about 4 or 5 lessons at Samsondale Music, but then realised that I must play bass. So, I kept bugging my dad, and he soon brought me home a 1972 Gibson EB-O." Spitz's earliest recollection of any formal band unit was the 9th grade combo Rockside. "This band was interesting, as our main repertoire was Black Sabbath." Attending the State University of New York at Geneseo, Spitz's next port of call would be the band Freeway, who roamed the upstate New York, Connecticut, and the Tri-State area performing at every high school, college, and bar that would take them. The repertoire comprised such weighty fare as Scorpions, The Who, Tull, Be Bop Deluxe, Zeppelin, Floyd and Sabbath. "I co-wrote all the originals, and we actually pressed a single ('Streamline' / 'Out On The Road'), which we used to sell at the shows."

It would be Dave's brother, future Anthrax guitarist Dan Spitz, who secured his next rung up the ladder with Americade and subsequent valuable contact with producer Jeff Glixman. "It was 1979–80, and I graduated college and remained upstate to keep gigging. My brother was living in Orangeburg, just outside New York City, and he was getting amazing on guitar. He started to meet a lot of people on the NY scene, as he was working on the famous 48th street in Manhattan at a guitar shop. One night he met a well-known drummer named Walt 'Wildman' Woodward, III. Walt was formerly in a group called Rachel which featured frontman Rhett Forrester, who later joined Riot. Walt told Dan about this hot, new band he was in called Americade, which was then looking for a bassist. Of course, Dan filled his ears with info about yours truly. Dan called me up, and he was actually my motivation to leave the upstate scene. So, I packed up my shit, and headed back to New York. Americade auditioned quite a few guys, but The Beast slid right in."

Americade, centred on the DeMarigney brothers Gerard and P.J., created quite a stir. It was well known in Rock circles that some serious money was being injected into the band, which may have proved their undoing. "The band was pretty hot, and people were talking. We still had no deal, so we hired a famous producer, Jeff Glixman, to produce the second record, 'Rock Hard'. They paid him some big bucks, and we trekked off to Atlanta to record at Axis Studios." Spitz and Glixman hit it off instantly. The producer could see the bassist's potential but had serious misgivings about Americade and in particular singer P.J.

This is where Spitz's path crossed that of White Lion, giving him his first real step up into the limelight. The band, Danish born singer Mike Tramp with the Staten Island duo of guitar hot shot Vito Bratta and drummer Nicki Capozzi had cut an album in Germany at Dieter Dierks studio with Angel's Felix Robinson supplying bass and Peter Hauke handling production. With Robinson out of the frame and exhaustive auditions to find a replacement failing to locate the desired bass partner Spitz's introduction came as a godsend. "The band needed an aggressive bass player with chops, who could play the complicated heavy riffs and complement Vito's stunning guitar work. White Lion rehearsed in the basement of L'Amour, and during the audition, Vito tried his best to screw me up; to no avail, as I kept throwing curves at him and Nicki. We ended up jamming for hours, and Vito sent the other hopefuls home. Beast was in."

The promise of White Lion, including a deal with Elektra courtesy of label president Bob Krasnow would start to show signs of faltering though. Losing their A&R representation the band discovered to their abject horror that the 'Fight To Survive' album, despite a genuine media buzz, was to be shelved. The group toured the East Coast with Krokus, Twisted Sister, Wendy O'Williams, Blue Oyster Cult, Foreigner but still the album languished. Unexpectedly White Lion got a welcome injection of publicity courtesy of Steven Spielberg no less. The band was picked by director Richard Benjamin for the Tom Hanks and Shelley Long movie 'The Money Pit', performing the original track 'Web Of Desire'.

In the midst of shooting 'The Money Pit' Spitz's old acquaintance Jeff Glixman secured his services for Tony Iommi. The producer, reminding Spitz of an earlier promise to call him once an opportunity arose, telephoned to inquire if the bassist would like to play with Tony Iommi. Spitz informed his White Lion colleagues he needed to take a break down to Los Angeles. "They were pretty nervous because we were set to start filming the movie, and we had numerous dates booked. Tony had cut some demos with Glixman at the helm, and he was engaged to Lita Ford at this time, so he ended up using Eric and Gordon Copley as the rhythm section. When Gordon had to split to Hawaii to write with Lita, the bassist spot opened up. Sure enough, Glixman had remembered me from the Americade situation, and recommended me to Iommi. So, I flew in to LA, and I was picked up at the airport by Richard Cole." The Beast soon struck up a lasting friendship with the notorious ex-Led Zeppelin road manager.

Spitz describes his introduction to Tony Iommi and Eric Singer. "We chatted about all kinds of stuff that first night. He was very intense, and there was a cool vibe brewing, although I must admit I was a bit nervous meeting the master. I think it was the next evening that we went to jam at some really dark studio. I remember first plugging in, and noodling around bending strings and slamming some bass chords and such, and Tony looked over at me and smiled. I think we just started jamming on a riff that Tony threw out, and this jam went through all kinds of permutations and changes for a while. I don't remember if we actually played any Sabbath songs, but we jammed there for hours, having a blast. I got the word the next day that Tony wanted me to stick around."

Next in line would be Glenn Hughes. Considered to have godlike qualities by his many admirers, the Glenn Hughes legend was fostered with stints in both the Staffordshire Funk based Rockers Trapeze and the mighty Deep Purple. Indeed, the man can be heard on the Trapeze albums 'Trapeze', 'Medusa' and 'You Are The Music… We're Just The Band' as well as Deep Purple albums 'Burn', 'Stormbringer', 'Come Taste The Band', 'Made In Europe' and 'Last Concert In Japan'. Although Hughes has a quite uniquely rich and soulful vocal style he has pursued a diverse range of R&B, Funk and Soul for a growing catalogue of solo endeavours. The singer suffered during the mid eighties from excesses instigated in the seventies but has spent over a decade in full health much to the admiration of his global fan base.

The singer, as so often with the most uniquely talented, was blissfully unaware he was in possession of a set of platinum lined pipes until chance accident forced him up to the microphone. Hughes was performing in a formative act known as The Hookerlees. With the regular singer on vacation and a debut gig looming the band members decided Glenn should give it a go. That concert made a striking impression on Glenn's father, having a drink at the bar that night. "He told me that he heard the voice of an angel, he turned around and saw it was his son. I don't think either of us had any idea I could sing until then" he says humbly. It would be with Trapeze that the calibre of Hughes' voice really came into play, sending reverberations around the world. "Again, that was a bit of an accident too" Glenn motions. "Johnny Jones left the band and once again it came down to me to have a go at singing. I was really thrown in at the deep end there too. It was 'Medusa' where I felt that I was really cutting it, songs like 'Coast To Coast' and 'You Are The Music'. That album made a big difference to us, it's very much full of Glenn-isms that would later surface on 'Burn'."

Whilst a member of Deep Purple, Hughes contributed lead vocal to bassist Roger Glover's solo concept album 'The Butterfly Ball' and also two tracks on Eddie Hardin's 'Wizard's Convention' eponymous album in 1976. Hughes had already been planning his solo career whilst still a member of the by now fragmenting Deep Purple and, initially, no less a figure than David Bowie had agreed to produce the first solo album, but further touring with Deep Purple put these plans on ice. Still, Hughes' debut solo foray turned up in 1978. Titled 'Play Me Out', the album was much more of a Soul record than Rock yet featured his old cohorts from Trapeze drummer Dave Holland, guitarist Mel Galley and keyboard player Terry Rowley. Additional drums were supplied by ex-Rainbow drummer Mark Nauseef. Following completion of the album Hughes rejoined Trapeze for an American tour, but quit before its finish having also contributed lead vocals to the 4 On The Floor project comprising of guitarists Jeff Baxter and Al Kooper. It was this guitar duo that had originally worked up a pre-Sabbath band fronted by Ronnie James Dio. Once Dio had secured the Black Sabbath post he passed Hughes on to Baxter and Kooper.

In 1982, after five years as a virtual recluse, Hughes made his comeback with the critically acclaimed 'Hughes–Thrall' album recorded with Automatic Man and Pat Travers Band guitarist Pat Thrall and ex-Ragamuffins drummer Frankie Banali. This was the first of Hughes post Deep Purple projects to come to fruition as he had previously attempted to establish bands with Ray Gomez and Soul man Narada Michael Walden, but ultimately to no avail. The 'Hughes–Thrall' album, handled initially by former producer Bob Fraboni but finished by Andy Johns, remains a cult classic to this day. Banali joined Quiet Riot midway through recording and the album also has contributions from drummers Gary Ferguson of Black Rose and Steve Miller Band man Gary Mallaber. Hughes/Thrall debuted with live dates supporting Santana in America on which drummer Tommy Aldridge sat in on the drum stool prior to leaving for the Ozzy Osbourne band despite laudable press attention the album failed to sell well. Hughes next appeared contributing vocal tracks to the first 'Phenomena' concept album in 1984, which saw the singer reuniting in the studio once more with Mel Galley. In early 1985, following an offer to re-form Trapeze with Galley and ex-Michael Schenker Group drummer Ted McKenna, Hughes joined Gary Moore's band for a brief if volatile period, recording the two tracks 'Reach For The Sky' and 'All Messed Up' on his 1985 'Run For Cover' album.

Glenn expands upon the historical tradition of friendship and camaraderie that placed him in the frame for 'Seventh Star'. "Trapeze and Black Sabbath had been on the same circuit locally for years. All around the West Midlands Trapeze would be playing the exact same clubs as Black Sabbath so we had known each other for years and years. That whole crowd—John Bonham, Robert Plant, us and Black Sabbath. Although the music was very different, because we had that loose Funk thing going on and Sabbath was kind of ultra heavy we had a basic respect for each other. Because the bands were so different we could afford to be friends too because Trapeze was no competition to Black Sabbath but we had common bonds. We all hung out together, I would go to Ozzy's house, he would come to my place and we were just good friends. I lived in Penkridge in Cannock and Ozzy lived just down the road. As the years went on I always kept an eye on what they were doing just because they were local."

Glenn is happy to add some depth to these recollections. "Yeah, I was around at Ozzy's house a lot in '77 when he was first trying to put that Blizzard Of Ozz band together. We spoke quite a bit about forming a band too but I don't think we could ever really get beyond the fact that we were both singers so could not find a way of making it work. I was also working on my solo record 'Play Me Out' too, I had just come out of this huge Rock band Deep Purple and really wanted to do my own thing. I could see Ozzy needed to go it alone too but I guess he was looking for some support from a friend. We were both young then and, in truth, both completely screwed up too.

Tony I've always liked. He's a very giving, generous person. I know it's not in keeping with the whole Black Sabbath image but Tony Iommi is truly a wonderful, friendly guy. I think his generosity and his desire to just play has been abused by various people in the past but that's what he is all about really—the guy just wants to play. Tony invented a certain type of guitar playing which is now so overlooked because so many people have copied him. What you have to remember is that when those first two Sabbath albums came out he was doing something unique. He plays these really weird notes that people at the time just didn't get. There was nobody writing riffs like that, he kind of took a whole new lateral way of thinking into putting riffs together. Of course now everyone does it but he was the first."

This mutual respect would finally see the artistic gap being bridged by circumstances in both parties careers. After Glenn Hughes critically acclaimed 'Hughes–Thrall' project album had failed to sell, despite being revered as an underground classic, the singer hit a deep furrow in his life and had shied away from the public eye for many years. He had been coaxed back from reclusion and into the limelight by the Irish guitar maestro Gary Moore. Not only did Glenn deliver his toughest work to date with the 'Run For Cover' album but the upfront press coverage for the album had reminded the Hard Rock industry and the public that the man was still in possession of a world beating voice. Unfortunately Glenn's well documented substance abuse problems came to a head with Gary Moore resulting in an abrupt departure. Allegorical reports of surreptitious midnight feasts on 'Mars bars' might have confused the fans but told insiders all they needed to know.

"I had big problems then but I was being put into impossible situations" a defiant Glenn reckons. "Gary is a genius on the guitar, an absolute genius but he has this way of working that is extremely pedantic. Very regimented. Anyone who has been in his band will tell you the same thing. Everything has to be just so and it is very difficult to deliver any feeling in that situation. I did the 'Phenomena' album too at that point and when the press started appearing for that Gary just blew up. He was furious about that. His Hard Rock career was on an up and maybe he felt I had hindered his progress but he went about dealing with it in all the wrong ways. There was a lot going wrong for me at that point. I had problems yes, but nothing like some of the things I read about afterwards. It was a great shame because we had been such great friends. His manager at the time was just fucking unbelievable. He even had me followed!"

Being tracked by minders on a daily basis, combined with the quite vicious barbs being flung his way via the medium of magazine print, ultimately proved too much to handle. The much vaunted union fractured and Hughes found himself out in the cold. Only one figure was to extend the hand of friendship. "When it all fell apart I was actually thankful that Tony Iommi asked me to get involved because a lot of doors were shut in my face because of Gary's revenge. He said a lot of things about me which were not just wrong but cruel. Things designed to harm my career which is exactly what happened. The worst thing was that things were said not only in magazines but behind closed doors too. A lot of potential opportunities simply evaporated because nobody wanted to work with Glenn Hughes. Not a happy time."

Importantly though, on record Glenn had made a valuable Hard Rock statement, just as Tony Iommi was thinking along more Blues based themes and edging back from the traditional Doom workouts of Black Sabbath. The musical chasm decreased enough for the two to make a link. "The record that Tony first told me about was a solo album" Glenn continues before stressing "If Tony had called me to say would I like to sing on a Black Sabbath record I would have said 'no' because musically that is not where I am at." Glenn demonstrates this by expanding upon the possibility of him being asked at any previous time to join Black Sabbath. "Well, no because I'm sure Tony knew that Heavy Metal was not my thing. Naturally I sing in a Soul style which is certainly not Black Sabbath. I was around quite a bit when they were recording but never asked before because I was never the kind of singer Black Sabbath needed. With the solo thing though, I could see that it could work well."

The vocalist remembers the whole process as being hasty. "We did the record really quickly, starting in July. The whole thing at Cherokee was completed in a matter of days actually. I wrote a lot of stuff for 'Seventh Star' and so much stuff was put down Tony wanted to use most of it. So I ended up doing the whole thing because Tony was really happy. I must stress that all the way through this I was being told this was Tony's solo record. The idea was to call it just 'Tony Iommi' which I was happy with too." The pairing worked together well in the studio, Glenn describing Tony Iommi as "A real joy to work with." It would, as history unfolded, be seen as a becalming and deceptive tranquility before the unleashing of the mother of all storms. "The studio work was just fine, we had a blast. Tony and I really gelled and the whole feeling of the album was very, very positive. I am really proud of the 'Seventh Star' album" he records.

Geoff Nicholls is eager to give Glenn Hughes due credit for his work on 'Seventh Star'. "Glenn just has one of those totally unique voices. He has possibly one of the greatest Rock voices I have ever heard and it was just great for me to work with that. I'm serious, ask anybody in this business and they will all tell you the same thing—Glenn Hughes has one of the greatest voices in the world. For me, it is such a shame that he has yet to be really recognised outside of the Hard Rock field. I guess his reputation has put a lot of major players off. I really rate him as the very best. Because he was singing a lot my words I sometimes asked to put a bit more gravel on or try this or that but very little really. Some of the stuff he could do was just amazing. He didn't even stand up in the studio! He could hit these incredible notes when sitting down in a chair. With vibrato, he could double take it and get it perfect on the very first take. Absolutely amazing."

When Hughes was incorporated into the proceedings, music had already been written with Geoff Nicholls laying down lyrics and melodies as Iommi, 'Beast' Spitz and 'Earache' Singer worked the tracks up ready for final vocals. The new singer never heard any of the Jeff Fenholt material and it was never discussed. "I didn't know until recently that Jeff had been involved to such an extent actually. I've met Jeff and he's a lovely, sincere guy. He never told me had done so much before I got there" he avows. "You see, that's interesting that I was never given that information about Jeff's involvement. If he says he was told he was working on a Black Sabbath record, knowing Jeff, I would believe him. I wasn't singing on a Black Sabbath album though because it was a big point of concern to me that I wouldn't do that. I can well imagine things being changed as it went along. These things are pretty common place. When I came in an awful lot of it was already written, by Tony and Geoff. I put a lot into the writing of three songs including 'No Stranger To Love'. I was obviously unaware of a lot that had gone on previously but we worked so well on that first lot of songs I think that Tony, who really is a creature of habit and always looking for a comfortable option, decided that was it for him."

"Both Tony and Jeff Glixman wanted Glenn involved. Jeff really rated Glenn and with good cause" records Eric Singer. "We worked well, Glenn is such a great, great singer. Absolutely world class. We scrapped all the Fenholt vocals and started afresh. Geoff Nicholls was contributing ideas for lyrics. I just strictly played the drums." The drummer also documents just how convoluted these sessions became, with both Dave Spitz and Gordon Copley being credited for bass, the latter on 'No Stranger To Love'. "Looking back the recording process was all over the place. That's why some original demo stuff with Gordon playing bass ended up on the record. In fact a lot of what actually made it to the album was intended just for demo purposes."

Dave Spitz explains the technicalities, or precise lack thereof, that resulted in Copley's bass parts remaining on 'No Stranger To Love' yet rerecorded for the rest of the album. This is a point of detail, which has often puzzled Sabbath historians. Why rerecord all of the bass lines except for just one song? "Apparently, Tony and Gordon had just tuned up the guitars to each other, rather than using an established tuner. So, the actual tuning was not precisely at concert pitch, was not a half-step down, or at any other discernable interval. During the recording of the basic tracks for 'Seventh Star', Glixman and I spent countless hours trying to match up the tuning so I could re-cut the bass. At first, we thought it was us, that we were too tired, or too fucked up. We would match it up in certain spots, and then it would sound like shit. There was such a great vibe between Tony's guitar and Eric's drums that Tony really wanted to keep it. So, eventually we gave up and used Gordon's bass part for just that song."

Eric Singer reminisces on all this chopping and changing of material and believes that for his debut recording experience it was pretty unique. "What I remember was the album almost being thrown together. There was a lot of tape cutting, cut tape all over the floor. There were no click tracks, we played live as a band so a lot of it didn't hook up. But, you know what? It sounds just great! When I did that record it was my first. I had very little studio experience, just the demo stuff with Lita really. If I told you the money I got paid you would say oh my God ... The thing was though that the album just kind of all came together despite the circumstances. For my first experience of the recording studio environment it was a revelation and since of course I have discovered that it was far from the ideal way of putting a

Black Sabbath—Dave 'The Beast' Spitz, Glenn Hughes, Tony Iommi, Eric Singer, Geoff Nicholls.

record together. I learned a lot from it, probably as much as if I had made three regular albums."

Dave Spitz too records the initial sessions as being unconventional. "When we cut the basic tracks to 'Seventh Star' there was no singer and the arrangements were based upon what we thought would be an intro, verse, B-section, chorus, solo, etc. There were no vocals, or vocal arrangements at all. Plus, this was an analog 2-inch recording; there was no digital Pro-Tools abilities to cut and paste, like we have now. However, I know that Glixman busted out his razor in some spots for manual splicing." Despite his misgivings as to the methodology employed in scoring the original tracks to tape Eric Singer does have fond memories of these times. "Tony was great to work with. He is a great guy and although he's quiet he has an incredible sense of humour. People see the man in black, the 'bad guy' moustache and the whole Black Sabbath image but he really is a very funny guy. His sense of humour is very British, very dry. You would never guess it but being holed up in the studio with Tony is actually quite a fun experience."

This lack of cohesion that Singer and Spitz were dealing with was also felt by others with more invested in the endeavour. Geoff Nicholls records the whole process as less than a united front and admits to difficulties in working with the producer. "We just did not click and I always felt he was sticking his oar in too much. All those songs were very precious to me so I was possibly over protective but, the way I saw it, I knew Tony and I knew what he wanted. Glix just kept trying to change things away from the Sabbath sound. I know Tony wanted to branch out a bit but a lot of what Glix was suggesting was all a bit airy fairy and not necessary for the songs. He just didn't understand how Tony and I worked I guess."

To illustrate this Geoff picks the song 'Turn To Stone', relating a particularly satisfying conclusion to an artistic dispute with the producer. "That's very much my song. I wrote the riff on a keyboard then gave it to Tony to work into a guitar riff. Most of the time I came up with chords on the keyboard and Tony would then plonk a big fat riff of his own on top but on this particular occasion I had thought of the main riff and Tony was keen to use it. After all, if it is good why change it? Anyhow, this one time Tony was going through this riff and it wasn't coming out quite right. Just as I was saying to Tony "No, you need to roll it like this" Jeff Glixman walks in and says to me "You can't tell Tony how to play a riff." Of course he didn't realise it was my riff so I thought, OK, I'll just shut up here and see what develops. Glixman tried to get Tony to make it more

Geoff Nicholls at Cherokee Studios.

The nearly bride to be in black. Tony Iommi and Lita Ford.

jazzy which didn't work at all. Tony went back to the original."

Once the tracks had been laid down both Dave Spitz and Eric Singer would effectively become free agents once again leaving Iommi, Hughes and Nicholls to polish off the album. The rhythm section was called back into the band at a later date. The pair, at first, did not relocate too far though as Spitz explains. "Once Eric and I completed the basic tracks for 'Seventh Star', Lita Ford was so impressed with our rhythm work that she asked us to play on her next record and begin rehearsals immediately. So, I had to phone the White Lion guys in New York who were frantically waiting for me to return, and tell them I'm not coming back yet! Long story short, Eric and I began rehearsals with producer Ashley Howe. However, during this extra three weeks, Lita rarely showed up, and was not getting along with the producer. He was a perfectionist who arrived with a suitcase full of 15 micro-cassette recorders, and was trying to organize every riff and every bar of music! He drove us nuts, and Lita fired him. Since her album was then in limbo, I split back to New York."

Lita's highly anticipated 'The Bride Wore Black' stalled in the studio. Quite why has always remained a mystery as the lady certainly had a major fan base awaiting the record. 'The Bride Wore Black' still languishes in a record company vault. With 'The Money Pit' movie in the bag, White Lion reinstalled Spitz and resumed touring. "We did some kick-ass shows with Krokus on the East Coast. White Lion eventually garnered some heavy interest with JVC Japan, who agreed to buy us out of the Elektra deal, and amazingly put up a bunch of cash for a video of 'Broken Heart'. This was a three-day shoot, and after the first day, my phone rang again."

Tony Iommi and Don Arden had tracked him down, putting a proposal to the bassist to join the touring band, now billed as 'Black Sabbath featuring Tony Iommi'. It was no easy decision for Spitz, sensing White Lion was on the verge of something very big indeed. "Of course, this was a difficult time" states the bass man, obviously torn between two loyalties. "White Lion had finally received the go-ahead on our long-overdue album, and now had a video. I remember being on the phone with Vito Bratta and Mike Tramp for several hours, as they really did not want me to leave. However, I decided that playing with Tony, the inventor of Heavy Metal, was the smart move for myself."

Prior to regrouping with Spitz the group had finished up at Cherokee and relocated to Georgia, Atlanta on 22nd August to finalise the sessions. Further new music would be added at this eleventh hour too with 'Angry Heart' and 'In Memory' being cut. "I'm not sure why we added that one later" ponders Glenn. "I played bass on those last recordings too. I'm not credited but that's my bass on there not Beast's."

Oddly, 'Angry Heart' would be a battleground for a lyrical tug of war. Geoff Nicholls had provided a set of lyrics inspired directly by the death of his mother. Jeff Glixman had also weighed in with a collection of words in homage to his recently deceased ... dog. "I had that song written and the words were pretty special to me at the time for obvious reasons" states the keyboard player. "There was always this power struggle going on with Jeff over everything—instruments, riffs, words. Anyway, he had these lyrics about his

Tony Iommi at the piano in Cherokee studios.

dog that had just died. Tony wanted to use my lyrics and told Glixman he thought the original version of the song was just brilliant so to leave it alone. Anyway, we ended up recording two versions of that song, one with my words and one with Glixman's. Tony picked mine for the record."

Some lyrical explanation is due for some of the other 'Seventh Star' material too. The rush of the g-force inducing album opener 'In For The Kill' is remembered by Geoff for its 7/4 timing, making it decidedly awkward to wrap a melody around. As with most Sabbath songs it hosts a double storyline, dealing with both Vlad the Impaler and the accountability humanity will face in the Armageddon of Revelations.

On the opposite end of the pace scale, but probably 'Seventh Star's most majestic track, is the glorious Blues work out 'Heart Like A Wheel'. This song pleased many Iommi fans by providing a platform for a quite evocative and extended Iommi solo. Lyrically, Nicholls had been directly inspired by a movie he had just watched that told the tale of a female racing driver's fight for equality in her sport, hence the wheel imagery, blending these images into a standard Blues lost love scenario. As a last minute add on embellishments were tacked on to a second version of the single 'No Stranger To Love'. Nicholls complimented the track with layered keyboards with Hughes putting in more backing harmonies and dropping in further vocals.

With the record being completed during September some unwelcome news was to come Glenn's way some time later in December. "I got a call telling me that Don Arden and Warner Bros. had got together and decided the album was going to be called Black Sabbath!" The singer was nothing less than mortified to learn that the status of the album was subject to change. "It put me into a situation that I really did not want to be involved in" he sighed wearily. He struggles somewhat in quantifying his feelings at that time. "How can I explain this? I'm speaking about all of this in hindsight now you understand. Tony Iommi and I are very good friends now. It was a difficult time in my life and the way I was living my life is completely different to how it is now. I was drinking non stop and the people I was associating with then had no motive to help me out of that problem. I have in fact been completely clean for a number of years now and I can view these events from a safe distance. I have re-established my friendship with Tony too so that I'm speaking about all of this in the past sense.

For years I have been being pushed into this Heavy Metal / Hard Rock bracket and it's something I have constantly fought against. My background is Soul, it's Funk, it's Pop, R&B, it's groove music. I have much more in common with James Brown than Black Sabbath. Trapeze was not Heavy Metal and neither was Purple when I was in the band. The 'Hughes–Thrall' album wasn't Heavy Metal yet all my life I have been pushed into this direction. I had just come out of the Gary Moore nightmare too so musically I was really keen to distance myself from it. As an artist I have never, until very recently, been able to follow my own instincts so it has been a battle. I could have made, and have been offered, a lot of money to fall back on the Hard Rock scene. My voice, although a true blessing, is a curse too because I can pretty much sing just about everything you care to name. Unfortunately for too long people just saw Glenn Hughes—Deep Purple—Long Hair—Heavy Metal.

So when I learned that Don Arden and the record company had this wonderful idea of calling the album Black Sabbath I was really shocked. Even Tony was shocked and disappointed too I think. In fact, I know he was. I don't know what went on there really but it came out of the wash as some kind of awkward compromise as 'Black Sabbath featuring Tony Iommi'. I was horrified because the very first thing I can remember thinking was 'Oh no, I have to go out on tour as the singer for Black Sabbath'. I was dreading it. I really, really did not want to do it. It was not only that I had no desire to do it I knew in my heart that I simply couldn't do it. Try taking the bass away from Paul McCartney or Sting and you'll get the picture. I need my bass for the gut rhythm. I knew of course that Tony had Dave Spitz so I wasn't going to be playing bass and that I would be asked to sing Ozzy songs too.

Y'know, I've said this before—and meaning absolutely no disrespect to Ronnie, Ray and Tony—but Sabbath is Ozzy. Always has been, always will be. Those others guys did great, they're wonderful

Glenn Hughes and Geoff Nicholls.

singers, but to me Ozzy is Sabbath. There was no way I wanted to go out and attempt to replace him. I was just thinking "How am I going to explain this to Ozzy?" Remember, Ozzy was a close friend. It was nothing short of my very worst nightmare. It was asking too much."

With juicier targets on display regarding the status of the band and its singers nobody seemed to question the significance of the album title upon its release, the cryptic title being completely overlooked. So why 'Seventh Star'? The most common reference to 'Seventh Star' is in Revelation. It is not directly named as such but the prophet Yahushúa speaks of seven stars, cities or churches, of Asia ('Star Of India'?). The Seventh Star is named as Laodicea, recorded as having a population ambivalent in their devotion to God. For such token deference they were, according to Yahushúa, spat out of the mouth of God. Many latter day Christian analysts equate 'Seventh Star' with the fall of man or the fallen, morning star— Lucifer. An explanation which certainly ties in with the lyrical content of the title track.

The lyrics for the song 'Seventh Star' were written by Geoff Nicholls, inspired by texts from a book that would come to lend great weight upon this and future albums. "I have always had a great interest in ancient mysteries, biblical prophecies and theology" the songwriter confesses. "I have many, many books but one particular one I would use a lot for source material, just to fire off ideas. I can remember using it for the track 'Seventh Star' which was an idea from ancient times about the coming of Armageddon when seven stars lined up. They did a film about it recently too I recall. Anyway, that was roughly where 'Seventh Star' came from. It was quite a mixing pot of ideas on that one because there was a bit of Egyptology thrown in for good measure too." But 'Seventh Star' as the fallen Lucifer? "Well, yes—that too. All that stuff. It all ties in quite neatly" he admits. "There is a story about that book I used too. I used it all the time and I had marked off pages and references that could be good song ideas. Well, when I was working with Ray Gillen later on I made the mistake of lending it to him and the bugger nicked it when he did a bunk!"

'Seventh Star', complete with unwieldy title and questionable line-up, was offered to the world in February of 1986. Taken out of its political environment the record was a stately piece of work. Glenn Hughes had turned in a masterly performance and the wider span of Iommi's material stood up well. If the album had been able to rid itself of its shackles the reception would probably have been much kinder. Undoubtedly the clumsy herald of 'Black Sabbath featuring Tony Iommi' had seriously backfired. Rather than discuss the merits of the music the Rock magazines globally took the spur and devoted acres of print to everything Tony Iommi did not want to be talking about. Visually the portents did not bode well either. The album cover, Iommi alone, downcast and forlorn in an empty desert lit only by a weak sunset, seemed to say it all. The photographer was probably after a something a bit moodier and reflective. What he got had fans wondering if the guitarist was glumly contemplating the end of a career.

In keeping with the cryptology evident on Black Sabbath albums Iommi martyred himself in full public view with artwork that was to adorn the inner album sleeve, tour tee shirts and even backstage passes. The disturbing woodcut in question saw an unfortunate individual held aloft, suspended by demons in the guise of monstrous beetles and mutated winged beasts. Often mistakenly attributed to Albrecht Durer, it is in fact the work of Lucas Cranach the Elder (1472–1553). It was executed in 1506, whilst Cranach was enjoying patronage as court painter to Frederick the Wise in Wittenberg, and depicts 'The Temptation Of St. Anthony'. This celebrated aesthete underwent torment in the desert by the Devil himself, the lord of flies presenting himself in the form of a beautiful temptress and various animals, all in a futile yet torturous attempt to sway Anthony from his path of piety. The parallels were stark indeed. Two Anthony's exiled in the desert, centuries apart yet equally tormented.

Confirming these assumptions to a degree Geoff Nicholls adds a dash of much needed humour into this bleak equation. "There was a double implication, yes. Black Sabbath liked to do little things like that, things the public wouldn't get. The photo of Tony used for the front cover was actually from the video shoot from 'No Stranger To Love'. The whole artwork and video thing was rushed through very quickly. We used Bing Crosby's niece Denise as an actress in the video and they had me dressed up as an LA policeman. Yes, shades of George Michael—I know. Anyway, when the video came out they had chopped my bloody head off. Bloody marvellous!"

At least, this time around, Geoff got his face in the official band photographs as well as being credited as a full band member. Previously Nicholls had been cloistered behind the onstage scenery. This time around he was to man his keyboards from his very own upfront and grandiose pulpit. "I think I had got myself so pissed off with being shoved into the background yet again on 'Born Again' I made a point of telling Tony Iommi exactly what I thought" states a belligerent keyboard player. "With 'Born Again' they had put the 'focus' argument forward again and told me it was a priority for the press to

Black Sabbath in downtime during the 'No Stranger To Love' video shoot.

Geoff Nicholls (complete with head) as LA cop.

concentrate on Ian. I'd had enough though. I told him straight, look—I've written most of these bloody songs, melodies, words, everything. I should be in the photos and I should be onstage. It wasn't really something he could argue against. If I was going to play my songs I wanted to actually be on the stage this time—not stuck in the bloody corridor."

The issue of photos as official records of the band's composition had only recently become important to Nicholls for another reason too. "I had always been told that the band needed to be shown as a four piece for this or that reason but later on Bill Ward then told me something really interesting which came as quite a shock. If you are in the photos they have to pay for your rights to use your image. I never knew that before. Obviously if I wasn't in the picture I didn't get paid. I had been thinking all these years that by stepping out of the pictures I was helping the band out. I was led to believe it was all for the good of the band. I was so into Black Sabbath, probably more than most of the band members at most times,

Phil Soussan, photographer Mark Weiss, Jake E. Lee and Randy Castillo.

'Seventh Star' album promotion. Note positioning of band members and misspelling of "Geoff Nichols".

that I just went along with it thinking I was helping. When Bill told me I was really pissed off because obviously it had all been to do with just money."

Notwithstanding the physical and cerebral trials crafting 'Seventh Star' had placed on all concerned Warner Bros. held out very high hopes for the album. It was not to be. That very month Ozzy grabbed all of the magazine front covers with his 'Ultimate Sin' album. Nowhere near Ozzy at his best, the record was described internally within the Ozzy entourage as the 'Ultimate Din'. So disparaging were they of this record Ozzy even deemed it unworthy of reissue in subsequent years. The competition was not up to the grade when matched against 'Seventh Star' on musical merit but that simply didn't matter. By that stage Ozzy was unassailable.

Behind the scenes, Ozzy too had been having his own problems on the song-writing front. Bob Daisley would be recalled yet again to do the honours. "Ozzy called me again less than six weeks later wanting some lyrics for 'The Ultimate Sin'" Bob confides. "Of course, I ended up doing it. I did some demos and wrote the lyrics for 'The Ultimate Sin' album, which was a bit of an odd one because I don't think anyone in the band really liked it. I know Ozzy doesn't rate it—he calls it 'The Ultimate Din'! Ozzy and I had a verbal fallout though and Ozzy told me that we could not work together. So be it, I thought, and left." 'Ultimate Sin' was given impetus by far the standout track on the album, the bouncy Phil Soussan composed 'Shot In The Dark' single. Soussan, brought in to supplant Daisley, joined forces with David Donato's pal Randy Castillo on the drums to present an all new look for the Ozzy band where sequins and perms ruled.

Oddly, producer Ron Nevison, a man responsible for quite stellar outings by bands such as UFO and Heart, had served up 'Ultimate Sin' as a stodgy, plain meat n' two veg Heavy Metal album with little sparkle. It would surprise everyone by easily cruising to the million sales marker, going top ten in North America, the UK and Sweden. It was a crushing, even humiliating, blow. Wrapped in a cloak of confusion, the musically superior 'Seventh Star' scrambled its way into the lower reaches of the UK top thirty, just fell shy of the top ten in Sweden and made the barest of dents on the Billboard top 100, grazing the rankings briefly at No. 78. It was Black Sabbath's lowest ever USA chart placing.

Black Sabbath had lined up a typically monumental world tour to promote the 'Seventh Star' album. Fronting the band would be the reluctant figure of Glenn Hughes. To those outside the inner circle the obvious question has to be—why didn't Glenn simply decline? Apparently loyalty and a large dose of persuasion played a large part in the vocalist's decision. "Tony is a very sweet guy but he can also be very convincing. The way it was presented I didn't think that morally I had much of a choice" he concedes. "I really liked Tony and I didn't want to let him down. Both Tony and Don had a huge amount invested into the tour and the album so it was not easy to just walk away from. My judgement was severely clouded too because I was drinking a lot, I was medicating myself, I was fighting some horrible demons and mentally I was not firing on all cylinders at all. Although the prospect of what was in store was horrifying I also found myself in a situation where Tony was showing a lot of inspiration, kindness and love. Tony really cared and he was trying his best to help me out. I never had any of that in Deep Purple so I really did not want to let a good friend down. Tony and I spoke the same language if you understand my meaning, so I bit my tongue and got on with the job."

Glenn's discomfort was all too clear to the rest of the band too. Eric Singer has this observation. "You just couldn't get mad at Glenn. That was actually part of the problem we faced because at rehearsals he was just like a big kid, like a 9 year old. They were rough but ... we all kinda knew. Glenn was very overweight, he was bearded and was not looking his best. I remember at those production rehearsals the guys from Mötley Crüe and Quiet Riot came down and Glenn didn't sing well at all. He was really under pressure. When we got out to play live it was bad for him. I actually think, and I'm sure Glenn will agree, he found it very odd being up there without his bass. So that was strange for him and then he had to get to grips with all the old Sabbath songs, which was a nightmare for him. He was literally rewriting out all the lyrics so he could remember them. Glenn was struggling and his voice was having a hard time too. In fact he was not singing well at all and Glenn was really unhappy with the entire situation. The reviews were very bad, very critical."

Dave Spitz was concerned enough to voice his worries to Tony Iommi. He could see Glenn Hughes was being forced into an unnatural situation and judged there would be repercussions felt at a later, and probably more critical, date. "I don't think Glenn was ever comfortable fronting Sabbath; that is, being a frontman as opposed to playing bass and singing. He was heavy at the time, as he stated, so who wouldn't be self-conscious? In addition, even in Deep Purple, I believe he always played bass while singing on stage. Secondly, he was so wrapped up with his own affairs that he was not as motivated as the rest of us. But, we all loved Glenn, and this was a very difficult time for all; especially Eric and I, who not only admired Glenn, but were so psyched to be playing with Tony that we did not want any fuck-ups.

Glenn had many chances to make this gig work. The truth is, I saw it coming before the tour even started. I spoke with Tony and Don Arden about it, and that's when I first told them about Ray. I just didn't think that Glenn's heart was in it. The problem was that now we had Glenn's name and face out there on Sabbath's first new record, and video, in several years. Believe me, Tony and Don were quite nervous. But, they thought that he would prove us wrong and save the day. I guess the stars were just not lined-up properly for him during this period."

Just previous to the North American tour something quite incredible had happened. Although hushed up at the time Glenn Hughes suffered an injury which jeopardised the entire tour. Production manager John Downing punched Glenn in the face. Although this fact has been learned from Glenn in recent years he now reveals the true course of events which led up to this beating. "I've not wanted to say why this thing happened until now" Glenn admits. "Thinking about it, you are actually the first person to ask me Garry! So, OK, everyone knows I was punched in the face even though at the time they attributed what happened next to drugs, booze and everything else, which was, as everyone now knows, completely untrue. This is what happened. My girlfriend's Mother was there and she was, shall we say, a little disturbed. We had all been up all night and everyone was very high. This woman, the mother, was carrying a gun and she was really winding me up. I mean, seriously out of order. I can't go into too much detail here but it was getting very nasty.

Things got out of hand, I was angry I admit. Anyway, John Downing took me out of the bar and was manhandling me up towards my room. I was still angry at this stage and I will admit I probably threw the first punch. Not in any meaningful way because I was totally wasted. Anyhow, John, working for Black Sabbath and knowing there was a tour about to start, had a number of options of course. He could have just restrained me, hit me in the arm or the stomach or anywhere. I was no danger to him because I was a harmless drunk that just needed putting to bed. So what did he do? He hit me straight in the middle of the face! I was knocked out, saw stars—the whole thing. Let's just say his actions where inappropriate."

The vocalist's recollection is reinforced by Dave Spitz. "I wasn't there at the exact time but my room was close to Glenn's and I remember the noise going on. I went to see what was happening because I couldn't sleep. I walked in and said "What the fuck's going on?" By that stage Glenn was, I thought at the time, obviously very drunk. He couldn't stand up and they were trying to get him to go to sleep. In the morning Downing himself told me there had been a big scuffle and he had punched Glenn. He made no attempt to hide the fact.

There is something people should know about John Downing. He was a no frills kinda guy. He was big, had some strange habits and could certainly make people get things done. He was a sneaky bastard though and not on everybody's party list. There wasn't much respect for him. I'll give you an example; when we were staying at the Burbank I left him in the company of my girlfriend Sharice. When I got back Downing was feeding her blow and trying to get into her pants! I very nearly went for the guy. John Downing was most definitely a fucked up individual. Punching Glenn in the face was hardly logical."

When this version of events initially surfaced, it tended to be, along with stories of knee injuries, mental illness and other such bizarre fables, dismissed as damage control PR spin. A plethora of stories pinning the blame onto Glenn's drug abuse at the time were still in circulation until only recently. The very real blow delivered by John Downing though had serious repercussions and Glenn maintains this is the only reason he was forced out. "The drugs thing was just so easy" he allows. "To the fans it made sense after all the crap Gary Moore had said about me previously. I never got the chance at the time to tell my story. That punch was so heavy I was still wearing makeup after I had left the band to cover up the bruising where the bone had broken. When we did the media show before the tour I was caked in makeup and looked awful. I was carrying too much weight at the time because of my own problems but my face was very, very swollen too. I looked dreadful. Every picture you see of me from that time I'm wearing makeup to cover that bruise.

Technically, this is what happened. Rather stupidly I didn't treat it at first. I didn't see a doctor or apply any ice or anything. I was so hurt emotionally, spiritually and physically that I just couldn't deal with it in any way. The eye socket had been badly damaged and a piece of bone had lodged in my sinuses. It was horrible. Consequently everything was blocked up with dried blood. It was pretty gruesome. So for the next three weeks I tried to sing with my vocal chords blocked. When I first tried to sing it sound like a broken reed in a saxophone. A really strange, unnatural sound. It was pretty alarming. Previous to the punch I was rehearsing regularly, four to five hours a day, and singing like a bird."

Dave Spitz is firmly convinced the writing had been on the wall for a long time prior to the Downing punch. "Glenn was never right for Sabbath. He's a world class act but he was put into the wrong environment. Yes, John Downing did punch him, which certainly compounded things, but Glenn had extremely serious problems at the time. I mean really serious. Tony Iommi knew exactly what the score was. I'm just so glad Glenn eventually got through it all and came out the other end alive. There were times when it looked inevitable that he wasn't going to make it." Glenn Hughes was perilously fragile and with an expensive album to sell and a world tour booked a swift decision needed to be taken.

Chapter 15

Gillen Not Gillan

Ray Gillen, already having made his presence felt on the outer parameters of the Black Sabbath labyrinth with his involvement with Rondinelli, was quite a find. Ray had two qualities heavily in demand for that of singer with a major status Rock act. The first is that he could undoubtedly sing with a rare passion, range and distinct character. His second attribute, the undeniable fact that he looked every inch a 'Rock God', made his ascendancy all the more inevitable.

Ray was a native of Cliffside Park, New Jersey, born May 12th 1961. A strong athletic streak at school had given way for an all consuming love of classic Hard Rock and as a youngster the singer had schooled himself with an immersion in the sounds of Bad Company, Free and Deep Purple. He enrolled himself as a pupil with vocal coach Robert Fitzgerald, expanding upon his range and bringing his natural talent up to a consummate professional level. The early eighties had Gillen energetically working up David Lee Roth impersonations with his club band Harlett. It was from this act that Bobby Rondinelli had snatched him away for his new band during 1985. Rondinelli comprised of the two siblings Bobby and Teddy, the latter delegated the guitar and keyboard role, with James Lomenzo on the bass. Tommy Henriksen would later take the bass role.

Drummer Bobby Rondinelli records the band's progress. "We did a bunch of demos and people got pretty excited" he enthused. "We really worked hard at it because we rehearsed for what seemed like forever even before we took the band out live. The band did quite a few showcases for labels too. I've still got some great raw live in the studio tapes we cut for a producer. We just knocked them out. Boom, boom, boom. Sounded great. They might see a release one day, who knows? We were hot, the gigs were just great. There was a buzz on the band which resulted in a few offers being put on the table. Just as things were looking very promising for the band Sabbath swiped him!"

Having earlier described how Gillen was persuaded to join Rondinelli the drummer was open to speculation about their frontman's lineage and even his name. "I think there might have been some native American in him, not full blooded though. I never met anyone who looked more like a lead singer than Ray. He was Latin I guess. I did wonder about his name and I did ask him if it was real. I mean, Gillen. C'mon! It turned out it was his real family name though."

Just how the 24 year old was spirited away into the clutches of Black Sabbath during early 1986 has remained a mystery for many years. Bobby Rondinelli remembers Dave Spitz appearing at gigs but found out he had lost his prize asset second hand. "Somebody called me saying Ray had joined Sabbath. OK I thought, if he isn't man enough to tell me I'll just wait. Then later Ray himself called me, which I guess can't have been easy for him. I was really pissed off, I mean—really pissed off because I had just earlier turned down Whitesnake a few weeks earlier. Ray was with me at my kitchen table when I took the call and he said 'I can't believe you turned down a job with my favourite all time singer to stick with me!' I just told him I was committed to the band, that he was the singer I wanted to work with and that was that. Turns out Ray wasn't quite so committed! Of course, that next Whitesnake album sold in the millions so I guess I should have followed Ray's lead. Sometimes you make the right choice, sometimes the wrong one. Our band was very hot at the time, there was a nice feeling bubbling with the labels and Whitesnake had actually been struggling along for quite a while so it was nothing I could predict."

Dave Spitz though had actually first clocked Gillen as far back as 1984 when he was still involved with White Lion. He remembers being awestruck by the singer. "It was during this time period that I had seen Ray Gillen sing with Rondinelli, at L'Amour. Ray had left a lasting impression on me that night. Our managers owned the club, so I was hanging out in the back bar with some hotties when they went on. Ray commanded the stage and the large crowd, was bursting with charisma, and his tone and vocal ability was a marvel. At this point, my curiosity was

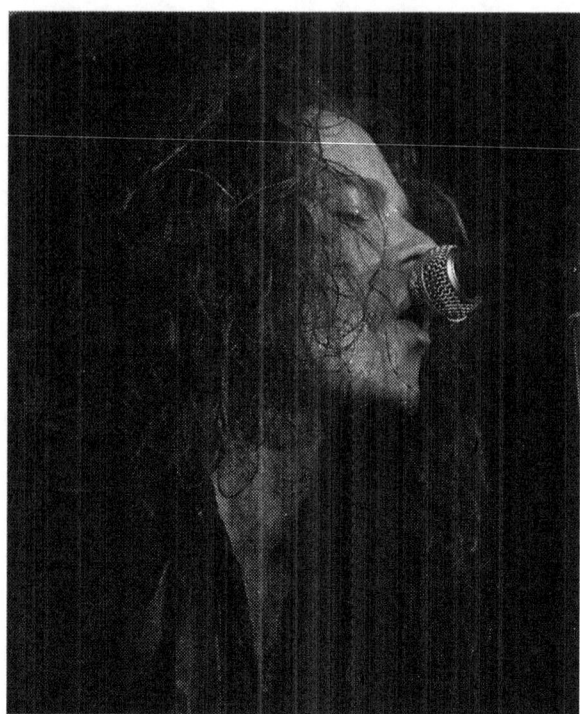

Ray Gillen. Pic: Matt Sampson.

piqued, so I made my way up closer to the stage. I'm pretty tough to blow away, but I remember thinking that this guy is a star, and what the hell is he doing in this family band? With all due respect to Bobby Rondinelli, who I truly admire (Rainbow's 'Straight Between The Eyes' is one of the greatest Rock albums ever made) the band wasn't very good and had no songs. Clearly the wrong vehicle for Ray Gillen. I watched the whole show, and made a mental note to keep this guy in mind for the future."

The question of compensation from Black Sabbath for stealing Gillen away ignites a gusty howl of laughter from Rondinelli. "Compensation for my loss? Ha Ha! No, he just fucked off and left. I was stupid for not having contracts signed. That was my fault so I only have myself to blame there. Ray was on a salary from us and he was living at my house. It was no casual association. No, Black Sabbath didn't do the decent thing. I never went to see Ray with Sabbath. I refused to go. We made up later, buried the hatchet so to speak but at the time I had been well and truly fucked."

Eric Singer remembers the excitement Ray's introduction brought to the band. "We all just knew the moment we heard him sing and of course he just looked great. In fact he looked English, like a classic English Rock God type of singer. Ray was a great package because obviously besides looking the part he sounded phenomenal. The thing was he had absolutely no experience at all. He didn't know any of the old Sabbath songs and the only Black Sabbath stuff he was familiar with was the Dio songs. We rehearsed for two days in Boston so that he could learn everything. Just before he joined us he was actually in line for the 'Cats' musical. He had a good Rock tradition though, we used to jam around a lot with songs like Deep Purple's 'Burn', stuff from Roger Glover's 'Butterfly Ball' album and Free. Ray was great at imitating Robert Plant and, ironically, Glenn Hughes."

The freshman had been plunged into a world beyond his wildest dreams. Geoff Nicholls recalls that Ray had difficulty containing his excitement. "Ray seemed like a nice guy. He looked absolutely brilliant, very young and he had a good voice but he was totally star struck. It was like talking to a fan sometimes. You could just tell he was thinking 'Wow!' all the time. He came across a bit shy but I think that's because he was intimidated to a certain degree."

The actual incorporation of Ray Gillen into the band poses some questions too. At the time the word was that Gillen, posing as a friend of Dave Spitz's, was covertly part of the tour entourage, finding his feet in the Sabbath fold and learning material. The North American 'Seventh Star' tour, eventually, got going in Cleveland on the 21st of March. Preceding this an initial run of gigs projected to commence in Chicago was cancelled at short notice. Support came from New York Thrashers Anthrax, featuring Dave Spitz's brother Dan on guitar, and Los Angeles shock Rockers W.A.S.P. promoting their 'Inside The Electric Circus' album. This latter act included the tattooed self styled 'mean motherfuckin' man', guitarist Chris Holmes, shortly after to date Iommi's former fiancé Lita Ford.

Glenn Hughes would only manage a total of five gigs. These being Cleveland Public Hall, Ohio, Detroit Joe Louis Arena, Michigan on the 22nd, East Rutherford Meadowlands Arena, New Jersey, Providence Civic Center, Rhode Island on the 25th and the Worcester Centrum, Massachusetts on the 26th.

Ray Gillen, publicly at least, first stepped up to the microphone on the 29th at New Haven, Connecticut. His first acknowledged liaison with Black Sabbath was at the Meadowlands Arena in New Jersey but it now becomes clear that the wheels of industry might just have been humming silently in the background for quite some time. It is possible that Gillen could have been discussed as a possible candidate for inclusion in the Sabbath entourage as early as February.

A pre-tour Los Angeles showcase gig, recorded at the old Lucille Ball / Paramount Desilu soundstage, had been especially laid on for the benefit of the press. There were many stars of the day loitering backstage such as Mötley Crüe, Quiet Riot and Ratt members all being present as Dave Spitz con-

A rushed publicity shot of Black Sabbath issued mid-tour with Ray Gillen. Ray Gillen, Eric Singer, Tony Iommi, Dave 'The Beast' Spitz and Geoff Nicholls.

Beauty and The Beast. Backstage, America 1986.

firms. "Eric and I were hangin' with Tommy Lee and a bunch of other LA stars. We were having a blast backstage, and were really excited to kick some ass in front of our peers. This was also the first time that we played the show utilizing the Birmingham stage set, lasers, and tunnel of doom, which Tony walked through in the beginning. It was held just a short time after Downing had clocked Glenn, and Glenn was certainly wearing some serious makeup that night, as well as very dark sunglasses. We all felt bad for him, and did not know what to expect. His singing was passable, but barely. However, we still tore it up, and the media and radio people really dug it. Tony's guitar and my bass were so fuckin' loud, the giant building was literally shaking. This was an exciting time. I had mentioned Ray to both Tony and Don as soon as I had started to feel uneasy with the way Glenn's problems were starting to be felt on the band. This was quite early on, before the tour."

Tony Iommi, when faced with the question of Gillen's incorporation delivered stock answers to the collective media claiming the youngster had been thrust into the spotlight mid tour and had effectively saved the day. This was the line he trotted out to the author backstage at the Leicester De Montfort Hall. Hindsight though lends new emphasis on Tony's carefully chosen words. "I'm not quite sure where Ray came from, somebody just found him out of the blue. Dave Spitz knew about him somehow and when we started to have problems with Glenn, well, more problems with Glenn shall we say…, we had to do something very quick. Ray turned up, we chatted, he sang for us and he was perfect. We had no choice but to take a chance because Glenn was going downhill fast and some of the feedback we were getting was horrible. Ray saved our bacon. He had to learn the material and then get straight onto the stage with us. The tour took on a new light after that. It was a huge relief. The guy is an amazing singer. It's difficult to believe he was unknown at the time."

W.A.S.P. frontman Blackie Lawless has a razor sharp mental picture of the pre-show shenanigans at the Meadowlands. "W.A.S.P. had just finished our sound check for the day, this would have been about 4 o'clock in the afternoon. So we walked back to our dressing room. Now, our rooms were exactly opposite Black Sabbath's and as soon as we got into the hallway we could hear singers running through a cappella scales. It was a little odd to say the least. Basically there were a bunch of singers in there tearing their asses off. I said to one of the crew 'What's happening' and he says 'They're holding auditions. Glenn is out'. I couldn't fucking believe it. 'You've gotta be fucking kidding me?' I said to this guy and he tells me 'No, they're really auditioning right now'. I don't how many people they put through their paces but it was certainly a few because both the W.A.S.P. crew and the Sabbath crew were walking up and down the hallway imitating these scales which was quite funny. Obviously I left my dressing room door open too so I could hear everything. How many singers? I don't know. Certainly a bunch."

This revelation is confirmed by Geoff Nicholls. "Being New York, there were a few singers that came down for a try out. Ray was the one doing all the scales because he was having singing lessons and liked to keep his voice warm. He didn't want to go straight into 'Neon Knights' cold. Although all the crew were sworn to absolute secrecy, Blackie is right—they did all keep wandering up the corridors practicing their scales too!"

Local boy Dave Spitz has good call to remember the nightmare of the Meadowlands show. "This show was a milestone for me personally, as I was born and raised in New York, and I had a plethora of guests that night. It was especially memorable, as Anthrax was invited to open the show for several dates, this being one of them. My parents, George and Irene Spitz, witnessed both my brother Dan, and myself playing this huge venue together! They were certainly proud of their boys that night. In addition, my White Lion brothers were there as well, with management. I spent some time with them in the private bar, and was quite busy backstage."

This relaxed atmosphere regrettably did not transfer to the stage that night. "Once we started the show, Glenn could barely sing a note. Tony and I kept glancing at each other, like, what the fuck is going on? We thought that Glenn had been rested, and was going to kill this crowd. As a black belt in traditional Goju-Ryu Karate, I summoned up all of my Goju spirit and restraint to prevent myself from literally kicking him off the front of the stage. The band was playing unbelievable, but Glenn just could not sing. There were some shenanigans backstage later between Tony and Glenn, and we all thought that Tony was going to kick his ass."

Ray Gillen, ostensibly masquerading as a friend of Dave Spitz, travel with the band on their bus whilst other arrangements were made for Glenn. Dave Spitz describes the method of subterfuge. "As far as anyone knew Ray was my friend just come down to check out the tour. Because we had him on the bus with us we got in some valuable time to catch his vibe, hang out with him and discuss material. There was no real talk of him being in the band as such as we were all hoping Glenn was going to see the tour out."

Spitz does concede though that Ray was installed as a back up. "Sure, Glenn was fragile and, yes, his days were certainly numbered. We all hoped he was going to complete the tour because, from a business point of view, Glenn's voice was on the record and his face was on the video. Tony Iommi and Don Arden had arranged for Doug Goldstein to come in and act as a kind of caretaker for Glenn. Basically Doug travelled separately with Glenn in order to keep an eye on him and make sure he was rested enough for the gigs. It's sad to say Glenn did need looking after at that point."

Glenn Hughes put in just two more shows, the last being the Worcester Centrum in Massachusetts, before leaving. At this last concert fans reported that Hughes was in such bad condition that Geoff Nicholls took over lead vocal duties from a lip synching Hughes in an effort to save the day. "That's right actually" Geoff confirms. "At one stage in the show Glenn just turned round to look at me and mouthed 'help!' His voice had just gone—completely. It was actually pretty saddening because, as everybody in the world knows, Glenn is an amazing singer. Yet here he was with nothing coming out of his mouth at all! So, for that last gig I actually sang most of the show. There was no choice because without the singer the show would musically fall apart. All the other musicians rely on the singer to tell them were they are in the song. For example, if you have a Sabbath song with 24 riff sections in it the drummer will only know if he is on part 20 or 22 from listening to the singer, otherwise he hasn't got a clue. I tell you, that was one heck of a show to get through."

Luckily, with Glenn's voice finally giving up the ghost Geoff Nicholls had the knowledge to get them through to the end of the gig. "Fortunately I knew the words back to front because I had written most of the 'Seventh Star' lyrics and knew the Ozzy stuff off by heart. I had been playing those songs for five years. Very often in rehearsals and sound checks, even recently with Black Sabbath, I'll do the vocals if Ozzy isn't around. I very often used to rehearse for 'Seventh Star' with just myself, Dave and Eric." Bootlegs recorded from the crowd testify much of the vocal work that night were handled exclusively by Nicholls.

It would certainly be a day the ailing Glenn Hughes will never forget. "That last show was without a doubt the most terrifying experience in front of an audience I have ever experienced" he reckons. "My voice by that stage had completely packed up—there was absolutely nothing left of it. My vocal chords were simply unusable, completely blocked up. It was the only time in my 30 year career I have ever gone through anything like that. Totally frightening."

Following the show the band retired to their hotel. As well as having a party laid on for Black Sabbath the hotel was also hosting other functions and parties on other floors. "The building was very crowded" remembers Dave Spitz. "We had our party going on with lots of friends and fans and other people were partying too. It was looking like it was going to be a great night. Somehow we ended up on another floor in someone else's room. This is when I noticed that as well as all the girls and friends hanging out Ray was in there too. I was in a corner of this room talking to some people, Ray was in another corner talking to some chicks, as always, and that's when I saw Glenn was there too. Of course, we all knew this whole thing was going to boil over soon and Glenn is no dummy. He knew something was going on but he didn't know what. Ray was just oblivious, he was just into his chicks but I just knew something was about to happen. Next thing I know time freezes because this girl suddenly points at Ray and says 'Hey look—that's the new singer with Black Sabbath!' Of course Glenn heard everything! Oh my God . . .

I literally ran out of that room and down to mine, phoned Bertie the tour manager and told him "Bertie—the shit has just hit the fan brother! Glenn knows!" You know what Bertie said? "Lock you door and put the fucking dresser up against it. Do it now!" So I did. I locked my door and piled furniture up in front of it and it's a good job I did. Within minutes Glenn was pounding on my door like a Grizzly bear. He was just in the most intense rage, pounding and pounding on my door! I just sat there and figured the best plan of action was to simply pretend I wasn't there. Glenn was so pissed he was going to do someone some serious damage. Finally he stopped the pounding. I gathered up my courage and peeked down the corridor. Glenn was there, he had calmed down and was at somebody else's door and they were just talking calmly. That's the very last time I saw Glenn."

Black Sabbath's lead vocalist would be dismissed in the most ignominious of fashions. "Do you know how they fired me?" he says, Glenn's voice still bearing a trace of incredulity after all these years. "They shoved a goddamn note and a plane ticket under my door! I couldn't fucking believe it. They couldn't bear to tell me themselves face to face. I tried to find them but they refused to speak to me. It was all very school-boyish. Doug Goldstein drove me to the airport and that was it. Bye bye Black Sabbath."

Blackie Lawless details how the switch in singers affected W.A.S.P. Apparently it would be fortuitous. "A few days of the tour were put off, which suited me fine because I needed to rest my voice on doctor's orders. So for us it was quite good timing. A few days later the tour gets back underway and there is Ray Gillen! The guy did great but was obviously finding it tough because he had his lyrics on the stage. It was a shame about Glenn though. I don't know what he was having to deal with at the time, but he has always been in my eyes one of the quintessential Rock stars. With Purple he had it all, the look, the moves, the voice. Total star quality."

In that brief window of down time Black Sabbath had rented out an old theatre to put Ray Gillen through his paces with a full set list. A set of brand new official band shots was rushed out to herald in the new era. Gillen looks exceptionally young and, with a heavy application of eyeliner, bordering on the feminine. In stark contrast the fatherly Tony Iommi, sporting distinguished silver sideburns and a grey tipped moustache, seems to have stepped straight out of a colonial Victorian hunting party. Such was the guitarist's expression and demeanour one could quite easily expect the photograph to have been sepia toned. Circulation of these pictures was not rapid enough though and the very first chance many Sabbath fans got to see Ray Gillen was in the flesh as he strode out from the dry ice, purposefully grabbed the microphone and roared like a young lion having just taken over the pride.

History would repeat itself though in an attempt to foil the new singer's debut. Just as Ian Gillan had found dry ice to be a curse so Ray Gillen found himself up against the same enemy. "Ray didn't come from that old Sabbs history and he actually didn't know a lot of the old stuff" says Dave Spitz. "The only way we could get around this problem in the short term was to give him cue cards. So, for the first gig all the front of stage monitors and every available space was filled with bits of paper with the lyrics to the songs. The stage was plastered and it actually looked kind of funny." As the haunting strains of the intro tape commenced and the lasers scythed across the stage Spitz recalls standing side stage with an exceptionally nervous singer. "Ray wasn't used to big shows. He had only ever done clubs so he was totally psyched up. He was full of nerves so I gave him a big hug and told him 'Go for the throat Ray!' That's exactly what he did. He strode out there and just did fucking great. He was barking into that microphone really loud. His vocals were just amazing.

What happened though was that the smoke was being pumped out onstage for the song 'Black Sabbath'. Ray needed his cue cards for that one because he didn't know it at all but they were getting covered in thick smoke! Ray was wafting this fog out of the way, trying to keep it looking cool, and they just kept cranking up the smoke. He got through it somehow. It was unfortunate it happened with 'Black Sabbath' though because that track is very important to Tony. I'm not sure if fans have ever noticed this but he doesn't want any showmanship when the band does that track. This is because he believes it epitomises everything the band stands for. You had to just stand your ground for that song and to be as intense as you can. It's an odd one because it's very freeform. Usually in quieter moments on songs the drummer can keep the time with a hi hat but Tony didn't even want that with 'Black Sabbath'. In rehearsals Tony had to put a lot of time in with Eric so he could get that just right. It was really difficult for Eric to hit those octave notes right on time. That's totally intense to play live. Overall though, for a first show, Ray was amazing. I can just remember thinking that he had this huge voice. It was electric out there. Ray was just roaring let me tell you."

Black Sabbath would be roaring musically too, once again as evidenced by Dave Spitz. "The volume level on stage throughout this tour was devastating. Tony's wall of sound was incredible, and I was using like six Ampeg SVT 8x10 cabinets, several Cerwin Vega 18" enclosures, and six Marshall 4x12's across the top of the SVT's. In addition, we were being blasted through the stage monitors, and the huge side fills."

Although Sabbath had quickly regained their poise Geoff Nicholls felt he personally had been dealt a blow by the whole fracas. "I was pinning a lot on 'Seventh Star' because I had written so much of it. I really thought of it as 'my' album. When we first started the TV and radio promotion for 'No Stranger To Love' was very strong and its exposure was rising. Things were looking very promising. When Glenn left the record company pulled all the promotion overnight. Basically we got fucked."

"It's a real shame, as our entire American Tour suffered big-time; especially since Sabbath was out of the public eye for a while after the 'Born Again'

record, and there was great anticipation for this album" thinks Dave Spitz. He too views the record as a lost opportunity both in terms of personal aspirations and the band's standing. "It was important to all of us to make a big impact when 'Seventh Star' came out. I still don't understand the decision to release 'No Stranger To Love' as the first single. It's a fucking great song, but it should not have been the first track the world heard with the new album and line-up. Man, it should have been the heaviest fuckin' track on the record! We really needed to go in with a sledgehammer. All in all, the recording of 'Seventh Star' was certainly unconventional, and Glixman fucked up the mix; except for the drums, which were quite big. I'm still pissed off about him ruining my bass sound; it turned out to be so muddy, not even close to my gritty, balls-out Bestial sound that hit the tape."

Glenn Hughes, in recovery from his facial injuries and contemplating his next career move, was bitter about the circumstances that forced his ousting but not the outcome. He tries to qualify his emotions, learning that he had been replaced as Black Sabbath frontman. "When Ray took over I was happy, relieved, glad they had got in a good singer. I liked Ray, I actually struck up a friendships with him before I even knew he was there to replace me! We became very good friends later and it was nice to see a young talent like that being given such a golden opportunity."

Glenn Hughes now had to face up to some very practical physical problems on top of any mental anguish resulting from his dismissal. "Afterwards I simply could not sing at all. Doug Goldstein, who was looking after me at the time and who now manages Axl Rose, took me to a doctor." In hospital Hughes had an operation to reconstruct his nose and sinuses, eventually solving the problem. It was a procedure well overdue. "It was pretty awful. They had to scrape a lot of stuff, dried blood and stuff, out of there. The doctor told me that not only could I not sing but that I had to not even talk for three months! I went around writing notes everywhere. That's why I couldn't give my side of the story. I heard all this crap about drugs and that I was supposedly mentally unbalanced but the truth was I was out of Sabbath due to an injury. At that stage I couldn't have done anything at all so I was no good to any band. Thankfully my voice came back and has actually been getting stronger with each passing year. I'm blessed."

Career wise, Glenn Hughes would now be staring wide eyed into an yawning abyss of his own making, an inescapable black hole that few return from. His colleagues could help him no longer and the music industry—his lifeline—had shut all the doors. "I went into a very dark place for the next two to three years. I felt utterly sorry for myself and just hid myself away. I was an egomaniac with a very low self esteem. In 1989 I prayed to God and began to deal with my obsession with drink and drugs. On Christmas of 1991 I had got sick enough to check myself in and deal with it. All of my friends and family had yelled at me, screamed at me and pleaded for me to sort myself out before I died but I just wasn't ready. I put people I love very much through some real pain, and I include Tony Iommi in this. Tony often tried to help me and I turned my back every time. He really cared. My parents were terrified but for a long time it just didn't matter. One day I woke up and realised I was on my way to becoming a statistic. I've been clean for 11 years now and each day has been wonderful. I'm only just learning what it is to be a real man."

Upon reflection Glenn realises he was the wrong man at the wrong time. His induction into the Black Sabbath roll of honour dictated more by way of friendship than design. "I should never have been the singer for Black Sabbath. That was all wrong. I still love the album and I am a great fan of Tony's work and his choice of singers since. Tony Martin is a wonderful singer and a great guy, lovely bloke and deserves so much more recognition. Ronnie James Dio is a master of his craft. I never got the Ian Gillan thing, that was too far out there for me. That to me wasn't Sabbath at all. My part in it? I made one album I'm very proud of. That I'm happy with. The story of Glenn and Tony isn't over yet."

It would not be such a happy ending for John Downing, the man who threw the punch at Glenn. There is a common train of thought that the production manager was murdered. "Nobody really knows what happened to John" Glenn wonders. "But, all we do know is that he got on a ferry, got into an altercation with some people on that journey and never made it off the ferry at the other end. Very sad."

Poignant too, would be the last date of the North American 'Seventh Star' tour in Dallas, Texas. Blackie Lawless remembers making an effort to see the Sabbath show and found himself dumbfounded. "I don't normally go out to watch the other bands too much but because this was the last gig I wanted to make sure I caught the whole thing. I can just remember Tony Iommi playing this phenomenal guitar solo, almost like he was possessed. For most of the show he just stared at the ceiling, there was no audience contact. For me, it felt like he was playing as if this was to be his last American show. He told me years later that he wasn't thinking that way but to watch him at the time was just incredible. He certainly had something on his mind that's for sure." A further run of U.S. Black Sabbath shows was projected and set in place but pulled. Once again a North American tour had been cut short.

Whilst Tony Iommi was coping with the tribulations of 'Seventh Star' Geezer Butler was still attempting to piece together his own band and by 1986 Welshman Carl Sentance had stepped into the role of frontman. Sentance had impressed many with his vocal prowess on the debut and, as it turned out only, Persian Risk album 'Rise Up'. That record also featured future Motorhead guitarist Phil Campbell. 'Rise Up' had stood proud amongst the plethora of post NWoBHM albums by virtue of the sheer quality of song-writing and Sentance's mature vocal style. The singer, realising Persian Risk was eking out a precarious living on borrowed time once Campbell had teamed up with Lemmy & co., got his tapes submitted to the Black Sabbath management. These recordings would, in turn, be exchanged between Gloria Butler and Smallwood Taylor who were handling the business affairs of the bassist's fledgling band.

Sentance pans out the sequence of events from there. "I got a phone call from Smallwood Taylor asking if I would be interested in an audition. They sent me a tape of about five songs to learn. Not what I expected because it was actually quite lightweight, even American styled AOR. Quite strange." Carl was put through his paces at the legendary Rockfield Studios in Monmouthshire, returned home and heard ... nothing. "It was quite a few weeks before I heard anything back so I didn't think anything was going to come of it at first. Finally I got the call and we got to work."

The band Geezer was working with incorporated Sentance, guitarist Pedro Howse, keyboard player Jezz Woodruffe and, at first, a drummer named 'John'. "The first drummer was a bit too progressive really for the kind of music. He was a bit too crazy for the songs. Gary came in and suited it perfectly." The percussive role would soon be filled on a more permanent basis though by Gary Ferguson, noted for his work with Gary Moore. "I loved working with Geezer" the vocalist says in praise of his erstwhile employer. "He is a bit out there at times but as a musician he's just great. He is the only bass player I know who can wildly overplay but still keep it solid. He's all over the neck all of the time but he keeps that rhythm spot on. I used to stand in amazement watching him."

The musical direction of the band surprised many in the industry but Carl explains the thinking behind it. "You have to remember that bands like Bon Jovi and Europe were huge at the time so I think that affected the way Smallwood Taylor were thinking. I thought that was a mistake. Even though I disagreed with the musical direction I just thought that the combination of Iron Maiden's manager and Black Sabbath's bass player must know what they were doing."

Apparently unknown to Carl Sentence though was another vocalist Geezer Butler worked with, albeit briefly. Right in the middle of Sentence's tenure the Geezer Butler band rehearsed with Chicago native Kyle Michaels. After just having had an album released by his band Ravage the singer was informed by Tom Mohler at Sanctuary Geezer was on the search for a singer. Michaels submitted his tape and waited. "First I heard I was in the top 250, then the top 10, then the final 3" reports Michaels. "The next phone call told me I was getting on a plane to Gatwick!"

The young hopeful was collected at the airport and driven to Rockfield Studios. His debut was far from impressive. "When I walked into the studio I was introduced to Geezer" says Michaels describing his entrance. "He was seated at a table eating soup. He looks up at me and, without saying 'Hello' or anything, the first thing he says to me is 'What's your favourite Black Sabbath album?' I said 'Born Again'. I had only just got that album and had been listening to it over and over again. I love Ian Gillan. That record was foremost in my mind just because I was playing it so much. Well, Geezer picks up his soup and, without a word, walks off! Someone says to me 'That's the worst possible thing you could of said. Geezer doesn't even consider that a Black Sabbath album.' Oh my God, what a way to start. It didn't get much better from there actually. The whole time I felt pretty uncomfortable."

Regardless, Michaels set to work rehearsing with a band unit incorporating Geezer, Pedro Howse, Jezz Woodruffe and Jay Schellen of Los Angeles band Hurricane on the drums. This variant of the band would only rehearse and never record anything. Michaels records the material as being Hard Rock, nowhere near as heavy as Black Sabbath, particularly noting a track entitled 'Lock Myself Away'. "It was cool, I was paid well and paid on time—which is unusual in this business" he states for the record. "The whole thing lasted maybe three weeks, a month at the most. I was told that Sanctuary was getting sued by Poison and it looked like Poison was going to win so the money dried up. I went home."

Michaels relocated to Los Angeles, uniting with erstwhile W.A.S.P. guitarist Randy Piper in his new venture Animal. Subsequently he would found Bird Of Prey with former members of Armored Saint before hooking up with guitarist Alex Masi to record a number of albums. "Whilst in LA I bumped into Jay again. He told me the whole Geezer band situation had just stopped. I never heard about Carl Sentence until now." It would seem Carl Sentence was none the wiser about Kyle Michaels either and dutifully maintained his role as frontman throughout this entire period.

Carl remembers a lack of finality to the proceedings. "Towards the end the budget started slipping with Smallwood Taylor so it fizzled out." During this time frame the band, working under a loose title of Ghost, undertook no live work at all. "It was very frustrating" admits Carl. "The rest of the guys just wanted to gig, to get on with something but all we did was showcase down at Tasco, cut some videos and demo. At my age, back then, I was just raring to go of course. When I joined the band I was a bit naive because I can remember thinking 'Wow! This is it!' but slowly but surely two years drifted by. There was a lot of political stuff, a lot of business meetings. It was all quite odd because I just sat at home for month after month doing nothing. All this time I was getting paid by them too."

As far as Sentence recollects the band fell apart when Geezer was welcomed back into the arms of his old comrade Ozzy Osbourne. "Right at the end I was really just thinking what the hell is going on? Nothing was happening. I had an offer from another band, Monroe. They were signed and gearing up for some work in Europe. That was it more than anything, I just wanted to work. I called Smallwood Taylor, told them I had this offer and that I didn't want to let them down. Surprisingly they said 'You may as well do it because Geezer is joining Ozzy's band'. That was the first I knew. I did regret the move over to Monroe because that simply didn't happen. The chemistry was all wrong."

With the Monroe situation collapsing Sentence bit the bullet and relocated to North America, forming an alliance with the former UFO guitarist Paul 'Tonka' Chapman in an outfit ironically enough billed as Ghost. The very same handle Geezer had toyed with. Chapman's Ghost, despite having only recently issued an album of archive tracks, succumbed to the same fate as Geezer's, eventually floundering. Sentence struck out on his own, resurrecting the Persian Risk band name for live work in Florida. That too faltered after the outfit got bogged down in the club covers circuit. Returning to the UK Sentence oddly found himself inducted into the lead vocalist role with Swiss veterans Krokus, recording one album 'Round 13'.

A rejuvenated Black Sabbath, buoyed by the enthusiasm injected by their eager new frontman, had high hopes for their British tour. "When we hit the UK we really had the wind in our sails" relates Eric Singer. "Ray was a great breath of fresh air for us all. He was just so desperate to get out there and sing." It seemed as though Black Sabbath had been pulled

Ray Gillen. Pic: Matt Sampson.

back from the brink. Ray Gillen had given the band everything they had desperately been searching for in a singer for over two years. He was young, lean, he looked sensational and had the belly roar of a leviathan.

Unfortunately advance ticket sales for the UK shows had been dismal. Since the David Donato episode the vast majority of Black Sabbath stories propagated by the UK Rock press had proven mocking at best and nothing short of vicious as the norm. The Glenn Hughes 'Mars bar' stories had all been raked over once again and journalists delighted in the fact that Ray Gillen was a complete unknown, the implications being that Sabbath was so washed up that a nobody was the only person ready to take the task on.

The anticipated walk up for the shows did not transpire and for many of the dates the band played out to an audience in the hundreds rather than thousands. It was undoubtedly grim but, to their credit, the band completed the entire tour of twelve dates, commencing in deepest Yorkshire on the 21st May at the Sheffield City Hall. Support for all dates would come from Zeno, an incompatible union at best. The German band, managed by the notoriously roguish, yet immensely likeable, figure of Dave Corke, had just scored a deal of immense proportions with EMI. Tour managing Zeno would, coincidently, be erstwhile Black Sabbath tour manager Albert Chapman. Having spent an entire year in the studio, going through three top name producers and a budget even Michael Jackson would choke at, Zeno were all set to promote their grandiose debut. Unfortunately for them the only tour available was Black Sabbath. It is highly unlikely that the presence of Zeno managed to entice more than a handful of extra punters to the entire tour.

At one of the latter staging posts, the London Hammersmith Odeon; scene of many a previous sell out four night run, the author discovered the well known Kerrang magazine writer Malcolm Dome leaning on a side aisle pillar. He was far from impressed. "Look at this audience. I mean, where is it? Where is it? This is Black Sabbath for God's sake!" he motioned flapping his arms about as if to further illustrate the void. Malcolm was right. The audience was sparse, thinner still for having been spread over a two night consecutive stint. Oddly, five large TV cameras were very much in evidence filming the event for a proposed commercial concert video. This film has yet to see the light of day.

At the Leicester De Montfort Hall gig on the 27th of May the author put in an interview with a surprisingly upbeat Tony Iommi. Unfortunately much of what was said would be strictly within the parameters of promoting the album. The guitarist had wised up to providing too much detail a long time before and was cautious in offering anything of substance.

Ray Gillen succumbed to the lure of the tape recorder on the very last show of the UK tour at the Nottingham Royal Concert Hall. The gig was far from sold out but still reeled in a respectable audience as Nottingham was, and always probably will be, a 'Rock' town. Interestingly the Leicester De Montfort Hall gig a matter of weeks before which had suffered an appalling attendance was a mere half hour's drive away suggesting that if the promoters had got their planning right and just put in the one gig it could well have been packed. In the bowels of the theatre, Ray emptied the room and proceeded to graze his way through a salad bowl as he answered the author's questions.

Now, let me get this straight because you are here, an unknown as yet, fronting Black Sabbath and many British fans are wondering who the Hell you are. It's an uncanny coincidence you very nearly sharing the same surname as another famous Sabbath singer— Ian Gillan.

"As coincidences go it's pretty wild isn't it? My name is spelt, like you say, just one letter different. Vocally we're nothing alike. I mean, I love Ian Gillan's voice, I grew up on it and I'll admit that I have sang along to most of the Purple records at some point. Ian's great but we are very different in style. Glenn Hughes was great too. Incredible singer, more my kind of thing. I just love that bluesy Rock style. Coverdale is cool too, Robert Plant, Paul Rodgers, that kind of thing—the old masters! I listen to a lot of Free, Bad Company, Zeppelin. Ha Ha. I'm definitely old school Rock. If it's cool or not I don't care. It's what I like."

What were you doing before Black Sabbath?

"I was with Bobby Rondinelli from Rainbow. We had a band, just called Rondinelli. Good band. Bobby and his brother Teddy. We were getting near a deal, a lot of interest, but Black Sabbath came along and so, ... sorry Bobby!"

I've seen quite a few shows on this tour now. How do you think it has progressed?

"I don't know about Great Britain because this is first time around for me. Tony tells me we are doing fine. OK, it's tough because I think the media here are giving us a hard time because the band seems to be changing all the time. People have told me that it's kind of a British thing too, to pull bands down. The fans like us, the press doesn't. That's OK because we are winning over the people that matter. People are telling me after the shows that they have been impressed. I'm sure they are being genuine too. This is a great, great band to sing for. Tony, Dave, Eric, Geoff are real talented people."

Let's not beat about the bush. There aren't many people coming to see you? It's a long time since I saw Hammersmith Odeon so empty.

"Really? Maybe you're right but I think those that came will go away and tell their friends and it will be different next time. Someone told me more girls were coming to the shows which is cool. It has been building, people coming to repeat shows in other cities they tell us. It's tough, the fans know Tony but not the rest of us. It will just take time I guess.

Maybe the other thing is that Sabbath need to make a point to a new generation of Rockers. There are people out there who think that by slapping on some makeup and teasing their high six foot hair that somehow constitutes Rock n' Roll but I don't think so. I don't have anything against those kind of bands, we are all here to entertain, but maybe the focus is too much in that direction right now. For me it's about the playing, the musicianship, the heart n' soul. Certainly is with this band anyhow. I think people are going to want that back."

I have to say this, and not just because you are sitting here, but I think you are right. I have been very, very impressed.

"There you go!"

I noticed the cameras at Hammersmith. Were they for a video?

"Yeah, that's right. Should be interesting."

Who's idea was it for the stage set?

"I have no idea."

What is it exactly? Looks a bit like a Victorian Satanic mill.

"I will have to take your word for that. Looks kind of industrial to me. Like a big Heavy Metal factory or something. It's cool but kind of obscure."

It's nice to see Geoff Nicholls on the stage for a change. Why the change?

"I don't know much about that. I know Geoff is happy though because he worked hard on the album. A lot of the 'Seventh Star' songs he wrote. I don't know how the band worked before I got involved but Geoff seems to be very much a part of the team. Maybe he didn't like being out front before? I don't know, I think it's good for him though."

In a strange kind of way, the fact that the venues have not been full has made a lot of people I've spoke to feel almost privileged to see you in action. I mean, your voice is just huge and it looks like you've been singing with the band for years.

"Thanks. It's nice to hear that. Onstage I just focus on the task. I hope those people tell their friends to come next time."

The American shows you just did must have been a very strange experience?

"Yes, strange in a totally positive way. It was the thrill of a lifetime every night. The audiences were great, very hot for the band. Everything happened so fast. There was a bit of confusion naturally. I got called 'Glenn' more than once! It was a rush for me personally, one I don't think I'll be able to repeat too quickly."

Just when and how did you come to join the band?

"Dave Spitz knew about me. Tony just phoned me up one day out of the blue and I was like 'This is a joke, right?' But it wasn't. It took a while for me to realise this thing was for real. It's not everyday you are asked to join Black Sabbath.

We met, we talked and then, it was all quite strange because Glenn was still around. It was scary but when we got the chance I sang for Tony and he just gave me this big smile so I kind of knew then. Glenn was very suspicious and it wasn't the best way of doing things but Tony really had no other choice."

How do you feel singing the old Sabbath material? Anything you would rather not sing?

"I like all of it, truthfully. It is almost like an honour for me to sing the songs that Glenn sang on the album. I'm hoping I do him justice there. The Ozzy stuff? Well, we are Black Sabbath so we can't get away with not playing it. It isn't easy, I'll admit to that. Ozzy sang on such a kind of one level approach which suits those songs perfectly. It's not my style and it's a challenge. You know, I didn't actually know too much of the old Black Sabbath stuff, a lot of it was new to me."

Really? You didn't know 'Paranoid'? C'mon.

"I knew of it, I had heard it plenty but it had never sank in because it just wasn't my thing. Sure, you hear Black Sabbath on college radio, in the car, at parties, but I never sat down to listen to a whole album. Dio, that's different. I love Dio with Rainbow and Sabbath. The Dio songs I knew word for word even before this whole thing came along. Now I'm learning to love Ozzy in a strange kind of way by performing these songs night after night."

What do you make of the comparisons people are making between you and Ozzy?

"I don't understand it. We are so different. I don't try to look like him, (Ray grabs his belly here!) I don't copy his stage moves and there is no way I can even begin to sound like Ozzy nor would I want to. In fact, if ever I begin to sound like Ozzy point me in the direction of a doctor! People should get over it, Black Sabbath moved on a long, long time ago. It's Tony's thing now, not Ozzy's.

I've heard comments from Ozzy and Ronnie about this band and all I can say is, hey, it's Tony's band to do with what he likes. I think that's very unfair. You guys bailed out and, OK, I have some very big boots to fill. I admit to that. Ronnie, he's like a hero. Ozzy, he can say what he likes. I just don't care.

The thing is this, Sabbath is a legend and it is easy to take a shot at, especially in times of change. I think all that will change for the better once we get a new record out."

How do you rate Zeno?

"Well, they're Germans ... Ha Ha Ha! Except Rod who just has a German name."

It's kind of different don't you think? They're not really suited for a Black Sabbath audience.

"It's not your regular Rock that's for sure. The guy has a great voice and Joe is great on guitar. Joe's cool, the keyboard guy is kinda strange though. I like the album, not what you expect. I think it's kind of Queen like. They're trying something a little different from everything else that is out there. It could be huge. You just can't tell. At least it's different so it gets my vote. They are getting a lot of money from somewhere so good luck to them."

How does it 'feel' to sing for Black Sabbath?

"Wonderful. Really. I want to make my mark here and I think this is the band to do it. Tony is such a wonderful, wonderful player. Just listen to the Blues solo he plays in the set. He doesn't get enough credit for how sensational a guitarist he really is.

I don't know how I come across to the fans yet. I'm learning on my feet still but I'm getting there and the guys are really helping me out with good advice. These audiences, they seem to stare at you like this ... (pulls very critical, screwed up face) ... as if they are thinking 'OK big shot, show me how good you really are'. That for me is new. I'm used to playing for people who go out for a good time not to judge you.

There is a certain amount of pacing myself I have to remember during the set too. The whole thing is a craft, but it's coming together."

What do you mean by pacing yourself? Like maintaining your energy?

"No, I mean more emotionally. Each song tells a story and you have to get into the whole vibe of the song to deliver it with conviction. That is what makes Ronnie so good, he can give himself to a song totally. Tony and Geoff have been guiding me and given me good advice there. It's OK to 'sing' a song but to make it really work, so the audience believes it, you have to pull from something deep down, really get into it. I have to do that but at the same time I need to project my persona too.

The way I am approaching each show is that I really have something to prove and each song is a way of reminding the audience that Black Sabbath has a new singer. I put my heart and soul into it and make an effort to deliver the goods every time. I would never say forget those guys because that would be both disrespectful and plain stupid. Ronnie, Glenn, Ian—they are legends."

Who is your favourite amongst those names?

"Can't choose. Ian has all those great, great Deep Purple songs. Just stack them up. It's a hell of an achievement. The guy has just sang on so many amazing songs. There's some cool stuff on 'Born Again', that album had a nice groove to it. Some of his vocals on that record are incredible.

Glenn too with Purple but I love his soulful style, he has a lot of R&B in him. Really gives himself to a song. Amazing singer with a great gift. Glenn makes everything look just so easy.

And Ronnie? He's a vocal God for sure. A very small vocal God but still a God! In Rainbow he was awesome. You kinda look at him and wonder where this huge voice is coming from and that's very cool. Love Ronnie's voice, love his songs. Singing these songs is an experience I tell you. Huge respect to Ronnie."

It must be tough to replace these people?

"This is an uphill battle for us now, we are realistic. It just makes me fight harder, I want to sing better to make sure people leave believing that Sabbath is back on the rails again. And it is, it really is. I feel some confidence coming back, I really do.

Tony tells people he is proud of this band and I believe it. I'm proud to be here. I view this like a God given opportunity because I was kind of plucked right out of the blue for this band. I love singing all these classic songs but right now I'm just itching to sing in the studio. I want to have my name on a Black Sabbath record. I want to have my friends walk into a record store, pick up a Black Sabbath album and see my picture on there. That's where my focus is now."

What were you told about the reasons you were being pulled into the band so quickly? There are a lot of rumours about Glenn. Can you clarify the situation?

"Glenn was having lots of problems. That is all I was told. Health problems. He'll be back on the scene soon I'm sure."

Has the band done any writing for a new album?

"No, just ideas, just talk. Tony is starting to think about a new record."

Any idea of musical direction?

"No, too early. I know Tony wants to make it very heavy. That's good with me."

Will it be called Black Sabbath?

"No, it will be called 'Ray Gillen featuring Black Sabbath'! Yes, it will be Black Sabbath. That last album, well, it should have been Tony's solo thing but the record company just thought it would sell better as Sabbath. Tony has told me it was a complete mess for him. It was confusing and it didn't work. 'Seventh Star' was very Blues focussed, some ballads, perfect for Glenn, so I think Tony wants to get a lot heavier again for the next record.

Black Sabbath fans, I think, want Tony to play in a particular way and as good as 'Seventh Star' is it does not really represent that because it was Tony trying something different. I love 'Seventh Star'. There is some great music on there. If it had been released as the 'Tony Iommi Band' or something I think the critics would have been kinder."

How stable is the band now? Are you in for the long run?

"I hope so. Tony says yes so ... who can say? I'll give it my best shot."

That sounds a little cryptic?

"So far, so good. If you are asking me if I want to sing for Black Sabbath then the answer is yes, I'm not some temporary fill in. The guys make me feel at home and the line-up feels stable. It's a great band, Tony's great, The Beast, Eric, Geoff. No weak links. This is a wonderful band to be in. We all get along but it's Tony's baby at the end of the day and he makes all the decisions."

You mentioned 'The Beast' there. Why is Dave Spitz called that?

"The guy is a complete animal on the bass. Plus he has all this hair—everywhere! He's got more hair on him than a wolf! I don't think you could call him anything else except 'The Beast'."

I guess this is pretty much Tony's band now so how democratic is it?

"It's Tony's call every time. Black Sabbath is his band, he's the only one who never gave in which makes him, in my eyes, tougher than the rest of them. I'm learning a hell of a lot about Black Sabbath now. Things that the fans never get to hear about because Ozzy is always pushing his side of the story. I tell you, Tony is the man. He is Black Sabbath. Of course we discuss things, and he listens but he's the guy who has to carry the burden. He's very wise y'know. He's

Tony Iommi, Leicester De Montfort Hall 27th May 1986. Pic: Matt Sampson.

seen a lot, done a lot more so I'm personally happy to listen to the voice of experience. I love listening to his stories about the old days."

With a knock on the door, actually the third intrusion prompting Ray Gillen to get himself ready for the night's action, the singer bade his farewells, stepping out for his last ever performance as frontman for Black Sabbath ...

By this stage of the game Black Sabbath was no longer under the wing of Don Arden. Their former manager's protective wing may have been that of a ruthless raptor but just what had they swapped it for? Conversing with the author in a hotel in Southern Germany during 2000 Ronnie James Dio was scathing in his condemnation of the band's next manager—Patrick Meehan. According to Ronnie the band had already suffered at the hands of the Meehan clan and had gone back for a second whipping. There was talk of houses and cars being repossessed at the very height of Black Sabbath's global domination. Unfortunately the author had a beer in his hand that night instead of a tape recorder but, rest assured, the normally affable Ronnie was far from kind.

This is how Eric Singer experienced the shift in management. He is also forthright. "Everyone knows Sabbath always had a tradition with Don Arden. Now, he's a tough guy with a reputation—a deserved one. The guy gets things done in his particular way

Sage advice over a pint. Pic: Dave Spitz.

Ray Gillen and Tony Iommi rehearsing in Monmouth. Pic: Dave Spitz.

and takes no shit. People in this business know Don Arden and if you choose to deal with him you should know what to expect. Forget Don Arden's reputation, the real thing is ten times harder. That was obviously too tough on Tony eventually because he then went with Patrick Meehan. So, there I was, my first record, all this shit going on. Welcome to the music business.

You know, Black Sabbath was my introduction into how Rock n' Roll really works. I was very green to all the fundamental aspects of the business side of things but I think I was very quick to grasp how things work. Let me say this, I met a lot of very cool people with Sabbath, Dave, Bob, Glenn, Geoff were all great people. Our crew were just stars. Tony was always very, very cool with me. He has my respect to this day. But behind the scenes? Fuck man, you would not believe what goes on. If fans who bought the records and see the shows knew what the musicians have to go through they might buy a few more records and tickets just out of sympathy.

With Sabbath, Tony was always engaged in survival tactics. That's how it looked to me. He had to watch his back from two angles, keeping an eye on what Ozzy's next move was but also dealing with the people that were supposed to be helping him. So, he's having to deal with all of this and still deliver onstage every night, keep his band together and then make a world class record. The thing that Tony had was the ace card. He owned Black Sabbath. That really pissed Ozzy and Sharon off I can tell you! Sometimes, just being the drummer is a very comfortable position to be in. How the fuck Tony dealt with all of that I cannot tell you."

Following the British tour the band rehearsed at Henley on Arden near Birmingham. There was discussion about a set of gigs in Hawaii, which fell by the wayside, and even shows in India. This last proposal had apparently been in place even when Jeff Fenholt was in the studio and relates to the original concept behind the 'Star Of India' song. However,

Tony and Geoff in Monmouth. Pic: Dave Spitz.

these notions did not materialise and so Black Sabbath indulged themselves in the tranquil British summertime to score new material. "The studio was in a barn in the middle of nowhere" says Eric. "The weird thing was we were near all these antique stores so we had to keep the volume down so as not to disturb the locals. I actually had my drums packed with blankets. Then we had a six week break before heading to Monmouth. One little incident I remember was that the building we stayed in was supposedly haunted. Well, I got this bat in my room, which gave me the frights. Tony caught it in a towel and let it out the window."

Out of the frontline, Black Sabbath rested up and then put their minds to writing. Dave Spitz believes that it was during this period that the cracks began to get a little deeper than he would have liked, both within the band organisation and with Ray Gillen. "We had a number of problems" he opines. "Firstly, Tony Iommi had stopped using Don Arden as his manager and, for some reason, hooked up with Patrick Meehan. Initially we were just chilling, gelling together as a band, jogging, growing beards and all that goofy stuff. We had some good times, spending far too much time in the local Chinese restaurant. In truth we got a bit too mellow and the work ethic drifted.

Then a reality kind of began to sink in. Nobody was getting paid. This was frustrating to say the least. Secondly, we were moving like snails. Basically nothing was happening and a lot of it was down to Ray. The guy had absolutely no experience whatsoever. I have memories of Geoff Nicholls, myself and I sitting out on the lawn on a fabulous sunny day desperately trying to get some songs out of Ray. We had lots of little pieces but no solid songs. We moved into this little red barn. We spent a lot of time in there trying to nail songs but it just wasn't happening. Let me tell you, when you are working on the same riff over and over again it gets to be a pain in the ass. I have tons of cassettes of that period and they are proof that what we were doing was like pulling teeth. Basically Ray couldn't write and it was really holding us back."

Those researching Black Sabbath have often got confused over the band's switch from the Meehan to Arden and back to the Meehan stables. Bob Daisley, soon to enter into the story, sheds some light. "There are two Patrick Meehans, senior and junior. In the early days the father managed the band and in 1987 it was the son. Now Patrick Meehan senior had a heavy reputation. I had heard all kinds of things about him, that he was from that whole London underground type of background and stuff like that. Those were the rumours. I believed it because that's how he came across to me. When you meet someone you just know. He never crossed me, we never fell out, but you 'just knew'. This is just my feeling of the guy you understand. People told me had a heavy background and he gave no reason to disbelieve it. Patrick Meehan senior was still involved the second time around with Black Sabbath because I met him at Antigua on my connecting flight to Montserrat to record the album. Mainly it was the son involved then though."

The bass player recalls a conversation with Ozzy about this very same subject. Apparently, when with Black Sabbath in the seventies, every time the singer received a royalty cheque he went out on a spending spree building up his car collection. "Ozzy used to tell me that was his security. He was very suspicious

Waterfall buddies—Eric Singer, The Beast and Ray Gillen. Guess which one is the singer?

of all the dealings. He filled his driveway up with brand new cars because, as he told me, when it all crumbled at least he will have a load of cars to show for it."

Meehan's game plan for Black Sabbath's would take both Eric Singer and Dave Spitz by surprise. When it was revealed, the bassist could not figure out the reasoning behind such a move. "Basically the band was broke. If it wasn't broke then Eric, Ray and I were getting shafted because we weren't getting paid a dime. The band was really hurting for money. Then we get told we are going to record at Montserrat—the most expensive studio in the world! I admit, we went with the flow and Montserrat was a once in a lifetime, gorgeous place. The studio was simply amazing—but all that fucking money!"

Montserrat, situated southeast of Puerto Rico, then played host to Air Studios. The 100 square kilometre island, actually one of the last remnants of the British Empire, was breathtakingly beautiful until the eruption in July 1995 of the Soufriere Hills volcano. The studio itself, utilised by some of the very biggest names in the Pop industry, was destroyed by hurricane a little over two years after the band had vacated. Into this temporary tropical Garden of Eden stole the almost Gollum like figure of a wounded and deeply troubled Black Sabbath ...

Chapter 16

Blacky Sabb: Caribbean Speedballs

Bob Daisley's introduction into the unfolding saga of Black Sabbath, in spite of its brevity, would be nothing less than revolutionary. For the very first time Tony Iommi welcomed a confidante of Ozzy Osbourne's into his inner circle. Although Daisley and Ozzy have had many spats and altercations over more than a decade the Australian four-stringer's talents both musically and as a songwriter would see him playing a sometimes pivotal role in Ozzy's career. There was possibly anticipation that the Australian's song-writing crafts could achieve for 'Eternal Idol' what had already been achieved with 'Blizzard Of Ozz', 'Diary Of A Madman' and 'Bark At The Moon'. Ozzy had swallowed his pride on numerous occasions over the years to enlist Daisley as a kind of song-writing fire brigade. To be blunt, Daisley was Ozzy's hit machine and Sabbath were hoping some of that magic might rub off on them too.

Eric Singer is candid regarding the reasoning behind placing the call to Bob Daisley. "We did 'Eternal Idol' with Bob Daisley because Dave was having personal problems. Y'know, Dave was a great guy and an awesome bass player but he just had stuff he had to deal with away from the band" he acknowledges before revealing his enthusiasm for working with Daisley. "For me it was just great because Bob is my all time favourite bassist, I loved all that stuff he did with Ozzy. Also, Bob had written a lot of Ozzy's hits too and was very strong on lyrics. Although Ray could sing anything he was not up to speed on writing so Bob was a bit of a godsend really."

The aforementioned revelations thrown up by the protracted Daisley / Kerslake versus Osbournes court case in regard to the writing credits and royalty payments have thrown some much needed light on the importance of a band's rhythm section, so sorely overlooked before. When questioned on the bass role within Black Sabbath Bob Daisley makes these observations. "Bass is central to Black Sabbath because Geezer really pushed himself forward on all those early songs. He wasn't a backroom boy in any sense. The band sound then was pretty primitive and Geezer drove those songs along as much as Tony's riffs. When it came time for me to play the Black Sabbath songs as part of Ozzy's band I didn't sit down and listen to the old records though. We just went for it and I played what I felt should be there in most cases. It seemed to work. Funnily enough when Geezer joined Ozzy he then had the opposite—he had to learn my bass parts! Ozzy told me once 'Ay Bob, Geezer thinks the sun shines out of your arse!' I guess that was a compliment!"

"The way I like to work on lyrics is by myself" Daisley discloses. "I can't write with someone else so I'll go home, or to my room, and come up with something on my own. That's the way I did it with Ozzy and Sabbath. I would write up the lyrics then hand them in to either Jeff Glixman or Ray Gillen. When I got there most of the songs had titles, 'The Shining', 'Ancient Warrior', 'Glory Ride'—they had all these already. Lyrically they didn't have much at all, just some ideas, a few lines really. Ray was a great singer but lyrics were not his strongpoint. So, for 'Eternal Idol' I would talk to Ray about his original ideas that he had then come up with lyrics to fit that so some of the songs are from Ray's idea and some from mine. Then we would work on them, changes get made inevitably because although words can look fine on paper sometimes they just don't 'sing' well if you know what I mean. Ray and Geoff had some good lines that we kept too."

In their working state, previous to the arrival of Bob Daisley, the 'Eternal Idol' tracks went under such cryptic provisional titles as 'The Boogie Song' ('Black Moon', also given the later provisional title 'Gypsy Warning') and 'One In The Box'. In their formative stages songs were often delegated working tags rather than song 1, 2 or 3. For example, 'Lost Forever' spent some time as 'Speedballs' and 'Ancient Warrior' as 'The Axeman', apparently in honour of George the chef, whose enthusiasm in carving meat made quite an impression on the band. Once tagged with proper song titles they had a base from which lyrical ideas could flow. In the early stages the album itself was given the, obviously, temporary handle of 'Blacky Sabb'.

"The thing with 'Eternal Idol' is that the band had song titles, Ray had ideas so I built those up to full songs" continues Daisley. "But then of course at a later stage Tony Martin came in, this was after I had gone so the lyrics got changed again. Tony copied Ray's vocal melodies to the note, probably just for speed's sake. Some of my original words got changed in that process, some by accident. That's obvious when you listen to the record, Tony maybe listened to what Ray was singing and got a few of the words wrong. Other stuff lyrically was changed completely and not for the better I think. Some of it ended up pretty tacky I have to say. All the lyrics I write are quite cryptic and ambiguous. I never make things too obvious and a lot of what ended up on 'Eternal Idol' was just that—obvious. It's interesting that they seem to have kept the first lines of my lyrics but started messing about with them toward the end of the song. A bloody mess really, change the lyrics, change the producer, change the singer. One band started recording that album and another finished it."

'The Shining' would be launched to radio and inexplicably fell flat on its face. Certainly one of the catchiest Black Sabbath songs for a long while the song oozed class and would have nestled comfortably within the grooves of 'Heaven And Hell' or 'Mob Rules'. Rooted as far back as the 1984 David Donato sessions it would ultimately prove itself a lost classic. Bob Daisley recounts the writing process for this underrated track. "Ray Gillen never regarded himself as a lyricist. He had some good ideas and a few lines down but that was about it. Don't get me wrong—Ray's ideas were good but he didn't really know how to express them in a set of lyrics. Basically they had an album with no words. I did a deal with Patrick Meehan where I simply said give me some dough upfront and I'll put down the bass and write some lyrics. You will notice I said 'upfront' there!

They already had the title 'The Shining', remember the film of the same name was not that old then. I think we tried to steer the lyrics away from the film a bit, make it more ambiguous. Ray had a few interesting lines for it already when I started but it has been changed since for the album. A lot of lyric writing was done in Montserrat Air Studios but when we got back to London I was still dropping lyrics off for them at the Air Studios in Oxford Circus. A lot of the lyrics for this song were replaced."

Bob is correct in surmising that the wording for 'The Shining', amongst other tracks, was changed but Geoff Nicholls believes that the lyrics were, rather than being revamped, reverted back to a more original form. "The problem with Ray Gillen was that he was a vowel singer" he explains. "By that I mean he had a lot of vibrato, like Ronnie James Dio, so he had to sing in a certain way. All singers have different techniques and a natural way of singing that you have to deal with in the studio. Now when Bob Daisley came in Ray was just totally in awe of him. Bob overwhelmed him, which actually didn't help because he was so star struck by the whole Sabbath thing anyway. Bob came in and was paid to write some stuff, which he did brilliantly, but the problem was that Ray simply couldn't sing a lot of it because of some of the words that Bob used. So, what we actually did was to go back to the old original working lyrics. Time became a big factor. It all became a bit of a blur so songs would end up with a little bit of Bob's words, some of Ray's and some of mine."

The second track was the majestic 'Ancient Warrior', Tony Iommi delving deep and drawing forth a riff of colossal proportions. "That one is much more mine" affirms Daisley. "The bit about a swollen sea of tears is definitely mine. It's about the futility of war. This being, the 'Ancient Warrior' throughout eternity has seen the stupidity of war. It's a bit abstract, a bit subtle. Basically he is saying 'Am I the only one who sees this?' There is a line further which describes a keeper of light, that's not necessarily Jesus. It's saying we all have the insight to stop the greed and stupidity. Most of those lyrics are mine, the band already had the title."

Bob analyses the up tempo 'Hard Life To Live' as follows. "The first line is Rays, I remember that. Then it goes into a lot of my words. That song might have been about my frustrations with Ozzy at the time because it's about people throwing their life away, people who are disrespectful of life by drink and drugs. Those people who have the attitude 'I'll worry about it later' but 'later' always comes. Then you have to pay. It's a bit of a warning song really." The bassist acknowledges that it would not be the first time these thoughts had been on his mind when penning lyrics either. "That was my second warning to Ozzy because I had written 'Suicide Solution' about him too. It's hard thinking back to remember some of these lyrics but rereading them that looks like what I was saying."

For 'Glory Ride' the band took an unexpected turn and one that will have certainly passed most listeners by. As Daisley discloses the thoughts behind the song though, the meanings behind the words become apparent. "It's about second world war pilots" says Bob. "Spitfire pilots in the Battle of Britain and the Japanese Kamikaze pilots. There are lots of lines in there about dogfights, killing other pilots and those that did not come home. Again, the band already had the name of the song but no words at all."

"The song 'Born To Lose' was a kind of positive / negative idea I seem to remember. Pretty basic, self explanatory about someone having a go at life.

Although it's called 'Born To Lose' it should really be 'Not Born To Lose' I suppose. Again, the basic idea was mine. I did a version of 'Nightmare' but its been changed quite a bit. I know I didn't use the word 'Satan' that is there later in the lyrics, I would never use 'Devil' or 'Satan'. Nothing tacky or as cheesy as that.

'Lost Forever' was, as the lyric reads really, about someone facing a death sentence. He is praying for his life, pleading innocence but they can tell he committed the crime because of the look in his eye. That was the idea there. I remember turning that famous phrase 'give 'em enough rope' into a line there. Again, some of it has been changed. There's a bit in there about 'burning with fire', That's not mine. Some more corny stuff about 'steel wheels'—again, not mine. I don't write all that kind of corny shit.

The track 'Eternal Idol' was a kind of philosophical thing I guess, about the world being ruled by the powers that be. A bit of a redemption song in a way. Some of it was changed later, the words in the middle section are all waffle, all that stuff about politicians is not mine. Patrick Meehan came up with the title. It's from a famous statue, the same one they used on the album cover."

As with 'Seventh Star' before many overlooked the significance of the album cover. Executed by the famed sculptor Auguste Rodin in 1889 the 'Idole Eternelle' sculpture was crafted during a twenty year period in which the artist was producing commissioned works for 'The Gates Of Hell', and indeed, the original proposal for the lead song from the album was intended at first to be set as 'The Gates Of Hell'. This was a series of works depicting aspects of Dante's 'Inferno' for a proposed museum which was never built. The two lovers depicted by the 'Eternal Idol' carving, originally entitled 'The Host', are supposedly locked in sin. What a lot of people have failed to recognise though is that the 'sculpture' on the album cover is nothing of the sort. Black Sabbath, none too surprisingly, had their request to use the Rodin piece turned down. In a spirit of ingenuity they conjured up the next best thing. Vocalist Tony Martin explains how they got around the problem. "Black Sabbath was not allowed to use the statue or any image of it" he insists. "They were very clear about that. So what they did was to get two people in as near that pose as they could and spray them with gold paint! They couldn't get it identical of course but they spent eight hours posing as this statue trying to get it just right. In the end the two models were taken to hospital with paint poisoning!"

When quizzed on the author's hypothesis that the Rodin inspiration was deeper than the aesthetic Martin is in confirmation. "Tony Iommi has never admitted any of that kind of stuff but, you're right, that statue was chosen for a reason. When they were told 'no' it was obviously important enough to them to try and get around that obstacle. They didn't only choose it simply because they liked the look of it."

Interestingly the title track would be the last to be recorded at Montserrat, everything else had been laid down before Bob's arrival but with 'Eternal Idol' itself the song was worked up from scratch in the late stages of the sessions. "Montserrat was a beautiful place to work in" Bob remembers fondly. "Absolutely lovely, we would drink from warm coconuts straight off the tree, we had a cuisine chef on hand and in the evening we would watch the sun sinking over the horizon, like something from the movies. Not very fitting with the Black Sabbath image I know but that's how it was. There were plenty of goats about but I think we were all too relaxed to actually bother with sacrificing any. The trouble is, although it was a bit of a paradise there was fuck all to do except work." Actually, there was something else to occupy idle minds ... "The coke was very good there!" the bassist laughs. "They flew the stuff straight in from Peru. It froze my whole face."

Eric Singer believes Bob Daisley was quite tempted to officially join the band during these sessions but could also understand the forces that held him back. "I think Bob was interested in joining the band full time but he was no rookie and keen to work everything out properly with Patrick Meehan and, of course, that never happened. So, there's no way Bob is going to join something without some firm commitments, plus, he had a good relationship with Gary Moore going on too which, from what he said, was an easy ride without the bullshit. Bob did the record, put down the bass, did a lot of writing, and that was it."

Bob finally puts the record straight on this issue. "I told people I couldn't join Sabbath because I was committed to Gary but in truth I could have done. Gary was resting up, there was plenty of time and I was a free agent so I could have left Gary. The trouble was with Sabbath that the band was good, I liked the songs and I liked the guys, Tony, Ray, Geoff and Eric were excellent people and we all got on fine—no problem there. Later, back in London, Tony Iommi and I got together at his place in London to write some more stuff and he told me I was the only writer that he felt relaxed and productive with since Geezer so that was quite a compliment. A shame really because the situation had a lot of pluses, I liked the people, I liked the songs. Ray was a great singer with a strong persona, Eric knew his stuff, we clicked well as a rhythm team, and Tony was a pleasure to work with. It was just too much of a mish mash, a big wishy washiness of managerial crap."

It wasn't the only kind of crap that Tony Iommi

Geoff Nicholls.

had to put up with. One day a suspicious package arrived at the studios which had everyone wrinkling up their noses in disgust. Bob Daisley describes exactly what the noxious delivery turned out to be. "It was a box of shit—quite literally a box of shit! It was addressed to Tony Iommi. I remember there was myself, Tony Iommi, Geoff Nicholls, Ray Gillen and Jeff Glixman there at the time when this shoebox arrived through the post. It reeked. Tony sniffed it and said 'That smells like shit!' Well, it was! Nobody could quite believe it. Tony opened it up and there was a note inside which said 'You've got to eat a lot of shit before you have a hit album in this business'. Obviously this was a huge mystery. Who on earth would dare send Tony Iommi a box of shit through the mail? Not only was it really offensive but of course the note just didn't make sense. Tony had obviously already had a ton of hit albums.

We all thought it was from Don Arden. I know Tony was convinced it was from Don for a long time afterward. Later, when I was working for Ozzy again Sharon told me she had sent it. At first I had visions of her squatting down over this box and unloading herself but then she saw what I was thinking and told me she had just emptied one of the babies nappies into a box. Still, bad enough." Bob believes the 'box' episode was designed as an exercise in kick 'em when they're down. "Oh, they loved the fact that Ronnie had walked and Sabbath was struggling. They were also very pissed off that I was working with them too."

This then was the highly stressed political and business climate in which Tony Iommi brokered a union with Bob Daisley. "They asked me to join but I was put off by the whole atmosphere. People were moaning about not getting paid, there was a lot of unhappiness in that regard. You just felt people were being dicked around. I didn't get that with Gary so the choice for me was obvious. The prospect of joining Black Sabbath was very tempting of course, it would have looked good for my career, but I was in a better situation with Gary Moore. It was a nice situation to be working closely with a musician I respected enormously who gave equal respect back. After all the Ozzy shit I felt I deserved it. I liked working with Gary, the albums were good, the pay was good, the tours were good and I knew where I stood. That was the thing, if I join Sabbath where is thing going to go? It looked shaky from the inside. I was still on good terms with the Osbournes at this time and beforehand I remember discussing this with Sharon, in case it rocked the boat with them. She said 'Whatever you do, if you're working with Black Sabbath or Meehan make sure you get paid up front'. So that's what I did. It wasn't a great amount but as I got involved and began to get a sense of how everyone was being messed around I was glad I took Sharon's advice there."

With Daisley declining Iommi's invitation the uncertainties already present in the remaining half of Black Sabbath's rhythm section would also come to a head. Eric Singer had worked well with both Dave Spitz and Bob Daisley and now both had gone. "This period is actually tough to talk about because I don't want to cast any negativity on Tony. The fact is I was on a minimal retainer, and I mean minimal, yet I wasn't getting paid. Meehan would not communicate and there was no money coming my way, no return calls. It was just bullshit. Much as I wanted to stay for Tony there was just too much other crap to deal with so of course when Bob Daisley called me to ask if I wanted to audition for Gary Moore I didn't hesitate. I flew to London and got the gig."

Unfortunately for Eric Singer the break from Black Sabbath may have been executed on a physical level but not a fiscal one. "Black Sabbath still had my drum kit so I wrote a letter asking for my kit back. No response. Finally this management guy calls up and they eventually paid me for playing on the record but I still had no kit. Well, I was still hanging out with Ray at this point, we were good friends, so I was getting all the inside information. I discovered my drum kit was in storage and the owners were not going to let it go until some major bills had been paid. Now, this situation was getting bad. I had a world tour to do with Gary Moore. I ended up using a loaner in the mean time, which I remember was packed in Cozy Powell's drum cases. The production manager for Gary Moore saved the day by getting me a brand new kit. I had to personally cut a deal with the storage company to get my kit back, for a substantial sum of money, and had it shipped out for the U.S. portion of the tour. I paid a lot of money to get my own drums back. It was a lesson well learned."

Once in the employ of Gary Moore the Daisley / Singer axis would later pay particular attention to the credits on the 'Eternal Idol' album. The drummer was more than a little mystified to see his credits being shared. "The 'Eternal Idol' record, I thought was very strong. There are some great songs on there. I never understood that credit for Bev Bevan for percussion though. I know my drum patterns and I know what I did in the studio and everything I hear is mine on the final thing. Percussion? What's that supposed to mean? Did he add a cowbell or a tambourine or something? I can't hear it if he did.

Y'know I think they might have added his name because he was in line to become the next drummer. Tony and Bev are big, big friends. So maybe that was it, to give some continuity. I think we all got caught up in mix ups, shall we say, on the credits. Dave Spitz is credited on bass but I'm sure that is all Bob's work.

Poor Ray never got a mention though. Tony Martin came in and sang Ray's lines note for note exactly. The vocal melodies were identical. Personally I think it sounded better with Ray, not knocking Tony Martin who has done some great singing on later records, but that was Ray's record and he had won back a lot of fans for Sabbath when they were really down. He deserved that record. Maybe if all the bullshit was not going down Ray would have stayed."

Bob Daisley too was disgruntled to find his input down played on the final product. "I keep reading all this stuff about Dave Spitz playing bass on the album and it's bollocks" maintains Daisley. "When I got there they had drums down, bass, Ray's guide vocals—just melodies really, along with rhythm and lead guitar. I told Jeff Glixman I didn't want to hear any of the original bass because I didn't want to have my ideas swayed in any way. Anyhow, I completely rerecorded all of the bass parts—everything. So, when I later read bass credits for both myself and Dave Spitz on the album I was a little pissed off for sure.

I was told Dave had gone back to America to sort out personal stuff. Whether that was financial, marital or what I don't honestly know. Someone obviously made the decision and I rerecorded the whole lot. It wasn't like the Tony Martin situation later, copying Ray Gillen's vocals, because I never heard any of Dave's stuff. I laid it down all brand new. It's the same thing with Eric getting stuffed on his credit for drums. I heard the drums in the studio and they sound exactly the same to me as on the finished album. I'm sure Bev Bevan didn't add drums."

Which of course has Sabbath fans scratching their heads as to why exactly credit those who were uninvolved? Dave Spitz is understandable, he did record those bass lines even if they were, mostly, later wiped. But Bev Bevan? Bob has this take on the whole scenario. "Sometimes bands like to credit people on the album sleeve like that in order to provide some notion of stability. Of course the most famous and unsubtle example of that is when my name and Lee Kerslake's were removed from Ozzy's 'Diary Of A Madman' album. I guess Black Sabbath put Dave and Bev on there because they thought at the time that would be the rhythm section that would be touring."

Although Dave Spitz does not appear on the album Bev Bevan, long thought to have been added on the credits simply to smooth things along, does in actuality make an appearance. The cameo instrumental 'Scarlet Pimpernel', recorded in London, features the lightest of cymbal splashes and for this contribution alone Bevan gains the 'Percussion' credit.

The actual recording sequence progressed as follows. Tony Iommi, Ray Gillen, Dave Spitz, Geoff Nicholls and Eric Singer laid down the initial tracks in Montserrat with producer Jeff Glixman. Spitz then returned home and Bob Daisley joined the team, on 30th September to be precise, rerecording all of the bass lines for the songs which made the album. Due to difficulties Gillen was having with Daisley's new lyrics, amongst other things, another producer, Vic Coppersmith, was brought in to specifically oversee Ray's work. With Ray Gillen's departure, and after the band had returned to London, Tony Martin then reconstructed the vocals for the entire album. This last stage was held under the auspices of a third producer Chris Tsangarides. Eric Singer decamped too but his drums remained in place. However, not all of the songs recorded stuck to this pattern. Geoff Nicholls provides the detail, solving a few little mysteries in the process.

"This is how I saw the whole recording process for that album. We began in Montserrat with Jeff Glixman. It was horrifically expensive but we got a lot done. The place was a very creative environment. The problems began when Glixman tried to take control of the whole Sabbath thing. That's how I saw it anyhow. He used to pick on Dave Spitz a lot, which I thought was quite petty. Spitz was a fucking incredible bass player. If you listen to 'In For The Kill' on 'Seventh Star' you will appreciate just how good he was. That is some very difficult stuff he's doing there.

I used to have the same problem with Glixman because he was a keyboard player so kept trying to push me to put in all these Kansas type keyboard flurries. Now, that's no problem for me to do but the thing is, it's not what Tony wants and it's not the Black Sabbath sound. As a guitarist I understood exactly what Tony wanted which was layered chords for the guitar to go on top of. So, I knew where Dave Spitz was coming from because Glixman had done the same to me earlier. Anyway, Dave was having girlfriend problems and because Glixman was giving him this constant grief he just packed in and left. We sent him home. I know how Dave felt and understood. Now, I should point out that Dave, even though he was young, was a great bass player. He didn't go for any musical reasons you understand."

Dave Spitz is keen to put the record straight regarding his mysterious departure, which as, until now, always been attributed to 'personal reasons'. "I don't mind discussing this even if some of it is a little embarrassing for me" he grants. "It's not as simple as it might have been portrayed though and there were a number of factors involved. Some of these things affected the whole band too. When we arrived in Montserrat it was all a little unreal. The place was total paradise. Soon though, some disturbing patterns started to emerge. First of all factions started to develop because Patrick Meehan, Jeff Glixman and Tony Iommi had a villa on one side of the island and the rest of us were stuck on the other side in another villa. That really didn't help the atmosphere.

The next thing was that my relationship with Glixman started to break down big time. I found this odd because, up until then, he had been a great friend and ally. Once in Montserrat though it all turned very sour. Whether this was down to money, drugs, or whatever I just don't know but Glix was, in the way I saw things, the catalyst for the whole fuck up. There was a very bad vibe going down and the entire unified band feeling started to crumble. From the very moment we started to lay down basic tracks Glixman was a complete pain in the ass. On top of Glixman being an asshole I found Patrick Meehan to be a complete prick. He had it in for people and loved bossing people around. Nobody could understand exactly why Tony had hired him. I had another thing to deal with. Basically I had found out from reading a Rock magazine that my girlfriend had been cheating on me with Eric Carr from Kiss. As you can imagine, I got rather fucked up by that."

The Caribbean isolation only compounded matters for Spitz and a TV report just added to his tribulations. "In our villa we had a TV that I think had just the one channel. Anyway, at the time my brother Dan was on tour with Anthrax in Europe. They were touring with Metallica. I see this news report that the tour bus had flipped over and that one of the guys in the band has been killed! The thing is though, they didn't say which band or who it was! So I'm thinking 'Is it Dan?' I was freaking out!

Now, one of the worst things about Montserrat then was the terrible phone system. You had to request an outside call and sometimes they would phone you back hours later and say 'OK, Mr. Spitz, we can place your call now'. It was madness. Anyhow, it took me quite a few days to discover my brother was safe. I weighed everything up. Glixman was being a schmuck, Meehan was just bad news and the album was getting stuck on the vocals. Money, or the lack of it, played a big part too. The thing with my brother had me desperate to get off the island too. I just left."

Enter Bob Daisley. "Glixman was very keen to get Bob involved, it was really his thing" Geoff reckons. "Now, this was interesting because Ray was completely in awe of Bob because of the Ozzy connection. He was star struck with the whole situation. Bob wrote a lot of new lyrics but the problem was that Ray, being your classic American vowel singer, couldn't sing them. Personally I felt that Bob's lyrics were good but a little grand if you know what I mean. I thought Sabbath needed something earthier. Some of the stuff was OK. The song 'Glory Ride' I remember Ray did a good job on but he was struggling with most of it. Anyway, that obviously presented a problem."

Enter producer number two: Vic Coppersmith. "There was another concern with Ray because he had absolutely no studio experience whatsoever so he had to be looked after a lot. In fact, and I don't like to say this but it's the truth, Ray didn't have a fucking clue! He was so naïve he didn't even know about basic overdubbing which really surprised us. Ray was a cool guy and a good singer and, I think because he died, there has been a bit of legend that has grown up around him. He did a great job taking over from Glenn on the road but it's one thing taking on the temporary role of singer to finish a tour but quite another to become a lead vocalist in the true sense. Ask Ozzy, Ronnie or Tony Martin. It's a whole different ball game because a lot of responsibility comes with that job. Singers take the brunt of everything the press wants to chuck at you. You need a big pair of balls to front Black Sabbath. We were getting the early signs in the studio that Ray maybe wasn't quite up to the job and also we were already at a stage when we couldn't afford this and couldn't afford that. That's why when Tony Martin came in later we all breathed a huge sigh of relief. He was a godsend.

To give you an example, Ray used to like a party and he would be out every night if he could, running to clubs and the like. He liked the girls, which was fine, but we were recording an album at the time and needed all hands on deck. There was no denying Ray was a very good looking bloke and, as such, a big asset to the band because of that. The girls used to drool over him and he made full advantage of it. He was actually living in a flat with me at the time because we were supposed to be concentrating on song-writing and I was put in there to gee him up a bit. Trouble is, every night he would say "I'm just going out for an hour" and then he would get back at four in the morning! When you are actually in the band it's very difficult to tell someone they should get themselves more focussed on the job in hand. We kept shouting at him but he wasn't paying much attention. So, it was solved by getting Vic Coppersmith in to keep an eye on him. Any musician will tell you that recording can often go right through the night but Ray just wanted to party. That's why Vic came in—to make sure Ray did his job."

Jeff Glixman would break away from the project at this juncture. "Glixman was really pissed off" Bob Daisley recounts. "I don't know if it was money or points or what or if he was rocking the boat. I got the impression he was dicked off about money, which, under the circumstances would have fitted in with the whole scenario then."

Without warning Ray Gillen then bailed out to join Blue Murder. "I was still in communication with Ray at that point" states Dave Spitz. "I knew he couldn't handle the vocal side of things but I also knew, because he told me, that he wasn't getting paid by Meehan and didn't even have basic money for food. He was ready to go." John Sykes had already been through a number of quality musicians in an attempt to assemble this band which by this stage of the game also numbered bassist Tony Franklin of The Firm and drummer Cozy Powell. Eric Singer takes this up. "Ray quit to join John Sykes in Blue Murder but John Kalodner didn't like him. Now, at that stage Cozy was playing drums so just think what the fans would have made of that record—Sykes, Cozy and Ray. That could have been huge. But Kalodner said no to Ray. After that Cozy said fuck it and left too."

Geoff Nicholls believes Gillen did not stay the course with Blue Murder for exactly the same reasons Black Sabbath had encountered. "I know what happened. Cozy obviously thought this guy looks great, can sing great and Sabbath was on rocky ground. Let's nick him! The thing was that Ray had of course told John Sykes he could write but when he got into the studio with Blue Murder it be-

'Eternal Idol' bootleg with Ray Gillen.

came clear very quickly he couldn't. That's why Ray was in and out of that band so quickly."

Next in line for Black Sabbath production duties would be Chris Tsangarides. "When we got to London the money issue really began to squeeze" Geoff acknowledges. "In fact there was one point when the album stopped because a whole lot of studio bills had to be paid before we could continue. We actually couldn't get the tapes back unless we coughed up. It was very tight. Chris Tsangarides rerecorded the two extra tracks with us, 'Some Kind Of Woman' and 'Black Moon', redid all the vocals with Tony Martin and mixed the entire album."

The final record would not meet the satisfaction of everybody. Bob Daisley was less than impressed. "I thought Jeff had done a great job on the album. It was very fresh, very raw. I have some board mixes that sound way better than the finished album. The original was much, much ballsier. That's what I thought when I heard the finished things. Where did all the balls go?"

When Eric Singer's stint with the Gary Moore world tour drew to a close the drummer would partake in a much vaunted supergroup with more than its fair share of Sabbath and Ozzy connections. The lynchpin of Badlands was guitarist Jake E. Lee, the man who had hugely impressed on the Ozzy albums 'Bark At The Moon' and 'The Ultimate Sin'. Jake not only looked the complete guitar God but played with an artistic abandon few could match. Quitting the Ozzy band the natural assumption from his many fans was that Jake's next move would have platinum plastered all over it. However, post Ozzy Jake would reportedly not touch a guitar for nearly six months. Flooded with offers from major bands Lee remained resolutely silent. When he did emerge again it was with no fanfare and as understated as could possibly be. In 1988 Lee put down tracks on the Japanese release 'Meiki' by Ann Lewis. With zero media coverage hardly any of his fans even noticed.

In the interim, and soon abandoned by John Sykes, it would be the ambitious Tom Galley concept record 'Phenomena II: Dream Runner' which was to host Ray Gillen's commercial recording debut in late 1987. Galley, brother of Whitesnake guitarist Mel Gally, had devoted his energies to the 'Phenomena' venture and had scored significant success with the original. The 'Dream Runner' follow-up pulled together such notable singers as Glenn Hughes, GTR's Max Bacon and Asia man John Wetton.

Chosen for bass with Badlands would be Steeler's Greg Chaisson, a man who had very briefly occupied the Ozzy bass position although it seems an earlier incarnation would include Terry Nails (later to cite his own Ozzy credits) on the bass. The Black Sabbath ties came courtesy of singer Ray Gillen and drummer Eric Singer. It was a seriously heavyweight line-up. It was originally intended to be even heavier as Dave Spitz relates. "After the whole Montserrat deal had gone down I went back to New York. I decided to catch up with a pal of mine named Pat Sciciliano. Everyone knows this guy, he was the guy who made things happen for Jet Records and Don Arden. Anyway, I knew Jake E. Lee had quit the Ozzy band. Jake was one of those guitarists with a rare gift. For someone who didn't use a whammy bar he got some pretty spectacular sounds out of his guitar. The guy looked great, he had the Ozzy credibility. In fact Jake was the whole package.

This was my idea, to put Jake with myself, Ray and Eric. I spoke to Pat about it and he loved it. It sounded like it could be huge. This was the very beginning of what would become Badlands. The trouble was I could not get hold of Jake. The guy never picked his phone up. This went on for weeks and because I couldn't speak to the guy I just let it go. Some time later I hear that Jake, Ray and Eric had got together anyway and were holding auditions for a bass player! Obviously this was not the best news I had heard. As it happened I was flying back to Los Angeles to attend a NAMM show so I decided to make the time to jam with my old friends Eric and Ray at Mates Rehearsals. Jake, Ray, Eric and I had a good jam session whilst Greg Chaisson was waiting outside in the hall."

Returning to the East Coast Spitz received the news that, despite being outvoted, Jake had insisted Greg Chaisson land the job. "I got the inside word. Apparently Greg and Jake had been in a band together in ancient times and Jake had given Greg a pledge that if he ever got big he would help him out. That's what happened. That was direct from source so I knew that is what had gone down. That's why Badlands became Gillen, Lee, Singer and . . . who?"

Musically Badlands opted to steer in a Blues Rock direction at a time when party flavoured Glam Rock ruled supreme. When Badlands signature to Atlantic Records affiliate Titanium was announced, anticipation was high. MTV rotation for the inaugural single 'Dreams In The Dark' was prominent. As the basics of the band was being formulated, Singer found himself with the space to have his feet in two camps. "I was actually playing with Badlands at night and The Cult during the day. It was tough but I was having a blast. Ian and Billy were in Los Angeles working up demos for what became the 'Sonic Temple' album. Les Warner had gone so they needed a drummer. It was working out fine and as a band we were really tight. The Cult actually wanted me to do the album. Both Bob Rock the producer and the band wanted me but they would need my undivided attention for six weeks and the Badlands management said no. A shame but Ian and Billy gave me a nice big thanks on the album."

The Badlands album was ushered in with great fanfare but progress soon stalled. The album appeared to have nearly everything—almost the pedigree, the sound and the musicianship. Everything that is except a set of quality songs. The cracks started to show and Eric Singer was shown the door, usurped by Jeff Martin from Phoenix, Arizona act Surgical Steel, for a second album 'Voodoo Highway'. Album sales soon slid away. "I voiced my opinion which is why I was fired from Badlands. Basically business fell flat. Although the first record was great and we drew a lot of enthusiasm the whole thing was just falling apart internally. In my opinion there were a lot of bad business decisions, poor choices regarding MTV, promotion, the record company and everything. Ray was ill too. He was playing both sides of the fence with me by saying Jake wanted me out but I found out afterward he wasn't the ally I thought I had. It didn't matter, within a week and a half I was playing with Alice Cooper which was very rewarding.

I saw all the interviews they did slagging me off, which was unnecessary, but y'know success is the best revenge. Alice Cooper and Kiss. I have a hell of a lot to be proud of. Jake E. Lee, he's a sensational player but what has he done since? His profile should tell you something. He should be a Rock star. There's a reason why he is not. Badlands got rotten very quickly. Even the bass player episode, that was one of Jake's calls that just should not have happened. I think they slagged me to get the first shot in, to make anything I said in future look like sour grapes. I kept my mouth shut and just got on and played." Badlands stumbled on. 'Voodoo Highway' was a mediocre offering at best and, although the group got into the studio to record a third effort 'Tribal Moon', the plug was pulled. 'Tribal Moon' was shelved, Gillen decamped and John West briefly took the vocal role. Eventually the project fizzled out.

Badlands—Singer, Gillen, Lee and Spitz... er... Chaisson.

Returning to London with the Tokyo incident a distant memory, practicalities for Phil Soussan and the next Ozzy Osbourne album became paramount. "Sharon and Tony Martell, head of CBS Records, had pulled me aside at our platinum album party in New York to tell me that they wanted me to start writing for the next album. I took a room in Sharon's Maida Vale offices and converted it into a studio and spent the next four months writing before going on to LA in the beginning of 1987 so we could start getting some songs into shape."

Once in California the elements of friction that had been developing around Jake began to seriously hinder progress. "Randy, John Sinclair and I would show up at rehearsal at midday as arranged and basically wait for Jake. This happened every day. Jake simply never showed. He had brought a new car and was working on that all the time. His roadie Spike would be there but for days Jake just would not arrive. I don't think that for a long time Ozzy knew about this because he was spending a lot of time promoting the 'Tribute' album."

Finally the errant guitarist did come to the rehearsal studio. "He showed up in the evening after we had been waiting for him all day" Phil says resignedly. "So, he arrives and the first thing he says is "I need a sleep." So he takes a nap! After he woke we tried to find a practical solution to this so we asked him what time he wanted to rehearse. '4' he said. So, next day we were there at 4 and he arrived at 8 and told us he was too tired to do anything! This unbelievably went for about three months. Well, of course, word eventually got back and Ozzy and Sharon laid down the law. If he wasn't there by one o'clock the next day he was fired."

Trying to keep the peace Phil telephoned Jake in an endeavour to instill some enthusiasm and drop a strong hint that he really was required to attend the next day's session. His conciliatory efforts received an unexpected reply. "As a favour I told him that he really needed to be there tomorrow and he had to be there on time" the bassist muses. "He told me in no uncertain terms that he ran this band and that was that. I've actually never seen him since." The next day Phil and Randy were instructed to meet up with Ozzy at the Westwood Marquee hotel and from there went onto a Mexican restaurant. During their four hour stop off there Sharon was elsewhere informing Jake he was no longer part of the band. Another era finalized. "I've heard that Jake kind of holds me responsible for his dismissal" opines Soussan. "I've never spoken to him to this day but I find it odd he thinks I had something to do with it. He credits me with too much power there I think."

In the wake of the Badlands crash n' burn, Lee would still be working with Ann Lewis contributing virtually all guitar parts to 1990's 'Rude', 1991's 'K-Rock' and the 1993 opus 'Rockadelic'. As with prior releases his many fans remained blissfully unaware of his contributions. The mid 90s did see Lee poking his head above the parapet, albeit nervously. Unbeknown to his fan-base internationally Lee also recorded a solo album for Japanese label Pony Canyon 'A Fine Pink Mist' which, rerecorded totally would be consigned to the vaults for many years. In 1994 a union with Mandy Lion, the outrageously over the top ex-WWIII vocalist, produced a bout of Stateside club touring under the banner Wicked Alliance. The same year Lee guested on the Air Pavilion Japanese album 'Sarrph Cogh', produced by his erstwhile Ratt colleague Juan Croucier.

In 1995 Lee committed to his first tribute album. The man cut a radical rework of Jeff Beck's 'Rice Pudding' for the 'Jeffology' release and the following year could be found on two Rush workouts 'Working Man' and 'By-Tor And The Snow Dog' for the 'Working Man' homage. The same year finally witnessed the release of his solo endeavour 'A Fine Pink Mist'. The record marked the commercial release of his teenage composition 'The Rapture' more than two decades after it was first penned. A whole slew of tribute affairs ensued. Lee marked his territory on Queen's 'Dragon Attack' offering 'Get Down Make Love' in 1997, on AC/DC's 'Thunderbolt' with 'It's A Long Way To The Top', Metallica's 'Metallic Assault' reforging 'Seek And Destroy' in 2000. The same year he united with his old sparring partner Ratt's Stephen Pearcy and Quiet Riot's Frankie Banali on a version of Van Halen's 'Running With The Devil'. Of greatest curiosity was Lee's inclusion on the Randy Rhoads tribute record cutting 'Crazy Train'—with Skid Row's Sebastian Bach and 'Revelation (Mother Earth)'— with Slaughter's Mark Slaughter. A third Badlands record, compiled from live tracks laid down in 1992, emerged too titled 'Dusk'. All told a pretty feeble collection of dabblings from one once regarded so highly.

With Jake E. Lee scrubbed from the Ozzy team sheet an earnest quest for a replacement was soon set in motion with Soussan and Castillo proving to be any budding wannabe's first line of redoubt. "We got through loads of guitarists, hundreds and hundreds. Auditioning really is a hell of a task" affirms the bassist. All the budding applicants had three songs to learn—'Crazy Train', 'Mr. Crowley' and 'I Don't Know'. Phil was delegated the task of sifting through a mountain of audition packages. Quite an endeavour as the Los Angeles grapevine had rapidly spread word of the hottest job in town. Among those who elevated themselves to the possibles listings were Steve Fister, who both Randy and Phil knew from previous jam sessions, Jake E. Lee's old Rough Cutt sparring partner Amir Derakh, Vinnie Moore, Chris Impelliterri, Joe Holmes and Nick Nolan. "A lot of the G.I.T. people" Phil laughs. "I think we must have seen them all."

Mitch Perry of MSG and Steeler was also a contender. "Mitch was in there too although I think he might have said something wrong which cost him his chance" declares Soussan. One potential candidate who would make it into the chosen few was Steve Fister. The young six-stringer had already made his mark by working with the former Detective and Silverhead vocalist Michael Des Barres (now of course an actor) and with hoary Psych Rocker pioneers Iron Butterfly. When the call to arms for the Ozzy position came Fister was working up his first solo album in collusion with the erstwhile David Lee Roth sibling partnership of Gregg and Matt Bissonette. Another project being pitched to record companies had Fister in alliance with former Ted Nugent singer Derek St. Holmes.

Steve describes how he got to hear about the tryouts. "At that time, you had a 'network' of friends, musicians, cocktail waitresses, music writers, record company people, etc.," he explains. "You just had to call and hang out, to find out who was looking for a guitar player. I had heard through that grapevine that Ozzy was looking for a new guitarist. So, I called a friend of mine at Jet Records for info about the auditions. I got an address to send a promo pack. I thought at least I'll get a shot at the gig. I learned 'Shot In The Dark' and another one. You also had to look the part, very important! In the next few weeks I waited for a call." The musician's wait would prove to be frustrating. Not only did he not get a call back but he had to endure the uninhibited glee of those who did receive an invitation.

"I guess every guitar player in the LA area was up for the gig! It seemed like anyone who owned a guitar and hung out at the Rainbow Bar and Grill got an audition!" Steve says with exasperation. However, the guitarist had the foresight to apply for another opening at the same time, which as coincidence would have it would land him at his originally intended destination. "During that time I heard Lita was also looking for a guitar player. I heard that she had been through 80 or more players. While waiting for the Ozzy call I got a call to audition for Lita." Lita Ford, often dictated by way of sheer talent as being the top ranking in the girl guitar league, had carved her name with pride as part of the original all girl teen brat pack The Runaways. It was Lita, who admits to having attended her first Black Sabbath concert at the tender age of 13, who lent The Runaways their metallic sheen.

The lady in black records just how the presence of Ozzy Osbourne had shaped her entire career. "My cousin took me to see Black Sabbath at the Long Beach Arena. It was my first ever gig and it totally changed my life!" she gushes. "The bands music was just so awesome, really dark and powerful. I remember Ozzy being hunched over with all his crosses—and all that hair! It wasn't just the music it was the whole atmosphere the band created. The smell struck me too. Thousands of kids smoking pot!" The teen Lita left that night with her life's mission clearly laid out in front of her. "Seeing Black Sabbath was an inspiration. It gave me my whole want for Rock n' Roll and made clear to me exactly what I wanted to do."

The Runaways had forced Lita's attentions onto the American consciousness but that flame, bright as it was, had flickered all too briefly. Squabbling tore the band apart leaving a cult legacy of proto Riot Grrrl teen spirit to be picked up by later generations. Now flying solo, Lita's explosive looks and supreme guitar skills had propelled her to the forefront of the Hard Rock scene again. The opening 1983 salvo of 'Out For Blood' was a mean statement of intent proving that girls could shred too and provided the impetus needed for the sophomore 1984 outing 'Dancin' On The Edge' to chart on both sides of the Atlantic. Drums on the 'Dancin'' opus had been handled by one Randy Castillo who after an excursion with Stone Fury, was now firmly entrenched in the Ozzy camp.

Gearing up for the launch of what would be her greatest commercial endeavour, the million selling 'Lita' album, her business affairs at this juncture were coincidentally handled by the intuitive figure of Sharon Osbourne. Such was the Metal queen's regency at the time of the auditions, the domain into which Steve Fister entered. "I went to Leeds Rehearsal in North Hollywood to play for her" Steve records. "I had learned 4 tunes. I remember there were 3 guys ahead of me, one of which was Scott Sheets from Pat Benatar's band. The holding room looked like a waiting room at a maternity hospital! Lots of raw nerves! I went in and played, and Lita asked me to hang around." His wait would not as expected be ended by Lita Ford though. "Half an hour later Ozzy and Sharon walk in! We played the songs again for them. In the last 3 weeks I could not buy an audition with him, and there I am playing Lita tunes with him sitting 3 feet in front of me!"

One can imagine what state Steve Fister's frayed nerves were in at this point. Further protracted waiting ensued. "After we played, Lita went into the office with Sharon, and I just hung out with Ozzy. Lita had introduced me as having just worked with Michael Des Barres. Ozzy was really nice, telling stories and such. Ozzy was funny and friendly. Fun to be around. The next day, I was officially hired on with Lita. As the rehearsals progressed I was made the 'musical director' in charge of rehearsing the band, making the set lists etc."

Steve's Fate had been dictated by the fact that both Ozzy and Lita were hungry for a new guitarist at the same juncture. Phil Soussan had recommended Steve for the Ozzy gig but his style of playing was deemed more suitable for Lita Ford's band. "Over the years I've played with both Phil and Randy on various sessions, gigs and jams. Phil told me that after he reviewed my package, they wanted to audition me for Ozzy." The Osbournes would have other ideas though and Lita's need was as great as Ozzy's. Steve soon found himself in at the deep end in his new band environment. It would, as history confirms, prove a fruitful relationship. "At that time Lita did lots of press and didn't have a lot of time. So I was appointed to run the rehearsals, pace the show, (always subject to her approval, but she gave me lots of room) write endings for the tunes, write the guitar harmony parts. Lita was cool, she let me play a lot of solos on the gig, we did a lot of harmonies and trade offs, and on some tunes she would just sing and I'd play all the guitar." As Lita Ford claimed her man the hunt for an Ozzy guitar slinger continued apace.

Meantime in the thick of the action in the Ozzy camp the Soussan / Castillo rhythm section cum judging panel developed their own system for weeding out the no hopers. "We had secret signals. If Randy dropped a drumstick that meant he was telling me the guy was no good and likewise if I 'accidentally' dropped my pick. It worked out fine because nobody got really upset but then we had this one guy who was just racing around the studio like a lunatic, running up and down and spinning around. He was obviously not right for the job because he wasn't a brilliant player but he was just so entertaining to watch I lost my concentration. Of course what I wasn't seeing was Randy dropping sticks behind me. In the end he threw a stick straight into the back of my head to force my attention. "Sorry, I dropped my stick" he said! He had dropped about 8 sticks before resorting to that move."

The bassist recalls another memorable candidate. "There was also some Swedish guy that was very good but didn't make it in the end. Actually, the reason he didn't make it was because he tried to tell us that we were all playing in the wrong keys which really pissed us off! When we played 'Flying High Again' with this guy Ozzy sang the first line with an appropriate change: "Got a crazy feeling I don't understand, get this cunt away from me!!" We cracked up!" There was another high calibre applicant who very nearly made the grade, the Kramer guitar endorsed Jimi Bell. The young guitarist had made an impression with his act Joined opening for Joan Jett's band. Indeed, Bell's playing had prompted both Kramer and Seymour Duncan to grant full endorsements and put the musician forward for a movie slot. Bell, alongside a cameo with Joan Jett, would wind up in the Michael J. Fox film 'Light Of Day'.

It was Kramer guitars who sent Bell's video to Sharon Osbourne hence securing the audition. As Jimi relates he made past the first hurdle. "From that point they flew me out to LA for auditions. The audition itself was a great experience for me. You had to play with Phil and Randy first. Then you were either told, "Thanks for coming!" or "We need you to stay." Sharon was there for my audition. She was a wonderful woman and was very nice to me. After I was done, they said they wanted Ozzy to hear me play. So about a day later, I auditioned with Ozzy."

Came the day of final reckoning Bell was just as nerve ridden as his predecessors at the trials. Witnessing Ozzy manifest his disdain for one unlucky soul who had stepped up before him did little to dampen his fears. "There was one person before me and he was butchering the 'Flying High' solo. Ozzy was standing behind him pretending to stab and strangle him. Of course this scared me because I was next to audition!" Fully committed though Bell took his turn. "As I started to play, Ozzy started to get into my playing. When ever I played a solo, he knelt down in front of my amp and listened. Some of the songs I played were, 'I Don't Know', 'Crazy Train', 'Suicide Solution', and a jam. When I was done, they were very impressed. They sat me down and Sharon said, "Well, it's between Zakk and yourself"."

The Osbournes invited Bell out for a meal that evening, an event during which Bell would experience Ozzy's wicked sense of humour at first hand. "While eating, I asked Ozzy if he wanted the tomatoes from my salad. He replied, "No!" So about a minute later while eating, he reached his hands into my salad and snatched the tomatoes. It was a funny experience to have Ozzy reaching into your plate like that!!" he laughs. "Then we went back to Ozzy's place. While I was there a Black Sabbath video came on TV and Ozzy grabbed his daughter Aimee and said, "Look Aimee there's daddy with his old band!" That night, Phil and Randy took me out to the Troubadour club in LA where they met up with Chris Impelliterri and Blackie Lawless. The next day I flew home waiting to hear the results."

Then came Zakk Wylde, suggested by the Rock photographer Mark Weiss. "Zakk, or Zachary Wylant (real name Jeffrey Weilandt) as he was known then, was flown in and I picked him up at the Hyatt" remarks Phil. "He was there hanging out with another good friend Adrian Vandenberg. He was totally wide eyed, just a laughing kid. We took him down to rehearsals and it was just so refreshing. Not only was he a really nice guy, really friendly but he could really play. The other really great thing about him was that he arrived and said "Let's go!", plugged himself into a Marshall and let rip. After Randy and I had been wasting time with all those jokers taking two hours to set up massive rack systems it was great to see just raw enthusiasm."

Zakk Wylde it appears was just glad to be given the opportunity. "He was so genuine. Zakk was having a blast and I don't think he realized how right he was for the job," recalls Phil. "He even got his albums out to get autographed. He said "I'll probably never see you guys again." He was the right guy for the job though. Ozzy liked him too because he reminded him of Randy, the enthusiasm and even the look to a degree." Another close contender was Terrif man and former Randy Rhoads guitar pupil Joe Holmes. His turn would come later on down the line. Of the other hopefuls Vinnie Moore and Chris Impelliterri would persevere with their solo careers whilst Amir Derakh would completely reinvent himself for the Nu-Metal age scoring platinum success in the millennium with Orgy.

Meantime, one of the final contenders pipped to the post by Zakk would not find his efforts had been in vain. Whilst awaiting auditions Bell had shared the same hotel as Zakk and the pair had often jammed together. "We got along really great. I knew later that he respected my playing because he mentioned it at a guitar clinic that he was doing." Much as Steve Fister had been manoeuvred over into the employ of Lita Ford so Jimi would find there was other Black Sabbath related work in need of his guitar skills. "After finding out they went with Zakk, I received a call from Geezer Butler who told me Sharon had recommended me for his new band. From there I flew to England to work with Geezer where Gloria Butler made me feel very much at home." The introduction of Bell provided the catalyst needed for a push into more familiar territory for both singer Carl Sentance and Butler. The vocalist explains the shift of emphasis in the musical slant of the band. "Geezer is into a lot of different styles of music too but, as we went on, especially when Jimi came in, the music got heavier and heavier and I felt more comfortable with that."

Jimi Bell had just been pipped to the post as Ozzy's guitar player by a certain Zakk Wylde. Bell had taken it down to the wire with Wylde, sharing a hotel room with his friendly rival whilst being put through his paces by Ozzy's rhythm section of bassist Phil Soussan and drummer Randy Castillo. Following this near miss Bell's deflated hopes would be raised

Phil Soussan, Ozzy Osbourne, Randy Castillo, Zakk Wylde.

again as he records. "After my audition with Ozzy, Sharon Osbourne gave a video of me performing to Geezer. About two weeks later I received a phone call from him." The budding guitarist was flown to St. Louis, Missouri. The Black Sabbath bassist broke the ice with a few beers at the airport before the family and managerial introductions. "Geezer was such a down to earth person, very fun to be around and not head strong at all considering he was in one of the biggest bands in the world. I then was introduced to his beautiful wife Gloria. She was one of the nicest people I have ever met. She treated me wonderful and went out of her way to make me feel at home. I also met Biff and James, Geezers two boys. They were just kids then. The walls in his home were covered with gold and platinum records upstairs and down. I always considered him to be the ultimate Rock bass player so this was a thrill for me."

A few weeks later Bell was flown out to England, introduced to the Smallwood Taylor management team and the rest of the band then put to work. Like Carl, Jimi remembers the excitement of being in the thick of the action with a potentially major band. "Carl was a great singer even back then. Jezz had been playing with Robert Plant's band and Gary was with Eddie Money and Glenn Hughes. It was a great band." Rehearsals for Jimi first took place at Tasco's, where the guitarist became acquainted with two aspects of uniquely British culture—warm beer and the Sex Pistols." The band shot a promotional live video and did a round of showcases for major labels. MCA Records took the bait. Further rehearsals saw a relocation South. "We then started rehearsing at an old air force base just outside of Brighton. Ozzy had just finished using it. We stayed there all the time. They even had an in house cook there!"

Tracks the band were working up included 'Take The Night Away', 'Guilty Of Love', 'Never', 'Heat In The Street' and ... 'Computer God'. The latter would, of course become a familiar title with Black Sabbath fans as a standout track on the Dio reunion 'Dehumanizer' opus. 'The song 'Computer God' did turn up on the 'Dehumanizer' album" confirms Bell. "But much different than what we recorded. I liked them both. The version of 'Computer God' that Sabbath did was much heavier. In fact, the only thing that remained the same was the title. The version that Terry wrote had strong keyboard parts in it, much more commercial."

Black Sabbath did not impinge too much on progress with Geezer's project and the guitarist only recalls one notable instance when Mr. Iommi was mentioned by his employer. "Geezer didn't say too much about Sabbath except for when one of Tony's records came out, I believe it was 'Eternal Idol'. Geezer said that he wrote part of a tune on there and wasn't mentioned."

In the throes of working up this new endeavour Geezer and Jimi managed to find time to catch a break. The Black Sabbath bassist instilled some English culture into the American with a visit to mediaeval stronghold of Warwick castle. Along with Butler's eldest son Biff (now a fine musician in his own right) a younger member of the Osbourne clan was along for the ride too. "We all went up to the castle lookout tower where we stayed for a while. In fact, Kelly Osbourne was supposed to go too but she had spilt red paint all over Gloria's carpet so was being punished. It was getting dark so we decided to go back down. As we headed down the stairs we didn't realise that there were no lights in the tower. It had a spiral staircase all the way down. So Geezer grabbed Biff and I took Aimee and carried her step by step to the bottom as I leaned into the circular wall of this old tower." The American guitarist was already envisaging his name in headlines next to that of Ozzy's like he had always dreamed of but this time for all the wrong reasons. "At this point, it was pitch dark and I started to pray, 'Oh my God, please don't let me fall with Ozzy's daughter in my arms!' This would be the end of me!" Aimee and Jimi arrived safely on the ground.

Unbeknown to Jimi at the time, a simple request from Geezer would bond the band project tighter into the Black Sabbath tapestry than he could have thought at the time. "We continued rehearsing for about three weeks. One night Geezer came to me and said I needed to write something with a hint of Black Sabbath to it. So, that's when I wrote 'Master Of Insanity'. We went to a studio in London called The Music Works. I recorded about five or six songs there."

Chapter 17

Idolatry

In May of 1987 with Zakk Wylde on board the Ozzy band set to work on the next record. The band spent a good portion of 1987 ensconced in the Hurricane whipped Music Farm—soon dubbed the beetle farm—working up songs which would eventually surface on 'No Rest For The Wicked'. One insider portrays the strengths Zakk brought to the team. "With Zakk in the band things got a lot noisier that's for sure" he laughs. "There were absolutely no doubts about Zakk at all, he was just so confident and totally into it. To tell the truth his playing was pretty awe inspiring and a bit of an inspiration to us all. I've seen it all, but when he started playing guitar my jaw just dropped. Amazing stuff straight from the top of his head." Zakk's resemblance to Randy had not passed by either. "He was a pretty Randy-ish type figure. Randy's influence was with us all the time and Zakk seemed to fit into that. When he first joined the band he was very much up on classical music. He would set up his music stand and simply practice for hours and hours—he's changed a lot!"

Phil Soussan was again asked to contribute to the songwriting process but this act in itself would lead to his opting out of the band. "I was writing songs for the album as requested but we were having difficult negotiations over the publishing arrangements. It's quite a normal thing in this game but it's also important for a writer to hang on to this because publishing for a writer eventually becomes his pension. This went on for about three months and basically I didn't want to sell so I quit."

Soussan's term of engagement would come to a close in March of 1988. "I didn't want to leave, I had friends there but it was time to move on. Randy Castillo thought I was an idiot and told me so. We had loads of arguments afterwards about it although we are still great friends to this day."

The bassist's next port of employ would again, just as with Ozzy, come along in the form of a co-incidence. "Randy Castillo and I went on a long holiday to Tahiti. We met Billy Idol on the beach there which led to me appearing on his next record. Randy planned to join Billy's band too but didn't in the end."

Phil Soussan would later co-found Beggars And Thieves with former New York session singer and ex-Centaurus frontman Louie Merlino. Also involved was guitarist Ronnie Mancuso who had first hooked up with Louie Merlino when the singer was in Modern Design, the band which included oft time Ozzy collaborator and Mr. Fixit Dana Strum. Rounding off the original formation of Beggars And Thieves was drummer Bobby Borg, later of Warrant. The band would issue one highly praised album for Atlantic Records before Soussan made his exit.

Following Soussan's endeavours with Beggars And Thieves the bass player, who had performed on the debut 1990 Beggars And Thieves album, would hook up with his old friend Vince Neil, now flying solo from Mötley Crüe. "I started writing songs for him and helped Vince put the band together. I even took record company meetings with him to get a deal." Soussan worked on the album which would become Neil's debut 1993 album 'Exposed' forming a rhythm section with erstwhile Enuff Z' Nuff drummer Vikki Foxx. Guitar was handled by another acquaintance of Soussan's, former Billy Idol man Steve Stevens.

"A lot of the earlier Ozzy stuff would resurface on the 'Exposed' album" Phil readily admits. "The songs 'Look In Her Eyes' and 'The Edge' are two which I had written specifically for Ozzy and which have very Ozzy characteristics." Unfortunately it was not to be the only echo of his Ozzy past that Soussan would encounter. The chosen producer was none other than Ron Nevison. After contributing his songs and producing the initial album demos Soussan's disappointment in working once again with Nevison presented him with no choice but to retire from the situation. The 'Exposed' album would chart high breaking the Billboard American top twenty. (Incidentally, the ever present figure of Dana Strum would later appear once more in the Vince Neil story when he would step in as live bassist following a physical altercation after the second 'Carved In Stone' album between Neil and Soussan's replacement Robbie Crane resulted in flying fists!). Meantime, Soussan would

Tony Martin. Pic: Michael Eriksson.

hook up with Johnny Halliday recording no less than four Chris Kimsey produced albums with the French superstar. Subsequently, the bassist formed an alliance dubbed The Odd Couple in union with Edgar Winter and Toto's Steve Lukather touring Europe. His songwriting skills too are still much in demand gaining credits on Steve Lukather's 'Luke' album as well as the latest Toto album 'Mindfields'.

With 'Eternal Idol' not yet finalised and the band unit having fragmented, Black Sabbath was in a precarious situation. With a hugely expensive album ripe for the obligatory round of touring they suddenly found themselves singer-less. There was no question of shelving the record, what was required was a makeshift quick fix. What's more it had to be cheap—very cheap. This ruled out the big guns. Just like Ray Gillen before him Tony Martin was plucked from relative obscurity to be thrust into the harshest of spotlights.

Tony 'The Cat' Martin had been raised in Hall Green, Birmingham so the West Midlands held common ground with Tony Iommi. His first rungs on the Rock n' Roll ladder had been the traditional school band although not, as expected, in the role of vocalist.

"I started off as a guitarist" Tony elaborates. "My first school band was just mucking about, like most people's first bands I guess. I remember we were learning by doing covers of bands like Sweet, Led Zeppelin and T-Rex, that kind of stuff. Something really strange I remember from way back then was going to see Black Sabbath in Birmingham for the first time. I must have been about 14 and I took along my first girlfriend. I can remember saying to her 'If that singer collapsed right now or fell off the stage I'm going to get up there and sing every single song and finish the show'. Just a really stupid thing that a typical 14 year old would say trying to impress a girl but as things turned out I wasn't too far wrong!"

During his mid teens, besides picking up girls, he would also be picking a new stage name for himself. 'Tony Martin' is not his real name and, although it has already been revealed accidentally, his family name is something he chose to keep out of the spotlight. For very good reason as it turned out later on down the tracks. "The name 'Martin' came from a guy called Roland Martin who played bass in a cabaret band I had with my cousin Dave" he reveals. "I was about 15 at the time, they were quite a bit older, and we were playing cabaret covers to bring some money in. Quite a lot of money as it happens! Anyway, Dave and I were intrigued by this name Roland Martin, Lord knows why, so we all became the 'Martin's—Tony Martin, Dave Martin and Roland Martin. Just something as daft as that. Trouble was it just stuck so I kept on using it."

It would be this newly named optimistic novice that would quietly and unassumingly save Tony Iommi's proverbial bacon over the course of the next ten years. It is a quite remarkable feat that Tony Martin's resolve to make Sabbath work that he never cancelled a show in that entire period. No vocal nodes, no throat infections, no 'nervous exhaustion' so rampant in most major league acts. Tony Martin's determination, alongside the ever reliable stoicism of Geoff Nicholls, provided a valuable foil, indeed a veritable lifeline of stability that would anchor Iommi's vessel in the stormiest of waters.

Martin's contribution fronting Black Sabbath has never received the justice it deserves. Not only did he offer continuity in sometimes the most adverse of circumstances but he lent the proceedings an undeniable class. Tony Martin was undoubtedly Black Sabbath's untarnished diamond in an unrelenting dust storm of controversy that would consume the band for the next decade. The pinnacle of Black Sabbath's vocal achievements surely has to be found on the authoritative 'Headless Cross' and it's codicil 'Tyr' album, Martin surpassing all previous incumbents claims to fame with the quite edifying 'When Death Calls' and the ethereal malevolence of 'Kill In The Spirit World'.

Speaking of those sessions in later years Cozy Powell, interviewed by the author, would be enthusiastic in praise for Martin. "When I first discussed this whole Black Sabbath idea with Tony Iommi I was very keen to keep Tony Martin. The 'Eternal Idol' album was good and continuity, from the fans point of view, is very important. I think on 'Headless Cross' he surpassed himself. He did things on that record which really surprised all of us. With 'Tyr' he has expanded his range that bit further too. I wouldn't want anyone else singing for Sabbath. The best singer Black Sabbath has ever had is Tony Martin and that's a fact he has proved three times over now."

To get technical for a moment, Tony Martin is in possession of a five octave range although he adds a note of caution here. "Five octaves but two of them are bloody useless. Some of my range I keep just for party tricks y'know? Some of what I can do is either so low or so high it's a squeak that they are next to useless. Three octaves is what I tell everybody." For someone capable of almost superhuman vocal histrionics it comes as a surprise not only to learn that Martin's preferred choice was guitar and not vocals but that he does not find his natural talent blessed with a confidence normally associated with a lead singer. This is clear when Martin is asked if he can pinpoint the exact moment he realised he was in possession of a rare gift. "I still haven't realised!" is his light hearted riposte. "Seriously, it is still a real struggle for me sometimes. I guess it was a band called Legend that sparked it off. I went to audition as a guitarist and they said 'Can you sing?' I think I said 'a bit' or something like that so I just sang a bit and they turned around and said 'OK, forget the guitar—you're our singer!' That's when I thought, OK, there might be something there. I had never really thought about it before."

Legend pursued a distinctly American melodic Rock sound. The band did achieve a Radio One session but, as Tony concedes, "It was a bit of a nothing band really. Vocally it wasn't anything like Sabbath at all. We did try to get some stuff out there but that's about as far as it went." The budding singer's preceding act to Legend had been Orion, a shift in musical direction and home of 'The Cat' sobriquet. Even early Black Sabbath press releases still referred to the singer with his feline adjunct. "Orion was kind of Punky in a way" expounds Martin attempting to pin some definition on the band. "This would have been the late 70s, maybe 1980. We recorded enough material for an album but it never got out there. Very different to Legend, almost like the Nu-Metal of today but a lot less refined. Very raw.

That's where I got the name 'The Cat' from. We managed to get ourselves on a really good gig with Motorhead and Twisted Sister in Wrexham. It was at the football ground which could hold about 20,000 people. Only trouble was that about 3,000 punters turned up. Anyway, that's where I first met Lemmy and where I got this name from. Some journalist, from NME or Sounds, I can't remember, reviewed Orion and said we were good but that the band's singer looked Catweazle! I suppose it was true, at the time I remember I had this big baggy shirt on with these huge sleeves, very long hair and a monster of a beard! I was way ahead of my time! When the guys in the band saw this review they just thought this was hilarious so from that point on they kept calling me 'Cat' and it just stuck." For those not in the know, 'Catweazle' was a quirky and very eccentric children's TV character, a dishevelled hermit who lived in an old water tower.

Antecedent to his Black Sabbath tenure it was The Alliance that gave Tony Martin his closest shot to stardom. The band reaped a deserved reputation locally although successive show cases for labels and a run of demos failed to snag an elusive deal. The Alliance would derive from a former act billed as Space Race that included Ace Kefford and Barry 'Spence' Scrannage. The credibility of this pairing, the troubled Kefford with The Move and Scrannage with Judas Priest guitarist Glenn Tipton's formative unit The Flying Hat Band as well as The Starfighters, was to place Martin with valuable experienced, if eccentric, veterans. Scrannage was also an acquaintance of Ozzy Osbourne, even sitting in on once on the drums when Ozzy was building up his Randy Rhoads version of the Blizzard Of Ozz band.

It was through Kefford and Spence that Martin first met Albert Chapman. This renowned figure on the Birmingham music scene boasted a strong tradition with Black Sabbath and had tour managed the band throughout much of the seventies. "Albert had gone to school with all those guys in Sabbath" Tony relates. "Ozzy and Albert even worked in an abattoir together. In fact it was Albert who first sang for them when they were just doing Rock n' Roll covers in the very early days." Now, Albert Chapman was very 'old school' management, an affable giant sporting a barrel chest with an expanse to rival outer Mongolia. Chapman's trademark gold scorpion necklace told you, as if you needed telling, he meant business. He always looked like he was about to do you some personal serious harm but generally the only damage inflicted was to his wallet as he offered you a pint.

Chapman's clout and experience allied with Martin's talent seemed like an obvious partnership in the making and so a deal was struck. "Albert managed me for many, many years and made a lot of situations happen for me. The only real agreement was that when Albert was negotiating for me, one of the conditions was that I was able to work with other people too. It seemed to work well. He's a very 'big' character in both senses of the word. A lovely guy,

Orion at The Railway, Curson st, Birmingham. Tony Martin on left with guitar. Note pre-Sabbath light show . . . .

we became good friends. Albert was great if you were on the right side of him, which I was, but if you weren't . . ."

Space Race would gradually erode its membership to such a degree that only Martin was left standing in an all new guise as The Alliance. Albert Chapman fired both Ace Kefford and Spencer Scrannage and new faces drawn into the ranks included guitarist Adrian Dawson (who conjured up the band name 'The Alliance'), bass player Tim Kelly and Eddie George on keyboards. "We must have worked at it for 3 or 4 years with The Alliance with various members including a keyboard player that joined after Eddie George left who's name escapes me, but went on to join T'Pau. The drummer's name was Mitch Archer, a great drummer and a very funny guy." Tony reminisces. "It just kind of fizzled out, the guys got day jobs, they just got tired of it I think. I recall that everyone was tired of trying to make the band work and not having any money. There was always lots of promise but we could never get it to that next step. It was always a struggle financially. Anyway, in the end I was the only one going into the studio to do anything—it had got to that point. So, Albert put the feelers out."

Tony was introduced to former Whitesnake guitarist Bernie Marsden with a view to fronting his Alaska band project. The signs looked promising but the singer was "pulled out" by his manager. Although The Alliance was grinding to a halt the band's music was set to live on. Tony Martin utilised The Alliance songs for a project involving guitarist Misha Calvin. Unfortunately this latest endeavour did not turn out the way the singer wished for as he elaborates. "Misha Calvin was, in truth, a bit of an oddball. It is the only musical project that I have been associated with that I have an active dislike for now for a number of reasons. Misha had deserted from the Yugoslavian army and had somehow got into Britain and got himself a British passport. Don't ask me how he did it. He did something else which was quite incredible too because when he came to Britain he could barely play a note. Within eighteen months he had become this super fast guitar demon. Quite incredible really. Misha got fixed up with The Alliance somehow but in reality all he wanted was to project himself as the next guitar hero. We didn't actually take him that seriously and it soon all went wrong. I wasn't into it at all but the next thing I knew he had this album out."

Misha Calvin's 'Evolution' record surfaced in 1993, Tony Martin sharing vocals with Ian Parry. Martin was less than amused when he received a copy of the record. "It was outrageous. Calvin had taken all

The Alliance. Adrian Dawson, Tim Kelly, Tony 'The Cat' Martin, Marten Barter & Mitch Archer.

these songs from The Alliance and credited them to Martin / Calvin. He didn't write them—The Alliance did. None of the other guys in the band even got a mention. We kicked up a bit of a stink about it at the publishers Warner Chappel but nothing got done. No one got a penny from that record, including me."

With Martin decamping, The Alliance offered the vacant vocal spot to another well known Birmingham based singer, Al Atkins, former frontman with the original Judas Priest. Atkins declined the offer and The Alliance finally crumbled. Subsequently Eddie George made an impression with the Robin George band and as tour stand in for Magnum when Mark Stanway's parallel Grand Slam schedule conflicted.

Martin formed a brief association with Tobruk. A Birmingham based band then managed by the Light And Sound Design company, which as well as providing lighting and staging services to the world's biggest Rock acts, including Black Sabbath (where in the warehouse Tony Iommi was known by one and all as 'Tony Wyoming'!), had branched out into band management.

A true local success story Light And Sound Design not only fostered Birmingham talent but put it on the world stage. Catering to both ends of the musical hierarchy many a 'between jobs' muso has worked the floors at LSD in their time. During the mid 80s LSD, together with erstwhile Judas Priest manager Dave Corke, founded a host to nurture bands such as UFO, Zeno and Tobruk. At that juncture in early 1987 Tobruk had just lost their deal with EMI Records and were on the hunt for a new label. Unfortunately their longstanding singer Snake had bailed out to Idol Rich and a voice was needed for demos. Their drummer Eddie Fincher had skipped class too but this was not to hinder progress. "I wasn't there with Tobruk for long" motions Tony. "I just put vocals down on a few tracks, that was it really. They had no drummer so we had to use a drum machine. Albert came down to the studio and said, in all seriousness, 'The drummer's great but the band is crap!' That was the end of my dealings with Tobruk!"

It would be Adrian Vandenberg that nearly put Martin beyond Tony Iommi's reach, in more ways than one. Renowned for a triumvirate of slick, guitar driven melodic Rock mid eighties albums and predicted for bigger and better things by the industry, the esteemed Dutch guitarist invited Martin over to Holland to discuss the assembly of a new band project. "Adrian Vandenberg was a lovely bloke but he very nearly killed me!" Martin reveals. "I went over to stay with him at his house in Holland to discuss putting a new band project together. Basically it was a song-writing session and to see if we got along. The vibes were good and Adrian was a fantastic guitarist and very easy to get along with. Adrian was obviously very keen and he said to me 'Do you want to do a gig?' OK I thought, thinking I would have to work this out. 'When?' I asked him. 'Tonight!' he laughed. He was playing that night and wanted me to get up onstage with him to knock out some covers. I think we decided on Free's 'All Right Now".

The next thing I know we are tearing down the autobahn but we only got a few kilometres down the road. The thing that happened was that we were both trying to put a cassette into the tape player. We were actually arguing about it, he was trying to put it in one way and I was saying 'No, it goes in like this' and we were fighting over this tape. Of course neither of us was looking at the road so the next thing I know, I look up and we hit the central reservation. The crash was huge. The bonnet came off, the doors came off and smoke was billowing out everywhere. We were going fast and it's a miracle that we survived it let alone escaped uninjured. We eventually got the car off the autobahn and got back to Adrian's place. He jumped straight into his Dad's car and we razzed off to the gig!"

The Vandenberg / Martin liaison was curtailed by an intervention from a certain Mr. Coverdale. "I've still got a photo of Adrian on the phone when Coverdale asked him to join Whitesnake" Tony Martin confides. "Bugger!"

Albert Chapman's next appointment would be with Tony Iommi. A visit to the guitarist's house produced the news that Black Sabbath needed a singer—fast. Tony Martin journeyed down to London to try out for the position and was filled in on the details. "I was told they had the album done and needed the vocals rerecording exactly as they were. I knew I could do it because I have a very versatile voice. Whatever type of band I've been involved with, from light Rock to Reggae, I can make my vocals suit the situation. I'm a bit of a chameleon that way. I didn't know why Ray had gone, I was privy to none of the details. When I got down to

Adrian Vandenberg takes a call from David Coverdale. "Oh bugger!" thinks photographer Tony Martin.

the studio I was asked to sing 'The Shining'. They gave it to me line by line. I did as I was asked and after one track, they said 'You're in'." Eschewing the usual round of hammering out contracts between heavyweight managers and lawyers Tony Martin's introduction into one of the very biggest band's in the world would be casual in the extreme. "The Sabbath thing was done on handshakes. That's how simple it was."

Tony Martin, fortunate to enjoy the protective services of his own personal manager Albert Chapman throughout his tenure in Black Sabbath, nevertheless soon discovered that Patrick Meehan loomed large in his day to day dealings with the band. "Patrick was a heavy guy of that you had no doubt. He used the full force of his money to do exactly whatever he wanted to do. He was very hands on, right in there making decisions, at the studio and the gigs. He even approved what I wore onstage. Patrick was one of the reasons that talks kept breaking down with Geezer. I remember once we met up with Geezer at Trader Vics in London for a meal, to talk about him coming back into the band. Geezer would have none of it because he hated Meehan. His exact words were

'No fucking way'. Geezer said he'd been burnt before and he wasn't stupid enough to fall for it again. The money thing? It was all very vague. From what I was told Black Sabbath made so much money that they didn't even know how much had gone or where it had went. It's a familiar tale with most major artists. When you look back at that's obviously why all the wives got involved—Wendy, Gloria, Sharon. It's all a matter of trust. Tony was the odd one out—always looking for a manager who wouldn't rip him off. These were all things I would learn as each day passed."

The prospect of having his name engraved in succession into the annals of Black Sabbath history after such illustrious predecessors as Ozzy Osbourne, Ronnie James Dio, Ian Gillan and Glenn Hughes would certainly be felt by the young singer. "The job was huge" says Martin humbly. "The rewards were potentially enormous but as we got into it, it became just another career step for me. The strange thing for me was that I was younger by a good decade than Tony, Geezer, Geoff and Bev. I was also being introduced into a band that had a set way of doing things. It became obvious that Geoff Nicholls was Tony Iommi's right hand man, almost his soul buddy. They did absolutely everything together.

There was a job to be done though and I think we all realised that Black Sabbath needed picking up again and that it was going to be far from easy. The truth is that at that stage nobody really wanted to work with them. There were huge bills everywhere and the band had been a bit of a mess for years."

It would be a daunting task that faced the newly inducted singer. The 'Eternal Idol' album had been completed in Montserrat at huge cost and a drastic face lift was required in double quick time. In fact, Tony Martin recorded all of his vocals in just 8 days. Outside the studio, in an ominous portent, the full force of an unprecedented hurricane was lashing through the London streets. The intensity of the sessions would leave an indelible mark on Martin. "I had to duplicate Ray's vocals exactly—whether I could hit the note or not. They really, really pushed me to get it exact note for note. It was pretty gruelling. They wouldn't let me change anything, not the slightest thing. We also had to do it quick because the album had already cost them an arm and a leg. They were getting further and further into debt. They were really short of both time and money."

"When I started all of the songs were totally complete" illustrates Martin. "My job was made very clear. I was given no choices. I had to learn each song and sing exactly what was there, if it was in my key or not. That was what the audition had been all about, to see if I could replicate what was there exactly. The funny thing was that although the vocals I had done on 'Eternal Idol' were so rigid when I got the chance to change things, on the 'Headless Cross' album, I didn't want to. I had used all the features of my voice on 'Headless Cross' to full force, and when asked if I was maybe pushing it too hard I was sure it was the right thing to do, so I didn't want to change it."

Understandably the singer had mixed feelings about erasing Ray Gillen's vocals. "Ray had a great sounding voice" he says with obvious admiration. "If it wasn't me with the job of recording over it I would have liked to hear Ray's singing on that album. Trouble was he had buggered off so what could they do?" Bob Daisley would be quick to spot that the rush job had seen a few casualties in the lyric department, particularly in the song 'Nightmare'. "There is a line of mine that was changed 'Don't get fooled by the Devil's hand' was originally 'pulled' not 'fooled'. It doesn't make sense with the way they changed it."

Tony Martin is not surprised. "The thing was, I was given a sheet of words and told to sing them exactly the same. Some of it I was unsure of though because Ray's diction sometimes wasn't too great. A lot of singers are the same, particularly Americans. You listen to it and you think 'What the fuck are they saying?' That's probably how 'pulled' got changed to 'fooled'. When I teach people how to sing nowadays I'm very careful about diction. You have to emphasis each individual word otherwise it all gets mushed up. My understanding was that Bob Daisley had written a lot of lyrics and Geoff Nicholls had got involved too. Tony Iommi never wrote lyrics, in the old days that was all left to Geezer. I did ask Tony why he wasn't interested in lyrics. I guess it just isn't his thing. Still, 'Eternal Idol' wasn't too bad seeing as it was just 8 days start to finish."

Time, and money, were of the essence. "The band was really short on money when we were in London" admits the vocalist. "It did make me think a bit because obviously, joining a big name band, you expect different." Most thought that Tony Martin had done an effective job in completely eradicating Ray Gillen's recorded legacy. That was not quite the case as Gillen does in fact still feature on the 'Eternal Idol', courtesy, strangely enough, of Tony Martin himself. "On the track 'Nightmare', toward the middle, there is this evil, satanic laugh. I was asked to do my own laugh but I really didn't want to. I didn't think I could do it actually so I said 'Let's leave Ray's laugh on there. No one will know'. Well, they still wanted me to rerecord it but I won that little battle. So, Ray does still appear on the album. His evil laugh was better than anything I could do!"

With the bulk of 'Eternal Idol' in the bag the band took the opportunity to cement two more tracks 'Some Kind Of Woman' and 'Black Moon'. These would subsequently prove of huge interest to Sabbath collectors as neither appeared on the album itself, only on the B-side to the 12" format of 'The Shining' single and as 'Black Moon' as a completely reworked version for the 'Headless Cross' record. Recording the songs would provide a further challenge for Tony Martin. "Tony had these tracks that were a little off the wall. He told me that he couldn't find anyone to sing over them. Tony told me they had been kicking around for ages. They were pretty outrageous actually but I listened to them and thought 'yeah, I can do this'. I told him 'I'll have a go' so we did it. I wrote all the lyrics for those tracks and at first Tony was a bit 'er, I don't know about this ...' but they turned out fine. I remember that, as raw guitar tracks, they were too much to sing over, even impossible I would say, so Geoff Nicholls padded them out with keyboards chords over the top. Once Geoff had done that I could tackle them."

The keyboard player shines some light on the origin of these two songs. "We first did 'Black Moon' with Chris Tsangarides. The lyrics for that one are mine. I played all the bass and keyboards on that one too. I think that is the only time I have performed bass on a Sabbath song that made it onto record. 'Some Kind Of Woman' was recorded in Montserrat with Dave Spitz but both of these songs only got finished later when Tony Martin put the vocals on."

With recordings finally wrapped up a bit of light relief was doled out from an unlikely source. "Tony Iommi had this Irish gardener" chuckles Martin. "This guy had heard the record and when he spoke to Tony about it he said "I really like that new record Tony, that 'Eternal Ee-jut', fucking great!" Tony of course said 'It's not the 'Eternal Idiot' it's the 'Eternal Idol'! 'Oh yes' he says, 'That's the one, the 'Eternal Ee-jut', fucking great!' From that point on everyone in the band called that album the 'Eternal Idiot'."

The new look Black Sabbath, Tony Martin, Tony Iommi, Geoff Nicholls and Bev Bevan, geared up for an anticipated world tour. Tony Martin is unsure of Geezer Butler's involvement at this juncture. "I recall that talks were held with him in London but Geezer wasn't happy because their old manager Patrick Meehan was still involved and he disliked him intensely. The story goes that Meehan was, allegedly, responsible for ripping off the band for 6 million pounds and they never got it back."

Black Sabbath's return to live action however, did not to start off smoothly. A festival in Southampton was scheduled to witness the rebirth of the band although circumstances would dictate otherwise. "There was a gig before Greece ... well nearly" affirms Tony Martin. "We flew down to Southampton with Captain Sensible on a private jet for this festival. I remember it had been organised by two women who had both put up their houses as collateral on the whole thing. Unfortunately they lost everything as I was told. Only about 200 people turned up. I don't think anyone knew the gig was happening. It was a huge anticlimax for me of course. The gig didn't take place obviously so we flew back."

With the convoluted sessions to bring 'Eternal Idol' now at a close and the Southampton debacle behind them the band put in a run of noteworthy, if controversial, shows. The band roster though was far from stable as Tony Martin reveals. "At this stage we knew about the South African shows and Geezer was totally adamant he would not get involved with that. He just said 'No, it's wrong, I'm having nothing to do with apartheid' and that was that. There was no persuading him at all. One day Dave Spitz turned up out of the blue so he did the gigs with us."

In his time away from Black Sabbath Spitz, after his role as catalyst for Badlands, had delved into the world of law, putting himself through two semesters of schooling in business law in New York. "I just got a call one day asking if I could come back for some more touring. Despite everything, I had loved working with Tony Iommi. He had never let me down so I agreed with certain conditions. The first was that I get all my gear flown out to New York. After Montserrat all of my Spectre basses and the rest of my gear had been impounded in storage lockers because they hadn't paid their bills. Eric got his gear back by buying it back personally but I was in no position to do that at the time. OK, they agreed to that and I got my gear back. Next, I insisted on being paid half my fee upfront and the other half upon immediate conclusion of the tour. They sent the contract, I signed and I went to the UK. That's when I first met Tony Martin. The band had a cool vibe—people were even being paid!"

Incorporating the reinstated Dave Spitz, Black Sabbath, still incorporating Bev Bevan, played a unique gig at the Panathenaikos Stadium in Athens, Greece on the 20th of July. The show, due to inadequate security, was brought to a premature close as fans clambered onto the stage rigging. It was a portent of what was to come. "God that gig!" sighs Tony Martin. "They let the kids in during the sound check so we were all thinking 'What the fuck is going on here?' It was mayhem. With that as my first gig I should have realised what I was letting myself in for. Tony was so furious he had the promoter up against a wall and was whacking him! He's quite handy that way is Tony and that was the first time I saw him in action so to speak. We were right in at the deep end."

Dave Spitz had clocked the potential danger signals before the show. "The gig was quite strange. It was a big outdoors theatre like an old colosseum

Black Sabbath feel the heat before the very first 'Eternal Idol' gig in Greece. This line-up only performed this one show. L–R: Tony Martin, Dave Spitz, Geoff Nicholls, Tony Iommi and Bev Bevan.

with an arch of stone seating. The stage itself was in the middle of a field. It was also hellishly hot. Greece was going through some kind of once in a lifetime heat wave and people were dropping like flies. That heat probably contributed to the madness later. It took our crew forever to set up because they had to keep resting every five minutes because of the heat. The backline they used was the worst thing I had ever seen. All kinds of amps just piled up on top of each other. We had only brought our basic gear out with us, just guitars and drums really. The other thing I noticed was that the security guys looked as if they would be useless. They just sat around smoking cigarettes, doing nothing."

Tony Martin too went into the show with an air of trepidation but was determined to make his first entrance onto a Black Sabbath stage count. "So, my first gig with Black Sabbath and all this was going off around me. I did get to speak to Tony beforehand though and I said 'Listen, I'd like to try and get the crowd going a bit first so if you see me at the front of the stage just carry on'. 'OK' says Tony so on we go ... When we started with 'Children Of The Grave' I went to the front of the stage as planned, the band was playing and ... I forgot the words! Of course I had told Tony though to keep playing so he just kept on with the riff, giving me a strange look as if to say 'What the fuck is he doing?' The words just escaped me completely so I stood there for an eternity but they just didn't come. I ran over to Geoff Nicholls and shouted 'I've forgotten the words!' He tried to prompt me but of course it was just too loud. I couldn't hear him so I shouted back at him 'Fuck!' and he shouted back at me 'Fuck!' I then ran over to Tony Iommi and shouted 'I've forgotten the words!' and he mouthed back at me 'Fuck!' He solved it by going into straight into the chorus and from then on I was alright!"

Tony Martin may have been alright but the atmosphere was anything but. Dave Spitz reckons the familiar strains of 'Black Sabbath' acted as the trigger. "The really strange thing about that gig was that when we started there were a few stragglers up at the front and the rest were way back, all seated on these stone steps. Between them was a big space. There were quite a few houses and apartments overlooking the venue too so we had these people hanging out of windows looking to see what was going on too. It was pretty wild. I have to say the show, what there was of it, was rough. Bev Bevan didn't know the songs and it was sounding pretty bad. It stayed like that until we opened up 'Black Sabbath'. As soon as the riff to that song started the kids went nuts! People came out of nowhere! Suddenly everybody rushed to the front and started trying to get onstage. It was like a zoo. These security guys just stood there ignoring the whole situation so I had to resort to literally kicking people off the stage! That's how bad it was. Next thing I know is that the kids were scaling these lighting poles either side of the stage and these things are starting to sway dangerously!"

"Some kids did get injured which was a shame" sighs Tony Martin. "There were kids hanging like monkeys in the rigging while we were playing. Bloody dangerous. What a way to start your career!" Evidently the situation became too unpredictable. "Tony Iommi looked at me and shouted 'Let's get the fuck out of here!' I chucked my bass to my roadie and we just ran!" says Spitz. "It wasn't that easy though because there was no barrier between us and these kids and we had to run across a field at the back of the stage to our dressing room. This mob was after us, pulling at our clothes, and if they had pulled us down we would have been trampled. We just made it into the dressing room where we got locked in! The promoter came in to see us, gave us a crate of vodka and told us to stay put because there was a riot going on outside. It took quite a while to calm things down so it was safe enough for us to leave."

After the Greek debacle Bev Bevan backed out. Cozy Powell's services were requested but he was, somewhat ironically, involved in the very same Blue Murder project Ray Gillen was now involved in. With the sands of time slipping by Black Sabbath hastily pulled in Terry Chimes, formerly with The Clash, to man the drums. "We went through three or four drummers" Tony Martin recalls. "One of them used to play for Showaddywaddy! Another one was a born again Christian and as he walked in he said 'You don't play anything evil do you?' There was talk of Cozy again at that stage too. He was probably caught up in something he couldn't get out of."

Geoff Nicholls reveals how Sabbath broke the boredom of auditioning an endless cycle of drummers. "Tony would give everyone a signal and we would start the song in the wrong key. It was interesting to see how the person being auditioned would react when we burst out laughing. Auditioning drummers was always quite a task, just finding people who could keep time y'know? I can remember we asked people to play 'War Pigs' and the amount of drummers who tried to play it in a straight 4 / 4 was amazing. It's a 3 / 4 waltz, it's in swing time. If they didn't know that they didn't stand much of a chance and you would be amazed by how many didn't have a clue. That's why Bill was always so good. He had all that nailed."

Chimes had just come from the Cherry Bombz, a Pop Rock outfit led by the former Hanoi Rocks team of guitarist Andy McCoy and Nasty Suicide, fronted by the quite delectable Anitah Chellemah. Besides his tenure with The Clash, Chimes too had been involved with Generation X and Hanoi Rocks, filling the void left by Razzle, the band's late sticksman killed as a victim of 'vehicular manslaughter' when as a passenger in a high speed car smash by Mötley Crüe's Vince Neil.

With Chimes name most commonly associated with The Clash many saw the match as an ill fit but the drummer had no such reservations. "The Cherry Bombz was over and I was looking for another job at the time. I had heard about the Black Sabbath opening and I told my manager to get me in there. I really wanted it. People couldn't see the connection between the Punk stuff I was known for and Black Sabbath but that was the kind of music I grew up on as a kid. My whole reason for playing the drums was John Bonham and I applied that equally to The Clash and Black Sabbath. I really wanted the job so

I put a lot of time in beforehand working everything out very, very carefully."

Despite having schooled himself in the songs up-front of the audition Terry's first impressions did not bode well though. "I think I gave them a shock with the size of my kit—or the lack of it" he laughed. "I just put the basics into my car thinking I wouldn't need to take along a whole kit. I didn't think that whole palaver was necessary. Well, I walked in with this little set up and they said 'What the hell is that?' Obviously they were expecting the full drum kit! Anyhow, we got playing and it was alright. I got along with them all straight away and I could tell I could fit in with the band. I did find the whole situation a bit strange though because, unlike the other bands I had been in, these guys were people I had looked up to since I was a kid. Joining a band and making a record is one thing but joining a band that you have bought their records as a kid is a whole different ball game."

Next on the agenda would be another first for Black Sabbath—South Africa. The band, minus Bevan who like Geezer Butler also steadfastly refused to perform in South Africa, played a series of week-end shows on both Saturday and Sunday for three weeks running at the 6,000 capacity Sun City Superbowl venue. The travel arrangements made for the 'band' certainly established the internal power strata within the organisation at this point. "Tony and Patrick Meehan were up on the top floor in first sipping champagne all the way" Martin registers. "The rest of us were down at the back with the goats and pigs. You certainly knew where you stood no mistake. That was made clear on the sleeve of the 'Eternal Idol' album too. Not many people picked this up but the whole thing of just Tony appearing in pictures was quite deliberate. That's also why he is credited as 'The Player' and the rest of the musicians were 'The Players'. Patrick Meehan got credited as executive producer too. There was a very real attempt to separate Tony from the rest of the band at that point in time."

Terry Chimes, anticipating his debut gig with the band had more to contend with than just the standard pre-gig nerves. When asked by the author if he encountered any teething problems the drummer, nowadays a practicing acupuncturist, bellowed out loud. "Teething problems? Well, yes you could say that. It's funny you use those words too because that is exactly what I had—teething problems quite literally! Just before going to South Africa I had a new bridge fitted in my mouth. The thing was though, was that the dentist made me up this temporary one cemented in, just to get a fit. He put it in my mouth and it felt fine but when he came to take it out it was stuck fast! He pulled and pulled but it wouldn't

budge. So, I went to Sun City with this temporary ceramic bridge stuck there.

Anyhow, just before the first gig I was cleaning my teeth with dental floss and this thing just fell out of my mouth, bounced off the sink and smashed to pieces on the tile floor! It was about an hour before my first Black Sabbath gig and it looked like I was about to do the show with no teeth! Luckily I found a fantastic lady at the pharmacy in the hotel who super-glued the teeth back together and put them back in. So, I was playing the gig, concentrating obviously on what Dave Spitz was up to but conscious of my teeth all the way through. Tony Iommi made me laugh during that first gig though because he turned around to look at me and he had a guitar plectrum balanced on his nose like a performing seal! I couldn't laugh because I was afraid my teeth would go flying again! I just stared at him stony faced so he must of thought I was a right miserable bastard! Not many people see the funny side of Tony like that."

Reports from a fan that attended one of those Sun City gigs suggested the group played far too loud. "True" confirms Tony Martin. "It was fuck off loud, really out there. I guess not that loud to us but those people would not have been used to it. It was OK for us onstage because all the bodies in the audience absorbed it. You have to remember that the sound out front is not in our control, and when people say the band played to loud, it's not like we have the volume control up on stage with us, it's out front with the bloke at the mixing desk."

Black Sabbath would not be alone in the whirlwind of political turmoil. Status Quo would endure similar grief for playing the same venue later that year and two years previous even Queen had performed at Sun City. Reports suggested that the band had been duped into the gigs by being told that Sun City was not in fact in South Africa at all but in a totally separate country. There is some credence to this as, officially, the resort was in the 'homeland' of Bophuthatswana during the apartheid years. What is beyond doubt is that Black Sabbath received generous monetary compensation for the trip. Did the band get paid well? Dave Spitz thinks so. "Tony Iommi was given a Rolls Royce for doing those shows. That was part of the whole deal."

"We got grief from the very first minute those shows were announced" reveals Tony Martin. "Before we went there was this lobby trying to stop us going. There was one idiot in particular who was really stuffed up, accusing us of all kinds of things in the press. That one guy got all of us very angry. It's not nice to be branded a racist. On the other hand the organisers in South Africa were doing their best to make sure we would go out and play the gigs.

Onstage in South Africa 1987. Tony Iommi, Tony Martin and Dave Spitz.

We even asked them if both black and white people would be allowed into the gigs and they said 'sure'. They kept their word because there were black people there, I've got the photos to prove it. Overall, I have good memories of those South African shows. The kids were obviously very grateful we played for them."

The band would receive a taste of what the local population was enduring though. At an interview session in Johannesburg the group was alarmed when a large blast rocked buildings just a few blocks away. "Someone had set a bomb off a few streets away" observed Dave Spitz. "It kind of reminded us of the real situation we were in. As we were leaving there was a huge ruckus, police vehicles everywhere. We hightailed it back to Sun City pretty fast."

Black Sabbath's singer does confess though to being both naïve as well as being carried along by events too. "I have to say that at that point I was still kind of floating along in my own private, tiny world, not really making any sense of it. I didn't have any political views one way or the other. For us it was just a gig. South Africa, Russia, China—who cares? I could see both sides of the argument. The promoters kept offering us more and more incentives to go as soon as the political storm brewed up." Terry Chimes echoes Martin's thoughts. "I just thought the whole thing was bizarre. Like, why were they so bothered?" he mused. "The band did get a lot of stick for it but did they really think Black Sabbath somehow held the key to the racial problems in South Africa? I couldn't understand why they were asking five musicians questions they should really have been putting to the United Nations and international bodies like that. We got a lot of unfair flak that's for sure. It was unwarranted. What the press didn't tell anybody was that the promoter of the show was black and that audience was a mix of black and white too. The press just saw something they could shout their mouths off about. If you told them the real story they just ignored it and printed something else."

Talking to 'Kerrang's Dante Bonutto in 1987 Tony Iommi had this to say on the matter. "Everyone was on about this whole apartheid thing. So I called up various people who had been there, Queen for example, and they all thought it was great. I mean, we're musicians, all we want to do is play, and they're really starved of music over there. It's a shame that music should have to be caught up in politics—music is for the world!" However, some five years later, Tony's thoughts had been coloured by hindsight. "We shouldn't have gone really. There was a lot of money on the table but we were not told all the details that's for sure. Apartheid—I can't ever condone it, it's wrong. Geezer told me not to do it and he was dead against it. At the time it did not seem like such a big deal. The shows were good, a lot of different people came to see us and we were treated like royalty. There were no political problems while we were there but when we got back home ... No, we shouldn't have done it."

Post Sabbath, Dave Spitz made a return to New York putting together a band unit led by singer Leo and guitarist Ernie Burns. This group journeyed to Los Angeles before stalling. The bassist received a call offering a place in the Impelliterri band. Chris

Impelliterri was a well known guitar hotshot from the Malmsteen school of speed. His 'Last In Line' album, fronted up by former Rainbow singer Graham Bonnet, was reaping healthy sales but he had just lost his rhythm section of bassist Chuck Wright and drummer Pat Torpey. Spitz, alongside Stet Howland, plugged the gap. A video, filmed atop the Houston Pacific building, scored regular rotation on MTV. The future looked bright but Spitz soon began to realise his days of dealing with 'erratic singer syndrome' were not yet over. "Graham Bonnet was a helluva a singer but, like Glenn Hughes, he had his own personal demons he was dealing with too. He actually disappeared on us without notice a few times. We lost a Blue Oyster Cult support tour because the guy just vanished one day. There were obvious problems and live work was minimal. We did get to play some amazing shows in Japan though."

Spitz's musical journey then took him to Slam Nation, working with Hellion guitarist Chet Thompson. Reuniting with his Black Sabbath colleague Eric Singer the bass man involved himself with Purple Heart, a group mentored by the esteemed Japanese guitarist Kuni Takeyuchi and featuring vocals from Dennis Feldman. Eventually Singer was superseded by Stet Howland and the new rhythm axis, together with singer Jack James, then set about the creation of an all new act entitled Big Richard. Another fresh project was then brokered billed as Insomnia, Spitz working in alliance with the hugely talented Paul Sabu, ex-Baton Rouge guitarist Lance Bullen and Kentucky native Jerry Lawson on drums. Despite the pedigree, Insomnia too came to naught. Great White would be next in line to secure The Beast's services. The band, riding high on the huge success of the single 'Once Bitten ... Twice Shy', hit a snag mid tour when bassist Tony Montana suffered a family bereavement. Not wishing to halt momentum Great White pulled Dave Spitz in to keep the tour going. "Doug Goldstein, the guy who had helped out Black Sabbath on the 'Seventh Star' tour, had set up a management company called Stravinsky Bros. with Alan Niven. They hit success straight away with Guns n' Roses and Great White. After filling in on tour for them I did the 'Psycho City' record."

Spitz then ducked out of Rock n' Roll for a period to concentrate on Goju-Ryu Karate. Rock n' Roll, or rather Thrash Metal, would soon entice him back into the musical arena. "I went back to New York and got involved with re-forming Nuclear Assault with drummer Glenn Evans." The band was Glenn, Karl Cochrane on guitar and original Nuclear Assault singer John Connelly. Following further financial disillusionment and a realisation that Metal was enduring a down turn in fortune Dave Spitz struck out in to the world of law.

With Dave Spitz returning to America and Geezer Butler immovable due to both the South African expedition and Patrick Meehan's grip on proceedings, the bass position was still unoccupied with just two weeks left before a European tour. The man who took on the task for the 'Eternal Idol' European shows was Jo Burt, for most Sabbath fans a complete unknown. As with most musicians involved in this story though Jo was no lucky fly by night and had worked with some of the music industries very biggest names before adding Black Sabbath to his curriculum vitae.

However, there had been approaches made to others, including one to Neil Murray of Whitesnake fame, then ensconced in Japanese Rockers Vow Wow. Tall for European stock Murray stuck out like the proverbial sore thumb amongst his oriental band members. He records this first inquiry from Black Sabbath as only semi-serious. "I was busy with Vow Wow, we had plenty of things coming up and at that stage it looked like exciting times were ahead for the band. It was not really a formal invitation as such I received from Sabbath at that time. I think the management just asked me if it would be of interest. I listened to 'Eternal Idol' and I'm afraid I wasn't terribly knocked out by it so it wasn't enough of a strong invitation for me, either musically or officially. I certainly didn't jump up and down shouting 'Oh wow—I must join!' Maybe that's what they were looking for. Maybe I should have done it, then I would have got to play on 'Headless Cross'. If they would have played me 'Headless Cross' instead of 'Eternal Idol' things might well have been different. I just didn't rate the album."

It was not Neil Murray's first brush with the Sabbath family though. During 1985 he had aided Ozzy Osbourne in the rehearsal studio. "I never really joined the band at all, I just helped them out. That's how I viewed it—just helping. Someone called me up and asked if I would like to rehearse with Ozzy for a few days to tide them through as they had no bass player at that point. It was Ozzy, Jake E. Lee and Jimmy DeGrasso on the drums. They were just trying out some songs, pretty casual actually. I ended it actually because I got a call to go down to the south of France to join David Coverdale and John Sykes to put together the Whitesnake '1987' album. I said 'Look Ozzy, I'm sorry but I've got to disappear'. That was that. I never went along with the assumption I was being tried out for the band unlike the first time around with Sabbath."

Before Burt stepped into the breech there was another, albeit fleeting, addition to the Black Sabbath roll call. Shooting a promotional video for 'The Shining' the band rather embarrassingly found themselves without a full compliment of band members. "The director, quite rightly, pointed out that we couldn't shoot a video without a bass player" says Tony Martin. "It was all a big cock up. A lot of phone calls were made but nobody we knew could do it at such short notice. What we did was ask one of the crew guys to go out into the street and find anyone with long hair, ask them if they could play and did they want to be in a video! That's how desperate we were. We sent this guy out and sure enough he returns with this bloke. He looked the part, long black hair, lots of blue stone jewellery. We said to him 'Do you know how to use a bass?' He said 'Yeah, I'm a guitar player'. So that's how we did it. I don't think anyone thought to even ask him what his name was. We auditioned him for the job of bass player but he was pretty useless actually. He didn't exactly do his chances much good when he also told us he was the reincarnation of a Red Indian chief!"

So Jo Burt it was. Most press reports, those that bothered, picked up on the fact that Jo had been involved with melodic Rock outfit Virginia Wolf, a band highlighted by the inclusion of a certain Jason Bonham on drums and given an enormous push by Atlantic Records. The group was managed by Phil Banfield, the long term business brains behind Ian Gillan's career. Virginia Wolf put out two albums of high calibre before nose-diving, leaving many puzzled fans behind. Immediately before Virginia Wolf beckoned Burt had been laying down bass lines for Freddie Mercury's album 'Mr. Bad Guy' and had also been in the studio working up a project with Queen's Roger Taylor and Status Quo's Rick Parfitt.

In 1985 the Queen drummer had just signed on to produce the debut Virginia Wolf record. "When Roger agreed to produce the album he approached me when Rhino went off to join the Quo and asked me to play on a couple of tracks" remembers Burt. When Virginia Wolf had dispensed with their original rhythm section of bassist Clive Corner and drummer Paul Johnson initial bass for the recording sessions had been laid down on the album by John 'Rhino' Edwards. "Once Phil had got the deal with Atlantic, and Jason was definitely going to stay, I agreed to join the band, finish the album and go on tour in the U.S."

The album was launched to glowing reviews and the band duly plunged into a major North American tour opening up for much vaunted former Led Zeppelin guitarist Jimmy Page and ex-Free singer Paul Rodgers band endeavour The Firm. Burt has vivid memories. "It was wild! With Jimmy Page in the headline act and Jason with us, Led Zeppelin fever was everywhere. I had done a lot of U.S. touring prior to this but never experienced the Zeppelin factor. There were banners everywhere saying Bonham lives and Jason was received like a God. Paul Rogers got upset because for an opening act we were pretty potent. Jason got a standing ovation for 8 bars of Moby Dick in his drum solo at The Philadelphia Spectrum. He was only 19 and I felt quite responsible for him. The rest of the band, all from Manchester, had little experience but thought they were in "the ultimate sweetie shop", and actually, for a while, coped with the pressure very well."

Both Atlantic Records and MTV were fully behind the band and album sales had provided a strong base for the future. As Burt reveals though the impact of the first album could have been much greater. "At a meeting at the Omni Park Hotel, New York, just prior to the Meadowlands show, Phil Banfield said we were due to be bumped onto a second tour opening for Van Halen. At this point Chris the singer stood up and said "I can't do it—gotta go home." He was homesick and missing his girlfriend. At this point I knew I should have bailed out!"

Burt returned to the UK to begin work on a second Virginia Wolf album. The band upped camp to San Francisco with producer Kevin Elson, fresh from his enormous global smash with Europe's 'The Final Countdown'. Atlantic Records believed this next effort could well be Virginia Wolf's 'big one' and pulled out all the stops but once the tape machines stopped rolling they lost some of their enthusiasm. "Atlantic Records was not happy and wanted to remix the album. Nick the guitar player, who felt his songs were sacred and never allowed anyone else's input, phoned the New York office one night on hearing of this idea and told them to "stuff the contract up their arse." End of career!"

Virginia Wolf's sophomore outing 'Push' still sold a healthy quarter of a million copies even without band and label support, an indicator perhaps of what might have been. Jo Burt got back to session work, putting in terms of duty with Brian Setzer of The Stray Cats and appearing at the Montreaux Jazz festival with James Reyne. Ian Gillan's manager, Phil Banfield, then took a further hand in the musician's career, suggesting he might be just the man Tony Iommi was looking for. Black Sabbath was corralled in Tasco's Woolwich rehearsal complex staring up a proverbial yet distinctly foul watered creek. The canoe was booked but the paddles had not arrived. Burt retraces the expedience of the situation. "They were already in production rehearsals and I just joined in—they didn't have much choice as the tour was to start in two weeks."

Although committed, the union was not an easy fit. "Tony Iommi wasn't happy with my bass sound—I had previously told my guitar tech to replace one of the amplifier heads because I thought it was broken. In fact, the pre-amp stage of the 3 Ampegs had been tampered with the get maximum distortion and this was the sound of 'Sabbath'. This was the first sign as to how out of place I was!"

This latest variant of Black Sabbath bowed in at the Essen Park Palace in Germany on the 22nd November. Evidence of the haste in which Burt was shoe horned in can be found in the official tour itinerary for band and crew members, the bassist not being listed as a band member but as part of the travelling crew. New material from 'Eternal Idol' was sparse with only 'Glory Ride', 'Born To Lose' and 'The Shining' putting in a showing. 'Die Young', gradually to evolve into a tour de force track for Tony Martin, would be dusted off for a return in a set that included no Ian Gillan era songs.

Jo Burt has cause to recall the opening night of this tour. "It was unforgettable. A huge curtain was draped across the stage about 2 metres in front of the drum riser and assorted stacks. The two Tony's and I stood there while they pumped dry ice from the wings until I couldn't see my hand in front of my face! All the time, a guitar choral soundtrack played until such time the curtain opened spilling all the smoke onto the stage. I played the first song not being able to see anything! When the mist finally cleared, a sea of fists clenched in the Sabbath 'Devil's sign' greeted me. What struck me strangest of all from my previous experience, was that the audience seemed to be primarily guys... and they all seemed to chant my bass parts... they knew them better than I did!"

This Heavy Metal tribalism was all new to Jo Burt, as it was for Terry Chimes. As the new boy the bassist came in for a fair amount of ribbing as can be expected. "I was never really a Sabbs fan and I struggled with so many riffs" he admits. "They sussed me out and I became the butt of so many tricks. Even the way I moved, I couldn't stand with my legs apart so I just shook my head!"

One particular jape delivered by Tony Iommi would test his nerve mid set. "Tony and I used to meet centre stage during one song. He pulled off his dummy fingers in front of my face. I nearly passed out—I didn't know!" Unbeknown to him tour photographer PG Brunelli captured the moment just after this jape, Burt on his knees in disbelief and Iommi sporting an uncharacteristic Cheshire cat grin. Tony Martin tells of another favourite pastime of Mr. Iommi's involving these digital prosthetics. "He would often alarm people by sticking them on his face" he giggled at the school boy humour of it all. "These false fingers he had were hollow so he would use the suction to stick them to his face. Because they were skin coloured it really did look quite bizarre!"

The rhythm section of Burt and Chimes gelled personally because of their common musical backgrounds. "What was strange about this particular line-up was that the rhythm section had come from the New Wave era, and he and I laughed about the irony of the situation, when things started to go pear-shaped" he relates. "I think with the benefit of hindsight, both Terry and I were slightly out of our depths on this tour because we were not from the Metal tradition. Cozy Powell who ultimately replaced him, and with whom I had no empathy, was much more within the Sabbath mould. Under all the circumstances, I thought Terry coped admirably."

Tony Martin confesses he too was still finding his sea legs as this most unique of vessels set sail into uncharted waters. Just as Ian Gillan had discovered before the Henry T. Ford school of thinking was still in force when it came down to fashion sense in Sabbath land. "The thing with Sabbath was that you had to wear black. It sounds ridiculous but if you weren't wearing black you were seen to be really letting the side down and they made sure you knew it. You could not wear blue jeans, only black ones.

They would not tell you that you couldn't wear another colour but they did make sure your life was made miserable until you conformed. They did this by constantly taking the piss out of you until it became so annoying you wore black just to have an easy life. I made a huge mistake of wearing a white scarf onstage early on. They didn't like that one bit so that soon went. Onstage I actually used to wear a lot of Tony Iommi's clothes. I didn't have any and he had wardrobes full of designer gear custom made in Los Angeles. I used to very often delve into his wardrobe before a show."

Supporting on the German leg of the tour was the grandiose American Metal band Virgin Steele. Germany was almost like a second home to singer David DeFeis and his cohorts having built a cult following up into an ongoing mainstream success. The band had only just completed one German trek, with Manowar, when the call came to open for Sabbath. "Black Sabbath were very kind to us" remarks DeFeis. "Tony Iommi had this thing about socks as I recall. Many, many times he would greet us in the morning and say "I've been up all night washing my socks." Isn't that odd? You go on tour with Black Sabbath and all I can remember is Tony's socks! He regaled us with some amazing stories of his past, particularly at a very, very remote gig called Walschutigen on Thanksgiving. He told me then that John Bonham was best man at his wedding I recall. The odd thing is that since then I have never come across that gig since and we have toured Germany a lot. I even tried to find it on the map because it was bothering me so much, it had echoes of 'The Twilight Zone'. I couldn't find it. The actual shows were great for us. Black Sabbath's crew treated us very well. Tony Martin and I got along great. I can remember doing some mad song-writing sessions with him backstage at Munich on the piano. Once his voice was giving him problems so I gave him some 'interesting' German herbs to sort it out. I don't know if it was my herbs or something else but that night he sounded great."

Having wrapped up the German leg Burt's birthday of 2nd December, a last German gig, "in the middle of nowhere with no facilities", offered another prime opportunity for tomfoolery at his expense. As Burt remembers, upon arrival the band personnel were dismayed to discover their venue for the evening was less than salubrious. "We were actually playing in a cattle shed! I was cheered up though when the promoter turns up with a blonde on each arm dressed as biker chicks and says 'Happy birthday Jo—these are for you!'" As is evident by photos of this Sabbath line-up, bearing in mind this was the eighties, the bassist's attention to his spiked and back combed hairstyle had obviously caught the attention of his other band members. The 'gift' was not all what it seemed. "Turns out they were hairdressers! They were going to give me a good seeing to in the hair department. So, with a superb hair do I hit the stage. Half way through the show the band stop the show to announce my birthday. The whole crowd was singing along to 'Happy birthday'. As I took my bow centre stage, unbeknown to me the entire crew had assembled behind me dressed in the old monks outfits from the wardrobe cases. I then had custard pies squashed in my face from every direction as the others took photos! With no showers at the gig I had to travel across the Brenner Pass into Italy still picking the cream out of my ears!"

The band, recording some shows along the way, continued the shows into Italy commencing in the cathedral city of Milan. Italy would prove memorable for all the wrong reasons. As their Len Wright tour bus drew up to their hotel in Rome the band and crew were staggered at the official reception they were seemingly afforded. They had the red carpet treatment quite literally—or so they thought. The pavements on both sides of the street had been overlaid in regal red carpeting and as they pulled up the coach was surrounded by a mass of gesticulating police officers. "Turns out the Pope was coming!" laughs Burt. "Sure enough, moments later he came through. The irony of the situation was not lost on me. I swear he waved at me!"

The police would also force a presence on the gig itself, providing stark recollections for Burt. "The police baton charges at our first Italian show upset me greatly, while all this was going on I was trying to remember the bass riffs! In Rome, the promoter had sold tickets for two shows when there was only one. The police opened fire on the dissatisfied crowd who all had valid tickets and were waiting outside.

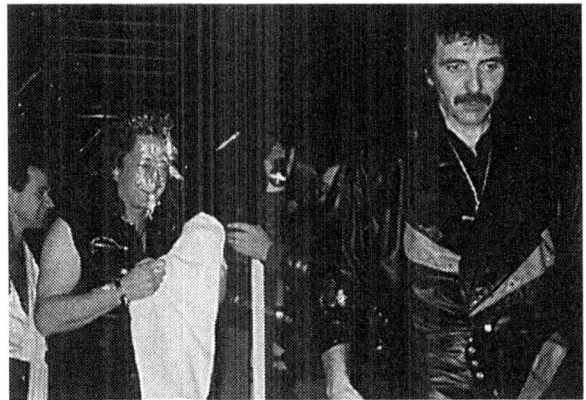

Jo Burt gets caked. Pic: David DeFeis.

We had to abandon our set and run for the buses in order to avoid the riot which ensued. The road crew had to deal with all this and more."

Prompted by Joe's memory Tony Martin lets us in on some of the background details to this gig. "Rome was a total disaster and actually the Pope was partly to blame bizarrely enough" he remonstrates. "What had happened was that originally we were booked into an auditorium that held roughly ten thousand people. There had been about seven thousand tickets sold. However, the Pope had just held a major religious meeting in this auditorium and the authorities thought that it would be some kind of blasphemy if Black Sabbath played in the same building as the Pope. So, what did they do? They moved the band to a 2,000 capacity theatre! Of course we arrived and discovered what was going on but there was absolutely nothing we could do. Joe is right, there was about twice the number of people there for just the one gig and they all had a valid ticket. Stupidly they tried to cram everybody in. There were kids packed in everywhere, pushed in here, shoved in there. All the standing room was taken and there were people hanging off things all over the place. They still couldn't get them all in and 3,000 fans were stuck outside demanding to get in.

Amazingly the gig went on but half way through someone said to me 'Listen Tony, we have to get you guys out of here quick. They are rioting outside and the kids are starting to attack the bus. Go and tell Tony'. I said 'I'm not fucking telling him—you tell him!' Anyway, I was persuaded. Can you imagine this—I walked up to Tony in the middle of a guitar solo and interrupted him. The look on his face! I thought he's going to clobber me! We were having this huge row in the middle of a gig in front of both the band and the audience. All this time the band kept playing looking at us and thinking what the fuck...? Finally I got to tell him 'Stop, we've been ordered out!' 'No way!' he says 'keep playing!' Finally, finally I convinced him. He threw his guitar down, literally, stopped the band and said 'OK lads, let's go!' We just ran out of there. Left all the gear—everything. Left it all to the poor crew to look after. It was terrible two kids were shot by the police outside. It really did get very bad."

Not wishing to put themselves through the indignity of a half full Hammersmith Odeon again the band scaled down their traditional two night run down to just one on December 28th, slating Gothic Rockers Fields Of The Nephilim as support act. It would be an indication as to how low the band's standing had dropped when this solitary gig, the only one announced for Great Britain, was pulled. Unfortunately the cancellation was so last minute coach loads of fans had actually turned up for the gig, many having travelled hundreds of miles for the event. Most rumours pointed to dismal ticket sales although stranger tales of 'tennis elbow' and 'Singapore flu' were also circulating. To add to their misery the press had the smell of blood in their nostrils and on a more practical note the band's gear was under house arrest at Tasco.

Band members saw things differently, as Jo Burt explains. "I was unaware of any press at the time, I was more concerned about the fact that cheques were bouncing in my bank account because we were not being paid. At this point, the Sabbath experience was forever spoilt. As the tour faltered and we flew home, it then became apparent that the bills for the trucks and the sound system all supplied by Tasco had not been paid. My guitars, FX rack and stage clothes were all impounded by Jo Brown (Tasco director) who insisted on payment before the release of any goods. All my pleas to the management fell on deaf ears. Finally, on my knees to Jo Brown, I reclaimed my bass guitar, but the rest of my equipment and belongings I have not seen since."

In speaking to Kerrang magazine Tony Iommi was not shy in addressing the various tribulations. "Yes, our equipment had to be impounded and I was suffering from a bout of what was thought to be tennis elbow, but on top of this I came down with Singapore flu while in Europe and got really ill. I couldn't shake it off and felt horrible. Even now, the after effects haven't completely worn off. It's awful. The last thing I wanted to do was to cancel the Hammersmith show—I was really looking forward to it. But we had no choice and all I can do is to apologise to the fans. But we do intend to reschedule this date as soon as possible, plus hopefully slotting in a couple of other British gigs."

They never got the chance. After 17 years Vertigo did the unthinkable and Black Sabbath's contract was not renewed. The last time Black Sabbath had come to the precipice of a contractual closure they had delivered 'Heaven And Hell'. This time, 'Eternal Idol', just scraping up to a lowly No. 66 in the UK album charts, simply wasn't enough. In that same Kerrang interview Iommi told Malcolm Dome "The situation with Patrick was unworkable. We could never find him when bills had to be paid and apart from one girl in the office, there was no one we could talk to about anything. It was a nightmare and eventually I was left with no option but to walk away and try to pick up the pieces. All I wanna do is be left alone to get on with playing music. I just wish all these problems would go away."

Tony Martin sheds some harsh light on the immediate aftermath of the Meehan years. "For a very brief time Terry Chimes had his manager help Tony out and they actually managed Tony Iommi for a very, very short period—probably a matter of weeks. It was all very fucked up though because of all the previous stuff that had gone down. Everything was such a bloody mess. When that relationship broke down Terry Chimes' manager took Tony Iommi's Rolls Royce as payment!

Tony Iommi was basically funding the band out of his own personal funds at that stage. He would pull out his personal credit card to pay for tour expenses loads of times. At the end of the 'Eternal Idol' tour he said 'This is the last fucking time!' You had to admire him for that. Tony was always sticking his hands in his pockets to keep the band going. He paid for a lot of the day to day stuff that really other people should have been paying for. I didn't envy him that. When Sabbath was at its lowest it was Tony who kept it going all the time. You know something? I never once heard Tony Iommi say 'I give in' or anything even remotely like that. I think he was always showing a brave face for the troops but we would have heard if he had confided those kind of thoughts to anyone. He never did. A lot of other people—most people—would have jacked it in. Every time he vowed it would be the last time. Every time it wasn't."

Besides Tony Iommi flashing his plastic more times than he would have liked there was also the flash of the blade to be wary of. The media knives had been out for much of the year and much like Caesar on the steps of the Senate the previously unassailable Black Sabbath put up no resistance. The Sun City debacle, a haemorrhaging of band members and the final slap in the face from Vertigo gave the press more ammunition than they had dared dream of. What was lost in the vitriolic nature of press reports was that the 'Eternal Idol' album was a damn fine effort and that with Tony Martin Black Sabbath had brought another world class singer to the fore.

Chapter 18

No Rest For The Headless

Former Ozzy drummer Fred Coury, by 1988 firmly ensconced in Cinderella with 6 million record sales behind him happened to find himself meeting up with Ozzy once more just upfront of recording for the 'No Rest For The Wicked' album. "I was actually in an elevator in this apartment block saying goodbye to a friend when Ozzy kinda 'kidnapped' me and took me to his room. So there I was, sitting with Ozzy and the comedian Sam Kinison having a real good time. Ozzy was just sitting there listening to old Black Sabbath records and I was just thinking to myself "This is the coolest!" I was flipping out. So, anyway, Ozzy asks me "Fred, What do you think of Mike Inez?" I replied that I didn't know who he was (Nowadays he's a very good friend but then I didn't know him) and Ozzy says "He's my new bass player."

Then Ozzy asks me "What do you think of Bob Daisley?" so I tell him the truth which is that Bob is by far the best bassist I've ever played with in my life. By then I had played with a lot of people. Cinderella had played with some big bands like Bon Jovi and everyone and we always got to jam but out of all them Bob was the best no question. The way Bob plays had such a groove that it made you a better drummer. I still think he is the best Rock bassist in the world." Two days later Fred received a surprise visitor at his door. "It was Bob Daisley" exclaims the drummer. "He came round to say thank you! I don't know how much influence I had with Ozzy just by saying what I did that night but it was a really nice thing for Bob to do. I guess Ozzy must have told him. He came to my room just to tell me that. Cool!"

Bob relates yet another saga in his life with Ozzy Osbourne. "I did the 'No Rest For The Wicked' record, writing lyrics and music and playing bass. I also wrote and performed fretless bass on a track that didn't make the album called 'The Liar'. It came out later on a 12" single. Geezer did the tour I think." Daisley would also record the 'Odyssey' album with Swedish guitar maestro Yngwie Malmsteen, the Scandinavian's biggest selling album to date. He would then delve back into the Black Sabbath camp when, alongside Ozzy, he played on drum-

Bill Ward & Bob Daisley.

mer Bill Ward's solo album 'Ward One—Along The Way'. Naturally it would not be Daisley's last tenure with Ozzy either.

In October of 1988 Ozzy served up 'No Rest For The Wicked'. The album sessions had begun with Roy Thomas Baker but would be completed by Keith Olsen. With the sanitized 'Ultimate Sin' having, despite the odds, racked up larger sales than anticipated the new album needed to be something special. Ozzy fans should not have feared, with Zakk Wylde Ozzy had found a foil every bit as arresting as his predecessors. Randy had the vision and Jake the groove but Zakk rudely observed no precedents. What you saw is what you got. And that was only one thing—the loudest, rawest most bitchin' guitarist on the planet. The lead single 'Miracle Man' proved to be a well aimed swipe at American TV evangelists, Ozzy seemingly delighted at bloodying the nose of Swaggert and his crucifix wielding cronies that had hounded him over so many road miles.

The Japanese really went to town in an exercise of marketing zeal. Besides the regular release the record was offered repackaged as 'The Bible Of Ozz' boasting an extra two tracks, a heavyweight belt buckle, an Ozzy logo patch, a Zakk patch and a book. The whole thing cased in packaging designed to give a Bible appearance. If there was one overriding factor about 'No Rest ...' it was that riffs ruled. 'Tattooed Dancer', 'Devil's Daughter' and the unsedated lunacy of 'Crazy Babies' rode riffs that seasoned rodeo vets would have difficulty hanging on to. Somehow though Ozzy not only maintained his grip but would perform the feat with a nonchalant ease. Of course the album itself could never fully hope to capture Wylde's untamed approach but it gave the youngster enough leeway to prime his audience. 'No Rest For The Wicked' was more a statement of intent, a warning if you will.

Zakk's zeal in stamping his authority knew no parameters. If he was Rockin' he was unstoppable until the curtain dropped. Ample evidence for which can be found by this eyewitness account from a backstage vantage point at London's Hammersmith Odeon.

"Zakk had got up on top of this pile of cabs for his solo spot. Unfortunately he had ripped the back of his trousers open so all I could see right in front of me was this dirty great pair of balls! It was not a pretty sight. Anyway, Zakk didn't care one bit—he just got on with the show so I had just had to stand with Zakk's balls swinging in front of me! He was soloing like there was no tomorrow with his hair swinging, his balls swinging and the kids just loving it."

Among those staying low in the trenches would be Tony Iommi. 1988 had been a grim year for Black Sabbath. Jo Burt too was facing bleak times. The bassist hung on though, assured that matters would be rectified. "Tony Iommi told me everything would be sorted. With no means of working, I hung on till February 1988 when summoned for an audition with new drummer Cozy Powell. We didn't gel. I got fired. They recruited Neil Murray who remains a good friend. Further attempts to get my money failed." Thus ended Jo Burt's sojourn into the world of Heavy Metal.

Early that year another candidate had a go at filling the Black Sabbath bass void. Steve Redvers had the image and could certainly deal a mean bass hand. At the time he formed up part of the then recently resurrected Starfighters, a notorious act on the Birmingham circuit. Founding members vocalist Steve 'Bertie' Burton and guitarist Stevie Young had, following two successful early eighties albums for Jive Records and extensive North American touring, recently rebuilt the band for another stab at glory. New members comprised guitarist Rick 'Rikdiculous' Sanford, bassist Steve Redvers and drummer Jamie Hawkins. Having recently demoed the band found itself in the almost unique situation of having virtually all of its musicians being absconded by name artists.

Rik Sanford was working on the side with Phil

Bill Ward fronting his solo band for a rare Los Angeles performance in July 1986. Pic: Rich Galbraith.

Mogg and Pete Way of UFO. Many of the demos laid down during Sanford's tenure later winding up on the 'High Stakes And Dangerous Men' album. Stevie Young meantime had been spirited off into AC/DC for their 'Blow Up Your Video' world tour. Not only was Stevie cousin to Angus and Malcolm but he could pass for a double of his better known rhythm guitarist relation. When Malcolm opted to sit out the tour in order to beat his alcohol problems Stevie was first on the list. Even if AC/DC had to pay for some new front teeth, lost to the baseball bat of an irate Birmingham bouncer, to make him presentable for media exposure!

Steve Redvers too hopped up a few leagues by working out with Black Sabbath in rehearsals at Rich Bitch Studios tucked into a discreet alley on Selly Oak's main street. For many years Rich Bitch Studios, an unsung creative landmark owned by Rob and Lynn Bruce, had been a familiar haunt of all the major Birmingham Rock acts. It would not be uncommon to walk into the coffee bar to be confronted by artists like Slade, Black Sabbath, Magnum, UFO as well as many well known Pop stars.

Tony Martin attests to Redvers brief stint with the band. "I think we did a few rehearsals with him, just working through some familiar stuff. At the time we were just keeping busy I think and, while he was good and a nice guy, Tony Iommi and the label were really looking for a name so that's probably why that situation didn't happen." After his Sabbs experience Redvers relocated to London to work with The Grip before joining up with the Deep Purple road crew.

Another try out on bass would be Alan Warner, known for his guitar work with The Foundations and heavy Rockers Pluto. Geoff Nicholls admits that the bass auditions, and indeed all sessions at Rich Bitch, became a bit of a blur. "I remember the guy from The Starfighters. He was good. Of course we knew Burtie because he was quite a character on the Birmingham scene from The Starfighters and The E Numbers. He even crewed for Sabbath at one point when his band wasn't working. He may well have tried out for the vocal position with Sabbath once too. I'm actually not too sure because Burtie is one of those guys who was always around. I have a mental picture of him in the rehearsal studio with us but whether he was holding a microphone or a bottle I can't remember! Lovely bloke and a great, rough edged bluesy voice but not typically Sabbath I don't think.

Tony Mills from Shy was suggested too because Rich Bitch Studios and Light And Sound Design were both involved with that band. He had a great voice I remember, big range but not as full as Tony Martin. I do remember at one stage we went through hundreds of bloody bass players. What used to really amaze us is that most of them simply couldn't get the basics right. They could do all the fancy stuff but when it came down to getting the simple rhythm of 'Heaven And Hell' right they just fell to pieces. The guys we did end up using were in a class of their own really."

Oddly, with band attending to priorities behind the scenes, the press had obviously relished their Sabbath baiting to such a degree that 'Kerrang' magazine could not resist another stab. So dull had Iommi's star dimmed in their eyes that in April a well-executed Kerrang! Magazine April Fools hoax ran with an 'exclusive' story related to plans for top Welsh crooner Tom Jones to join the band, the combination revealing their intention to record a concept album and undertake a tour based upon the dual subjects of bullfighting and Welsh coal mining. Although this concept was of course pushing surrealism right over the edge, what could not be denied that Tom Jones was in fact one of the handful of British singers with the range and power to actually handle the Sabbath catalogue!

Black Sabbath's second charity show came as a damp squib after the monumental 'Live Aid'. In Philadelphia the band had performed to 90,000 fans. At Oldbury Top Spot Club approximately 300 crammed into the working men's club on the evening of the 29th May 1988. Of those, probably a dozen at most were actual Sabbath fans, the author included. Many of the rickety tables, usually reserved for dominoes, were populated with the 'blue rinse brigade' making the average age of the crowd well into the pension bracket. Tony Martin explains that the event was ad hoc to say the least. "Tony Iommi got roped into that one somehow. I think he said 'yes' to someone then afterwards thought 'oh fuck . . .' We didn't know what we were supposed to do at all. We didn't even have a full band. We couldn't find a bass player so Geoff became our bassist. Terry Chimes played the drums. It was for the 'Children In Need' appeal which was a good cause. The problem later got to be that these charities became very fashionable and we kept being asked more and more. In the end I just said no to everything."

Black Sabbath, sporting the unique line-up of Tony Iommi, Tony Martin, Geoff Nicholls on bass and Terry Chimes on drums ran through a brief set including the only public airing to that date of 'Heart Like A Wheel'. Watching Iommi soloing away in obvious bliss it was curious to note this track had never made the regular live set. The affection for the song was apparent so why the exclusion? Tony Martin remembers the song fondly too. "'Heart Like A Wheel' was a song we always used to warmup with in sound checks. I love that song and it gave me an opportunity to pretend I was Glenn Hughes. I wish! I always wanted to be able to sing like Glenn so for us in sound checks and warmups we played it just to have a good time. When they told me we were going to do it that night I just went 'What?!!' Great song, love it. Just wish I could sing it like Glenn."

Whilst awaiting the result of negotiations between Cozy Powell and Tony Iommi in building a brand new band Tony Martin took another sojourn into the studio. The vocalist stepped into a vacancy just left, oddly enough, by Ray Gillen and found himself trying out material in the seaside holiday resort of Blackpool with Blue Murder, the new band being structured by the hotshot ex-Tygers Of Pan Tang, Thin Lizzy and Whitesnake guitarist John Sykes. When the guitarist's intentions were first unveiled many sensed a supergroup in the making. However, the process of building a band had proven arduous.

"That situation was hard to get attached to" the singer comments. "I gave it all I had got, and we achieved quite a bit. He liked my voice for sure. The evidence of that is my writing credit on the track 'Valley Of The Kings' on that first album. I have to say though that I should have received a lot more credit on other songs for that record. I did a lot more work on that than most people are aware of, stuff like vocal melodies and lyrics that stayed exactly the same on the record. All lost to history I guess. The stuff we did was really powerful. Sykes just sang my melody lines, exactly in a lot of cases."

In hindsight the debut Blue Murder album, their best selling effort, does bear many similarities with material Black Sabbath were delivering in the early nineties. 'Valley Of The Kings' in particular would have nestled nicely into the grooves of 'Headless Cross' or 'Tyr'.

Aspects of the Blue Murder project, and Sykes' personality, would not sit comfortably with the vocalist though. "He was a bit of an odd bloke I have to admit. He was obsessed with image, and in particular my hair. I was in the same room as him when he was on the phone talking to the record company man John Kalodner once and he was talking about me as if I wasn't there. He kept saying 'He hasn't got enough hair. Can we get him a transplant?' Very strange." With Martin embroiled in the Blue Murder project Tony Iommi had resolved to rebuild Black Sabbath. He was starting from the ground up after seventeen years having lost the support of the only record label he had ever known. He was Ozzy-less, Geezer-less and even contemplating the end for Black Sabbath.

Cozy Powell was involving himself in a bit of behind the scenes skullduggery too. Having first discussed the Black Sabbath project with Tony Iommi earlier in the year, he had worked with bassist Jo Burt in February of 1988, he then took himself off on tour with Gary Moore. These dates would probably be on contractual obligation to promote the record but still usefully filling the gap between his 'official' enrolment into Black Sabbath in October. He would also toy with an idea of working with Cream bassist Jack Bruce in the summer too. Was this for Black Sabbath or a completely different entity?

Geoff Nicholls describes how nebulous Sabbath had become at that point in time. "Tony and Cozy were talking which was looking very promising. Initially they discussed getting in another name singer. Both Ronnie James Dio and David Coverdale were mentioned again. Cozy was keen on David obviously but was ready to concede on Ronnie if that was on the cards. So, for quite some time, the original working idea was to get Ronnie in for 'Headless Cross'. Cozy and Ronnie didn't like each other even though they respected each other's abilities. Tony Iommi was keen on Ronnie again. Anyhow, when Cozy heard the original version of 'Black Moon' he changed his mind totally. He loved the way Tony Martin sang that track and then started to think some continuity would be a better approach. Once Cozy committed to Tony Martin he backed him 100% and there was no more talk of anyone else. Funnily enough, Ray Gillen and I had been working on an Egyptian type song for the next Sabbath album. When Tony Martin came back from Blue Murder I discovered he had used the title, 'Valley Of The Kings', for them!"

Ozzy would announce a touring line-up of Zakk Wylde, Randy Castillo and his old Black Sabbath cohort Geezer Butler on bass. The resulting world tour would be a triumph. Not only did Ozzy nick Iommi's bass man he would also (artistically speaking) nick his ex-bird too when he hooked up with Lita Ford for a monster hit single. It was plain to see who was winning this round.

As Sabbath crashed to an all time low 1988 would be the year that Ozzy Osbourne scored his biggest American hit single. What made the success of 'Close My Eyes Forever' the more remarkable though was that the track came together by happy accident, was initially resisted as a single choice by all the powers that be and to top it all was a duet with Lita Ford.

So, just how do you come up with a Billboard blockbusting ballad from two of the world's biggest Rock artists? Both Ozzy and Lita had been recently voted 'Best male Rock vocalist' and 'Best female Rock vocalist' respectively and both were managed by Sharon Osbourne. Surely the answer is obvious? The formula is not as scientific or calculated as might be expected as Lita Ford sets the scene. "It was a total accident" she confesses. "My band and I were in a North Hollywood recording studio trying to find some more songs for the 'Lita' album. We needed one or two more songs to complete the record."

The pressure of wrapping up an album was relieved in true Ozzy Osbourne style as he and Sharon arrived bringing along a new found friend. A strong but silent type with jet black hair, Ozzy's companion would make an immediate impression on Lita. "It was a life size inflatable gorilla from the San Diego zoo!" Lita howls at the memory of it. "Those things are big and this was actual size. I had just moved apartments and Sharon and Ozzy had brought me this gorilla as a housewarming gift. You should have seen this fucking thing. It was huge! So anyway, a couple of bottles of wine were opened and we started to play pool. Eventually Sharon got bored and left. At the studio there was this little room set off with guitars, keyboards and stuff so we got drunk and before we knew it we were writing a song. Ozzy has this great sense of melody, he's very inspired by The Beatles, and he's just a great singer. People often don't appreciate that about him. We carried on, completely drunk, until we had finished by that time it was daylight. We were pretty sloshed!"

The finished song, although a ballad, was far from stereotypical. "Ozzy's idea for the lyric was this vision of him standing on a mountain looking over the entire world but with his eyes closed, still able to see everything" Lita reveals. "Isn't it amazing what alcohol can do?! All I can say is that song must have been a gift from God" Sharon Osbourne was far from happy though. "Sharon was very upset with both me and Ozzy for staying out all night" Lita confides. "But hey, we had a song!"

A song was not the only thing Lita had. "I had to drive home—drunk—with a gorilla!" she laughs. "So, there I am in my black jeep with Ozzy's life size gorilla in the passenger seat with his seat belt on to keep him from falling out driving home thinking oh God please don't let me get pulled over. And, of course, I was pulled over. Even a drunk woman can do a lot by just batting her eyelids so I said "I live just over there, please let me go officer." What could he do? Ozzy Osbourne, a gorilla and Lita Ford. Who would make that up?"

The Mike Chapman produced 'Lita' album would be Ford's biggest album of her career. Kick started by the bouncy single 'Kiss Me Deadly' just missing out on a U.S. top ten slot but securing a heavy MTV rotation which brought Lita's vivacious curves to the masses. The songwriting calibre was high (Nikki Sixx had co-written 'Falling In And Out Of Love'), the guitar quota was high and even higher was the teenage male population of America's hormone levels. The album had it all and its tour de force had not even been unleashed yet.

"The radio hit on 'Close My Eyes Forever' even before anyone else" Lita admits. "Nothing was planned at all. It started to take off without any record company involvement. People everywhere were playing that song. One day the news must have finally sunk in because a guy from the record company called and said 'Lita, you're gonna have to do a video of that song'." This snowballing momentum would be questioned from an unlikely source though. "Sharon was against it at first" Lita informs. "She was very keen to promote Ozzy and I as completely separate artists. I think she thought we should leave it, not do it right now and try another track. The problem was the song kept on growing."

This opinion that Lita and Ozzy should be marketed as distinct separate entities even dictated the perception given out to the TV viewer from the promotional video. "We did it in an old train station but it looks like we are not even in the same room. That's the way it was shot. Although we were in reality together the video looks like we're not. I was on ground level and Ozzy was on this shelf type thing. We're never actually together in the video."

Divisive videos aside 'Close My Eyes Forever' duly delivered top ten on the Billboard charts and gave the Americans a refreshed look at the world of Ozzy Osbourne. The ballads had always been there, right from the Black Sabbath fave 'Changes', but clouded beneath the flotsam of decapitated doves, bats heads, tortured dwarves, tattooed werewolves and vampire fangs. Now Ozzy's more heartfelt renderings would be given more credence and acceptance opening up new markets later demonstrated by the acceptability of mainstream tracks such as 'Mama, I'm Coming Home'.

"The fans made it a hit" Lita reckons. "They wanted it and they forced it to happen, both my fans and Ozzy's fans. It wasn't the record company or anybody else just the fans."

With Lita now a platinum media darling and Ozzy sharing the same management stable a joint tour seemed inevitable. It was not to be. "I was very excited. We were riding high with a big hit single and then they put out Vixen on tour with Ozzy instead of me!" Lita says unable to hide her indignation. "Ozzy and I had this huge hit, all over radio and MTV, and they put fucking Vixen on!! Like, what's the whole idea? Don't get me wrong—I love Vixen, nothing against them as female artists—God knows we have to stick together in this game but where's the logic? I just could not see the sense. I was very, very hurt."

Lita Ford did manage just one show with Ozzy. "I did my hometown show at Long Beach Arena with Ozzy but I didn't get to see them or speak to them the entire day. I was ready to jam, I always am, but nothing happened. Strange." Ozzy and Lita would never get to sing 'Close My Eyes Together' live.

Lita Ford still has trouble reconciling those times. "Sharon was wonderful and I loved her. Ozzy was wonderful too. I mean, he was out there on occasion but he was a great, great guy and a fantastic singer too. You gotta love him. Sharon worked really hard for me, made me a platinum artist and she's one of the best people I've ever known but at the end it was a weird situation. We had the big hit but it just wasn't promoted for some reason. It would have been great for both our fans to see us do that song together live."

As Ozzy was snuggling up with Lita Ford her former fiancé set himself the task of, once more, rebuilding Black Sabbath from scratch. This time around Tony Iommi found a keen ally in Cozy Powell. This pairing would come tantalizingly close to propelling Black Sabbath back into the premier league. Cozy Powell (a.k.a. Colin Flooks) was a major name in Rock circles long before he took up the challenge of re-engineering Black Sabbath. He was a highly rated journeyman drummer, noted for his hard hitting virtuosity, onstage pyro displays and candid banter. In short, Cozy was grade A Rock star material.

Cozy Powell's CV reads like a 'Who's Who Of Rock'. Between stints for such hallowed institutions as Rainbow, the Michael Schenker Group, Emerson Lake & Powell and Whitesnake he put in a vast wealth of appearances as a session drummer on albums by the likes of Graham Bonnet ('Line-up'), Cinderella's ('Long Cold Winter') and even Robert Plant ('Pictures At Eleven'). Cozy also deservedly achieved solo

Cozy Powell.

success with various projects breaking into the UK singles charts in his own right on a number of occasions. The very fact that he had broken high into the British charts with drum compositions such as the imminently memorable 'Na Na Na Na Na' and 'Dance With The Devil' spoke volumes about his standing.

The man's career began in Cirencester with The Sorcerers sometime in 1965. Powell rounded out a band unit that comprised singer Ken Aston, keyboard player Pete Ball and bass player Roy Black. It would be this band that broke Cozy into the European touring circuit on extended jaunts onto the mainland which included gigs at USAF bases in Turkey before the drummer undertook a short diversion to Casey Jones & The Engineers in February of 1968. This union was short, lasting a matter of weeks, before Cozy returned to the familiar stomping ground of The Sorcerers in April of that year. The group opted for a new title of Young Blood, releasing a crop of singles but Cozy then decamped, his place being taken by a pre-Chicken Shack Mac Poole.

A further shift found the drummer re-establishing an alliance with his Sorcerers band colleagues brothers Dave and Denny Ball, in a new group entitled Ideal Milk. The potential displayed was enough to score the trio a valuable BBC session. This unit then added former Move star Ace Kefford to become the Ace Kefford Stand. Although this would be Cozy's first real act to push itself into the spotlight, Kefford being regarded as a bona fide Pop star, the whole edifice soon fractured. "Ace was a nice guy but ..., er. How do I say this?" the drummer prevaricated when quizzed on these early years. "OK, he was mad. You just couldn't work with him. A great shame."

Striving to force his way into the upper echelons of the Rock rankings a union with Colosseum guitarist Dave Clempson and bassist Dave Pegg did not get beyond rehearsals. Despite not bearing fruit by way of product or touring this set up did establish Cozy as a drummer of no mean standing and word of his prowess filtered down through the Hard Rock grapevine. Stints with Big Bertha, featuring the Ball siblings once more and led by the legendary Peter French of Leafhound acclaim, and high profile work with guitar legend Jeff Beck ensued. During 1970 Beck and Powell laid down a series of recording sessions, most of which have yet to see the light of day. Powell also appeared at the legendary 1970 Isle Of Wight festival backing Tony Joe White.

The drummer reacquainted himself with Big Bertha for a further round of dates in Germany before getting the call from Jeff Beck once again. This would be the transitional Soul influenced era of the guitarist's career. The band Beck had gathered up—vocalist Bob Tench, bassist Clive Chaman and keyboard player Max Middleton—would be tight but Cozy was soon hankering to Rock out once again. "I've always known that I've wanted to play Hard Rock and Heavy Metal Music" he qualifies. "To me a drum is an instrument that you need to hit as hard as possible. I have great respect for all the Jazz drummers and such like but I've got this animal aggression I can't seem to keep down. I'm just a big show off really! That was great playing with Jeff Beck in the early days, I learned a huge amount from him, but at the back of my mind I just kept thinking about putting a real Hard Rock band together which is where Bedland and Hammer came in." Cozy also enjoyed a brief spell with the masterly Californian Psychedelic Rockers Spirit in late 1972. Early 70s sessions included appearances on ex-Focus man Harvey Anderson's 1972 album 'Writer Of Songs', Ten Years After keyboard player Chick Churchill's 'You & Me', Donovan's 'Cosmic Wheels' and Murray Head's 'Nigel Lived'.

In 1973 Powell found himself a member of Bedlam alongside vocalist Frank Aiello, Dave Ball on guitar and bassist Denny Ball. The resulting album, 'Bedlam', was a marvellous display of Hard Rock that was sadly neglected. With Bedlam failing to take off Powell then participated in a brief supergroup including (once again) Colosseum guitarist Clem Clempson and bassist Greg Ridley titled Strange Brew. Endeavouring to strike out on his own terms, not to be seen as 'just a drummer', Cozy formulated a touring band, modestly titled Cozy Powell's Hammer together with keyboard player Don Airey in the mid seventies to promote his single successes. The drummer, along with Airey, was enticed into the ranks of Ritchie Blackmore's Rainbow during 1975. It would be here that Cozy Powell was launched onto the international arena, carving a huge reputation for himself in the process.

Cozy's first solo album, 'Over The Top' issued whilst still a member of Rainbow, was a collaboration with ex-Cream bassist Jack Bruce, his erstwhile Colosseum and Strange Brew colleague Clem Clempson, Whitesnake guitarist Bernie Marsden, Gary Moore and Don Airey. 1979 sessions included work with Gary Moore. He would quit Rainbow in 1980, performing his last gig at the inaugural 'Castle Donington' festival. At that momentous event Cozy Powell's departure from Blackmore's crew, a gargantuan extravaganza of fireworks and pyro, was an undoubted show stealer much to Blackmore's chagrin. He received word that Black Sabbath were interested in putting him through his paces but his next public engagement in 1981 was as a member of the much touted Michael Schenker Group. The drummer injected a good degree of credibility to that outfit and scored himself another major album for his trophy cabinet.

The parallel solo effort 'Tilt' went gold in Japan. Featured were familiar faces Moore, Marsden, Bruce and Airey along with Whitesnake bassist Neil Murray, saxophonist Mel Collins, Michael Schenker Group bassist Chris Glen, guitar maestro Jeff Beck and vocalists Elmer Gantry of Velvet Opera and Stretch alongside Bedlam's Frank Aiello. He was soon back with a major league act shortly after jettisoning from MSG by forming part of Whitesnake for two albums 'Saints n' Sinners' and 'Slide It In'. Other projects kept Powell's face in the spotlight as the drummer lent his talents to Graham Bonnet's 'Line-up', Jon Lord's 'Before I Forget' and Robert Plant's 'Pictures At Eleven'. He also appeared in Jonathon King's short-lived Metal 'supergroup' Gogmagog.

His 1983 solo album, 'Octopuss', charted only briefly although it featured contributions from Whitesnake's bassist Colin 'Bomber' Hodgkinson and guitarist Mel Galley, keyboard players Jon Lord and Don Airey alongside legendary guitarist Gary Moore on two tracks, namely 'Dartmoore' and 'Up On The Downs'. Unbeknown to the public it would be at this juncture that Cozy had declined on his second offer to join Black Sabbath.

Band activity witnessed duties with Gary Moore and the formation if the ill-fated Emerson, Lake & Powell. He also figured significantly in the 1985 'Phenomena II' concept album. Cozy would be back in the media spotlight with Forcefield a group forged with ex-Focus guitarist Jan Akkermann. During this period Powell sessioned on Danish Artist Sanne Salomonsen's 'Not Angel' album, German Metal band Warlock's 1987 'Triumph And Agony' and for Pop band Boys Don't Cry. The man was also in illustrious company featured as part of Spencer Davis Group drummer Pete York's ambitious 'Pete York Presents Super Drumming'. Powell became embroiled in the formative stages of Blue Murder before recording drum tracks for Cinderella's 'Long Cold Winter'. His last tenure before sinking his teeth into Black Sabbath was with Gary Moore, recording the 'After The War' album. This record would be of note for a myriad of Black Sabbath connections, sporting as it did Ozzy Osbourne guesting on vocals, bassists Laurence Cottle and Bob Daisley with keyboards courtesy of Don Airey. Mid tour, Cozy bailed. He would not be inactive for long.

In short, Cozy Powell had been in constant demand throughout his entire playing career and never short of offers. The full extent of the bands he might have been invited to join but had declined will probably never be revealed but is likely to be voluminous indeed. His track record though had been marred by perceptions, often false, that he was fleet of foot when it came from jumping from one high profile project to the other. Cozy wished to lay that particular misconception to rest and was actively seeking a stable, long term band in which to entrench himself. The problem was that the band he felt most kinship with was in dire straits.

"Tony did talk to me about starting up a completely new band. That's how bad it had got for him" sighed a realistic Cozy. The drummer had obviously been keeping tabs on just how much of a battering his friend Tony Iommi had been receiving over the years and, having suffered at the hands of journalists himself, keenly felt the injustices. "The whole 'Seventh Star' and 'Eternal Idol' period had really knocked the stuffing out of him. There were no other band names discussed or anything like that but Tony did say 'Shall I lay this to rest now and start something new?' We sat in his office for a good while, going through all the pros and cons of the situation. Tony had been totally stuffed by the press, the label and his manager. Other people have topped themselves for a lot less believe me. He had made some mistakes too. Some of the people he hired. All good musicians, but some of them just wrong for the band.

So yes, we did discuss knocking Sabbath on the head as a very real possibility, but the thing is, if it's a new band it's an even bigger financial risk and every interview would always ask about Black Sabbath. It's also difficult to sell to a label and there is always that thing where, no matter what the musicians really want, they'll just call it Black Sabbath anyway. Just look at 'Born Again' and 'Seventh Star'. That's exactly what happened there. Tony would never be able to shake that off. I've been there with Rainbow, Whitesnake, MSG, etc., etc., so I know. You know the question is coming.

We would also have to go out and play Black Sabbath songs because Tony's fans would demand it and then with my history they might be after Rainbow stuff or my solo singles. Then there is the no win situation with record companies and promoters. No matter what you want to call it they'll just turn around and tell you it has to be Black Sabbath because it's either that or we cut the budget and you can play clubs and pubs. So, no, let's keep it simple. Let's make Sabbath fans proud again."

Cozy, although later interviews with other band members showed otherwise, was keen to portray the new Black Sabbath as very much a solid and stable group. "The other very important thing for me was that I only agreed to come into the whole situation if it was a proper band unit. I didn't want to sit there as just the drummer. The last thing I wanted was that whole 'Eternal Idol' nonsense all over again. We needed to show some strength and stability. Tony Martin had proven himself brilliantly and I don't think Sabbath could have dared bring in yet another new singer at that point. Neil Murray was just so obvious. Geoff Nicholls has always been there, and is responsible for a lot more than people think, so that was that." Powell knew he faced an uphill battle. "It was a real spur for me to come in at that point" he said with an obvious determination. "When I got involved it was at it's lowest ebb ever, it couldn't have got any worse other than the band breaking up and I think Tony was very close to doing that."

One of the major obstacles that needed overturning was the British press. The Rock media had been pouring scorn upon every move Tony Iommi had made since Dio had packed his bags. They had hailed 'Holy Diver' as a masterpiece yet laid the boot in on 'Born Again', which had actually sold in far greater quantities, and been taking well aimed jabs at Sabbath ever since. The bully needed silencing and only a stable line-up of known faces and a world beating album could achieve that.

Speaking to the author at IRS Records in London for a 'Metal Forces' magazine interview the drummer was as frank as he could be with a tape recorder running. "They couldn't have been more slagged anymore than if the journalists were paid to slag 'em off" spat Cozy unable to hide his temper. "I saw some absolutely horrific articles from a press that had not only become hostile but malicious as well. I don't know if you can take these people seriously when you have one of the founding great British Rock bands being slagged that much. Why they got this tirade of abuse from the press I'll never know. Anyway, it gave us the incentive to prove everybody wrong and sometimes you need that spur. We worked very hard that year on material, getting it right, getting the manager sorted, the record company and then it's down to the band to deliver a great album.

You know, I really thought what the British press did was pretty awful, sheep mentality at its worst. It was like open season on Black Sabbath just because a few idiots found it funny. I don't mind criticism, I can take it. If you put something out there you expect a few knocks but they just went way over the mark. I'll take more notice when they can convince me they know what they're talking about. (Cozy named a well known UK Rock magazine here) Fuck 'em!"

With Tony Martin having made such an undeniable impact with the 'Eternal Idol' album Black Sabbath would count themselves lucky to snare the singer back into the fold. Sensing that Black Sabbath's grip on their new singer had been weakened by the drubbings from the press, lines were cast in the direction of a number of well known faces. It would be with obvious relief for both Tony Iommi and Cozy Powell to learn that Tony Martin would give Sabbath another shot.

'Headless Cross' is an important route marker on Black Sabbath's post Ozzy wanderings. With 1987 having been so harrowing financially many major labels that were interested in Black Sabbath the legend soon got goose bumps when they learned the full scale of any commitment required to pull this band out of an exceptionally deep hole. Black Sabbath had not only faced the abyss but they had fallen into it. The majors shied away but the colourful former head of the CIA, Miles Copeland, was intrigued. Miles, elder brother of The Police drummer Stewart, had recently set up IRS Records and was on the prowl for a Rock heavyweight to lend him some kudos. The proposed union held intriguing possibilities. With Copeland's standing Black Sabbath would not look to be stepping down into independent land and the prospect of a massive promotional push was alluring. IRS Records had a lot to prove and they would spend whatever it took to ram the message home.

The record itself was recorded, by Sabbath terms, fairly cheaply. With production credited to Tony Iommi and Cozy Powell the man behind the desk would be Sean Lynch, a man who would later develop the same crunch factor for Judas Priest. Laurence Cottle, a figure known for his Jazz Rock outings, commanded bass for the sessions and Tony Iommi's old pal Brian May lent his deft touch to the track 'When Death Calls'. Albeit executed on a budget on a par with Indie acts of the day it would still outshine 'Eternal Idol' on a sonic level so fans remained none the wiser. Tony Martin managed to inject a bit of local history into the album title 'Headless Cross'. The song is descriptive of the 'Black Death' plague that swept through Europe and ravaged Worcestershire, Shropshire and Staffordshire during 1349–50. Indeed various forms of plague would take their toll in the area until well into the 1640s. The lyrics are centred on the borough of Alvechurch just south of Birmingham. This village (originally 'Aelfgithecirce' in Anglo Saxon) suffered particularly at the hands of the contagion burying over half the local population in Pestilence Lane. Creative license saw the singer picking on the nearby Redditch town of Headless Cross for a suitable 'Sabbath-like' title. The town itself bears little in the way of sinister history as 'Headless' is an adoption of the local landowner Headley's title. Still, it sounded evocative enough.

"The band loved the title 'Headless Cross' when I suggested it" relates Tony Martin. "I had become very interested in the history of where I live and where I was brought up. We are surrounded by it here. The original idea came from the Birmingham M42 motorway because when they were planning where it was to go some historians brought up the subject of Alvechurch and the old mass graves there from sixteen hundred and frozen to death or whenever it was. There was a very serious concern that if they ploughed a motorway through it they might disturb these plague burials and release the bacterial spore and create a brand new plague. The bodies may well have rotted away but scientists had a theory that the virus that had killed those people might still be very much alive and of course nowadays there would be no vaccine for it at all. It was deadly serious at the time. I can just imagine some oik in the planning office having his week ruined because he had to redraw all of his plans to avoid a bloody plague pit!"

"The funny thing is that I still live in Headless Cross. What makes it worse is that I live next to a graveyard too!" says the exultant singer. "When the album came out I got slated by the locals, they were up in arms. Somehow they thought I had slurred the village although of course that was farthest from my mind." But, here's the thing. 'Headless Cross' could also be construed in a visual sense. Lopping the head off a classic crucifix leaves you with a 'T'. So is that a 'T' for Tony or a 'T' for 'Tyr'? The Norse God Tyr, so dominant on Black Sabbath's subsequent record was a stylised 'T', as made all too evident on the album sleeve. Just as Rodin left the caveat that opened the 'Gates Of Hell' for 'Headless Cross', was the 'T' sigil leading the path towards 'Tyr'? Just how deep does this go?

The album itself was put together in rapid fashion. Tony Iommi believed that the record benefited from this sense of purpose. "It was quite quick because we had fallen into the trap before of rotting in the studio. There have been times in the past when recording an album became endless and of course every day you are in there costs a lot of money. This time we made each day count. It was a fresh start and both Cozy and I were just keen to get in there and get it down. We didn't waste time trying to find a bass player either so we called Laurence up for the job. The songs came quite quickly and because we only had ourselves to fall back on for the production the responsibility was on us to get the record completed on time. It wasn't rushed in any way but I think the enthusiasm shows on this record. I'm proud of this one, there is a lot of passion gone into it which you can hear on the vocals and Cozy's drums too."

Tony Martin, the figure delegated to inject that front end passion Tony Iommi spoke of, reveals just how much effort went into these sessions to get the desired result. "The trouble with songs like 'Headless Cross' and 'When Death Calls' is that it's all very well pushing yourself like that in the studio to get those notes and hold them but live you very often just can't do it. Actually, live my vocals fail me a lot but unlike a lot of singers I can work around it. I've developed this way of dealing with things like that because the worst thing is to cancel a show. My voice has failed me both on stage and in the recording studio but I deal with it, I can go for a third or fifth either way. Hitting that perfect note, whilst I can do it, is not always guaranteed. I wish I had Glenn Hughes voice because he just seems so at ease with it.

So, a song like 'When Death Calls', that is like making a rod for my own back because then I have to do it live. Sometimes I think 'what the bloody hell did I do that for?' In the studio there were 50 bloody harmonies and live you just can't take a choir out on the road with you so that's where Geoff Nicholls box of tricks comes in. I actually wish it was a bit more like the old days when a band would spend a good degree of time on the live club rounds before recording. That way you know what's going to work and what won't. You need to get things tried and tested on the road. Generally that is why so many bands first albums are always their best. Nowadays, you do the album then rehearse the songs to see what you can do and what you can't. Then of course the fans always want the one bloody song on the album you can't do!"

These thoughts would be backed up by Tony Iommi, eager to get across his belief at the time that the industry was pushing bands too hard and too fast. "Bands should start out in the pubs and clubs like we did. Black Sabbath spent many years there and we slowly learnt our craft. When we started the fame side of things was at the very backs of our minds. All we wanted to do was make the best music we could and maybe get it onto vinyl that people could buy. Playing the clubs, learning the ropes, seems to neglected these days and I think bands are suffering for it. There are some great players out there but a lot of them seem to have lost the art of what they're doing. Technically it's great but it's all a bit cold. All of us in this band, even Tony Martin, have come up through that scene. It is the only way to get the experience you need to have a life time career in a band. I'm a bit worried that Rock bands are going for a Pop attitude towards success these days."

Although 'Headless Cross' was verbally undoubtedly populated by whole legions of demons the singer did not get to use the full scope of his vision on the album though as Cozy Powell revealed. "We've got a song on their called 'Nightwing'. It's about an owl funnily enough so I don't think the Devil crept into that one. Anyhow, Tony's guide vocal for that track were perfect. It was one of those rare moments where he just got the thing exactly right when actually he was supposed to be just really finding his way with it. He wanted to redo the vocals but we said no, leave it as it is, it's great. He argued like Hell about it but he came to like it in the end. There was some real spontaneity there which comes across."

A promotional video for the title track was shot at Battle Abbey near Hastings. It would be a gruelling ordeal according to Tony Martin's recollections. "Cold, very bloody cold" he sums up. "Cozy even had a bottle of Gordon's gin and Schweppes tonic down by his hi-hats to try and keep himself warm. I have a vivid memory of that video because it went on for ever. We started at seven in the evening and went on filming all night until seven in the morning. I kept pointing out to them that the sky was changing colour but they didn't seem to care. Consequently, when they edited the video, the sky keeps changing. The other thing was that they had these exploding crosses in the video too. They blew them up and then they started to burn. They thought it looked great but we said "Er, listen . . . stone isn't supposed to burn is it?" It was all looking a little 'Stonehenge' if you know what I mean. I think the reply was something like "This is Black Sabbath—we can do what we bloody well like!" But anyway, I still maintain that stone doesn't burn."

Hardships aside the video clip served them well. Cozy again. "That video was bloody murder to do but well worth it. It was nice to see the label come through on that because it got the song onto the TV all across Europe. They had done videos before of course but the label then just chucked them out and hoped for the best. With this one the IRS promotions people made damn sure it got played. I got quite involved in all of that side of things too."

With a solid tradition with Whitesnake and the Gary Moore band behind him Murray had spent much of the tail end of the eighties valiantly pursuing the cause of Japanese Hard Rock act Vow Wow. Always somewhat of an oddity in Europe Vow Wow, rooted back to their debut in 1975, had a lengthy history in their homeland and had racked up both considerable album sales and high status. They had also been armed with the extraordinary guitar talents of Kyoji Yamamoto and their 'Warning From Stardust' and 'Holy Expedition' outings had made a considerable dent on the import charts. However, this had been under the former title of Bow Wow, too close to comfort to Malcolm McLaren's newly constituted Bow Wow Wow Punk Popsters. A name change would also signal a concerted effort to break the band in the UK and with the departure of long-standing four stringer Kenji Sano some anglicised input was sought and found in Neil Murray.

Neil Murray explains his personal circumstances in early 1989 that eased inauguration into the Black Sabbath fold from his personal vantage point. "I was actually kind of in between things. I was with Vow Wow at the time and, not wishing to cast a bad light on them, but that band was not really going anywhere. The momentum and excitement we had built up had in fact crumbled pretty fast. The novelty factor in Britain had worn off and in actual fact the Japanese were losing interest too. I had some good times with the guys but I just couldn't see where it was going. So I had decided that Vow Wow for me was over. I had also just received my first royalty cheque from the Whitesnake '1987' album which gave me a greater degree of independence. It was time to move on."

Murray's last stand with Vow Wow was to be the creditable 'Helter Skelter' album. A great deal of pride and finance had gone into floating the Vow Wow dream but just like Loudness, Earthshaker and Ezo, all highly talented acts in their own right, the Western Rock audience simply didn't get it. Minus his services Vow Wow cut a further album 'Mountain Top', produced by Bob Ezrin and featuring American bassist Mark Gould, but echoing the British bassist's predictions the band folded shortly after. (They would ultimately retreat to the land of the rising sun, re-billing themselves Bow Wow once more where they remain active.) As Neil was contemplating his next step in his career his old mucker Cozy Powell caught him fortuitously off guard. "He rang up out of the blue" the bassist admits. "It was very simple, he was helping Tony put a new version of Black Sabbath together, they had recorded the album and did I want to get involved for the tour?"

In the interim the band auditioned a few other bassists but remained unsatisfied. Cozy got back on the blower to Neil again and persuaded his old comrade in arms it was worth a shot. To an outsider the reunion of the famous Whitesnake rhythm machine would seem a done deal but not quite as Neil relates. "I certainly had to audition. Yes, Cozy and I had always clicked. We knew each other's mindset when it comes to playing and we got on professionally and as friends very well but Tony had no experience of me whatsoever. I was told that Laurence, who had done the album, was more a kind of Jazz Fusion player and not interested in touring with Black Sabbath at all. Tony Iommi had never listened to me play with Whitesnake though. He had no particular reason to."

Some of the British press, hungry for the slightest morsel of gossip, thought they smelt a rat. "I had got myself quite a name for attending parties and clubs in London" laughs Murray. "I was forever being photographed 'ligging' with a drink in my hand. I had attended a launch party for the 'Headless Cross' album too. A journalist or two, spotting me hanging around asked me if I had joined Black Sabbath to which I truthfully answered 'no'. It was shortly after I was asked by Cozy so of course when it was announced that I was to join the band it made me look like I had been lying through my teeth. It was just coincidence."

Cozy Powell elaborated on the choice of Neil Murray for the job. "Neil was a pretty obvious choice, along with Geezer and Bob Daisley I suppose. Out of the available candidates those three guys are always your first choice and Neil and I are a proven team. Tony didn't know too much about him other than who he was. The big plus was that we had worked together in Whitesnake so we had already built up a rhythm rapport. Sometimes you can get the greatest drummer and the greatest bass player together but they just don't click so it's not always about getting hold of the star of the moment. Bass is very underrated in a band, almost like the backroom boy but it's the furthest from the truth. I can afford to be a bit flashy on the drums, as I have been known to on occasion, but bass binds the whole thing together. It's like the glue. Neil's good at that. He has his Blues foundation and his Jazz down to a tee too but he's solid. That's what you need.

It's difficult to put your finger on but you either click or you don't. You don't want to end up on the road stuck with a miserable bastard. People are people, for better or worse, and if I'm going to smell somebody's grotty socks for twelve months and get to learn all their disgusting personal habits I want to know I'm going to get on with them. You can audition some great bassists, really superb players but if it doesn't click then it ain't gonna work. You just know. A rhythm section has to become almost one person onstage and Neil and I had done more than enough work with each to reach that stage. The other thing was of course that he had a good name, which always helps. I like playing with Neil."

Murray, although not finding himself in such an alien environment as Jo Burt had earlier, would nevertheless take some time to get to grips with the desired 'Sabbath' bass sound. "We started rehearsals at Rich Bitch Studios and through the Sabbath contacts I got sorted out with an endorsement through Peavey" he records. "The Peavey gear was great I have to say but, and it was a very big but, it was a bit too good in some ways. It sounded 'new' and what I was after was something that sounded buggered. It took a long time for me to get that meaty, distorted sound that is right for Sabbath. Throughout the whole 'Headless Cross' tour I certainly didn't have the sound right. It was always work in progress. There was always lots of extra bits of equipment being brought in. In the seventies Geezer had defined the Black Sabbath bass sound which was nasty, distorted, loud and very full sounding. On 'Headless Cross' Laurence had recorded the bass much tighter, much cleaner. In truth it was a bit of a bugger.

The start of 'When Death Calls' I ended up making my own personal crusade. It's made up of very high hammers, quite complicated. Of course that was great for Laurence to do that in the studio but doing it live could have proven a complete nightmare because the intro is a totally opposite set up to the rest of the song. By the time we got to the 'Forbidden' tour much later on I conquered that by having two basses. I had a bass set up on a solo stand for the intro and my regular bass strapped on my back which I would whip round for the rest of the track. I noticed when Geezer came back he didn't even try and replicate the bass intro to 'When Death Calls'. He just used a sample! Bassists actually have it a lot harder than you would imagine. On a guitar you can distort by turning up the volume control to get it sounding distorted, compressed and squashed. On the bass that's very difficult to get that dirtier sound. It's a bit of a balancing act."

The bassist's commitment to getting 'When Death Calls' just right would not pass Tony Martin by either. "Neil put an enormous amount of work into getting that just right. He became very dedicated to it and he did get it right, exactly, night after night. It was a big thing for him and we all actually became quite

Black Sabbath 1989. Tony Iommi, Cozy Powell, Tony Martin and Neil Murray.

proud of him for achieving that. It was quite an achievement."

Cozy Powell harks back to the excitement felt by the band before the world tour. "We were really pumped up and eager to prove to the world that Sabbath was back. I know it was a big thing for Tony Iommi too because at last he had a solid band he could rely on and be proud of. This time around he wasn't wasting time explaining who everybody was. Before he had been answering too many questions like 'who's in your band this week?' and all that nonsense. We could actually get on with it for a change."

Just why 'Headless Cross' did so well in Germany might be attributed to the strengths lent by the Cozy Powell and Neil Murray pedigree and the fact that mainland Europe had, in the whole, been fairly immune to the stinging criticisms poured down upon 'Eternal Idol' in the UK. Also, Germany has, and probably always will be, a uniquely Rock orientated community and welcomes both new and established acts. Hard Rock and Heavy Metal in Germany is sustained by an enthusiastic media, a series of major summer festivals and a refreshing appreciation of talent over hype. Many mature Rock artists count on Germany as a financial lifeline. KK Downing, founder member of Judas Priest, once illustrated Germany's importance on the global market to the major players in the Metal field. "Germany is just so consistent once you've cracked it. If you make good records you can sell a lot of albums there, a lot more than the UK, and you can put on big tours. It doesn't seem to matter if your popularity goes up or down in America. Germany just seems to be great all the time. You only have to take a look at the audiences. They are obviously totally into it in a big way. Every time I get a royalty statement I can guarantee German sales always bring a big smile to my face!"

Miles Copeland, basking in the acquisition of such a household name, was keen to make it known to the world that Black Sabbath was a force to be reckoned with. The video for 'Headless Cross', complete with burning stone, had garnered healthy television rotation and the IRS Records promotion team had gone into overdrive putting the band through an intensive interview schedule to push the record. This was like candy to a baby for Cozy who revelled in the media environment.

"Cozy loved all of that" affirms Neil Murray. "He loved speaking to journalists and had a great rapport with them. A lot of his acquaintances had been in that game for a long time. Tony Iommi was not good at interviews because he was so reserved, Tony Martin too a bit I suppose, just liked to keep himself to himself. Both are hardly extroverts and not really keen on playing the media game. Cozy put an enormous amount of work into promoting 'Headless Cross' because he knew that Black Sabbath needed to have the press on their side this time. He really pushed IRS Records to get every opportunity possible. Cozy always gave a good interview."

In America though an about face in fortune saw the band floundering in some dismally attended venues throughout June of 1989. Support acts came in the shape of Kingdom Come and Silent Rage. It was a major let down and, reluctantly, the tour was pruned back sharply. "The American tour was a complete joke" Cozy said in obvious disgust. "The promotion of the tour was badly handled. There were ludicrous attempts at trying to advertise the shows at the very last minute. The shows we did were really good but it was obvious it wouldn't have been worth carrying on through the Midwest. The bloody awful support band we had, Kingdom Come, were no good at all for either ticket sales or as a band. Mercifully for everybody they broke up right after that. America was well tough last year for a lot of bands. We weren't the only ones to suffer."

Neil Murray records that the band only got a mere 8 gigs into their stride before pulling the plug. The blame, he believed, was not only to be laid at the doorsteps of the promoters. "The American shows were scheduled originally for six weeks I think but we ended up doing just a bit of the East Coast and got into Canada. We had to stop, there simply was no point in continuing into the Midwest as planned because it would have been financially disastrous. Yes, there was a lack of promotion and it was a case of people simply not knowing the band was playing which was very frustrating. There was something else too though. At the time there was apparently a lot of bad feeling between Sharon Osbourne and Black Sabbath. We certainly heard stories about people being paid to rip our posters down and promoters receiving telephone calls advising them we were not going to show up for the gig or that we had let other promoters down by not showing up. Lots of underhand stuff like that that. I just didn't understand why they were so concerned about us. Whether it was all true or just our paranoia I don't know but it was a genuine concern. I didn't understand it because Black Sabbath was of no threat to Ozzy. We were much father down on the ladder of success at that point."

Neil is harmonious with Cozy's thoughts regarding the support act too. "Well, it was a straight forward Led Zeppelin rip off wasn't it? The drummer was excellent, I do remember that. James Kottak did an impressive job and it is good to see he has gone onto better things. As a Hard Rock band they were OK I suppose but they didn't put bums on seats and they were obviously trying very hard to be Zeppelin. A bit of a waste of time really and not very compatible with Sabbath." Murray finishes philosophically "America just didn't get the message. It was a deflating experience but we more than made up for it later with the UK, Europe, Japan and Russia. The tour just got better and better so the USA disaster was quickly forgotten."

With 'Headless Cross' far exceeding sales expectations in Germany the band's European tour was conducted with a renewed flush of success. The German melodic Rock outfit Axxis supported in the UK during August, Black Sabbath kicking off their British dates at the Aston Villa Leisure Centre. Not a regular name on the touring circuit bands had come to use the Leisure Centre because Birmingham's central old warhorse, the Odeon, had been closed to bands the year before. The premier National Exhibition Centre venue, at the time, only catered for bands that could really guarantee an audience into five figures. Judas Priest had earlier tried to squeeze a major production into the Powerhouse club for their 'Ram It Down' hometown gig but, like Sabbath, would subsequently opt for the Leisure Centre next time around. Although out of the City Centre the venue must have proven like a home from home for the Aston raised Tony Iommi.

More traditional stamping grounds such as Liverpool's Royal Court, Sheffield's City Hall, Newcastle City Hall, Edinburgh Playhouse, Manchester's Apollo and Leicester's De Montfort Hall all boasted a respectable turn out and led up to a double barrelled brace of dates at London's Hammersmith Odeon. By scheduling two Hammersmith dates Black Sabbath were giving a display of optimism that would serve them well. On the last of these shows, the 10th of September, Brian May strolled on for the encores to an ecstatic crowd response. Axxis would remain as special guests throughout the Scandinavian and European leg, commencing at Stockholm's Solnahallen venue. The following night in the Danish capitol of Copenhagen Ian Gillan showed plenty of water had flowed under his particular bridge by gracing the stage for an encore of 'Smoke On The Water'. Needless to say, the bootleggers had a field day.

With virtually every Sabbath concert a target for eager tape traders Neil Murray is surprised that many prized moments passed the bootleggers by. "Tony Iommi loves to jam. That's one thing I soon discovered. We spent countless hours just jamming away at sound checks before a gig, playing all kinds of things just for the sheer enjoyment of it, improvising on songs, playing the Blues. It was our way of unwinding. I'm quite amazed that the bootleggers don't seem to have got much of that stuff."

Tony Iommi, Stockholm 1989. Pic: Michael Eriksson.

Germany was given priority treatment with a rash of gigs across the whole country before the band delved into Hungary, Yugoslavia and Italy. Also doing the rounds in Europe would be the Gary Moore band, complete with erstwhile Black Sabbath bassist Bob Daisley. "I remember meeting the guys from Sabbath in a bar in Germany" he records. "I was on tour with Gary Moore and we ended up in the same hotel. Cozy was there too, and he had not long worked with both I and Gary. Now, Gary and Cozy did not exactly see eye to eye. Gary prefers the exact same drum sound onstage as is on the album, no deviation whatsoever. This was difficult for Cozy because he would tend to drift a bit, he'd speed up and then he would pull it back down. Timekeeping was a big thing for him.

Anyhow, Gary had his ideas and Cozy had his ideas—problem was that it was Gary's band. About one week into the tour we did with Cozy I had phoned Gary and said 'Look, I really don't think this is going to work. Cozy is all over the place'. Gary said 'No, he's fine. It'll sort itself out'. By the second week we were still having the same problem. On the third week Gary phoned me! He said 'What are we going to do about this?' So, he had decided Cozy wasn't the man. Chris Slade came in and he was perfect, absolutely brilliant. We postponed a few gigs, rehearsed with Chris then got straight back on the road. Of course, in the meantime Cozy had joined Black Sabbath.

So, this was still fresh in the memory when Chris Slade and I walked into this bar. Tony Martin said to me 'Thanks for the lyrics on the album' which I thought was kind, especially as so many of them got changed afterward. The funny thing was that Cozy said 'Is Gary in the hotel?' 'Yeah' I said. I told him the room number and said he should go and say hello. Well, he went off to see Gary but before he had left the bar I said 'Oh, Cozy. When you knock on his door—don't speed up!'"

Regrettably a trip to Mexico for what was to be the band's inaugural live performances in that country disintegrated into comic book farce. "The dates got pulled for what we would call 'technical and logistics problems' but it was a little more involved than that" relays Murray. "I think the gig originally was planned to be in Guadalajara. When we arrived we stopped one night in a hotel in Mexico City. Just before the show, even on the day it was supposed to happen I think, we got told it had all been changed and that the gig was now somewhere else entirely. So, of course, the band starts to look at each other, thinking 'here we go ....' We should have known what was coming." The planned Guadalajara concert was transferred to Leon only to be moved almost immediately to San Luis Potosi and scheduled for the 28th of October.

"Anyhow, they flew us up into Northern Mexico and from that point it turned into a complete shambles. We soon discovered that the local authorities, the mayor and the Catholic church, had been trying to get the gig stopped claiming we were going to be conducting black masses, that we were practising Satanists and all that kind of crap so the omens weren't too good. Half the population thought we were instruments of the Devil whilst the other half were just fanatical about the gig. Because we knew it was all a bit fishy we sent the crew out to have a look at the venue for us. What we were told was a soccer stadium turned out to be a shabby playing field! The crew came back with their report which basically told us there was no security, no real equipment and in their opinion the gig simply wasn't happening. The whole thing felt as if it had been thrown together at the last minute so we made the decision not to play. It was just too risky. The problem became much worse than that though because our decision not to play had leaked to all the local fans waiting for us to play. We quite literally had to hightail it out of there with this mob coming down the street after us! They would have torn us apart if they had got their hands on us. We just about lost our pursuers by zooming off to the airport and just managed to get away."

Although physically out of harms way from an irate population Mexico itself would retain its grip on the individual band members for quite some afterwards though. Unfortunately that grip would be on Black Sabbath's bowels. "Yes, Mexico had its revenge that's for sure!" groans Murray at the memory. "Everybody in the band was struck by a vicious Montezuma's revenge so it was memorable if even for that. My condition got so bad I had to go to the doctor. If you wanted to find a member of Black Sabbath to talk to that week you were out of luck. We would have all been on the toilet! I can also tell you this. Despite our ailments there was a cruelly funny side to it because ..., well, we'll keep him nameless, but a certain member of the band had picked up a waitress at the Los Angeles Rainbow Bar & Grill and had taken her down to Mexico for the obvious reasons. They hardly knew each other but what was obviously planned as a bit of quick romance ended up with them both being in the loo all the time. I don't think she was too impressed!"

Not often given much consideration by the public, the perils of local water has in fact tarnished the glamour on many a world tour. "That is true" agrees the bassist. "When you are on a world tour you would be wise to heed the old advice of 'don't drink the water'. It's great playing all these exotic places but there can be a price to pay. Some countries are grottier than others. Places like Japan and Singapore are fine but I was very cautious in Russia later on with Black Sabbath I remember. With Whitesnake at the 'Rock in Rio' festival in 1985 it got the entire band too. We were all struck down with exactly the same thing. It was quite literally squirting out of both ends! The paying public don't see that side of things of course. Sometimes it's hard to maintain your dignity and put on the Heavy Metal hero act onstage when all you can think about is rushing to the loo!"

On August 12 and 13th of 1989, Ozzy played the Moscow Music Peace Festival. This gargantuan display of perestroika featured heavyweight acts such as Bon Jovi, the Scorpions and Mötley Crüe. The other bands were basically small club bands but of course Ozzy was a worldwide name and the crowd just went crazy when it was his turn to play. By coincidence Black Sabbath too would make a keen impression on Mother Russia that same year. By October the strong upward curve for Black Sabbath had been re-established as they made a welcome return to Japan, limbering up before the undoubted highlight of the world tour.

Mikhail Gorbachev's 'Glasnost' had opened the former Soviet union up to western artists for the first time. Artists such as Black Sabbath, Uriah Heep and the Scorpions all took advantage, aware that their popularity on the open black market had pushed album sales in the country into the many millions. Supported by Girlschool the band performed at the gigantic Moscow Olympic Hall before moving onto the Leningrad (later St. Petersburg) EKS Hall. All told Black Sabbath's Russian sojourn lasted little under a whole month, effectively becoming 'house band' at both venues performing back to back matinee and evening performances.

"Russia was an eye opener that's for sure" records Neil Murray. "It really was a big deal for them to get Black Sabbath. To the Russian public Black Sabbath was something almost mythical and I expect that no one there really expected to see a band like us in their lifetime. The interesting thing was that, although they obviously knew we were Black Sabbath, their knowledge of the band was pretty minimal. I am pretty sure that an awful lot of the people that came to shows thought that Tony was Ozzy and I was Geezer.

We did 10 gigs at a huge Moscow indoor sports arena, then more in St. Petersburg. Although it was a slightly smaller venue we were still playing to 15,000 people at each show there, two times a day. The intention was to record the gigs for a live album, just because it was such a huge event and the opportunity of playing so many gigs one after the other is rare. The problem was, although we recorded a lot of shows the Russian security prevented our people from getting the tapes!

The whole scenario was very surreal. Moscow in particular. The officials and dignitaries had got claim on all the good seats right in front of the stage and that's all we could see from the stage. The thing was, behind these stuffy officials the hall floor was empty. However, the real fans were stuffed right at the sides and the back of the arena, away in the distance, which was most bizarre. When we finished each song these sour faced officials would give us a reluctant clap but we could also hear this huge, and I mean huge, roar coming from the darkness of the back of the hall."

Tony Martin echoes these memories and, in typical fashion, has a bizarre personal recollection that at the time stopped him in his tracks. "Neil is right about the Moscow crowd" he confirms. "There was also the mass of people with guns there to keep an eagle eye on the crowd. They were not allowed to jump about or anything even vaguely 'Western' in behaviour. I mean, they even had water cannons manned. What I noticed about all the officials at the front was they had brought their extended families along. So there would be the kids picking their noses, aunties, uncles, grandads and grannies. At one gig, and I swear this is true, this old granny just sat their knitting while we were blasting out 'Iron Man'! I couldn't believe it. I said to the other guys 'Look, she's fucking knitting!' I could hardly sing for laughing. Stitching in time to 'Iron Man'. A world first."

"In St. Petersburg it was the exact opposite" maintains Neil. "The crowd were totally nuts, so nuts it got very dangerous in fact. They chucked everything but the kitchen sink at us onstage—crosses, sparklers, all sorts. It got so bad we had to keep stopping the show because we were bloody scared. It was like playing to a Greek or Italian crowd, very Latin in temperament. Although they were crazy they really appreciated us being there so it was a pleasure to play for them and we got really fired up from the adrenaline of it, a mixture of being terrified and pumped up. I don't know if they were actually listening to what we were playing. We could have played anything I think and they would have been happy just to see us." The warmth of the reception in Russia would be tempered by the extremes of the Russian Winter. "Why on earth we had to play in November and December is beyond me" Murray laughed. "I have never been so cold in all of my life. It was simply unbelievable how cold it got. After a while the whole experience lost its appeal and it just got incredibly boring I have to say. There wasn't a lot of fun to be had in Moscow either."

The intensive schedule also took its toll. "Matinee shows are tough" moans Martin. "They are tough on your spirit and on your voice. In Moscow the whole thing was so regimented. They would shove 40,000 people in, push them out and get the next 40,000 in. Day after day after day the same. Very militarised. The other thing was that it was so mind numbingly cold outside at minus 40 degrees, yet inside it was stiflingly hot, like a sauna. The heating was on full, all the time. We just could not get used to that. It actually really fucked my voice up, switching from one extreme to the other. You would get to the hotel and ask for a beer and it would be warm. You asked for a cold beer and they would say 'Impossible'. We said 'Just stick the bottle outside for 30 seconds'. 'Impossible' they would say. The band had a lot of stuff like that to put up with. We got out just the once into Red Square to sign some autographs. All the while with our escort keeping an eagle eye on us."

Tony Martin came to see the Russian shows as pivotal in his internal relationship with the band. "I think in Russia I finally felt I was coming into my own and that I really deserved to be there. I can remember being onstage, looking at Tony, Neil and Cozy and thinking 'My God, these are the very best players in the business and here I am singing for this band!' You can never tell when a moment like

Tony Martin, Stockholm 1989. Pic: Michael Eriksson.

that will strike because you are so preoccupied with getting on with the job in hand. It took a long time to get there in my own mind, probably because of the sheer hard work involved from the very first day I joined the band. In Moscow though it struck me—my God! This is Black Sabbath I'm singing for!"

Cozy Powell summed up his Russian experience in a more concise manner. "Wonderful people, amazing architecture but after a couple of weeks you can understand why they all look so bloody miserable on the TV. Not very Rock n' Roll but it was a once in a lifetime thrill. We should have done a live album there. It was the perfect opportunity. Don't know what happened to that because we really should have done it. The last live Sabbath album wasn't exactly amazing and here we were in about an ideal situation as you could get for a live recording. The band was tight as it was ever going to get, playing those songs twice a day, the audiences from the last shows would have sounded incredible. Russia should have been a live album." Fortunately at least some tapes from the Russian gigs would be rescued with two tracks, 'Heaven And Hell' and 'Paranoid', appearing on later B-sides.

Putting the missed opportunity of a live album to one side all in all the 'Headless Cross' tour had put Black Sabbath back on the map as a viable contender.

Acknowledging the progress made Neil Murray adds a practical note to the illustrate his predicament during these dates. "The world tour was wonderful really in terms of the places we got to see and the fact that the band had begun to cross back into major league where we all wanted to see it. Both Tony Iommi and Cozy were overall very happy. America was a disappointment but everywhere else had been very, very positive and we felt that America could be fixed next time around. The record had not been promoted well in America, unlike Europe, and the promotion for the tour was a sad joke really. Other than that the band did the business pretty much everywhere we went which was very gratifying. The trouble with the tour was that there were too many gaps along the way. Practically this meant two things for me—sitting around doing nothing and, most painful of all, not getting paid. I received a fee for my work on the road but in between I was left to my own devices but, of course, I had to wait around for the next leg which put me out of contention for other paying projects. It's par for the course in this game I'm afraid."

'Headless Cross' was akin to an unheralded renaissance for the band. Almost a silent revolution, if such a description could be used in context with such a loud piece of work. Reviews had been commendable, the line-up had truly gelled for once and hard sales had been rewarding. Indeed, 'Headless Cross' had given Black Sabbath their highest chart position in the Heavy Metal heartland of Germany for many, many years. "Everyone in America kept going on about the old band all the time but the 'Headless Cross' record was huge in Europe" remonstrates Geoff Nicholls. "The band was bigger there than at any time with Ozzy. Same went for Japan too, Black Sabbath was bigger than ever. For the first time it felt as though the band was being given a fair crack of the whip, being judged on the content for a change."

Not all the pieces of the puzzle were in place though as Cozy Powell explained. "The 'Headless Cross' album had done very good business overall but it seemed as though nobody seemed to know about it here" he mused at the time. "Put it this way—the accountants were happy because a big black hole suddenly had something going back into it. It was a big success in Europe particularly. OK, we had problems in America but still the general feeling was a good one. I can't remember seeing a bad review for the album either which, compared to 'Eternal Idol', was a big change this time around.

New label, new band, new album so it was a big challenge for us and one I thought, we all thought, we had come out of with flying colours. Sabbath was a dead duck before 'Headless Cross' but the new band proved a point. Everything we told the press and the Black Sabbath fans came true. Once we had finished touring the album we had a bloody big pile of albums sold which is, after all, what it's all about. Nobody in England seemed bothered though. It was just ... weird."

'Headless Cross' had crossed one of those boundaries that truly successful records need to break to achieve some longevity. Simply put, the album was developing a buzz with Rock fans recommending it to each other. Something 'Eternal Idol' fell short of. Cozy Powell agreed. "Some albums reach that stage and then you begin to see it reflected in royalty statements year after year. It sold a lot initially, which we know, and the acid test is to see if it keeps on selling. Word of mouth is so important. If an album is good it will keep bubbling along for years and years after it first came out. The CD revolution proved that. People had to replace all their old vinyl with CDs but of course they then had to make the decision of which albums to replace. Now, you're only going to replace the good ones aren't you? Musically the advent of CDs was great because it forced people to make decisions about music in their own homes without being swayed by advertising, hype or hairspray. It all boiled down to whether it was a good album or not. Of course what the labels discovered was that they were selling a lot of Rock music again. CD buyers didn't want the Pop stuff—they wanted Rock. Look at all the seventies Sabbath albums. They keep getting rereleased and they keep selling. Hopefully 'Headless Cross' will join them. To be honest, record sales in the UK weren't that clever but in Europe we had phenomenal sales, especially in Germany. Our sales in Germany exceeded everyone's expectations. I think for the UK we were still suffering from the bad press. Everywhere else the record did great."

Chapter 19

A Last Tyr Goodbye

As 1990 was ushered in, Ozzy found himself once again in need of a bass player. Called in for auditions would be Portland, Oregon native Todd Jensen. The four-stringer had made his mark with a series of local bands, such as Sequel, Harlow and Movie Star, but had come to the fore with Neal Schon's Hardline. It would turn out to be a week to remember for Jensen.

"If you can believe this, I had auditions for both David Lee Roth and Ozzy Osbourne in the same week. You can imagine how pumped up I was. I had auditioned for Dave a few days before seeing the Ozzy guys and that had gone very well for me. It was a set of musicians I really wanted to play with. Then I went to North Hollywood to audition for Ozzy.

There were a bunch of bass players coming in and out but I do remember Mike Inez being there. I think he was in just before me. Zakk Wylde and Randy Castillo were the guys doing the work. We played a few tunes, I remember 'Crazy Train' and 'Over The Mountain'. I thought it went great. It was very relaxed and we sat down and chatted for a good while afterward. I was confident.

The day after that, the David Lee Roth camp called and said the job is yours if you want it. Dave thinks you're the man. I really had made my mind up because of the musicians involved. I knew the band was going to be Joe Holmes on guitar, Brett Tuggle on keyboards and Greg Bissonette on the drums, so I said 'yes' with no hesitation. Then a few days later, Tony, Ozzy's assistant called me to say congratulations, you've made the short-list and we'd like you to come down again. Of course, I had to tell him I had taken the job with Dave!

So, I did that whole lap around the world with Dave and the irony was I was playing with Joe Holmes, who later replaced Zakk. Great, great guitarist so I could see why Ozzy wanted him."

Back in the Black Sabbath camp, and eager to cement the now proven Iommi / Martin / Murray / Nicholls / Powell line-up, the management and label soon had the group back into the studio. The resulting 'Tyr' album acted as a foil to 'Headless Cross' in much the same manner as 'Mob Rules' had serviced 'Heaven And Hell'. At last Tony Iommi must have been hopeful of some much need stability and a line-up with potential longevity.

Evident with 'Tyr' was the shift in lyrical values, not just to the Norse mini-conceptual segment of the record, but in its entirety. 'Headless Cross' bore one flaw only but it was a major one. The quota of verbalised 'Devils' and 'Satans' was to outweigh the musical and vocal merits to a degree. Cozy Powell had recognised this too and, whilst praising Tony Martin, also observed that changes had made been made. "What's a Black Sabbath album without the Devil? OK, 'Headless Cross' had too many, that we'll admit. There are a few tracks on there not about ol' Nick though but nobody complained in the early days did they? Maybe it's more noticeable now because the music is so much more refined than what it used to be. This is a completely different band after all. We did recognise it, which is partly the reason for the Norse mythology theme on this record. We wanted to get away from the death, ghouls and devils angle. I think we did more than enough of that on the last album.

He (Tony Martin) was obviously very naive when he joined Sabbath, even before I was involved. He was coming into an area of music, which he wasn't particularly familiar with having done a lot of commercial projects before. Coming in to sing for a band like Sabbath is not easy. I mean, you have to follow in the footsteps of Ozzy, Dio and Gillan, three real big names and I know he took it on real well. In fact I love the way he sings the old stuff. It's nice that he is able to assert his identity on the band. I think he's really developing fast as one of the contender singers. You've got people like Ozzy who are great characters and frontmen. You've got people like Lou Gramm and Joe Lynn Turner who are singers in their own right and Tony is coming out as a truly great singer. I've worked with some great singers like Ronnie James Dio, Graham Bonnet and Robert Plant, and they are all good, but Tony Martin has got that own little distinctive edge on his voice. It's nice that he's come to the fore."

Neil Murray would, in hindsight, be critical of the 'Tyr' album. "I think it served the people who had got into 'Headless Cross' very well" he surmises. "At the time we thought it was very strong. There are some excellent songs on there. Possibly, because of the adverse reaction to the lyrics on 'Headless Cross', the Viking thing was overdone a bit. There was nothing really about Satan or Black Masses. Tony Martin did a spectacular job on the vocals and the record had a good mix of material from the very heavy, to the epic, to the commercial."

Indeed, the pendulum swung so far in the opposite direction that the 'Devil' quota on 'Tyr' came tumbling down to zero. Tony Martin did manage to squeeze in a mention of Lucifer on closing track 'Heaven In Black' although that track's subject matter was historically based and prompted by their earlier Russian trip. "That song is about the builders of St. Basil's cathedral in Moscow's Red Square" describes the vocalist. "The story goes that after they had the thing built they asked them if they could build another, to which they replied 'yes'. So they blinded them. They dragged them back a few years later and asked him the same question. Again they gave the answer 'yes' so they were killed."

The spectacular cathedral of St. Basil the Blessed is such an icon that it is very often mistaken for the Kremlin. Built in 1552 by the architects Postnik and Barma the edifice was constructed at the orders of Czar Ivan IV, 'Ivan the terrible', to celebrate the Russian victory of the Mongols. "That song 'Heaven In Black' a good example of us consciously getting away from the whole Devil thing. We had a very commercial radio track on there, 'Feels Good To Me', the Norse trilogy and 'The Sabbath Stones' which is actually about the ten commandments. We just felt our audience had matured along with us at that point and we had some more interesting stories to tell too."

'The Sabbath Stones' was worked up from an idea tagged 'Lunchbox' by Cozy and Geoff "Because it was so meaty!" It also spent some time in the studio entitled 'Fire And Water' prior to Tony Martin completing his biblical narrative.

It is worth taking a note of just how Black Sabbath crafted those songs. As expected, everything started with the Riffmeister Pursuivant. "Tony Iommi always started everything off with a riff" Tony Martin exemplifies. "That would nearly always be building block number one. Sometimes Geoff Nicholls came up with some melodies and chord patterns and Tony would plonk his riff down on top of that. It would be a problem sometimes deciding which riffs to pick because there were just so many of them. There must be hundreds of tapes of classic riffs we never

Neil Murray and Cozy Powell working the desk.

had the chance to develop up into a song. Anyhow, once I had the riff it would be given to me to chop and change around, start getting the basic building blocks into a song, to make it work. I would always try and come up with three completely separate versions, present them to the band and say 'Take your pick'. One would be chosen then to complete. Sometimes we would work out the demos without Tony Iommi being there. I would put the guide guitar down and Neil and Cozy would do their thing. Geoff used to contribute a lot here too as he has a great ear for melody." One such track that did not make the album would be 'Wings Of Thunder'. It was demoed up, with Tony Martin on guitar, but never worked on for subsequent product.

Neil Murray, precious regarding his particular contribution to the album, was a tad deflated with the final result. "Personally, I was never happy with the bass sound. It simply wasn't loud enough and Sabbath has always had a tradition of loud bass on its albums. Geezer insisted on it and it is part of the trademark Sabbath sound. I didn't understand that as it is simply a case of pushing up one fader in the studio. The drums were always loud because of Cozy's involvement of course but some more bottom end wouldn't have hurt it. Possibly 'Tyr' was a little too polished, a bit too 'epic' like."

What 'Tyr' had undoubtedly achieved was the affirmation that the Black Sabbath line-up 'most likely' had passed that vital second album marker. Although 'Headless Cross' had not been recorded by Murray most viewed his association with its promotion as adequate in making it 'his' record. 'Tyr', just like 'Mob Rules' a decade previous, signalled a statement of much needed solidity. 'Headless Cross' and 'Tyr' can, and often are, viewed together in much the same way as the original Dio era studio records. There is a significant set of Sabbath fans that proclaim the pair to be amongst the very best from any band that bore the Black Sabbath name.

The actual identity of the album was, throughout the recording process, far from a foregone conclusion. In fact the band had given the record a working title of 'Anno Mundi' whilst laying down the tracks but this notion fell out of favour. "It all looked very well planned didn't it?" Tony Martin says mischievously. "The truth was that we were totally bloody desperate for a name for the album. It got down to the wire, the very last day on which we had to decide. It could have easily ended up as one of the song titles. 'Heaven In Black' for example, which have then given us a Russian theme. Phil Banfield came up with 'Tyr' and the whole Nordic thing. All the album visuals followed after that."

The 'Tyr' world tour got rolling in the hometown West Midlands gig of Wolverhampton Civic Hall on 1st September 1990, the venue having taken over from the now defunct Birmingham Odeon for acts of major status. Black Sabbath would be ably supported on this trek by the American biker Rock Circus Of Power. The tour, when first scheduled, had the band roaming further a field into the outer reaches of the UK with gigs in Wales, Carlisle and three shows in Scotland but unfortunately the last week of dates would be pulled. This must have been a personal setback for Cozy Powell who had pushed the promoters for a lengthier set of British dates as he outlined just before the tour.

"I said to the agency that the amount of shows we did last time wasn't enough" he motioned. "We need to reach more people in this country. I don't think a lot of kids can afford to come down to Hammersmith and it applies to other outlying areas." Unfortunately the drummer's particular preferences would be the very gigs that ended up being pulled. "For example, kids in Carlisle have generally got to get to Newcastle or come down to Manchester and it's a long way. I think it's important to take the show to a wider audience. We're trying to play as many venues as we can. We're doing eighteen dates in the UK and twice as many gigs in Europe as we did last time. This has all been generated from the success of the 'Headless Cross' album and it means we are going to be playing for a solid eight months in Britain, Europe, Scandinavia, Russia, Japan, Australia and America." Sadly that eight months that Cozy was looking forward to would be optimistic. The cancellation of British shows would only be the first of many.

"I don't know what they told the press" wonders Neil Murray. "The fact of the matter was the band simply wasn't selling enough tickets so rather than waste more money on trucking and everything else they pulled the tour. The furthest we got in the UK was Leeds. Shame, I like playing Scotland but it was not to be. I remember Tony Iommi getting particularly despondent at this time. Pulling a UK tour was quite a humbling experience I imagine. He did tell me he felt like he was knocking his head against a wall. It did pick up a lot as soon as we got to Europe though but that just illustrated the intense frustration. Black Sabbath was on a rise in Europe but the two territories where it really, really mattered to Cozy and Tony—America for the money and Britain for more personal reasons—just were not happening. In America we felt a lot of that could be laid at the record company's doorstep but Britain was a bit of an odd one."

By the close of September Black Sabbath was back in Italy for an extensive run of dates before winding through Switzerland and Austria then launching into a full two weeks worth of shows in Germany. "Germany was very strong as usual" observes Murray. "The album had sold relatively well and the audiences were glad to see us back. I think we did feel a bit as though we were preaching to the converted though." A quick dash into Scandinavia pre-empted yet another foray into the German heartland.

During this tour Neil Murray discovered his solo spot was enjoying a little more impact than he had imagined. "There were venues were my bass solo could cause some serious damage to the buildings. It did knock down ceiling tiles and things like that because the sub bass vibrations I used would give the ceilings and walls a good old shake." Of course, if Neil could give the place a good shaking down, Cozy would naturally have to go one better though. In Amsterdam, at the Jaap Edenhall, he brought the roof down—literally.

"We had been banned from using Pyro's at this particular gig and was warned some time previous that we weren't gonna be able to use them. So he had an amazing idea to use compressed air in great fuckin canisters 5 feet tall!!" laughs Tony Martin, reliving the moment as if it were yesterday. He goes on to explain the ad hoc Heath Robinson device the inventive drummer had concocted to get around the ban. "Cozy had a series of pipes and tubes laid around the kit in a square formation with jet nozzles at appropriate places. The idea was that when he did his 1812 drum solo his drum tech would open the valves on these compressed air canisters and all hell would let loose upward around the kit. So we tried it at a rehearsal and sure enough it was quite spectacular great jets of steam rising out of the kit! Wow!

OK, so that was agreed but then a quiet voice of concern from behind the kit. The drum tech couldn't turn the fuckers off because compressed air freezes when it comes out at that velocity and the valves stuck, along with his skin I might add, to the canister. He thought it was still possible if he wore industrial gloves. So, we tried again and it worked OK".

Tony Iommi. Pic: Michael Eriksson.

Come the actual gig an air of trepidation held both nervous band and crew members in its grasp. "When it was time for the solo we all stood in the wings watching and waiting for this thing to go off. The time came, the tech shoved the lever on the canisters and the force of the jets took out the ceiling completely! All kinds of shit came out of the roof that had been up there since the building was erected, and for a time it was difficult to breath. When the dust settled I went out front and applauded the audience for bringing the roof down. We were subsequently banned from the gig. In fact I don't think anyone ever played there after that because of the unsafe ceiling."

"After the European tour we went to the Philippines and Singapore" records Neil. "Then things went quiet, very quiet. You must have heard the phrase 'The phone stopped ringing'. I called the management because I had vague suspicions of what was obviously going on. Earlier in the tour, at Hammersmith, Geezer had got up and jammed and went down an absolute storm."

This gig, the first in a two night stand on the 8th and 9th of September, would see Geezer treading the boards with Black Sabbath for the first time since the 'Live Aid' extravaganza some five years previous.

Also putting in an appearance for the encore would be Iommi's guitar buddy Brian May. "There was definitely some kind of magic there—you couldn't deny it" Murray concedes. "So, after that gig I started to think 'Aaaah, OK ...' Tony and Cozy were getting a bit frustrated too, especially because the band was making very little headway in the States and that had always been their prime objective really. If America had opened up like Europe it would have been a very different story. I think they thought the public perception, of seeing Black Sabbath playing in crummy places in America, was damaging the band and they had to do something about it. I know they were starting to feel a bit crushed by America, putting on a gig and people not being bothered enough to come and see the band. The truth was that Black Sabbath was not making enough money. Both 'Headless Cross' and 'Tyr' had been steps forward in Europe but it didn't matter because America wasn't interested. There was a realisation that IRS Records simply did not have the muscle to promote the band in the States.

You have to remember that although 'Headless Cross' was a big plus from the days of 'Eternal Idol' it was nothing compared to what Black Sabbath had been. They were a mega huge band during the seventies on a par with Led Zeppelin and Deep Purple—certainly within the top three Rock bands in the world. They used to be absolutely enormous which naturally generated a quite enormous amount of money. Any other band out of Britain at that time would probably have been as pleased as Punch with the sales of 'Headless Cross' and 'Tyr' but Tony had experienced ten times that before and that's what he wanted again.

So, it was all pretty clear to me what was about to happen. Ozzy was out of the picture so they patched up the differences with Ronnie. Of course, his career needed a boost too because his sales had been slipping dreadfully. The first few Dio albums had given him a good jump start but then everything kind of started to sound a little boring and dreary. Sabbath needed Dio and Dio needed Sabbath and, of course, once someone high up at Warner Bros. starts to figure that one out the next logical step in the formula is to get Geezer too. I soon discovered that Geezer was coming back into the band although nobody had bothered to tell me of course. It was no surprise. Tony in particular was yearning to get back up there naturally. Cozy too had big visions."

The drummer most certainly did hold ambitions for both himself and Black Sabbath. Promoting the 'Tyr' album when asked about the band's prospects for the long term future he had this to say. "All the signs are there that say Sabbath are going to regain their rightful status. I don't think Sabbath will be in profit for another year or so yet but it will happen. To put a show on worldwide is expensive, but in the long run it'll be worth it. I'm certainly committed. I just want Sabbath to build and build, which we are doing. I've no limit on it and I would honestly be happy to still be in Sabbath in ten years time. We feel that supporters of the band have renewed confidence in this long-term line-up and we hope we can justify that support by turning out some great albums in the future. Black Sabbath definitely mean business, we're not one of those old bands who are a pathetic shadow of their former selves. We go out there and we mean it." Cozy did indeed go out there. Los Angeles to be precise, along with Tony Iommi and Geezer Butler, to meet up with a former comrade. Back in Birmingham Tony Martin and Geoff Nicholls would, at first, be blissfully oblivious to goings on across the Atlantic.

In 1990 Ozzy aided his old mucker Bill Ward on his inaugural solo outing 'Ward One—Along The Way'. Released on the independent Chameleon label the album would witness Ozzy donating lead vocals to two tracks 'Jack's Land' and 'Bombers (Can Open Bomb Bays)'. Unfortunately due to the nature of its release the album received little attention and those not quick off the mark enough at the time to purchase it will be disappointed. A rerelease is projected but with the two Ozzy fronted songs excised. Ozzy would also turn up in a more unlikely combination with comedian Billy Connelly and boxer Frank Bruno the same year delivering 'The Urpney Song' for inclusion on the 'Dreamstone' cartoon series.

With the gap widening between Ozzy product a stop gap release was hastily convened. No new material was as yet on the table so mobile recording studios attended some of the last gigs of the tour. These tapes would be issued as the mini album 'Just Say Ozzy', a record which would only serve to mystify fans and critics alike. Featuring four Ozzy numbers and renditions of Sabbath's 'War Pigs' and 'Sweet Leaf' it did at least capture the Wylde / Butler combination in flow but achieved little outside of that. Puzzled fans were far from impressed and 'Just Say Ozzy' snuk timidly into the gutter of the Billboard rankings before hastily skulking out again.

In a 'Metal Forces' magazine interview Geezer Butler had this to say about the record. "It's just one of those record company things, and the record company pointed out we hadn't released anything for about fourteen months, and the new album won't be out for about a year, and they wanted some product. It was kind of like "What haven't we done?" Ha Ha. The record company took over at that point. It's just to shut them up really."

The next manoeuvre in the grand game plan would be as predictable as it was unimaginative. As Dio's solo career progressed the impetus provided by the meisterwerk that was 'Holy Diver' would serve him well. 'The Last In Line', the 1984 second effort, actually sold in greater quantities in both North America and the UK. 1985's 'Sacred Heart' again charted prominently but was the first record to draw the detractors out of the woodwork. It also signalled the closure of a chapter with Vivian Campbell. The inspiring Irishman later made his name most noticeably with Whitesnake and Def Leppard, leaving Dio to struggle on. Craig Goldy, fresh out of the Driver project, was pulled in but the sales and chart positions began to dip with 'Dream Evil'. On tour, Dio's visual arsenal added a monstrous mechanical spider to compliment an unreliable hydraulic dragon. With 'Lock Up The Wolves' a large contingent of fans found the band to be treading water, rehashing tired themes and losing inspiration.

Black Sabbath meantime had demonstrated they could still generate a sharp upward curve in album sales and respectability in Europe but in America, the land where it really counted, the career graph was looking decidedly flaccid. If Ozzy wasn't about to play ball the Warner Bros. execs reasoned Dio might just do the trick. However the PR agents wanted to dress it up, a marriage of convenience was affected.

Belief in the project was high enough to draw in producer Mack, noted for his multi-platinum works with Queen and Billy Squier, and extend the recording budget by a few naughts. Originally the band had begun work with Max Norman, the man famed for his clutch of Ozzy albums amongst others, at the desk but the results were unsatisfactory and would be scrapped. Ronnie James Dio knew of Mack from the producer's formative years working as assistant to Martin Birch.

Cozy Powell would be forced out of this formula in the most unpredictable of circumstances, his horse collapsing from under him and breaking the drummer's hip. Sadly the horse, one of Cozy's favourites, did not survive and for a period things looked decidedly bleak for Cozy too. His friend Geoff Nicholls was extremely concerned. "At one stage they were even saying Cozy might not be able to walk again but Cozy just shrugged that off. It took him a while but he got there. I felt really sorry for him but he was always in high spirits and determined to get back on the kit. His energy level was always pretty amazing. Cozy's whole life was music. He had this old barn next to his farmhouse that was just full of records. I mean thousands and thousands of them. He had about three or four rows of vinyl that went around the entire inside of the building. He had just collected all these over the years from record companies. I often wondered what happened to that collection."

"That's the way I live my life" the drummer offered. "Cars, bikes, horses, Rock Music. That's me, I'm not hiding anything. It's not a predictable hum drum life, if you'll excuse the pun. When the accident happened it came at a bad time, but looking back, it was possibly for the best because in actual fact I never agreed with the whole Ronnie thing. I felt it was a bit of a smack in the face to Tony Martin, Neil Murray and the fans that had stuck with us with 'Headless Cross' and 'Tyr'. They were bloody good albums that had sold well. We were on the up so I just didn't see the need to go back to the past.

I voiced my opinion but the label boys had already made the decision. The money was huge. I had the choice of course. I could have backed out with no problem because, let's face it, I've never been short of work. Sabbath was very special to me though. They wanted the 'all star' package again. Those kinds of people aren't interested in the fact that two band members won't even share the same room together so long as they stand next to each other in the photos. That's how I felt and the atmosphere between Ronnie and I was not cordial shall we say. There were difficulties. I personally had given a lot to Black Sabbath and it was paying off. Black Sabbath was deep in the red when I joined and through sheer bloody hard work we got it back in the black. The line-up was stable, which was a first, and the band had got back a lot of the credibility it had lost. When Ronnie came back, we just lost it all again. Threw it all away. That's how I felt."

As widely reported Cozy Powell and Ronnie James Dio were incompatible personalities. The frictions had already begun to rub in the prototype stages of the new band. Geoff Nicholls sums the two characters up as fire and water. "The thing with Cozy is that he was a straight talker. A lot of people respected him for that. He couldn't stand egos and I never heard him talk about people behind their backs. Like of all of us sometimes he got things wrong but if he did he would apologise and get on with it. There were a few times when his initial line of thinking on something turned out to be not quite right but he would still apply himself 100% to get the job done. I really admired him for that. Likewise, if he was right he would tell you straight and them commit himself until the job was done. Cozy drove other people along with him. He was a great team player.

In my experience, Ronnie wasn't a straight talker. I've heard him slagging Tony and Geezer off which wasn't right. I've been in situations where things have been said that were really unnecessary. You never got that with Cozy. He told you straight whether you liked it or not. If it's out in the open Cozy reasoned you could then deal with it. That probably sounds a little more malicious than intended. The whole culture of Sabbath, being a Birmingham band, was that things needed to be said just the once. That's how Tony Iommi, Geezer and Ozzy are. All Brummies are like that. So, if Tony says something—that's it. He sees no reason to keep on dragging up the same old subject again and again. Ronnie never understood this at all and thought that because things were not being spoken about that there were secrets and plots going on, which half the time simply weren't happening. Of course the other thing to bear in mind is that Black Sabbath is Tony Iommi's band. He has the final say on absolutely everything so that didn't sit well with Ronnie either. So there was always that friction of misunderstanding too on top of the fact that there was this personal thing with Cozy too. The thing was never going to work.

When that version of the band was first put together there was definite embitterment between Ronnie and Cozy. The truth was they hated each others fucking guts but I guess Warner Bros. thought money would smooth everything over. I got the impression that something big had gone down in Rainbow. At one stage Cozy got so pissed off he told me "I can't work with this fucking little midget!" Ronnie, I remember, always wanted to work with a drum box at his house which I found a bit odd to say the least when he had one of the world's best drummers at his disposal.

Ronnie could be very difficult to work with I have to say. I know he has said some things about me in the past, in print as well, which were unkind and not representative of my input. What happened with 'Dehumanizer' was that they asked me to work on the vocals with Ronnie because he was having difficulties with some stuff. What I did was to get these songs he was struggling with, add some keyboard chords and then said to him, OK, now try this. It was a method Tony Iommi and I had tried before with other singers that had worked very well. He said he couldn't do it. I played it to everybody else then put my vocal ideas on top. Tony Iommi said "That sounds really good, let's do that" but of course Ronnie wouldn't have it. Anyway, he went away then came back with a vocal line that was very similar to the one I had done. Now, if that had all been conducted with a team attitude, like a band, it would have been fine but it wasn't. The band lost out because of that too because of course Geezer was sitting there and he had written all of the classic Ozzy lyrics. Every classic Sabbath song lyric that Ozzy ever sang was written by Geezer. Yet Ronnie and Geezer never collaborated. I never understood that."

'Dehumanizer', without doubt, struck out on a new lyrical path. Geezer's recent excursions with his latter solo material made their presence felt in bringing the record right up to date. This is something Ronnie James Dio is happy to clarify. "At first I was writing words in my fantasy style actually. These were being submitted and Tony Iommi was not too happy with it. We spoke about it and he said he wanted to change a few things. What he actually said was 'You've used all that before'. OK, I took that on the chin because Tony was probably right. Then we had to decide what he did want. It seemed at one stage as if he was asking me to come up with a whole new language, Sanskrit or something. Eventually we determined the fantasy stuff was out. I started to write in a very stark, black and white kind of way. It was about as heavy as you could possibly get. Geezer had quite a few things too. He had a great idea for 'Computer God' so I came up with some more stuff to go around that. 'Computer God' was probably the song that started us off into the direction we ended up with."

According to some, the piecing together of 'Dehumanizer' would not run a smooth path. Personalities soon divided. "There were some very strange things going on" reckons Geoff Nicholls. "Ronnie used to rehearse with an Octa-divider on his voice for example because he didn't want us to hear his real voice. I never fucking figured that one out! The whole thing was weird and eccentric. Ronnie was very fragile and I just felt like we spent too much time stroking his ego when we should have been making an album."

Ronnie James Dio, talking in 1998, acknowledged that the band was trying to fit together a lot of broken pieces. "It wasn't exactly easy. I think that the thing I learned, or they way I came to look at the situation, was that this was the same set of people but the setting and the circumstances were very, very different. That's why we didn't make 'Heaven And Hell part II'. It had been a decade since we had spoken really. Since we broke up they had really struggled. I mean, the last Sabbath album that did anything was 'Born Again'. I had three very successful records since then too."

A measure of cynicism suggested that Dio and Sabbath needed each other, both having to swallow equal portions of Humble Pie. Was the suggestion made by the money men or was it a true creative union? In promotion for the album in 1992 Ronnie ducked this one. "I guess we are both at that point in our careers when it is advantageous for us to do this. I'm not going to try and hide that. What I will say though is that I had put Dio on hold for this, which is a big sacrifice. It's a sacrifice both in terms of my own artistry and money if you want to be so crude. When the idea was first put forward my whole take on it was can we make a good record? That's all I care about. We discussed future albums, future tours and Black Sabbath existing as a band again rather than a circus with Tony Iommi as ringleader. If people say the record is worthwhile then I'm happy."

The singer must have been conscious of a stream of thought from both media and fans that, given past experience and the iron willed personalities of those involved, this venture was doomed to implode at some point. He didn't see it that way. "We're older and wiser" he maintained. "Circumstances and personalities have changed. There have been a lot of apologies from both sides about the things that were said in the past. If nothing else it has been good to finally rid ourselves of those things. When we did 'Heaven And Hell' Black Sabbath was out for the count—truly. Right now it's had a beating but I respect Tony's determination and resilience in never throwing in the towel. I think we can do something here I really do. We're not going to recreate that era because we have all moved on from there but the songs we have are very, very strong. Some of the toughest material I have ever sang on believe me. This is a very heavy, dark record with a modern edge. There is nothing old about 'Dehumanizer'."

As this most delicately balanced of alliances was being pieced together the band's former singer was, for a time, blissfully ignorant of the preparations for his departure. "I found out about Ronnie in the

Ronnie James Dio.

usual Sabbath fashion" says Tony Martin affording himself a wry laugh. "I was just leaving my house to go to rehearsal as normal when, just as I got to the door, the phone rang. It was Albert who said 'I think you'd better sit down son'. What he actually said was quite incredible. Albert told me they were rehearsing with Ronnie Dio and they didn't want me there. If I turned up at rehearsals they wouldn't let me in! I was a bit stunned to say the least. What gets me though, still to this day, is that they never told me I was fired. Nothing was ever said. Just 'Don't come to rehearsal'. On that morning I was gutted but I soon accepted it and got on with my life."

Neil Murray looks back on the closing of his first chapter of the band philosophically. "It was just business pure and simple" he maintains. "Warner Bros. offered them a huge great deal to get back together with Ronnie. It must have been very tempting. At the time we all knew we were onto a good thing with the line-up we had. It was working but obviously not fast enough for those that mattered. There were some questions about Tony Martin's stage presence, that it was a bit lightweight for the music. Not his singing, everyone was agreed that there were no problems in that department. It wasn't a musical issue though. Tony Iommi was not, as I recall, in any mad rush to get back with Ozzy at that moment in time because of all the sabotage attempts on the Sabbath name over the years. We can all look back now and say, OK, that line-up that did 'Headless Cross' and 'Tyr' should have done a third album. I would have stuck around for that. If Geezer had not come back I think I would have stayed. I don't believe Bill Ward was really in any fit state of health to play. If he was they would have asked him."

The culling of Black Sabbath's revival line-up raised many questions with Geoff Nicholls too. "I never understood it at all. There was a huge optimism generated with that line-up. Cozy was an absolute ball of energy and enthusiasm and there were a lot of promises being made for the next album. Everything was on an upward curve. I mean, the band was great. Not just the fact that we had Cozy and Neil there, which really helped add some credibility, but Tony Martin had really proved himself too. We were getting that whole invincible 'band' feeling too. There was no hatred and back stabbing. We had a friendly, family unit. The sales figures in Europe were evidence enough that it was all heading in the right direction. Another album with Tony Martin, Neil and Cozy was discussed and I think everyone just kind of assumed it would happen. Cozy was totally committed and I'm sure Neil would have been involved too. Everyone had really took a big risk on that line-up, invested a lot of time and effort. The third album was always promised as the financial payback too so when it didn't happen there were a lot of pissed off people."

Free agents once again, Murray and Powell set to work on a Cozy Powell solo album 'The Drums Are Back'. Cozy's '92 album featured such luminaries as Brian May and John Deacon from Queen, Deep Purple's Jon Lord, Steve Lukather of Toto and Mr. Big bassist extraordinaire Billy Sheehan. Geoff Nicholls also donated his song-writing skills to four tracks. Neil Murray gives some background on these sessions. "Don Airey was originally very heavily involved in Cozy's album. Cozy put some tracks down in Los Angeles and then set about putting a band together. Don Airey found the guitarist Mario Parga. With that line-up we did quite a bit of rehearsing but then Cozy and Don fell out about something trivial. I can't honestly remember what it was. Don went, which Cozy said he was happy about because he wanted to keep the size of the band down. Then a friend of Cozy's from one of his seventies bands got involved. That didn't work at all."

Tony Martin felt that he had finally managed to free himself from the shackles of Black Sabbath and make a musical statement in his own right. "I was well into my solo album 'Back Where I Belong'. The deal with Polydor Records was good and things were looking very, very positive. The whole Ronnie thing I had pretty much put behind me and I was just getting on with my life." 'Back Where I Belong' was lent weight by a veritable roll call of specially invited guests including Queen's Brian May, Black Sabbath colleagues Neil Murray, Geoff Nicholls and Neil Murray and Saxon drummer Nigel Glockler. For good measure Martin also included a rework of the Black Sabbath song 'Jerusalem'.

The singer's new found status as a solo artist though had engendered a number of inquiries from other interested parties. "Yngwie was quite persistent for a time" Tony Martin insists. "In fact, the barrage of phone calls from his management and his friends really made me a bit wary. They were so keen it got a little too weird for me actually which put me off. It was very difficult to diplomatically tell them that, although I was appreciative of being asked, my solo album was in the works and far too important for me to stop. Being my first solo thing it was extra special and I really wanted to see it through. There were others too, even some talk of Journey at one point. Just a brief conversation. I didn't audition for anyone or follow anything up really because the 'Back Where I Belong' album was my priority."

There would be one telephone call though that did change his focus. The most unexpected one of all—Black Sabbath. "It was only two months after getting Ronnie in though that they asked me back. Well, I was stuck and told them so. Look, I said, I've got my solo thing going so it's really difficult. Anyhow, I went to have a meeting with Tony Iommi. There were no problems between us, never has been, it was all very professional. He wanted me back but when I asked what the problem with Ronnie was he just clammed up, just made lots of 'Errrr' and 'Ummm' type noises. The result of it all was that I couldn't do it because I was so deep in with Polydor at the time."

It would not be the only hiccup in the reconstituted Mk III line-up. Within a few months Tony Iommi was back on the telephone to Tony Martin yet again. "This was about four months later" Martin calculates. "Tony told me they just didn't know where they stood with Ronnie. Apparently Tony and Geezer had put down all the music and lyrics but Ronnie wasn't contributing and no vocals were getting put down. They thought he was being very secretive with his contributions and wouldn't leave anything in the studio. Basically they couldn't finish the songs and he could not see an end to the album the way it was recording."

At Iommi and Geezer's request Tony Martin made his way down to the familiar pastures of Rockfield Studios in Monmouthshire. "I knew Ronnie had been there only recently because when I walked into the studio there was a microphone stand set up at half-mast, about my shoulder height!" scoffs Martin. Long term followers of the band will attest that microphone stands had been the bane of Ronnie James Dio's life. Many a time Dio concert audiences have enjoyed the hilarity of seeing Ronnie's mic set up before a show at an almost gnome like level by a merciless leg pulling road crew.

"Basically they wanted me to redo the vocals for the 'Dehumanizer' album" states Tony matter of factly in a revelation that will no doubt shock many Sabbath and Dio fans. "Well, I'm just a singer so I thought OK, I can do my thing here. I've done it before. I did have a few reservations, which I spoke to Albert about but he assured me the situation was different this time. We put down vocals on some of the 'Dehumanizer' songs and it was sounding good. Obviously we had to start from scratch on all of the vocal melodies and lyrics to redevelop everything. In fact it was sounding very good. There were a lot of happy, relieved people in the room."

With both Tony's solo effort 'Back Where I Belong' and 'Dehumanizer' in the bag the decision was made to re-recruit Martin back into the fold. The vocalist was doubly cautious. He that knew Ronnie James Dio, residing in the West Midlands town of Henley on Arden at that time, had no knowledge of his clandestine session and had been told by Iommi and Butler they had needed a short break. Ronnie indeed was none the wiser. "Y'know, I heard some rumblings about this after the event. Did I know they got someone else in at the time? No. They must have been pretty sneaky."

Tony Martin felt he was back on familiar yet dangerous ground. "You know that expression 'Once bitten twice shy'? I don't know how many times I had been bitten by that stage of the game! There were a few more heated discussions, arguments if you will, between myself and Albert. I was very, very wary but strangely Albert, for a change, was very much on their side this time around. That was very unlike Albert because he usually could see a conspiracy around every corner with Sabbath. My point of view was that I had been fucked over so many times they must be wondering what kind of a sucker I am but Albert said "No, this time it's different. I've spoken to them, they desperately need you and it will be different this time. They're telling the truth—believe me." Because my manager was so convincing I was basically convinced too that everything really would be fine this time around. So, I rejoined Black

Dehumanizer.

Sabbath and as soon as Polydor Records found out they dropped me! That's the reason 'Back Where I Belong' only came out in Germany and Japan.

What happened after that was that it was decided that 'Dehumanizer' should be put out with Ronnie's vocals. We fucked that stuff off that I had sung on, which was a shame because those tapes sound just great believe me. There must have been a lot of label pressure, contracts and stuff. Time was a very big issue I remember. So, I stopped work on the 'Dehumanizer' songs and, because at that stage Ronnie was still out of the picture, we started to get brand new material together because it was decided it would be much quicker to do it that way round. This is where 'Cross Purposes' started. We were actually getting basic 'Cross Purposes' songs together in the studio before Ronnie joined back up with them to do the 'Dehumanizer' tour of America. You can imagine how everyone was feeling at this time. It was pretty strained between Tony, Geezer and Ronnie."

"It was a money thing pure and simple" affirms Geoff Nicholls. "Warner Bros. had given the band a huge advance for 'Dehumanizer'. Believe me, when I say huge I mean it. Anyway, they were picking up all the bills so they wanted a big name and that meant either Ronnie or Ozzy. Tony was happy with Tony Martin back in because that meant he could jam and play music again which is all he wanted to do. Ronnie never jammed which frustrated him. Warner Bros. didn't care. They wanted Ronnie for the name and that was it. The label was banking on another 'Heaven And Hell' and Black Sabbath selling a million albums again. The last time the band had done that was with Ronnie so in their eyes it must have looked simple."

Ronnie James Dio towed the PR line when asked how the album was assembled. "I love that album," Ronnie enthused. "I really thought it had a good modern sound, lots of very heavy riffs, very heavy songs. The whole album had an edge. I liked the fact that we were dealing with some good topics too, not the expected Sabbath subjects. Geezer pulled some interesting stuff out there. I think the fans loved it but the press couldn't see past the fact that it was me singing, or that it wasn't 'Heaven And Hell' part two, but who cares. Both Geezer and Tony came up with some great stuff for that record. I think it's a hugely underestimated record."

Others closer to home also had an interest in the album as former Geezer Butler band singer Carl Sentence explains. "That song 'Master Of Insanity' made me sit up and take notice" he says. "Two thirds of the vocal melody of that is mine. I was well disappointed. Jimi Bell worked a hell of a lot on that song too. I'm sure he even thought of the name. It's a brilliant song and Dio does it very well but he even sings some of the very same vocal melodies that I came up with. I've still got my original tape of that song, it's very close. It happens, I'm not bitching about it but I should have been given a credit where it's due I think." Geoff Nicholls remembers the song being put forward. "I've still got the tape of 'Master Of Insanity' with Carl singing it. It was always a great track. The original was a little more commercial but essentially exactly the same song. I had no idea Jimi Bell wrote it. What a bummer eh?"

Jimi Bell backs up Carl's assertions regarding 'Master Of Insanity'. During 1990 he received a further telephone call from Gloria Butler. It would be bitter sweet. "Gloria called me and said that Sabbath was getting back together again with Ronnie Dio and they were going to record 'Master Of Insanity'. I was thrilled until she told me I couldn't be listed as the writer. That was a bad blow to me considering I wrote all the music for that song and even came up with the title. She said that my name would appear in Geezer's credit, which it does. Gloria promised me that when the 'Dehumanizer' tour was over, I would receive payment for the song. I never saw a dime. I still should have gotten paid something. When Sabbath was touring with Dio, I got to see them two or three times. They even played my song live which made me both happy and disappointed at the same time. I got to meet Ronnie Dio. He was a very nice person, great to talk to. In fact, Ronnie had told me on the phone one time that he knew I wrote that song and he knew I wasn't getting paid."

The Ozzy, Wylde, Butler and Castillo line-up would remain in force for recording of what would, eventually, turn out to be the 'No More Tears' album. However, Butler would then make a hasty exit leaving the bass role vacant. This gap would be plugged by Terry Nails, a man pivotal in the crafting of the album but often neglected by biographers.

Nails had forced his presence onto the Californian club scene with Killerwatt. Session duties then ensued which led to a project with Quicksilver Messenger Service guitarist John Cipollina. Nails would also aid in live production type work with some of the early Bay area Punk bands like The Avengers, The Nunns, The Mutants and The Ready Mades. During this period some of Nails clients were booked to open for no less than the Sex Pistols. It was here Nails struck up a keen friendship with Sex Pistols guitarist Steve Jones.

Another colleague, bass player Mike Varney of The Nunns (now owner of influential guitar label Shrapnel Records) would hook Nails up with his next assignment Tommy Tutone. "I still have a hard time believing I even got that gig" he confesses. "I was actually a professional skate boarder at the time and my playing hand was in a cast due to a skate boarding accident and I was only able to play with one finger of my fretting hand, it was really bizarre. Tommy said he really liked my playing because I didn't over play!"

A six year tenure with Tutone was broken by relocating to Los Angeles and an endeavour with drummer Matt Sorum and guitarist Danny Stag. The bassist readily admits that at this juncture in his life he had also instigated a re-evaluation when it came to traditional Rock n' Roll recreation. "Most of my time was taken up by just getting sober, which I'm glad to say I still am. And that's how I got hooked up with Jonesy and where I met Ozzy. We were all trying to do the same thing. I must say that we were all in pretty fabulous shape at the time. I could barely remember where I lived, I'm not sure whether Jonesy actually had a place and Ozzy was really fed up and pretty damn unhappy with the way his life was going. A very lovely crew we were . . ."

It would be a colourful and notorious crowd Nails was hanging with at the time. Both he and Jones, whilst performing together as a band, would also be temping off and on with The Cult. "Steve and I and the guys were doing gigs with The Cult and actually played a couple of gigs as temporary members of The Cult. It was me and Steve and our drummer Pete Kelly—awesome drummer, real power house, with Ian and Billy, talk about fun! Wow! It was a real hoot. Steve and Billy sounded great together. It was like playing with family because Billy, Ian, Steve and myself spent a lot of time together when we weren't playing. Besides us, there was another part of the gang that included Charlie Sexton, Julian Lennon, Mickey Rourke, James Caan and Mickey's brother Joey, oh yeah, and Randy Castillo when he was in town, which wasn't that often cause he was out on tour so much. Later on Phil Soussan was part of that group also. We all hung pretty tight back in those days cause we all had bikes and we all rode together."

It would be Castillo who put in the invite to try out with Ozzy. "I was out sort of club hopping one night on my bike with my teenage daughter Willia, when I ran into Randy coming out of a club we were just going into. He came over to us while I was parking the bike too say hello and asked me what I was doing tomorrow. I told him I didn't have anything planned, so he said "do you want to do some playing with us." Now you gotta' understand something about Randy. He loves to play and is always playing with somebody, so I wasn't sure just who the "us" he was talking about was. So I said "sure, who are we playing with?" He told me Geezer and Ozzy had a tiff and that Geezer had split and they needed someone to fill in for him till he came back, which he didn't do till years later.

Needless to say, I was pretty stunned, I mean after all playing with Ozzy was probably one of the best gigs, if not the best gig in the country as far as I was concerned. The next morning Sharon Osbourne called me and told me where the studio was and asked me if I needed anything and thanked me for helping them out. She was so nice it just blew me away, and that's how I got hooked up with Ozzy. There is one other person that might have recommended me and that's Bill Ward, the drummer for Black Sabbath. I worked with him for awhile when he was getting ready to do his solo album. That was a lot of fun too. Bill's a great guy."

A somewhat nerve ridden Nails arrived at Frank Zappa's rehearsal complex Joe's Garage the next day. "Geezer had walked either earlier that day or maybe the evening before. It may have just been a case of being in the right place at the right time. When I got to the studio the next day the equipment that Geezer was using was still set up and plugged in, so I think it was pretty spur of the moment." Fortunately for the new enlistee his friend put him at ease. "When I got there I went in and got set up straight away. I think the only person there was Randy, which made things a bit easier cause we were pretty good friends already. Everyone filtered in fairly soon afterwards."

Then came the bombshell. "Someone, I think it was Zakk, suggested that we warmup with a Black Sabbath song. Well I figured I was screwed right then and there because I had to admit to everyone including Ozzy that I didn't know any Black Sabbath songs because I never really listened to them. "Well there goes that gig" I thought, but all Ozzy and the guys did was laugh. Everything started out pretty good as Randy and I started going through a bunch of old songs that we grew up listening to like Blue Cheer's version of 'Summer Time Blues' and some other stuff."

Indeed, the new band unit gelled quickly enough to reap some cast iron results from this early union. "We took a short break and I came back in to the room early to warmup." Nails explains the sequence of events. "I was just kinda playing this heavy sort of groove when Randy came in and started playing this thuggish type of drum beat with me, then Zakk came in and started playing also and the thing just sorta took off by itself. Then I noticed Ozzy standing there with this little memo tape recorder in his hand recording what we were doing. He then walked up to the mic and started making up lyrics on the spot, something about a hell raiser and that's how the song 'Hell Raiser' got started."

The streak of good fortune was about to be abruptly curtailed though in spectacular and embarrassing fashion. "Everything was going really good until we started working on 'Zombie Stomp'. It was at that point that I somehow completely fried and I do mean fried, Geezers amp. It kinda sounded like a series of gigantic nuclear farts. Zakk told me later on that he had listened back to the rehearsal tapes months later and that he was rolling on the floor laughing when he heard it. At the time I was just thinking, "Shit! How am I gonna pay for this now?"

Needless to say that cut everything short for the day. When we left I didn't know whether I was coming back or not, but I thought what the heck, at least I got to play with them once and, hell, it was really a lot of fun." A couple of days later Nails received a telephone call from Sharon Osbourne asking if he would mind coming back in to play some more. "Mind? Would I mind coming in and playing more bass? I thought; sure, I'd love to. How much do I have to pay you? I told her I could probably manage it and asked when and where and she said tomorrow at the same place. She then asked what kind of equipment I would like them to rent for me—since I had obviously just ruined Geezers rig—and I said that I'd like to ruin, I mean ... use my own if that was OK. So they arranged to have my stuff picked up the next day."

The bassist found himself in the midst of a long drawn out process that the 'No More Tears' album sessions had stagnated into. The recording and writing was becoming protracted ebbing and flowing with each new personality's arrival and departure. Nails got the impression the team had reached stalemate and needed some reinvigoration to get the ball rolling once again. "Why? I don't honestly know. There seemed to be a lot going on behind the scenes that I just wasn't a party to. Ozzy seemed to be doing really good for awhile and then sort of fell off, if you know what I mean. I don't really mean to be telling stories out of school, but I just don't know how else to put it.

From what I had been told, they had been in the

studio for over a year trying to get the songs for the album worked out and were at a sort of stalemate with the whole thing when I came into it. After that things started to move pretty fast. Ozzy told me that if Geezer didn't come back that he wanted me to take his place and I did for awhile. I think that the bringing in of someone new to the project changed the vibe enough to get things going again. But then again, who knows? It could have been the weather for all I know..."

Despite the surrounding turbulence Nails was quick to recognise the calibre of the players involved. "One of the things I remember most is how blown away I was by Zakk's playing. He was just fucking amazing!! Zakk was a complete madman. A really great guy and an insane guitar player. One of the best I've ever seen, completely one with his instrument. Someone who would constantly push the limits and make everyone a better player because of it. Randy is a great drummer and a good friend, rock solid player. Ozzy? What can I say about him? I love Ozzy, it's that simple."

With the album taking so long to commit to tape and a myriad of players involved the goals appeared to have been temporarily lost. As so often happens in studio scenarios such as this the attention to detail clouded the initial nature of the songs as Nails clarifies when discussing the original demo takes. "I'd say that they were a lot more ballsy when they were recorded the first time. They had a spontaneity and energy that seemed to be lacking on the later album. I don't mean all the songs just certain ones like 'Same Old Desire', 'I Don't Want To Change The World' and 'Zombie Stomp'. To me the songs sounded like they had been rehearsed too many times."

The actual recording process would be far from smooth though. "When we did the demos—the stuff that you hear on the 'No More Tears, The Demo Sessions' CD—we had this guy who did a good job for us, but he kinda fucked things up for himself when we started the album the first time. It seems that he had a bass player friend that he wanted to get to do the bass on the album and he started trying to manipulate the situation. He ended up finding himself out of a gig as well as probably being contributing factor to the reason I found myself out of a gig as well. At least that's what the other guys told me they think happened. From what I understand the guy actually came in played and Ozzy was so unhappy with the situation that he decided to scrap the whole project till a later date."

With 'No More Tears' requiring salvage Bob Daisley's literary skills would be in demand again. Having assembled the Mother's Army band with another Ozzy veteran drummer Carmine Appice alongside former Rainbow / Deep Purple and Yngwie Malmsteen colleague Joe Lynn Turner and Night Ranger guitarist Jeff Watson a familiar call interrupted proceedings. Although things did not work out according to plan. "Typically I got a call from Ozzy asking me to leave for Los Angeles the next day. I think I made it a few days later and started recording straight away. I wrote all of the lyrics for all of the songs on 'No More Tears' and they were accepted" he determines. "We even shook on it. Then they changed their minds. All the song titles stayed the same but they got in different lyric writers to redo them all."

On hand during this period of revision would be none other than Lemmy of Motorhead. A man whose literary skills are oft overshadowed by the hyperblast of the music that surrounds them. Terry Nails recalls Lemmy's involvement. "It was great to have Lemmy involved cause he's just fun to work with and very professional. He wrote most of the lyrics for the album. Ozzy would give him an idea about what he wanted and Lemmy would come back the next day with a finished lyric sheet and that's what you hear on the album. Lemmy had been a friend of mine for awhile so it was just that much more of a comfortable atmosphere in the studio. Besides, I love Motorhead."

One of those tracks Lemmy is credited for 'Hellraiser' would be included not only on the Ozzy product but rather cheekily on Motorhead's own 1992 'March Or Die' opus. Nails is undiplomatic. "Their version of 'Hellraiser' was by far the best..." Ozzy returned the favour to Lemmy by lending his distinctive vocal tones to another 'March Or Die' track 'I Ain't No Nice Guy'.

As the sessions drew toward a close one question was still left unanswered. What to call the album. Proposed album titles such as 'Hello To Heaven' and 'Don't Blame Me' leaked into the public domain. It certainly was no forgone conclusion as Nails illustrates. "Was the album intended to be called "No More Tears" from the beginning? I don't think so. Ozzy asked me to come over one night and listen to a tune that he had that didn't have any lyrics and asked me if I'd like to help write lyrics for it. He said he would send me a copy of it the next day—which unfortunately didn't happen—and the tune is what later became the song 'No More Tears'. I'm pretty sure that was the last song written for the album."

Did any of Nails lyrical work end up on the finished record? The bassist is not credited on the sleeve notes. "Let me put it this way, some of the songs were very different when I first came in and the way they sounded after I came in is the way they got recorded on the album." He says gingerly. "Don't get me wrong, I knew what I was dealing with when I got into it and I didn't expect anything, although it would have been nice to get a thank you on the album. Aside from that, they took care of me very, very well. I sure would have liked to have done the album but that's not the way the cards played out. It sure was fun while it lasted though ..." As for the eleventh hour re-induction of Daisley on bass Nails has this to offer. "I'm not surprised that Bob got the call to do the album. That seems to be the way things went. Nobody ever seemed to know what was going to happen next, including Ozzy. Bob was definitely the right man for the job, he's simply a great player."

The story does not end for Terry Nails there though. Besides his port of employ with Steve Jones the bassist was also busying himself with a side venture Bone Angel. This band unit was fronted up by former Alien and Four Horsemen vocalist Frank C. Starr and included ex-Dio and Rough Cutt guitarist Craig Goldie with Impelliterri man Mark Bistany on drums. "We did a couple of gigs under the name Hardluck and then Craig and Mark got busy with other projects so we asked Randy to come in and play." Randy Castillo would induct guitarist John Lowery into the fold. It was this unit that would witness a second term of studio involvement with Ozzy.

The bass player unfolds the scenario. "Just before the album came out a year or so later, Ozzy and—I think it was Zakk, were at logger heads over publishing on the album. Neither of them was about to budge on the issue, so Ozzy said fuck it and decided to start all over again from scratch and asked the Bone Angel guys to come in and start writing a new album. So we did, for about a week, until he was able to work things out with Zakk and then that was it."

To promote the album Epic Records undertook the unprecedented move of releasing to radio a promotional sampler entitled 'The No More Tears Demo Sessions'. Backed up by an interview narrative with Ozzy the disc contained working versions of 'I Don't Want To Change The World', 'Desire', 'Time After Time', 'Won't Be Coming Home' and 'Mrs. J'. The penultimate track would, with a change of lyrics, evolve into 'S.I.N.' whilst 'Mrs. J' is a Zakk Wylde acoustic guitar showcase. It is not only the music and the rarity of this disc that makes it a highly prized item as a print of an original painting by Ozzy himself graces the cover.

The 'No More Tears' album itself barged into the Billboard top ten during October of 1991. Fans found it on the whole a more introspective, even gloomier, work than previous fares. Highlights would be the comparatively upbeat 'Mr. Tinkertrain' and the maudlin title track itself. 'I Don't Want To Change The World' would soon become locked into the live

Zakk Wylde. Pic: Artemis Records.

set and the ballad 'Mama, I'm Coming Home' gave the man a further hit single to add to the trophy collection.

In later years John Lowry of course would go on to work with Judas Priest vocalist Rob Halford on his Two venture prior to morphing into 'Johnny 5' as part of the Marilyn Manson band. These days Terry Nails is living on the East Coast and known as T. Goodman in literary circles and on the cover of his 'Conspiracy Of Light' book. "Its sort of a comparative religion / metaphysical / comedy book ... Just writing books and music ... and surfing a lot."

Chapter 20

No More Dio

'No More Tears' echoed into 'No More Tours' and Ozzy limbered up for a last hurrah offering to the collective press that the time had come to hang up his crucifixes and become the family man. This last round of farewell dates saw Ozzy flanked by Zakk Wylde, Mike Inez on bass and Randy Castillo. The familiar if usually discreet personage of keyboard player John Sinclair was not involved, having been enticed away, albeit with the Osbourne's blessings, to join The Cult on the road as their 'Sonic Temple' arena shows. Selective dates on the 'No More Tours' campaign would be captured on tape for a subsequent double album 'Live And Loud'.

Black Sabbath, with Ronnie James Dio back at the helm, used South America as the first staging post in the 'Dehumanizer' world tour. During June the band performed to enormous audiences in Sao Paulo, Porto Alegre and Rio De Janeiro just upfront of the album release. Stalling at No. 44 in the Billboard charts in mid July it was hardly the much vaunted resurrection Warner Bros. had hoped for.

The group used Florida as an inception point from which to launch their first leg of the USA, the Gothic Rock n' Roller Danzig lending suitable support. Cruel jibes that Dio had insisted on a support band that had a singer shorter than him were dismissed by crew members with a barely stifled grin. Chuck Billy's Thrash vets Testament provided the guest honours for a round of British shows in September.

Black Sabbath provided their fans with yet another dose of Thrash as they got stuck into the second round of U.S. shows in October as San Francisco's Exodus paired up with German's Skew Siskin to act as support. In the main Sabbath were performing on the Theatre circuit to a few thousand people a night and whilst packed halls looked convincing it was hardly the arenas of yesteryear.

Ronnie was surprisingly candid about the whole Costa Mesa affair. Asked if he thought the episode looked shambolic to fans on the outside of the situation the singer agreed. "Shambolic, yes. Actually a bloody mess. It could have all been avoided, I had told them I would never do it but after I had made it

Sabbath's Dehumanizer line-up: Vinny Appice, Geezer Butler, Ronnie James Dio and Tony Iommi.

very clear it seemed to be forgotten. I never forgot but they seemed to. It wasn't raised again and so we carried on with the tour as if nothing had happened, nothing had been said. So they left, they buried their heads maybe hoping that once we got there I would be forced into changing my mind because it was too late to do anything else. We just never spoke about it for months, all the time we were on the 'Dehumanizer' tour. There was no way I was going to sing for Black Sabbath as a support act to Ozzy. They must have known that as soon as the subject was raised. Tony and Geezer didn't communicate on it at all so that's why it ended up a bloody mess for them, a big last minute panic. It's what they do, if they don't like something they stick their heads in the sand and hope someone else will clear the mess up. I saw some press that said it was down to me, pulling out at the last minute but actually we all knew a long time before that."

So when did the crunch come? When did Tony and Geezer realise Ronnie was not going to do the shows? "Well they should have realised when I told them first because, as a rule, if I make a decision I stick to it" states a recalcitrant Ronnie. "If I say it I mean it and I'll stand by it. Everybody knows that's how I am and they knew that too. I'm very black and white in that way. I had decided and I told them. I never once changed my mind. I thought it was a bloody stupid idea and that it would reflect badly on the band. In the end I think I was right. I knew exactly why the whole show was being planned that way, it was obvious. It was a big charade to announce the reunion with Ozzy so of course I wanted absolutely no part of it. Upon reflection I still find it amazing they thought I would ever do it. I mean, we know each other very well for better and worse, none of us had changed, so I cannot imagine they ever really thought I would do it. For me it was casting me as some kind of stooge, like I was the one who upset the party, but it was a pride thing for me. Not just my personal pride but also that of Black Sabbath and the good feeling we had built with 'Dehumanizer'."

Did he think it was demeaning to 'Dehumanizer', almost to say forget that album? "Yes, but also to Dio too. Remember I had given up my band to do Black Sabbath so it kind of cheapened both achievements in my eyes. I had sacrificed Dio for Black Sabbath. I had an assurance that it was a band effort so to admit to your fans that you would throw it all away just because Sharon Osbourne called and they're all jumping around like little kids again. Ozzy claps his hands and Tony and Geezer jump. That's how it is. I felt it was a slap in the face to those fans who had bought the album, bought the tickets and were expecting us to deliver more. 'Dehumanizer' was about the best album we could made at that time, I loved it. I was very proud of that album and the tour was good, we were getting an excellent response so to shoot it like a lame horse at the end was insulting. That's what I thought they were doing."

As support act, Exodus was all too aware of the divisions backstage throughout the tour. "Ronnie and Vinny had their dressing room and Tony and Geezer had theirs" observed Exodus guitarist Gary Holt. "I think just about everybody knew half way through the tour that Ronnie was not going to appear at those final shows so things were always pretty tense backstage.

We got on great with Ronnie James Dio. He was a perfect gentleman and one of the most genuine people I have ever met in Rock n' Roll. I had only met him for the first time about a month before the tour. I had introduced myself at the steps of the Foundation Forum and we spoke for just about five minutes. When we hooked up for the tour he remembered my name which really surprised me. Ronnie was always the perfect host. He never let us buy a drink and for a man who, to put it mildly, is not exactly a giant, he used to drink the whole band under the table! I think the first time we went out to a bar with him he just killed us on the drink. We were playing pool, too drunk to even see the ball and Ronnie was still drilling them!" Exodus had plans to entice Ronnie out on stage for their final gig in Oakland but it was not to be. "Yeah, we asked Ronnie to come out onstage and do 'Long Live Rock n' Roll' but he thought that Tony and Geezer wouldn't like it. Shame."

Ronnie James Dio put in his swan song with Black Sabbath on the 13th of November at the Henry J. Kaiser Convention Center in Oakland, California. He would not let the show go down as a damp squib, injecting some unexpected humour into the proceedings courtesy of Vinny Appice's elder brother Carmine. Probably one of the most high profile drummers on the American Rock circuit Carmine had already carved out a formidable reputation with Vanilla Fudge and Ozzy Osbourne. This latter alliance sparked Ronnie's mischievous streak and he collared Carmine backstage.

"Ronnie had this great idea" relates Carmine. "He asked me if I wanted to have a jam that night so of course I said 'yeah, sure' but thinking to myself something was up because Black Sabbath is not known for being a jamming type of band. Ronnie had it all planned though. I would substitute for Vinny on 'Paranoid'. Of course the track was a breeze for me because I used to play it every night with Ozzy. Ronnie didn't tell Tony and Geezer though so during the encore I switched with Vinny. We start playing 'Paranoid' and we're having a blast. I was really enjoying myself up there and Vinny and I just thought this was so funny. Tony and Geezer still didn't know what was happening so Vinny goes over to the sound monitor at stage left where Geezer sees him of course. Much to his surprise! He turned around, looked at me with just the biggest look of shock on his face. Then he recovers and goes to tell Tony. We just rocked harder from that point! The crowd thought it was great and both Tony and Geezer had a good laugh about it. I took my bow with the rest of the band at the end of the show. That was a special night."

Mirth making aside, with Dio adamant he would not do the gig Black Sabbath was, yet again, in a quandary. Geezer describes the situation. "Ronnie just wouldn't do it so it left us in a hole. We were going to get Tony Martin back in but he couldn't make it so that really forced us to start thinking of someone from outside of the Sabbath family so to speak. I think Rob's name was the first to come up and after a little bit of thought we just said, yeah, it's obvious isn't it? The guy is from Birmingham so had that going for him plus of course we all knew Rob has an amazing voice. With Black Sabbath we have always had singers with great character but Rob has that as well as a range that means he can sing pretty much everything we have ever done easily. When we got hold of him it turns out that he really didn't need to learn too much because he had all the albums already. The guy lives and breathes Heavy Metal. He lived only a few hours away too so everything locked into place there too. He saved our bacon on the day."

Rob Halford, since shocking legions of fans by severing ties with Judas Priest at the close of their immensely successful 'Painkiller' tour was working up his back to basics Metal band Fight. "As I recall the telephone call came completely out of the blue" says Rob. "As I was told, Sharon, Tony and Ozzy had put their heads together and came up with my name. I guess there was some bad blood between Ronnie and Ozzy about the whole reunion thing. Ronnie was adamant he wasn't going to share the same stage and he was looking for a way out. The guys came down to my hometown of Phoenix, Arizona and we soon had something worked out. It was actually very straight forward."

From Rob Halford's vantage point it no doubt was as clear cut as that. Prior to placing the call to the former Judas Priest man though, on the other side of the Atlantic the celebrated Black Sabbath wheels of confusion had been grinding yet again, threatening to catch Tony Martin's coat tails in the mincer. "What a farce! What a fucking joke!" is Martin's good humoured riposte when the inquiry is made as to his thoughts regarding Costa Mesa. "That whole thing still brings tears of laughter to my eyes every time I think about it. Gloria Butler phoned me up and offered me Costa Mesa. I just thought here we fucking go again ... So, Albert and I sat down once again to talk about the same old thing. Albert really convinced me this time though. He said something like he thought they had learned their lesson now. That all the scheming was finally over. I can remember saying to him 'Hey Albert, didn't you say that before ...' Anyhow, 'OK' I said 'Let's give it a go. Phone them and say I'll do it'.

Albert phoned them up and everything was sorted. I was going to Costa Mesa. Then we get another phone call later on from Gloria which was quite unbelievable. Incredibly she told me that I 'wasn't allowed' to do the gig. I said 'What do you mean 'not allowed'? What does that mean?' Gloria said that Ronnie's manager, Wendy Dio—it's all the wives y'see—was refusing to sign the visa for me to do the show. Apparently Wendy Dio was completely in charge of the Black Sabbath side of things for the gig. Sounds incredible I know and how much truth is in this whole thing I just don't know but it's what I was told. Gloria said that if I turned up at the gig Wendy would have me arrested. I wouldn't get as far as the gates!"

"I put it to Tony that it might be a nice idea to dig

Rob Halford. Pic: Garry Sharpe-Young.

up some Sabbath songs from the past, some stuff that had not been done in a long time" motions Rob Halford. "Tony liked the idea so we went through the set list two or three times until we got something in order. I just thought it would be a nice gesture to give the fans something a bit different to what they would generally expect."

Rob Halford and Black Sabbath retired to Vintage Studios in Phoenix to hone the set. "It felt really special y'know?" enthuses the singer. "The studio was just a very small room where we had demoed the Fight material. We just ran through it once and it sounded great. Afterwards we all looked at each other and said 'well that's it then isn't it? We don't need to do it again' It was that easy to lock in. Next night we did the same thing in front of 20,000 people. I wish that, looking back, we had captured that moment in the studio on video or something. It really was a special moment."

It is common knowledge that Halford had nailed the lyrics in just two days. What has been previously overlooked though is that Rob had the words to many of those songs ingrained into his mercurial metallic lined brain for nigh on twenty years. "Learning the songs was easy" he admits. "I have all the albums in my collection. The reason I was so thrilled to be approached for the event in the first place was because I am, and always have been, a massive Black Sabbath fan. I look up to people like Ozzy, Ronnie and Glenn Hughes just like anybody else does. I'm no different in that respect."

This admission of humility from the man his fans hail as the 'Metal God' would serve him well when the day came. Costa Mesa, probably out of all the gigs Black Sabbath had performed since 1979 really should have been the occasion where that well worn 'Lights, Camera—Action' came into play. Oh, there was action aplenty but the only cameras whirring were palm cams in the hands of Billy Bootlegger and lights ... Let Rob Halford entertain you with a story of light out of the black. "I knew the band had an intro tape, so, when I thought it was time to go we all assembled backstage. The problem was we were four musos dressed in black and we were behind this huge black scrim drape behind the drum riser, all the lights were off so ... we actually lost each other! I have to tell you I had huge nerves, the anticipation was enormous so realising I was on my own was just the worst."

The hapless Halford then was forced into making an initiative. "They were pumping huge plumes of dry ice out onto the stage at this point and I thought to myself 'Is that me? Is this where I go on? I couldn't see Tony or Geezer to get a signal from so I thought surely that has to be me. So, I casually strode out there, wading my way through the smoke and stood there centre stage—and nobody else was there! I was way too early, standing there feeling a complete plonker! This huge crowd was cheering and there I was just thinking to myself that I had just made a complete prick of myself. I couldn't do anything so I just stood there taking some deep breaths to calm myself down.

I was rooted to the spot, I couldn't turn around and go back because that would look ridiculous. I can remember thinking to myself 'Well these Sabbath fans are now going to think I must really love myself for having put on such a grand entrance!' I was waiting for what seemed like an eternity. My nerves were right on the edge but, actually, although it was a blunder on my part it actually looked pretty cool at the end of the day, like part of the show. In reality what the audience thought was part of the show was a big mistake."

At least Rob had got his obligatory freshman faux pas out of the way and could now just get on with the show. Or so he thought ... "I fucked up again didn't I?" he laughs. "I came in four bars too early for the first song for which I got a kick on the leg from Tony. I always laugh when I see that on the bootleg video. No more mistakes after that and it was all plain sailing. Singing those songs, tracks I had grown up with, was a total blast. Black Sab-

bath had always been there throughout my entire career with Judas Priest, they were always releasing albums and touring when we were. Especially 1980 because we had scored a big hit with 'British Steel' and Sabbath had come back with Dio and 'Heaven And Hell'. I suppose I took more interest because they are a Birmingham band and you always like to see your own doing well. I loved every second of it and the way the audience seemed to acknowledge my ... I was going to say authority but that's the wrong word. What I mean is that the Black Sabbath fans seemed to just accept me instantly which after following in the footsteps of Ozzy and Ronnie made me feel just great. Besides putting my energy into the show it was just a breeze with the fans. To share a stage with Tony and Geezer just felt wonderful."

For the first night of the 14th of November Black Sabbath ripped through a set triggered by the standard fare of 'Mob Rules' and, somewhat surprisingly, 'Computer God' off the 'Dehumanizer' album. From there the set notably contained a shift toward more Dio-era orientated material such as 'Children Of The Sea', 'Die Young', 'Heaven And Hell' and 'Neon Knights'. Of course, 'N.I.B.' and 'Symptom Of The Universe' were dusted off too as well as a welcome 'Into The Void'. On the second night Rob did his thing and then handed over the microphone to Ozzy Osbourne for 'Black Sabbath', 'Fairies Wear Boots', 'Iron Man' and 'Paranoid'.

"At the time I think we all just were preoccupied with getting the job done" ponders Halford. "I guess we all have this West Midlands attitude of not making too much of something but of course that was wrong because soon after it became obvious that what had occurred was something very special indeed. It's a typical Birmingham way of thinking, we'll do it for the knock, have a good time regardless and not make too much of a fanfare. West Midlanders and Black Country folk are very humble about self promotion, always have been. They work harder than most but are reluctant to be praised for it. For some reason nobody at the time thought about getting the event onto film or tape which was a great shame, to have nothing official. It really should have been a live album and video, that whole event. That's quite amazing really when I sit and think now about how many management parties were involved."

Not everyone with a Black Sabbath affiliation found the extravaganza so edifying though. Cozy Powell, on tour with Brian May of Queen at the time, held a view askew to the common voice. "I actually missed the actual Costa Mesa thing but when I got to know the details I just felt sorry for them. It was a circus and Ozzy ... Well, Ozzy got exactly what he wanted out of it didn't he? Ever since he left the band Ozzy and Sharon have been trying to mess things up for Tony and trying to say that Ozzy WAS Black Sabbath. With 'Headless Cross' and 'Tyr' we proved that wasn't the case. We had stopped the rot. We had a good thing going there. Rob Halford's good, he's very good, nice guy and all that, but the whole show was about rolling over for Ozzy. Of course there is no way Ronnie would have done that. The two people that profited from that gig were Ozzy and Rob. Black Sabbath? Nah, I thought it looked desperate for Tony and Geezer. They didn't need to do that. I didn't agree with Dio coming back into the band in the first place but they never stuck with it. When they ditched him just because Sharon Osbourne clicked her fingers, which is obviously what happened, I just thought I was so glad to be out of it at that point."

These behind the scenes machinations would be lost on the Heavy Metal public though who simply saw Costa Mesa as another landmark to rank alongside Castle Donington and the San Bernadino U.S. Festival. Quite simply history had been created. Even though officially the opportunity was let slip naturally the bootleggers had a keener eye on the ball. The Costa Mesa tapes of Black Sabbath and Rob Halford had soon circumvented the planet making many a fan of both Judas Priest and Black Sabbath persuasion very happy indeed.

"I've got a copy of the bootleg" admits Rob. "I'm glad I have it too. These things are getting very sophisticated, it's very well made. I just wish something official could have been done. Someone dropped the ball there." Halford's summary of Costa Mesa, bearing in mind Tony Martin's comments about not "being allowed" to do the gig, give cause to ponder. One assumes here that Rob is asking us to read between the lines. "Ronnie and I are good friends. He is a truly wonderful singer, one of the very, very best in the business. I'm grateful for his understanding on the whole Costa Mesa thing so that the thing could actually take place."

Dio puts an interesting slant on Halford's comment although stops short of confirming some kind of legal smoothing over was necessary to effect the union. "I've known Rob for years and years. He always turned up backstage to see us and I'm proud to count him as a true friend. I care a lot for the guy and he will always have a true ally here. When we did the Hear n' Aid record Rob moved his entire schedule to do that for us. I can remember asking him and thinking to myself that it might not happen because Judas Priest was busy but Rob basically said 'Anytime, anywhere—just call me'. The Children Of The Night fund was very important to him and he made it priority. That's exactly what he did too.

When the whole Costa Mesa mess hit the band was frantically trying to find singers to do it. That I do know. It was interesting being an observer on the outside of that picture. Anyhow, they sorted something out with Rob. He called Wendy and I and said 'Listen, I've been asked to do these Black Sabbath shows but I really don't want to lose our friendship. If it is going to upset things between us I'll decline'. Now, Rob didn't need to do that all but he's a true gentleman so he did the right thing. I wouldn't say Rob needed our permission but he wanted our blessing, not that he needed it, and he got it. It didn't matter to me at that stage who was going to do it but I was glad it was Rob and I thought some of the song choices were interesting too. I knew everything about what was going on. I would see Vinny in the mornings and I would say "Going to rehearsals?" and Vinny would say "Yeah, going to rehearse with Rob." It was all out in the open."

With Costa Mesa having been elevated to such a degree of notoriety there would soon generate a whisper trail indicating that the obvious next move, creatively and financially, would be to unite the Halford / Sabbath team in something of a more permanent fixture. After all, Ozzy had officially 'retired', Rob Halford was a free agent, Black Sabbath needed a singer and Ronnie James Dio was off the Christmas card list once again. Black Sabbath fronted by Rob Halford would have proven a lucrative proposal indeed.

"We did speak about it and it did seem to be a very obvious thing for a short while" confesses Rob in the first unqualified acknowledgement that such conversations did take place. "Tony and I discussed it a few times but at the time both our worlds were in chaos and turmoil so we never got the chance. Possibly we should have both pursued it more seriously. Tony is a great person, a good guy to hang out with so there were never any personal issues in the way to prevent a union like that happening. Glenn Hughes was in there too. I'm a huge fan of Glenn, terrific bass player and wonderful singer."

Geoff Nicholls allows himself to be more candid on this subject. "That was definitely the big plan, to get Rob into the band and sing on the next Black Sabbath album. Costa Mesa was like one big test, which the guy passed with flying colours. For quite some time there was a lot of excitement in the air because we all thought Rob was going to do it. Discussions got to the point where he was going to be the next Black Sabbath singer and we all knew that could produce a monster of an album.

Rob had everything. He could hit all those high notes, which meant that he could sing absolutely every song Tony Iommi had ever written; the first time that had ever happened. He had a reputation, he had his own fans, he was a Brummie, his stage presence too was just awesome. What more could you ask? Both Tony Iommi and I really liked Rob's look then too, with that whole Bela Lugosi Nosferatian thing going on. I think Rob with Sabbath and the full show would have put us back on the map for sure."

The erstwhile Sabbath trio of Martin, Powell and Murray were also out on the road although not in such grand circumstances. During the Autumn of 1992 Murray hooked up with his old friend Brian May for a series of North American dates before re-establishing contact with Cozy. "By that time he had combined forces with Tony Martin so it was like getting the old team together."

In fact another stab at Cozy Powell's Hammer was tried in 1992 with vocalist Peter Oliver. This line-up only lasted one gig and soon erstwhile Tony Martin was drafted. The band switched handles to Tony Martin & Friends to tour Germany as Neil Murray describes. "We did some gigs, very, very small gigs mostly. In Germany we were using a guitar synth and I was playing samples triggered from foot pedals. We did two ridiculously pointless gigs in the UK calling ourselves Cozy Powell's Hammer. It was all a bit of a damp squib."

In actuality the prospect of two former Sabbath men promoting solo product at the same juncture had raised the possibility of a joint promotion effort with one show designed to sell two albums. For the European dates Martin, Parga, Murray and Powell ran through a set that incorporated an eclectic breadth of material. "Those shows were very tough on my voice" admits Tony Martin. "It was an odd mix of very diverse material which had me really stretched. Some bright spark had the idea of compiling a set which represented each person involved, each era and each band. Consequently we found ourselves playing Black Sabbath songs, Whitesnake songs, Rainbow songs as well as solo stuff from my album and Cozy's. It was bloody tough as well as long—nearly two hours. In fact it was so hard on my voice that, for the first time ever, I lost my voice in Germany. Mario Parga was a very gifted guitarist I have to say. He could construct all these strange shapes on the guitar with his hands that you really weren't supposed to be able to do. He would often play TV themes, stuff like 'Crossroads' and other silly stuff, in Flamenco style. Nice guy, very unassuming and not in the least bit flash."

The band, as Neil Murray has pointed out, was earlier billed as Cozy Powell's Hammer but this title had really been settled on so as not to labour any further discussions. Tony Martin recalls half a day's rehearsal time being devoted to the subject of a band name. "I suggested The Cage actually, which is what I called my later project with Dario Mollo. There were a lot of suggestions such as calling it 'Martin, Murray & Powell' or other such variations on our names. We settled on Cozy Powell's Hammer just to end the discussion really."

The German arm of Polydor proved enthusiastic in promoting Martin's 'Back Where I Belong' album. "They were so bloody keen to sell that record it got embarrassing. They insisted on having tee shirts and CDs on sale at the shows which got up Cozy's nose a bit. I think he was thinking, probably rightly, that my record was being promoted better than his. What really tipped it over the edge for all of us was these cardboard cut outs they had made of me—life size!

It was so embarrassing—having these things by the merchandise stand and outside the gig. We had to drag these things around with us too so they travelled with us in the van. At one gig Cozy was driving around the town when he saw some kid walking down the street with the cardboard cut out version of me tucked under his arm. He had obviously nicked it from outside the gig. Cozy pulled up in his car, obviously giving this kid the fright of his life and says "Ere! Where are you going with that?" The kid told him he thought they were giving them away and promised to take it back. Obviously he didn't so it's probably a dartboard in someone's bedroom now."

With virtually every arm of the Black Sabbath octopus thrashing about on the world stage it would seem strange that one of its brightest potentials had slipped off the radar. For many years Ray Gillen, the charismatic youngster that had been instrumental in pulling Black Sabbath back from the brink of disaster, had been strangely absent from Rock's frontrunners. Although Badlands had failed to deliver Gillen's obvious talents and potential seemed destined for much greater things. A career fronting a major Rock band seemed so obvious that the lack of such a move had his many fans voicing concern. Then the rumours started. "I knew he was ill" sighs Bobby Rondinelli. "I saw him a few times and he didn't look right. Had no idea what it was though. We kind of did the Sun Red Sun thing together but physically missed each other. I laid down my parts and then went off to do Sabbath. Ray came in later to do his vocals."

Sun Red Sun was a genuine all star line-up created by New York guitarist Al Romano. Others involved included Irish ex-Ozzy Osbourne and Gillan guitarist Bernie Tormé (going under the pseudonym Arthur Guitar), Belladonna, Ace Frehley band and McCoy man Mike Sciotto, Artension's John West, Savatage guitarist Chris Caffrey, Gillan and Mammoth bassist John McCoy as well as Alice In Chains drummer Mike Starr. Former Anthrax frontman Joey Belladonna also contributed on the song-writing front and even guitar guru Yngwie Malmsteen added a deft touch to the tracks 'Deadly Nightshade' and 'Big Misunderstanding'. These were to be Gillen's last recordings.

Ray Gillen. Pic: Matt Sampson.

Further Sun Red Sun sessions and rehearsal tapes were issued in 1999 under the Ray Gillen banner. At the time Gillen's illness was being attributed to a whole swathe of ailments, including stomach cancer. In truth the singer had caught the HIV virus.

Drummer Eric Singer, Gillen's erstwhile colleague in both Black Sabbath and Badlands, knew all was not as it seemed. "The Badland's management told me Ray was very sick. Well I had a lot of loose ends to still sort out as I was still signatory to a lot of contracts so that's when I discovered Ray's life insurance company had requested an AIDS test in 1990. The band said he got pneumonia once because a tour was pulled but I think we all knew. Y'know, Ray was my friend in Sabbath but he became someone else. He knew he was ill and, I knew his lifestyle and what kind of guy he became. He was very irresponsible in his affairs. I don't want to speak ill of Ray because he once was my friend and he was a truly gifted singer but what he did, knowing how ill he was then, was very, very wrong. He told people he was clean, he told his partners he was clean. It upset me greatly. It's not something I can understand at all. I'm sure other people must have been affected. One tragedy is enough y'know?"

British Badlands shows in mid 1992 had band leader Jake E. Lee announcing that Gillen was out of the band and that female vocalist Debbie Holliday had usurped his position. Gillen responded publicly and angrily but fans of the band were mystified by a series of oblique press statements from both sides. Lee claimed that Gillen had backed out of the tour because he had "A boil on his neck." However, such was the outcry from British fans that the band was forced to reinstate their original frontman. Upon return to Los Angeles though Gillen was ousted and John West took over the vocal mantle. The singer's friends watched him suffer throughout this period. "Ray was in total denial which must have been a terrible thing for him to live with" insists Glenn Hughes. "A lot of people don't know that Ray and I were very good friends for a long time. There had been this rumour going around that Ray had contracted AIDS and Ray was telling everybody this was false and coming up with proof that he was HIV free. He even showed me a medical report giving a clean blood test. Obviously he had showed this to quite a few people too but it was all part of the deception. The paper work wasn't his, it belonged to his brother in law. The rumours wouldn't go away though so one day I just told him that it didn't matter to me if he had AIDS but he denied it again. I opened my heart and soul to him but he just couldn't face it. He was very believable. He must have been very scared."

Dave Spitz too was kept in the dark by his friend. Gillen never confided in him although the bassist knew he was very ill. "I last met Ray in Los Angeles. I had this jam band with Jeff Duncan from Armored Saint where we used to do the clubs playing Sabbath numbers. Anyway, Ray came to one of these gigs shortly before he died. He was wearing a bandana because his hair was going and the guy just looked very ill. It was quite a shock to see him like that because Ray is one of those very few people that had a magnetic aura. Real stars have this, people are drawn to them. Tony Iommi has it too. With Ray, this meant he was surrounded by girls all the time. Man could that guy pull the chicks! So, to see him like that was really very sad. I had heard all the rumours on the scene about his illness but AIDS was never mentioned. It was covered up pretty well. I heard about stomach ulcers and blood diseases. Ray told me he was checking into hospital because he had stomach problems."

Ray Gillen, aged just 32, died of AIDS on December 3rd, 1993 although some reports suggest the actual date was December 1st, coincidentally, the date now recognised as World AIDS Day.

Glenn Hughes was instrumental in organising a benefit concert to honour Ray. Held in New York at the Irving Plaza, during February of 1994, Glenn had re-formed Trapeze for the night. "It was terrible to lose him. It was only after he had died that I was told

Ray Gillen tribute concert poster.

he did in fact have AIDS. I told people, important people, that Ray didn't have AIDS because I believed that to be true at the time. Even his mother told me he did not have AIDS so of course I believed it. What else was I supposed to do? I even went on MTV and said that too. It could have been any one of us. When I think back to the days of Deep Purple, the way we used to live and how lucky so many of us are to get through that with mind and body intact. Ray was a great loss. He had a great voice, great looks and was so young. He had the world at his feet God bless him."

Chapter 21

Vai–able Options

As soon as Ozzy had loosened the reins Zakk Wylde founded Pride & Glory, a deep Southern based Power Metal triumvirate with Wylde handling both guitar and lead vocals. Pride & Glory was essentially the bastard offspring of three of the guitarist's all-time favourite acts Black Sabbath, Lynyrd Skynyrd and The Allman Brothers. Indeed, whilst with Ozzy, Zakk had dabbled with an extracurricular cover band named Lynyrd Skinhead! The resulting eponymous 1994 album took many by surprise. Wylde had cleverly harked back to the golden days of the balls to the wall power trio era of Cream and The Experience. There the nostalgia ended though and Wylde's sense of the raw dynamic took centre stage.

In early 1993 with Ozzy officially out to pasture word filtered through that retirement was not all that Ozzy had maybe thought it to be and he had a hankering for the bright lights once again. Ozzy poked his head above the parapet by lending his vocals to Irish act Therapy?'s take on 'Iron Man' for a Black Sabbath tribute 'Nativity In Black'. His colleague Geezer Butler would also figure on the same album as part of the Bullring Brummies, led by ex-Judas Priest frontman Rob Halford. Soon on the hunt for a guitarist once again, Ozzy got wind of a young Newcastle guitarist Jimi Savage, who had scored some favourable press with a solo album. Savage confirms he was approached. "I had to send lots of info to Sharon as they were in the States at the time. I sent off pro photos along with my instrumental CD 'Trinity Heights'. All was going well and I was going to head off to the States for a rehearsal. Then I got notified Steve Vai got the audition and everything was cancelled for me". Ozzy got around to sending Jimi a letter of appreciation roughly a year later.

With Ozzy "retired", a fresh project was in the making. There was even a projected album title 'X Ray' being bandied about and deeper rumblings that Ozzy's new campadré was plucked from the very cream of the elite—former David Lee Roth, Whitesnake and solo star in his own right Steve Vai. Having just come off the adulation afforded to his 'Sex And Religion' album Vai was hot property. Indeed, Vai's

Jimi Savage's letter from Ozzy.

profile was at such a peak there was a very real possibility of the proposed venture going out under a different title.

"We thought about calling it a name, X Ray, and maybe a one off for Ozzy" confirms the guitarist. "Ozzy had been working on a CD with his band and they finished about half of it. They then decided to pair Ozzy up with various people to write some additional stuff. My name came up and Ozzy came to see me play while I was on tour in Europe with Aerosmith. We got together after that tour and hit it off very well. We wrote and cut demo's for about 15 or so songs."

The rhythm section for this project found Vai locating a bass man by utilising the David Lee Roth grapevine of musicians, being directed to Todd

Jensen, the same guy Ozzy lost out to with David Lee Roth in 1990. The timing was opportune, as Jensen had just completed a world tour with ex-Free singer Paul Rodgers, as had drummer Deen Castronovo.

"This whole period lasted some two months" recalls Jensen. "It was exciting because not only was this Steve Vai and Ozzy Osbourne but Deen and I had been playing in bands with each other since we were kids. We're from the same town so we had a great bond. Steve Vai telephoned me and asked me if I wanted to get involved. It was that simple. There was no band name around at this time and we all approached it like a writing exercise. We were there just to see what songs would result.

The material was signature Ozzy for the most part I would say. A lot of heavy chord progressions, very aggressive but with that classic Ozzy melody. There was also some offbeat Steve Vai things going on too. Much of the time was spent just searching through ideas, jamming and trying to find some common ground between Ozzy and Steve."

These writing sessions would be conducted at Steve Vai's own private home studios. "A typical day would see Tony, Ozzy's assistant, dropping Ozzy off at Steve's house then loading in an endless supply of diet Pepsi. Ozzy drank that stuff non-stop. Ozzy and Sharon were holed up at the Four Seasons at this time. We certainly worked at the project. We all got together several times each week but really only got a half a dozen songs together, which I thought was a slow pace."

Why did the Osbourne / Vai / Jensen / Castronovo union not progress? The bassist sheds some light. "I was a bit disappointed we only got six songs together but it was happening. I guess they just took a break because the cheques stopped! I went straight into Steve Perry's band from there and did another world tour."

With the introduction of new blood it was determined that a familiar face might provide the right grounding to see the project through. "I got a call from Sharon in 1994" Bob Daisley relates. "I was in the middle of the Mother's Army project at the time. Anyway, I then found myself in the studio with Ozzy, drummer Deen Castronovo and Steve Vai. What had happened was that someone had decided to recreate the atmosphere and sound of the first two albums. That's why they got Steve in who was of course a well known and genuine guitar hero. They had apparently tried working with someone else on bass but then the suggestion was made that if they were really trying to capture that particular sound then they should get me back."

Although Steve Vai was a musician of unquestionable repute the leap of imagination required to transport Vai's skills displayed on work with Roth, Whitesnake and Alcatraz et al. is quite wide when one considers the sheer heaviness required for Ozzy's music. More importantly did the guitarist catch wind of the attempt to recapture past glories and the quest for a 'Randy Rhoads' aura? "It was a very creative process. I obviously approach things different from Randy but there was a great vibe for sure. Yes, it was much different. Everything was tuned down to C and I was using an Octave divider on a lot of stuff. Very, very heavy."

Vai recalls the sessions with Ozzy with obvious fondness. "Working with him was a complete pleasure and a blast. He is one of the most unique and interesting people I have ever met. Sort of like the Godfather of Metal. You would never believe how funny he is. Just the way he talks and explains things and the extraordinary stories he would tell constantly were historical delights. He's pure Rock music and he's not in the least bit stupid or anybody's fool. He knows exactly what he wants and there is an honesty and realness to him that is undeniable. He has no circuit breaker between his head and his mouth and he speaks what he is feeling the moment he feels it. He acts the same around his musicians as he does with his family. He's very real. It was refreshing to have the opportunity to work with him for 3 months and it's an experience in this business I will cherish and remember for ever. After working with him I know why his fans are so loyal and why they feel the way they do about him. They have good reason to."

The course of events did not pan out as Daisley, and probably Vai, envisaged though. "We went to New York to rehearse at the Sony studios" Daisley records. "We were actually getting on great, doing some great work but right in the middle of this we were told that Sony had pulled the plug on the project. Frankly I did not believe it. I cannot imagine Sony cancelling a project that had two top selling artists involved."

The guitarist saw things differently. "We liked working together and felt like we should make a whole record together but the record company ended up feeling that he should take some of the best stuff from what we had done and complete the CD he started with his band. It was not a money issue. I would almost consider working for free to work with Ozzy. He's ... Ozzy! Like I said, the record company felt that he should finish what he started and I believe the new producer Michael Bienhorn was not very keen on working with me."

Steve got back to what he knew best and rapidly set to work on his next solo venture 'Alien Love Secrets' leaving fans of both camps wondering just what might have been.

Meantime, Bob Daisley felt his assumptions were

proven correct and explains the pattern of events after Ozzy had parted ways with Vai. "Deen was gutted and he was wondering what to do. I told him in my opinion that this whole thing was a ploy to get Steve out of the picture and that we would get a call in a few days time saying it was all on again but with another guitarist. The very next day that call came saying "We still want you and Deen." Well, that was OK but they kept me hanging on for months. It ended up with us in London working with these outside songwriters!"

The experience of hit songwriters Mark Hudson (Aerosmith) and Jim Vallance (Bryan Adams writing partner) was brought to bear on the endeavour but Bob Daisley is scathing. "It was bloody ridiculous. They wanted to get back the original sound and were asking these songwriters to come up with those kind of songs when one of the blokes that had written them was just sitting there playing bass! I got fed up and left. I think Geezer took over again."

The acquaintance struck up in the earlier aborted Ozzy / Vai project would signal another venture that Daisley is proud of. "Steve Vai was doing a track for a Jimi Hendrix tribute called 'In From The Storm'. The whole thing was being produced by Eddie Kramer. Steve recommended Kramer to get me in which was nice of him. We had quite a band with Steve, myself, Paul Rodgers from Free and Tony Williams on drums who is sadly no longer with us. A great session."

Bobby Rondinelli, already having figured in the Black Sabbath labyrinthine jigsaw by hosting a pre-Sabbath Ray Gillen back in the eighties, was now set to step up to the block as drummer number seven. The genial mop topped New Yorker had come to the fore with one of Ritchie Blackmore's most commercially successful incarnations of Rainbow. Just how the young Brooklyn native had got himself embroiled in Rock n' Roll in the first place though was a hair raising experience—quite literally.

As with so many of his generation it would be a certain Liverpool fab four that triggered his interest in music. "The Beatles came out when I was a kid so that just did it for me. I always felt drawn to the rhythm. I decided pretty much there and then that I wanted to be a drummer. My parents though had other ideas because we lived in Brooklyn apartments that were very close together so drums didn't seem that practical. So, my parents got me a guitar and got me guitar lessons. That is when it got interesting because I didn't want to play guitar and the next thing I know is this teacher is saying 'Now we're going to teach you how to sing'. Sing? Nobody said anything about singing! I never signed on for that!

Anyhow, I was so nervous about this I started losing my hair. For real. I was just a ten year old kid. It was just falling out by the roots and I could tear great clumps of it out. My parents got me to see this female doctor who asked me if I was doing anything I didn't want to do? Of course I thought she was talking about abuse or something so then I was getting even more freaked out. When we had worked out nothing like that was going on I told her I just wanted to play drums and I was being forced into learning guitar. My parents got the message and within six months I got a drum kit. My hair grew back too thankfully. I was eleven years old."

Bobby Rondinelli's first band experience echoes that of Mick Fleetwood. Both had been caught unawares bashing seven shades of the proverbial out of their kit when curious passers by were stopped in their tracks outside, knocked on the door and changed their lives forever. In Bobby's case it was a bunch of eighteen year olds calling themselves The Wanderers.

"These guys heard me playing on my kit as they were walking past and asked me to join their band. That's how simple it was. I was still eleven, maybe twelve and these guys were eighteen so they seemed like grown up men to me. We used to rehearse every Sunday. I would put my drum kit on the train and travel to this big old school and practice. I loved it, I thought I was at Madison Square Gardens or something. That's how I got on the first rung of the ladder."

Rondinelli's prominent tour of duty with Rainbow was preceded by a stint with an oddball act by the name of Samantha. "Samantha was certainly odd that's for sure" agrees Bobby. "I had just broken up a band with my brother Teddy and was really just looking to play but without the commitments. Samantha caught me when I was available. We did some strange stuff from 'Iron Man' to a whole range of diverse and crazy songs. The singer of Samantha was a nut. In the middle of a live set, without warning, he would stop the entire band, point at me and shout 'Drum solo—now!' and I would have to do it on command. Then he would point again and yell 'Stop!' Crazy band but that's how I bumped into Ritchie which was a bit of a bizarre tale in itself."

Doing the rounds of the New York clubs with Samantha, Rondinelli had heard that two major openings were looming—Rainbow and Kiss. He went for both. "I auditioned for Kiss and out of 2,000 applicants it came down to the wire between me and Eric Carr" he says modestly. "The thing was, I wasn't really that interested in Kiss because a friend had told me Rainbow was looking for a drummer too and that was much more my kind of thing. There was a friend of mine, he owned a recording studio, and someone he knew was connected to Ritchie Blackmore. Well, this guy wanted some studio time so my friend cut him a deal, which was to get me an audition with Ritchie in exchange for 30 hours free studio time. The guy agreed to hook me up with Rainbow but in the interim my band, Samantha, had all of our gear—including my kit—stolen out of our truck. It was just the worst time.

Now, a really cool thing happened. Friends of ours in bands like Twisted Sister and Zebra put on a benefit concert to raise us the money back to buy new gear. At the sound check for this gig the drummer from Twisted Sister asked me show him a particular lick. So, I sat down at his kit and showed him this lick. At that very precise moment a friend of Ritchie came in and saw me play. Now, here is where the craziness begins because this guy was actually in jail and had been let out on a day pass. So anyway, he goes back and tells Ritchie what he's seen and heard.

A week later I'm doing a gig on this crappy borrowed kit. This guy comes up to me and says 'I'm a friend of Ritchie Blackmore and he would like to meet you' so I say 'I've been trying to get hold of Ritchie too'. Anyway, turns out Ritchie was there at the back of the club. He shook my hand and said 'I really like the way you play'. Cool! He knew about the Kiss situation and said that if I didn't get that gig would I try out for Rainbow? We hit it off really well. Ritchie wanted to know what would happen if Kiss gave me the call but I told him straight, I wanted the Rainbow gig."

Bobby's port of entry into Rainbow corresponded with a flush of commercial good fortune for the band. Headed by the former Fandango singer Joe Lynn Turner the Rainbow that had thrilled the post Purple die hards had been transformed into a radio compliant hit machine with the 1981 'Difficult To Cure' album. The single 'I Surrender', written by Russ Ballard, had just lost out by a hair's breadth from securing the British No. 1 position. 'Spotlight Kid' and 'Can't Happen Here' too transferred well to radio. The follow-up 'Straight Between The Eyes' trimmed away the Pop pretensions but still fared well, going top 30 in the USA, after which Rondinelli was usurped by Chuck Burgi. His Rainbow tenure had served Rondinelli well, elevating him into the upper echelons of respected Rock drummers. However, a greater portion of the next few years would be spent formulating his own Rondinelli act, closing the decade with a session on Doro's 'Force Majeure' opus.

"I took a call from a good friend of mine Robert Gambino" states Bobby describing the first steps that led to his enrolment into Black Sabbath. "It was funny because Robert had worked for Tony Iommi for a very long time but they had fallen out for some reason and weren't speaking to one another at this point. Anyway, he still knew what was going on with Sabbath, still had all the connections, so he rings up one day and left this message on my machine 'Bobbeee... Tony's looking for a drummer, here's his number. Gambino'. That was it!

No one keeps track of Tony's phone number because he changes it every five minutes. Eventually I got it from the manager or the agent or someone. So I rang him and spoke to his wife and left a message. Ten minutes later Tony was on the phone and I was on my way to rehearsals in England."

Those rehearsals, after an audition at Tasco, took place in Henley on Arden, scene of many a Black Sabbath limbering up in the past. "It was kind of casual because Tony had said I was in but of course I still had to play with the guys in the band but I wasn't worried about that. I guess there are a number of musicians, drummers in particular, who have a reputation and a track record and I'm fortunate to be in that group of people. Tommy Aldridge, Carmine, Vinny, Cozy—all those guys. It's a pretty small network really. We're all very different in our approach. We each have our particular style live and in the studio so anyone with any experience can pick the style of drummer they want for a particular project. The rest is a character test.

Drummers are a breed apart. We'll actually help each other out too, which you don't get with singers and guitarists. There is an observation that I've made, at trade shows like the Frankfurt Music Fair or the NAMM show. In the Hilton bar you will always find twenty or more drummers hanging out socialising but at the other end of the bar will be a miserable guitarist all on his own! Your social life is better if you're a drummer that's for sure. We share info, we network and recommend each other for jobs we know are going.

Putting a band together is a lot more than finding the most talented people. You don't want some asshole in the band just because they can play better than anyone else. People have to work and get along together. If you hire me you know what you're going to get even before I walk in the door. I'm reliable, I hit hard, I'm a fun guy to be around and I have a loud mouth. That's me."

With his position freshly confirmed Bobby took an unexpected phone call from an old friend, not offering wise words but something altogether more appealing if only in jest. "It was Cozy Powell" he laughs. "He said 'How are you doing Bobby?' Great I said. How are you Cozy? 'I'm great too' he said. Then he goes 'Listen Bobby, I'm going to give you the telephone number of my girlfriend'. So I start to smile and of course I took the bait and asked why. 'Because I've given you everything else so you may as well have her!' That was just so Cozy! What a great guy he was. Loved him to bits."

Bobby was pleased to discover he had entered the proceedings at a formative stage. One where he could make a difference. "When I arrived they had just begun to start getting some ideas for songs down which was a good thing for me because we spent a long time just jamming through stuff. There were some songs already done but for some stuff Tony had some riffs but nothing complete so it was good for me to get involved at that stage of the process. It showed them I wasn't just a drummer, that I could contribute ideas too. It all felt very comfortable because these are all top league players. We had some good times there even before I was fully accepted into the band I suppose. It was all pretty intensive because we rehearsed, we got the songs together then demoed them for the album."

The drummer gelled quickly with his compatriots and was quietly impressed with the individual skills being displayed. "Tony Martin has a great voice, he's certainly very underrated. He would pull out some sensational stuff which really surprised me. He lives under that cloud of Ozzy and Ronnie which is very unfair because, in my opinion, the guy is up there with the very best. With Sabbath he lived under the shadow of Ozzy all the time, just like Ronnie did and everyone else. If you look at it though he stuck it out longer than any of them so he should get some respect for that. He's never got his due."

Geezer too offered this about working with Tony Martin on 'Cross Purposes'. "He was great to work with in the studio because he just wants the best for the songs and the band. Tony puts a lot of effort in and I can see why Tony Iommi has really enjoyed working with him in the past. He's willing to adapt and listen to suggestions without having a tantrum. We've had to deal with all of that from singers in the past so working with Tony was refreshing. We worked well on the lyrics together too. For a singer he's actually fairly humble. You don't get many like that. Most of them have singers disease if you know what I mean."

Conversely, Bobby Rondinelli's rhythm partner too comes in for some praise. "Geezer is a great bass player. He does a lot of stuff, quite busy but he drives it along. He is also a very funny guy. There was a very good atmosphere in the band at that point and a lot of that was down to Geezer. As a drummer you have to try and keep pace with him whereas with Neil Murray, he's more a traditional type player in that he follows the drums. When Geezer starts up you just have to go along with the flow. I loved playing with the both of them."

Unbeknown to the general public, and even members of the band it seems, 'Cross Purposes' almost came to the very same crossroads that 'Seventh Star' had dithered on before taking a wrong turning. The album hit the shelves sporting the Black Sabbath moniker but according to Geezer Butler, interviewed some three years later, it was initially designed as a project piece. "I wasn't happy with that at all" he protested. "That album was not supposed to be Black Sabbath. It wasn't Black Sabbath because at the time the whole reunion with Ozzy was under discussion. I never viewed it as Black Sabbath. We were talking to Ozzy. How could it be Sabbath? It was the same old thing though. It has happened so many times."

Butler's viewpoint is at huge variance to his team mates. "No fucking way" Bobby Rondinelli objected. "I was asked to join Black Sabbath. We recorded a Black Sabbath album and then we toured as Black Sabbath. A Geezer / Iommi album? That doesn't make any fucking sense."

Tony Martin too was, it appears, kept in the dark. "Wow, I never knew that. We all thought it was a Black Sabbath album when we were recording it" he laughs. "It is possible that Geezer and Tony had something else in their minds because Black Sabbath was, of course, the master of deception. Geezer, lovely guy though he is, does have a habit of saying some odd things at times. Maybe there was some scheme we were kept in the dark about. Maybe there could have been some pressure from the Osbournes but that was not the kind of information Tony Iommi would ever pass on. I can't see it though because it was far from a 'Seventh Star' situation. The music sounded like Black Sabbath to me. The other thing is that the name Black Sabbath carries so much weight, something Tony discovered of course with 'Seventh Star' and the way that whole thing backfired. Tony Iommi owns the name Black Sabbath, Ozzy doesn't. There's no way he would give that name up.

There was something else too which makes me find the whole 'not Black Sabbath' thing a bit weird. That was very much Gloria Butler's baby. She had a very clear picture of how all the photographs were going to look, the artwork, everything, even before we started. When it was finished it looked exactly like Gloria had said it would. So, if it wasn't Black Sabbath you would think Geezer's wife might have known about it."

Tony Martin has pleasant memories of this period. "That time with Sabbath, 'Cross Purposes', it felt good. I was a little more wise to their antics but I had Albert to keep his eye on things there. The good thing for me in having Albert involved was that because he had known them so long they couldn't bullshit him. Basically for 'Eternal Idol' I was chucked in at the deep end, 'Headless Cross' and 'Tyr' were essential to keeping Black Sabbath alive and then they really fucked up by bringing Ronnie back in. That is not meant as a go at Ronnie, who I love, but they were offered a great opportunity and blew it. Sorry if I'm

Black Sabbath—Tony Martin, Tony Iommi, Bobby Rondinelli, Geezer Butler.

a little bitter about it but we really worked at that line-up and a lot of promises were made which just evaporated. Neil, Cozy and I deserved better than the treatment we got at the end. We were all in 100%. It wasn't just a paying job with those albums because we were all on the same wavelength, let's make this happen, let's get Black Sabbath back up there.

A huge amount of money was spent on 'Dehumanizer' so what should have been five steps forward ended up being two steps back. They asked me back—again—for 'Cross Purposes' and that felt good. Tony said to me that, in hindsight, we should have all just carried on after 'Tyr'. The team was good. There were a few ups and downs but generally it was working. Tony got a load of money put onto the table to do the Ronnie thing and that can cloud your perception."

Guesting, albeit very low key, on 'Cross Purposes, would be the hugely respected figure of Eddie Van Halen. So low key in fact that the world renowned guitar maestro is not even credited on the album, all tracks being credited to Iommi / Butler / Martin. "Tony Iommi is good mates with a lot of those kind of people" the vocalist observes. "I just turned up at the studio one day and there he was. He was very enthusiastic I remember, he really pushed us along to get that song done. As well as co-writing 'Evil Eye' he actually played on it too."

Surprisingly very few Sabbath aficionados failed to recognise the very un-Iommi like opening guitar break on this track. Geoff Nicholls prefers to leave an air of mystery hanging over this issue though. "Eddie came down to rehearsals because he was playing at the Birmingham N.E.C. Tony went and picked him up in his car and brought him down. What actually happened was that Eddie quickly worked up this song, 'Evil Eye', and put quite a bit of work into it. When he had to go, Tony reworked the track, basically learning the parts Eddie had put down for the real recording. I don't think that first solo is Eddie because Tony redid that again and again so probably just duplicated what Eddie had done before. Tony was at this stage trying out different guitar sounds too which is why it probably doesn't 'sound' like Tony. Then again, Tony might just have left Eddie's little bit on there. Let's leave it a mystery shall we?"

So, with the exception of the unexpected studio guest, for Tony Martin it was business as usual even if he did afford a few more over the shoulder glances than usual. Oddly, Ronnie James Dio seemed to be, internally at least, excised from band history for a second time. "Tony Iommi just never spoke about it so I didn't ask" opines Martin. "I know that might sound ridiculous but, as I've said before, that's how Black Sabbath operates. Tony just said they didn't get on, it was the same as the old days and that he hadn't changed one bit. That's all that was ever said about Ronnie."

When he received his first pressing of 'Cross Purposes' singer Tony Martin was horrified to see his name on the writing credits. Stories of injustices of being unaccredited for song-writing abound in Rock n' Roll but for Martin the situation had become cruelly reversed. He was fully credited—but under his real family name. "I was furious" he seethed. "I had spent years and years trying to keep my family name completely out of the business and for very good reason. It was Gloria Butler who apparently gave them my real name. An honest accident I'm sure but it had major repercussions for me. I had been receiving death threats, God knows why because in the whole Sabbath scheme of things I didn't think I was that important, but nevertheless I had received threats. It's not a very nice feeling believe me.

One or two people picked up on it but I could not make a fuss about it because that would only draw attention to the problem. I didn't want press releases and such going out. I had people going to my school and trying to get to my kids so they could find me. It was horrifying. To this day I don't know why I was a target but suddenly, with my family name out there, I was open for any nutter who wanted to track me down through the electoral roll, my family, etc. That was one major fuck up."

It was not the only bugbear. The lack of formality and contract that had smoothed the way for Tony Martin's entrance into Black Sabbath in 1987 had been sitting uncomfortably for many years. "Albert got very, very frustrated with them. They would just ignore him, which is the normal day to day way Black Sabbath works. If there's a problem they just don't talk about it. I still have all these faxes from Albert to them and if you could shout in a fax, that's what Albert was doing! In the end the communication got down to 'What the fuck are you doing?', 'Where the fuck are you?', 'Answer my fucking faxes!' Getting me the job with Black Sabbath was probably the worst thing Albert could have done for himself."

Promoting 'Cross Purposes' in America Black Sabbath were now in possession of two strengths they had been sorely lacking for a long time. Despite Neil Murray's Whitesnake pedigree it was Geezer Butler the die hard Sabbath fans wanted back onstage and that's what they got. The second major plus was that the band was heading up an exceptionally strong billing with special guests Motorhead and the satanically charged Death Metal veterans Morbid Angel—both acts more than capable of pulling healthy ticket sales in their own right. Whilst Lemmy's vehicle for sonic excess had long since passed into the annals of Rock n' Roll legend, Morbid Angel was probably only the extreme Death Metal band on the planet that could proudly boast one million album sales and counting.

The package was strong, unified and most importantly compatible. All three acts could be appreciated by fans of each artist whilst each band also drew upon fans from varied quarters too. As Black Sabbath limbered up in Connecticut during early February the omens looked decidedly black. That is of course black as in Black Sabbath, Lemmy's jeans and undiluted Black Metal. On this tour Black was to be celebrated, black a good thing.

Six weeks hooked up with this treble bill of tribulation closed in Florida as Motorhead took their own path snaking across the United States of America whilst Black Sabbath boarded a plane across the Pacific to Japan. By mid April the band was back on European soil ploughing their way through the UK with Lee Dorrian's doom laden Cathedral and Americans Godspeed. By now Black Sabbath was being hailed by three popular music movements—Grunge, Stoner and Doom. Cathedral, as displayed on a run of impressive albums, were about as close to genetically engineered clone of Black Sabbath as you could get. In 1994 the band, another product of the industrial West Midlands, were brandishing 'The Ethereal Mirror' album and their endeavour to pursue all things Sabbath now saw them incorporating guitarist Victor Griffin and drummer Joe Hasselvander from The Cult underground seventies U.S. act Pentagram into their line-up. They took the whole thing one step closer to lunacy by sporting distinctly retro seventies stage gear including bell bottoms! Cathedral were the undisputed Doom leaders in the UK and securing the support slot to Black Sabbath was, for them, akin to sitting at the feet of God and inhaling on the omnipotent one's very own Bong pipe. Cathedral subsequently released 'The Carnival Bizarre' album, produced by Kit Woolven. The track 'Utopian Blaster' featured guest guitar from none other than Tony Iommi.

Black Sabbath's next album would be culled from these dates. Captured on film at London's Hammersmith Odeon the band delivered the 'Cross Purposes Live' package, a video / CD package rush released to virtually no promotion whatsoever. So low key was the release that it took many die hard fans several years to discover the damn thing had even been released at all. 'Cross Purposes Live' is somewhat of an anomaly in the catalogue. The obvious strain affecting Tony Martin's vocals and the very manner of its issue demonstrates a distinct lack of forward planning. In retrospect though, fans have come to

Tony Iommi. Pic: Sean Denomey.

regard the outing as a valuable historical record of the Iommi / Martin / Butler / Nicholls / Rondinelli line-up. In spite of his affliction Martin's command of Dio's 'Time Machine' and 'Mob Rules' is impressive and Tony Iommi gives a fluid demonstration throughout. Unfortunately, once again, the album packaging completely failed to mention Geoff Nicholls.

Geezer Butler found the reverential status afforded Black Sabbath by the Grunge and Stoner movement somewhat alarming. "We had spent two decades being the uncoolest band on the entire planet and suddenly there was this huge turnaround" he insists. "I can't remember when it struck me exactly but I gradually became aware that this whole new breed of bands was talking about Black Sabbath all of the time. To be that influential after such a long time was odd. We were used to everybody hating us, now, here they were, all worshipping everything we had ever done. It started in the late eighties with Metallica and then this whole Grunge thing exploded and suddenly it became very cool to like Black Sabbath. Of course we had a completely different perspective on things because we had been in the middle of this thing for so long. Black Sabbath had made millions and lost millions. We got ripped off so many times it is a wonder the band carried on for so long.

When all these bands started talking about us it took a while for us to get it. I think it was when they started looking like we did and sounding like we did we got the picture. Those first Black Sabbath albums were being hailed as masterpieces but to us they were pretty basic. I mean, we are all very proud of them of course but Black Sabbath is essentially a very simple band at heart. We were just too close to it and couldn't see the way the outside world viewed what we were doing. We never, ever thought we would influence anybody!"

Outside influences were certainly making an impression on Black Sabbath though. "There was this ongoing discussion between Geezer and Tony Iommi about musical direction all the time" recalls Geoff Nicholls. "Geezer was very keen on pushing for a more modern sound but Tony's argument was always seen from the viewpoint that Sabbath shouldn't be influenced by bands that were really just bad copies of Black Sabbath. It just didn't make sense. There was always this tug of war going on about the music and the name."

'Cross Purposes' was also ably supported throughout the Festland with the traditional lengthy glut of shows in Germany and short stabs into the Czech Republic, Poland, Hungary, Italy and Austria. In the town of Lienz in Austria on the 25th of May, the band was subject to a revisitation of Catholic fun-

Tony Martin. Pic: Sean Denomey.

damentalism they had not experienced for many a year. It seems the point of contention was the 'Cross Purposes' album cover. "We suddenly encountered all this religious stuff down in Austria which really felt weird. We hadn't had to put up with any of that nonsense for a long, long time so it kind of took us all by surprise." Tony Martin relates. "It seems they were upset about the fire on the angel's wings on the album cover. They really got quite upset about it and they banned all our gig posters in the town." Reluctant to forgo their local advertising the posters were altered in accordance with the wishes of the diocese magnates. It would result in a surreal quick fix. "Things got very weird from that point on. They got some guy with a big stencil of a crocodile's mouth to go around town and paint this thing on top of all the posters. God knows where this idea came from. The crocodile covered up the flames. Apparently it was bad to set angels on fire but it was quite alright to have large reptiles eating them!"

The Baron Munchausen world into which the band had unwittingly entered would prevail for the gig itself. "If you can believe this, because we didn't at first, the Bishop of Fulda sent an emissary down to check out the gig! This guy, in a long white trench coat was there all night acting as an official observer in case we got up to anything naughty. In the audience was this lone guy with this placard 'Save your souls—Turn to Jesus!' I asked the crew to turn a spotlight on him and said to the audience 'Please give this guy a huge round of applause because he's got the biggest bollocks of anyone here tonight!' The bloke got a big cheer."

Attendance ratings in general, not counting clergy, for the tour were healthy across the board but, for the first time, Tony Martin voiced his dissatisfaction. "For the 'Cross Purposes' tour the set consisted mainly of older tracks. 90% of it was either Ozzy or Ronnie songs, I considered walking out at that point because I felt like we should be moving on from that, but I gave my word that I would see it through and so I carried on. It was sometimes very hard to be enthused about the whole thing."

As Finland said goodbye to Black Sabbath another casualty was added to the roll of honour. "After the European tour things got fucked up for me because I had this girl manager at the time" reckons Bobby Rondinelli. "The band was talking about doing another record with me, they said they wanted me and I knew Tony liked the way I played because he kept

Cross Purposes tour pass.

telling me. But she asked for too much money. Of course they said "Fuck off!" Managers ..."

Minus Rondinelli the 'Cross Purposes' tour would extend itself by wending its way down to South America, the band supporting Kiss in Chile, Argentina and Brazil. These dates would herald the very welcome return of Bill Ward, apparently something the moustachioed ones had been plotting for some time. "They had been planning on getting Bill back for a long time" affirms Tony Martin. "That's how they worked, decide upon getting someone but get someone else in for the meantime. There were a lot of people in Black Sabbath that were history before they knew it! They wanted Bill back so they made it happen. I really enjoyed working with Bill I have to say. He is a great bloke so I could see why they were so determined to get him back into the band.

We did some rehearsals in Birmingham with Billy. He hadn't played the Sabbath repertoire for years and years so it was a bit of a gentle coaxing really. When he actually got to perform live I was giving Billy a lot of cues for the drums, telling him what was next. He was still great, he had just been out of the game for so long. He soon got back into the swing of it. Lovely rhythm. I know Tony and Geezer were very glad to have him back."

South America would not be all the band expected as the singer reveals. "Some of the gigs were big outdoor events and some were fairly small indoor theatres. We were supporting Kiss which was an odd experience because their fan base down in those countries is just absolutely fanatical. All the kids would be in the Kiss makeup and they would chase our car around everywhere. It got quite intimidating. I think they expected quite a bit more out of South America because they had been down there earlier with Ronnie James Dio for the 'Monsters Of Rock' and then it was just huge. This time it was all a bit of a let down."

Black Sabbath opened these gigs on August 27th at the Sao Paulo Estádio do Pacaembú 'Monsters Of Rock' show. Delivering a pared down set the band performed before Kiss and, oddly, Slayer. Other acts on the billing comprised Suicidal Tendencies and local fare the fast rising Prog-Metal band Angra with Dr. Sin and Viper. "We had a hell of a lot of technical problems, equipment failure and all of that kind of thing" Tony Martin grimaced. "To give you some idea, they had no radio mics or transmitters. Well, the last time I had used a mic with a wire was at least eight years before that. Consequently I got myself into a right bloody mess. I got the bloody thing wrapped around the lights, around Tony's legs, everywhere. It was a major stress. We actually had to alter the stage show because of it, ditching the front of stage lights and moving all the monitors. Oh well, the show had to go on as they say." Sabbath, Kiss and Suicidal Tendencies continued on through Santiago in Chile and put in a brace of shows in Buenos Aires, Argentina.

In early 1995 Wylde was beckoned back into the Ozzy camp to complete the 'Ozzmosis' record. The album included contributions form Rick Wakeman reforging a link back to the keyboard maestro's assistance afforded to Black Sabbath during the 70s. With Daisley gone it would be Geezer Butler handling bass chores and Castronovo on drums. The only evidence of Steve Vai's involvement being a co-write credit on the cut 'My Little Man'.

The stability Ozzy sought though was not to transpire. Zakk Wylde was being courted by the leviathan that was Guns n' Roses and, although virtually impotent for the past few years, the spell woven by the Axl Rose led supergroup had proven enticing. The comeback tour would not even attempt to gloss over the fact that Ozzy had changed his mind. Dubbed the 'Retirement Sucks' trek, the band was originally slated to include Wylde in the line-up. However, the guitarist's public dalliances with Guns n' Roses and the indecision surrounding any commitment ignited a further round of auditions.

During periods of inactivity Geezer and Castronovo convened G//Z/R with Fear Factory vocalist Burton C. Bell and Midlands guitarist Pedro Howse for the uncompromisingly raw 'Plastic Planet' album.

Chapter 22

Skol?

Joe Holmes first made his presence felt as founder member of an act assembled on the reputation of ex-Angel vocalist Frank Dimino in the mid 80s following the singer's first post Angel act The Ruffians had disintegrated. Moving to Portland, Oregon, Dimino put a new group together entitled Terrif featuring guitarist Joe Holmes, bassist Emil Lech Brando and drummer Tom Cosmo. Demos were recorded before Dimino, frustrated at the lack of progress, moved back to Los Angeles. Dimino and his former Angel colleagues Punky Meadows and Barry Brandt united again in late 1985 in an attempt to resurrect Angel.

Lech promptly joined Sound Barrier before stints with Joshua for their 'Speed Of Light' record and by 1989 Driver. Holmes meanwhile joined theatric Metal act Lizzy Borden for their 1987 album 'Visual Lies' before quitting that band to recreate Terrif. This second version of the band numbered Holmes, Cosmo, erstwhile Lizzy Borden bassist Mike Davis and vocalist Dana Freebarin.

Terrif folded once more when in October of 1990 Holmes landed the job as six-stringer for David Lee Roth, featuring in the same line-up as bassist Todd Jensen. As Rock stars go you couldn't get much bigger than David Lee Roth. Fronting the all American multi platinum dream ticket that was Van Halen Roth's outrageous sense of showmanship and bravado had put even Eddie Van Halen's guitar prowess in the shade. Upon leaving Van Halen, Roth's career had been even more explosive with a clutch of hit albums, hit singles and extravagant videos blessed with the patented Roth mixture of wacky humour, supreme musicianship and a larger than life ego. Roth was limbering up to promote the 'A Little Ain't Enough' album but had switched guitarists used for that record, Steve Hunter and Jason Becker. For touring purposes ex-D'Molls man Desi Rexx alongside New Jersey's Joe Holmes. The duo was added after Becker was tragically stricken with Lou Gehring's Disease that would leave the promising young star in a wheelchair.

Fred Coury recalls being asked his advice on the Terrif man at the time. "The owner of Mates Rehearsals had known Joe for years and years so that's how I got to know him too. Joe is a truly fantastic guitarist and a really nice guy too. Anyway, someone from the Roth organization, I think it was Pete Angelus, called me to tell me they were looking for another guitarist. Then Dave himself got on the phone and said "You seem to know everyone. Who's a really hot guitarist?" We had a talk about styles and I said "Well, there is only one guy—Joe Holmes." Two weeks later I saw that he was in the band."

By the close of the nationwide tour Holmes had bailed out. Roth would struggle visibly without him. The Nile Rodgers produced 'Your Filthy Little Mouth', with Steve Hunter and Terry Kilgore supplying guitars, was released in early 1994 and failed to capture the sparkle of previous outings. Holmes got back to what he knew with a new look Terrif made ready for launching. Occupying the vocal slot this time around was Ray Gillen. The singer's term of duty with Terrif would last a matter of months with only basic demos cut. With Gillen's departure Holmes adopted a new style for Terrif and morphed the unit into Dog-Ma and then subsequently Alien Ink.

However, during 1995 upfront of Joe Holmes securing the position Ozzy, unbeknown to most, would try out another guitarist. To cut in with a personal anecdote, in conversation with Gloria Butler, wife and manager of Geezer Butler, one day, she happened to drop a heavy hint to the author it would be well worth my while getting down to Nottingham Rock City that night. Naturally intrigued, it seemed as though my curiosity would have to be tempered though as I already had an interview with Lemmy from Motorhead in Birmingham that very same evening. Well, there was only one course of action to take—do both! The very moment Motorhead closed their show in Birmingham it was a desperate motorway dash up to Nottingham. Just as soon as I had walked through the entrance to the club—literally those very few seconds—Ozzy and band march onstage. Rock City that night was honoured with a clandestine Ozzy gig but this was no average warmup. The man on guitar was Alex Skolnick.

Skolnick had made his mark as a quite electrifying player with his early work for Bay Area Thrashers Testament before a leap to more refined, if no less heavy, pastures new with Savatage. Indeed, the guitarist had carved out such a name for himself that he was already being revered by fans of both bands as the hottest guitarist to go through the ranks of either. The surprised Rock City audience lapped it up and we were collectively of the opinion that the throng had witnessed the debut of Ozzy's new right hand man. The gig was intense to say the least and Skolnick had seemed at ease throughout, Ozzy being happy to introduce him to the crowd by name repeatedly. It was not to be though.

An anonymous Ozzy insider sheds some light. "Yeah, I was there at that gig" he confirms. "You weren't seeing things—it was Alex. I was actually quite surprised when we came to rehearsal. Alex was a really nice guy, really into it. He really thought that after that show in Nottingham he had got the gig but it just didn't work for some reason. I remember him being quite shocked. One minute he was there the next he wasn't and we just carried on as normal."

Catching up with Alex himself puts the whole thing into context. "In seven years you're the first person that's contacted me about that gig!" the guitarist says by way of introduction. Illustrating just how easily other Ozzy histories have wiped the slate of this incident. Post Savatage Skolnick was pursuing his own Jazz Rock endeavour Exhibit A.

"I had left Testament in 1992. In 1991, I started playing with different artists and realized I wanted to stretch out musically. I recorded with Primus Bassist Les Claypool then toured with bassist Stuart Hamm, both in 1991. In 1993 I recorded with bassist Michael Manring on his album "Thonk." In '94 I recorded with Savatage on their album 'Handful Of Rain', and toured the U.S. and Japan with them. I also had my own band, called Exhibit A, but it wasn't having much luck getting a record deal. Towards the end of 1994, I was one of three guys called in to audition for the Spin Doctors and came in second."

Meanwhile, in New York Ozzy had tried run throughs with Ritchie Kotzen of Poison and Warren De Martini of Ratt fame. Neither exactly slouches on the guitar but obviously the Ozzy 'X' factor was to be found elsewhere and Deen Castronovo thought he knew just the man. Alex, then just arriving home to Berkeley, California from guitar clinic demonstrations in Texas, records just how eager the Ozzy camp was to establish contact.

"There were a lot of messages on my answering machine. The first one said "Alex, this is Deen Castronovo. I'm playing drums with Ozzy. We need a guitar player. I think you'd be perfect. Give me a call as soon as you can." He left his hotel number. Apparently he had called just when I'd left town a week earlier. The next message was also from him, trying to reach me again. Then there was a message from someone at Sharon Osbourne's office, and another message from Deen. I wondered if the next message would be from Ozzy! By the time I called Deen had checked out of his hotel, so I called Sharon's office. I was informed that they didn't have a guitarist yet, and that I should expect a call from Sharon. She called a short time later and asked if I'd like to come to London."

Skolnick mailed Ozzy's office video footage of Savatage in Japan and Testament recordings. In return a rather large parcel winged its way from the Osbournes to Alex. Inside was a copy of every Ozzy album and a list of twenty tracks to learn—most of the 'Live And Loud' album plus two from 'Ozzmosis' including 'Perry Mason'. "I was told to expect a call in a few weeks, when Ozzy finished his vocals in the studio (for Ozzmosis). It was hard to keep it a secret, but I held it in. A few weeks later I got a call early in the morning from the office asking if I could be on a plane to London the next day. And off I was."

Once in London Alex was put through his paces with a formal audition. It would prove a somewhat intimidating process. "Deen filled me in on all the details. Yes, this was an audition, but I was highly recommended and they liked the materials I had sent so I had a very good shot. I also met a couple guitar techs who were coordinating the auditions. I was told to make sure I'm in tune, don't waste any time and be prepared to launch from one song right into the other!" Alex had his instructions and the collectively assembled waited on the appearance of Ozzy.

"I guess it went really well. I had been told to be ready to play as soon as Ozzy walks in. So he comes in, waves hello to everyone, gets behind the mic and asks what I want to play. We launch into "I Don't Know" and during the solo, Ozzy is staring at me from behind dark glasses. It was a bit intimidating. But he starts slowly nodding his head, and gives the thumbs up sign. We finish the song and a second later he calls out the next song, "Crazy Train." During the solo, he has the same reaction. As soon as we're done he looks at me and says "Great! Can you come back at noon tomorrow?""

"Sure" I said. What else was I going to say? He left and everyone in the room started cheering. "Was it okay?" I asked? "Are you kidding?" said Deen. "That was awesome. I can't believe he asked you back after just a couple songs! That's unheard of. Way to go!"" Indeed, Alex's audition had proven so positive an immediate live test was deemed necessary. The guitarist would be quite taken aback to learn that he would be playing a full blown gig within days.

"I got back to the hotel and was told that it went so well that they've decided to book an unannounced show at Rock City in Nottingham, where ironically I had played a few years earlier with Testament. So the next day, we played ten songs. It had much more of a feel of a rehearsal than an audition. Sharon was there, as were the kids. A couple days later, we moved to a rehearsal studio in Birmingham. We did a few rehearsals, but they were without Ozzy, just instrumental. I remember he had come down with a bad cold and almost had to cancel the show, but he got well just in time for the gig."

Ozzy, happy to introduce Alex by name at that gig had seemingly found his man. As an eye witness the author can confirm that not only did the crowd warm to Ozzy's new candidate but that Skolnick seemed in his element. Ozzy was beaming smiles and made damn sure the audience knew who was up on stage by reinforcing Alex's presence with named introductions on a number of occasions throughout the show.

For Skolnick the gig made an indelible mark on the memory. "It was absolutely amazing. Definitely one of the loudest gigs I've ever played; I didn't wear ear plugs because I was afraid it would affect my performance. My ears rang all night! All the songs felt like I imagined, but with even more of an intensity. I really liked playing the Sabbath tunes too. Even though it was short, it was still a great experience and I wouldn't trade it for the world."

Ozzy's band for the day featured Alex, Geezer Butler on bass, John Sinclair on keyboards and Deen Castronovo on drums. The Nottingham Rock City crowd thought they had just been privileged to see Ozzy's new line-up for the forthcoming tour. But it was not to be. Alex takes up the story from his vantage point. "It is a mystery worthy of the show "Unsolved Mysteries." After the show, Ozzy gave me a big hug, and said "Alex, you've got the gig."

Guys in the crew were thanking me, saying they haven't heard it sound that good since they could remember, and they could finally go home. One of them said he hadn't seen Ozzy look so happy in a long time. Also I had figured out a way to play the multiple guitar harmonies in 'Mr. Crowley' live, and someone said "Man, when you played that, we were all floored. Even Randy didn't do that."

I had been in London a total of about ten days. I flew back home the day after the show. Even though Ozzy said I was hired, I knew enough not to count on anything happening until contracts were signed and an itinerary received. Even then, nothing is certain. A short time later, I was informed I wasn't doing the tour. It was a little disappointing, but I think it worked out for the best. There was no detailed explanation. I asked Sharon if there was anything I could have done differently. She said absolutely not, it was fabulous and I could have worked out great. But the fact was they had someone who they felt better fit the group right now, who turned out to be Joe Holmes. I made it clear I would have loved to have stayed on, but I understood that they had to make the decision that they felt was best. I said they could still call me anytime I'd be happy to work with them again. That's still true. But I guess it wasn't meant to be and I'm just thankful for the opportunity I had, short as it was!"

After his fleeting tenure with Ozzy Alex got down to his music in serious fashion. "In retrospect, everything seems to have turned out for the better. I had always had a secret desire to go back to school and get my music degree (inspired by Randy), and perform and study improvisational music, from John Coltrane, The Brecker Brothers, Weather Report, Miles Davis and John McLaughlin. I always knew of the risks of being more of a "Jazz" artist, but decided that if nothing else, I could play in small clubs, continue my studies, get my musicianship to the highest possible level. So immediately after the Ozzy gig, I enrolled myself in school and started working as a Jazz and World music guitarist in clubs, restaurants and private events. A few years ago, I moved to New York to complete my studies at New School University, one of the top music programs in the country. Since moving here, I've been busy as a sideman, session guitarist, composer and leader of my own groups."

Latterly Alex has been prominent in the seasonal Savatage offshoot Trans Siberian Orchestra and his own Attention Deficit. His next release will certainly be of interest to Ozzy fans, not just down to the gig connection but the subject matter. Alex is interpreting Rock and Metal standards in a Jazz Rock format. "Ironically, the title track of my album is the one Ozzy song we do, Goodbye To Romance!"

Once Black Sabbath had laid the 'Cross Purposes' tour to rest, Geezer Butler duly hopped beds and nestled in with the Ozzy Osbourne camp once again. During a gap in the double O's schedule the bassist pulled enough momentum to finally get his debut solo product out into the world. It had been a long time coming yet sounded nothing like his previous attempts. The odds were against it, the bassist and nephew Pedro Howse having been hammering away at a myriad different combinations of the Geezer Butler Band for well over a decade with not a scrap of material aired for public consumption and barely a handful of club gigs to its name. That span of time had caught Geezer's solo meanderings ranging from U.S. style, soft melodic Rock to what was now being presented as G//Z/R—raw, caustic Metal.

Butler would be upfront about incentive behind

Plastic Planet.

forging the solo venture. "I have been writing material for years and it has just been collecting at home. A lot of it wasn't suitable for Sabbath and some of it I also wanted to keep for myself because I really have not been happy with the way Black Sabbath has been going for a long time. I always like working with Tony but some of those records should never have been called Black Sabbath but the record company always gets their own way. Now I've got the space to do this so I wanted to make the heaviest record I possibly could. The last thing I wanted to do was come out with something tired and old. I think the aggression on this album has surprised quite a lot of people."

The 'Plastic Planet' record fused the Geezer and Howse partnership with drummer Deen Castronovo and Fear Factory vocalist Burton C. Bell. The bassist was in the thick of the action in an 'Ozzmosis' tour of duty and had little trouble in convincing Ozzy's sticksman Deen to come along for the ride. Getting the right singer had proven much more of a task though. "Getting Burton in was a relief because I had auditioned quite a few people and not really got anywhere close to what I wanted" he told the author. "I knew the sound and attitude I wanted, which was very heavy and aggressive but with a sense of melody. A lot of the singers we looked at had either one or the other but not both. I really didn't want go down the predictable old Rock way of thinking either so I was out to get a singer that was current. It's all too easy to get on the phone to a lot of familiar faces and get them into the studio. I don't want to work with people I've been seeing on the road over the past twenty years. I guess it's what people expect but the music called for something different.

Scott (Koenig), who manages Fear Factory, was helping me out looking for singers and he also sent me over a Fear Factory CD. I listened to Burton and thought to myself that's exactly what I wanted but of course didn't ever think he would have the time to do it. When Scott said he would be up for it and they had a gap in their schedule I was quite surprised. Fear Factory were due out on the road so we got the album done in a very short space of time, a matter of days really."

'Plastic Planet' took the industry by surprise not only for its undiluted and brazen cutting edge heaviness but its very existence. Geezer Butler had been shopping his solo band for so long 'Plastic Planet' had been akin to bursting a monstrous, persistent boil. When the thing finally did pop it was very nasty indeed. Not just the music, the lyrics to 'Giving Up The Ghost' could not have been any less cutting. Surely he would not deny that song was written about Tony Iommi? "Is it that obvious?" he laughed heartily. "No, not so much Tony, the whole Black Sabbath thing. I've been saying the same thing for years but it just keeps dragging on. It's flogging a dead horse really."

True, Geezer had been voicing his deep dissatisfaction for years but there were also many instances when he too had formed up part of the line-up that bore the title Black Sabbath. So how did he qualify his involvement on such occasions? "When you have known people that long you always want to believe. You get told things so you go in thinking, OK, this time it will be different but it never is. I spent a lot of time working on my own songs, some of which got used on Black Sabbath albums, 'Dehumanizer' and 'Cross Purposes'. I have been trying to get some space between us for a long time. They keep phoning me up though!"

'Plastic Planet' was aimed fairly and squarely at the youth Metal market, Geezer obviously trying to distance himself from the perception of languidity slowly but surely paralysing through the Sabbath fold. The band put in a smattering of club shows, in between Ozzy dates, and reaped complimentary press coverage. The record, it has to be said, was far from spectacular but it served a purpose. Geezer was reserving his coup de grace for his next outing. When pressed on his relationship with Tony Iommi the bassist was forthright. "I haven't spoken to him because I have no reason too. I don't like what has happened with Sabbath in recent years. It just became a joke."

Did he think Tony was planning on resurrecting Black Sabbath with Rob Halford or Glenn Hughes? "I don't care. It wouldn't surprise me at all. So long as I'm not involved. Rob's a good singer, Glenn's a good singer. It's not Sabbath though is it? It hasn't been Black Sabbath for a long time and I just wish Tony would give it a rest and come up with a different name."

Of interest as a snapshot of time, Geezer's response to the question of a full scale, original Black Sabbath re-formation was uncharacteristically scathing. "Nah, I don't wanna do that. Sabbath is done. It's over for me. Let Tony do whatever he's doing with it. I'm not interested." Not even if Ozzy was onboard? "It's not going to happen. If it does, I'm not involved. Ozzy doesn't want to do it. Bill can't do it. Tony is the only one really. It's been talked about for so long and there are just too many things in the way. I'm bored with talking about it. Black Sabbath was something great we achieved a long time ago. You can't recapture that. Let's all be sensible and just leave it there were it belongs shall we?"

When asked if he felt torn between two loyalties, with Ozzy and Tony, the bassist reflected. "I suppose you could say that. Yeah. Which is why it was time to do my own thing. I like working with Ozzy and I like working with Tony. The mistake Tony made is in putting out albums with people that were not Black Sabbath. In my mind, if it's just two of us left then it's not Sabbath anymore. You never knew who was in the band and the name deserves more than that. There are too many people out there telling everyone they are 'ex-Black Sabbath'. I didn't think 'Cross Purposes' should have gone out as a Black Sabbath album. That wasn't right."

Chapter 23

A Forbidding Farewell

In 1995 the author spoke to Cozy Powell once more. Not only was it our fourth Sabbath related chat but it was also Cozy's second time occupying the Black Sabbath drum stool. Having wrapped up our previous interview at the IRS boardroom in London it was plainly obvious that the drummer was gushing pride on behalf of his new band and the 'Tyr' album and was and predicting a solid future for the band. Of course it did not pan out that way and Black Sabbath plunged back into the abyss. Had Cozy's enthusiasm not been enough to hold the whole edifice together?

"I remember that and I remember what I told you" he sighed before collecting himself for the reply. "I told every journalist that at the time because I really believed it. In fact I probably came across a bit too happy about the whole thing to the press because I, as well as the rest of the band, really wanted to get that message home—that this band had sorted itself out and was here to stay. We had a point to prove because the years leading up to the 'Headless Cross' album were an embarrassment and Sabbath's name was in the mud. There's no denying that if you are realistic. It had hit an all time low. We all had a mission back then, I had a mission too, to give the band its credibility back. So, when I said those things I meant 100% of every word.

It's difficult because you, as a journalist, expect me to say those things "This is our best album", "This is the best line-up", "We're best mates", etc., etc., and of course you've heard me say it about Rainbow, and Gary Moore, and Whitesnake and Michael (Schenker) too.

A lot of people, and I saw this in magazines, said "oh, there goes Cozy hopping onto his next band" but it was the complete opposite in reality. Joining Black Sabbath was no easy ride believe me. If I told you how much money the band owed at that point you would think I was insane for even thinking about joining. I joined because I could see a challenge, which I thrive on, and I felt some injustice had been done. I saw a lot of the press and it made me angry. Black Sabbath is part of Rock history and I just thought that what they were saying was disgusting.

Our problem was that Tony and I really believed in it. It was a different situation. 'Headless Cross' and 'Tyr' were both world class albums and our judgement with those songs paid off because, believe it or not, not only did we hold onto the fans the band had but we won back quite a few and pulled in some new people too. To achieve what we did was actually a bit of a minor miracle. Getting it across was hard though. All the intentions were there.

The job we have now is to keep this line-up solid. The Dio thing was a mistake and it's not a coincidence that I'm back where I belong, Tony Martin is singing again and Neil is there on bass. Tony Iommi asked us back personally so I think he knows, well—he does know, that we've got some ground to make up. It feels good to be invited back and I'm sure Tony had to swallow some pride to do that because after my accident I was actually fired. There was a lot of behind the scenes stuff, some things that should not have been said, which I won't bore you with. For this album Tony phoned me, told me he thought that we should get the whole 'Headless Cross' team back together again and asked if I wanted to be involved. I think he knows that the band had achieved a lot before and that it could work again. It's very obvious to the fans of the band and everyone else which band works and which doesn't."

Naturally Cozy Powell had kept up his playing between Sabbath terms. He was keen to discuss other band ventures. "While I was away I did some things with Glenn Tipton from Judas Priest. Great songwriter. So I put drums down on his album. That was fun, we both have a very similar sense of humour so that was very enjoyable, very relaxed. Glenn is just itching to get out there again and do something. Priest can't find a singer though so ... I'm working with a singer called John West too so something will hopefully come of that. Right now though I am totally committed to Black Sabbath but I have a cushion there of my solo album if needs be. John is a great singer, a bit of an undiscovered talent. Maybe me, John, Glenn and Neil Murray. That would be quite a band. It could happen."

Neil Murray would be back by personal invitation too. "Yes, in the summer of 1994 Tony Iommi got back in touch. Myself and Cozy had been pretty busy in the meantime with Brian May, supporting Guns n' Roses in the USA. Tony was keen for me to get back involved, he was very gracious about the whole thing. He basically said that, although he had loved playing with Bobby Rondinelli he thought, that because Cozy was coming back, it would be good to get me back to make that team back up. Tony was in fact more than happy to carry on working with Bobby Rondinelli on the drums but I believe there was quite a bit of pressure to reunite the 'Tyr' line-up from the management side. Very often you see it's not about the individual players but how people work together—the band, the management and the label.

The thing that struck me immediately was that it was not a straight forward step back into time. The internal politics within the band had changed a great deal. Before the band had been Tony and Cozy's. Now it was very clear that Cozy was just the drummer and Tony had the total control. So in that sense it wasn't the 'Tyr' line-up again even though it had the same faces. Same people but different roles."

Echoing Neil Murray's observations is Geoff Nicholls. The keyboard player soon realised Cozy was rapidly becoming disillusioned. "Neil is right about that. Cozy thought he was coming back into the old way of doing things but it didn't take him long to figure he was now just the drummer. He didn't like it and I don't blame him because that deal he had with Tony before 'Headless Cross' had worked."

Neil expands upon the very real artistic tug of war being conducted at the time. "Cozy wanted 'Headless Cross' part III but the record company were very resistant to that. Tony Iommi didn't want that either. He thought that style was all a bit old hat and eighties. Cozy was fighting a bit of a battle he couldn't win and it was difficult seeing him back in the band but being seriously demoted. There were some outside pressures too because the first time around the musical environment had been very different. Now we were faced with a Rock industry that had since come to hail Black Sabbath as Grunge Godfathers. Those outside elements came to bear on what happened next. All that kind of thinking certainly played a part in the thinking behind the 'Forbidden' album. I thought it was a mistake, Cozy thought it was a mistake. There were a lot of glum faces."

Caught in the midst of these tribulations Cozy sought to defend his standing and place the revised band formula in context. "Are we friends? Ahhh ... we respect each other. We get along fine, probably better than a lot of bands out there. I'm here because Tony needs me. Same for Neil, same for Tony Martin. I'm sure I've said this before but the only really stable Black Sabbath line-up since Ozzy was when we did 'Headless Cross' and 'Tyr'. We accomplished a hell of a lot and we were all thinking about what was to come next, the album after 'Tyr'. At least I was. That band never let Tony Iommi down once. That kind of loyalty is hard to find believe me. We have to build that camaraderie back I think. I learned a long, long time ago about this business. Friends count for nothing. As soon as a secret deal comes in through the back door it's goodbye. It happens to all of us. You saw it with Dio at Costa Mesa. We're professionals so we just get on with it. Nothing personal."

'Forbidden' caught many Sabbath fans by surprise. Just as the second Dio wind had promised a return to majesty of the early eighties but fell short of expectations so 'Forbidden' proved a further deflatory disappointment. The Iommi / Martin / Murray / Powell combination was strong, of that there was no doubt. Behind the scenes the fiscal haemorrhaging had been stemmed too and Tony Martin would be glad to see that many of Tony Iommi's financial problems were now in check and now in capable hands. "For years Tony had been trying to find someone he could trust with his band and money. The team he got together was completely different to every other management team he had worked with."

The team comprised Ernest Chapman—also Jeff Beck's manager, Phil Banfield—long time personal manager of Ian Gillan, and Ralph Baker. "Ernest Chapman is a really good bloke" states Martin. "I doubt you will find anyone with a bad word to say about him. He's a shrewd businessman and when he says something will happen it does. Thing is he doesn't have to get heavy to achieve things. Everything is done in a very gentlemanly, professional manner. He is very well respected in the industry. Phil Banfield has some wacky ideas sometimes, 'Forbidden' was one, but he's a worker. Always doing stuff, always arranging things and very practical. Ralph Baker is very quiet and considerate, but still another guy who makes things happen. Tony was very, very lucky to get such a good team. If he had got them involved ten years earlier things would have been very, very different."

The quality of the songs themselves, bar the odd sparkle of 'Guilty As Hell' (which featured an uncharacteristic Tony Martin use of the 'F' word!), left much to be desired but it was really the production that shocked many. Parchment dry, the thing bore all the hallmarks of a glorified demo. Cozy Powell's drum sound could only be described as polite and Martin

Black Sabbath 'Forbidden' line-up: Cozy Powell, Neil Murray, Tony Iommi and Tony Martin.

was never given the space to fly.

'Forbidden' had been produced by Ernie C., guitarist with Body Count. Just why and how this incompatible alliance had manifested itself was never adequately explained. Were Sabbath merely chasing the coat tails of a fad? For many observers it seemed that way. During the mid nineties the Metal world was awash with over hyped hopefuls virtually all of whom would nosedive into obscurity. Body Count's contribution to the world of Rock Music was like that of a briefly prominent but annoying zit. What on earth was Tony Iommi thinking? Word was that Body Count main man Ice T was slated to act as guiding hand in the studio but delegated the duty down a rung to his guitarist Ernie C. Nevertheless, the famed rapper cum gangster cum actor does appear on the opening track 'The Illusion Of Power'. This was a first for Black Sabbath to pander to a guest singer but actually does little to redeem the song.

Tony Martin feels finally able to give the full story. "Phil Banfield came up with the idea of getting in Ice T. He had this notion that it was to be like an Aerosmith—Run DMC type thing which would resurrect the band's career. How he could see Black Sabbath in the same light as Aerosmith I just don't know. Everyone else just thought it was bloody stupid. Cozy was dead against it and said so. I can remember him telling the manager when he found out 'Are you sure?' We even thought it might be a very bad joke at first. Cozy argued like Hell about it, which went on and on. In the end though he just gave up.

The thing is, 'Forbidden' was the last album under contract so Tony wanted to get it away so he could get on with the reunion. I just could not get any straight answers out of anybody. Was Ice T going to sing half the album? Or the whole album? Were we going to do a duet? I was kept in the dark. Nobody gave me a clue and on the very first day I went into the recording studio I still had no idea how much of the album I was supposed to be doing. You can tell that from the album. There's no conviction or energy in those songs whatsoever. I can't stand to listen to the thing."

Both Cozy Powell and Tony Martin, holed up in the studio and utterly exasperated at the situation couldn't believe what they were hearing. "When we learned about this Rap guy we just looked at each other," says Tony Martin, "and together we both said 'This is bollocks!' That was probably the only light relief we got doing that record. Everybody was trying to put a brave face on it but we all knew it was the end. It was the lead up to the Ozzy reunion and the break from IRS. Everyone knew but nothing was being said. It was clear the Ozzy thing had been bubbling along for quite some time. Tony was really keen. Sabbath owed millions when I joined way back and we had got through that and turned it around. It had been a big battle but it seemed like all that counted for nothing now."

Ultimately 'Forbidden' smacked of carelessness. Even the cartoon sleeve, complete with IRS Records chief Miles Copeland as a winged devil noticeably overseeing the band, came across as an exercise in self-mockery. The figures represented on the artwork has presented a minor mystery in itself. Besides the band members, including Tony Martin with suitable 'Cat', both Ice T and Ernie C. are present, the artists themselves are represented and even Tony Iommi's ex-wife Val. Others are yet to be solved.

As Tony Martin has revealed to be true, speculation was rife that 'Forbidden' was a quick fix contractual effort to seal the lid on a contract that once closed would provide one less stumbling block on the way to a full blown Ozzy re-formation. At the time the band members, naturally, tried in vain to convince journalists and fans that 'Forbidden' was actually a worthy piece of work.

Neil Murray, in hindsight, is uncharacteristically blunt. "Ernie C. was not a good producer it has to be said. Looking back it seems daft because it was a wasted opportunity. The four of us had made a good album before and we could have done it again with little difficulty. It's that whole Black Sabbath thing of not speaking up until it's all too late I suppose. A lot of what was going on was half hearted and Cozy was obviously unhappy with the whole thing. Some people wanted to go more nineties Metal, to be a bit different. The production was all wrong though."

Cozy Powell had this to say. "The record is far less polished than the others I've worked on that's for sure" he admitted. When told that the record was a let down for the author the drummer conceded. "OK, some people will like it, some won't. It's a very modern sound. Ernie has a completely different viewpoint to the rest of us and I think it was hoped that would really give us an extra push in the studio. I think this is probably the heaviest thing he has ever done. I don't know quite how he got involved. Actually, yes I do. It was the record company. They wanted an outside view, someone who wasn't tainted by the whole Black Sabbath tradition. They didn't even want Tony getting involved. Ernie is a guitarist so he approached the album from that angle. I didn't agree with all of his ideas and decisions I have to say. I'm not ecstatic about the drum sound. If you listen to 'Headless Cross', the drums on there—that's my

'Forbidden' album insert—spot Tony Iommi, Cozy Powell, Neil Murray, Tony Martin, Geoff Nicholls and IRS label boss Miles Copeland.

production. There is a big difference. I came in a bit late for this one so basically just went in and did my thing, kept my mouth shut."

One of the major plus factors in Sabbath's arsenal to have been nullified on 'Forbidden' was the quite enormous range of Tony Martin. The breathtaking display he had put down on 'Headless Cross' and 'Tyr' had been replaced with a more 'experimental direction', incorporating no harmonies, which sat uneasy on the ear. Was this a conscious decision, to rein Martin's abilities in for some reason? "It was what the songs called for I guess" Cozy mused in an attempt to paper over some very big cracks. "Tony Martin is a fantastic singer. Probably in fact the very best singer I have ever worked with in terms of his range and power. He really matured back in the 'Headless Cross' days, put a lot of work in and pulled himself up quite a few notches. He now goes out onstage and has a good time, builds that audience rapport quickly. That took him a while but he did it so credit to him. He's great to work with. I suppose for 'Forbidden' that was just another of those things. Y'know, let's try something different this time to see if it works."

This was certainly not the same proud and determined self styled ambassador for Black Sabbath I had encountered previously. When questioned on his guarded enthusiasm Cozy offered this. "I don't know if this production will work. I had to let the reins go. Some people are totally convinced by it. I don't know. Only time will tell us I guess. It's not me. If I had produced it 'Forbidden' would sound very different. It is getting people talking though which can only be a good thing. We've just got to get out there now and deliver it live. That's where it counts."

Neil Murray observed another aspect to the synergy within the band and the producer. "Cozy was not happy jamming the songs. That I remember. Ernie wanted a more organic thing going on, whatever that meant, but … there is theory and there is practice. What I guess I'm trying to say is that it didn't work. Cozy wanted to work the songs out then play them. He didn't want to spend hours every day messing about and it was getting like that. The other thing with Cozy at that point is that he simply didn't have the power he had before. A lot of the energy had gone and that was made worse by the fact that I don't think he really wanted to be there.

Tony Iommi and Cozy were no longer on the same wavelength. Before, with 'Headless Cross' Black Sabbath had been Tony and Cozy's band no question. Now Cozy was there as a hired gun. There was also a very strange feeling around the whole album, too many fingers in pies. People who should not have really been there because, if we had been left to get on with it in our own way the record would have been better. There was the whole political thing too, we all knew what was coming."

A large part of the musical content of 'Forbidden', including the album title, was once again down to Geoff Nicholls. The keyboard player provides the background to some of the album tracks. "The title 'Forbidden' was an idea I had. Tony Martin liked the idea and wrote the lyrics accordingly. As it states, it's about all the supposed good things in life being forbidden. I think it was chosen as the album title because it had a darker edge and it also had that double meaning, which is more in line with the Sabbs thing.

'Sick And Tired' was another song name I came up with that both Tony Martin and I put the words to. Again, it's a Blues song with a double meaning. It's about a relationship that we have probably all been through but also about all the music business bullshit too. 'Rusty Angels' was more historical. That was about the aeroplanes that had dropped the atomic bomb and were now left in scrap yards, rusting away in the desert. Tony Martin came up with those lyrics."

The question was put it to Cozy that the Grunge phenomenon and the success of the 'Nativity In Black' album, which had married newer artists such as Megadeth, Sepultura, Type O Negative, Biohazard and White Zombie with familiar, classic Sabbath tunes, played any part in the concept of 'Forbidden'. Dare I say IRS even looked for a 'current' artist of similar stature they could rope in to repeat the formula? "That's record companies for you" he said resignedly. "Of course we were aware of 'Nativity In Black'. It was quite a surprise, the success of that thing. You might be closer than you think."

The 'Nativity In Black' collection hosted a number of interesting liaisons. Amongst them would be the Irish Alternative Rock act Therapy?'s less than successful rendition of 'Iron Man', complete with a guesting Ozzy Osbourne on lead vocals, and giving vent to 'The Wizard' a project known as the 'Bullring Brummies'. This purely studio band comprised Geezer Butler, Bill Ward, vocalist Rob Halford and The Cult figure of Wino from Stoner lords The Obsessed. Intriguingly, when questioned on Halford's involvement with this session his personal manager John Baxter replied "Rob did his vocals in a studio in the USA and sent them over. It was a studio project so Rob did his vocal tracks here and Tony did his guitar parts in the UK."

The band was hardly in the best of spirits to conduct a world tour as Tony Martin illustrates. "We hated the album and we all knew what was in store for us at the end of the tour. Tony was going to walk off into the sunset arm in arm with Ozzy and a big cheque and we were going to be out of a job. We were not happy one bit."

Keeping tabs in the press on his former band mates Bobby Rondinelli could not help Cozy's lack of enthusiasm and suspected he might receive an olive branch from Tony Iommi in the near future. "Cozy was very open in his criticism of the album and the whole situation" Bobby suggests. "He was very open about it. I liked Cozy, there never was any bullshit with him. We were good friends. When he started to talk about 'Forbidden' like that it was obvious what was coming."

Plans were afoot to replace Cozy at an even earlier stage as Bobby Rondinelli reveals. "I knew before the U.S. tour" he affirms. "Tony called me and we went for dinner in Manhattan. He told me the score with Cozy and said he really wanted me in the band, that he enjoyed playing with me, and that Cozy wasn't working out.

After a couple of weeks Tony asked me to come back into the band. I flew down to the Universal Amphitheatre in California to catch the last show. Cozy knew all about it, there was nothing secret, no hard feelings. It was more like an exchange than a replacement, nothing sly. Cozy just said to me 'Look Bobby, I'm done here. Best of luck with it'. He just wanted to go. We then went to Europe. I got in a few days rehearsal to learn the 'Forbidden' songs and off we went on tour again."

"I'm pretty certain it was Cozy himself who suggested Tony Iommi ask Bobby Rondinelli back in" surmises Geoff Nicholls. "I think Cozy was just knackered you know? He had his solo thing going on, he

Forbidden tour pass.

was working with Brian May and with Yngwie too so to add Sabbath to that was just pushing him too far. He had taken too much on. He told me he felt totally burnt out and the Sabbath schedule didn't allow for much time off. I know he really didn't want to play in Europe. America was always OK but in Europe it can get a bit arduous and cramped. There was also talk of Eastern European shows too and Cozy didn't want to sleep in crap hotels and ride around on poxy buses."

All this is verified by Tony Martin. "Cozy was having a tough time of it physically. He had asked Tony Iommi for longer gaps between songs so he could get his breath back but Tony said no, he liked the songs close to one another. Cozy was struggling, trying to catch his breath between songs. It wasn't good. He told us in California, those two shows in Los Angeles and San Francisco. I was sad to see him go, because we really did get on well, but at least that time everything was out in the open. Cozy and Bobby really liked each other so there were no hard feelings. Cozy always joked with Bobby. He even claimed that Bobby would get to jump in his coffin before he did! Bobby came in with Cozy's blessing and we carried on as if nothing had happened."

Neil Murray echoes these observations. "Cozy wasn't happy and he was struggling physically that's true. I just think his heart wasn't in it because the whole band structure and purpose had changed. It was more of 'just a job' at that stage. Tony said that Cozy wasn't playing onstage the way he wanted him to play. Much as I liked Cozy things got noticeably better when Bobby came onboard for the European shows."

As a precursor to a sixteen week European mainland slog the new line-up was broken in with a brace of Austrian festival appearances at the 'Rock At The Border' event in Gmund on the 19th August and the 'Arena Open Air' in Vienna on the 20th. The band would then break away from the mainland for a one off gig on the Mediterranean island of Malta at the Orpheum Theatre on the 25th. Renowned for having its entire population being awarded the George Cross medal during the war, having endured at great loss an unrelenting bombing campaign and siege, the small holiday rock has, aptly enough, been a haven for Hard Rock and Heavy Metal for well over a decade. Oddly though it is rarely visited by international bands. Those that have played there, including Deep Purple, have come away pleasantly surprised at this isolated bubble of Metal appreciation. In typical fashion the Malta gig did not run as smoothly as the band would hope for.

"Malta really stood out for me because of the unique circumstances of that gig" says Bobby Rondinelli. "It was one of my first gigs since coming back but I remember it because the local population were just insane. I swear to you, when we landed at the airport we were mobbed by hundreds of fans. It was just like The Beatles. When we landed we were in the plane looking out at these hundreds of kids who had been waiting for us and thinking 'what the fuck?' It just got better. They couldn't do enough for us. If I said to someone 'where can I buy some cigarettes?' two seconds later there would be a pack in front of me and they refused to accept our money. The Maltese treated us real well. I tell you, any bands that get offered a gig in Malta should grab it. Wonderful country."

Malta was a standout gig for Neil Murray too. "Malta was a special gig for a number of reasons" he records. "A lot of gigs tend to all become a bit of a blur when you're on tour but this was a one off, our first memorable show with Bobby and it was so unbelievably hot. I have never been so hot on stage in my entire life. It was like a sauna.

You learn to get a little sceptical about gigs in out of the way places because they generally promise you anything and everything to get you there and when you arrive you find they've lied through their teeth. That happens more than you think. Malta though was different. The gig itself wasn't too great, it was an old dilapidated theatre as I recall, but the people that came to the gig were just totally fanatical which made the whole enterprise very worthwhile. They were totally over the top.

The heat during the actual show gave me some very real problems. Over many years I have built up calluses on the ends of my fingers from playing bass. If you play a lot you get lumps of hard skin building up to protect the ends of your fingers. That show was so hot and sweaty though that those calluses, which are normally hard, started to go soft. It was like being in a hot bath. They went soft so actually playing the bass for me that night was like crunch, crunch, crunch. Very difficult indeed."

"Neil is right about that" affirms Bobby. "That gig was hotter than Hell. I remember too that the PA system they expected us to play through was suitable maybe for a wedding reception but not Black Sabbath. Fortunately, because we were there for about four days in all, our crew had time to organise something a bit bigger. I think we ended up commandeering every PA system and piece of sound equipment on the entire island just for that one gig."

For some involved the entire 'Forbidden' world tour was little more than an exercise in deceit. The Sabbath name and the credibility generated by the individual players themselves had stretched the dates out to an arduous nine month expedition. Paradoxically one of Black Sabbath's most effective world tours would be to prop up one of its weakest albums. As the months rolled on Tony Martin's belief that wheels were turning within wheels once more was confirmed. A potentially valuable run of November shows in Australia and New Zealand was regrettably cancelled but the band still had some lucrative outposts in the Far East to conquer. As Neil Murray resigned himself to get on with the job in hand because "Everyone just knew", the singer felt it was not his place to acquiesce.

"I went to Tony Iommi and said 'Look, I just don't understand. Can you fill me in on what's happening here?' As usual I got no answers because Tony just cannot deal with confrontation like that when it's to do with the band. By that stage I had become used to Tony's personality when it came to dealing with important issues. It was quite confusing at first because Tony Iommi has taken his fist to those outside of the band that have upset the applecart, I've seen it, but would never even talk to the guys that really mattered about the real important stuff. There was one side of confrontation that didn't phase him at all and another, which he did everything possible to avoid.

This all came at a time when the tour was just snaking ahead and they were loading on more and more shows closer together. Now, remember, I had never missed a show and I said 'guys, look, if you keep on putting gigs so close together I'm going to fuck my voice up and you'll end up pulling shows. Just give me a breather won't you?' That fell on deaf ears. I gave up, got very angry and just did the best I could every night from that point on.

Very shortly after that conversation I got a fax from Phil Banfield basically saying stop whinging, we're doing the gigs and by the way 'The band will not be staying in the same format'. Those were the exact words. Not 'you're fired' or 'Tony has made it up with Ozzy, sorry mate' but all very typically Sabbath-like and cryptic.

While I was starting to get my head around that they then asked me to sign on for some more gigs. We ended the tour but they had more gigs to add in places like Bali and a few others. What a fucking cheek! The onus was then being put on me to do the gigs but I just felt like that was the very final straw. I didn't feel guilty in the slightest and told them to fuck off."

Black Sabbath—Tony Iommi, Tony Martin, Neil Murray, Geoff Nicholls and Bobby Rondinelli performed at the Singapore Harbour Pavilion venue on the 12th of December then put in their last performance on two days later at the Bangkok Capital Music Hall, Phoebus Amphitheatre complex. A further show, at the Manila Araneta Coliseum on the 16th was curtailed due to government objections to supposed "Satanic" lyrics. The band would only learn this once they had arrived in the city. It would be an ignominious exit. The wheel had turned full circle, Tony Martin's first scheduled gig back in 1987 cancelled and here they were languishing in the South Pacific with another gig pulled from under them.

This time it really was over for Tony Martin. Returning home to Birmingham he felt as if, proverbially at least, he had been exiled a few miles North East to Coventry. "Nobody rang me after the tour from that day to this. Isn't that amazing? The only people that have kept in touch have been Geoff Nicholls and Neil Murray. This is how they treat people all the time. Thankfully I can now deal with the fact that Sabbath is finally over."

Joe Holmes meanwhile, courtesy of yet another tip off from Deen Castronovo, had entered the world of Ozzy Osbourne. The opening had been created when Zakk Wylde reportedly had found himself on the receiving end of a tempting offer from Guns n' Roses. Unable to decide firmly which camp to settle on, and with a series of conflicting signals to contend with, the decision was made for him. As it transpired the Guns n' Roses post would evaporate into thin air leaving Wylde temporarily high and dry.

Auditioning in Los Angeles, Holmes kept quiet about having had Randy Rhoads as a guitar tutor fearing it would jeopardise his chances. He still got the gig and Ozzy's new band of Holmes, Butler, Sinclair and Castronovo embarked on the self effacingly titled 'Retirement Sucks' tour. Joe Holmes was the antithesis of the 6 foot blond maned Zakk Wylde. Blessed with an incredible degree of control and fluidity to his playing style he would soon find favour with Ozzy fans. From the audience the initial percep-

Ozzy Osbourne 1995. Pic: Gene Kirkland.

tion of Holmes was of a slight dark haired figure lost in his own world faithfully churning out a structured but dynamic regime that had Ozzy purists reeling in admiration.

Opening dates for the 1995 Ozzy world tour started in Chile. Following a handful of gigs Castronovo was out (later turning up as a member of AOR stalwarts Journey) and Randy Castillo, pulled from his act Juice 13, was back behind the drum stool. The 'Ozzmosis' album proved to be Osbourne's most successful for nearly a decade, debuting in the American Billboard album charts at Number 4 and selling over 127,000 copies in its first week of release. Mid way through the dates Geezer returned home and Mike Inez, on his second Ozzy call up, took the position.

A third single was lifted from 'Ozzmosis' in the form of 'I Just Want You' with an accompanying video. The single was timed perfectly to coincide with an American tour commencing in May. Ozzy's band for this jaunt was made up of Joe Holmes, Robert Trujillo of Suicidal Tendencies and former Faith No More drummer Mike Bordin. The previous occupant of the drum stool, Randy Castillo, had leap frogged onto another major act supplanting the errant Tommy Lee in Mötley Crüe. Support acts for Ozzy at various stages found Sepultura, Filter, Type O Negative and Henry Rollins as openers.

Chapter 24

Reunion

During April 1996 Tony Martin's manager Albert Chapman received a telephone call from Phil Banfield informing him of the release of an IRS Records compilation entitled 'The Sabbath Stones'. Out of sixteen songs, the vast majority were fronted by Tony Martin. The Black Sabbath camp, deep in negotiation with Ozzy Osbourne, camouflaged this activity by claiming all was still well with Tony Martin, denying a split with Martin as late as December of 1996. The singer would even be contacted to explain the exact meaning of the title song in order for Iommi to lend some authority to this in interviews. It was all a sham according to the singer "The interview was to give the impression that all was still well, but it wasn't and I never heard from any of them again."

An Ozzy-less Black Sabbath had not totally been put out to pasture though. Talks were still delicate and the house of cards was liable to collapse as it had done many times before. Glenn Hughes confirmed he had been elicited by Tony Iommi to consider a lead vocal role with the band as late as January of 1997. "As the whole Ozzy reunion thing was being talked about Tony had this idea as a back up plan or possibly something to lead into it" affirms Geoff Nicholls. Very simply, the proposed venture was put forward as a touring Black Sabbath family tree, the band being fronted for each era spanning such vocalists as Ronnie, Glenn Hughes, Rob Halford, Tony Martin and others. "It was a guy at a record company in London who put the idea to Tony. He was very keen to get Glenn Hughes back with Sabbath because he was nuts about the 'Seventh Star' album. A lot of people still rate that as the best album we did despite what was going on at the time. Tony was keen and started to plot a few things out, made some calls. It might have been quite nice because the IRS Records thing was over and it would have made a good entrance into the Ozzy thing too. I'm sure a tour like that would have done very well indeed."

Ronnie James Dio remained unaware of these notions and is dismissive. "Nobody asked me and if they had they would have been disappointed. After 'Dehumanizer'? After Costa Mesa? C'mon ... I wouldn't have done that kind of thing unless it was for a charity—maybe! By then the whole thing was going on of trying to remove me from the band history too so I don't think I would have been too accepting of any approach. I'm not pointing any fingers but to try and erase someone from the history books and then turn around and ask them back out of convenience is more than a slap in the face.

I think that kind of idea would have tarnished the importance of what I gave to Black Sabbath. I mean, look at it. I did three albums with the band and what did those other guys do? Glenn's album wasn't exactly a world beater. What was that album again? How many did it sell? Rob just did two shows. They're great singers but in the world of Black Sabbath their contribution pales compared to mine.

I'm sorry but I hold my impact upon the band to be much more special than that. Now, that's going to come across as me being big headed again but I don't mean it in that way. For me to give myself to something I have to be involved wholeheartedly so that I can give the audience what they deserve. I cannot give 40% of my energy to something. It's everything or nothing.

In that kind of circus I don't think I could have done that. My contribution to the band and the album warrants much more than that kind of dumb idea. Do you think Tony Iommi would join in a Dio extravaganza with Ritchie Blackmore, Vivian Campbell, Tracy G and Craig Goldy? Of course he wouldn't. He's like Ritchie—too special. So am I."

It then transpired that Tony Iommi was once more working with vocalist Rob Halford and former comrade Glenn Hughes for an album project, although the former Judas Priest vocalist still had commitments to his newly established Industrial project Two. These discussions were subsequently put on hold, and despite rumours to the contrary, no sessions eventuated. "No, we never got into the studio, never wrote anything, never rehearsed" affirms Halford. "The idea was great and there was a lot of talk between us and for a while it was all looking very

The Dio band.

promising. There were too many management issues to deal with. It could of happened, but it didn't. One of those things where you wish you could turn back the hands of time."

When pushed on the subject Halford appears to acknowledge that something very special had slipped through their fingers. "You can never tell in this game. So many maybes all the time but it all makes sense doesn't it? I mean, Tony, Glenn and I are all from the same area. We've all played the same clubs when we started out and we've all enjoyed a fair degree of success. We have all pursued similar paths and made something of ourselves in this crazy profession. The synergy from the fans of Tony and I seemed to be there too. The bridge between Judas Priest and Black Sabbath was there in terms of style so that was no worry. Maybe it should have happened."

With everything up in the air once more Tony Iommi's mind duly wandered back to his very first choice for a post Ozzy singer—Glenn Hughes. By this time the consensus was leaning toward another solo venture. The experiment promised much but would ultimately leave a sour taste for the singer.

"That whole episode was fucking awful" cringes an obviously disgusted Glenn Hughes. "The project itself was just great, a really nice vibe but the way it got leaked was outrageous." The singer goes on to explain the circumstances of the union. "I was living in Sweden at the time, I got a call through to Stockholm from Tony's manager Ralph Baker telling me Tony was looking to put a new band together. Now, of course, I've heard this before and 'Seventh Star' is one of those memories that stays with you so I asked if this really was the case. This wasn't going to turn into Black Sabbath again was it? I got my assurances and we got to work."

As evidenced by subsequently (illegally) released recordings the music put down was relaxed, moody and evidently oozing with class. Hughes Trapeze band mate Dave Holland, better known these days for a ten year tenure with Judas Priest, manned the drums whilst another old ally Don Airey gave the proceedings colour on the keyboards. Geoff Nicholls would also be in attendance. Recordings took place at the Cabin Studios in Coventry and DEP Studios in Birmingham with Mike Exeter and noted producer Kit Woolven acting as engineers.

"It was a nice atmosphere" Glenn remembers fondly. "We were just four musicians having a blast, getting some music worked up and it all felt very good. There were a lot of differences to this situation as opposed to last time Tony and I had been in the studio. I had been sober and clean for a good 6–7 years so I was a different animal all around. Tony already had a million riffs ready to go so we very soon had seven songs worked up into demo format. Everything got worked up to the ideas stage with those songs and then the plan was for us to get some more tracks together, we were aiming for about 30 I seem to recall."

Geoff Nicholls saw a different side to the Glenn Hughes he had worked with back in the eighties during these recordings. "He had got back to that old Stevie Wonder type stuff!" he laughs. "I liked those songs. We didn't get too far with it though which was a shame because it was very different to a lot of the stuff Tony had done previously."

Leaving the project in suspension to reconvene work in progress on his solo career, Glenn would be disappointed when the summons did not come to complete the sessions. "It was a shame but I think the manager stepped in or something. Quite some time after I received a package in the mail with those sessions on CD. I was mortified! I still don't know who did it. What's interesting is that the songs on the bootleg are a very different mix to the ones I have so those are not the definitive tracks."

When quizzed about this bootleg drummer Dave Holland was incredulous. "You are joking aren't you?" he exclaimed in disbelief. "I never even knew that. I can't think of anyone who could have done that because it was just the band working on those songs."

Surfacing in Japan, the cannily titled 'Eighth Star' album, even mimicking the 'Seventh Star' jacket design, caused a furore amongst hardened Black Sabbath traders and copies were keenly snapped up. The songs were titled by obvious guess work as 'Not The Same', 'I'm Gone' (actually, according to Glenn simply 'Gone'), the oriental 'Real World', 'Don't You Tell Me', 'I'll Be Fine' and the ballads 'From Another World' and 'Through The Rain'. The aforementioned 'Gone' would make it into the public arena, nestled amongst tracks on Glenn's superb 2000 solo album 'Return Of Crystal Karma' (aka 'R.O.C.K.'). Tony Iommi also rejigged the main riff from 'Don't You Tell Me' as the skeleton on which to hang 'Black Oblivion' on his 2000 'Iommi' record.

By August Ozzy was back in the UK quite uniquely acting as a joint headliner alongside Kiss at the prestigious 'Monsters Of Rock' festival, Ozzy's third appearance at the event. Dates promoting 'Ozzmosis' would continue throughout the year, with a further run of American shows winding up in Honolulu, Hawaii on 11th November.

Eighth Star bootleg.

With major name Rock acts struggling to fill stadiums nationwide Sharon Osbourne's next venture would seemingly fly in the face of all logic but would succeed in not only bolstering Ozzy's reputation but also turned the U.S. touring circuit on its head and provided the catalyst for what had for an age seemed unthinkable—a full blown classic Black Sabbath reformation. Initially, the 'Ozzfest' extravaganza would signal the debut of a concept many felt ambitious in the extreme. The event arrived in two massive outdoor shows on October 26th in Phoenix, Arizona and the following day in San Bernadino, California. Backing up Ozzy for these gigs was Slayer, Fear Factory, Coal Chamber and Neurosis. In March of 1997 the 'Ozzfest Live' album and video arrived in stores on the short lived Red Ant label. Live cuts from all the bands appearing on the day were topped off with Ozzy's 'Perry Mason'.

1996 closed in confusing fashion for Black Sabbath. Word had been delivered that October stating Tony Martin had officially been let go. However, in December both Martin and Iommi were stating that this was not the case, and that further product was planned. In reality, at this juncture Iommi's Black Sabbath was a dispirited and dispersed force. However, in true Mordor-esque fashion, something very big, and very black was stirring beyond the horizon.

"I think had just finished up the 'Black Science' album when Ozzy called me up out of the blue" Geezer reminds himself. "I was quite surprised when Ozzy told me he was working with Tony again because there had been so many blocks put on that in the past. Before, anything like that had taken months of negotiations and playing the game with lawyers, managers, labels, accountants—everybody. What usually happened was that months went by, people outside the band made a lot of money for their 'services', I suppose you would call it, and it would never happen. So, every time this got mentioned I had learned to be sceptical.

The difference was that this time it was all very quick so I was surprised. Ozzy said they were getting on with each other like the old days again so I felt reassured that this could happen finally. Once I had figured out that this thing really was going to happen, and not fall apart again, I just said 'yeah, OK'. After that it all went very quickly.

We met up in Los Angeles and the old friendships were still there. There were no personality problems, no business hassles so we just got on with rehearsing which felt great. I was a little wary because, although Ozzy and Tony are lifelong friends, we have all had a go at each other in the past for the most stupidest of things—me included. But that didn't happen. By the end of a week we were all still feeling the same way. Nobody had fallen out and the whole thing felt very positive. I think we are all at that point now where if it doesn't feel right it is just too much to try and put something together for any other reason. It felt good so we did the Ozzfest."

It was a good environment to re-launch Black Sabbath Mk I. Ozzy's 1997 album 'The Ozzman Cometh' had neatly included a clutch of rare 'basement' Sabbath tracks. Geezer's second solo album 'Black Science' had been one of the revelations of the year and had affirmed his status as a songwriter. 'Black Science' bristled with bulldozing, high quality tracks, all imbued with some of the quirkiest lyrics to ever grace an album. Many Americans were utterly mystified as to just what message was being put across. The author had a prior insight into this though through a chance meeting with Geezer.

Ashamed to admit it, but I attended a Sci-Fi toy fair in Birmingham to help out my brother in law with his Star Trek stall. Surrounded by thousands of Trekkies (and desperately trying to look out of place!) my somnambulistic state was broken by a familiar face.

Geezer was at the stall with son Biff. We engaged in a brief conversation in which he confessed he was on the look out for classic British Sci-Fi merchandise. Now, Daleks, Joe 90, Thunderbirds and Cybermen I could relate to. So, when 'Black Science' first hit my deck I understood. In a subsequent interview Geezer seemed relieved that someone had 'got' the record.

'Black Science' was littered with references to the Gerry Anderson Sci-Fi puppet series such as 'Stingray', 'Thunderbirds', 'Joe 90', 'Fireball XL5' and 'Captain Scarlet'. Obviously 'Dr. Who' put in an appearance too as did Elvis Presley and The Cult comedian Norman Wisdom. Geezer even managed to include two songs about his beloved Aston Villa Football Club. Geezer, having just tried to explain these references to a stream of nonplussed American

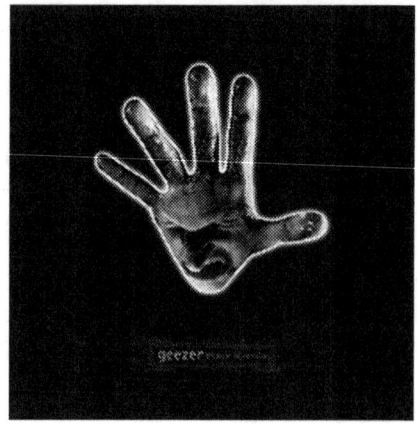

Black Science.

journalists, revelled in his enthusiasm for the record.

Utilising guitarist Pedro Howse and drummer Deen Castronovo once again the choice for vocalist fell on an unknown. Clark Brown turned in a monstrous vocal performance that was both emotional and supremely melodic. Oddly, little has been heard of him since bar whispers of projects in the works. Dealing with the Football connection first, the track 'Trinity Road' was obviously a geographical Villa reference but the hallowed ground had inspired another song too it seems in the form of the sinister 'Number 5'.

"Aston Villa is a big part of my life from when I was a kid. In Aston it was all we had really. Obviously 'Trinity Road' is about Villa but so is 'Number 5'. When I was young I used to catch the number 5 and number 7 bus to get to the ground. That's why 'Number 5 and 7, took me to my heaven'. I just thought it would be nice to capture a bit of my heritage while I had the chance. It's quite funny because a lot of people have been trying to decipher the lyrics to this album. It's all actually quite simple if you had the same kind of upbringing as me. I had three obsessions—TV, football and then music."

The mellow 'Northern Wisdom' had me foxed because at first I thought Clark was singing 'Norman Wisdom'! (Wisdom is a giant among British comedy, having starred in a marvellous series of classic 50s and 60s movies).

"You were right there. When we were working on the song it was called 'Norman Wisdom' just for a laugh. We do that a lot with songs, give them temporary working titles while we build up the music and the lyrics to go with it. So yeah, originally that song was called 'Norman Wisdom'. There was just a slight change at the end."

So, would I be correct in thinking that the lyric line for 'Among The Cybermen' was originally Dr. Who?

"Dead right. Originally the line was 'Dr. Who lies

dead among the Cybermen'. Again we just changed it a little bit. I grew up on 'Dr. Who'. It used to scare the living daylights out of me."

The opening track 'Man In A Suitcase' appears to be a bit of a mix. It looks like there are a number of subjects going on there with one reference to the Rock n' Roll lifestyle and another to something else entirely.

"That song is about being on the road. Literally living in a suitcase. It has always been a kind of odd lifestyle, very unsettled. The other thing is another TV thing. There was a spy character that was in a suitcase. I always found that quite bizarre."

Sadly tour work to push 'Black Science' was far from extensive. Geezer had created a cult classic and conjured up a record so unique that any attempt at genre tagging simply failed. The record was gloriously melodic, quirky and undoubtedly exceptionally heavy. There was absolutely nothing old school about the album despite it hosting storylines harking back thirty years and more.

What 'Black Science' had achieved, where 'Plastic Planet' had fallen short, was to pinpoint Geezer Butler as an up to the minute, forward thinking songsmith. Virtually every other attempt by musicians of, shall we say, a certain age had failed dismally. Often embarrassingly so. Geezer showed he could not only ride the wave but control it too.

Meantime, nearly a decade passed before Bill Ward's next solo outing. For 1997's 'When The Bough Breaks', which saw Ward handling lead vocals, his band comprised guitarists Keith Lynch and Spencer Sercombe, former Earl Slick bassist Paul Ill and ex-Riverdogs drummer Ronnie Ciago. Sercombe, besides having once tried out for Ozzy's band, had of course made his name with The Sharks, Shark Island and Riverdogs. Once again this album came with two versions of sleeve art, the first with a rose design and the second with an archive picture of Bill.

Whilst 'Black Science' was an undoubted musical triumph for Butler and 'When The Bough Breaks' had rekindled interest in Ward's activities, the reunion leviathan jaws were awning and personal projects were cast aside. There would be bigger fish to fry.

The first inklings of a reunion started to filter through in March of 1997. Oddly, Bill Ward would need feature in the equation, the drummer famously discovering his non-involvement via an MTV news broadcast.

As it transpired Ozzy Osbourne band sticksman Mike Bordin, a man having made his name with the highly inventive Faith No More, was to man the tubs for live work. However, the old ties nearly pulled Bobby Rondinelli back into the picture too.

"Tony often used to tell me before that he was planning on reuniting with Ozzy and that he thought

When The Bough Breaks.

Ozzy would be open to myself being involved. His exact words were 'Ozzy is going to love you, it'll be great'. I thought that was pretty cool. I knew Bill was physically unable to do it at that point so it looked like it was going to develop into something interesting.

Later I found out about the re-formation with Ozzy, Geezer and Bill on MTV. I had been waiting around for six months. Tony could have at least phoned me and I would have been cool about it but he didn't so I lost six months income. There are no sour grapes now, but at the time it didn't feel too good. Tony should have called."

The New Yorker was obviously still potentially part of the Iommi grand plan though. "I was asked to do the 'Ozzfest' dates for Black Sabbath" Bobby reveals. "I was in Blue Oyster Cult at the time so it was tricky. Tony Iommi told Sharon that he either wanted Bill or Bobby which was a nice compliment. The thing was I would have to arrange a fill in for Blue Oyster Cult for a gig. I didn't mind doing that, but I was loyal to the guys in The Cult and no way wanted to jeopardise that situation. I think they would have understood but when it came down to it Sharon offered me such a ridiculously small amount of money for the Ozzfest thing I declined. It simply wasn't worth harming the relationship with Blue Oyster Cult".

Does the drummer believe his days on the Sabbath drum stool are well and truly over? "You can never tell with Tony!" he laughs heartily. "That phone call could come out of the blue. That's generally how it works in this game. Blue Oyster Cult is occupying all my time right now. I've been with them six years and it feels like home. I enjoyed playing with Black Sabbath though, it was a fun time."

The Ozzfest concept solidified its standing with its first proper run of dates stretching from late May through the summer, headlined quite spectacularly by a Black Sabbath line-up of Ozzy, Tony Iommi, Geezer Butler and stand in Mike Bordin on drums the show saw Ozzy doubling up appearing with his own band too. Other featured artists were Pantera, the newly controversial ticket of Marilyn Manson, Type O Negative, Machine Head and Fear Factory on the main stage. A secondary stage was occupied by the Osbourne managed Coal Chamber, Powerman 5000, Downset, Vision Of Disorder, Slo Burn and feisty Swedish femme fatales Drain (known as Drain S.T.H. in America). An unqualified success all round the only potential fly in the ointment came when the Ozzfest June 5th gig in East Rutherford, New Jersey was put in jeopardy after Marilyn Manson's antics prompted local authorities to try and ban the show in its entirety. The Osbournes threatened to counter sue and the show went ahead.

Ozzy would also unite in the studio with one of the major 'Ozzfest' attractions Type O Negative cutting a version of 'Pictures Of Matchstick Men' for the 'Private Parts' hit movie centred on over the top shock jock Howard Stern. With no new original Ozzy album product in the pipeline the welcome compilation offering 'The Ozzman Cometh' saw a release on November 11th. No ordinary cash in collection 'The Ozzman Cometh' dug up archive Black Sabbath basement demo versions of 'Fairies Wear Boots', 'Behind The Wall Of Sleep', 'War Pigs' and 'Black Sabbath' with a previously unused Ozzy track 'Back To Earth'. With no fresh material as such the album still made platinum status. Eagle eyed Ozzy fans spotted an undercurrent of ill feeling in the accompanying credits though with Bob Daisley credited as 'Bob Daisy', Rudy Sarzo as 'Trudy Sarzo' and Phil Soussan as 'Bill Susan'.

The year rounded off with the realization of a dream that had kept the Rock world salivating since the all too brief 1985 Live Aid performance. On 4th and 5th December, the original Black Sabbath, Ozzy Osbourne, Tony Iommi, Geezer Butler and Bill Ward, joined forces for two blockbusting shows in their hometown of Birmingham. The gigs, held at the cavernous National Exhibition Centre, would be captured for historical record on the 'Reunion' album. The Black Sabbath resurrection would recommence in late May of 1998 with a full scale European tour taking in Germany, Hungary, Austria, Italy, the Czech Republic, Poland, Sweden, Finland and Norway. Unfortunately, Bill Ward's health failed him during pre-tour rehearsals that May and he suffered a heart attack. The tour still got underway with Vinny Appice making a temporary return to the fold.

With the original Black Sabbath reunited, those who had played a part in the intervening years had cause to reflect. Tony Martin, although not having weathered the full two decades like Geoff Nicholls, had manned the helm longer than any other singer. Since leaving the band Martin has amassed a cat-

Bill Ward.

alogue of solo material and figured on a number of album projects, such as Dario Mollo's Cage ventures. He has turned down more offers than he has accepted, believing the current Euro trend for 'Rock Opera' concept albums to smack of desperation. He is keen to plough his own furrow.

Looking back he still betrays the unease he felt upon very first joining Black Sabbath. "The vast difference in experience between me and the rest of the band was a constant thorn, that kind of prejudice is quite formidable. I was put in my place 2 or 3 times quite firmly by Tony Iommi or Cozy because of things I'd done that were seen by them as unprofessional or embarrassing. Usually my manager Albert was able to point out that they had done the same stuff when they were younger, in some cases many times anything I had done. Usually it was something like getting drunk and doing something stupid. I'm 12 years younger than they are and that seemed part of it.

I'm aware that some people thought that I just wasn't up to the job, they may be right. It certainly felt uncomfortable most of the time because I was never really part of the inner circle. I was always looking over my shoulder or reading between the lines to try and figure out what came next."

Tony Iommi's two shoulders to lean on throughout that time frame would unquestionably be Geoff Nicholls and Tony Martin. The keyboard player as a close friend and personal ally whilst Martin was the man that could always lend class to the proceedings in the studio and not fail him on the road. The singer is very clear in his own mind as to why he was chosen above all others. "My voice was really what kept me in favour, and I was the only singer that was able and mostly willing to cover all the songs from the entire history of the band. It was my suggestion to do songs like 'Sweet Leaf' and 'Changes' in the set for example. Songs like these had never been played live before so it was a great thing to be able to do. I encouraged Tony Iommi to play keyboards in 'Changes' on the 'Forbidden' tour but things like this were the only moments that I was able to influence. Mostly it felt like the material I appeared on wasn't as important somehow. In any case the only chance I had of getting my "Era" across was by being there so I had to get on with it and hope that I could work it out as we went along. No one can change the fact I appeared on six albums from 'Eternal Idol' in 1987 to 'The Sabbath Stones' in 1997, a span of 10 years, so in that respect I'm pleased. I'm pretty certain we never released anything unworthy of ourselves during that time. One or two albums might not have been up to par but there was some bloody good stuff in there too. Those albums I know Tony Iommi is really proud of. I feel that despite the personal battle of being in the band, I was able to bring something positive to Black Sabbath."

Recent events have, as Tony Martin admits, soured the Black Sabbath experience. "I was watching a TV documentary about Black Sabbath the other day and they never even mentioned my name" he exclaims. "I sat there thinking to myself, hang on, I was there wasn't I? That is my voice on those albums isn't it? I mean, that ten years was real wasn't it?"

Glenn Hughes was interviewed at length for that very same programme, aired in December of 2002 and made by Central TV, but in retrospect wishes he had declined the offer. "It put me off ever talking about Black Sabbath again. I was interviewed for five hours and they used about 30 seconds, which, of course, was about drugs. Those fucking people! They did the same with Tony Iommi. The only quote you saw from him about me was to do with drugs but of course he said a whole lot more on the positive side which was just cut out. It's like a revision of history that has gone on with Black Sabbath ever since Ozzy left. Don't these people realise this is the Internet age? You can't hide anything anymore."

Geoff Nicholls too was more than a little aggrieved by the very same documentary. "They came up here for two days, came to my house, asked me lots and lots of questions then when I sat and watched the thing I wasn't even included! Not one bloody second. I just sat there speechless. They had a quote from Don Airey which implied he had been Black Sabbath's keyboard player and not me.

Sometimes I feel like I've been the ghost in this whole thing. I've been there for every rehearsal, every gig, every album. I wrote a lot more than people know about yet the only real time Tony Iommi gave me just credit was for 'Seventh Star'. Y'know Ozzy paid me a great compliment in a TV interview once and that meant a hell of a lot. When the reunion happened, we spent about 3 or 4 weeks writing material for a new studio album. We were coming up with some good stuff and I was contributing heavily on the song-writing. Ozzy did a TV interview and actually said the songs were great and that I was doing the writing. He didn't need to say that but he did. It makes all the difference. It was a pleasant surprise for me to hear Ozzy say that because I was so used to being cut out of the picture. He's a hugely generous person and such a big star he doesn't need to concern himself with the politics of stuff.

Both Ozzy and Sharon I have always found to be very straightforward, honest people. Sharon is extremely protective of course but the whole thing is done out of a love for Ozzy and her family. Sharon tells it straight whereas with Sabbath before every question was either answered in such a way as to hide things or was just ignored. Every time they released a band photo without me of course the first question a journalist would ask Tony was 'Where's Geoff?' So it all kept backfiring.

Obviously there are many, many things in the Black Sabbath history, business, family and private stuff, that I am privy too and will always remain secret. That will never change. All the stuff about band line-up changes, who wrote the songs and who didn't make the auditions is of huge interest to fans though. I can see that. Jeff Fenholt is a good example. Why deny he was there? Just tell the truth. He was a bloody good singer and deserved to be there at that time. Tony Iommi never chose crap singers because to be in Black Sabbath you had to be the absolute best. Keeping things like that under wraps never works. I can see that and as part of all that I think it's about bloody time my contribution was recognised. Even with riffs. Tony Iommi is a genius at riff writing and 90% of the riffs are his. But, and this is a big but, some of them are mine too. I'm a guitarist and a songwriter but nobody says to me 'Cool riff Geoff'. I'm not detracting anything from Tony Iommi, because he is the man, he is Black Sabbath. Sometimes though it would have been nice for him to say 'Yeah, Geoff wrote that one'.

It seems odd to say but once I made my mind up to

stick with Black Sabbath, and put my energies into the overall good of the band, I kind of forgot about promoting myself until it was too late. The years drifted by so quickly because it was just so intensive all the time. I should have spoken up and I should have put my foot down when it came down to songwriting credits and royalties but I'm a Brummie y'see. I work hard and I don't like to make a fuss.

I did wonder sometimes why I was so laid back about the whole Sabbath thing. For much of that twenty years I really was Iommi's right hand man. We shared flats, wrote songs together, planned things together—all for the good of the band. I contributed a lot behind the scenes too, smoothing over band arguments and providing a shoulder to cry on too. I played a big part in keeping the band intact quite a few times. I know what part I played and it is no coincidence I kept getting asked back again and again. Every time there was a new line-up the only person who knew all the songs, could play the songs and wrote half of them was me. Yet now, I look at the photos and I'm not there!"

Tony Martin concedes that it has been difficult for him dealing with the reality of his seven years with the band as opposed to what the media machine wanted the fans to believe. "Sometimes I'm just ambivalent about the whole thing, sometimes it really gets to me. I don't understand this policy they seem to have of rewriting history because surely they must have learnt by now that if you create a mystery people just want to know the real story much more than they ever did before. If you try to keep a lid on things it always explodes in your face. It's not like I forced my way into Black Sabbath—they asked me. And they kept on asking me!

Why? Because I knew all the songs, I was one of the very few singers that could actually sing the entire Black Sabbath catalogue and Tony Iommi knew he would never have any reliability issues with me. You know there are some songs that both Ozzy and Ronnie can't do. I can do the lot and I proved that time and time again. I can do all of their tracks but they can't do mine."

For a significant period during the mid nineties the Tony Martin era albums dropped off the distribution lists. Frustrating for fans who had recently cottoned onto the quality of these records and conversely impacting upon band members quarterly pay checks. Although the IRS label had gone belly up, Tony Martin surmises that Machiavellian forces were in play to keep such a lucrative catalogue kept out of stores.

"For quite some time, after IRS Records had been shut down, those Black Sabbath albums were difficult to get hold of. Then EMI rereleased them all but with the Ozzy reunion suddenly they became very scarce again. It's all politics. I think they didn't want anything out there on the shelves that had any other singer on except Ozzy. Anyhow, 'Headless Cross', 'Tyr' and the rest are all available again and I've noticed a significant leap in royalty statements so people are buying them."

Ronnie James Dio, the man who pulled Black Sabbath up by its bootstraps, has also questioned this revisionism. In a compelling interview given to Jeff Kerby at KNAC.com he explained his position. "Well, I don't concern myself with it. I'm a very aware and observant person, and it's quite easy to discern that my part of Black Sabbath has been attempted to be quashed. You hear no mention from the Black Sabbath camp that those things even existed. That 'Heaven Or Hell' or 'Mob Rules' or 'Dehumanizer' or the 'Live Evil' album every really existed. It doesn't concern me one bit at all though because I know that the only person keeping any of those albums alive of course is me. With Dio, we do some of those songs because I like these songs and not because I'm trying to sell more of that old product—I just think they're necessary to do. Every time we do 'Heaven And Hell' it shows you how important those songs are. They cannot ever be quashed because people who like that music will never let that happen. I have seen the direct attempt for that to happen though."

Dio, talking to the author in 1998, also illustrated some of the difficulties he faced when selecting Black Sabbath material for his Dio live set. "It gets more difficult every tour because we have to promote a new record each time we go out" he says practically. Agreeing that the band, not to mention the label, are keen to air the new tracks he concedes that Black Sabbath will always play a part in his live show. "I don't think we could ever get away with not playing Black Sabbath or Rainbow. The choice is always which Sabbath songs to play not if. I don't view those songs as tired or less fun to play in any way. I love those songs, I wrote the words, the melodies—they're very much a part of me. I always have a great time singing those classic songs which the audience wants to hear. They expect it and we're glad to deliver. One of the interesting things for me recently has been fans asking us to play Elf songs!"

Just how inevitable was the reunion with Ozzy? Just how far, if at all, did Tony Iommi manage to pull out of the suction generated by the Ozzy black hole? Eric Singer saw Ozzy as omnipresent. "The rest of the guys did get this sense from Tony that the Ozzy thing was a major burden. The competition was certainly there even though it was never really voiced. Everything we did was, eventually, compared to Ozzy's album or Ozzy's tour. When I got to know Tony a bit better it became clear that it was not the Sabbath–Ozzy split where this was all coming from,

Dave Spitz & Ronnie James Dio.

which of course the Rock magazines loved to play up on, but it went way, way deeper.

Tony and Ozzy had known each other since childhood and that competition was there from day one. Tony Iommi actually used to bully Ozzy! Can you imagine that? Tony beating up Ozzy! Tony is not a great communicator, he lets other people sort things out for him generally so the dynamic between him and Ozzy is a very special one. I think it must be hard for Tony having everyone else tell him that to be successful he needs Ozzy. He kind of proved otherwise with Ian Gillan and Ronnie James Dio but still that Ozzy thing just won't go away.

I see similar kind of relationship patterns in Kiss with Gene and Paul, not that they beat each other up but they fire the other one up. That way they excel, they want to always do better. Fortunately Gene and Paul can coexist within the same band quite comfortably. It's odd, these people, Gene and Paul, Tony and Ozzy, the dynamic from childhood stays the same. Doesn't matter how successful they are, how many records they sell, how old they get—it's just the same as when they were kids, it'll never go away."

Ronnie James Dio has no misconceptions when it comes to the inevitability of a reunion with Ozzy. "Reuniting with Ozzy has always been like some kind of holy grail to Tony and Geezer, they follow it blindly," he reckoned. "After every album and every tour they start talking about getting back with Ozzy and of course Sharon and Ozzy just lap it up. They've been doing it for fifteen years and it's kind of desperate.

I think the only time Tony really wasn't interested in getting Ozzy back was after 'Heaven And Hell' because that album really proved a big point. Black Sabbath took a big step forward into a new generation, we sold a million albums, the concerts were great and there was a lot of pride there. After that, after I went the slide began. Their obsession since that day was in getting Ozzy back and it showed in their decision making. You know, they had some good singers in that period, people I have no problem in giving due respect, but they were all put into impossible situations so, of course, the result was always inevitable. I'm proud of what I achieved with both Black Sabbath and Rainbow. A lot of people, the fans that buy the records, tell me both of those bands peaked at those times. That's enough of a legacy for me."

Bassist Jo Burt confirms this undercurrent of thought within the band back in 1987. "It's an odd experience playing in a band who constantly talk about re-forming with the original members, and this was the first time I experienced what it felt like to be replaced at any moment (by Geezer Butler). My good friend, Phil Soussan played bass guitar with Ozzy Osbourne at exactly the same time and we often compared notes. I remember Ozzy slagging off Tony to me in the Sunset Marquee Hotel, Los Angeles, sometime after my departure and me defending Tony. Such is life ... !"

Tony Martin, probably the Black Sabbath member that has dwelt longest in the shade of both Ozzy and Dio felt the competition all too keenly. "The Ozzy thing was always there but, as a Black Sabbath fan going back to when I was a kid, I always knew it would be. I went in with my eyes open. Personally, I felt the Ozzy thing was illogical because he is such a larger than life and genuinely loved character that I didn't see the need for a lot of things that happened. The band that Black Sabbath became—with Ronnie, Ian Gillan and Glenn Hughes was so different from the seventies. So, you see, it wasn't the band Ozzy and Sharon had a problem with. It was the name.

I can remember once their promoter put Ozzy on in the same town in Germany as we were playing. All it did was destroy the attendance for both gigs as the attendance was drastically reduced for both of us. That kind of petty stuff was going on a lot but you learned to somehow ignore it.

Tony Iommi was, and is, always very, very careful about what he says. He keeps a lot to himself. There is still a lot I don't know about him and that's after ten years of working with him. He has to be one of the most private individuals I have ever met. The subject of Ozzy within the band was never really discussed although we all knew what was going on. Ozzy probably thought that Tony Martin was a complete wanker. What do I care? I was there to do my job and I did it the best I could.

There was no way that Ozzy was ever going to rejoin the band during the eighties and early nineties so I can't see what difference the Black Sabbath albums and tours made to him. The thing is though, we did get to him and Sharon. We must have needled them. From what I understood it was simply the fact that Tony Iommi owned the name and was daring to release albums and tour as Black Sabbath. Ozzy and Sharon believed Sabbath was their thing, not Tony's.

That was obvious because of a lot of the stuff being said. I can remember talking to Tony about this on the plane going to America for a tour. I told him straight, if Ozzy wants to come back just keep me in the picture. That's all I ask. The trouble was though that I don't think anyone in that band, besides Tony, was ever kept in the picture. When I think about it, the secrets that Tony Iommi must have kept—that I know he kept—must have been a huge burden really. You just never knew from day to day.

Tony always wanted Ozzy back. It was not voiced but it was no secret. Everybody involved with the band knew it, even when things were looking great for us with 'Headless Cross' and Cozy. If Ozzy clicked his fingers it would have all collapsed I'm sure. I can remember Tony being asked in an interview if there were plans to bring Ozzy back. I thought the interviewer had a bloody cheek because I was sitting right next to him at the time. I sat there in amazement thinking 'Do I exist? Shall I hit him?' Just amazing cheek. Tony replied 'There are absolutely no plans to bring Ozzy back … at … this … moment'. I looked at him gobsmacked but of course I was in no position to say anything. He could never just say 'No'. He was always very careful about the words he picked because he knew anything he said in an interview could be seen by Sharon. Those kind of statements were made a lot, so Tony always left the door wide open for Ozzy.

With Ronnie, that was different to Ozzy. He was a bit of a musical hero so, to me, his boots were much bigger to fill. I loved what he did on 'Heaven And Hell' and 'The Mob Rules'. As a singer I got into that stuff far easier than the old Ozzy songs. Technically and creatively I loved the challenge of those songs. I mean, 'Paranoid'. That song never made a blind bit of sense to me. I would sing it and not know what I was singing about. Geezer explained it to me once and I was still none the wiser.

I grabbed Ronnie at a gig once and had a good chat. I don't think he liked me much but I hopefully got across to him the degree of respect I had for him. That was important to me personally. Glenn Hughes too, my favourite singer of all time. A wonderful, wonderful voice."

Summing up his tenure Tony Martin encapsulates it all succinctly. "I was stepping into someone else's shoes—not one pair either but four of them. Those shoes were huge. They were in fact so fucking big I spent a decade tripping over myself in the bloody things!"

With the Ozzy led Black Sabbath making the news, Neil Murray soon gravitated back toward Cozy Powell, the rhythm partners providing a valuable foil for Blues guitar supremist Peter Green. After many troubled years away from the music scene Green had, by a way of a series of bizarre circumstances (including an impersonator come chicken farmer landing a major record deal!), come back to the fore. Mainstream interest was high in the man that had penned such legendary tracks as 'Albatross', 'Man Of The World', 'Black Magic Woman' and 'Green Manalishi'. Powell and Murray, together with guitarist Nigel Watson and keyboard player Spike Edney, formed up the Peter Green Splinter Group. This outfit cut an eponymous live album befittingly comprised of Blues standards by the likes of Robert Johnson, Elmore James and Otis Rush.

Powell would decamp but Murray stayed the course for Green's next work 'The Robert Johnson Songbook'. The former Sabbath men would unite once more for Queen guitarist Brian May's album 'Another World' in 1998. Powell performed drums on seven tracks for this record in 'Business', 'China Belle', 'Why Don't We Try Again', 'Slow Down', Jimi Hendrix's 'One Rainy Wish', Mott The Hoople's 'All The Way From Memphis' and 'The Guv'nor'.

A second tragedy struck the Black Sabbath family in 1998. The seemingly indestructible Cozy Powell, a man whose career trajectory had appeared to be stretching infinitely over the horizon, was killed. It was a massive shock to friends, fans and the music community.

Business had been brisk for Cozy in the preceding years having given Yngwie Malmsteen a boost by appearing on his 'Facing The Animal' album. Cozy's inclusion on that album had done much to bolster the Swede's credibility, particularly in Japan. He had also featured heavily on material cut for Judas Priest guitarist Glenn Tipton's solo record 'Baptism Of Fire'. There was concerted talk of a full blown classic Rainbow reunion too, instigated by a huge offer from a Japanese label, pulling together Messrs. Blackmore, Dio, Bain and Powell.

On April 5th 1998, Cozy Powell met his untimely death in a car crash, his Saab going off the road at a reported 120mph plus, smashing into the central reservation on the M4 near Bristol. Reports were sketchy but it was determined the drummer had been using his car phone when the accident happened. Cozy succumbed to his injuries in hospital. He was just 50.

SABBATH BLOODY SABBATH: THE BATTLE FOR BLACK SABBATH

Ironically, prior to the fatal accident, Cozy had been forced to pull out of his appearance on a Japanese tour with Yngwie Malmsteen because he had injured his foot in a minor motorcycle accident. In a twist of fate Japan's massively influential 'Burrn' magazine had already gone to print with their reader's polls for the previous year. Powell had been voted number 1 drummer.

Brian May paid tribute by withdrawing his planned single, a costly affair as they had already been pressed, quickly issuing a remixed version of his album cut that featured Cozy prominently 'The Business' (Rock On Cozy mix). Powell's last recorded work came with Colin Blunstone's 1998 album 'The Light Inside' which found him back at Silvermere Sound Studios in Surrey, where had recorded 'The Drums Are Back', in the familiar company of old friends engineer Sean Lynch, Don Airey and Neil Murray. Recorded during February of 1998 Powell performed on six tracks for the record.

Powell's fourth solo record, an on off affair that had been ongoing for a number of years also hit the stores. The record, laid down with singer John West, guitarist Mike Casswell, bassist Neil Murray and keyboard player Lonnie Parks was re-titled 'Especially For You' and issued in Japan. The Japanese fans in particular mourned the loss of Cozy and two tribute albums 'Rest In Peace—Thanks Cozy' and 'Cozy Powell Forever' were also released in quick succession. The latter featured Loudness guitarist Akira Takasaki, Vow Wow keyboard player Rei Atsumi, Carmine Appice and Tony Franklin.

In the small spa town of Buxton in Derbyshire's Peak District musicians of distinction gathered at the Opera House Theatre on May 1st to pay tribute to Cozy. In attendance would be Brian May, Tony Martin, Bobby Rondinelli, Neil Murray and Geoff Nicholls running through numbers such as 'Headless Cross' and 'Long Live Rock n' Roll'.

Tony Martin remembers the event well. "As we were going on stage, Cozy's lady came to me and said, "He's really with you tonight." I thought OK, I can get my head round that. Spiritually I guess he could be watching over us I suppose. So I thanked her and went on stage. When I came off she was stood there with his urn of ashes! She had him placed under the kit riser, so he really WAS on stage with us. I thought it was amazing. I feel sure Cozy would have thought it hilarious but at first it was a heart stopper!!"

Geoff Nicholls abiding memories of Cozy Powell are of a public figure unphased by fame and always on the look out for a positive angle to any situation. "Cozy just had so much energy and enthusiasm. When he joined the band he gave Tony Iommi a real lift. Sabbath had taken a good kicking with 'Eternal Idol' and Cozy took the bull by the horns and helped Sabbath turn it around again. The guy had a great sense of humour too and clicked with Tony Iommi. Both of them loved to play jokes all of the time which really kept everyone in the band on edge!

Tony Martin at the Cozy Powell tribute gig in Buxton.

Very often you would find your hotel bed dismantled so that as soon as you had got into it the thing collapsed under you. Lots of other stuff I can't repeat too! Tony had this wonderful trick he played on Bobby Rondinelli. Bobby used to wear these grey tracksuit bottoms a lot so, while Bobby was asleep on the bus, Tony would rub chocolate on the backside. When he put them on it would look like Bobby had bad skid marks! I don't think Bobby actually ever caught on to that!

Tony Iommi had always loved a good practical joke but when he got together with Cozy it just got completely crazy. Tony and Cozy were always scheming on things like that. When they were together it was terrible. You made sure all your doors, windows and suitcases were all firmly locked at all times. Nobody was safe from either of them. It got so bad in the end Cozy and Tony had to call a truce because they were causing so much damage to hotels.

I guess that's one aspect of Black Sabbath the fans never got to see. The whole thing from the outside must have looked very doomy and secretive but in reality we were having a ball. Tony Iommi was always up to something and when he was put together with personalities like Ian Gillan or Cozy Powell life got totally crazy. It's a shame there aren't more photos of us having a good time because, for most of the time, we were really enjoying life. Whenever a photographer appeared though all the dour faces came out!"

Stepping into the breach to promote Brian May's 'Another World' opus would be none other than erstwhile Black Sabbath man Eric Singer. The Brian May Band, numbering Murray, Singer, guitarist James Moses with keyboard player Spike Edney trekked throughout Europe in September of 1998 proffering their wares.

By 1999 the circle had been closed for Neil Murray. Having enjoyed some of his greatest successes with Whitesnake an alliance with former allies from the 'MTV unfriendly' version of the band was on the cards. Thus, in early 1999 the Company Of Snakes was born, the bassist hooking up with former snake charmers Micky Moody and Bernie Marsden, the journeyman keyboard veteran Don Airey and former Bad Company singer Robert Hart.

'Ozzfest' was back bigger and better for 1998 spanning the United States from its inception in New Jersey on the 5th of July to its grand finale in the nation's capitol Washington D.C. on the 2nd of August. On the 20th of June 'Ozzfest' had reached the UK and the Milton Keynes National Bowl. Black Sabbath and Ozzy would be joined by such contemporaries as the Foo Fighters, Korn, Pantera, Soulfly, Slayer, Fear Factory, Coal Chamber, Life Of Agony, Limp Bizkit, Entombed, Human Waste Project, Pitchshifter and Neurosis. To everyone's amusement Osbourne welcomed Bill Ward on stage then pulled the drummer's trousers down in front of 60,000 bemused onlookers. The tour continued into Europe stopping off in Spain, Denmark, Switzerland and Belgium before repeating the whole process over again for American fans in Holmdel, New Jersey on July 3rd.

With media attention firmly focused on the founding four, the group was put under pressure to deliver a brand new studio album. Black Sabbath did enter the studio but, although tracks were laid down, the process stalled. Geoff Nicholls was present at the sessions. "The band put down quite a few songs but not a full album. I contributed most of the lyrics too. I felt it was sounding good but it just kind of fizzled out."

'Reunion' would be issued on 20th October, just two days after Ozzy's infamous appearance on the notorious 'South Park' cartoon. 'Reunion' gave Black Sabbath something they had been lacking for 18 years—a million selling platinum album. Not only would 'Reunion' satisfy fans desire for live material but it would also offer up two brand new studio

Geoff and Ozzy.

recordings in 'Psycho Man' and 'Selling My Soul'. Before October was out, Ozzy and Black Sabbath had put in an appearance on the 'The Late Show With David Letterman', performing 'Paranoid'. It had been 23 years since the last Sabbath TV showing. The year signalled another personal landmark for Ozzy, a lifelong and vocal fan of The Beatles, with his vocal inclusion on the title track of Ringo Starr's 'Vertical Man' album.

Black Sabbath was back on the road in the USA on New Year's Eve in Phoenix, Arizona. Bill Ward had thankfully regained his strength and performed each show. Vinny Appice was also in the entourage as back up in case of any problems, even having his kit set up behind Ward's each night, but fortunately the situation never arose. The only dates cancelled would be those caused by recurring throat problems assailing Ozzy.

1999 would see no let up in the schedule. By late May 'Ozzfest' had recommenced with the added tag of 'The Last Supper', an indicator that these were in fact to be the last ever Black Sabbath shows. For this run of shows John Sinclair would find himself deputizing with Black Sabbath too. Kicking off on the 25th of May at the Coral Sky Amphitheatre in West Palm Beach, Florida and running through until the closing date in California at the suitably titled Devore Blockbuster Pavilion in late July. 'Ozzfest', grossing a gargantuan $19.4 million, would yet again defy all trends and come out on top as one of the most heavily attended touring packages of the year.

Along for a ride on the 'Ozzfest' rollercoaster for this round would be Rob Zombie, Deftones, Slayer, Primus, Fear Factory, System Of A Down, Godsmack, Slipknot, Puya, Hed(P.E.), Drain S.T.H., Static X, Flashpoint, Pushmonkey and Geezer Butler's son Biff's band Apartment 26. Right at the tail end of the 'Ozzfest' a further show was tacked on that Mike Bordin's prior commitments precluded him from attending. Stepping into the breech would be former Ugly Kid Joe drummer Shannon Larkin. 'Ozzfest' had morphed into so much more than a trend defying touring package it was rapidly becoming a proven nurturing ground for new talent.

1999 would also be marked with a guest appearance for the famed Yes keyboard player Rick Wakeman. In an ambitious move Wakeman reconvened his leviathan 'Journey To The Centre Of The Earth' saga that had reigned supreme among Pomp in the seventies recording a sequel 'Return To The Centre Of The Earth'. Amongst an all star international cast Ozzy contributed lead vocals to the track 'Buried Alive', which also surfaced as a single.

As 2000 drew in, and with a lull in Ozzy's activities, Holmes, Trujillo and Bordin founded a fresh, yet short-lived act Mass Mental fronted by ex-Dub war vocalist Benji. As for Ozzy he was soon back in the public eye collaborating with Wu Tang Clan on the track 'For Heaven's Sake' and putting in a cameo in the 'Little Nicky' comedy. In keeping with the tradition of musical chairs, Ozzy announced his drummer for the 2000 'Ozzfest' series to be ex-Thorn, Crisis, Soulfly and Pale Demons man Roy Mayorga. However, within weeks drummer Brian Tichy, a man with a diverse CV stretching the spectrum from Zakk's Pride & Glory to a recent stint with Foreigner, was on the drum stool.

Despite previous claims that the Birmingham December 1999 gigs were the very last, Black Sabbath did reunite for a summer 2000 show although after the event they probably wished they hadn't. A surprise performance after an Ozzy gig at the Anaheim 'Weenie Roast' festival ended in debacle when a revolving stage snagged the band's gear resulting in a long embarrassing silence and lengthy delays. In more of a low key vein, other live activities included Iommi taking time out to perform with impromptu Midlands club act Belch, a band that featured his ex-Sabbath friend Bev Bevan and comedian Jasper Carrott on vocals.

Iommi also finally got around to issuing his first solo album proper simply credited to 'Iommi'. Notably, both Osbourne and Ward were included on the track 'Who's Fooling Who'. The Iommi solo album also featured a multitude of guest artists including Osbourne, Pantera's Phil Anselmo, Smashing Pumpkins Billy Corgan, Foo Fighters Dave Grohl, Henry Rollins, Type O Negative's Pete Steele, ex-Soundgarden drummer Matt Cameron and former White Zombie drummer John Tempesta. Hardened, longstanding fans found the material worthy but the guest inclusions more in keeping with ill advised marketing rather than what his followers actually

Iommi.

wanted. Eagle eared devotees spotted a rehashed riff from the 'Eighth Star' bootleg from the song 'Don't You Tell Me' turning up in the track 'Black Oblivion'. Ward meantime, was still endeavouring to complete his third solo album provisionally titled 'Beyond Aston'. A projected reissue of his first album 'Ward One—Along The Way' was shelved when two songs that featured Ozzy on lead vocals created business complications.

Long time ally Geoff Nicholls found the 'Iommi' album confusing. "Tony Iommi can't make a bad record, he's just too classy for that, but I found his solo stuff a bit bewildering. I think he was listening to too many people that really don't understand what Tony is about, or what his fans want. I guess it was part of this drive to sound modern, which had always failed Sabbath in the past. When Sabbath just got on with things you had records like 'Heaven And Hell' and 'Headless Cross', when we started listening to other people you get 'Forbidden'. A lot of those singers on that album I think were very lucky to be associated with Tony Iommi. The whole thing was very confusing.

What's strange is that Tony, gifted as he is and with his reputation, is very often unsure of himself. We've had endless jam sessions and afterwards we've both thought the same thing—if that was on a record the fans would love it. I've always thought a Tony Iommi solo album should be just that, a true solo record with maybe a couple of guest singers but mostly instrumentals. That's what his fans want. I've seen it time and time again in concert. When Tony plays a solo the audience are mesmerized by what he's playing. So, why not give them what they want rather than giving them something that just confuses them? I've given Tony tons of material to play over for solo things that never happened, a lot of Santana style stuff and all kinds of styles that I'm sure his fans would love. The thing is, that's what Tony is into himself too, stuff like The Shadows instrumentals we used to do with Sabbath, the stuff we jam at soundchecks. At the end of the day it's all about sales and Tony's fans want to hear him soloing, not some bird they've never heard of screeching!"

Launched on 2nd of July in Palm Beach, Florida the 'Ozzfest' event still retained Ozzy as overall headliner despite several murmurings the event would carry on without Ozzy at the helm. The main stage would also be graced by heavyweights Pantera, Incubus, Godsmack, Tommy Lee's Rap Rockers Methods Of Mayhem, P.O.D., Static-X and Stoners Queens Of The Stone Age. As before a second stage provided further diversions with industrialists Ministry along with the all girl Nu-Metal sounds of Kittie together with Taproot, Primer 55, Nottingham's own Pitchshifter, Disturbed, Crazy Town, The Deadlights, Shuvel, Slaves On Dope and Pumpjack.

Rumours surfacing toward the tail end of 2000 via Internet reports on KNAC's website had Ozzy's new band slated as Zakk Wylde returning on guitar, a reinstatement of Geezer Butler on bass and the surprisingly newsworthy inclusion of erstwhile Mötley Crüe drummer Tommy Lee. This roster was then swiftly denied, in typically colourful language, but an Ozzy insider subsequently confirmed that the leaked band unit had been motioned. The projected album would not actually transpire and the band that eventually set to work could not be more different. Joe Holmes was still holding down the guitarist slot, Robert Trujillo had kept his place and on drums was the young Brooks Wackerman of Suicidal Tendencies, Trujillo's old band. Preproduction for a new album began in earnest but soon faltered when the band and slated producer Toby Wright apparently simply didn't gel.

During April of 2001 the Ozzy rhythm section of Bordin and Trujillo would back up erstwhile Alice In Chains guitarist Jerry Cantrell for live dates whilst Trujillo, along with his Pale Demons colleague and ex-Ozzy drummer Roy Mayorga, would be found guesting on the debut Insolence album. The summer of 2001 had Ozzy topping the bill on the international 'Ozzfest' once again back in place with Black Sabbath. A totally unexpected surprise in the Sabbath set would be the brand new song 'Scary Dreams'. Zakk Wylde meantime featured his act Black Label Society, promoting a live album which featured Zakk's version of 'No More Tears', on the bill also.

Just prior to this round of concerts, Black Sabbath entered a U.S. studio with an objective of crafting new material for a proposed album. "We spent a couple of weeks in the studio putting about half a dozen new songs together" says Geoff Nicholls. "That's where 'Scary Dreams' came from. Most of the songs only got to the stage of having working titles

Ozzfest 2001.

but there was a good one called 'He's Back Again' I remember. I wrote most of the lyrics for them all. Actually, one of the hook lines got used later for an Ozzy album in the song 'Black Illusion'. That song is from those Sabbath sessions."

Decades of mayhem, madness and album and concert ticket sales stretching into the millions and yet Ozzy has still not spent his final shot. As testimony to his enduring staying power the 'Down To Earth' album, released on the 16th October 2001 broke top 5 in both America and the UK, debuting at Number 4 on the Billboard charts shifting over 150,000 copies in the process. The album even gave his Ozzness his first ever Swedish Number 1. Ozzy's new single, 'Gets Me Through', was announced for a September 2001 release but would actually arrive in stores on 1st October. Japanese copies boasted an extra track 'No Place For Angels'. Notably, amongst inclusions on the songwriting front would be Black Sabbath keyboard player Geoff Nicholls on 'Facing Hell' and 'Black Illusion' whilst 'Running Out Of Time' was co-penned by Foreigner guitarist Mick Jones. Meantime, it was also announced that Ozzy had lent his voice to a track called 'Iron Head' on a forthcoming Rob Zombie album.

However, the subsequent 'Merry Mayhem' tour, with support acts Rob Zombie, Mudvayne and Soil would not run so smoothly. Ten dates, commencing 9th of November at the Compaq Center in Houston, would be postponed when Ozzy suffered a stress fracture in his leg. The injury had come about when Ozzy had reportedly slipped in the shower prior to a gig in Tucson. The singer, apparently unaware of the severity of the damage to his leg, continued to perform until the pain became unbearable and doctors diagnosed the fracture. Ozzy recovered to resume action by the 29th of November in North Dakota.

Japanese shows in early 2002 would be recorded for a live album and DVD 'Live At Budokan', mooted to also contain a number of new studio recordings. The UK leg of the 'Ozzfest' tour would be put in at the world famous Castle Donington site on May 25th, Ozzy heading a bill over Tool, System Of A Down, Slayer, Black Label Society and Cradle Of Filth. The American leg of 'Ozzfest' would feature a revised billing with Ozzy topping System Of A Down, P.O.D., Black Label Society, Drowning Pool, Adema, Rob Zombie, Meshuggah, Apex Theory, Lostprophets, Pulse Ultra and Neurotica amongst others. Robert Trujillo would double up duties with both Ozzy and Black Label Society.

While all this road activity was going on millions of TV viewers would be tuning into the "fly on the wall" six part documentary 'The Osbournes', a quite hilarious peak at the private life of Ozzy and Sharon Osbourne at home. This show, which rapidly climbed to the status of MTV's most successful show, took Ozzy's star status to unprecedented levels. 'The Osbournes' also heralded the arrival of another part of the Osbourne clan into the music world when Ozzy's daughter Kelly cut a version of Madonna's 'Papa Don't Preach' backed by Californian Hip Hop Rockers Incubus.

Sadly, former drummer Randy Castillo lost his long battle against cancer on March 26th 2002. As little as two months before his passing Castillo was full of optimism, believing he had beaten the disease. "There's nothing as painful as the radioactive, red hot fire going through your veins. But I'm beating this motherfucker!" Castillo's funeral would naturally prove to be a star studded affair. Unfortunately the event also made news when Sharon Osbourne, according to Phil Soussan, gave the former bassist a kick. The ex-Ozzy bass player was at the time engaged in a legal dispute with the Osbournes.

The long running battle between Osbourne and his early 80s rhythm section of bassist Bob Daisley and drummer Lee Kerslake was given new impetus when it was learned that quite incredibly the 'expanded' reissues of the 'Blizzard Of Ozz' and 'Diary Of A Madman' albums had the original bass and drum parts excised and replaced by that of Robert Trujillo and Mike Bordin. Fans were universally outraged that such a monumental slice of Rock history had been tampered with so brazenly.

Bob Daisley in particular was horrified. "I heard they were going to reissue the albums and I just thought to myself, OK, there are some more royalties I won't get to see for a long time. Then I had an email from someone telling me that my bass parts and Lee's drum parts had been removed. Honestly, I just could not believe it because it was such an outrageous thing to do.

I really cannot understand the motive. It deprives Lee and I of performance credits, which is probably the reason. So now we have gone from being not credited on the originals to being totally removed. The crazy thing is that all of Ozzy's fans know we played on those albums and there has been so much press about the whole thing they also know exactly what happened. Of course the big picture is much worse because it is immensely disrespectful to the memory of Randy Rhoads. I know his mother is just as angry as Lee and I about it.

The worst thing is that the fans suffer. People who go to replace their original vinyl albums now can't get what they want because it does not exist anymore. They have tried to rewrite history. You cannot reproduce that magic. Fans know this too. It's a unique, creative thing when a bunch of musicians make something really special. I've not seen one good report from the fans at all. It looks like Ozzy alienated a lot of fans by doing that."

Lee Kerslake, who had his drums removed from the new editions, was equally saddened. "At first I was angry but then I just felt so sad. Not for Bob or me but for Randy and the fans of those original records. I feel Randy's name has been tarnished and I don't see what he has done to deserve that. Ozzy knows how those records were recorded, he knows who wrote the songs, who put the arrangements together, who wrote the lyrics. He knows this. I still have not heard those new versions and I don't want to."

With 'The Osbournes' rating as the highest rated MTV show it would come as no surprise that a further two series were secured with the famous family netting a reported $20 million for the privilege. Ozzy would also land a cameo role in the latest movie from the Austin Powers series, 'Goldmember'. Also released in June would be a compilation album culled from 'The Osbournes' billed as 'The Osbournes Family Album', comprising of music from the show. Included would be Ozzy's own 'Crazy Train', 'Dreamer' and 'Mama, I'm Coming Home' alongside crooner Pat Boone's take on 'Crazy Train', Kelly Osbourne's 'Papa Don't Preach', The Kinks 'You Really Got Me', System Of A Down with Black Sabbath's 'Snowblind', John Lennon's 'Imagine', The Cars 'Drive', Starsailor 'Good Souls' and Eric Clapton's 'Wonderful Tonight'. The strength of the TV series was demonstrated when this record landed in the top 20 of the Billboard charts. Yet further spin offs from the TV show included a merchandise deal which not only saw the prospect of Ozzy figurines but Sharon, Jack and Kelly dolls too. Back on the musical front with Ozzy himself a double live album recorded at the Tokyo Budokan, and set to include new studio cuts, was announced for the Summer.

Ozzy pulled out of the Irish 'Ozzfest' event on the 26th of May due to an undisclosed illness. Further troubles hit the European leg of Ozzfest as Zakk Wylde reportedly fell ill, citing mental and physical exhaustion, necessitating a rapid return to America. The events in Zurich, Copenhagen, Stockholm, Helsinki and Russian shows in St. Petersburg and Moscow were all cancelled. Some consolation was afforded by the fact that Ozzy was deemed by many critics to have stolen the show at the Buckingham Palace concert to celebrate the 50th anniversary of Queen Elizabeth II's reign. Ozzy triumphed with a rendition of the perennial 'Paranoid' which included a guest showing from Tony Iommi. The rhythm section for this esteemed one off band comprised of the renowned session bassist Pino Palladino and Genesis drummer Phil Collins.

The first two North American 'Ozzfest' dates, Bristow, Virginia on July 6th, and Pittsburgh, Pennsylvania on July 7th, would be rescheduled when it was learned Sharon Osbourne was to undergo surgery for what was described as a "treatable" cancer. Shortly after Ozzy withdrew from ten 'Ozzfest' dates in order to be at his wife's side as she underwent chemotherapy, planning on a return for the Denver leg of the tour. During the interim System Of A Down would extend their set to cover the absence. However, in actuality Ozzy would only miss two 'Ozzfest' dates.

The subsequent 'Ozzfest 2002' album not only boasted track inclusions from the event roster such as White Zombie, Meshuggah, P.O.D., Adema, Hatebreed and Drowning Pool but also led off with Ozzy's own 'War Pigs'. Zakk Wylde would be in evidence with his own Black Label Society's 'Berzerkers' and also as guest for Soil. Even Kelly Osbourne got in on the action, duetting with Andrew W.K. on the closeout track 'She Is Beautiful'.

By September it would seem that Kelly might be in line to rival her father in the future as 'Papa Don't Preach' debuted in the UK singles charts at a healthy No. 3. Ozzy put in a solo show with a marked difference on October 25th at The Palms Casino in Las Vegas, Nevada. The promoters even went so far as to honour the event by producing Ozzy gambling chips in $5, $25 and $100 denominations. Ozzy would then be the subject of further rumours in late November, just as a second series of 'The Osbournes' was aired on TV to over 6.6 million viewers, suggesting his next album was to be comprised entirely of cover versions. There would also be talk of a Hollywood movie based on Ozzy's life, with talk of no less than Johnny Depp as a preferred candidate for the lead role.

Ozzy recorded guest lead vocals for the track 'Stillborn' on Black Label Society's April 2003 album 'The Blessed Hellride'. Robert Trujillo teamed up with Black Label Society for subsequent touring. A matter of days after this liaison was confirmed Trujillo was confirmed as the new Metallica bass man. Another Ozzy headlined 'Ozzfest' extravaganza was scheduled for the summer in North America commencing on June 28th at the San Antonio, Texas, Verizon Wireless Amphitheatre. Various supporting acts included Korn, Marilyn Manson, Cradle Of Filth, Chevelle and Disturbed.

In an unexpected and curious turn of events Robert Trujillo joined Metallica in February whilst former Metallica and current Voivod bassist Jason Newsted teamed up with Ozzy's band a matter of weeks later. Trujillo's last performance with Ozzy's band came on 14th March at the Hard Rock Hotel in Las Vegas, Nevada. The new look Ozzy band debuted with a run through four tracks, 'War Pigs', 'Believer', 'No More Tears' and 'Crazy Train' on March 17th at a Los Angeles media showcase. Closing a 23 year relationship Ozzy left the Sony Music stable in May.

The 'Ozzfest' trek once again did brisk business, defying trends in its usual fashion. However, Ozzy was forced to pull out of one gig at Marysville, California when he contracted severe laryngitis. Also in July it was revealed that Ozzy had rerecorded the Black Sabbath ballad 'Changes' as a duet with daughter Kelly.

With Ozzy recovered from laryngitis the singer reclaimed his headlining slot on the 'Ozzfest' dates. Unfortunately sad news arrived on July 24th when the singer's longstanding tour manager, Bobby Thompson, was found dead in his Detroit hotel room. Although still acting as Ozzy's personal tour manager Thompson had been battling throat cancer. Ozzy led a mid set silence and dedicated both 'Goodbye To Romance' and 'Mama, I'm Coming Home' to Thompson at his Independence Township, Michigan show. Ozzy pulled out of another show due to illness, making a non appearance at the PNC Bank Arts Center in Holmdel, New Jersey due to what reports described as a mild case of pneumonia. Mid tour Ozzy's last album, 'Down To Earth', received a platinum award for one million U.S. sales.

An interesting aside came with the knowledge that the erstwhile 'Blizzard Of Ozz' rhythm section of bassist Bob Daisley and drummer Lee Kerslake had formed up part of a much vaunted 'supergroup' billed as Living Loud with strong Deep Purple, Uriah Heep and Ozzy connections. Spending the Summer months recording in Florida, the duo was joined by Deep Purple guitarist Steve Morse, Australian vocalist Jimmy Barnes and the Black Sabbath, Deep

Living Loud in Australia. Don Airey, Steve Morse, Jimmy Barnes, Lee Kerslake and Bob Daisley.

Purple and Ozzy Osbourne credited keyboard maestro Don Airey to cut an album entitled 'Relentless' comprising five new songs and no less than six Ozzy tracks.

Ozzy's UK and European tour dates were postponed, the singer undergoing an operation on his foot. Although the gigs were rescheduled to commence 22nd October in Dublin, Ireland, and run through until 5th December in Munich, Germany these shows too would be curtailed under doctor's advice. Reports emerged that Osbourne was suffering from a severe tremor which required medication. Successive statements in the Los Angeles Times newspaper revealed that a Beverley Hills physician, Dr. David A. Kipper, was under investigation for oversubscribing medicine to the star.

Jason Newsted stepped out of the group and the band rehearsed with Fear Factory's Christian Olde Wolbers for a period. The European gigs, seeing Ozzy's band joined by bassist Rob Nicholson (a.k.a. 'Blasko'), a man holding a wealth of credits with such acts as Cryptic Slaughter, Rob Zombie, Suffer, Drown, Prong, Danzig and The Death Rays, would be announced for a third attempt during 2004, these new dates including Ozzy's debut in Croatia at the Dom Sportova in Zagreb.

However, once more the live schedule would be put in jeopardy when Osbourne put himself out of action, crashing his quad bike at his Buckinghamshire home. The singer, apparently having to be revived by his on hand security guard Sam Ruston, broke eight ribs, a collarbone and a vertebrae in his neck. Part of the singer's treatment included the fitting of an internal 7 inch steel device to strengthen his spine. Just as this setback came about more positive news came with the entry of Ozzy's remake of Black Sabbath's 'Changes' entering the UK singles charts at the UK No. 1 spot, his first ever top position in his homeland. Osbourne was released from intensive care just prior to Christmas.

Backing up this daily press onslaught in regard to Ozzy's accident and the success of 'Changes' press teasers leaked to whet the appetite for the official Osbourne's book 'Ordinary People' had Sharon Osbourne apparently revealing indiscretions with the late Randy Rhoads. More concrete facts came as Billboard delivered figures detailing that the 'Ozzfest' festivals had racked up a staggering $146 million over 236 shows and drawing 3.8 million fans since their inception.

In early March of 2004 Osbourne filed an official complaint with the Medical Board of California, claiming that Dr. David Kipper had prescribed a cocktail of over 40 pills a day including opiates, tranquilizers, amphetamines, antidepressants and an antipsychotic, which had adversely affected his mobility and speech to such an extent it had shocked viewers of 'The Osbournes' TV series. Kipper, who had charged Osbourne over $650,000 for his services, had begun treating the singer for drug addictions in June of 2002. He was fired in September of the following year.

2004 witnessed a further coincidence in the labyrinthine catalogue of fate that envelops Black Sabbath when former singer Ronnie James Dio suffered an incident that harked back to Tony Iommi's pre-Earth machine accident. Unfortunately the severity of the injury would be more than outweighed by the circumstances as Dio revealed he had been the victim of a real life "bizarre gardening accident" in true Spinal Tap fashion. Compounding the tale would be the identity of his assailant.

"It was a killer garden gnome" the singer says in earnest. "I'm not joking, although I certainly wish I was. What happened was that I was in my yard trying to place this garden gnome on a slope. This is a seriously heavy piece of garden ornament, probably 60lbs or so. Anyway, it fell over, I fell into the shrubbery and then began to slide down to the bottom of the hill. I was trying to stop myself with my feet but put my hand out at the wrong moment. You can understand this all happened in a split second. My hand landed on a rock, and the gnome landed on it, squashing my thumb between the rock and the gnome. Basically it was crushed and took the end of my thumb off. I just looked at my hand and the first thought that flashed into my mind was 'How on earth am I going to make my devil horn sign now? That's my trademark!' I wasn't worried about the injury, more concerned with my career."

Did it enter your head that you had been struck by the ultimate Rock n' Roll irony of a bizarre gardening accident?

"Oh of course it did. I was imagining all the headlines in my head. It had every comedy element and more."

How did you deal with it practically?

"I just picked up the end of the thumb, went back into the house, washed the nub of my thumb then got myself down to the hospital. It was quite surreal because I had one hand with this crushed thumb, basically just red meat and miniscule bits of bone, and I was holding the end of the thumb in my other hand. It was quite fascinating. It's not too often you get to see inside your thumb.

I got a shock when I arrived in the emergency room because a nurse took a look at it first and said "No, I don't think we can save this." I had to wait a while then for a doctor, all the time praying that he would come up with a different evaluation. Anyhow, he did thankfully. He said he could sew it back on. 'Please do!' I said, and that's exactly what he did."

Was there any pain or was it totally numbed out?

"Totally numb, no pain whatsoever. I think all the nerves got crushed or something. It looked like it should be painful, but it wasn't. After it was sewn back on they did a proper job of it and now it's OK. It looks a little distorted and the nail has not grown fully back yet but I'm thankful I still have my thumb and I can still do my horn sign."

What happened to the gnome? Did you take revenge?

"Ah no, he's still there. Only now he is on a very sensible level piece of ground. It wasn't his fault, he's an inanimate object but sometimes I look at that face and think ... Y'know, he just has one of those faces! Put it this way, if I'm involved in another gardening accident you won't have far to look. There was I suppose some kind of suppressed 'shock', but at the time, when it is actually happening, I think I automatically went into a kind of primal survival mode. I saw the end of my thumb, I picked it up and got it sewn back on. It really was that simple. There was no panic, just an immediate thought to how I could solve this. Out on the edge of my mind though, the comedy was starting to creep in though I have to admit."

Thankfully Ronnie's thumb was repaired and he would soon be back flashing his trademark devil horns to the world promoting the exceptionally dark 'Master Of The Moon' album.

Once again announcing he was to headline the 2004 'Ozzfest', over fellow Brummie veterans, the recently re-formed Judas Priest, Slayer, Slipknot, Norwegian Black Metal combo Dimmu Borgir, Superjoint Ritual and naturally Zakk Wylde's Black Label Society, a press announcement revealed that Ozzy was planning on having a team of doctors travel with him. In addition, Ozzy was to have use of "several well-placed chairs and poles to assist him if he should need to sit or stand during performances." As was by now tradition, the rumour mill soon was sparked up once more by the advent of 'Ozzfest' in regard to a full blown Black Sabbath re-formation.

By March Tony Iommi was in negotiation with Osbourne and as the month closed speculation arose that Geezer Butler had supplanted Rob Nicholson as bassist in Ozzy's band. Indeed, just hours later Nicholson confirmed that he was out and intent on pursuing new music with his project The Death Riders. Ozzy would auction off some famous pieces of onstage memorabilia in aid of the Sharon Osbourne Colon Cancer Foundation in May, namely his custom designed water guns and 'Down To Earth' backdrop.

As predicted, Osbourne would indeed head up the 'Ozzfest' festivals by fronting Black Sabbath once again. Unbeknownst to fans, Iommi had only agreed to join the 'Ozzfest' formation just days before the first show. What fans were very much aware of though was the non-presence of Bill Ward and keyboard player Geoff Nicholls. When Sabbath's confirmation with 'Ozzfest' was first confirmed on 26th May, it was set to be Mike Bordin back behind the drum kit. Outraged fans soon took up an Internet campaign which, backed by some heartfelt words from Bill Ward himself, duly forced the issue, resulting in Ward's welcome return to his rightful position being confirmed on 2nd June. Nicholls, engaged in film score work, was replaced by Adam Wakeman, son of Rick Wakeman, thus ending his 24 year unbroken tenure with the band. Apparently, the new keyboard man had been contracted for Ozzy's band before Black Sabbath had been mooted and subsequently exercised his contract.

Geoff Nicholls, by then a staunch veteran of 25 years service, sums up his tenure with these words. "I have been incredibly lucky to have experienced everything I have. I have worked with some true creative geniuses which is a reward in its own right. Because Tony Iommi has always had a top bracket band I have lived the life of a multimillionaire, travelling in private planes, stretch limos and staying at the very best hotels. When they got back together with Ozzy and Sharon my lifestyle just got even better! How many people can say that? I've got no complaints whatsoever.

I have very, very few regrets. I would have loved to have seen 'Seventh Star' do well because I wrote so much of that. I guess that was just circumstances really. That would have made me a nice pension! The other regret is seeing Cozy forced out of the picture because he really was a true gentleman and he had put his heart and soul into it. That line-up should have done another record really.

I love recording, writing and composing but much more than that I just love life on the road. Some people can't stand it but for me it's wonderful. Touring has never been a chore for me, always the opposite. I have seen the entire world because of Black Sabbath."

Geoff's sense of industry was unabated, the keyboard player working on solo projects for Tony Martin and building up a name as a screen writer.

The opening show of the 'Ozzfest' dates in Hartford, Connecticut on 10th July witnessed a hour long set of classics, controversially including a film backdrop for the track 'War Pigs', which included president George W. Bush wearing a superimposed red clown nose cruelly juxtaposed with images of Adolf Hitler. Bill Ward was quick to distance himself from the film, stating that it did not represent his personal views towards President Bush and claiming the video was made without the drummer's "prior knowledge or consent." The offending segment of film would shortly afterwards be removed.

On 26th June Ozzy, and daughter Kelly, performed at a free Rod Stewart headlined concert in London to mark the arrival of the Olympic flame in Britain. With 'Ozzfest' thundering on across North America, Ozzy's health gave out, forced out of action by an attack of bronchitis. With a packed audience awaiting Black Sabbath at their 26th August stop in Camden, New Jersey, a quick fire replacement saw Rob Halford once again manning the microphone much to the delight of both Judas Priest and Sabbath fans.

Meantime, word of Tony Iommi's shelved 1996 album would be back in the news when earlier plans to release the Iommi / Hughes sessions as an Internet download album were revised. Now scheduled as a regular album to be delivered through Sanctuary Records, the sessions had been somewhat reworked under the Iommi handle. The guitarist had re-cut some of the main riffs and two songs had new bass guitar work added by Iommi's former Black Sabbath colleague Neil Murray. Alarmingly, in the interim original drummer Dave Holland had been convicted of sexual offences and although no official word was forthcoming as to his absence his drum work had been wiped and replaced by that of the Paul Rodgers band and M3 credited Jimmy Copley. The record emerged in September 2004 under the billing 'The 1996 DEP Sessions'.

As 'Ozzfest' once again pulled in major audiences across North America, on a somewhat smaller scale former Ozzy guitarist Brad Gillis took an unexpected diversion as he hooked up with the "greatest Ozzy impersonator on Earth" Peter Marrino, a man noteworthy for having fronted Le Mans and Cacophony, to form up the tribute band Ozzy Unauthorized. Also on the tribute front a whole host of Spanish bands, including Hamlet, Sober, Saratoga, Soziedad Alkoholika, Baron Rojo and Mago De Oz contributed tracks to a Ozzy tribute collection organised by producer Jorge Escobedo for El Diablo Records.

Taking the Black Sabbath tribute concept into new realms would be the 'Everything Comes & Goes' issued through Temporary Residence. Assembled by names unfamiliar in the Heavy Metal world the record included the likes of 'Reversible Sabbath', a composition from Japanese Noise mongers Ruins that involved a mesh of eight different Sabbath songs played in reverse. Four Tet delivered an acoustic version of 'Iron Man', Grail's committed an entirely instrumental version of 'Black Sabbath' whilst Electronica duo Matmos rendered 'F/X' into a "barely audible jumble of electronic chirping".

Another Sabbath player came back to the fore as the year closed too as Tony Martin set 'Scream' as the

The 1996 DEP Sessions.

title of his solo record, revealing it was to include two archive tracks, 'Raising Hell' and 'Wings Of Thunder', both featuring Cozy Powell. Strangely, the official press statement claimed these songs were Cozy Powell's Hammer tracks whereas in fact they were Black Sabbath outtakes from the 'Tyr' and 'Headless Cross' albums. Geoff Nicholls featured prominently on the sessions, which found Martin not only singing but performing guitar, bass, drums and even electric violin.

Returning to studio work, the New York Post reported that Ozzy recorded a theme song for a new TV show 'Dog the Bounty Hunter'. MTV signed up Sharon and Ozzy for a fresh reality TV series 'Battle for Ozzfest' based upon a talent contest for bands, the main prize being a slot on the 2005 'Ozzfest' festival, touring money, equipment and a possible record deal. Meantime erstwhile Alice In Chains guitarist Jerry Cantrell made public the fact he, alongside Chris Wyse, bassist for Cantrell's "jam" band the Cardboard Vampyres and The Cult, were recording music for an Ozzy box set. Manning the drums would be Mike Bordin with Jim Cox on keyboards. Additional guitar solos and steel guitar came courtesy of Robert Randolph.

It was subsequently learned that this collection was to include cover versions of The Beatles' 'In My Life', Buffalo Springfield's 'For What It's Worth', the Rolling Stones' 'Sympathy For The Devil', Arthur Brown's 'Fire' and King Crimson's '21st Century Schizoid Man'. Featured on a take of Mountain's 'Mississippi Queen' would be guitarist Leslie West. Ozzy would also share a lead vocal with Ian Hunter on Mott The Hoople's 'All The Young Dudes'. The box set sold over 30,000 copies in its first week of U.S. sale to land at No. 36 on the Billboard charts. October found Ozzy back in the U.S. Billboard charts in a fashion as Southern hip hop pioneer Trick Daddy's (a.k.a. Maurice Young) single 'Let's Go', top five in the Rap charts and top twenty on the national singles charts, featured a sample of 'Crazy Train'.

Ozzy was thrust back into the international headlines in November when he grappled with a burglar at his Surrey mansion in Chalfont St. Peter, Buckinghamshire. Despite catching the intruder in a headlock, the thief, taking an estimated $3.2 million of Sharon Osbourne's jewellery, escaped by jumping out of a third storey window. Both Osbournes were unhurt in the drama. Sharon Osbourne subsequently appeared on the UK 'Crimewatch' television programme in an effort to track down the jewels.

Ozzy's only UK live appearance of the year was to come on 14th December at the star studded 'Royal Variety' show held at the London Coliseum in the presence of Prince Charles. However, the star would withdraw in order to undergo a further operation to ease pain caused by a metal plate that had been inserted after his quad bike accident. Ozzy was also announced as appearing at an all-star Tsunami relief concert at Arrowhead Pond in Anaheim, California, but pulled out of this event too the day beforehand citing a "family emergency."

First signs of Black Sabbath activity for 2005 would be confirmation of an appearance at Denmark's Roskilde festival. As further gig announcements rolled in, including an appearance at the UK's 'Download' festival, filmed for DVD release, German shows opened by Soulfly and Scandinavian shows supported by Velvet Revolver, Osbourne dropped hints that another Black Sabbath album was probable. Meantime, the band, seeing Adam Wakeman once again installed on keyboards, headed up another series of U.S. 'Ozzfest' events backed by Iron Maiden and a supporting cast including Velvet Revolver, Rob Zombie and Mudvayne. Ozzy fronted up Black Sabbath once again for a Summer 2005 'Ozzfest' tour across North America.

In June the Recording Industry Association of America revealed Ozzy Osbourne had sold over 28 million albums in the USA, incredibly a full 13 million more albums than Black Sabbath. Thankfully, fans were rewarded with further product as Tony Iommi hooked back up with Glenn Hughes to craft the 'Fused' album. This highly commendable effort arriving shortly after Geezer Butler's latest GZR solo outing 'Ohmwork', prompting rumours of a joint tour. "I'm all up for a tour with Tony on this album" stated Hughes. "There's a very positive atmosphere around the whole thing and I see this as just the first step. I'm sure there will be more records in the future, because this band is just so damn good. People have to see it live."

Iommi also reforged ties with another Black Sabbath singer, prompted by a documentary film to celebrate Ian Gillan's four decades of Rock n' Roll. Amongst many other luminaries, the movie includ-

Glenn Hughes and Tony Iommi.

Fused.

ing contributions from both Tony Iommi and Ronnie James Dio. Working with producer Nick Blagona, the singer travelled to a Buffalo, New York studio to cut an album, entitled 'Gillan's Inn' to coincide, this featuring reworks of tracks spanning his entire career, including Black Sabbath. "We dubbed it 'The Nipple Farm' because it was so cold your nipples would drop off and shatter on the floor" says Gillan of the recording environment. Iommi featured on a remake of 'Trashed' from 1983's 'Born Again' opus, backed by the Deep Purple rhythm section of bassist Roger Glover and drummer Ian Paice. It had taken longer than expected, but Black Purple had finally arrived. "How could I resist? Look, I love that record and have nothing but great, great memories of my time with Black Sabbath. Tony was really busy but got his solos to me at the last minute as he promised and they are just fantastic. I think Black Sabbath fans will be over the moon when they hear what he's done. As for Roger and Ian, well, they just sound great on this song so it really did become 'Black Purple'. Personally, I love the irony of it all."

'Ozzfest' ran without a hitch until the 27th July Holmdel, New Jersey PNC Arts Center, which saw Black Sabbath cancelling due to illness afflicting Ozzy. The band did perform an abbreviated set at Tweeter Center in Tinley Park, Illinois on 30th July but then pulled out of the Noblesville, Indiana Verizon Wireless Music Center show and a date at the Germain Theater in Columbus, Ohio. With Ozzy revealing he was suffering from "acid reflux" problems, the scheduled 7th August 'Ozzfest' at Float Rite Park in Somerset, Wisconsin was postponed to 10th September. At this juncture it was revealed that the singer was being coaxed through the shows by Ron Anderson, a retired opera singer, who monitored Ozzy's diet, lifestyle and even spoke directly to him on stage through an earpiece.

Black Sabbath's 11th August gig at White River Amphitheatre in Auburn, Washington had fans witnessing the severity of Ozzy's ongoing vocal problems when his voice gave way in the midst of the track 'Dirty Women'. Ozzy threw his microphone down in disgust but was eventually coaxed out to struggle through the remainder of the set. The following day the singer made an official announcement "After 10 years, the 'Ozzfest"s name and reputation have been established. It's time for me to move on and do other things." Ozzy put out an official call for a new guitarist for his solo band shortly afterward, this prompting speculation that long-term ally Zakk Wylde was no longer in the frame.

Ozzy, together with a band including guitarist Zakk Wylde and drummer Mike Bordin, put in an unannounced performance of 'Crazy Train' in Foxboro, Massachusetts for ABC's NFL Kickoff show leading into the season opener between the New England Patriots and Oakland Raiders at Gillette Stadium. Ozzy showed his allegiance by donning a Patriots jersey.

Ronnie James Dio stunned Black Sabbath fans in mid October with a casual remark during a BBC Radio 2 "Masters of Rock" radio interview by stating "Tony Iommi and I are going to write a couple of tracks together for a project that I think is called 'Black Sabbath—The Dio Years'." With fans clamouring for solid details on this possible thawing of the ice between Dio and Iommi, it transpired this move was in regard to polishing off previously unreleased material for an intended Dio era box set. Also on Dio's agenda would be another high profile venture, portraying the character of Dr. X on Queensryche's grandiose 'Operation Mindcrime II' opus.

Back in the news and out on the road too would be another Sabbath singer—Tony Martin. His 'Scream' album, issued through the German label MTM Music, had taken many hardcore fans by surprise, not only due to its undeniable quality but its marked similarity to classic 'Headless Cross' and 'Tyr' era Black Sabbath. 'Scream' gave the long suffering Sabbs devoted exactly what they wanted and a brief burst of European dates drew positive reaction all around. Wisely, Tony Martin gave the faithful exactly what they had been clamouring for in the live set.

Geoff Nicholls formed part of the live band and was surprised by the enthusiasm shown the band. "We didn't do that many shows to start off with but it was very heavy and the fans just loved it. I spoke with Tony Martin beforehand about the set and that we should down tune too to keep it really heavy. We played most of the 'Scream' album but we also played all the Sabbath stuff that people really wanted to hear too, like 'Devil And Daughter', 'Headless Cross', 'The Shining' and 'Eternal Idol'. Tony's voice was really strong too and all the journalists were just loving it. Most importantly the band had a blast too. There were no moaners onboard so we had a great time doing those gigs!"

In November both Ozzy and Black Sabbath were inducted into the UK 'Music Hall of Fame' alongside Bob Dylan, The Kinks, The Who, Jimi Hendrix and Pink Floyd. During Black Sabbath's live performance at the ceremony, held at the Alexandra Palace in London, Ozzy made headlines one more time. Disgusted by the apathetic and muted reaction to the evening celebrations by the celebrity guest list he responded in typical fashion by mooning the audience.

Just how has Ozzy stayed the course? Our anonymous insider provides a fitting finale:

"Ozzy is the same performer now that he ever was. Offstage he can be very quiet and unassuming. He's a very thoughtful person too, very articulate which is something the public don't see. He has an intense interest in history which he loves to share with people and he paints a lot too. The other thing of course is that he is a family man. It's a whole different side to him the public don't see because all they want after all is 'Ozzy' the product not 'Ozzy' the man.

Onstage he is someone else of course. There are always the two Ozzy characters. It's never false though, it's the show but it is him as well and it just kicks in as soon as he gets onstage. Everyone is very understanding of how the whole thing works on the road too. He actually has a very strong personality as he has to in order to deal with it. You see, everyone else in the organisation and the band can get on with it, do their work and have a great time as part of this character world built around Ozzy but he has to deal with it in his own head. I think he has suffered with it in the past but he has been able to do that now for a long time because he knows his own person very well."

When asked just when Ozzy might just one day really, truly, once and for all retire the same source counters with a quote from Ozzy. "I asked him this once. Ozzy just looked at me and said "What else can I do? Go and grow fucking marrows?""

Throughout 1979–1997 the creative glue that held Black Sabbath together was undoubtedly the quite awesome catalogue of riffs generated by Tony Iommi. Without Iommi's distinctive input Black Sabbath would have always been 'just another band'.

Glenn Hughes sees Tony Iommi as nothing less than an innovator. "The man is a giant on the guitar" he avows. "The thing with Tony Iommi is that passage of time has concealed a lot of what he did back in the early days. He invented a certain style of playing on those first two records. Nobody really got it back then but he had developed something new.

Tony Iommi and Glenn Hughes.

The way he constructs his riffs, the notes he uses is actually pretty unusual. It has been a bit lost unfortunately because everyone from that point on copied him. I remember when we were working back in 1996 he would have at least five or six new riffs for me to listen to everyday. I was lost for choice!"

Eric Singer is in agreement. "Tony is uniquely talented a guitarist. Nobody writes heavy riffs like Tony. What's interesting is that virtually everything out there on the heavy end of the Rock field is directly influenced by Tony. You can speed it up, slow it down, distort the Hell out of it but you can't hide the Black Sabbath influence.

A lot of what these guitarists forget when interpreting what Tony does, and trying to make it their own, is that Tony is a great Blues player. He has the foundation to build on that and come up with his own great riffs and solos."

Singer's rhythm partner Dave Spitz is equally effusive when it comes to praising his former employer. "Most Rock people don't have a clue how amazing Tony actually is. Let me be perfectly clear: Tony Iommi absolutely invented Heavy Metal, i.e., the sound of the heavy guitar, and the pedalling, or chunking. No one else did this: not Hendrix, Clapton, Beck, Page, Garcia, Kaukonen, or any other human (I dare any soul to challenge me on this).

Tony is masterful on flute and jazz guitar, and he totally blew me away when he sat down at the piano. I honestly could not believe what I was hearing. His musical soul emanates from great knowledge and inspiration from many earlier musicians.

We had many, many late night talks and jams—Tony, Geoff and myself—where we played stuff that could never be on a Sabbath record. We used to blast off into these amazing jazzy, Django Reinhardt pieces."

Judas Priest guitarist, fellow Brummie and 'Rockbroker' belt resident KK Downing is eager to reinforce these views. "I don't believe there is a Heavy Metal guitar player around that hasn't benefited from either being a fan or subjected to the riffs and guitar playing of Tony Iommi. I think it goes without saying that everyone considers Tony to be the number one supreme riff maker that there has ever been and probably will ever be! Needless to say his influences have covered the planet since the beginning of anything pertaining to rock music as we know it."

Alvin Lee, the man who Tony Iommi cites as a direct inspiration, where it really all started from, returns the compliments. "Tony is undoubtedly unique in his field. I know he has said some nice things about my playing but I can't really hear anything I've done in his style. Tony just came up with his own thing and that is such a rarity. Only a handful of guitarists have ever done anything unique and he's one of them. He has a very Jazz approach and the fact that he can do what he does despite his false fingertips is pretty amazing. His injury probably forced him into a different style of playing so in a strange way that accident he had has helped him in the long run. I often used to joke with him that maybe I should cut the ends off my fingers and use some false tips too. It's certainly less wear and tear!"

Ozzy Osbourne 2005.

Tony Iommi. Pic: John McMurtrie.

Appendix A

Discographies

A.1 Black Sabbath

ALBUMS

BLACK SABBATH, Vertigo VO 6 (1970). Black Sabbath / The Wizard / Behind The Walls Of Sleep / N.I.B. / Evil Woman (Don't Play Your Games With Me) / Sleeping Village / Warning. Chart positions: 8 UK, 23 USA.

PARANOID, Vertigo 6360 011 (1970). War Pigs / Paranoid / Planet Caravan / Iron Man / Electric Funeral / Hand Of Doom / Rat Salad / Fairies Wear Boots. Chart positions: 1 UK, 2 GERMANY, 5 NORWAY, 12 USA.

MASTER OF REALITY, First Stereo 6360 050 (1971). Sweet Leaf / After Forever / Embryo / Children Of The Grave / Orchid / Lord Of This World / Solitude / Into The Void. Chart positions: 5 GERMANY, 5 UK, 8 USA, 12 NORWAY.

VOLUME 4, Vertigo 6360 071 (1972). Wheels Of Confusion / Tomorrow's Dream / Changes / FX / Supernaut / Snowblind / Cornucopia / Laguna Sunrise / St. Vitus' Dance / Under The Sun. Chart positions: 7 NORWAY, 8 UK, 11 USA.

SABBATH BLOODY SABBATH, WWA WWA 005 (1973). Sabbath Bloody Sabbath / A National Acrobat / Fluff / Sabbra Cadabra / Killing Yourself To Live / Who Are You? / Looking For Today / Spiral Architect. Chart positions: 4 UK, 6 NORWAY, 11 USA, 49 GERMANY.

SABOTAGE, Vertigo 9119 001 (1975). Hole In The Sky / Don't Start (Too Late) / Symptom Of The Universe / Megalomania / Thrill Of It All / Supertzar / Am I Going Insane (Radio) / The Writ / Blow On A Jug. Chart positions: 6 NORWAY, 7 UK, 9 AUSTRIA, 28 USA, 33 NEW ZEALAND.

TECHNICAL ECSTACY, Vertigo 9102 750 (1976). Back Street Kids / You Won't Change Me / It's Alright / Gypsy / All Moving Parts (Stand Still) / Rock n' Roll Doctor / She's Gone / Dirty Women. Chart positions: 13 UK, 51 USA.

NEVER SAY DIE, Vertigo 9102 751 (1978). Never Say Die / A Hard Road / Junior's Eyes / Shock Wave / Johnny Blade / Air Dance / Breakout / Swinging The Chain / Over To You. Chart positions: 12 UK, 37 SWEDEN, 69 USA.

HEAVEN AND HELL, Vertigo 9102 752 (1980). Neon Knights / Children Of The Sea / Lady Evil / Heaven And Hell / Wishing Well / Die Young / Walk Away / Lonely Is The Word. Chart positions: 9 UK, 22 NORWAY, 25 SWEDEN, 28 USA, 44 NEW ZEALAND.

LIVE AT LAST, NEMS BS001 (1980). Tomorrow's Dream / Sweet Leaf / Cornucopia / Wicked World / Killing Yourself To Live / Snowblind / Children Of The Grave / War Pigs / Paranoid / Cornucopia. Chart positions: 5 UK, 26 SWEDEN.

MOB RULES, Vertigo 6302 119 (1981). Turn Up The Night / Voodoo / The Sign Of The Southern Cross / E5150 / The Mob Rules / Country Girl / Slipping Away / Falling Off The Edge Of The World / Over And Over. Chart positions: 12 UK, 29 USA, 45 NEW ZEALAND.

LIVE EVIL, Vertigo SAB 10 (1983). Children Of The Sea / Black Sabbath / Paranoid / Neon Knights / Iron Man / Children Of The Grave / E5150 / Heaven And Hell / Voodoo / Sign Of The Southern Cross / War Pigs / Mob Rules / NIB. Chart positions: 13 UK, 15 SWEDEN, 34 NEW ZEALAND, 37 USA.

BORN AGAIN, Vertigo VERL 8 (1983). Trashed / Stonehenge / Disturbing The Priest / The Dark / Zero The Hero / Digital Bitch / Born Again / Hot Line / Keep It Warm. Chart positions: 4 UK, 7 SWEDEN, 39 USA, 44 NEW ZEALAND.

SEVENTH STAR, Vertigo VERH 29 (1986). In For The Kill / No Stranger To Love / Turn To Stone / Sphinx (The Guardian) / Seventh Star / Danger Zone / Heart Like A Wheel / Angry Heart / In Memory .... Chart positions: 11 SWEDEN, 27 UK, 78 USA.

THE ETERNAL IDOL, Vertigo VERH 51 (1987). The Shining / Ancient Warrior / Hard Life To Love / Glory Ride / Born To Lose / Nightmare / Scarlet Pimpernel / Lost Forever / Eternal Idol. Chart positions: 66 UK, 168 USA.

HEADLESS CROSS, IRS EIRSA 1002 (1989). Gates To Hell / Headless Cross / Devil And Daughter / When Death Calls / Kill In The Spirit World / Call Of The Wild / Black Moon / Night Wing. Chart positions: 22 SWEDEN, 23 SWITZERLAND, 31 UK, 115 USA.

TYR, IRS EIRSA 1038 (1990). Anno Mundi / The Lawmaker / Jerusalem / The Sabbath Stones / The Battle Of Tyr / Odin's Court / Valhalla / Feels Good To Me / Heaven In Black. Chart positions: 12 GERMANY, 24 UK, 24 SWEDEN, 24 SWITZERLAND, 24 AUSTRIA.

DEHUMANIZER, IRS EIRSCD 1064 (1992). Computer God / After All (The Dead) / TV Crimes / Letters From

Earth / Masters Of Insanity / Time Machine / Sins Of The Father / Too Late / I / Buried Alive. Chart positions: 7 AUSTRIA, 12 SWEDEN, 13 SWITZERLAND, 14 GERMANY, 28 UK, 44 USA.

CROSS PURPOSES, IRS 07777 13222 2 8 (1994). I Witness / Cross Of Thorns / Psychophobia / Virtual Death / Immaculate Deception / Dying For Love / Back To Eden / The Hand That Rocks The Cradle / Cardinal Sin / Evil Eye. Chart positions: 32 GERMANY, 41 UK, 41 SWITZERLAND, 122 USA.

CROSS PURPOSES LIVE, PMI 7243 491314 3 9 (1995). Time Machine / Children Of The Grave / I Witness / Into The Void / Black Sabbath / Psychophobia / Wizard / Cross Of Thorns / Symptom Of The Universe / Headless Cross / Paranoid / Iron Man / Sabbath Bloody Sabbath.

FORBIDDEN, IRS 7243 8 30620 2 7 (1995). The Illusion Of Power / Get A Grip / Can't Get Close Enough / Shaking Off The Chains / I Won't Cry For You / Guilty As Hell / Sick And Tired / Rusty Angels / Forbidden / Kiss Of Death. Chart positions: 35 GERMANY, 48 SWITZERLAND, 71 UK.

REUNION, 20th Century Masters 491954-9 (1998). War Pigs / Behind The Wall Of Sleep / NIB / Fairies Wear Boots / Electric Funeral / Sweet Leaf / Spiral Architect / Into The Void / Snowblind / Sabbath Bloody Sabbath / Orchid / Lord Of This World / Dirty Women / Black Sabbath / Iron Man / Children Of The Grave / Paranoid / Psycho Man (Studio) / Selling My Soul (Studio). Chart positions: 5 CANADA, 11 SWEDEN, 11 USA, 40 GERMANY, 41 UK, 65 FRANCE.

PAST LIVES, Sanctuary 84561 (2002). Tomorrow's Dream / Sweet Leaf / Killing Yourself To Live / Cornucopia / Snowblind / Children Of The Grave / War Pigs / Wicked World / Paranoid / Hand Of Doom / Hole In The Sky / Symptom Of The Universe / Megalomania / Iron Man / Black Sabbath / NIB / Behind The Wall / Fairies Wear Boots. Chart position: 114 USA.

SINGLES/EPS

Paranoid, Philips SFL-1300 (1970) (Japanese release). Paranoid / The Wizard.

Iron Man, P.101 (1970) (Thai release. Split 7" single with CHRISTIE, CHICORY TIP & NEIL REID). Iron Man.

Evil Woman (Don't Play Your Games With Me), (1970) (Japanese release). Evil Woman (Don't Play Your Games With Me) / Wicked Woman.

Paranoid, Vertigo 6226003 (1970) (Portuguese release). Paranoid / Evil Woman (Don't Play Your Games With Me) / Wicked World.

Evil Woman (Don't Play Your Games With Me), Vertigo (1970) (Spanish release). Evil Woman (Don't Play Your Games With Me) / Wicked World.

Paranoid, Vertigo 6059 010 (1970) (Israeli release). Paranoid / The Wizard.

The Wizard, Vertigo 6059 005 (1970) (French release). The Wizard / Evil Woman (Don't Play Your Games With Me).

Evil Woman (Don't Play Your Games With Me), Philips SFL-1282 (1970) (Japanese release). Evil Woman (Don't Play Your Games With Me) / Black Sabbath.

N.I.B., (1970) (Thai release). N.I.B. / Behind The Wall Of Sleep / The Wizard.

Paranoid, Vertigo 6059 014 (1970) (French release). Paranoid / Rat Salad.

Paranoid, Vertigo 6276 009 (1970) (Australian release). Paranoid / Black Sabbath / Tomorrow's Dream / Changes.

Evil Woman (Don't Play Your Games With Me), Fontana TF 1067 (1970). Evil Woman (Don't Play Your Games With Me) / Wicked World.

Paranoid, Vertigo 6059 010 (1970). Paranoid / The Wizard. Chart positions: 1 GERMANY, 4 UK, 61 USA.

Sweet Leaf, (1971) (Thai release). Sweet Leaf / Lord Of This World.

Paranoid, Vertigo 6276 004 (1971) (Mexican release). Paranoid / Rats Salad / Electric Funeral.

Paranoid, Track FT.955 (1971) (Thai release). Paranoid / Sweet Leaf / Iron Man / N.I.B.

After Forever, 4 Track M.023 (1971) (Thai release). After Forever / Faeries Wear Boots.

Sabbath Bloody Sabbath, Vertigo SFL-1833 (1972). Sabbath Bloody Sabbath / Changes.

Paranoid, NEMS SP06-5 (1972) (Japanese release). Paranoid / Snowblind.

Snowblind, Cashbox KS 13014 (1972) (Thai release). Snowblind / St. Vitus Dance / Tomorrow's Dream / Supernaut.

Wheels Of Confusion, IT IT-012 (1972) (Thai release). Wheels Of Confusion / Tomorrow's Dream / Snowblind.

Changes, P.129 (1972) (Thai release. Split single with MARY HOPKIN, ROD STEWART and CLIFF RICHARD). Changes.

Tomorrow's Dream, Vertigo (1972) (Japanese release). Tomorrow's Dream / Laguna Sunrise.

Under The Sun, M M.153 (1972) (Thai release. Split single with SLADE and BLOODROCK). Under The Sun.

Paranoid, Vertigo 6276 003 (1972) (Portuguese release). Paranoid / Wicked World / Evil Woman (Don't Play Your Games With Me).

Wicked World, Vertigo SFL-1345 (1972) (Japanese release). Wicked World / Iron Man.

Tomorrow's Dream, Vertigo 6059 061 (1972). Tomorrow's Dream / Laguna Sunrise.

Sabbath Bloody Sabbath, Thai Nokorn KS 235 (1973) (Thai release). Sabbath Bloody Sabbath / Killing Yourself To Live.

Sabbath Bloody Sabbath, Vertigo (1973) (Norwegian release). Sabbath Bloody Sabbath / Changes.

Sabbath Bloody Sabbath, Vertigo 6165001 (1973) (French release). Sabbath Bloody Sabbath / Changes.

Sabbath Bloody Sabbath, Vertigo S 53726 (1973) (Yugoslavian release). Sabbath Bloody Sabbath / Changes.

Sabbath Bloody Sabbath, Vertigo 6165 001 (1973) (Portuguese release). Sabbath Bloody Sabbath / Changes.

A.1. BLACK SABBATH

Paranoid, Vertigo 6276 009 (1973) (Australian release). Paranoid / Black Sabbath / Changes / Tomorrow's Dream.
Sabbath Bloody Sabbath, Warner Bros. S 2695 (1973) (USA release). Sabbath Bloody Sabbath / Looking For Today / Sabbrta Cadabra.
Children Of The Grave, Vertigo DJ005 (1973) (Split single with STATUS QUO—Promotion release). Children Of The Grave.
Sabbath Bloody Sabbath, WWA WWS 002 (1973). Sabbath Bloody Sabbath / Changes.
Iron Man, Warner Bros. WB 7802 (1974) (USA release). Iron Man / Electric Funeral.
Sabbath Bloody Sabbath, Vertigo 6299003 (1975) (Brazilian release). Sabbath Bloody Sabbath / Rat Salad / Fluff / Paranoid.
Am I Going Insane (Radio), Vertigo SFL-2060 (1975) (Japanese release). Am I Going Insane (Radio) / Hole In The Sky.
4 Top Hits From England EP—Vol. 5, Young 302.1030 (1976) (Brazilian release. Split single with GENO WASHINGTON, PROCUL HARUM & SCARFACE). Changes.
Gypsy, Vertigo 6079 102 (1976) (Dutch release). Gypsy / She's Gone.
Gypsy, Vertigo 6079 102 (1976) (Yugoslavian release). Gypsy / She's Gone.
Am I Going Insane (Radio), NEMS 6165 300 (1976). Am I Going Insane (Radio) / Hole In The Sky.
It's Alright, Vertigo 6079 100 (1976) (Dutch release). It's Alright / Rock n' Roll Doctor.
Paranoid, NEMS NES 112 (1977). Paranoid / Snowblind.
Paranoid, NEMS SRS 510.044 (1977) (Dutch release). Paranoid / Tomorrow's Dream.
Hard Road, Vertigo 6079 104 (1978) (German release). Hard Road / Symptom Of The Universe.
Never Say Die, Vertigo 6079 103 (1978) (German release). Never Say Die / She's Gone.
Hard Road, Vertigo (1978) (Japanese release). Hard Road / Symptom Of The Universe.
Paranoid, NEMS 26550 (1978) (Belgian release). Paranoid / Tomorrow's Dream.
Never Say Die, Vertigo (1978). Never Say Die / She's Gone.
Hard Road, Vertigo SAB 002 (1978). Hard Road / Symptom Of The Universe. Chart position: 33 UK.
Never Say Die, Vertigo SAB 001 (1978). Never Say Die / She's Gone. Chart position: 21 UK.
Paranoid, NEMS NES 121 (1978). Paranoid / Snowblind. Chart position: 14 UK.
Lady Evil, Warner Bros. 49549 (1980) (USA release). Lady Evil / Children Of The Sea.
Hard Road, Vertigo SFL-2355 (1980) (Japanese release). Hard Road / Symptom Of The Universe.
Neon Knights, Vertigo 7PP5 (1980) (Japanese release). Neon Knights / Children Of The Sea.
Neon Knights, Vertigo SAB 3 (1980). Neon Knights / Children Of The Sea (Live). Chart position: 22 UK.

Paranoid, NEMS BSS 101 (1980). Paranoid / Snowblind.
Die Young, Vertigo SAB 4 (1980). Die Young / Heaven And Hell (Live). Chart position: 41 UK.
Paranoico, NEMS 165 0090 (1981) (Spanish release). Paranoico / Rats Salad.
Mob Rules, Vertigo 60 00 763 (1981) (Spanish release). Mob Rules / Voodoo.
Mob Rules, Vertigo SAB 5 (1981). Mob Rules / Die Young. Chart position: 46 UK.
Turn Up The Night (Live), Vertigo SAB 6 (1982). Turn Up The Night (Live) / Lonely Is The Word (Live). Chart position: 37 UK.
Paranoid, NEMS (1982). Paranoid / Iron Man / Fairies Wear Boots / War Pigs.
Paranoid, NEP 1 (1982) (Limited edition Picture Disc). Paranoid / Iron Man.
Trashed, WEA 7 294347 (1983) (USA release). Trashed / Stonehenge.
No Stranger To Love, Vertigo 884 532-7 (1986) (Dutch release). No Stranger To Love (Remix) / Angry Heart.
No Stranger To Love, Vertigo 884 532-7 (1986) (Spanish release). No Stranger To Love / Angry Heart.
Classic Cuts From The Vaults, That's Original TOF 101 (1986). Paranoid / Iron Man / Black Sabbath / War Pigs (Live).
The Shining, Vertigo 888 997-7 (1987) (Dutch release). The Shining / Black Moon.
No Stranger To Love, Vertigo 884 532-7 (1987) (Dutch release). No Stranger To Love / Angry Heart.
The Shining, Vertigo 888 997-1 (1987) (Dutch release). The Shining / Some Kind Of Woman / Black Moon.
Paranoid, Castle CD 3-5 (1988). Paranoid / Iron Man / War Pigs.
Call Of The Wild, IRS 24 1025-7 (1989) (German release). Call Of The Wild / Devil And Daughter.
Call Of The Wild, IRS IRS 241025-3 (1989) (German release). Call Of The Wild / Devil And Daughter / When Death Calls.
Paranoid, Old Gold OG 6129 (1989). Paranoid / Electric Funeral / Sabbath Bloody Sabbath.
Headless Cross (Extended Version), IRS IRS 241006-2 (1989). Headless Cross (Extended Version) / Headless Cross / Cloak And Dagger.
Headless Cross, IRS EIRS107 (1989). Headless Cross / Cloak And Dagger. Chart position: 62 UK.
Devil And Daughter, IRS EIRS 115 (1989) (One sided single). Devil And Daughter.
Paranoid, Old Gold OG 9467 (1990). Paranoid / Iron Man.
Feels Good To Me, IRS (1990). Feels Good To Me / Paranoid (Live) / Heaven And Hell (Live).
Feels Good To Me, IRS EIRS 148 (1990). Feels Good To Me / Paranoid (Live).
TV Crimes, IRS EIRSP 178 (1992). TV Crimes / Letters From Earth. Chart position: 33 UK.
Master Of Insanity, IRS (1992). Master Of Insanity / TV Crimes (Live) / Neon Knights (Live).

Master Of Insanity, IRS CDEIRS180 (1992). Master Of Insanity / Die Young (Live) / Children Of The Sea (Live).

TV Crimes, IRS (1992). TV Crimes / Letters From Earth / Mob Rules (Live).

TV Crimes, IRS (1992). TV Crimes / Letters From Earth / Heaven And Hell (Live).

TV Crimes, IRS 8 80130-2 (1992) (German release). TV Crimes / Letters From Earth (Alternative version) / Time Machine (Wayne's World version).

Back To Eden, IRS DPRO 10747 (1994) (Promotion release). Back To Eden / The Hand That Rocks The Cradle.

Get A Grip, IRS CDSP111 (1995). Get A Grip.

Selling My Soul, Sony ESK 41767 (1998) (USA promotion release). Selling My Soul (Danny Saber remix edit) / Selling My Soul (Album version).

Psycho Man, Epic SAMPCS 5513 (1998) (Promotion release). Psycho Man (Radio edit) / Psycho Man (Danny Saber remix edit).

Paranoid (Live), Sony ESC-666999-2 (1998) (German release). Paranoid (Live) / Psycho Man (Radio edit) / Psycho Man (Danny Saber remix).

Black Mass EP, NMC (1999). Paranoid / Black Sabbath / Iron Man / Blue Suede Shoes.

Paranoid, (2004) (USA promotion release. Paranoid / Iron Man.

A.2 Ozzy Osbourne

ALBUMS

BLIZZARD OF OZZ, Jet JETLP 234 (1980). I Don't Know / Crazy Train / Goodbye To Romance / Dee / Suicide Solution / Mr. Crowley / No Bone Movies / Revelation Mother Earth / Steal Away (The Night). Chart positions: 7 UK, 21 USA, 47 NEW ZEALAND.

DIARY OF A MADMAN, Jet JETLP 237 (1981). Over The Mountain / Flying High Again / You Can't Kill Rock n' Roll / Believer / Little Dolls / Tonight / S.A.T.O. / Diary Of A Madman. Chart positions: 14 UK, 16 USA, 42 NEW ZEALAND.

SPEAK OF THE DEVIL (LIVE), Jet JETLDP 401 (1982). Snowblind / Symptom Of The Universe / Black Sabbath / N.I.B. / Fairies Wear Boots / War Pigs / Sabbath Bloody Sabbath / Iron Man / Children Of The Grave / Paranoid / The Wizard / Sweet Leaf / Never Say Die. Chart positions: 14 USA, 21 UK.

BARK AT THE MOON, Epic EPC 25739 (1983). Rock n' Roll Rebel / Bark At The Moon / You're No Different / Now You See It (Now You Don't) / Waiting For Darkness / So Tired / Spiders / Forever. Chart positions: 9 SWEDEN, 19 USA, 24 UK, 50 NEW ZEALAND.

THE ULTIMATE SIN, Epic EPC 26404 (1986). Secret Loser / The Ultimate Sin / Thank God For The Bomb / Never Know Why / Lightning Strikes / Shot In The Dark / Killer Of Giants / Fool Like You / Never. Chart positions: 4 SWEDEN, 6 USA, 8 UK, 21 NEW ZEALAND.

TRIBUTE, Epic 450 475-1 (1987). I Don't Know / Crazy Train / Believer / Mr. Crowley / Flying High Again / Revelation Mother Earth / Steal Away The Night / Suicide Solution / Iron Man / Children Of The Grave / Paranoid / Goodbye To Romance / No Bone Movies / Dee. Chart positions: 6 USA, 13 UK, 17 SWEDEN, 36 NEW ZEALAND.

NO REST FOR THE WICKED, Epic 462581 1 (1988). Miracle Man / Devil's Daughter / Crazy Babies / Breaking All The Rules / Bloodbath In Paradise / Fire In The Sky / Tattooed Dancer / Demon Alcohol. Chart positions: 13 USA, 18 SWEDEN, 23 UK.

JUST SAY OZZY (LIVE), Epic 465940-2 (1990). Miracle Man / Bloodbath In Paradise / Shot In The Dark / Tattooed Dancer / Sweet Leaf / War Pigs. Chart positions: 58 USA, 69 UK.

NO MORE TEARS, Epic 46795 (1991). Mr. Tinkertrain / I Don't Want To Change The World / Mama, I'm Coming Home / Desire / S.I.N. / Hellraiser / Time After Time / Zombie Stomp / A.V.H. / Road To Nowhere. Chart positions: 7 USA, 12 NEW ZEALAND, 17 UK, 25 SWEDEN.

LIVE AND LOUD (LIVE), Epic 4816762 (1993). Paranoid / I Don't Want To Change The World / Desire / Mr. Crowley / I Don't Know / Road To Nowhere / Flying High Again / Suicide Solution / Goodbye To Romance / Shot In The Dark / No More Tears / Miracle Man / War Pigs / Bark At The Moon / Mama, I'm Coming Home / Crazy Train / Black Sabbath / Changes. Chart positions: 22 USA, 34 NEW ZEALAND, 44 SWEDEN, 60 GERMANY.

OZZMOSIS, Epic 481022-2 (1995). Perry Mason / I Just Want You / Ghost Behind My Eyes / Thunder Underground / See You On The Other Side / Tomorrow / Denial / My Little Man / My Jekyll Doesn't Hide / Old L.A. Tonight. Chart positions: 4 USA, 22 UK, 26 NEW ZEALAND, 30 GERMANY.

DOWN TO EARTH, Epic 63580 (2001). Gets Me Through / Facing Hell / Dreamer / No Easy Way Out / That I Never Had / You Know ... (Part 1) / Junkie / Running Out Of Time / Black Illusion / Alive / Can You Hear Them? Chart positions: 1 SWEDEN, 2 CANADA, 4 UK, 4 USA, 4 CZECH REPUBLIC, 9 FINLAND, 15 GERMANY, 38 DENMARK, 104 FRANCE.

LIVE AT BUDOKAN, Epic 86525 (2002). I Don't Know / That I Never Had / Believer / Junkie / Mr. Crowley / Gets Me Through / No More Tears / I Don't Want To Change The World / Road To Nowhere / Crazy Train / Mama, I'm Coming Home / Bark At The Moon / Paranoid. Chart positions: 28 CANADA, 38 AUSTRIA, 45 SWEDEN, 55 GERMANY, 70 USA.

PRINCE OF DARKNESS, Epic 5189002 (2005). I Don't Know (Live) / Mr. Crowley / Crazy Train / Goodbye To Romance (Live) / Suicide Solution (Live) / Over The Mountain / Flying High Again (Live) / You Can't Kill Rock And Roll / Diary Of A Madman / Bark At The Moon (Live) / Spiders / Rock And Roll Rebel / You're No Different / Dee / Ultimate Sin (Live) / Never Know Why (Live) / Thank God For The Bomb (Live) / Crazy Babies / Breaking All The Rules / I Don't Want To Change The World (Demo) / Mama, I'm Coming Home (Demo) / Desire (Demo) / No More Tears (Single version) / Won't Be Coming Home (Demo) / Perry Mason (Live) / See You

A.2. OZZY OSBOURNE

On The Other Side (Demo) / Walk On Water (Demo) / Gets Me Through (Live) / Bang Bang (Demo) / Dreamer / Iron Man (Ozzy with THERAPY?) / N.I.B. (Ozzy with PRIMUS) / Purple Haze / Pictures Of Matchstick Men (Ozzy with TYPE O NEGATIVE) / Shake Your Head (Let's Go To Bed) (Ozzy with WAS NOT WAS) / Born To Be Wild (Ozzy with MISS PIGGY) / Nowhere To Run (Vapor Trail) (Ozzy with CRYSTAL METHOD, DMX, 'OL DIRTY BASTARD & FUZZBUBBLE) / Psycho Man (BLACK SABBATH) / For Heavens Sake (Ozzy with TONY IOMMI & WU TANG CLAN) / I Ain't No Nice Guy (Ozzy with MOTORHEAD) / Therapy (Ozzy with INFECTIOUS GROOVES) / Stayin' Alive (Ozzy with DWEEZIL ZAPPA) / Good Times / 21st Century Schizoid Man / In My Life / Mississippi Queen / For What It's Worth / Fire / Working Class Hero / Sympathy For The Devil / Changes (Ozzy with KELLY OSBOURNE). Chart positions: 24 CANADA, 33 GREECE, 36 USA, 54 SWEDEN.

UNDER COVER, Epic 82876743142 (2005). Rocky Mountain Way / In My Life / Mississippi Queen / Go Now / Woman / 21st Century Schizoid Man / All The Young Dudes / For What It's Worth / Good Times / Sunshine Of Your Love / Fire / Working Class Hero / Sympathy For The Devil. Chart positions: 26 GREECE, 43 CANADA, 50 SWEDEN, 67 UK, 69 CZECH REPUBLIC, 95 SWITZERLAND, 134 USA.

SINGLES/EPS

Mr. Crowley, Jet JET 7003 (1980) (USA release). Mr. Crowley / You Said It All (Live).

Mr. Crowley Live EP, Jet EXP 37640 (1980). Mr. Crowley / You Said It All (Live) / Suicide Solution (Live).

Crazy Train, Jet JET 197 (1980) (USA release). Crazy Train / You Looking At Me, Looking At You.

Over The Mountain, Jet JET 7017 (1981). Over The Mountain / I Don't Know.

Flying High Again, Jet PD 02 2 (1981) (12" single). Flying High Again / Medley: Over The Mountain / You Can't Kill Rock n' Roll / Believer / Little Dolls / Tonight / S.A.T.O. / Diary Of A Madman.

Pre-Release Montage, Jet AS1317 (1981) (US promotion release). Pre-Release Montage / Flying High Again.

Crazy Train, Jet / CBS Associated ZS6 02079 (1981) (USA release). Crazy Train / Steal Away (The Night).

Flying High Again, Jet 12107 (1981). Flying High Again / I Don't Know (Live).

Little Dolls, Epic 02707 (1982) (USA release). Little Dolls / Tonight.

Symptom Of The Universe (Live), Jet P7 030 (1982). Symptom Of The Universe (Live) / N.I.B. (Live).

Symptom Of The Universe (Live), Jet 12 030 (1982). Symptom Of The Universe (Live) / N.I.B. (Live) / Children Of The Grave (Live).

Revelation (Mother Earth), Jet (1982). Revelation (Mother Earth) / Iron Man (Live).

Paranoid (Live), Jet JET-810 (1982) (Dutch release). Paranoid (Live) / Symptom Of The Universe (Live).

Iron Man (Live), Epic 03302 (1983) (USA release). Iron Man (Live) / Paranoid (Live).

Bark At The Moon, Epic 04318 (1983) (USA release). Bark At The Moon / Spiders.

Bark At The Moon, Epic TA 3915 (1983) (Silver vinyl single). Bark At The Moon / One Up The B-Side / Slow Down.

Bark At The Moon, Epic A 3915 (1983). Bark At The Moon / One Up The B Side. Chart position: 21 UK.

So Tired, Epic A 4260 (1984). So Tired / Forever (Live).

So Tired, CBS ZS4 04383 (1984) (USA release). So Tired / One Up The B Side.

So Tired, Epic TA 4260 (1984). So Tired / Forever (Live) / Waiting For Darkness / Paranoid (Live).

So Tired, Epic A 4452 (1984). So Tired / Bark At The Moon (Live). Chart position: 20 UK.

So Tired, Epic DA 4452 (1984) (Double pack single). So Tired / Bark At The Moon (Live) / Waiting For Darkness / Paranoid (Live).

So Tired, Epic WA 4452 (1984) (Gold vinyl single). So Tired / Waiting For Darkness / Paranoid (Live) / Suicide Solution (Live).

Shot In The Dark, CBS 07SP938 (1986) (Japanese release). Shot In The Dark / You Said It All.

The Ultimate Live Ozzy EP, CBS 9Z9 40532 (1986) (Picture disc). The Ultimate Sin (Live) / Never Know Why (Live) / Thank God For The Bomb (Live).

The Ultimate Sin, Epic ZAS 2385 (1986) (Promotion release). The Ultimate Sin / The Ultimate Sin.

Shot In The Dark, Epic TA 6859 (1986). Shot In The Dark / Rock n' Roll Rebel / Never Know Why.

Shot In The Dark, Epic A 6859 (1986). Shot In The Dark / Rock n' Roll Rebel. Chart position: 20 UK.

Shot In The Dark, Epic (1986) (USA Promotion). Shot In The Dark / Shot In The Dark.

Shot In The Dark, Epic 05810 (1986) (USA release). Shot In The Dark / You Said It All (Live). Chart position: 68 USA.

The Ultimate Sin, Epic A 7311 (1986). The Ultimate Sin / Lightning Strikes. Chart position: 72 UK.

Shot In The Dark, Epic 08463 (1987) (USA release). Shot In The Dark / Crazy Train.

Prince Of Darkness, Jet 20AP-2887 (1987) (Japanese release). You Looking At Me / One Up The B Side / Slow Down / Bark At The Moon (Live).

Lightning Strikes, Epic (1987) (USA Promotion). Lightning Strikes / Lightning Strikes.

Crazy Train, Epic (1987). Crazy Train / Crazy Train (Studio).

Back To Ozz EP, Epic 652 875 6 (1988). The Ultimate Sin / Bark At The Moon / Mr Crowley (Live) / Diary Of A Madman. Chart position: 76 UK.

Shot In The Dark, Epic 08463 (1988) (USA release). Shot In The Dark / Crazy Train. Chart position: 68 USA.

Miracle Man, Epic 653063-0 (1988). Miracle Man / Crazy Babies.

Miracle Man, Epic 653063-6 (1988). Miracle Man / Crazy Babies / The Liar.

Miracle Man, Epic 08516 (1988) (USA release). Miracle Man / You Said It All.

Crazy Babies, Epic 68534 (1989) (USA release). Crazy Babies / The Demon Alcohol.

Close My Eyes Forever, RCA PB 490049 (1989) (with LITA FORD). Close My Eyes Forever / Under The Gun. Chart positions: 8 USA, 47 UK.

The Urpney Song, Adventure ADVTS102 (1990) (with BILLY CONNELLY and FRANK BRUNO). The Urpney Song.

No More Tears, Epic 657440-6 (1991). No More Tears / S.I.N. / Party With The Animals.

No More Tears, Epic 657440-7 (1991). No More Tears / S.I.N. Chart positions: 32 UK, 71 USA.

Mama, I'm Coming Home, Epic 657517-7 (1991). Mama, I'm Coming Home / Don't Blame Me. Chart positions: 28 USA, 46 UK.

Mama I'm Coming Home, Epic 657517-8 (1992). Mama I'm Coming Home / Don't Blame Me / I Don't Know / Crazy Train.

Mama, I'm Coming Home, Epic 657517-6 (1992). Mama, I'm Coming Home / Don't Blame Me / Time After Time / Goodbye To Romance.

Changes (Live), Epic 659340-6 (1993). Changes (Live) / Changes / Desire (Live) / No More Tears (Live).

4 From Ozzmosis EP, Epic XPCD 741 (1995) (UK promotion release). Thunder Underground / Perry Mason / Tomorrow / I Just Want You.

Perry Mason, Epic 662412-2 (1995) (German release). Perry Mason (Edit) / Perry Mason (Album version) / Living With The Enemy / The Whole World's Falling Down.

Ballads Of Ozz, Epic SAMP 3143 (1995) (German Promotion release). See You On The Other Side / Ghost Behind My Eyes / I Just Want You / Old L.A. Tonight.

Perry Mason, Epic 662639-7 (1995) (Picture disc). Perry Mason / Living With The Enemy. Chart position: 23 UK.

Perry Mason, Epic 662412-2 (1995). Perry Mason / Living With The Enemy / The Whole World's Falling Down.

Perry Mason, Epic 662639-5 (1995). Perry Mason / No More Tears / I Don't Want To Change The World / Flying High Again.

See You On The Other Side, Epic ESK 7631 (1996) (Promotion release). See You On The Other Side (Long version) / See You On The Other Side (Short version).

I Just Want You, Epic 663570-2 (1996). I Just Want You / Aimee / Mama, I'm Coming Home.

I Just Want You, Epic 663570-6 (1996) (One sided etched single). I Just Want You / Aimee (Demo) / Voodoo Dancer (Demo). Chart position: 43 UK.

I Just Want You, Epic 663570-5 (1996). I Just Want You / Voodoo Dancer (Demo) / Iron Man (With THERAPY?).

I Just Want You, Epic ESK 7904 (1996) (Promotion release). I Just Want You.

See You On The Other Side, Epic 662778-2 (1996). See You On The Other Side (Edit) / See You On The Other Side (Album version) / Voodoo Dancer / Aimee.

See You On The Other Side, Sony SRCS 7962 (1996) (Japanese release). See You On The Other Side (Edit) / Voodoo Dancer / Living With The Enemy / Perry Mason (Edit).

Walk On Water, Famous Music PRO-CD-1050 (1996) (US Promotion release). Walk On Water.

Back On Earth, Sony 665049 2 (1997). Back On Earth / Walk On Water / I Just Want You.

Back On Earth, Epic ESK 3228 (1997) (US Promotion release). Back On Earth (Edit) / Back On Earth (Album version).

Gets Me Through, Epic ZSS7965 (2001) (US release. Double sided single). Gets Me Through / Gets Me Through.

Gets Me Through, Epic ESK-16793 (2001) (US promotion release). Gets Me Through (Edit) / Gets Me Through (Album version).

Gets Me Through, Sony 671888 2 (2001). Gets Me Through / No Place For Angels / Alive. Chart position: 89 GERMANY.

Gets Me Through, Epic SAMPCS105721 (2002) (UK promotion release). Gets Me Through.

Dreamer, Sony SME 672 341 2 (2002). Dreamer. Chart positions: 6 DENMARK, 8 SWITZERLAND.

Dreamer, Sony XDCS93499 (2002) (Japanese promotion release). Dreamer.

Dreamer, Sony SICP-83 (2002) (Japanese release). Dreamer / Dreamer (Acoustic version) / Black Skies (Unreleased version).

Mama I'm Coming Home, Sony SME 673 504 2 (2003). Mama I'm Coming Home / Mama, I'm Coming Home (Live) / Crazy Train (Live). Chart position: 63 SWITZERLAND.

In My Life, BMG 82876743112 (2005) (UK release). In My Life (Radio Edit) / Dreamer (Acoustic Version) / In My Life (Video).

A.3 Dio

ALBUMS

HOLY DIVER, Vertigo VERS 5 (1983). Stand Up And Shout / Holy Diver / Gypsy / Caught In The Middle / Don't Talk To Strangers / Straight Through The Heart / Invisible / Rainbow In The Dark / Shame On The Night. Chart positions: 13 UK, 18 SWEDEN, 43 NEW ZEALAND, 56 USA.

LAST IN LINE, Vertigo VERL 16 (1984). We Rock / The Last In Line / Breathless / I Speed At Night / One Night In The City / Evil Eyes / Mystery / Eat Your Heart Out / Egypt (The Chains Are On). Chart positions: 4 UK, 6 SWEDEN, 23 USA.

A.3. DIO

SACRED HEART, Vertigo 834 848-2 (1985). King Of Rock n' Roll / Sacred Heart / Another Lie / Rock n' Roll Children / Hungry For Heaven / Like The Beat Of A Heart / Just Another Day / Fallen Angels / Shoot Shoot. Chart positions: 4 UK, 6 SWEDEN, 13 AUSTRIA, 29 USA.

INTERMISSION, Vertigo VERB 40 (1986). King Of Rock n' Roll (Live) / Rainbow In The Dark (Live) / Sacred Heart (Live) / Time To Burn / Rock n' Roll Children (Live) (incl. Long Live Rock n' Roll / Man On The Silver Mountain / We Rock (Live). Chart positions: 22 UK, 70 USA.

DREAM EVIL, Vertigo 832 530-2 (1987). Night People / Dream Evil / Sunset Superman / All The Fools Sailed Away / Naked In The Rain / Overlove / I Could Have Been A Dreamer / Faces In The Window / When A Woman Cries. Chart positions: 4 SWEDEN, 8 UK, 15 AUSTRIA, 43 USA.

LOCK UP THE WOLVES, Vertigo 846 033-2 (1990). Wild One / Hey Angel / Between Two Hearts / Night Music / Lock Up The Wolves / Evil On Queen Street / Walk On Water / Born On The Sun / Twisted / My Eyes. Chart positions: 23 SWEDEN, 28 UK, 61 USA.

STRANGE HIGHWAYS, Vertigo 518486-2 (1993). Jesus, Mary And The Holy Ghost / Fire Head / Strange Highways / Hollywood Black / Evilution / Pain / One Foot In The Grave / Give Her The Gun / Blood From A Stone / Here's To You / Bring Down The Rain. Chart positions: 79 GERMANY, 142 USA.

ANGRY MACHINES, SPV Steamhammer 085-18292 CD (1996). Institutional Man / Don't Tell The Kids / Black / Hunter Of The Heart / Stay Out Of My Mind / Big Sister / Double Monday / Golden Rules / Dying In America / This Is Your Life.

DIO'S INFERNO-LAST IN LIVE, SPV Steamhammer 085-18842 (1998). Intro / Jesus, Mary And The Holy Ghost / Straight Through The Heart / Don't Talk To Strangers / Holy Diver / Drum Solo / Heaven And Hell / Double Monday / Stand Up And Shout / Hunter Of The Heart / Mistreated / Guitar Solo / The Last In Line / Rainbow In The Dark / Mob Rules / Man On The Silver Mountain / Long Live Rock n' Roll / We Rock.

MAGICA, Spitfire 6-702114-5020-2 (2000). Discovery / Magica Theme / Lord Of The Last Day / Fever Dreams / Turn To Stone / Feed My Head / Ebeil / Challis / As Long As it's Not Love / Losing My Insanity / Otherworld / Magica / Lord Of The Last Day / Magica Story. Chart positions: 40 GERMANY, 52 SWEDEN.

KILLING THE DRAGON, SPV (2002). Killing The Dragon / Along Came A Spider / Scream / Better In The Dark / Rock And Roll / Push / Guilty / Throwaway Children / Before The Fall / Cold Feet. Chart positions: 24 SWEDEN, 30 GERMANY, 194 UK, 199 USA.

MASTER OF THE MOON, SPV 08569912 (2004). One More From The Road / Master Of The Moon / The End Of The World / Shivers / The Man Who Would Be King / The Eyes / Living The Lie / I Am / Death By Love / In Dreams. Chart positions: 16 FINLAND, 62 GERMANY, 159 UK.

EVIL OR DIVINE, Spitfire SPITCD253 (2005). Killing The Dragon / Egypt / Children Of The Sea / Push / Drum solo / Stand Up And Shout / Rock And Roll / Don't Talk To Strangers / Man On The Silver Mountain / Guitar solo / Long Live Rock n' Roll / Lord Of The Last Day / Fever Dreams / Holy Diver / Heaven And Hell / The Last In Line / Rainbow In The Dark / We Rock. Chart position: 33 GREECE.

SINGLES/EPS

Rainbow In The Dark, Warner Bros. 29527 (1983) (USA release). Rainbow In The Dark / Gypsy.

Rainbow In The Dark, Mercury 15PP41 (1983) (Japanese release). Rainbow In The Dark / Holy Diver / Evil Eyes / Stand Up And Shout (Live) / Straight Through The Heart (Live).

Rainbow In The Dark, Mercury DIO 2-12 (1983). Rainbow In The Dark / Stand Up And Shout (Live) / Straight Through The Heart (Live).

Holy Diver, Mercury DIO 1-12 (1983). Holy Diver / Evil Eyes / Don't Talk To Strangers.

Holy Diver, Vertigo DIO 1 (1983). Holy Diver / Evil Eyes. Chart position: 72 UK.

Rainbow In The Dark, Vertigo DIO 2 (1983). Rainbow In The Dark / Stand Up And Shout (Live). Chart position: 46 UK.

We Rock, Vertigo DIO 3 (1984). We Rock / Holy Diver (Live). Chart position: 42 UK.

Mystery, Vertigo DIO 4 (1984). Mystery / Eat Your Heart Out (Live). Chart position: 34 UK.

Mystery, Warner Bros. 29183 (1984) (USA release). Mystery / We Speed At Night.

Mystery, Vertigo 15PP45 (1984) (Japanese release). Mystery / We Rock / Eat Your Heart Out (Live) / Don't Talk To Strangers (Live).

We Rock, Mercury (1984) (USA promotion). We Rock / Breathless.

Mystery, Vertigo DIO 4-12 (1984). Mystery / Eat Your Heart Out (Live) / Don't Talk To Strangers (Live).

We Rock, Vertigo DIO 3-12 (1984). We Rock / Holy Diver (Live) / Rainbow In The Dark (Live).

King Of Rock n' Roll, Vertigo (1985). King Of Rock n' Roll / Sacred Heart.

We Rock (Live) /, Warner Bros. (1985) (USA promotion). We Rock (Live) / Like The Beat Of A Heart (Live).

Rock n' Roll Children, Vertigo DIO 5-12 (1985) (12" single). Rock n' Roll Children / Sacred Heart / We Rock (Live) / The Last In Line (Live).

Rock n' Roll Children, Vertigo DIO 5 (1985). Rock n' Roll Children / We Rock (Live).

Rock n' Roll Children, Vertigo DIOW 5-12 (1985) (White vinyl 12" single). Rock n' Roll Children / We Rock (Live) / The Last In Line (Live).

Hungry For Heaven, Vertigo DIO 6-12 (1985) (12' single). Hungry For Heaven / Holy Diver (Live) / Rainbow In The Dark (Live).

Hungry For Heaven, Vertigo DIO 6 (1985) (7" single). Hungry For Heaven / Holy Diver (Live). Chart position: 72 UK.

Hungry For Heaven, Vertigo DIOW 6-12 (1985) (White vinyl 12" single). Hungry For Heaven / Holy Diver (Live) / Rainbow In The Dark (Live).

Stand Up And Shout, Crash (1986) (Free split flexi with ACCEPT for 'Crash' magazine). Stand Up And Shout.

Hide In The Rainbow, Vertigo DIO 712 (1986). Hide In The Rainbow / Hungry For Heaven / Shame On The Night / Egypt (The Chains Are On). Chart position: 56 UK.

When A Woman Cries (LP version), Mercury (1987) (USA promotion). When A Woman Cries (LP version) / When A Woman Cries (Edit).

I Could Have Been A Dreamer, Warner Bros. (1987) (USA release). I Could Have Been A Dreamer / Overlove.

I Could Have Been A Dreamer, Vertigo DIO 8 (1987) (7" single). I Could Have Been A Dreamer / Night People. Chart position: 69 UK.

Night People, Vertigo (1987) (Promotion). Night People / Sunset Superman.

I Could Have Been A Dreamer, Vertigo DIO 8-12 (1987) (12" single). I Could Have Been A Dreamer / Night People / Sunset Superman.

All The Fools Sailed Away, Vertigo (1987). All The Fools Sailed Away / Overlove.

Hey Angel, Vertigo DIO 9-12 (1990) (12" single). Hey Angel / Walk On Water / Rock n' Roll Children / Mystery.

Hey Angel, Vertigo DIOP 9-12 (1990) (12' picture disc single). Hey Angel / Walk On Water / We Rock / Why Are They Watching Me.

Hey Angel, Vertigo DIOCD 9 (1990) (CD single). Hey Angel / Walk On Water / Rock n' Roll Children / We Rock.

Hey Angel, Vertigo DIO 9 (1990) (7" single). Hey Angel / Walk On Water.

A.4 Bill Ward

ALBUMS

WARD ONE ALONG THE WAY, Chameleon 01 74816 (1989). (Mobile) Shooting Gallery / Short Stories / Bombers (Can't Open Bomb Bays) / Pink Clouds An Island / Light Up The Candles (Let There Be Peace Tonight) / Snakes And Ladders / Jack's Land / Living Naked / Music For A Raw Nerve Ending / Tall Stories / Sweep / Along The Way.

WHEN THE BOUGH BREAKS, Cleopatra CL9981 (1997). Hate / Children Killing Children / Growth / When I Was A Child / Please Help Mommy (She's A Junkie) / Shine / Step Lightly / Love & Innocence / Animals / Nighthawks Stars & Pines / Try Life / When The Bough Breaks.

SINGLES/EPS

Straws, (2003). Straws.

A.5 Geezer

ALBUMS

PLASTIC PLANET, Rawpower RAWCD 105 (1995). Catatonic Eclipse / Drive Boy, Shooting / Giving Up The Ghost / Plastic Planet / The Invisible / Seance Fiction / House Of Clouds / Detective 27 / X13 / Sci-clone / Cycle Of Sixty.

OHMWORK, Sanctuary (2005). Misfit / Pardon My Depression / Prisoner 103 / I Believe / Aural Sects / Pseudocide / Pull The String / Alone / Dogs Of Whore / Don't You Know.

BLACK SCIENCE, Eagle EAGCD001 (1997). Man In A Suitcase / Box Of Six / Mysterons / Justified / Department S / Area Code 51 / Has To Be / Number 5 / Among The Cyberman / Unspeakable Elvis / Xodiak / Northern Wisdom / Trinity Road.

A.6 Tony Iommi

ALBUMS

IOMMI, Priority 27857 (2000). Laughing Man (In The Devil Mask) / Meat / Goodbye Lament / Time Is Mine / Patterns / Black Oblivion / Flame On / Just Say No To Love / Who's Fooling Who / Into The Night. Chart position: 43 GERMANY.

THE 1996 DEP SESSIONS, Sanctuary (2004). Gone / From Another World / Don't You Tell Me / Don't Drag The River / Fine / Time Is The Healer / I'm Not The Same Man / It Falls Through Me.

FUSED, Sanctuary 06076-84759-2 (2005). Dopamine / Wasted Again / Saviour Of The Real / Resolution Song / Grace / Deep Inside A Shell / What You're Living For / Face Your Fear / The Spell / I Go Insane. Chart positions: 25 GREECE, 39 FINLAND, 43 SWEDEN, 92 GERMANY.

SINGLES/EPS

Goodbye Lament, Virgin IOMDPRO1 (2000) (UK promotion release). Goodbye Lament.

Index

Aaron Gilstrom, 155
Abominog, 60, 152, 153
AC/DC, 35, 45, 47, 63, 194, 216
Adam Wakeman, 297, 298
Adrian Vandenberg, 196, 203
Aerosmith, 77, 255, 257, 273
AIIZ, 57
Air Studios, 184, 186
Al Atkins, 203
Al Kooper, 17
Alan Clark, 1
Albert Chapman, 10, 179, 201–204, 279
Alex Skolnick, 265
Alexandra Palace, 300
Alice Cooper, 27–31, 128, 148, 192
Alice In Chains, 252, 292
Alvin Lee, 8, 64, 127
Angel, 29, 265
Angel Witch, 35
Anthrax, 158, 172, 174, 190, 252
Apartment 26, 290
Armageddon, 125, 126, 137
Arthur Sharp, 33, 38, 56, 101
Atlantic Records, 192, 199, 211
Atomic Rooster, 73, 74
Attention Deficit, 267
Australia, 3, 40, 154, 235, 277
Axxis, 227

Bad Company, 84, 116, 149, 171, 179, 290
Badaxe, 23–25, 30–32
Badlands, 191, 192, 194, 206, 252, 253
Bandy Legs, 12–14
Bark At The Moon, 95, 97, 112, 115, 185, 191
Barry Dunnery, 3
Barry Gibb, 22
Barry Scrannage, 34
BBC, 60, 152, 220, 300
Behind The Wall Of Sleep, 284
Bel Air, 17, 22
Bernie Marsden, 202, 221, 290
Bernie Tormé, 73–75, 77, 81, 84–88, 252
Bev Bevan, 104, 107, 110, 118, 121, 128, 189, 205–207, 291
Beyond Aston, 291
Bible Black, 137, 138
Bill Branch, 3

Bill Hunt, 39
Bill Ward, 1–3, 10, 13, 22, 49, 94, 101, 104, 110, 118, 121, 125, 147, 149, 166, 215, 237, 241, 244, 264, 275, 283, 284, 290, 297
Billboard, 9, 23, 59, 91, 94, 112, 167, 199, 218, 219, 237, 246, 247, 278, 292, 293, 295, 298
Billy Connelly, 237
Billy Corgan, 291
Billy Sheehan, 147, 241
Biohazard, 275
Black Label Society, 292–294, 296
Black Moon, 205
Black Oak Arkansas, 23, 28, 39, 59, 81
Black Science, 127, 282, 283
Black Widow, 2
Blackie Lawless, 119, 174, 175, 177, 196
Blas Elias, 32
Blizzard Of Ozz, 6–8, 38, 43, 45, 51–55, 59, 61, 67, 74, 76, 89, 120, 160, 185, 201, 293, 294
Blood, Sweat & Tears, 17
Bloomington Metropolitan Sports Center, 49
Blue Murder, 31, 118, 191, 207, 217, 218, 221
Blue Oyster Cult, 7, 36, 48, 50, 84, 102, 138, 154, 158, 210, 283
Bob Catley, 139
Bob Daisley, 8, 32, 33, 36, 38–41, 45, 51, 52, 56, 58–61, 90, 94, 112, 114, 115, 147, 148, 150, 151, 153, 167, 184–191, 205, 215, 221, 225, 228, 245, 256, 257, 284, 293, 294
Bob Ezrin, 128, 129, 224
Bob Geadreau, 23
Bob Geldof, 142, 148
Bob Krasnow, 158
Bobby Rock, 31, 32
Bobby Rondinelli, 135, 138, 171, 172, 180, 252, 257, 259, 263, 272, 275–277, 283, 289
Body Count, 273
Bon Jovi, 177, 215, 229
Bophuthatswana, 208
Born Again, 101, 102, 104, 106, 107, 111, 120, 126, 144, 222, 299
Boston, 18, 73
Brad Gillis, 83, 85, 87–89, 94, 297
Brazil, 264
Brian May, 14, 25, 128, 223, 227, 236, 241, 250, 252, 272, 276, 288–290
Brian Tichy, 291

Brooks Wackerman, 292
Bruce Brookshire, 65
Bruce Payne, 16, 137
Budgie, 54, 73, 88, 89
Bullring Brummies, 275
Bullrush Cottage, 6
Burton C. Bell, 264, 268

California Jam, 3
Capitol Records, 137
Captain Beyond, 24
Carlos Cavazo, 25
Carmine Appice, 86, 112, 113, 115, 245, 289
Castle Donington, 40, 95, 251, 293
Cathedral, 261
CBS Records, 193
Chalfont St. Peter, 298
Cheap Trick, 47
Cherokee Recording Studios, 32, 139
Chicken Shack, 32, 33, 220
Children Of The Grave, 54, 64, 149, 207
Children Of The Sea, 14, 17, 35, 36, 63, 250
Chris Holmes, 26
Chris Overland, 151
Chris Slade, 149, 228
Chris Tsangarides, 43, 189, 191, 205
Christopher Guest, 152
Chrome Molly, 154
Chrysalis Records, 32, 89
Chuck Weissner, 97
Cinderella, 148, 215, 219, 221
Cliff Burton, 154
Close My Eyes Forever, 218, 219
Coal Chamber, 281, 284, 290
Colin Flooks, 219
Computer God, 197, 239, 250
Connecticut, 16
Copperfield, 12
Costa Mesa, 247, 249–251, 272, 279
Country Girl, 56, 63
Cozy Powell, 38, 40, 44, 50, 101, 189, 191, 200, 207,
    212, 216–219, 221, 222, 224–226, 230, 231,
    233, 235, 238, 241, 250, 252, 258, 271–274,
    288–290, 298
Cradle Of Filth, 293
Craig Goldy, 142, 146, 237, 279
Craig Gruber, 18, 19, 137
Crazy Angel, 130
Crazy Train, 30, 41, 45, 54, 55, 73, 82, 97, 147, 194, 196,
    266, 293, 294, 298, 300
Criteria Recording Studios, 20
Cross Purposes, 242, 259–264, 267–269

Dana Strum, 23, 25, 29–32, 38, 96, 120, 122, 147, 199
Danny Peyronel, 152
Dante Fox, 97
Danzig, 247, 295
Dario Mollo, 252, 284
Dave Corke, 4, 179, 203
Dave Holland, 159, 280, 281, 297
Dave Potts, 38, 41

Dave Spitz, 140, 157, 161–164, 168, 169, 171–176, 180,
    182–184, 188–192, 205–210, 253, 301
Dave Tangye, vi, 6
Dave Walker, 9
David 'Rock' Feinstein, 15
David Arden, 53, 55, 76, 82
David Carruth, 23
David Coverdale, 14, 101, 118, 134, 135, 151, 210, 218
David DeFeis, 212
David Donato, 123, 125, 126, 128–130, 133, 146, 167,
    179, 186
David Lee Roth, 9, 31, 118, 171, 194, 255, 265
De Montfort Hall, 127, 173, 179, 227
Deen Castronovo, 256, 266–268, 277, 282
Deep Purple, 2, 3, 8, 14, 16, 24, 73, 88, 101–103, 108,
    110, 111, 116, 118, 126, 127, 134, 135, 159,
    160, 164, 168, 171, 172, 181, 217, 237, 241,
    245, 254, 276, 294, 295, 299
Def Leppard, 35, 63, 67, 100, 115, 237
Deftones, 290
Dehumanizer, 197, 239, 242, 243, 247, 248, 250, 260,
    268, 279, 286
Dennis McCarten, 3
Dennis Wheatley, 2
Devil And Daughter, 300
Diamond Head, 35, 108, 109
Diary Of A Madman, 55, 58–61, 66, 67, 74, 76, 89, 91,
    185, 189, 293
Die Young, 36
Digital Bitch, 105, 107
Dimmu Borgir, 296
Dio, 246, 286
Dirty Tricks, 7, 8, 14
Dirty Women, 300
Disturbed, 292
Disturbing The Priest, 104–107, 126
Django Reinhardt, 11, 301
Doc Holliday, 65, 66
Dokken, 23, 25, 26, 96, 153
Don Airey, 44, 52, 60, 68, 70, 74, 77, 78, 81, 83, 85–88,
    117, 118, 152, 221, 241, 280, 285, 289, 290,
    295
Don Arden, 3, 7, 20, 30, 31, 38, 101, 102, 107, 109, 110,
    126, 139–142, 163, 164, 168, 174, 182–184,
    188, 192
Don Costa, 97, 99
Doobie Brothers, 17
Doug Goldstein, 174–176, 210
Down To Earth, 292
Downset, 284
Drain S.T.H., 284, 290
Drew Forsyth, 28
Driver, 118, 146, 265
Drowning Pool, 293

E5150, 63
Earl Slick, 85, 86
Earth, 1
Eddie Kramer, 257
Eddie Money, 23, 152, 197
Eddie Van Halen, 9, 260, 265

INDEX

Edinburgh Playhouse, 227
Eighth Star, 281, 291
Electric Gypsies, 74
Electric Light Orchestra, 7, 39, 54, 104, 107, 118
Elf, 16, 123, 286
Entombed, 290
Epic Records, 32, 246
Eric Carr, 190, 257
Eric Clapton, 136, 293
Eric Dillon, 152
Eric Singer, 133, 139, 140, 143, 144, 147, 157, 158, 161–163, 168, 172, 178, 182, 184, 185, 187–189, 191, 192, 210, 253, 286, 290, 301
Ernest Chapman, 272
Ernie C., 273, 274
Eternal Idol, 198, 201, 204–206, 208, 214, 221, 222, 285
Exodus, 247, 248

Fairies Wear Boots, 284
Faith No More, 278
Faster Pussycat, 23
Fastway, 89, 90
Fat Mattress, 152
Fear Factory, 264, 268, 281, 284, 290, 295
Firehouse, 32
Flying High Again, 82, 85, 89, 147, 195
Fontana Records, 2
Foo Fighters, 290, 291
Forbidden, 225, 272, 274, 275, 277, 285
Foreigner, 158, 291, 292
Fran Sheehan, 18
Frank Bruno, 237
Frank Hall, 3–6
Frank Sinatra, 128
Frankie Banali, 30, 38, 159, 194
Fred Coury, 147, 150, 215, 265

G-Force, 24
Gary Driscoll, 16, 135, 137
Gary Holt, 248
Gary Holton, 152
Gary Moore, 24, 39, 44, 59, 60, 77, 88, 112, 128, 159, 160, 164, 169, 177, 187–189, 191, 218, 221, 224, 228, 271
Gary Shea, 31
Geezer Butler, 1, 10, 15, 18, 19, 22, 34, 55, 102, 104, 106, 111, 121, 125, 127, 130, 140, 146, 149, 151, 177, 178, 196, 205, 208, 210, 218, 237, 243, 255, 259, 261, 262, 264, 265, 267, 268, 275, 283, 284, 287, 290, 292, 296, 298
Gene Simmons, 123, 133, 155
Geoff Nicholls, 9, 10, 12, 14, 15, 17, 20, 22, 35, 45, 47, 49, 50, 55–57, 93, 101, 102, 105, 106, 108–111, 120, 122, 123, 126, 129, 134, 139–141, 144, 157, 161–163, 165, 166, 172, 174, 176, 180, 184, 186, 188, 189, 191, 200, 204, 205, 207, 217, 218, 222, 223, 231, 234, 237–239, 241–243, 251, 260, 262, 272, 275, 277, 279–281, 284, 285, 289, 290, 292, 297, 298, 300
George Lynch, 25, 26, 97
Gerry Bron, 40

Gillan, 35, 73, 74, 252
Girl, 33
Glasgow Apollo, 54
Glen Buxton, 27
Glenn Hughes, 5, 8, 14, 15, 24, 30, 122, 126, 134, 140–142, 144, 157, 159–161, 164, 165, 167–169, 172, 174–176, 179, 192, 197, 204, 210, 217, 223, 250, 251, 253, 268, 279–281, 285, 287, 298, 300
Glenn Tipton, 201, 271, 288
Gloria Butler, 130, 177, 196, 243, 249, 259, 261, 265
Godsmack, 290, 292
Gordon Copley, 133, 134, 139, 140, 142, 157, 158, 161
Graham Oliver, 48
Graham Wright, vi
Great White, 23, 25, 210
Greg Bissonette, 31
Greg Chaisson, 119, 121, 150, 192
Greg Hildebrandt, 58
Guns n' Roses, 23, 106, 210, 264, 272, 277

Hammersmith Odeon, 47, 54, 57, 65, 90, 91, 154, 179, 180, 214, 216, 227, 261
Hanoi Rocks, 108, 153, 207
Headless Cross, 200, 201, 205, 210, 218, 222–227, 230, 231, 233–238, 241, 251, 259, 271, 272, 274, 275, 286, 288, 298, 300
Hear n' Aid, 251
Heart Like A Wheel, 142, 164, 217
Heaven And Hell, 14, 15, 17–20, 34–36, 40, 45–47, 49–52, 56, 57, 63, 95, 107, 109, 137, 186, 214, 217, 230, 233, 239, 242, 243, 250, 286–288
Heaven Or Hell, 286
Heavy Metal Kids, 60, 152
Henley on Arden, 183, 242, 258
Henry Rollins, 291
Hirsh Gardner, 31
Holy Diver, 95, 96, 222, 237
Honolulu Stadium, 50
Human Waste Project, 290
Humble Pie, 2, 239

Ian Gillan, 74, 76, 82, 101–111, 118, 120, 136, 144, 175, 177–179, 204, 211, 212, 227, 272, 287, 290, 298
Ice T, 273, 274
Incubus, 292
Iron Butterfly, 60, 194
Iron Maiden, 35, 73, 90, 115, 146, 178, 298
Iron Man, 2, 25, 52, 54, 82, 102, 143, 149, 230, 250, 255, 257, 275, 297
IRS Records, 222, 226, 227, 236, 274, 279, 286

Jaap Edenhall, 235
Jackie Lynton, 152
Jake E. Lee, 96, 99, 112, 120, 147, 151, 154, 191, 192, 194, 210, 253
Jason Newsted, 294, 295
Jasper Carrott, 291
Jeff 'Skunk' Baxter, 17
Jeff Beck, 113, 194, 220, 221, 272

Jeff Fenholt, 135–144, 146, 157, 161, 183, 285
Jeff Glixman, 134, 137, 139, 141, 157, 158, 161–163, 185, 188–191
Jerry Cantrell, 292, 298
Jesus Christ Superstar, 135–137, 139, 143
Jet Records, 23, 24, 26, 31, 33, 34, 43, 52, 63, 73, 75, 77, 101, 192, 194
Jethro Tull, 2, 44, 88, 127, 128
Jezz Woodruffe, 3, 177, 178
Jim Simpson, 1, 3, 39
Jimi Bell, 196, 243
Jimi Hendrix, v, 113, 257, 288, 300
Jimmy Ayers, 150, 153
Jimmy Bain, 95
Jimmy Barnes, 294
Jimmy Copley, 297
Jimmy DeGrasso, 148, 151
Jimmy Nail, 152
Jimmy Page, 49, 127, 128, 148, 149, 211
Jimmy Phillips, 1
Jimmy Waldo, 31
Jo Burt, 210–212, 214, 216, 218, 225, 287
Joe Holmes, 194, 196, 265, 267, 277, 278, 292
Joe Lynn Turner, 126, 233, 245, 258
John Allen, 67
John Baxter, 275
John Bonham, 8, 47, 159, 207, 212
John Fraser Binnie, 7
John Lennon, 57, 86, 293
John McCoy, 73, 252
John Sinclair, 60, 151, 153, 193, 247, 267, 290
John Sloman, 101
John Sykes, 77, 95, 118, 151, 191, 192, 210, 217
John Tempesta, 291
John Thomas, 54
Johnny Neal & The Starliners, 12
Journey, 31, 47, 278
Judas Priest, 1, 2, 4, 23, 35, 66, 88, 115, 134, 201, 203, 223, 226, 227, 246, 249–251, 255, 271, 279, 280, 288, 296, 297, 301
Junior's Eyes, 9
Just Say Ozzy, 237

Kalamazoo Wings Stadium, 48
Keith Olsen, 215
Kelly Garni, 27–31, 63, 73, 94
Kelly Osbourne, 198, 293, 294
Kerrang, 88, 106, 107, 125, 129, 179, 209, 214, 217
Kevin DuBrow, 25, 28, 30, 61
Kevin Elson, 211
Kick Axe, 120
King Crimson, 298
Kingdom Come, 227
Kiss, 23, 31, 128, 130, 257, 258, 264, 287
Kit Woolven, 280
Kittie, 292
KK Downing, 226
Korn, 290
Krokus, 123, 158, 163, 178
Kyle Michaels, 178

L.A. Guns, 23

Larry Mazar, 137, 141
Larry Page, 152
Lars Ulrich, 154
Laurence Cottle, 221, 223
Lawrence Archer, 150
Le Parc Hotel, 24, 25
Led Zeppelin, 47, 113, 119, 127, 134, 149, 158, 200, 211, 227, 237
Lee Kerslake, 33, 40, 41, 54, 58–60, 152, 189, 293, 294
Lemmy, 177, 201, 245, 261, 265
Leslie West, 2, 27, 28, 298
Life Of Agony, 290
Light & Sound Design, 107
Light And Sound Design, 203, 217
Limp Bizkit, 290
Lindsey Bridgwater, 52–54, 56, 59, 61, 71, 88, 89, 99, 115, 116, 152
Lita Ford, 121, 126, 133, 134, 139, 142, 150, 158, 163, 172, 194–196, 218, 219
Little Feat, 17
Live Aid, 142, 148, 217, 236, 284
Live At Budokan, 293
Live Evil, 94, 286
Lostprophets, 293
Louie Merlino, 23, 31

M-80, 99
Mötley Crüe, 23, 25, 115, 120, 153, 168, 172, 199, 207, 229, 278, 292
Machine Head, 284
Madison Square Garden, 66, 84–87
Madonna, 112, 144, 293
Magnum, 63, 108, 149, 203, 216
Mainline Riders, 17
Malcolm Cope, 11–14, 104
Malta, 276
Marilyn Manson, 246, 284, 294
Mario Parga, 241, 252
Mark Bistany, 246
Mark Free, 31
Mark Nauseef, 24
Mark Slaughter, 31, 32
Marquee club, 2, 4, 59, 152
Mars Studios, 30
Martin Birch, 19, 35, 56, 58, 238
Mass Mental, 291
Master Of Insanity, 198, 243
Master Of Reality, 3
Matt Cameron, 291
Max Norman, 44, 55
MCA Records, 197
Megadeth, 148, 275
Melody Maker, 52, 152
Meshuggah, 293, 294
Metal Forces, 222, 237
Metallica, 154, 190, 194, 262, 294
Mexico, 126, 228, 229
Michael Des Barres, 23
Michael Schenker, 77
Michael Schenker Group, 45, 159, 219, 221
Michelle Meyer, 29

INDEX

Mick Box, 40, 60, 152
Mick Ronson, 25, 28
Mickey Lee Soule, 16
Mickie Most, 152
Mike Bordin, 278, 283, 291, 293, 297, 298, 300
Mike Inez, 215, 247, 278
Mike Jensen, 97
Miles Copeland, 222, 226, 274
Misha Calvin, 202
Mitch Perry, 97, 119, 194
Mob Rules, 56–58, 63, 66, 91, 104, 233, 250, 262, 286
Molly Hatchet, 47, 49, 50
Monsters Of Rock, 40, 95, 264, 281
Montserrat, 204
Morbid Angel, 261
Moscow, 229, 230, 234, 294
Mother's Army, 245, 256
Motorhead, 35, 67, 89, 108, 115, 177, 201, 245, 261, 265
Mott The Hoople, 28, 33, 116, 288, 298
Mr. Crowley, 39, 40, 45, 52, 53, 55, 82, 83, 153, 194, 267
MTM Music, 300
Mudvayne, 292, 298
Music Machine, 1
Mythology, 1

N.I.B., 2, 51, 250
Nassau Coliseum, 100
Nativity In Black, 275
Necromandus, 3–7, 14
Neil Carter, 70
Neil Murray, 148, 151, 210, 216, 221, 222, 224–227, 229, 231, 234, 235, 238, 240, 241, 252, 259, 261, 271, 272, 274–277, 288–290, 297
Neon Knights, 22, 36, 40, 63, 110, 121, 130, 174, 250
Neurosis, 281, 290
Never Say Die, 9, 10, 14, 19, 35, 44, 149
New Zealand, 3, 277
Newcastle City Hall, 227
Nick Tauber, 74
Nicky Moore, 101
Night Ranger, 83, 84, 95, 245
Nightmare, 205
Nikki Sixx, 219
No Bone Movies, 41
No More Tears, 73, 153, 243, 245–247, 294
No Rest For The Wicked, 199, 215
Nottingham Rock City, 265, 267
Nuclear Assault, 210
NWoBHM, 10, 35, 38, 47, 75, 95, 177

Ohmwork, 298
Ossie Hoppie, 40, 60
Over The Mountain, 70, 82, 87, 89, 147
Ozzfest, 131, 281, 283, 284, 290–300
Ozzmosis, 264, 266, 268, 278, 281

P.O.D., 292–294
Painkiller, 88, 249
Panathenaikos Stadium, 206
Pantera, 284, 290–292
Paranoid, 54, 64, 91, 115, 134, 149, 230, 248, 288

Pat Thrall, 84, 85, 159
Pat Travers, 39, 77, 147
Patrick Meehan, 3, 182–184, 186, 187, 190, 204, 205, 208, 210
Paul Chapman, 67, 69, 70, 79, 81, 82, 90
Paul Clark, 58
Paul Rodgers, 149, 179, 211, 257, 297
Paul Samson, 73
Paul Shortino, 96
Pedro Howse, 130, 177, 178, 264, 267, 282
Perry Mason, 266, 281
Persian Risk, 177, 178
Pete Steele, 291
Pete Way, 53, 67, 69, 77, 88–90, 97, 150
Peter Green, 288
Peter Mensch, 77
Phil Anselmo, 291
Phil Banfield, 74, 76, 102, 211, 235, 272, 273, 277, 279
Phil Collins, 7, 294
Phil Mogg, 67, 129, 216
Phil Soussan, 31, 149–151, 153–155, 167, 193, 195, 196, 199, 243, 284, 287, 293
Pink Floyd, 2, 128, 300
Pitchshifter, 290, 292
Plastic Planet, 264, 268, 283
Poison, 23
Polka Tulk Blues Band, 1, 17, 127
Polydor Records, 241, 242
Powerman 5000, 284
Praying Mantis, 38, 39
Pretty Maids, 107
Pride & Glory, 255, 291
Primus, 290
Psycho Man, 290

Quartz, 9–14, 17, 104
Queen, 14, 25, 194, 209, 211, 241, 250, 288
Queens Of The Stone Age, 292
Queensryche, 154, 300
Quiet Riot, 23, 25, 28–30, 32, 59–61, 96, 110, 118–120, 123, 142, 159, 168, 172, 194

Rachel Youngblood, 70
Rainbow, 16, 19, 33, 35, 44, 54, 81, 95, 96, 123, 126, 135, 138, 159, 221, 222, 245, 252, 257, 258, 271, 286–288
Rainbow Bar & Grill, 17, 26, 229
Ralph Baker, 272, 280
Randy Castillo, 126, 129, 130, 134, 147, 148, 150, 167, 195, 196, 199, 218, 243, 246, 247, 278, 293
Randy Rhoads, 24–26, 28, 29, 34, 38, 44, 52, 54, 60, 61, 63, 67, 68, 70, 71, 73, 74, 78, 82, 84, 85, 89, 91, 94, 96, 119, 120, 194, 196, 201, 256, 277, 293, 295
Rare Breed, 1
Ratt, 23, 25, 96, 97, 133, 154, 172, 194, 266
Ray Gillen, 123, 138, 141, 165, 171, 172, 174, 175, 179, 182, 184–186, 188, 189, 191, 192, 200, 205, 207, 217, 218, 252, 253, 257, 265
Ray Gomez, 85, 86, 159
Record Plant, 57, 58

Reunion, 290
Revelation Mother Earth, 45, 53, 82, 87
Rich Bitch Studios, 216, 217, 225
Richard Branson, 104, 106
Richard Cole, 158
Richie Hayward, 17
Rick Parfitt, 28
Rick Wakeman, 3, 4, 264, 291, 297
Ridge Farm, 43, 51, 56
Ringo Starr, 57, 290
Ritchie Blackmore, 16, 20, 33, 45, 49, 60, 108, 135, 137, 221, 257, 258, 279
Rob Halford, 122, 134, 135, 246, 249–251, 255, 268, 275, 279, 297
Rob Nicholson, 295, 296
Rob Zombie, 290, 292, 293, 295, 298
Robbie Crane, 32
Robert Fleischman, 31
Robert Gambino, 258
Robert Plant, 8, 14, 101, 127, 134, 139, 148, 159, 172, 179, 197, 219, 221, 233
Robert Trujillo, 278, 292–294
Robin George, 149, 203
Rockfield Studios, 38, 177, 178, 242
Rockwell Studios, 43
Rodger Bain, 2, 3, 7, 39
Roger Glover, 137, 159, 172, 299
Roger Myers, 7
Rolling Stones, 2, 12, 27, 64, 77, 298
Ron Keel, 119–123
Ron Mancuso, 31
Ron Nevison, 151, 167, 199
Ronnie and The Red Caps, 15
Ronnie Dio and the Prophets, 15
Ronnie James Dio, 10, 14–16, 18, 19, 22, 23, 33, 35, 45, 47, 49, 51, 52, 56, 58, 93–96, 103, 123, 127, 135, 143, 159, 177, 182, 186, 204, 218, 233, 238, 239, 242, 247, 248, 251, 260, 264, 279, 286, 287, 296, 299, 300
Rough Cutt, 95, 96, 114, 194, 246
Roy Lemon, 17
Roy Mayorga, 291, 292
Roy Thomas Baker, 215
Royal Concert Hall, 179
Rudy Sarzo, 29, 59–61, 70, 77, 81, 88, 118, 142, 146, 284
Russ Ballard, 258
Rusty Angels, 275

S.A.T.O., 56
Sabbath Bloody Sabbath, 3, 46
Sammy Hagar, 48
Sanctuary Records, 297
Sandy Pearlman, 18, 36, 58, 102
Savatage, 252, 266, 267
Savoy Brown, 9, 152
Saxon, 35, 47, 48, 223, 241
Scary Dreams, 292
Scorpions, 158, 229
Scott Shelly, 27
Sean Lynch, 222, 289
Sebastian Bach, 101, 194

Sepultura, 275, 278
Seventh Star, 140, 142, 144, 146, 157, 159, 161–165, 167, 172, 174–177, 180, 182, 187, 190, 210, 221, 222, 259, 279–281, 285, 297
Sex Pistols, 197, 243
Shannon Larkin, 291
Sharon Arden, 17
Sharon Osbourne, 63, 70, 82, 86, 142, 150, 195–197, 218, 227, 244, 248, 251, 266, 281, 293–296, 298
Sheffield City Hall, 48
Shot In The Dark, 153, 194
Silent Rage, 227
Singapore, 229, 236
Skew Siskin, 247
Slade, 6, 28, 40, 90, 216
Slayer, 264, 281, 290, 293, 296
Slipknot, 290, 296
Slo Burn, 284
Smallwood Taylor, 177, 178, 197
Smashing Pumpkins, 291
Smoke On The Water, 107, 108
Snowblind, 3, 293
Some Kind Of Woman, 205
Soulfly, 291, 298
Soundgarden, 291
South Africa, 208
Speak Of The Devil, 94, 97
Spencer Proffer, 119, 120, 122, 123
Spencer Scrannage, 202
Spinal Tap, 107, 152, 153, 296
St. Petersburg, 229, 230, 294
Stacey Morland, 23
Star Club, 12
Star club, 1
Star Of India, 139, 140, 142, 165, 183
Starfighters, 63, 201, 216, 217
Startling Studios, 57
Starwood Club, 25, 29, 96
Starz, 23
Static X, 290
Status Quo, 2, 12, 28, 149, 152, 208, 211
Steve Fister, 194–196
Steve Humphries, 152
Steve Marriott, 28, 139
Steve Vai, 118, 255–257, 264
Steve Ward, 23
Steve Webb, 152
Steven Hatfield, 5
Stoking The Fires Of Hell, 14
Sugar Rain, 13
Suicidal Tendencies, 264, 278, 292
Suicide Solution, 45, 115, 186, 196
Sun City, 208, 209, 214
Sun Red Sun, 252
Superjoint Ritual, 296
Sweet Leaf, 237, 285
Sydney, 55
Symptom Of The Universe, 250
System Of A Down, 290, 293

Tasco, 178, 197, 211, 214, 258

INDEX

Technical Ecstasy, 3, 35
Ted Templeman, 95
Ten Years, 38
Ten Years After, 108, 128
Ten Years Later, 64
Terrif, 196, 265
Terry Chimes, 207–209, 212, 214, 217
Terry Horbury, 7
Terry Nails, 192, 243, 245, 246
Testament, 266, 267
The Alliance, 202, 203
The Beatles, 1, 12, 57, 136, 143, 218, 257, 276, 290, 298
The Black Panthers, 1
The Boyz, 25, 26
The Cult, 56, 192, 243, 247, 261, 275, 282, 283, 298
The Electric Elves, 15
The Lemon Tree, 12
The Obsessed, 275
The Ozzman Cometh, 284
The Prophets, 15
The Prospectors, 1
The Rest, 1
The Sabbath Stones, 279, 285
The Shining, 128, 185, 186, 204, 205, 210, 212, 300
The Ultimate Sin, 148, 153, 155
Therapy?, 275
Thin Lizzy, 24, 35, 44, 77, 108, 217
Tim Bogert, 113
Tim Kelly, 32
Tobruk, 203
Toby Wright, 292
Todd Jensen, 233, 256
Tokyo, 55, 155
Tom Allom, 2, 66
Tommy Aldridge, 39, 59–61, 69, 75, 81, 84–86, 88, 90, 94, 97, 112, 115, 118, 142, 146, 147, 159, 258
Tommy Lee, 173, 278, 292
Tony Martin, 200–206, 208, 212–214, 216–218, 223, 225, 228–230, 233, 234, 237, 241, 242, 248, 252, 259, 261, 263, 264, 272, 274, 276, 277, 279, 281, 284–289
Tony Mills, 217
Tony Newton, 24
Top Of The Pops, 13, 32
Trans Siberian Orchestra, 267
Trapeze, 5, 8, 134, 135, 159, 164, 253, 280
Trashed, 104
Trevor Bolder, 153
Twisted Sister, 90, 108, 158, 201, 258
Type O Negative, 275, 278, 284, 291
Tyr, 200, 201, 218, 223, 233–238, 241, 251, 259, 260, 271, 272, 274, 286, 298, 300

U.S. Festival, 99, 251
UFO, 35, 53, 67–71, 77, 78, 89, 90, 129, 151, 152, 203, 216
Ugly Kid Joe, 291
Uli Jon Roth, 44, 149
Uriah Heep, 8, 33, 40, 41, 54, 60, 139, 149, 152, 153, 229, 294

Van Halen, 23, 211, 265

Vanilla Fudge, 31, 113, 133, 248
Velvet Revolver, 298
Vertigo Records, 2
Vince Neil, 32, 199, 207
Vinnie Vincent, 31
Vinny Appice, 50, 57, 86, 95, 248, 284, 290
Vintage Studios, 249
Violet Fox, 27
Violinski, 7
Virgin Steele, 212
Virginia Wolf, 211
Vision Of Disorder, 284
Vivian Campbell, 95, 96, 118, 237, 279
Vixen, 219
Volume 4, 3
Voodoo, 63–65, 192
Vow Wow, 210, 224, 289

W.A.S.P., 23, 26, 97, 119, 172, 174, 175, 178
War Pigs, 2, 9, 207, 237, 284, 294, 297
Warner Bros., 20, 36, 47, 56, 57, 95, 122, 130, 164, 167, 237, 238, 240, 242, 247
Warner Chappel, 203
Warrant, 23
Waysted, 90, 91, 150
Wendy Dio, 96, 249
When Death Calls, 200, 223, 225
White Lion, 157, 158, 163, 171, 174
White Tiger, 125, 130
White Zombie, 275, 291, 294
Whitesnake, 35, 44, 88, 101, 118, 134, 146, 148, 151, 171, 192, 202, 203, 210, 217, 219, 221, 222, 224, 225, 229, 237, 252, 255, 256, 261, 271
Widowmaker, 33, 41
Willy Daffern, 24
Wings Of Thunder, 234, 298
Wolverhampton Civic Hall, 235

Y&T, 115
Yardbirds, 113, 125
Yngwie Malmsteen, 119, 138, 146, 215, 245, 252, 288, 289
You Said It All, 55
You, Looking At Me Looking At You, 55

Zakk Wylde, 196, 199, 215, 218, 246, 247, 255, 264, 277, 292, 294, 296, 300
Zeno, 88, 179, 181, 203
Zero The Hero, 104, 106, 107, 110, 111

www.ingramcontent.com/pod-product-compliance
Lightning Source LLC
Chambersburg PA
CBHW060310240426
43661CB00059B/2716